Advances in Secure Computing, Internet Services, and Applications

B.K. Tripathy
VIT University, India

D.P. Acharjya
VIT University, India

A volume in the Advances in Information Security, Privacy, and Ethics (AISPE) Book Series

Information Science REFERENCE
An Imprint of IGI Global

Managing Director:	Lindsay Johnston
Book Production Manager:	Jennifer Yoder
Development Editor:	Austin DeMarco
Assistant Acquisitions Editor:	Kayla Wolfe
Typesetter:	Mike Brehm
Cover Design:	Jason Mull

Published in the United States of America by
Information Science Reference (an imprint of IGI Global)
701 E. Chocolate Avenue
Hershey PA 17033
Tel: 717-533-8845
Fax: 717-533-8661
E-mail: cust@igi-global.com
Web site: http://www.igi-global.com

Library of Congress Cataloging-in-Publication Data

Advances in secure computing, internet services, and applications / B.K. Tripathy and D.P. Acharjya, editors.
       pages cm
  Includes bibliographical references and index.
    ISBN 978-1-4666-4940-8 (hardcover) -- ISBN 978-1-4666-4942-2 (print & perpetual access) -- ISBN 978-1-4666-4941-5 (ebook) 1. Computer networks--Security measures. 2. Computer security. I. Tripathy, B. K., 1957- II. Acharjya, D. P., 1969- TK5105.59.A3834 2014
   005.8--dc23
                                2013038883

This book is published in the IGI Global book series Advances in Information Security, Privacy, and Ethics (AISPE) (ISSN: 1948-9730; eISSN: 1948-9749)

British Cataloguing in Publication Data
A Cataloguing in Publication record for this book is available from the British Library.

For electronic access to this publication, please contact: eresources@igi-global.com.

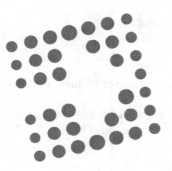

Advances in Information Security, Privacy, and Ethics (AISPE) Book Series

ISSN: 1948-9730
EISSN: 1948-9749

MISSION

In the digital age, when everything from municipal power grids to individual mobile telephone locations is all available in electronic form, the implications and protection of this data has never been more important and controversial. As digital technologies become more pervasive in everyday life and the Internet is utilized in ever increasing ways by both private and public entities, the need for more research on securing, regulating, and understanding these areas is growing.

The **Advances in Information Security, Privacy, & Ethics (AISPE) Book Series** is the source for this research, as the series provides only the most cutting-edge research on how information is utilized in the digital age.

COVERAGE

- Access Control
- Device Fingerprinting
- Global Privacy Concerns
- Information Security Standards
- Network Security Services
- Privacy-Enhancing Technologies
- Risk Management
- Security Information Management
- Technoethics
- Tracking Cookies

IGI Global is currently accepting manuscripts for publication within this series. To submit a proposal for a volume in this series, please contact our Acquisition Editors at Acquisitions@igi-global.com or visit: http://www.igi-global.com/publish/.

Titles in this Series

For a list of additional titles in this series, please visit: www.igi-global.com

Research Developments in Biometrics and Video Processing Techniques
Rajeev Srivastava (Indian Institute of Technology (BHU), India) S.K. Singh (Indian Institute of Technology (BHU), India) and K.K. Shukla (Indian Institute of Technology (BHU), India)
Information Science Reference • copyright 2014 • 279pp • H/C (ISBN: 9781466648685) • US $195.00 (our price)

Advances in Secure Computing, Internet Services, and Applications
B.K. Tripathy (VIT University, India) and D.P. Acharjya (VIT University, India)
Information Science Reference • copyright 2014 • 340pp • H/C (ISBN: 9781466649408) • US $195.00 (our price)

Trust Management in Mobile Environments Autonomic and Usable Models
Zheng Yan (Xidian University, China and Aalto University, Finland)
Information Science Reference • copyright 2014 • 288pp • H/C (ISBN: 9781466647657) • US $195.00 (our price)

Security, Privacy, Trust, and Resource Management in Mobile and Wireless Communications
Danda B. Rawat (Georgia Southern University, USA) Bhed B. Bista (Iwate Prefectural University, Japan) and Gongjun Yan (University of Southern Indiana, USA)
Information Science Reference • copyright 2014 • 595pp • H/C (ISBN: 9781466646919) • US $195.00 (our price)

Architectures and Protocols for Secure Information Technology Infrastructures
Antonio Ruiz-Martinez (University of Murcia, Spain) Rafael Marin-Lopez (University of Murcia, Spain) and Fernando Pereniguez-Garcia (University of Murcia, Spain)
Information Science Reference • copyright 2014 • 427pp • H/C (ISBN: 9781466645141) • US $195.00 (our price)

Theory and Practice of Cryptography Solutions for Secure Information Systems
Atilla Elçi (Aksaray University, Turkey) Josef Pieprzyk (Macquarie University, Australia) Alexander G. Chefranov (Eastern Mediterranean University, North Cyprus) Mehmet A. Orgun (Macquarie University, Australia) Huaxiong Wang (Nanyang Technological University, Singapore) and Rajan Shankaran (Macquarie University, Australia)
Information Science Reference • copyright 2013 • 351pp • H/C (ISBN: 9781466640306) • US $195.00 (our price)

IT Security Governance Innovations Theory and Research
Daniel Mellado (Spanish Tax Agency, Spain) Luis Enrique Sánchez (University of Castilla-La Mancha, Spain) Eduardo Fernández-Medina (University of Castilla – La Mancha, Spain) and Mario G. Piattini (University of Castilla - La Mancha, Spain)
Information Science Reference • copyright 2013 • 373pp • H/C (ISBN: 9781466620834) • US $195.00 (our price)

DISSEMINATOR OF KNOWLEDGE

www.igi-global.com

701 E. Chocolate Ave., Hershey, PA 17033
Order online at www.igi-global.com or call 717-533-8845 x100
To place a standing order for titles released in this series, contact: cust@igi-global.com
Mon-Fri 8:00 am - 5:00 pm (est) or fax 24 hours a day 717-533-8661

Dedicated to

My beloved mother Smt. Sasikala Tripathy
B. K. Tripathy

My beloved mother Smt. Pramodabala Acharjya
D. P. Acharjya

Table of Contents

Detailed Table of Contents

Section 1
Data Mining and Security

Chapter 1

Granular Computing has emerged as a framework in which information granules are represented and manipulated by intelligent systems. Granular Computing forms a unified conceptual and computing platform. Rough set theory put forth by Pawlak is based upon single equivalence relation taken at a time. Therefore, from a granular computing point of view, it is single granular computing. In 2006, Qiang et al. introduced a multi-granular computing using rough set, which was called optimistic multigranular rough sets after the introduction of another type of multigranular computing using rough sets called pessimistic multigranular rough sets being introduced by them in 2010. Since then, several properties of multigranulations have been studied. In addition, these basic notions on multigranular rough sets have been introduced. Some of these, called the Neighborhood-Based Multigranular Rough Sets (NMGRS) and the Covering-Based Multigranular Rough Sets (CBMGRS), have been added recently. In this chapter, the authors discuss all these topics on multigranular computing and suggest some problems for further study.

Chapter 2

During the last few decades, there has been a considerable growth of interest in pattern recognition in the field of robotics. An application of pattern recognition in robotics includes mobile robots and service robots. Visual and signal recognition of patterns enables the robots to perform a variety of tasks such as object and target recognition, navigation, grasping, and manipulation, assisting physically challenged people. This chapter surveys trends in robotics with pattern recognition that focuses more on the interaction between robot assistive device and human with signal pattern recognition. This interaction helps to enhance the capability of people in rehabilitation and in the field of medicine. Finally, this chapter includes the application of pattern recognition in the development of a prosthetic hand.

#### Chapter 3

The information technology revolution has brought drastic change in the way data is collected or generated for decision mining. The accumulated data has no relevance unless it provides certain useful information pertaining to the interest of an organization. The real challenge lies in converting high dimensional data into knowledge and to use this knowledge for the development of the organization. On the other hand, hiding an organization's sensitive information is a major concern. Much research has been carried out in this direction. This chapter discusses various privacy preservation techniques that can be employed in an information system to safeguard the sensitive information of an organization. This chapter also highlights sensitive fuzzy association rules that can be generated from an information system. The authors provide illustrations wherever necessary to give a clear idea of the concepts developed.

#### Chapter 4

High dimensional databases are proving to be a major concern among the researches to extract relevant information for futuristic decision making. Real world data is high dimensional in nature and comprises of irrelevant features, missing values, and redundancy, which requires serious concerns. Utilizing all such features can mislead the results for emergent prediction. Therefore, such databases are critical in nature to determine optimal solutions. To deal with such issues, the authors have developed and implemented a Cluster Analysis Study Behavior of School Children from Large Databases (CABS) framework to retrieve effective and efficient clusters from high dimensional human behavior datasets for school children in US. They have applied feature selection technique and hierarchical agglomerative clustering technique to discover clusters of vivid shape and size to retrieve knowledge from large databases. This study was conducted for Health Behavior in School-Aged Children (HBSC) using Correlation-Based Feature Selection (CFS) technique to reduce the inconsistent data records and select relevant features that will eventually extract the appropriate data to merge similar data and retrieve clusters. However, predictive analytics can facilitate a more thorough extraction of knowledge to facilitate better quality and faster decisions. The authors have implemented the current framework in R language where the clustering was emphasized using pvclust package. The proposed framework is highly efficient in discovering hidden and implicit knowledge from large databases due to its accessibility to handling and discovering clusters of variant shapes.

Intrusion Detection and Prevention Systems (IDPS) are being widely implemented to prevent suspicious threats in computer networks. Intrusion detection and prevention systems are security systems that are used to detect and prevent security threats to computer networks. In order to understand the security risks and IDPS, in this chapter, the authors make a quick review on classification of the IDPSs and categorize them in certain groups. Further, in order to improve accuracy and security, data mining techniques have been used to analyze audit data and extract features that can distinguish normal activities from intrusions. Experiments have been conducted for building efficient intrusion detection and prevention systems by combining online detection and offline data mining. During online data examination, real-time data are captured and are passed through a detection engine that uses a set of rules and parameters for analysis. During offline data mining, necessary knowledge is extracted about the process of intrusion.

Section 2
Project and Knowledge Management Infrastructure

This chapter introduces the framework and causal model of organizational culture, organizational learning, knowledge management, and job satisfaction. It argues that dimensions of organizational culture, organizational learning, and knowledge management have mediated positive effect on job satisfaction. Knowledge management positively mediates the relationships between organizational culture and job satisfaction and between organizational learning and job satisfaction. Organizational culture is positively related to organizational learning. Furthermore, the author hopes that understanding the theoretical constructs of organizational culture, organizational learning, knowledge management, and job satisfaction through the use of the framework and causal model will not only inform researchers of a better design for studying organizational culture, organizational learning, knowledge management, and job satisfaction, but also assist in the understanding of intricate relationships among different factors.

In the present economy, both at national and international front service sector, is playing a pivotal role as a major contributor towards the GDP. The importance of service sector necessitates the efficiency measurement of various service units. The opening of Indian economy (Liberalisation – Privitisation – Globalisation) has affected every segment of Indian industry and service sector, education being no exception. Today, management education is one of the most sought after higher education options for Indian students. Management education in India has also undergone many changes in the last decade or so, meeting the need of industries. Meeting this growing demand has lead to proliferation of management institutions, and in many a cases the quality of education is compromised. Some popular Indian magazines and journals started ranking the Indian B-Schools intending to give information to all the stake holders involved. All these methods either use weighted average or clustering method to rank the institutes. This chapter proposes an alternative method based on efficiency analysis using Data Envelopment Analysis to rank the Indian B-Schools. The B-schools are observed over multiple periods of time, and the variations of efficiency are used to draw a conclusion about the performance of B-schools. Window analysis is used to compare the performance of B-schools over the period of time.

The MIDAS project began in 2006 as collaboration between Endesa, Sadiel, and the University of Seville. The objective of the MIDAS project is the detection of Non-Technical Losses (NTLs) on power utilities. The NTLs represent the non-billed energy due to faults or illegal manipulations in clients' facilities. Initially, research lines study the application of techniques of data mining and neural networks. After several researches, the studies are expanded to other research fields: expert systems, text mining, statistical techniques, pattern recognition, etc. These techniques have provided an automated system for detection of NTLs on company databases. This system is in the test phase, and it is applied in real cases in company databases.

Chapter 9

This chapter focuses primarily on Graphical Evaluation and Review Technique (GERT), one of the intriguing techniques used for network-based management. It is a stochastic network technique and has many advantages over the conventional Critical Path Method (CPM) and Programme Evaluation and Review Techniques used for project management. The formulation of the GERT network for linear situation can be development by analytical techniques (such as signal flow graph theory); thus for a non-linear and other complex conditions, the Q-GERT (included Queueing Concepts) is used. To reinforce the importance of GERT and Q-GERT, a firm study is carried out on the limitations of the CPM and PERT. Thus, a solid comparison of GERT network with the CPM and PERT network is done not only to emphasize the applicability of the network but also to validate of the network. The scheduling of concrete formwork systems are considered for the comparison.

Section 3
Distributed Computing and Network Management

Chapter 10

Distributed heterogeneous computing is being widely applied to a variety of large-size computational problems. These computational environments consist of multiple heterogeneous computing modules; these modules interact with each other to solve the problem. The load balancing problem in the Heterogeneous Distributed Computing System (HDCS) deals with allocation of tasks to computing nodes, so that computing nodes are evenly loaded. The complexity of dynamic load balancing increases with the size of HDCS and becomes difficult to solve effectively. Due to the complexity of the dynamic load balancing problem, the majority of researchers use a heuristic algorithm to obtain near optimal solutions. The authors use three different type of resource allocation heuristic techniques, namely greedy heuristic, simulated annealing, and genetic algorithm, for dynamic load balancing on HDCS. A new codification suitable to simulated annealing and the genetic algorithm has been introduced for dynamic load balancing on HDCS. This chapter demonstrates the use of the common coding scheme and iterative structure by simulated annealing and genetic algorithms for allocating the tasks among the computing nodes to minimize the makespan. The resource allocation algorithm uses sliding window techniques to select the tasks to be allocated to computing nodes in each iteration. A suitable codification for simulated annealing and genetic algorithm for dynamic load balancing strategy are explained along with implementation details. Consistent Expected Time to Compute (ETC) matrix is used to simulate the effect of the genetic algorithm-based dynamic load balancing scheme compared with first-fit, randomized heuristic, and simulated annealing.

    D. H. Manjaiah, Mangalore University, India
    P. Payaswini, Mangalore University, India

Fourth Generation wireless networking (4G network) is expected to provide global roaming across different types of wireless and mobile networks. In this environment, roaming is seamless and users are always connected to the best network. Moreover, 4G networks will be packet switched systems entirely based on the IPv6 protocol. The essentiality of Quality of Service (QoS) and the heterogeneous nature of 4G pose high demands onto the mobility management technology. Due to this, one of the most challenging research areas for the 4G network is the design of intelligent mobility management techniques that take advantage of IP-based technologies to achieve global roaming among various access technologies. In order to address the issue of heterogeneity of the networks, IEEE 802.21 working group proposed Media Independent Handover (MIH). The scope of the IEEE 802.21 MIH standard is to develop a specification that provides link layer intelligence and other related network information to upper layers to optimize handovers between heterogeneous media. The IEEE 802.21 group defines the media independent handover function that will help mobile devices to roam across heterogeneous networks and stationary devices to switch over to any of the available heterogeneous networks around it.

    Pabitra Mohan Khilar, NIT Rourkela, India

Genetic Algorithms are important techniques to solve many NP-Complete problems related to distributed computing and its application domains. Genetic algorithm-based fault diagnoses in distributed computing systems have been a feasible methodology to solve diagnosis problems recently. Distributed embedded systems consisting of sensors, actuators, processors/microcontrollers, and interconnection networks are one class of distributed computing systems that have long been used, staring from small-scale home appliances to large-scale satellite systems. Some of their applications are in safety-critical systems where occurrence of faults can result in catastrophic situations for which fault diagnosis in such systems are very important. In this chapter, different types of faults, which are likely to occur in distributed embedded systems and a GA-based methodology to solve these problems along with the performance analysis of fault diagnosis algorithm have been presented. Nevertheless, the diagnosis algorithm presented here is well suitable for general purpose distributed computing systems with appropriate modification over system and fault model. In fact, this book chapter will enable the reader not only to study various aspects of fault diagnosis techniques but will also provide insight to build robust systems to allow for continued normal service despite the occurrence of failures.

Section 4
Neural Network and Applications

Chapter 13

Paramartha Dutta, Visva-Bharati University, India
Varun Kumar Ojha, Visva-Bharati University, India

Computational Intelligence offers solution to various real life problems. Artificial Neural Network (ANN) has the capability of solving highly complex and nonlinear problems. The present chapter demonstrates the application of these tools to provide solutions to the manhole gas detection problem. Manhole, the access point across sewer pipeline system, contains various toxic and explosive gases. Hence, predetermination of these gases before accessing manholes is becoming imperative. The problem is treated as a pattern recognition problem. ANN, devised for solving this problem, is trained using a supervised learning algorithm. The conjugate gradient method is used as an alternative of back propagation neural network learning algorithm for training of the ANN. The chapter offers comprehensive performance analysis of the learning algorithm used for the training of ANN followed by discussion on the methods of presenting the system result. The authors discuss different variants of Conjugate Gradient and propose two new variants of it.

Chapter 14

Raja Das, VIT University, India
M. K. Pradhan, Maulana Azad National Institute of Technology, India

The objective of the chapter is to present the application of Artificial Neural Network (ANN) modelling of the Electrical Discharge Machining (EDM) process. It establishes the best ANN model by comparing the prediction from different models under the effect of process parameters. In EDM, the motivation is frequently to get better Material Removal Rate (MRR) with fulfilling better surface quality of machined components. The vital requirements are as small a radial overcut with minimal tool wear rate. The quality of a machined surface is very important to fulfilling the growing demands of higher component performance, durability, and reliability. To improve the reliability of the machine component, it is necessary to have in depth knowledge of the effect of parameters on the aforesaid responses of the components. An extensive chain of experiments has been conducted over a wide range of input parameters, using the full factorial design. More than 150 experiments have been conducted on AISI D2 work piece materials using copper electrodes to get the data for training and testing. The additional experiments were obtained to validate the model predictions. The performance of three neural network models is discussed in the evaluation of the generalization ability of the trained neural network. It was observed that the artificial neural network models could predict the process performance with reasonable accuracy, under varying machining conditions.

Chapter 15

Neural Network Model to Estimate and Predict Cell Mass Concentration in Lipase
David K. Daniel, VIT University, India
Vikramaditya Bhandari, Shasun Pharma Solutions Limited, UK

Lipase is an industrially important enzyme with major use in food industries. The demand of lipase
is increasing every year. An online prediction of cell mass concentration is of great value in real time
process involving the production of lipase. In the current work, the use of a back-propagation multi-
layer neural network to predict cell mass during lipase production by Rhizopus delemar NRRL 1472 is
targeted. Network training data with respect to time is generated by carrying out experiments in laboratory. The fungus is grown in erlenmeyer flasks at initial pH of 5.6, temperature of 30°C, and at 150 rpm.
During the experiments, readings for cell mass growth are collected in specific period of time. By the
training data, an artificial neural network model programmed in MATLAB for Windows is trained and
used for prediction of cell mass. The Levenberg-Marquardt algorithm with back-propagation is used in
the network to get the optimized weights. The optimum network configuration with different activation
function and the number of nodes in the hidden layer are identified by trial and error method. Sigmoid
unipolar activation function is 2-5-1, whereas logarithmoid and sigmoid bipolar is 2-3-1. These are
chosen according to the values of Sum of Square of Errors (SSE), Root Mean Square (RMS) training
and testing. The sigmoid unipolar activation function gives a good fit for estimated value with network
configuration 2-5-1, which could be used for generalization.

Chapter 16

Prediction of Structural and Functional Aspects of Protein: In-Silico Approach
Arun G. Ingale, North Maharashtra University, India

To predict the structure of protein from a primary amino acid sequence is computationally difficult. An
investigation of the methods and algorithms used to predict protein structure and a thorough knowledge
of the function and structure of proteins are critical for the advancement of biology and the life sciences
as well as the development of better drugs, higher-yield crops, and even synthetic bio-fuels. To that end,
this chapter sheds light on the methods used for protein structure prediction. This chapter covers the
applications of modeled protein structures and unravels the relationship between pure sequence information and three-dimensional structure, which continues to be one of the greatest challenges in molecular
biology. With this resource, it presents an all-encompassing examination of the problems, methods,
tools, servers, databases, and applications of protein structure prediction, giving unique insight into the
future applications of the modeled protein structures. In this chapter, current protein structure prediction
methods are reviewed for a milieu on structure prediction, the prediction of structural fundamentals,
tertiary structure prediction, and functional imminent. The basic ideas and advances of these directions
are discussed in detail.

Preface

The vast amount of data collected by different organizations all over the world across a wide variety of fields today has no utility unless these are analyzed to get useful information. This necessitates the development of techniques that can be used to facilitate the process of analysis. The development of powerful computers is a boon to implement these techniques leading to automated systems. On the contrary, security is of paramount importance with network proliferation through wired, wireless, and mobile computing. Therefore, security is a foremost goal for many real life and software applications, especially those that involve network interactions at different levels of various reference models. In addition, other security issues with the technology in use need to be addressed too. A short time ago, security attacks were made against various organizations such as Sony, Facebook, Twitter, Apple, etc. With all such growing attacks, it is very important to make sure that we are safe.

Our intention in editing this book is to offer concepts and various techniques that are employed in secure computing, Internet services, management infrastructure, and project and knowledge management in a precise and clear manner to the research community. In editing the book, our attempt is to provide frontier advancements in secure computing, distributed systems, and Internet services, as well as the conceptual basis required to achieve in depth knowledge in the field of computer science and information technology. This book will comprise the latest research from prominent researchers from all over the world. Since the book covers case study-based research findings, it can be quite relevant to researchers, university academics, computing professionals, and probing university students. In addition, it will help those researchers who have interest in this field to keep insight into different concepts and their importance for applications in real life. This has been done to make the edited book more flexible and to stimulate further interest in topics.

The topics to be discussed are recent work and research findings in the areas of secure computing, Internet services, granular computing and knowledge representation, data mining, project and knowledge management infrastructure, artificial neural network, and their applications. Hybrid intelligent computing techniques and real life applications that stress the basic knowledge on secure computing techniques, Internet services, and their development stages to present day technology is also discussed in different parts of the edited book. These parts capture a number of applications of secure computing. The challenges faced and solutions proposed by different researchers in this area are discussed.

Data mining automates the process of finding predictive information in large databases. Questions that traditionally required extensive hands-on analysis can now be answered directly from the data. A typical example of a predictive problem is targeted marketing. Data mining uses data on past promotional mailings to identify the targets most likely to maximize return on investment in future mailings. The most commonly used techniques in data mining such as artificial neural network, privacy preservation, genetic algorithm, data envelopment analysis, clustering techniques, evolutionary algorithms, and rule induction will be stressed.

The book is comprised of four sections. The first section is an attempt to provide an insight on data mining and security. It presents a variety of real life applications based on data mining and privacy. The second section discusses project and knowledge management infrastructure, whereas section three provides information on distributed computing and network management. The final section discusses protein structure and various applications of artificial neural networks. Each section provides the current research trends in the concerned field of study.

Granular computing is an upcoming conceptual and computing pattern of information processing. It has been strongly encouraged by the urgent need for processing practical data in an intelligent manner. Such processing is now commonly available in a humanly manageable abstract form. In other words, granular computing offers a platform to transit from the current machine-centric to human-centric approach to gather information and knowledge. Basic rough set theory introduced by Pawlak is single granular from the granular computing point of view. However, Qian et al. in two steps introduced two types of multi-granulation: the optimistic multigranulation and the pessimistic multigranulation. Chapter 1 discusses various topological and algebraic properties of these two types of multigranular rough sets. The algebraic properties of the two basic multigranular rough sets shed light on the reduction of multigranulation to single granulation and the comparison of various types of multigranular combinations. Many real life examples are provided to illustrate the multigranular approach. In addition, discussions have been made on extensions of these two basic multigranular rough set models, like the Covering-Based Multigranular Rough Sets (CBMGRS) and the Neighborhood-Based Multigranular Rough Sets (NMGRS).

During the last few decades, there had been a considerable growth of interest in pattern recognition in the field of robotics. An application of pattern recognition in robotics includes mobile and service robots. Chapter 2 discusses the application of pattern recognition in identification of intended motion from myoelectric signals in the application of robotics. Various techniques used in pattern recognition have been discussed in respect to myoelectric control of a prosthetic hand. The pattern recognition techniques that have been used in identifying the intended limb motions of the subject are successfully implemented through the computer-based actuation of the drive as well as digital signal controller-based drive. Further, EEG-based brain controlled robots are being developed that necessitate the application of pattern recognition in order to support disabled people in daily activities.

Information technology revolution has brought drastic change in the way data is collected or generated for decision mining. The accumulated data has no relevance unless it provides certain useful information pertaining to the interest of an organization. The real challenge lies in converting high dimensional data into knowledge and to use this knowledge for the development of organization. On the other hand, hiding sensitive information of an organization is a major concern to provide privacy of an organization. Chapter 3 discusses various privacy preservation techniques that are generally employed in an information system to safeguard the organizational data. It also discusses an algorithm to hide sensitive fuzzy association rules in a quantitative information system after reducing superfluous attributes from the information system. Finally, a case study is presented to illustrate the fuzzy association rule-hiding algorithm.

Extracting knowledge from high-dimensional databases is a tedious task. As real world databases consist of irrelevant features, missing values, and redundancy, it further aggravates the situation. More often, conclusions drawn from such databases may not be dependable. In order to deal with such issues, a CABS framework is developed and implemented in chapter 4. The methodology retrieves effective and efficient clusters from high-dimensional human behavior datasets for school children in the US.

The techniques used here are the feature selection technique and hierarchical agglomerative clustering technique to discover clusters of vivid shape and size to retrieve knowledge from large databases. Further, the current framework is implemented, and it has been observed that the proposed framework is highly efficient to discover hidden and implicit knowledge from large databases due to its accessibility to handle and discover clusters of variant shapes.

Intrusion Detection and Prevention Systems (IDPS) are security systems that are used to detect and prevent security threats to computer systems and computer networks. The inadequacy of Intrusion Prevention Systems (IPS) to prevent suspicious threats led to the development of Intelligent Intrusion Prevention Systems (IIPS), which refer to any technology or strategy that allows us to detect and prevent the attempted compromise of our systems and information, and as before, preserve the CIA (Confidentiality, Integrity, and Availability) of the information and infrastructures. Chapter 5 discusses these concepts in detail and their advantages and disadvantages are focused. In addition, the results of simulation are presented for an efficient intrusion detection and prevention system by combining online detection and offline data mining.

Chapter 6 introduces the framework and causal model of organizational culture, organizational learning, knowledge management, and job satisfaction. It argues that dimensions of organizational culture, organizational learning, and knowledge management have mediated positive effect on job satisfaction.

Growing markets and institutions of several companies have underlined the importance of management education at the higher education level. Management education in India has also undergone a change in order to meet the need of industry. Meeting this growing demand has led to proliferation of management institutions, and in many cases, the quality of education is compromised. Chapter 7 analyzes data envelopment analysis technique for ranking these management institutions. This method and the subsequent analysis made over a period of time is supposed to provide useful information to aspirants for taking admission into management schools.

The Non-Technical Losses (NTLs) in power utilities are defined as any consumed energy or service that is not billed because of measurement equipment failure or ill-intentioned and fraudulent manipulation of said equipment. Chapter 8 describes advances developed for the MIDAS project. It proposes a framework to analyze all information available about customers by using the concepts of data mining, text mining, expert systems, statistical techniques, regression techniques, etc.

The Graphical Evaluation Review Technique (GERT) network, a stochastic network analysis technique that allows for conditional and the probabilistic treatment of the logical relationships between the project's activities following a randomly determined sequence of observations appears to be an excellent launching pad for carrying out the data visualization and categorization of data and modeling and analysis of the complex networks. Chapter 9 discusses this technique in detail with its superiority over other early existing techniques.

The load balancing problem on Heterogeneous Distributed Computing Systems (HDCS) deals with allocation of tasks to computing nodes, so that computing nodes are evenly loaded. In chapter 10, a suitable codification for simulated annealing and genetic algorithm for dynamic load balancing strategy is introduced, and the effect of genetic algorithm-based dynamic load balancing scheme has been compared with first-fit, randomized heuristic, and simulated annealing.

A 4G system is expected to provide a comprehensive and secure all-IP-based solution where users are allowed to roam between different types of access networks. It will have broader bandwidth, higher data rate, and smoother and quicker handoff. 4G services will be end-to-end quality of service, high security, available at anytime, anywhere with seamless mobility, affordable cost, and one billing. It is about convergence of networks and technologies, applications and of services, to offer a personalized and pervasive network to the users. The 4G network will be an umbrella of technologies. In chapter 11, the characteristics, objectives, key components, challenges and issues, overview of mobility management, mobility management at different layers, requirements for mobility management, and role of mobile IPv6 in 4G Mobility Management of 4G-Networks are critically analyzed and presented.

Fault diagnosis is another important problem in distributed computing systems to locate the faulty node. This is required to identify a set of fault free nodes on which normal function of distributed systems can be successfully executed. As the results of applications are vital and sometimes safety critical, reliable results will assert in providing correct decision. As the distributed embedded systems become smarter by including multiple electronic components, they become more complex. Chapter 12 discusses the design and implementation of fault diagnosis algorithms for distributed embedded systems. The chapter also presents the fundamentals of fault diagnosis and distributed embedded systems. Emphasis is given on the requirement, design, and implementation perspectives of fault diagnosis algorithms for detecting and diagnosing different faults in important components in safety-critical distributed embedded systems.

Manholes, the access points across sewer pipeline systems, contain various toxic and explosive gases. Hence, predetermination of these gases is imperative. The problem is treated as a pattern recognition problem. Chapter 13 offers comprehensive performance analysis of the learning algorithm used for the training of artificial neural network followed by discussion on the methods of presenting system result, and demonstrates the application of these tools to provide solutions to the manhole gas detection problem.

The Artificial Neural Network (ANN) is one of the earliest models to capture uncertainty in data. Its origin is to develop a model as close to the human brain as possible so that the functioning of the human brain can be realized through machine. Numerous applications of this model to different real life situations have been obtained over the years. More importantly, it can perform intelligently. Chapter 14 highlighted an application of artificial neural networks to the modeling of the Electrical Discharge Machining (EDM) process.

Within the area of process engineering, process design and simulation, process supervision, control, estimation, process fault detection, and diagnosis rely on the effective processing of unpredictable and imprecise information. The fundamental behavior of these processes can be understood by modeling that proves useful for online process control and optimization. Artificial neural networks provide a potential solution strategy for problems, which require complex data analysis. Chapter 15 generates data by carrying out batch experiments for various initial concentrations in shake flasks. These data were used to construct an optimum neural network model as well as to train and test the network. Feed forward neural network with three layers were used. In addition, four activation functions were used to select best suitable activation function. The prediction of the neural network was compared by changing the hidden nodes for different activation functions. By trial and error method, the optimized network with optimized nodes and activation function was identified. The results obtained on application of neural network for prediction of cell mass growth for lipase production were encouraging. The success depends largely on good, representative data for training and statistical validation. The results clearly showed that the neural network computation is well suited for prediction and estimation in industrial scale lipase production.

A thorough knowledge of the function and structure of proteins is critical for the advancement of biology and the life sciences as well as the development of better drugs, higher-yield crops, and even synthetic bio-fuels. Chapter 16 discusses on examination of the problems, methods, tools, servers, databases, and applications of protein structure prediction and provides some insight into the future applications of the modeled protein structures.

We made an effort to keep the book reader-friendly. By a problem solving approach, we mean that researchers learn the material through real life examples that provide the motivation behind the concepts and their relations to real world problems. At the same time, readers must discover a solution for the non-trivial aspect of the solution. We trust and hope that the book will help readers to further carryout their research in different directions.

B. K. Tripathy
VIT University, India

D. P. Acharjya
VIT University, India

Acknowledgment

While writing, the contributors referred to several books and journals; we take this opportunity to thank all those authors and publishers. In addition, we are thankful to VIT University, India, for providing facilities to complete this project. We are extremely thankful to the editorial board and reviewers for their support during the process of evaluation. Last but not least, we thank the production team of IGI Global for encouraging us and extending their cooperation and help in timely completion of this edited book.

B. K. Tripathy
VIT University, India

D. P. Acharjya
VIT University, India

Section 1
Data Mining and Security

Chapter 1
Multi–Granular Computing through Rough Sets

B. K. Tripathy
VIT University, India

ABSTRACT

Granular Computing has emerged as a framework in which information granules are represented and manipulated by intelligent systems. Granular Computing forms a unified conceptual and computing platform. Rough set theory put forth by Pawlak is based upon single equivalence relation taken at a time. Therefore, from a granular computing point of view, it is single granular computing. In 2006, Qiang et al. introduced a multi-granular computing using rough set, which was called optimistic multigranular rough sets after the introduction of another type of multigranular computing using rough sets called pessimistic multigranular rough sets being introduced by them in 2010. Since then, several properties of multigranulations have been studied. In addition, these basic notions on multigranular rough sets have been introduced. Some of these, called the Neighborhood-Based Multigranular Rough Sets (NMGRS) and the Covering-Based Multigranular Rough Sets (CBMGRS), have been added recently. In this chapter, the authors discuss all these topics on multigranular computing and suggest some problems for further study.

INTRODUCTION

Granular computing is an upcoming conceptual and computing pattern of information processing. It has been strongly encouraged by the urgent need for processing practical data in an intelligent manner (Pedrycz, 2007; Pedrycz et al, 2002, Yao et al, 2013). Such processing need is now commonly available in vast quantities into a humanly manageable abstract knowledge. In other words, granular computing offers a platform to transit from the current machine-centric to human-centric approach to gather information and knowledge. Granular computing as opposed to numeric computing is knowledge oriented. Numeric computing is data oriented. The origin of granular computing is in the context of fuzzy sets (Zadeh, 1965). But,

DOI: 10.4018/978-1-4666-4940-8.ch001

there are many other theories like interval analysis, rough set theory and probabilistic approach, which follow this approach.

Framing a hierarchical model for a given complex problem is the basic task of granular computing. The core components of granular computing include granules, a web of granules and granular structures. In general, a complex system was usually comprised of many interconnected and interactive modules. For such system each module can be considered as a granule and therefore it resulted with group of granules as a representation for the entire complex system. The description about the individual modules can be obtained from the specific granule whereas the web of granules provides us a clear and complete picture about the complex system. We treat granules as a primitive idea of granular computing. From this core idea other ideas could be derived since granules were an abstract notion. In planning, a granule can be a sub-plan.

In programming, a granule can be a program module. Generally speaking, information granules are collections of entities that usually arranged together due to their similarity, functional or physical adjacency, indistinguishability etc.., or in other words information granulation involves partitioning a class of objects into granules, with a granule being a bunch of objects which are drawn together by indistinguishability, similarity or functionality.

It encourages an approach to data that recognizes and makes use of the knowledge present in data at various levels. It includes all methods which provide flexibility and adaptability in the resolution at which knowledge or information is extracted and represented. A granule can be either simple or composite. A simple granule either cannot be further decomposed or formed by other granules, where as a composite granule consists of group of its interconnected and interacting granules. A granule is interconnected to other granules by its dual roles. A granule can be considered as an entire one when it is viewed as a part of another

granule. A granule is considered to be a group of interconnected and interacting granules when some other granules are viewed as its parts. We need to differentiate granules by a minimum set of properties. It includes

- Internal properties of a granule
- External properties of a granule
- Emergent properties of a granule
- Contextual properties of a granule

The internal properties of a granule generally deal with its organizational structures, its relationships and about the interaction among the elements (Yao, 2008). The external properties of a granule reveal its interaction with other granules (Yao, 2008). The emergent properties of a granule may be viewed as one type of external property (Yao, 2008). In most of the cases, both the internal and external properties of a granule were found to have certain dynamic changes with its related environment. The contextual properties of a granule show its relative existence in a particular environment (Yao, 2008). All the above said types of properties together give us a better understanding towards the notion of granule (Yao, 2008). The knowledge obtained based on granules although approximate but may be good enough for practical uses.

DIFFERENT VIEWS OF GRANULAR COMPUTING

There are several views of granular computing. These are

- Philosophical perspective of granular computing or structured thinking
- Methodological perspective of granular computing or structured problem solving
- Computational perspective of granular computing or structured information processing

In the following sections we discuss on these views in detail.

GRANULAR STRUCTURE

The granular structure not only integrates the above said components but also represents the real world at multiple levels of granularity. All are components are unified in such a way that each view supports the other two perspectives. In the philosophical perspective, granular computing deals with structured thinking where it attempts to extract and formalize human thinking (Yao, 2007; Yao, 2008). It concerns about structured problem solving and also aimed at study of methods and techniques for systematic problem solving.

STRUCTURED THINKING

Granular computing as structured thinking combines two the traditional reductionist thinking and more recent systems thinking. These two were usually viewed as two complementary philosophical views. It stresses the importance of thoughtful effects in thinking with hierarchical structures. In the methodological perspective, granular computing concerns structured problem solving. It wants to study methods and techniques for systematic problem solving (Yao, 2007; Yao, 2008).

STRUCTURED PROBLEM SOLVING

Structured thinking leads to structured problem solving and hence the process of understanding real world problem in terms of multilevel and multi-view representations has become more valuable. Such a perception plays an important role in problem solving. Granular computing is a structured problem solving guided by structured thinking.

The effectiveness of granular computing can be achieved by following the structured problem solving method and techniques. A convincing way to show such effectiveness is to present a set of principles and to demonstrate the working of these principles in real world applications. The following are such principles

- The principle of multilevel granularity
- The principle of focused effort
- The principle of granularity conversion

The first principle emphasizes the importance of prototyping in terms of hierarchical structures. Once such structures are obtained the second principle calls for attention on the focal point at a particular level of problem solving. The last third principle links the different stages in this process.

Even though the principles of granular computing were named differently in different principles they are indeed the same at a more abstract level. The computational view deals with structured information processing and it usually addresses the problems of information processing in the form of machines, abstract etc (Yao, 2007; Yao, 2008). More importance on granular structures was often provided by the granular computing and hence granular computing leads to structured solutions to real world problems.

STRUCTURED INFORMATION PROCESSING

Granular computing works with a pyramid consisting of different sized information granules in the information processing paradigm (Yao, 2007). This structured information processing is a necessary feature of any knowledge intensive system and also structured information processing is a stepwise refinement process. Two core ideas of structured information processing are representation and process (Yao, 2008). Here representation is a formal system that makes certain explicit entities and a specification of how the system does it. The result is called as a description of the entity in the representation. A process can be interpreted as set of procedures for carrying out information processing tasks. The effectiveness of processes was usually determined by the representation of granules. A representation of granules must capture their essential features to prove such effectiveness. The processes of granular computing may be broadly classified into two categories namely granulation and computation with granules. Granulation processes involve the construction of the core building block and structures namely granules, levels and hierarchies. Computation processes systematically look at the granular structures. This involves two way communications in the hierarchy level as well as switching between levels. Out of two levels, at a higher level some form of approximate, partial or a schematic solution would be obtained and at a detailed lower level more precise and complete solution would be obtained. This process of obtaining complete solution in more than one level proves that the structured information processing is a stepwise refinement process.

By emphasizing on granular structures, granular computing leads to structured solutions which further leads to real-world problems. The ability of granular computing can be fully appreciated from the philosophical perspective as structured thinking, from the methodological perspective as structured problem solving and from the computational perspective as structured information processing (Yao, 2007; Yao, 2008).

ROUGH SETS AND GRANULAR COMPUTING

Most of the datasets available now a day have impreciseness inherent in them. To represent such data many imprecise models have been put forth. One of the latest additions to this list of imprecise models is the notion of rough sets

introduced in (Pawlak, 1982). The basic rough set model introduced by Pawlak was dependent upon the notion of equivalence relations due to mathematical reasons as they induce a partition or classification on the universe and the rough set philosophy is based on the observation that human knowledge depends upon the capability of human beings to classify objects.

Let U be a universe of discourse and R be an equivalence relation over U. By U/R we denote the family of all equivalence classes of R, referred to as categories or concepts of R and the equivalence class of an element $x \in U$ is denoted by $[x]_R$. By a knowledge base, we understand a relational system $K = (U, P)$, where U is as above and P is a family of equivalence relations over U. For any subset $Q (\neq \phi) \subseteq P$, the intersection of all equivalence relations in Q is denoted by IND(Q) and is called the indiscernibility relation over Q. Given any $X \subseteq U$ and $R \in IND (K)$, we associate two subsets, $\underline{R}X = \left\{ x \in U \, / \, [x]_R \subseteq X \right\}$ and $\overline{R}X = \{ x \, / \, [x]_R \cap X \neq \phi \}$, called the R-lower and R-upper approximations of X respectively. The R-boundary of X is denoted by $BN_R(X)$ and is given by $BN_R\left(X\right) = \overline{R}X - \underline{R}X$. The elements of $\underline{R}X$ are those elements of U, which can certainly be classified as elements of X, and the elements of $\overline{R}X$ are those elements of U, which can possibly be classified as elements of X, employing knowledge of R. We say that X is rough (Pawlak, 1982; Pawlak, 1991) with respect to R if and only if $\underline{R}X \neq \overline{R}X$, equivalently $BN_R\left(X\right) \neq \phi$. X is said to be R-definable if and only if $\underline{R}X = \overline{R}X$ or $BN_R(X) = \phi$.

The equivalence classes induced by an equivalence relation on a universe are called the granules of knowledge represented by the relation. Since the early model was depending upon a single equivalence relation taken at a time, from the point of view of granular computing it is called single granulation. However, this notion was extended in (Qian et al, 2006) when they introduced the concept of multigranulation, when they took two or more equivalence relations simultaneously to define granulation of objects in a universe. Later on they introduced another similar concept, which they called the pessimistic multigranulation (Qian et al, 2010) and the first one was then renamed as the optimistic multigranulation.

Several properties of the two types of multigranulations have been established which are similar to the corresponding properties of the single granulation case. Also, the concept of multigranulation has been extended to some generalised models called the neighbourhood based multigranulation (NMGRS) (Lin et al, 2011) and the covering based multigranulation (CBMGRS) (Liu et al, 2013). In this chapter we shall discuss on all these models, their properties and examples for illustration. In the next section we start with the basic rough set model on single granulation.

MULTIGRANULATION

In order to more widely apply the rough set theory in practical applications Qian et al. extended Pawlak's single granulation rough set model to a multigranulation rough set model where the set approximations are defined by multiple equivalence relation on the universe.

There are two types of multigranulations have been found in literature. After the introduction of the second one these are now called as optimistic multigranulation (first one) and pessimistic multigranulation (second one). The two types are defined as follows:

Definition 1: *Let $K = (U, \mathbf{R})$ be knowledge base, $\mathbf{R}$ be a family of equivalence relations, $X \subseteq U$ and $R, S \in \mathbf{R}$. We define the optimistic multigranular (Qian et al, 2006) lower approximation and optimistic multigranular upper approximation of X with respect to R and S in U as*

$$\underline{R + S}\, X = \{\, x \mid [x]_R \subseteq X \text{ or } [x]_S \subseteq X \} \qquad (1)$$

and

$$\overline{R + S}\, X = \; \sim (\underline{R + S}(\sim X)). \qquad (2)$$

Definition 2: *Let $K = (U, \mathbf{R})$ be a knowledge base, $\mathbf{R}$ be a family of equivalence relations, $X \subseteq U$ and $R, S \in \mathbf{R}$. We define the pessimistic multigranular (Qian et al, 2010) lower approximation and pessimistic multigranular upper approximation of X with respect to R and S in U as*

$$\underline{R * S}\, X = \{\, x \mid [x]_R \subseteq X \text{ and } [x]_S \subseteq X \} \qquad (3)$$

and

$$\overline{R * S}\, X = \; \sim (\underline{R * S}(\sim X)). \qquad (4)$$

REAL LIFE APPLICATION OF MULTIGRANULAR ROUGH SETS

When we say about the practical view of multigranulation rough sets then the equivalence relations must be with finer and finer detail in the form of equivalence classes.

Example 1

Let us consider all the cattle in a locality as our Universe named as U. We define an equivalence relation R over C by xRy if and only if x and y are cattle of same kind. Let S be another equivalence relation and defined as xSy if and only if x and y are of the same size.

U = {Cow, Buffalo, Goat, Sheep, Bullock}

We have two equivalence classes in the first equivalence relation as defined below:

U/R = {{Cow, Buffalo, Bullock}, {Goat, Sheep}}

As per the second equivalence relation we get three equivalence classes as

U / S = {Small, Middle, Large}.

These are defined as Large = {Buffalo, Bullock}, Middle = {Cow} and Small = {Goat, Sheep}.

Let us arbitrarily take X = {Cow, Bullock}

Then for any subset X of the cattle in the society, we have

$\underline{R + S}X$ = It is the set of cattle whose category is completely in X or all the cattle of its size are contained in X.

$\underline{R * S}X$ = It is the set of cattle whose category is completely in X and all the cattle of its size are contained in X.

$\overline{R + S}X$ = It is the set of cattle whose category has nonempty intersection with X or whose size has nonempty intersection with X.

$\overline{R * S}X$ = It is the set of cattle whose category has nonempty intersection with X and whose size has nonempty intersection with X.

$\underline{R + S}X = \phi$ or {Cow} = {Cow}

$\overline{R + S}(X) = \sim (\underline{R + S}(\sim X))$

　　　　$= \sim$ (Goat, Sheep) = {Cow, Buffalo, Bullock}

$\underline{R * S}X = \phi$ and {Cow} = {ϕ}

$\overline{R * S}(X) = \sim (\underline{R * S}(\sim X))$

　　　　$= \sim$ (Goat, Sheep) = {Cow, Buffalo, Bullock}

Example 2

Let us consider the example of toys given by Pawlak (Pawlak, 1991). Here, U = $\{x_1, x_2, x_3, x_4, x_5, x_6, x_7, x_8\}$ be a universe of toys with three equivalence relations R, S and T representing "same colour as", "same shape as" and "same size as" be defined by the equivalence classes $\{\{x_1, x_3, x_7\}, \{x_2, x_4\}, \{x_5, x_6, x_8\}\}$, $\{\{x_1, x_5\}, \{x_2, x_6\}, \{x_3, x_4, x_7, x_8\}\}$ and

$\{\{x_2, x_7, x_8\}, \{x_1, x_3, x_4, x_5, x_6\}\}$ respectively over U. Taking $X = \{x_2, x_3, x_4, x_5, x_6\}$, we find that

$\underline{R + S}X = \{x_2, x_4, x_6\}$ = Set of elements of U all of whose colour toys are in X or all of whose shape toys are in X.

$\overline{R + S}X = U$ = Set of elements of U atleast one of the same colour toys is in X or atleast one of the same shape toys is in X.

$\underline{R * S}X = \phi$ = Set of elements of U all of whose colour toys and all of whose shape toys are in X.

$\overline{R * S}X = U$ = Set of elements of U atleast one of whose colour toys and atleast one of whose shape toys is in X.

Similarly,

$\underline{R + S + T}X = \{x_2, x_4, x_6\}, \overline{R + S + T}X = U.$

$\underline{R * S * T}X = \phi, \overline{R * S * T}X = U.$

TOPOLOGICAL PROPERTIES OF ROUGH SETS

Topological properties deal with the structure of sets as a whole. In this section we shall deal with such properties of multigranular rough sets. Before doing so we discuss on topological properties of basic rough sets in the next section.

TOPOLOGICAL PROPERTIES OF BASIC ROUGH SETS

An interesting characterization of rough sets was introduced by Pawlak, namely the topological characterization or classification of rough sets (Pawlak, 1983; Pawlak, 1991). This topological characterization is found to be an additional one to the characterization of rough sets by means of numerical values in the form of accuracy coefficients. While differentiating the topological characterization and accuracy coefficient Pawlak expressed that "The accuracy coefficient expresses how large the boundary region of the set is, but says nothing about the structure of the boundary, whereas the topological classification of rough sets gives no information about the size of the boundary region but provides us with some insight as to how the boundary region is structured" (Pawlak, 1991). In general, topological properties of sets deal with the internal structures of sets. The following four types were defined by the Pawlak. Basing upon the topological structure of lower and upper approximations, a rough set can be classified into following four classes:

Type 1: If $\underline{R}X \neq \phi$ and $\overline{R}X \neq U$, then we say that X is roughly R-definable. (5)

Type 2: If $\underline{R}X = \phi$ and $\overline{R}X \neq U$, then we say that X is internally R-undefinable. (6)

Type 3: If $\underline{R}X \neq \phi$ and $\overline{R}X = U$, then we say that X is externally R-undefinable. (7)

Type 4: If $\underline{R}X \neq \phi$ and $\overline{R}X = U$, then we say that X is totally R-undefinable. (8)

The physical interpretations for these four types of rough sets were provided in (Pawlak, 1991). The union and intersection of rough sets have importance from the point of view of distribution of knowledge and common knowledge respectively. In this context, the study of types of union and intersection of different types of rough sets has enough significance. For example, if two rough sets are roughly R-definable (Type 1), then basing upon the available information, there are some objects in the universe which can be positively classified as belonging to each of these sets. Now, one would like to know about elements in the universe which can be positively classified to be in both. If the intersection is of Type 1/Type 3, then one can obviously conclude this. On the contrary, if the intersection is of Type 2/Type 4, then no such element exists. Similarly, for each of such sets there are some other elements which can be negatively classified; that is, being outside these sets with the available information. One may be interested to know about the existence of negatively classified elements with respect to the union of these sets. If the type of union is Type 1/Type 2, then we are sure of such elements. On the other hand, if it is of Type 3/Type 4 no such elements exist. Basing upon these observations, the properties of union, intersection and complement of different types of rough sets and their extensions were obtained in (Tripathy et al, 2010; Tripathy et al,2012a, Tripathy et al, 2012b; Tripathy et al, 2013). In the next subsection we shall present the extensions of all these results to the setting of multigranular rough sets.

Incomplete rough set model based on multi-granulations was introduced in (Qian et al, 2007) by taking multiple tolerance relations instead of multiple equivalence relations. Several fundamental properties of these types of rough sets have been studied (Qian et al, 2006; Qian et al, 2007; Qian et al, 2010).

TOPOLOGICAL PROPERTIES OF MULTIGRANULAR ROUGH SETS

The topological characterisations for basic rough sets have been extended to the setting of multigranular rough sets and their properties have been studied (Tripathy et al, 2012a, Tripathy et al, 2012b; Tripathy et al, 2013).

Next, we present the definitions of types of multigranular rough sets. These definitions are in the expected lines.

TYPES OF OPTIMISTIC MULTIGRANULAR ROUGH SETS

Let U be a universal set and R and S be two equivalence relations over U. Then the four types of optimistic multigranular rough sets are defined as follows. Here, we neither mention that these are for multigranulation nor that these are for optimistic case as these are evident from the definition itself.

Type-1: If $\underline{R+S}X \neq \phi$ and $\overline{R+S}X \neq U$ then we say that X is roughly R+S-definable.

(9)

Type-2: If $\underline{R+S}X = \phi$ and $\overline{R+S}X \neq U$ then we say that X is internally R+S- definable.

(10)

Type-3: If $\underline{R+S}X \neq \phi$ and $\overline{R+S}X = U$ then we say that X is externally R+S-definable.

(11)

Type-4: If $\underline{R+S}X = \phi$ and $\overline{R+S}X = U$ then we say that X is totally R+S-definable. (12)

Example 3

In this section we provide some examples of the four types of optimistic multigranular rough sets. Let us take U $= \{e_1, e_2, e_3, e_4, e_5, e_6, e_7, e_8\}$. We define two granulations P and Q on U as follows.

$U/P = \{\{e_1, e_2, e_7\}, \{e_4, e_5\}, \{e_3, e_6, e_8\}\}$ and $U/Q = \{\{e_2, e_3, e_4, e_5\}, \{e_1, e_7, e_8\}, \{e_6\}\}$. Then taking $X = \{e_4, e_5\}$, we have

$\sim X = \{e_1, e_2, e_3, e_6, e_7, e_8\}$. So that $\underline{P+Q}(X) = \{e_4, e_5\} \neq \phi$ and $\overline{P+Q}(X) = \{e_4, e_5\} \neq$ U. Hence, X is of type-1.

Taking

$X = \{e_1\}, \underline{P+Q}(X) = \phi$ and $\overline{P+Q}(X) = \{e_1\} \neq U$

So, X is of type-2.
Taking

$$X = \{e_1, e_4, e_5, e_6\}, \underline{P+Q}(X) = \{e_4, e_5\} \neq \phi$$
$$and \ \overline{P+Q}(X) = U.$$

So, X is of type-3.
Finally, taking

$X = \{e_1, e_3, e_8\}, we\ have \underline{P+Q}(X) = \phi\ and\ \overline{P+Q}(X) = U$

So, X is of type-4.

TYPES OF COMPLEMENT FOR OPTIMISTIC MULTIGRANULAR ROUGH SETS

In Table 1 we provide the types of the complement of a set with respect to the types of the original set under optimistic multigranulation.

TYPES OF UNION OF TWO OPTIMISTIC MULTIGRANULAR ROUGH SETS

In Table 2 we provide the types of union of two optimistic multigranular rough sets from the types of the individual ones.

We see that the ambiguous cases can actually occur. For example, we consider the cell (1, 1).

Table 1. Table for types of complement of an OMGRS

X	Xᶜ
T-1	T-1
T-2	T-3
T-3	T-2
T-4	T-4

Table 2. Table for types of union of two OMGRSs

∪		Type of Y with respect to P+Q			
Type of X with respect to P+Q		T-1	T-2	T-3	T-4
	T-1	T-1 / T-3	T-1 / T-3	T-3	T-3
	T-2	T-1 / T-3	T-1/T-2/T-3/T-4	T-3	T-3 / T-4
	T-3	T-3	T-3	T-3	T-3
	T-4	T-3	T-3 / T-4	T-3	T-3 / T-4

Taking

$$X = \{e_4, e_5\}, \text{we have } \underline{P+Q}(X) = \{e_4, e_5\} \neq \phi.$$
$$\text{Also, } \overline{P+Q}(X) = \{e_4, e_5\} \neq U.$$

So, X is of type-1.
Taking

$$Y = \{e_1, e_6\}, \underline{P+Q}(Y) = \{e_6\} \neq \phi$$
$$\text{and } \overline{P+Q}(Y) = \{e_1, e_6, e_7, e_8\} \neq U.$$

So, Y is of type-1.
Here,

$$X \cup Y = \{e_1, e_4, e_5, e_6\} \text{ and so } \overline{P+Q}(X \cup Y) = U$$
$$\text{and } \underline{P+Q}(X \cup Y) = \{e_4, e_5\} \neq \phi$$

So, $X \cup Y$ is of type-3.
Again, taking

$$X = \{e_3, e_6, e_8\}, \underline{P+Q}(X) = \{e_3, e_6, e_8\} \neq \phi$$
$$\text{and } \overline{P+Q}(X) = \{e_1, e_2, e_3, e_6, e_7, e_8\} \neq U.$$

So, X is of type-1 and taking

$$Y = \{e_6\}, \underline{P+Q}(Y) = \{e_6\} \neq \phi$$
$$\text{and } \overline{P+Q}(Y) = \{e_6\} \neq U.$$

So, Y is of type-1. But,

$$X \cup Y = \{e_3, e_6, e_8\}, \underline{P+Q}(X \cup Y) = \{e_3, e_6, e_8\} \neq \phi$$
$$\text{and } \overline{P+Q}(Y) = \{e_3, e_6, e_8\} \neq U.$$

So, $X \cup Y$ is of type-1.

TYPES OF INTERSECTION OF TWO OPTIMISTIC MULTIGRANULAR ROUGH SETS

In Table 3 we provide the types of intersection of two optimistic multigranular rough sets with respect to the types of the individual ones.

We shall show through the following example that actually ambiguities can occur in the above table. Again we consider the cell (1, 1).
Taking

$$X = \{e_1, e_2, e_6, e_8\}, \underline{P+Q}(X) = \{e_1, e_2\} \neq \phi$$
$$\text{and } \overline{P+Q}(X) = \{e_1, e_2, e_6, e_7, e_8\} \neq U.$$

So, X is of type-1.
Taking

$$Y = \{e_1, e_8\}, \underline{P+Q}(Y) = \{e_8\} \neq \phi$$
$$\text{and } \overline{P+Q}(Y) = \{e_1, e_2, e_6, e_7, e_8\} \neq U.$$

So, Y is of type-1.
But,

Table 3. Table for types of intersection of two OMGRSs

$\cap$		Type of Y with respect to P+Q			
Type of X with respect to P+Q		T-1	T-2	T-3	T-4
	T-1	T-1 / T-2	T-2	T-1/T-2	T-2
	T-2	T-2	T-2	T-2	T-2
	T-3	T-1 / T-2	T-2	T-1/T-2/T-3/T-4	T-2 / T-4
	T-4	T-2	T-2	T-2/T-4	T-2 / T-4

$X \cap Y = \{e_1, e_8\}$. So, $\underline{P+Q}(X \cap Y) = \{e_8\} \neq \phi$

$and \overline{P+Q}(X \cap Y) = \{e_1, e_2, e_7, e_8\} \neq U$

So $X \cap Y$ is of type-1.

Again, Keeping X same as above but taking

$Y = \{e_1, e_3, e_4, e_5\}, \underline{P+Q}(Y) = \{e_3, e_4, e_5\} \neq \phi$

$and \overline{P+Q}(Y) = \{e_1, e_2, e_3, e_4, e_5\} \neq U,$

Y is of type-1.
But,

$X \cap Y = \{e_1\}$. So, $\underline{P+Q}(X \cap Y) = \phi$

$and \overline{P+Q}(X \cap Y) = \{e_1\} \neq U.$

So, $X \cap Y$ is of type-2.

TYPES OF PESSIMISTIC MULTIGRANULAR ROUGH SETS

Let U be a universal set and R and S be two equivalence relations over U. Then the four types of pessimistic multigranular rough sets are defined as follows. Here, we neither mention that these are for multigranulation nor that these are for optimistic case as these are evident from the definition itself. The original notations used for pessimistic multigranular rough sets was different from the one used in this chapter. This notation is simple and also more appropriate than the notation used by Qian et al. As was done for the optimistic case, we

can define the types of pessimistic multigranular rough sets as follows:

Type-1: If $\underline{R*S}X \neq \phi \ and \ \overline{R*S}X \neq U$
then we say that X is roughly R*S-definable.

(13)

Type-2: If $\underline{R*S}X = \phi \ and \ \overline{R*S}X \neq U$
then we say that X is internally R*S- definable.

(14)

Type-3: If $\underline{R*S}X \neq \phi \ and \ \overline{R*S}X = U$
then we say that X is externally R*S-definable.

(15)

Type-4: If $\underline{R*S}X = \phi \ and \ \overline{R*S}X = U$
then we say that X is totally R*S-definable.

(16)

We note that the topological properties for the three operations of complementation, union and intersection remain same. So, avoid presenting them.

MULTIGRANULAR ROUGH SETS ON INCOMPLETE INFORMATION SYSTEMS

Rough sets on incomplete information systems were introduced in (Kryszkiewicz, 1998) and she studied their properties. Here, we define the corresponding notion for pessimistic multigranular rough sets. The definition for optimistic multi-granular rough sets is similar.

Definition 3: *An information system is a pair S = (U, A), where U is a non-empty finite set of objects, A is a non-empty finite set of attributes. For every $a \in A$, there is a mapping $a : U \rightarrow V_a$, where V_a is called the value set of a.*

If V_a contains a null value for at least one attribute $a \in A$, then S is called an incomplete information system. Otherwise, it is complete.

Definition 4: *Let S = (U, A) be an incomplete information system, $P \subseteq A$ an attribute set. We define a binary relation on U as follows*

$$\text{SIM}(P) = \{(u,v) \in U \times U \mid \forall a \in P, a(u) = a(v)$$
$$\text{or } a(u) = * \text{ or } a(v) = *\}. \tag{17}$$

In fact, SIM(P) is a tolerance relation on U, the concept of a tolerance relation has a wide variety of applications in classifications (Kryszkiewicz, 1998, Pawlak and Skowron, 2007b).

It can be shown that $\text{SIM}(P) = \bigcap_{a \in P} \text{SIM}(\{A\})$.

Let $S_p(u)$ denote the set $\{v \in U \mid (u, v) \in \text{SIM}(P)\}$. $S_p(u)$ is the maximal set of objects which are possibly indistinguishable by P with u.

Let U/SIM(P) denote the family sets $\{S_p(u) \mid u \in U\}$, the classification or the knowledge induced by P. A member $S_p(u)$ from U/SIM(P) will be called a tolerance class or an information granule. It should be noticed that the tolerance classes in U/SIM(P) do not constitute a partition of U in general. They constitute a cover of U, i.e., $S_p(u) \neq \phi$ for every $u \in U$, and $\bigcup_{u \in U} S_p(u) = U$.

Definition 5: *Let S = (U,A) be an incomplete information system, $P, Q \subseteq A$ two attribute subsets, $X \subseteq U$, we define a lower approximation of x and a upper approximation of x in U by the following*

$$(P * Q) X = \bigcup \{x \mid \text{SIM}_p(x) \subseteq X$$
$$\text{and } \text{SIM}_Q(x) \subseteq X\} \tag{18}$$

and

$$\overline{(P * Q)}(X) = ((\underline{P * Q})(X^c))^c \tag{19}$$

Definition 6: *A Multi-granulation Rough Set can be classified into following four types*

If $\underline{(P * Q)}(X) \neq \phi$ and $\overline{(P * Q)} \neq U$, then we say that X is roughly P*Q-definable $\tag{20}$

If $\underline{(P * Q)}(X) = \phi$ and $\overline{(P * Q)} \neq U$, then we say that X is internally P*Q-undefinable $\tag{21}$

If $\underline{(P * Q)}(X) \neq \phi$ and $\overline{(P * Q)} = U$, then we say that X is externally P*Q-undefinable $\tag{22}$

If $\underline{(P * Q)}(X) = \phi$ and $\overline{(P * Q)} = U$, then we say that X is totally P*Q-undefinable $\tag{23}$

We note that all the tables above remain same. Table 4 presents a table which provides the types of P*Q rough sets from their individual types.

TOPOLOGICAL PROPERTIES OF ROUGH FUZZY SETS

In this section we shall introduce the topological properties of multigranular rough fuzzy sets. We focus on incomplete information systems. First we shall introduce the notion of rough fuzzy sets.

Table 4.

P*Q	Type of X with respect to Q				
Type of X With Respect To P		T-1	T-2	T-3	T-4
	T-1	T-1	T-1	T-1	T-1
	T-2	T-1	T-2	T-1	T-2
	T-3	T-1	T-1	T-3	T-3
	T-4	T-1	T-2	T-3	T-4

Rough Fuzzy Sets

Let us denote the set of all functions from U to the unit interval [0, 1], is called the fuzzy power set of U and is denoted by F(U). It follows that $P(U) \subseteq F(U)$.

It was established in (Dubois and Prade, 1990) that the two theories of fuzzy set and rough set complement each other and they developed the hybrid models, called fuzzy rough sets and rough fuzzy sets. Rough fuzzy sets are defined as follows.

Let (U, R) be an approximation space. Then for any $Y \in F(U)$, the lower and upper approximations of Y with respect to R are given by

$$(\underline{R}Y)(y) = \inf_{x \in [y]_R} Y(x), \text{ for all } y \in U \qquad (24)$$

and

$$(\overline{R}Y)(y) = \sup_{x \in [y]_R} Y(x), \text{ for all } y \in U. \qquad (25)$$

Multi-Granular Rough Fuzzy Sets Model

The concept of multi-granular rough sets was extended to define rough fuzzy sets based on multi-granulation in (Wu and Kou, 2010) as follows:

Definition 7: *Let K = (U, R) be a knowledge base, R be a set of equivalence relations on U and A, $B \in R$. Then $\forall Y \in F(U)$, the lower approximation $\underline{A + B}(Y)$ and upper approximation $\overline{A + B}(Y)$*

of Y based equivalence relations A, B are defined as follows:

$$\forall y \in U, \underline{(A + B)}(Y)(y) = \inf_{x \in [y]_P} Y(x) \vee \inf_{x \in [y]_Q} Y(x), \qquad (26)$$

$$\forall y \in U, \overline{(A + B)}(Y)(y) = ((A + B)(Y^C))^C (y). \qquad (27)$$

If $\underline{(A + B)}(Y) = \overline{(A + B)}(Y)$ then Y is called definable, otherwise Y is called a fuzzy rough set with respect to multi-granulations A and B. The pair $(\underline{(A + B)}(Y), \overline{(A + B)}(Y))$ is called a MG-fuzzy rough set on multi-granulations A and B. It has been illustrated in [36] that fuzzy rough sets based on multi-granulations and fuzzy rough sets based on single granulations are different. The following properties of MG-fuzzy rough sets on multi-granulations were established in (Tripathy et al, 2011).

MGRS in Incomplete Information Systems

A target information system (TIS) is a five-tuple (U, ATT, I, Dec, J), where A is a nonempty, finite set of attributes, I: $U \rightarrow Dom_a$, for any $a \in ATT$ Dec is a nonempty finite set of attributes called the decision attributes, J: $Dec \rightarrow Dom_d$ for any $a \in ATT$. Here, Dom_a and Dom_d are the domains of any attribute 'a' and a decision attribute 'd' respectively.

If the value of any attribute in a TIS is unknown then such a value is represented by '*'. Regular attributes are those attributes which do not have '*' as any domain value. Otherwise, it is called incomplete.

Definition 8: *A system in which values of all attributes for all objects from U are regular (known) is called complete and is called incomplete otherwise.*

An information system is a pair S = (U, ATT, I, Dec, J) is called an incomplete target IS if values of some attributes in ATT are missing and those of all attributes in D are regular (known), where ATT is called the set of conditional attributes and D is the set of decision attributes.

Definition 9: *For an incomplete information system (U, ATT, I) and B ⊆ ATT, we define a binary relation S(B) on U as*

$$S(B) = \{(x, y) \in U \times U \mid \forall p \in B, p(x) = p(y) \text{ or } p(x) = * \text{ or } p(y) = *\}. \quad (28)$$

If the attributes B ⊆ ATT are numerical attributes, the relation S(B) is defined as:

$$S(B) = \{(x, y) \in U \times U \mid \forall p \in B, |p(x) - p(y)| \leq \alpha_p \text{ or } p(x) = * \text{ or } p(y) = *\}. \quad (29)$$

It is easy to verify that S(B) is a tolerance relation and that

$$S(B) = \bigcap_{p \in B} S(\{p\}). \quad (30)$$

We denote the set $\{y \in U \mid (x, y) \in S(B)\}$ by $S_B(x)$ and it consists of the objects which are possibly indistinguishable from x with respect to B.

Let U/S(B) = { $S_B(x) \mid x \in U$}, the set of tolerance classes induced by B, which is also called the set of information granules. This set forms a cover of U. A cover is a set of nonempty subsets of U such that their union is U.

The incomplete MGRS on two Granulation Spaces is defined as follows.

Definition 10: *Let (U, ATT, I) be an incomplete information system and A, B ⊆ ATT be two attribute subsets. Then for any V ⊆ U, the optimistic lower and upper approximations of V with respect to the two granulations A and B are defined as:*

$$\underline{(A + B)}(V) = \bigcup \{x \mid S_A(x) \subseteq V \text{ or } S_B(x) \subseteq V\} \quad (31)$$

and

$$\overline{(A + B)}(V) = ((\underline{A + B})(V^C))^C. \quad (32)$$

The rough set of V with respect to A+B is given by the pair $((\underline{A + B})(V), \overline{(A + B)}(V))$ and its boundary region or the uncertainty region, denoted by $B_{(A+B)}(V)$ is defined as

$$B_{(A+B)}(V) = \overline{(A + B)}(V) \setminus \underline{(A + B)}(V) \quad (33)$$

MGRFS in Incomplete Information Systems

In this section we generalise both the MGRFS and MGRS on incomplete information systems to introduce the concept of MGRFS in incomplete information systems.

Let (U, ATT, I) be an incomplete information system and A, B ⊆ ATT be two attribute subsets. Then for any V ⊆ U, the lower and upper approximations of V with respect to the two granulations A and B are defined as:

$$\underline{(A + B)}(V)(x) = \inf_{y \in S_A(x)} V(y) \vee \inf_{y \in S_B(x)} V(y), \forall x \in U;$$

$$\tag{34}$$

$$\overline{(A + B)}(V)(x) = ((\underline{A + B})(V^C))^C(x), \forall x \in U.$$

$$\tag{35}$$

Definition 11: *The rough set of V with respect to A+B is given by the pair* $((\underline{A + B})(V), \overline{(A + B)}(V))$ *and its boundary region or the uncertainty region, denoted by* $B_{(A+B)}(V)$ *is defined as*

$$B_{(A+B)}(V) = \overline{(A + B)}(V) \setminus (\underline{A + B})(V) \tag{36}$$

Topological Properties of MGRFS in an Incomplete Information System

It has been noted by Pawlak that in the practical applications of rough sets two characteristics are very important. These are the accuracy measure and the topological characterization. The topological characterisation of rough sets depends upon the four types of rough sets. Following this approach, we define below four types of MGRFS in an incomplete information system. Here, we denote by the strict zero cut of a fuzzy set A by $A_{>0}$ and it contains all the elements of U which have positive membership value.

Definition 12: *A MGRFS in an incomplete information space can be classified into following four types*

If $(\underline{A+B}(V))_{>0} \neq \phi$ and $(\overline{A + B(V)})_{>0} \neq U$, then we say that V is roughly A+B-definable (Type-1). $\qquad$ (36)

If $(\underline{A+B}(V))_{>0} = \phi$ and $(\overline{A + B(V)})_{>0} \neq U$, then we say that V is internally A+B-undefinable (Type-2). $\qquad$ (37)

If $(\underline{A+B}(V))_{>0} \neq \phi$ and $(\overline{A + B(V)})_{>0} = U$, then we say that V is externally A+B-undefinable (Type-3). $\qquad$ (38)

If $(\underline{A+B}(V))_{>0} = \phi$ and $(\overline{A + B(V)})_{>0} = U$, then we say that V is totally A+B-undefinable (Type-4). $\qquad$ (39)

When we consider X as a crisp set instead of a fuzzy set then the above definitions reduce to their counterpart in the crisp rough set concept.

Note 1: *We would like to mention that the tables for complement, union and intersection of optimistic multigranular rough fuzzy sets remain same as the tables for the crisp version.*

INTUITIONISTIC FUZZY SETS, ROUGH INTUITIONISTIC FUZZY SETS AND MULTIGRANULATION

The notion of intuitionistic fuzzy sets was introduced in (Atanassov, 1986) as an extension of the notion of fuzzy sets. It has been found to be more realistic as the non-membership function is independent of the membership function but both are related to each other through a constraint. In fact, we have the following definition.

Intuitionistic Fuzzy Sets

In the intuitionistic fuzzy set approach every member x of a set $X \subseteq U$ is associated with a grade of membership and a grade of non-membership, which we denote by MX(x) and NX(x) respectively. Both MX(x) and NX(x) are real number lying in [0, 1], such that $0 \leq MX(x) + NX(x) \leq 1$ for all $x \in U$. The set of all functions from U to J, where J = {(m, n) | m, n $\in$ [0, 1] and $0 \leq m + n \leq 1$}, is called the intuitionistic fuzzy power set of U and is denoted by IF(U). It follows that P(U) $\subseteq$ F(U) $\subseteq$ IF(U).

The function $HX(x) = 1 - (MX(x) + NX(x))$ for all $x \in U$ is called the hesitation function for X. It is easy to see that for a fuzzy set X, $NX(x) = 1 - MX(x)$ and $HX(x) = 0$, for all $x \in U$.

For $X, Y \in U$, some operations on intuitionistic fuzzy sets are defined as follows:

$M(X \bigcap Y)(x) = \min\{MX(x), MY(x)\}$
and $N(X \bigcap Y)(x) = \max\{NX(x), NY(x)\}$,
for all $x \in U$;   (40)

$M(X \bigcup Y)(x) = \max\{MX(x), MY(x)\}$
and $N(X \bigcup Y)(x) = \min\{NX(x), NY(x)\}$,
for all $x \in U$;   (41)

$(MX^c)(x) = NX(x)$ and $(NX^c)(x) = MX(x)$
for all $x \in U$;   (42)

$X \subseteq Y$ iff $MX(x) \le MY(x)$ and $NX(x) \ge NY(x)$,
for all $x \in U$ (43)

$M(X \backslash Y)(x) = \min\{MX(x), NY(x)\}$
and $N(X \backslash Y)(x) = \max\{NX(x), MY(x)\}$,
for all $x \in U$ (44)

Rough Intuitionistic Fuzzy Sets

Extending the notion of rough fuzzy sets introduced in (Dubois and Prade, 1990), rough intuitionistic fuzzy sets can be defined as follows.

Let (U, R) be an approximation space. Then for any X IF(U), the lower and upper approximations of X with respect to R are given by

$M(\underline{R}X)(x) = \inf_{y \in [x]R} MX(y)$
and $N(\underline{R}X)(x) = \sup_{y \in [x]R} NX(y)$
for all $x \in U$ (45)

and

$M(\overline{R}X)(x) = \sup_{y \in [x]R} MX(y)$
and $N(\overline{R}X)(x) = \inf_{y \in [x]R} NX(y)$
for all $x \in U$.   (46)

Rough Intuitionistic Fuzzy Sets Model Based on Multi-Granulations

In this section we extend the concept of rough fuzzy sets on multigranulation in (Wu and Kou, 2010) to introduce rough intuitionistic fuzzy sets on multigranulation as follows.

Definition 4.6.3.1: *Let K = (U, R) be a knowledge base, R be a family of equivalence relations on U and P, Q $\in$ R. $(\underline{P+Q})((\overline{P+Q})(X))$*

For $\forall X \in IF(U)$, the lower approximation ($\overline{P+Q}$)(X) and upper approximation $(\overline{P+Q})$(X) of X based equivalence relations P, Q are defined as follows. For $\forall x \in U$,

$M(\underline{P+Q})(X)(x) = \inf_{y \in [x]P} MX(y) \bigvee \inf_{y \in [x]Q} MX(y), N(\underline{P+Q})(X)(x) = \sup_{y \in [x]P} NX(y) \bigwedge \sup_{y \in [x]Q} NX(y)$ (47)

$\forall x \in U, M(\overline{P+Q})(X)(x) = (M(\underline{P+Q})(X^c))^c(x)$
and $N(\overline{P+Q})(X)(x) = (N(\underline{P+Q})(X^c))^c(x)$.   (48)

$(\underline{P+Q})(X)(x) = (M(\underline{P+Q})(X)(x), N(\underline{P+Q})(X)(x)),$ $(\overline{P+Q})(X)(x) = (M(\overline{P+Q})(X)(x), N(\overline{P+Q})(X)(x)).$ (49)

If $(\underline{P+Q})(X) = (\overline{P+Q})(X)$ then X is called definable, otherwise X is called an intuitionistic fuzzy rough set with respect to multi-granulations P and Q. The pair $((\underline{P+Q})(X), (\overline{P+Q})(X))$ is called a MG-intuitionistic fuzzy rough set on multi-granulations P and Q (Tripathy et al, 2012).

We define below four types of MGRIFS. Here, we denote by the strict one cut of an intuitionistic fuzzy set A by $A_{<1}$ and it contains all the elements of U which have non-membership value strictly less than one. It may be noted that in the case of a fuzzy set, this is equivalent to the support set of A, which comprises of elements having positive membership value.

Definition 13: *A MGRIFS can be classified into following four types*

If $(\underline{P+Q}(X))_{<1} \neq \phi$ and $(\overline{P+Q}(X))_{<1} \neq U$, then we say that X is roughly P+Q-definable (Type-1). $\qquad$ (50)

If $(\underline{P+Q}(X))_{<1} = \phi$ and $(\overline{P+Q}(X))_{<1} \neq U$, then we say that X is internally P+Q-undefinable (Type-2). $\qquad$ (51)

If $(\underline{P+Q}(X))_{<1} \neq \phi$ and $(\overline{P+Q}(X))_{<1} = U$, then we say that X is externally P+Q–undefinable (Type-3). $\qquad$ (52)

If $(\underline{P+Q}(X))_{<1} = \phi$ and $(\overline{P+Q}(X))_{<1} = U$, then we say that X is totally P+Q –undefinable (Type-4). $\qquad$ (53)

It is worth noting that when we consider X as a crisp set or a fuzzy set instead of an intuitionistic fuzzy set then the above definitions reduce to their counterpart in the crisp rough set or fuzzy rough set concept respectively.

Note 2: *We would like to note that the tables for the types of complementation, union and intersection remain same for Optimistic Multigranular Rough Intuitionistic fuzzy sets.*

Algebraic Properties of Multigranular Rough Sets

Algebraic properties generally deal with elements and study of the relationship of elements. Lower approximations of rough sets and upper approximations of rough sets are having their similarity with mathematical morphology in the operators used. Lower approximation involve subset operation as like erosion and opening, while upper approximations involve set intersection as do dilation and closing (Bloch, 2000). Applying algebraic erosion, dilation, opening and closing for defining the corresponding approximations of rough sets lead to the concept called algebraic rough sets (Bloch, 200). Hence the morphological operators seem to be a good tool for defining lower and upper approximation of rough sets. Moreover these operators lead to a generalization of rough sets. In this concept we extended the concept of algebraic properties of general rough sets in view with multigranulation rough sets.

In general rough set theory some of the interesting properties were studied and obtained on intersection and union of rough sets of different types (Tripathy et al, 2010). This study has been further extended to multigranulation rough sets to find out the validity of other algebraic properties like associativity and commutativity (Tripathy et al, 2013). We have provided theorems with sufficient condition for equality to hold in some of the inclusions of the properties of multigranular rough sets. Also some of the theorems on approximations of classification in multigranulations were established along with corollaries for both optimistic and pessimistic multigranular rough sets. We also introduced two measures of uncertainty namely accuracy and quality measures which describes vagueness of multigranular approximation of classifications.

In rough set theory role of classification of universes were considered to be more important due to its usage in ability to classify objects. The concept of approximations of classifications was introduced and studied in (Busse, 1988). In his work (Busse, 1988) he revealed some important and interesting results. After analysis it has been found that not all the properties of basic rough sets can be extended to the category of classifications. In (Busse, 1988), Busse established four theorems as properties of classifications and the obtained results could be used in rule generation.

The unification process of the four theorems of Busse was done in (Tripathy et al 2010) in the idea that they established two theorems of the necessary and sufficient type, from which several results including the four theorems of Busse can be derived. Also, their results confirm to the prediction of Pawlak. From the view of information systems, the role of these four theorems was found to be useful in deriving rules from such systems. It was observed that only five cases were considered by Busse out of eleven cases as far as the types of classifications, on the other hand, the other types of classifications reduce either directly or indirectly to the five cases considered by Busse. Another interesting aspect of the results in (Tripathy et al, 2010) is the enumeration of possible types (Pawlak, 1983; Pawlak, 1991; Tripathy et al, 2010) of elements in a classification, which is based upon the types of rough sets introduced by Pawlak (Pawlak, 1991) and carried out further by Tripathy et al (Tripathy, 2009; Tripathy et al, 2010).

We have extended the results of [Tripathy, 2009; Tripathy et al, 2010) to the multigranulation context. In (Tripathy et al, 2013) the study about the types of basic rough sets was done from the view of optimistic multigranulation rough set and from the pessimistic multigranulation point of view was done in (Tripathy et al, 2012c). In this work, we find out the conditions under which the two types of multigranulations reduced to single granulation. Also, sufficient conditions for two inclusions to be equalities in the optimistic multigranulation case, which are equalities under single granulation are obtained and were shown to be not necessary.

PROPERTIES OF MULTIGRANULATIONS

We present below some properties of multigranulations which shall be used in this work to establish the results.

Properties of Optimistic Multigranular Rough Sets

The following properties of the optimistic multigranular rough sets were established in (Qian et al, 2006).

$$\underline{(R + S)}(X) \subseteq X \subseteq \overline{R+S}(X) \tag{54}$$

$$\underline{(R + S)}(\phi) = \phi = \overline{(R + S)}(\phi), \tag{55}$$

$$\underline{(R + S)}(U) = U = \overline{(R + S)}(U) \tag{56}$$

$$\underline{(R + S)}(\sim X) = \sim \overline{(R + S)}(X) \tag{57}$$

$$\underline{(R + S)}(X) = \underline{R}X \cap \underline{S}X \tag{58}$$

$$\overline{R+S}(X) = \overline{R}X \cup \overline{S}X \tag{59}$$

$$\begin{cases} \underline{(R+S)}(X) = \underline{(S+R)}(X), \\ \overline{(R+S)}(X) = \overline{(S+R)}(X) \end{cases} \tag{60}$$

$$\underline{(R + S)}(X \cap Y) \subseteq \underline{(R + S)}X \cap \underline{(R + S)}Y \tag{61}$$

$$\overline{R+S}(X \cup Y) \supseteq \overline{R+S}(X) \cup \overline{R+S}(Y) \tag{62}$$

$$\underline{(R + S)}(X \cup Y) \supseteq \underline{(R + S)}X \cup \underline{(R + S)}Y \tag{63}$$

$$\overline{(R + S)}(X \cap Y) \subseteq \overline{(R + S)}X \cap \overline{(R + S)}Y \tag{64}$$

Properties of Pessimistic Multigranular Rough Sets

The following are parallel properties for the pessimistic multigranular rough sets.

$$\underline{(R * S)}(X) \subseteq X \subseteq \overline{(R * S)}(X) \tag{65}$$

$$\underline{(R * S)}(\phi) = \phi = \overline{(R * S)}(\phi), \underline{(R * S)}(U) = U = \overline{(R * S)}(U) \tag{66}$$

$$\underline{(R * S)}(\sim X) = \sim \overline{(R * S)}(X) \tag{67}$$

$$\underline{(R * S)}(X) = \underline{R}X \cap \underline{S}X \tag{68}$$

$$\overline{(R * S)}(X) = \overline{R}X \cup \overline{S}X \tag{69}$$

$$\underline{(R * S)}(X) = \underline{(S * R)}(X), \overline{(R * S)}(X) = \overline{(S * R)}(X) \tag{70}$$

$$\underline{(R * S)}(X \cap Y) \subseteq \underline{(R * S)}X \cap \underline{(R * S)}Y \tag{71}$$

$$\overline{(R * S)}(X \cup Y) \supseteq \overline{(R * S)}X \cup \overline{(R * S)}Y \tag{72}$$

$$\underline{(R * S)}(X \cup Y) \supseteq \underline{(R * S)}X \cup \underline{(R * S)}Y \tag{73}$$

$$\overline{(R * S)}(X \cap Y) \subseteq \overline{(R * S)}X \cap \overline{(R * S)}Y \tag{74}$$

In fact we find out the conditions under which the two types of multigranulations reduced to single granulation.

Algebraic Properties of Multigranulations

The following theorem provides interesting conditions for the cases under which the two types of multigranulations reduce to single granulation rough sets. The algebraic properties of multigranulation of both the types established here are of utmost importance for the development of the theory and can reduce the efforts needed to establish the properties of multigranulation established in many papers. We can derive from the results that the properties which are not true for single granulation cannot be true for multigranulation

and the results which are true for multigranulation must be true for single granulation. Also, we would like to point out that there is no necessity to consider more than two granulations in establishing properties of multigranulation(Both the optimistic and the pessimistic cases) as whatever results are true for two granulations will be true for any finite number of granulations because of the associativity and commutativity of the two types of multigranulation.

Theorem 1: Let R and S be two equivalence relations on U and $X \subseteq U$. Then

$$\underline{R + S}X = \underline{R}X \text{ and } \overline{R + S}X = \overline{R}X \quad \text{when} \quad S = U \times U \tag{75}$$

$$\underline{R * S}X = \underline{R}X \text{ and } \overline{R * S}X = \overline{R}X \text{ when } S = \{(x, x) \mid x \in U \}. \tag{76}$$

Theorem 2: With the same notations as in previous Theorem, the following algebraic associative and commutative properties are satisfied by '+' and '*' type of multigranulation rough sets.

$$\underline{R + S}X = \underline{S + R}X \text{ and } \overline{R + S}X = \overline{S + R}X \tag{77}$$

$$\underline{(R + S) + T}X = \underline{R + (S + T)}X \text{ and } \overline{(R + S) + T}X = \overline{R + (S + T)}X \tag{78}$$

$$\underline{R * S}X = \underline{S * R}X \text{ and } \overline{R * S}X = \overline{S * R}X \tag{79}$$

$$\underline{(R * S) * T}X = \underline{R * (S * T)}X \text{ and } \overline{(R * S) * T}X = \overline{R * (S * T)}X \tag{80}$$

Next, we prove two theorems which provide sufficient conditions for equality to hold in two inclusions in the multigranulation case, which were true without any condition in the single granulation case.

Theorem 3:

$[\overline{RX} \cap \overline{SY}] = \phi$ *and* $[\overline{RY} \cap \overline{SX}] = \phi$

is a sufficient but not necessary condition for $\overline{R + S}(X \cup Y) = (\overline{R + SX}) \cup (\overline{R + SY})$.

Theorem 4: $\underline{R}X \cup \underline{S}Y = U$ and $\underline{R}Y \cup \underline{S}X = U$ is a sufficient but not necessary condition for $\underline{R + S}(X \cap Y) = \underline{R + SX} \cap \underline{R + SY}$.

Let us denote the pessimistic Multigranular rough sets and the optimistic rough sets associated with R and S by $R * S$ and R+S respectively.

Theorem 5: For any $X \subseteq U$ and two equivalence relations R_1 and R_2 defined over U, we have

$$\underline{R_1 * R_2}X \subseteq \underline{R_1 + R_2}X \subseteq \underline{R_1 \cap R_2}X \subseteq \overline{R_1 \cap R_2}X$$
$$\subseteq \overline{R_1 + R_2}X \subseteq \overline{R_1 * R_2}X \tag{81}$$

Note 3: *All the inclusions in the above theorem can be strict. Examples have been provided in (Tripathy et al, 2012; Tripathy et al, 2013) to establish this.*

Corollary 1: For any $X \subseteq U$,

$$BN(R_1 \cap R_2)(X) \subseteq BN(R_1 + R_2)(X)$$
$$\subseteq BN(R_1 * R_2)(X).$$

Corollary 2: For any $X \subseteq U$, X is rough w.r.t $R_1 \cap R_2 \Rightarrow$ X is rough w.r.t $R_1 + R_2 \Rightarrow$ X is rough w.r.t $R_1 * R_2$.

Corollary 3: For any $X \subseteq U$, X is crisp w.r.t $R_1 * R_2. \Rightarrow$ X is crisp w.r.t $R_1 + R_2 \Rightarrow$ X is crisp w.r.t $R_1 \cap R_2$.

We can extend the above results to the case when the number of granulations is more than two. For this we shall use the following notations:

Let $P_1, P_2, ...P_m$ be m number of equivalence relations over U. Then we use the notations:

$\sum_{i=1}^{m} P_i$ for optimistic multigranulation,

$\prod_{i=1}^{m} P_i$ for pessimistic multigranulation, and

$\bigcap_{i=1}^{m} P_i$ for indiscernibility multigranulation.

Corollary 4: For any $X \subseteq U$ and $P_1, P_2, ..., P_m$ being equivalence relations on U, we have

$$\underline{\prod_{i=1}^{m} P_i}X \subseteq \underline{\sum_{i=1}^{m} P_i}X \subseteq \underline{\bigcap_{i=1}^{m} P_i}X$$
$$\subseteq \overline{\bigcap_{i=1}^{m} P_i}X \subseteq \overline{\sum_{i=1}^{m} P_i}X \subseteq \overline{\prod_{i=1}^{m} P_i}X. \tag{82}$$

Theorem 6: Let $S = (U, A)$ be an incomplete information system where U denotes a universe of objects and A denotes an attribute set respectively. Let $R_1, R_2 \subseteq A$. Then for any $X \subseteq U$ we have the following:

$$\underline{R_1 * R_2}X \subseteq \underline{R_1 + R_2}X \subseteq \underline{R_1 \cup R_2}X \subseteq \overline{R_1 \cup R_2}X$$
$$\subseteq \overline{R_1 + R_2}X \subseteq \overline{R_1 * R_2}X. \tag{83}$$

Corollary 5: Let U be an incomplete IS. Then for any $X \subseteq U$,

$$BN(R_1 \cup R_2)(X) \subseteq BN(R_1 + R_2)(X)$$
$$\subseteq BN(R_1 * R_2)(X). \tag{84}$$

Corollary 6: Let U be an incomplete IS. Then for any $X \subseteq U$, X is rough w.r.t $R_1 \cup R_2 \Rightarrow$ X is rough w.r.t $R_1 + R_2 \Rightarrow$ X is rough w.r.t $R_1 * R_2$.

Corollary 7: Let U be an incomplete IS. Then for any $X \subseteq U$, X is crisp w.r.t $R_1 * R_2. \Rightarrow$ X is crisp w.r.t $R_1 + R_2 \Rightarrow$ X is crisp w.r.t $R_1 \cup R_2$.

Let $S = (U, A)$ be an incomplete information system where U denotes a universe of objects and A denotes an attribute set respectively. Let $R_1, R_2, ...R_m \subseteq A$. Then for any $X \subseteq U$ we have the following:

Corollary 8: We have

$$\underline{\Pi_{i=1}^m R_i X} \subseteq \underline{\Sigma_{i=1}^m R_i X} \subseteq \underline{\cup_{i=1}^m R_i X} \subseteq \overline{\cup_{i=1}^m R_i X}$$
$$\subseteq \overline{\Sigma_{i=1}^m R_i X} \subseteq \overline{\Pi_{i=1}^m R_i X}. \tag{85}$$

Multigranular Approximations of Classifications

We recall that a classification $F = \{X_1, X_2, ..., X_n\}$ of a universe U is such that $X_i \cap X_j = \phi$ for $i \neq j$ and $\overset{n}{\underset{k=1}{\cup}} X_k = U$.

The approximations (lower and upper) of a classification F was defined by Busse as

$$\underline{RF} = \{\underline{RX_1}, \underline{RX_2}, ..., \underline{RX_n}\} \text{ and}$$
$$\overline{RF} = \{\overline{RX_1}, \overline{RX_2}, ...\overline{RX_n}\}. \tag{86}$$

For any two equivalence relations R and S over U, the lower and upper optimistic multigranular rough approximations and pessimistic multigranular approximations are defined in a natural manner as

$$\underline{R + S}F = \{\underline{R + S}X_1, \underline{R + S}X_2, ..., \underline{R + S}X_n\}$$
$$\text{and } \overline{R + S}F = \{\overline{R + S}X_1, \overline{R + S}X_2, ...\overline{R + S}X_n\} \tag{87}$$

$$\underline{R * S}F = \{\underline{R * S}X_1, \underline{R * S}X_2, ..., \underline{R * S}X_n\}$$
$$\text{and } \overline{R * S}F = \{\overline{R * S}X_1, \overline{R * S}X_2, ...\overline{R * S}X_n\} \tag{88}$$

Theorems on Approximations of Classifications in Multigranulations

We use the notation in this section as $N_n = \{1, 2, 3, ...n\}$.

We use F, U, R and S as defined in 3.6 in the following theorems and corollaries.

For any $I \subset N_n$, I^c denotes the complement of I in N_n.

Theorem 7: For any $I \subset N_n$

$$\overline{R + S}(\underset{i \in I}{\cup} X_i) = U \text{ if and only if}$$
$$\underline{R + S}(\underset{j \in I^c}{\cup} X_j) = \phi. \tag{89}$$
$$\overline{R * S}(\underset{i \in I}{\cup} X_i) = U \text{ if and only if}$$
$$\underline{R * S}(\underset{j \in I^c}{\cup} X_j) = \phi. \tag{90}$$

Corollary 9:

(i) If $\overline{R + S}(\underset{i \in I}{\cup} X_i) = U$,
   then $\underline{R + S}(X_j) = \phi$ for each $j \in I^c$.

(ii) If $\overline{R * S}(\underset{i \in I}{\cup} X_i) = U$
   then $\underline{R + S}(X_j) = \phi$, for each $j \in I^c$.

Corollary 10: *For each* $i \in N_n$,

(i) $\overline{R + S}(X_i) = U$ *if and only if*
   $\underline{R + S}(\underset{j \in i}{\cup} X_j) = \phi.$

(ii) $\overline{R * S}(X_i) = U$ *if and only if*
   $\underline{R * S}(\underset{j \in i}{\cup} X_j) = \phi.$

Corollary 11: *For each* $i \in N_n$

(i) $\quad \underline{R+S}(X_i) = \phi$

$\quad$ *if and only if* $\overline{R+S}(\bigcup\limits_{j \neq i} X_j) = U$.

(ii) $\quad \underline{R*S}(X_i) = \phi$ *if and only if*

$\quad \overline{R*S}(\bigcup\limits_{j \neq i} X_j) = U$.

Corollary 12:

(i) $\quad$ *If there exists* $i \in N_n$ *such that* $\overline{R+S}X_i = U$

$\quad$ *then for each* $j(\neq i) \in N_n$, $\underline{R+S}(X_j) = \phi$.

(ii) $\quad$ *If there exists* $i \in N_n$ *such that* $\overline{R*S}X_i = U$

$\quad$ *then for each* $j(\neq i) \in N_n$, $\underline{R*S}X_j = \phi$.

Theorem 8: For any $I \subset N_n$,

(i) $\quad \underline{R+S}(\bigcup\limits_{j \in I} X_j) \neq \phi \Leftrightarrow \bigcup\limits_{j \in I^C} \overline{R+S}X_j \neq U$.

(ii) $\quad \underline{R*S}(\bigcup\limits_{j \in I} X_j) \neq \phi \Leftrightarrow \bigcup\limits_{j \in I^C} \overline{R*S}X_j \neq U$.

Corollary 13: *For each* $I \subset N_n$,

(i) $\quad \underline{R+S}(\bigcup\limits_{i \in I} X_i) \neq \phi \Leftrightarrow \overline{R+S}X_j \neq U$ *for*

$\quad$ *each* $j \in I^C$.

(ii) $\quad \underline{R*S}(\bigcup\limits_{i \in I} X_i) \neq \phi \Leftrightarrow \overline{R*S}X_j \neq U$ *for*

$\quad$ *each* $j \in I^C$.

Corollary 14: For each $i \in N_n$,

(i) $\quad \underline{R+S}X_i \neq \phi \Leftrightarrow \overline{R+S}(\bigcup\limits_{j \neq i} X_j) \neq U$.

(ii) $\quad \underline{R*S}X_i \neq \phi \Leftrightarrow \overline{R*S}(\bigcup\limits_{j \neq i} X_j) \neq U$.

Corollary 15: *If there exists* $i \in N_n$ *such that*

(i) $\quad \underline{R+S}X_i \neq \phi$ *if and only if for each*

$\quad j(\neq i) \in N_n$, $\overline{R+S}X_j \neq U$.

(ii) $\quad \underline{R*S}X_i \neq \phi$ *if and only if for each*

$\quad j(\neq i) \in N_n$, $\overline{R*S}X_j \neq U$.

Corollary 16: *For all* $i \in N_n$,

(i) $\quad \underline{R+S}X_i \neq \phi \Leftrightarrow \overline{R+S}X_i \neq \phi$ *for all* $i \in N_n$.

(ii) $\quad \underline{R*S}X_i \neq \phi \Leftrightarrow \overline{R*S}X_i \neq \phi$ *for all* $i \in N_n$.

Some properties of these measures were established in (Raghavan et al, 2013). We find that the same proofs work for both the multigranular cases. So, we only state below the results without any proof. We need the following additional definition.

Definition 14: *(i) We say that a classification F is (R+S)-definable if and only if* $\underline{R+S}F = \overline{R+S}F$ *or equivalently* $\underline{R+S}X_i = \overline{R+S}X_i$; $i = 1, 2, \dots n$. *(ii) We say that classification F is (R*S)-definable if and only if* $\underline{R*S}F = \overline{R*S}F$ *or equivalently* $\underline{R*S}X_i = \overline{R*S}X_i$; $i = 1, 2, \dots n$.

SOME PROPERTIES OF MEASURES OF UNCERTAINTY

In this section we introduce two measures, which describe inexactness of multigranular approximate classifications. These are extensions of the corresponding concepts used in the single granulation case.

We follow the same notations as used in the previous sections.

Accuracy of Multigranular Approximations

The accuracy of optimistic multigranular approximation of F by R and S is defined as

$$\beta_{R+S}(F) = \frac{\sum_{i=1}^{n} \text{card}(\underline{R+S}X_i)}{\sum_{i=1}^{n} \text{card}(\overline{R+S}X_i)}. \qquad (89)$$

The accuracy of pessimistic multigranular approximation of F by R and S is defined as

$$\beta_{R*S}(F) = \frac{\sum_{i=1}^{n} \text{card}(\underline{R*S}X_i)}{\sum_{i=1}^{n} \text{card}(\overline{R*S}X_i)}. \qquad (90)$$

As in the single granulation case, this measure expresses the percentage of possible correct decisions when classifying objects employing the knowledge of R and S taken together (optimistic or pessimistic manner).

Quality of Multigranular Approximations

The quality of optimistic multigranular approximation of F by R and S if given as

$$\gamma_{R+S}(F) = \frac{\sum_{i=1}^{n} \text{card}(\overline{R+S}X)}{\text{card}(U)}. \qquad (91)$$

The quality of pessimistic multigranular approximation of F by R and S if given as

$$\gamma_{R*S}(F) = \frac{\sum_{i=1}^{n} \text{card}(\overline{R*S}X)}{\text{card}(U)}. \qquad (92)$$

As in the single granulation case, this measure expresses the percentage of objects which can be correctly classified to classes of F employing the knowledge of R and S taken together (optimistic or pessimistic manner).

Theorem 9: For any classification F in U,

(i)   F is (R+S)-definable if and only if
$$\beta_{R+S}(F) = \gamma_{R+S}(F) = 1.$$
(ii) F is (R * S)-definable if and only if
$$\beta_{R*S}(F) = \gamma_{R*S}(F) = 1.$$

Theorem 10: For any classification F in U and equivalence relations R and S on U,

(i) $0 \leq \beta_{R+S}(F) \leq \gamma_{R+S}(F) \leq 1.$
(ii) $0 \leq \beta_{R*S}(F) \leq \gamma_{R*S}(F) \leq 1.$

COMPARISON PROPERTIES OF ROUGH SETS BASED ON MULTIGRANULATIONS AND TYPES OF MULTIGRANULAR APPROXIMATIONS OF CLASSIFICATIONS

As mentioned earlier in this chapter, the process of extending the idea of single granular rough sets have been introduced and resulted with two new concepts of multigranulation rough sets called the optimistic multigranular rough sets and the pessimistic multigranular rough sets. Several properties of these multigranular rough sets have been obtained in several papers ([Qian et al, 2006; Qian et al, 2010; Raghavan et al, 2011; Tripathy et al, 2012a; Tripathy et al, 2012b; Tripathy et al, 2013). Some algebraic properties were obtained for multigranular rough sets recently in (Tripathy et al, 2012), by the way of comparing the two types of multigranular rough sets along with the IND rough set obtained through the intersection of a set of equivalence relations and also the union of a set of tolerance relations in case of incomplete information systems. Also a useful concept of reduction oriented validation, including the cases when two types of multigranulations reduce to single granulation was introduced in (Tripathy et al, 2013a). In addition to this some more algebraic properties of multigranular rough sets were also obtained in (Tripathy et al, 2013a). A theorem which provides some sufficient conditions on multigranular approximation of classification was established in (Tripathy et al, 2013a). In this work we showed that the result was both necessary and sufficient type. There were eight relations between the upper and lower multigranular approximations of union and intersections of rough sets. Here, we proved that out of these two are actually equalities and for other six cases we have provided examples to show that proper inclusions hold true. The various types of rough sets provide more insight view into the topological structures of rough sets to explore their internal structure and also to introduce such types in the view of multigranular rough sets. Here, we carry our research in (Tripathy et al, 2013a) further by establishing a theorem on multigranulations, which extends a corresponding theorem on single granular approximations of classifications.

Multigranular Approximations of Classifications and Properties Needed for Comparison

The following properties of optimistic multigranular rough sets are well known.

$$\underline{(R + S)}(X \cap Y) \subseteq \underline{(R + S)}X \cap \underline{(R + S)}Y \quad (93)$$

$$\overline{(R + S)}(X \cup Y) \supseteq \overline{(R + S)}X \cup \overline{(R + S)}Y \quad (94)$$

$$\underline{(R + S)}(X \cup Y) \supseteq \underline{(R + S)}X \cup \underline{(R + S)}Y \quad (95)$$

$$\overline{(R + S)}(X \cap Y) \subseteq \overline{(R + S)}X \cap \overline{(R + S)}Y \quad (96)$$

The following properties of pessimistic multigranular rough sets are well known.

$$\underline{(R * S)}(X) = \underline{R}X \cap \underline{S}X \quad (97)$$

$$\overline{(R * S)}(X) = \overline{R}X \cup \overline{S}X \quad (98)$$

$$\underline{(R * S)}(X \cap Y) \subseteq \underline{(R * S)}X \cap \underline{(R * S)}Y \quad (99)$$

$$\overline{(R * S)}(X \cup Y) \supseteq \overline{(R * S)}X \cup \overline{(R * S)}Y \quad (100)$$

$$\underline{(R * S)}(X \cup Y) \supseteq \underline{(R * S)}X \cup \underline{(R * S)}Y \quad (101)$$

$$\overline{(R * S)}(X \cap Y) \subseteq \overline{(R * S)}X \cap \overline{(R * S)}Y \quad (102)$$

Comparison Results

The inclusions (99) and (100) have been established in (Qian et al, 2010). But we establish below that actually these two inclusions can be replaced with equalities.

Theorem 11: Equality holds true in the inclusions (99) and (100).

Taking examples into account the following result has been established in (Tripathy et al, 2012c).

Theorem 12: The inclusion relations in (93) - (96) and (101) and (102) we cannot replace inclusions by equalities.

Types of Multigranular Classifications

Classifications are of great interest in the process of learning from examples and deriving rules from classifications generated by single decisions. The types of multigranular approximations of rough sets were introduced in (Raghavan et al, 2011) and their properties were studied. We present below the types of rough sets.

Basic Types of Classifications

Let R and S be equivalence relations on U and F $= \{X_1, X_2, \dots X_n\}$ be a classification of U. We extend the five basic types of classifications introduced in (Grzymala Busse, 1988) as follows:

Definition 15: *We say that F is strongly R+S {R*S respectively} definable weak in U if and only if there exists a number* $i \in N_n$ *such that* $\underline{R + S}X_i \{\underline{R * S}X_i\} \neq \phi$.

Definition 16: *We say that F is roughly R+S{R*S respectively}-definable strong in U (or of Type-1) if and only if* $\underline{R + S}X_i \{\underline{R*S}X_i\} \neq \phi$ *for each* $i \in N_n$.

Definition 17: *We say that F is internally R+S {R*S respectively}- undefinable weak in U if and only if* $\underline{R + S}X_i \{\underline{R*S}X_i\} \neq \phi$ *for each* $i \in N_n$ *and there exists* $j \in N_n$ *such that* $\overline{R + S}X_j \{\overline{R*S}X_j\} \neq U$.

Definition 18: *We say that F is externally R+S {R*S respectively}-undefinable strong in U (or of Type-2) if and only if* $\underline{R + S}X_i \{\underline{R * S}X_i\} \neq \phi$ *and* $\overline{R + S}X_i \{\overline{R*S}X_i\} \neq U$ *for each* $i \in N_n$.

Definition 19: *We say that F is totally R+S {R*S respectively}-undefinable in U (or of Type-4) if and only if* $\underline{R + S}X_i \{\underline{R*S}X_i\} = \phi$ *and* $\overline{R + S}X_i \{\overline{R * S}X_i\} = U$ *for each* $i \in N_n$.

Further Types of Multigranular Classifications

A beautiful analysis of the types of classifications is provided in (Tripathy et al, 2010) and it has been found there that only five of these have been considered by Busse, where as all the other six types either reduce directly or transitively to one of these five cases. We see that the logic and properties of lower and upper approximations used there in remains same for both types of multigranulations. So, the conclusions remain same in case of multigranulations. Only for completeness we state below the other six types of classifications.

Definition 20: *We say that F is internally R+S (R*S)-undefinable (weak-1) in U if and only if* $\exists i$ *such that* $\underline{R + S}X_i(\underline{R * S}X_i) = \phi$ *and* $\exists j$ *such that* $\overline{R + S}X_j(\overline{R * S}X_j) \neq U$.

Definition 21: *We say that F is internally R+S (R*S)-undefinable (weak-2) in U if and only if* $\exists i$ *such that* $\underline{R + S}X_i(\underline{R * S}X_i) = \phi$ *and* $\forall j$ $\overline{R + S}X_j(\overline{R * S}X_j) \neq U$.

Definition 22: *We say that F is internally R+S (R*S)-undefinable (weak-3) in U if and only if* $\forall i$ $\underline{R + S}X_i(\underline{R * S}X_i) = \phi$ *and* $\exists j$ *such that* $\overline{R + S}X_j(\overline{R * S}X_j) \neq U$.

Definition 23: *We say that F is of T-4 with respect to R+S (R*S) in U if and only if* $\forall i$ $\underline{R + S}X_i(\underline{R * S}X_i) = \phi$ *and* $\forall j$ $\overline{R + S}X_j(\overline{R * S}X_j) \neq U$.

Definition 24: *We say that F is totally R+S (R*S)-undefinable (weak-1) in U if and only if* $\exists i$ *such that* $\underline{R + S}X_i(\underline{R * S}X_i) = \phi$ *and* $\exists j$ *such that* $\overline{R + S}X_j(\overline{R * S}X_j) = U$.

Definition 25: *We say that F is totally R+S (R*S)-undefinable (weak-2) in U if and only if* $\forall i$ $\underline{R + S}X_i(\underline{R * S}X_i) = \phi$ *and* $\exists j$ *such that* $\overline{R + S}X_j(\overline{R * S}X_j) = U$.

GENERAL RESULT ON TYPES OF CLASSIFICATIONS WITH RESPECT TO MULTIGRANULATIONS

The following theorem provides the number of possibilities from each of the five basic forms of classifications with respect to the types of elements in them. Since the proof is similar to that of the basic one, we avoid presenting it here.

Theorem 13: Let $F = \{X_1, X_2, ..., X_n\}$ be a classification of U. Then for $n \geq 3$, the number of possibilities in terms of types of elements $X_i, i = 1, 2, ... n$ with respect to both the types of multigranulations (optimistic and pessimistic) is $2(n+1)$.

Approximate Equalities Using Multigranulations

The equality of sets used in the mathematical sense has very little applicability in real life situations and have been found to be too stringent. Novotny and Pawlak (Pawlak, 1991) proposed three types of approximate equalities using rough sets. Even these notions are not far away from the equalities of sets in the mathematical sense as shown in (Tripathy et al, 2008; Tripathy, 2009). So the notion of rough equivalence was introduced. Further a complete study was done on approximate equalities in (Tripathy, 2011), where two more approximate equalities were introduced and a comparative study of these four approximate equalities based on rough sets have been made. Recently, all these results have been extended to the setting of multigranulation in (Tripathy et al, 2013b; Tripathy et al, 2013c). A complete discussion of these results has been done in a chapter (authored by B.K.Tripathy), in volume 1 of the edited volumes of these two editors. So, we avoid duplication of efforts.

NMGRS AND CBMGRS

Recently two extensions of basic multigranular rough sets have been proposed. These two are basing upon two types of extensions of basic unigranular rough sets; the neighbourhood systems and the covering based rough sets. These are the neighbourhood based multigranular rough sets (Lin et al, 2012) and the covering based multigranular rough sets. However, it may be noted that the notions are not unique. To be precise, four kinds of covering based multigranular rough sets have been introduced and studied (Tripathy et al, 2013). In this section we introduce these two types of multigranular rough sets and would like to mention that not much work has been done in this direction and enough of research on their basic properties and most importantly applications in real life situations are awaited.

Neighbourhood Based Multigranular Rough Sets (NMGRS)

This concept was introduced and studied in (Lin et al, 2012) recently. In order to introduce this, we first need to discuss on basic neighbourhood based rough sets.

Neighborhood-Based Rough Sets

In order to make Pawlak's rough set deal with the information system with heterogeneous attributes, (T. Y. Lin et al., 2012) gave the concept of neighborhood and proposed neighborhood-based rough sets. Since then, many researchers further studied the theory of the neighborhood-based rough set(Hu et al,2008a; Hu et al, 2008b; Hu et al, 2008c;Hu et al, 2010; Jin et al, 2006;,Lin, 1989; Wang,2006; Yao, 1998). In this section, we especially introduce some concepts of neighborhood-based rough sets proposed in (Hu, 2008c). In this section, we take the definitions as it is mentioned in (Lin et al, 2012).

Definition 26: *Let S = (U, AT, f) be an information system with heterogeneous attributes, X ⊆ U and A, B ⊆ AT are categorical and numerical attributes, respectively. The neighborhood granules of objects x induced by A, B, A ⋃ B are defined as*

$$n_A(x) = \{x_i \in U \mid d_A(x, x_i) = 0\}; \quad (103)$$

$$n_B(x) = \{x_i \in U \mid d_B(x, x_i) \leq \delta\}; \quad (104)$$

$$n_{(A \cup B)}(x) = \{x_i \in U \mid d_A(x, xi) \\ = 0 \wedge d_B(x, x_i) \leq \delta\}, \quad (105)$$

where d is a distance (Hu et al., 2008c; Lin et al., 2012) between x and y, δ is a nonnegative number, and "∧" means "and" operator. (1) is designed for numerical attributes; (2) is designed for categorical attributes, and (3) is designed for heterogeneous attributes, namely, categorical and numerical attributes.

A neighborhood relation N on the universe can be written as a relation matrix $M(N) = (r_{ij})_{n \times n}$, where

$$r_{ij} = \begin{cases} 1, & d(x_i, x_j) \leq \delta, \\ 0, & otherwise. \end{cases} \quad (106)$$

Accordingly, we say *(U, N)* a neighborhood approximation space. If there is an attribute subset in the system generating a neighborhood relation on the universe, we can regard this system as a neighborhood information system, denoted by *NIS = (U, AT, N)*, where U is a nonempty finite set and AT is an attribute set. In particular, a neighborhood information system is also called a neighborhood decision information system if we distinguish condition attributes and decision attributes, denoted by *NIS = (U, AT ⋃ D, N)*.

Definition 27: *Let (U, N) be a neighborhood approximation space. For any X ⊆ U, the lower approximation and upper approximation of X in U are defined as:*

$$\underline{N}X = \{x \in U \mid n(x) \subseteq X\}, \quad (107)$$

$$\overline{N}X = \{x \in U \mid n(x) \cap X \neq \phi\}. \quad (108)$$

One calls $(\underline{N}X, \overline{N}X)$ a neighborhood rough set. Obviously, $\underline{N}X \subseteq X \subseteq \overline{N}X$. The *boundary region* of X in the approximation space is defined as $Bn(X) = \overline{N}X \setminus \underline{N}X$.

The size of boundary region reflects the degree of roughness of set X in the neighborhood approximation space *(U, N)*. In the neighborhood rough set, δ can be considered as a parameter to control the granularity level at which we analyze the classification task.

Neighborhood Multigranulation Rough Sets

In this section, we extend the classical MGRS to neighborhood-based multigranulation rough sets (NMGRS). We propose two types of neighborhood multigranulation rough sets according to different representations of neighborhood information granules by Definition 9.1.1.2. In the first case, a granular space induced by a neighborhood relation on the universe can be regarded as a set of mixed information granules induced by both a similarity relation and an indiscernibility relation in the view of granular computing (Yao, 2001). If the approximations of a target concept are described by these mixed information granules, we call this rough set a 1-type neighborhood multigranulation rough set in this paper, denoted by 1-type NMGRS. In the second case, if the approximations of a target concept are described by multiple neighborhood relations, we call this rough set a

2-type neighborhood multigranulation rough set, denoted by 2-type NMGRS.

In the following, we will give the definitions of optimistic 1-type NMGRS and optimistic 2-type NMGRS and the definitions of pessimistic versions, respectively. Conveniently, we mainly discuss the properties of the optimistic versions. The pessimistic versions can be done similarly. We hence omit them in this paper

1-Type Neighborhood Multigranulation Rough Sets (1-Type NMGRS)

As we know, the incomplete MGRS is based on multiple tolerance relations, which sometimes can be also regarded as a neighborhood relation (Hu, 2008b). However, these existing multigranulation versions still cannot deal with data sets with heterogeneous attributes. Therefore, it is necessary to develop a new rough set based on multiple neighborhood relations to deal with hybrid data. Simply, we first investigate the approximation of a target set induced by mixed granules on the universe, which can be regarded as a simple neighborhood multigranulation rough set, just 1-type NMGRS.

Definition 28: *(1-type NMGRS): Let NIS = (U, AT, N) be a neighborhood information system, A ⊆ AT a categorical attribute set, B ⊆ AT a numerical attribute set, A ∪ B ⊆ AT a mixed attribute set; U/A, U/B, and U/(A ∪ B) represent a partition and two coverings of the universe U, respectively. For any X ⊆ U, the optimistic multigranulation lower and upper approximations of X with respect to A, B in U are defined in the following:*

$$\underline{(A+B)}X = \{x \in U \mid n_A(x) \subseteq X \vee n_B(x) \subseteq X\} \tag{109}$$

$$\overline{(A+B)}X = \sim \underline{(A+B)}(\sim X). \tag{110}$$

By Definition 9.1.2.1.1, we can see that the lower and upper approximations of X of optimistic 1-type NMGRS satisfy duality property, i.e., the upper approximation can be defined by the complement of the lower approximation. The area of uncertainty or boundary region is defined as

$$Bn(A+B)(X) = \overline{(A+B)}X \setminus \underline{(A+B)}X. \tag{111}$$

We call $(\underline{(A+B)}X, \overline{(A+B)}X)$ an optimistic 1-type NMGRS. Obviously, the optimistic 1-type NMGRS can degenerate into the original optimistic multigranulation while $\delta = 0$. The original MGRS is a special instance of 1-type NMGRS.

The topological properties for this type of rough sets and the approximate equalities based on them have been studied by (Nagaraju et al, 2013).

Covering Based Multigranular Rough Sets (CBMGRS)

In this section we introduce the four types of covering based multigranular rough sets and would like to state that there are only a few papers have been published on this topic. Besides their basic properties, their topological properties have been worked out (Liu et al, 2013).

Basics of Covering Based Rough Sets

Basic rough sets introduced by Pawlak have been extended in many ways. One such extension is the notion of covering based rough sets, where the notion of partitions is replaced by the general notion of covers (Yao et al, 2012). In this section we discuss the basics of these sets.

Definition 29: *Let U be a universe and C = {C₁, C₂,....., Cₙ} be a family of non-empty subsets of U that are overlapping in nature. If ∪C = U, then C is called a covering of U. The pair (U, C)* is called covering approximation space. For any $X \subseteq U$, the covering lower and upper approximations of X with respect to C can be defined as follows

$$\underline{C}(X) = \cup\{C_i \subset X, i \in 1, 2, \ldots, n\} \qquad (113)$$

$$\overline{C}(X) = \cup\{C_i \cap X \neq \emptyset, i \in 1, 2, \ldots, n\} \qquad (114)$$

The pair $(\underline{C}(X), \overline{C}(X))$ is called covering based rough set associated with X with respect to cover C if $\underline{C}(X) \neq \overline{C}(X)$, i.e., X is said to be roughly definable with respect to C. Otherwise X is said to be C-definable.

Definition 30: *Given a covering approximation space (U, C) for any $x \in U$, sets $md_c(x)$ and $MD_c(x)$ are respectively called minimal and maximal descriptors of x with respect to C,*

$$md_C(x) = \{ M \in C \ / \ x \in M$$
$$\text{and } (\forall N \in C \text{ such that } x \in N$$
$$\text{and } N \subseteq M) => M = N\} \qquad (115)$$

It is a set of all minimal covers containing x where a minimal cover containing x be one for which no proper sub cover containing x exists.

$$MD_C(x) = \{ M \in C \ / \ x \in M$$
$$\text{and } (\forall N \in C \text{ such that } x \in N$$
$$\text{and } N \supseteq K) => M = N\} \qquad (116)$$

It is a set of all maximal covers containing x where a maximal cover containing x be one for which no proper super cover containing x exists.

Basics of Covering Based Multi Granular Rough Sets

We would like to recall that the two types of multigranular rough sets are defined as follows.

Definition 31: *Let K= (U, **R**) be a knowledge base, **R** be a family of equivalence relations, $\in$ **R**. We define the optimistic multi-granular lower approximation and upper approximation of X in U as*

$$\underline{M + N}(X) = \cup\{x \ / \ [x]_M \subseteq X \text{ or } [x]_N \subseteq X\}$$
$$\text{and } \overline{M + N}(X) = (\underline{M + N(X^C)})^c \qquad (117)$$

Another kind of multi-granular rough sets called pessimistic multi-granular rough sets was introduced in (Qian et al, 2009). Now, they call the above type of multi-granular rough sets as the optimistic multi-granular rough sets.

Definition 32: *Let K= (U, **R**) be a knowledge base, **R** be a family of equivalence relations, $X \subseteq U$ and $M, N \in$ **R**. We define the pessimistic multi-granular lower approximation and upper approximation of X in U as*

$$\underline{M * N}(X) = \cup\{x \ / \ [x]_M \subseteq X \text{ and } [x]_N \subseteq X\}$$
$$\text{and } \overline{M * N}(X) = ((\underline{M * N})(X^C))^c \qquad (118)$$

Multi-granulation rough sets extended to covering approximation space. By employing minimal and maximal descriptor four types of CBMGRS are possible. The definitions of four types of CBMGRS are given as follows (Liu et al, 2013).

Definition 33: *Let (U, C) be a covering approximation space, $C_1, C_2 \in$ **C** be covers in C, for any $X \subseteq U$, its first type lower and upper approxima-*

tions with respect to C_1 and C_2 are defined as follows

$$\underline{F_{c_1+c_2}}(X) = \{x \in U \ / \cap md_{c_1}(x) \subseteq X \\ or \cap md_{c_2}(x) \subseteq X\} \tag{119}$$

$$\overline{F_{c_1+c_2}}(X) = \{x \in U \ / \ (\cap md_{c_1}(x)) \cap X \neq \varnothing \\ and \ (\cap md_{c_2}(x)) \cap X \neq \varnothing\} \tag{120}$$

Definition 34: *Let (U, C) be a covering approximation space, $C_1, C_2 \in C$ be covers in C, for any $X \subseteq U$, its second type lower and upper approximations with respect to C_1 and C_2 are defined as follows*

$$\underline{S_{c_1+c_2}}(X) = \{x \in U \ / \cup md_{c_1}(x) \subseteq X \\ or \cup md_{c_2}(x) \subseteq X\} \tag{121}$$

$$\overline{S_{c_1+c_2}}(X) = \{x \in U \ / \ (\cup md_{c_1}(x)) \cap X \neq \varnothing \\ and \ (\cup md_{c_2}(x)) \cap X \neq \varnothing\} \tag{122}$$

Definition 35: *Let (U, C) be a covering approximation space, $C_1, C_2 \in C$ be covers in C, for any $X \subseteq U$, its third type lower and upper approximations with respect to C_1 and C_2 are defined as follows*

$$\underline{T_{c_1+c_2}}(X) = \{x \in U \ / \cap MD_{c_1}(x) \subseteq X \\ or \cap MD_{c_2}(x) \subseteq X\} \tag{123}$$

$$\overline{T_{c_1+c_2}}(X) = \{x \in U \ / \ (\cap MD_{c_1}(x)) \cap X \neq \varnothing \\ and \ (\cap MD_{c2}(x)) \cap X \neq \varnothing\} \tag{124}$$

Definition 36: *Let (U, C) be a covering approximation space, $C_1, C_2 \in C$ be covers in C, for any $X \subseteq U$, its fourth or last type lower and upper approximations with respect to C_1 and C_2 are defined as follows*

$$\underline{L_{c_1+c_2}}(X) = \{x \in U \ / \cup MD_{c_1}(x) \subseteq X \\ or \cup MD_{c_2}(x) \subseteq X\} \tag{125}$$

$$\overline{L_{c_1+c_2}}(X) = \{x \in U \ / \ (\cup MD_{c_1}(x)) \cap X \neq \varnothing \\ and \ (\cup MD_{c_2}(x)) \cap X \neq \varnothing\} \tag{126}$$

Several fundamental properties of these four types of CBMGRSs have been studied in (Liu et al, 2013). Also, recently the topological properties of these CBMGRSs in the form of their types, the types of their complements, union and intersection have been studied in (Nagaraju et al, 2013).

PROBLEMS FOR FURTHER STUDY

Multigranular rough set concepts are relatively new. A lot of work needs to be done in this direction. However, we would like to specify some directions here.

10.1. Rule generation in the context of multigranulation needs to be focused more and real life applications where these rule generation techniques can be applied may be found out.
10.2. NMGRS is only a little more than a year old. Besides fundamental properties not much has been done. The basic rough set concepts can be worked out and once again applications of these concepts can be found out. Particularly it is felt that this theory has enough potential to be applied in social network modeling and analysis.
10.3. CBMGRS is the latest addition to the realm of multigranular rough sets. Except for two papers which have been accepted for publication not much work has been done. So, a lot of works can be done in this direction.

CONCLUSION

Granular computing is an upcoming conceptual and computing pattern of information processing. It has been strongly encouraged by the urgent need for processing practical data in an intelligent manner. Such processing need is now commonly available in vast quantities into a humanly manageable abstract knowledge. In other words, granular computing offers a platform to transit from the current machine-centric to human-centric approach to gather information and knowledge. From the granular computing point of view rough set theory is only unigranular. Several attempts have been made in order to extend the unigranular concept to multigranular stage. Two of the earlier attempts are the notions of optimistic multigranular rough sets and the pessimistic multigranular rough sets. In this chapter we talked about the topological and algebraic properties of such sets. Some of the results like the reduction of multigranulations to unigranulations are very interesting and correlates these two notions. We also presented the extensions of these basic concepts to the context of fuzzy sets and intuitionistic fuzzy sets and studied their topological properties. Also, we discussed on the latest additions in this direction that is the notions of NMGRS and CBMGRS. A lot of research work can be done in these directions.

REFERENCES

Atanassov, K. T. (1986). Intuitionistic fuzzy sets. *Fuzzy Sets and Systems*, *20*, 87–96. doi:10.1016/S0165-0114(86)80034-3

Bloch, I. (2000). On links between mathematical morphology and rough sets. *The Journal of the Pattern Recognition Society*, 1487 – 1496.

Chan, C. C., & Grzymala Busse, J. (1989). Rough set boundaries as a tool for learning rules from examples. In *Proceedings of the ISMIS-89, 4ᵗʰ Int. Symposium on Methodologies for intelligent Systems*, (pp. 281 – 288). ISMIS.

Chan, C. C., & Grzymala Busse, J. (1991). *On the attribute redundancy and the learning programs ID3, PRISM and LEM2*. Lawrence, KS: University of Kansas.

Dubois, D., & Prade, H. (1990). Rough fuzzy sets model. *International Journal of General Systems*, *46*(1), 191–208. doi:10.1080/03081079008935107

Fayyad, U. M., Shapiro, G. P., Smyth, P., & Uthurusamy, R. (Eds.). (1996). *Advances in knowledge discovery and data mining*. Cambridge, MA: MIT Press.

Grzymala Busse, J. (1988). Knowledge acquisition under uncertainty- a rough set approach. *Journal of Intelligent & Robotic Systems*, *1*, 3–16. doi:10.1007/BF00437317

Hu, Q. H., Liu, J. F., & Yu, D. R. (2008b). Mixed feature selection based on granulation and approximation. *Knowledge-Based Systems*, *21*, 294–304. doi:10.1016/j.knosys.2007.07.001

Hu, Q. H., Pedrycz, W., Yu, D. R., & Lang, J. (2010). Selecting discrete and continuous measures based on neighborhood decision error minimization. *IEEE Transactions on Systems, Man, and Cybernetics. Part B, Cybernetics*, *40*, 137–150. doi:10.1109/TSMCB.2009.2024166

Hu, Q. H., Yu, D. R., Liu, J. F., & Wu, C. X. (2008c). Neighborhood rough set based heterogeneous feature selection. *Information Sciences*, *178*, 3577–3594. doi:10.1016/j.ins.2008.05.024

Hu, Q. H., Yu, D. R., & Xie, Z. X. (2008a). Neighborhood classifiers. *Expert Systems with Applications*, *34*, 866–876. doi:10.1016/j.eswa.2006.10.043

Jin, W., Tung, A. K. H., Han, J., & Wang, W. (2006). Ranking outliners using symmetric neighborhood relationship. In *Proceedings of PAKDD*, (pp. 577–593). PAKDD.

Kryszkiewicz, K. (1998). Rough set approach to incomplete information systems. *Information Sciences, 112*, 39–49. doi:10.1016/S0020-0255(98)10019-1

Liang, J. Y., & Li, D. Y. (2005). *Uncertainty and knowledge acquisition in information systems*. Beijing: Science Press.

Liang, J. Y., & Shi, Z. Z. (2001). The information entropy, rough entropy and knowledge granulation in rough set theory. *International Journal of Uncertainty. Fuzziness and Knowledge-Based Systems, 12*(1), 37–46. doi:10.1142/S0218488504002631

Liang, J. Y., Shi, Z. Z., Li, D. Y., & Wireman, M. J. (2006). The information entropy, rough entropy and knowledge granulation in incomplete information system. *International Journal of General Systems, 35*(6), 641–654. doi:10.1080/03081070600687668

Lin, G., Qian, Y., & Li, J. (2012). NMGRS: Neighborhood-based multigranulation rough sets. *International Journal of Approximate Reasoning, 53*, 1080–1093. doi:10.1016/j.ijar.2012.05.004

Lin, G. P., Qian, Y. H., & Li, J. J. (2011). A covering-based pessimistic multi-granulation rough set. In *Proceedings of International Conference on Intelligent Computing*. Zhengzhon, China: IEEE.

Lin, T. Y. (2001). Granular and nearest neighborhood: Rough set approach. In *Granulation computing: An emerging paradigm* (pp. 125–142). Berlin: Physica-Verlag. doi:10.1007/978-3-7908-1823-9_6

Lin, T. Y. (2003). Neighborhood systems: Mathematical models of information granulations. In *Proceedings of 2003 IEEE International Conference on Systems, Man & Cybernetics*, (pp. 5–8). IEEE.

Liu, C. (2013). On multi-granulation covering rough sets. *International Journal of Approximate Reasoning*.

Liu, C. H., & Miao, D. Q. (2011a). Covering rough set model based on multi-granulations. In *Proceedings of Thirteenth International Conference on Rough Sets, Fuzzy Set, Data Mining and Granular Computing* (LNAI), (vol. 6743, pp. 87 – 90). Berlin: Springer.

Liu, C. H., & Wang, M. Z. (2011b). Covering fuzzy rough set based on multi-granulation. In *Proceedings of International Conference on Uncertainty Reasoning and Knowledge Engineering*, (vol. 2, pp. 146 – 149). Academic Press.

Liu, C. L., Miao, D., & Quain, J. (2012). On multi-granulation covering rough sets. *International Journal of Approximate Reasoning*.

Magnani, M. (2003). *Technical report on rough set theory for knowledge discovery in data bases*. Bologna, Italy: University of Bologna.

Nagaraju, M., & Tripathy, B. K. (2013). Covering based multi granulation rough sets and study of their topological properties. In *Proceedings of CCIIS 2013*. VIT University.

Pawlak, Z. (1982). Rough sets. *International Journal of Computer and Information Sciences, 11*, 341–356. doi:10.1007/BF01001956

Pawlak, Z. (1983). Rough classifications. *International Journal of Man-Machine Studies, 20*, 469–483. doi:10.1016/S0020-7373(84)80022-X

Pawlak, Z. (1991). *Theoretical aspects of reasoning about data*. London: Kluwer Academic Publishers.

Pawlak, Z., & Skowron, A. (2007a). Rudiments of rough sets. *Information Sciences-An International Journal, 177*(1), 3–27. doi:10.1016/j.ins.2006.06.003

Pawlak, Z., & Skowron, A. (2007b). Rough sets: Some extensions. *Information Sciences-An International Journal, 177*(1), 28–40. doi:10.1016/j.ins.2006.06.006

Pawlak, Z., & Skowron, A. (2007c). Rough sets and Boolean reasoning. *Information Sciences-An International Journal, 177*(1), 41–73. doi:10.1016/j.ins.2006.06.007

Pedrycz, W. (2007). Granular computing: The emerging paradigm. *Journal of Uncertain Systems, 1*(1), 38–61.

Pedrycz, W., & Bargiela, A. (2002). Granular clustering: A granular signature of data. *IEEE Transactions on Systems, Man, and Cybernetics. Part B, Cybernetics, 32*(2), 212–224. doi:10.1109/3477.990878 PMID:18238121

Qian, Y. H., & Liang, J. Y. (2006). Rough set method based on multi-granulations. In *Proceedings of the 5th IEEE Conference on Cognitive Informatics*, (Vol. 1, pp. 297 – 304). IEEE.

Qian, Y. H., Liang, J. Y., & Dang, C. Y. (2007). MGRS in incomplete information systems. In *Proceedings of IEEE Conference on Granular Computing*, (pp. 163 – 168). IEEE.

Qian, Y. H., Liang, J. Y., & Dang, C. Y. (2010a). Pessimistic rough decision. [RST.]. *Proceedings of RST, 2010*, 440–449.

Qian, Y. H., Liang, J. Y., & Dang, C. Y. (2010b). Incomplete multigranulation rough set. *IEEE Transactions on Systems, Man, and Cybernetics. Part A, Systems and Humans, 40*(2), 420–431. doi:10.1109/TSMCA.2009.2035436

Raghavan, R., & Tripathy, B. K. (2011). On some topological properties of multigranular rough sets. *Journal of Advances in Applied Science Research, 2*(3), 536–543.

Raghavan, R., & Tripathy, B. K. (2013). On some comparison properties of rough sets based on multigranulations and types of multigranular approximations of classifications. *International Journal of Intelligent Systems and Applications, 6*, 70–77. doi:10.5815/ijisa.2013.06.09

Tripathy, B. K. (2009a). On approximation of classifications, rough equalities and rough equivalences. In *Rough set theory: A true landmark in data analysis*. Springer Verlag. doi:10.1007/978-3-540-89921-1_4

Tripathy, B. K. (2009b). Rough sets on fuzzy approximation spaces and intuitionistic fuzzy approximation spaces. In *Rough set theory: A true landmark in data analysis*. Springer Verlag. doi:10.1007/978-3-540-89921-1_1

Tripathy, B. K. (2011). An analysis of approximate equalities based on rough set theory. *International Journal of Advances in Science and Technology, 31*, 23–36.

Tripathy, B. K. (2012). On some topological properties of pessimistic multigranular rough sets. In *Proceedings of the UGC Sponsored National Conference in Seemanta College*. UGC.

Tripathy, B. K., & Mitra, A. (2010b). Topological properties of rough sets and their applications. *International Journal of Granular Computing. Rough Sets and Intelligent Systems, 1*(4), 355–369. doi:10.1504/IJGCRSIS.2010.036978

Tripathy, B. K., & Mitra, A. (2013b). On approximate equivalences of multigranular rough sets and approximate reasoning. *International Journal Information Technology and Computer Science, 10*, 103–113. doi:10.5815/ijitcs.2013.10.11

Tripathy, B. K., & Mitra, A. (2013c). On the approximate equalities of multigranular rough sets and approximate reasoning. In *Proceedings of 4th IEEE Conference on Computing, Communication and Network Technologies*. Tamil Nadu, India: IEEE.

Tripathy, B. K., Mitra, A., & Ojha, J. (2008). On rough equalities and rough equivalence of sets. In *Rough sets and current trends in computing (LNAI)* (Vol. 5306, pp. 92–102). Berlin: Springer. doi:10.1007/978-3-540-88425-5_10

Tripathy, B. K., & Nagaraju, M. (2011). Topological properties of incomplete multigranulation based on fuzzy rough sets. In *Proceedings of ObCom 2011 Conference*. VIT.

Tripathy, B. K., & Nagaraju, M. (2012a). On some topological properties of pessimistic multigranular rough sets. *International Journal of Intelligent Systems and Applications, 4*(8), 10–17. doi:10.5815/ijisa.2012.08.02

Tripathy, B. K., & Nagaraju, M. (2012b). A comparative analysis of multigranular approaches and on topological properties of incomplete pessimistic multigranular rough fuzzy sets. *International Intelligent Systems and Applications, 11*, 99–109. doi:10.5815/ijisa.2012.11.12

Tripathy, B. K., Panda, G. K., & Mitra, A. (2012c). Some concepts of incomplete multigranulation based on rough intuitionistic fuzzy sets. *Advances in Intelligent and Soft Computing, 166*, 683–694. doi:10.1007/978-3-642-30157-5_68

Tripathy, B. K., & Raghavan, R. (2013a). Some algebraic properties of multigranulations and an analysis of multigranular approximations of classifications. *International Journal of Information Technology and Computer Science, 7*, 63–70. doi:10.5815/ijitcs.2013.07.08

Wang, H. (2006). Nearest neighborhood by neighborhood counting. *IEEE Transactions on Pattern Analysis and Machine Intelligence, 28*, 942–953. doi:10.1109/TPAMI.2006.126 PMID:16724588

Wu, M., & Kou, G. (2010). Fuzzy rough set model on multi-granulations. In *Proceedings of the 2nd International Conference on Computer Engineering and Technology*, (Vol. 2, pp. 72–75). IEEE.

Yao, J. T., Vasilakos, V., & Pedrycz, W. (2013). *Granular computing: Perspectives and challenges*. IEEE Transactions on Cybernetics.

Yao, Y. Y. (1998). Relational interpretations of neighborhood operators and rough set approximation operators. *Information Sciences, 111*, 239–259. doi:10.1016/S0020-0255(98)10006-3

Yao, Y. Y. (2005). Perspectives of granular computing. In *Proceedings of 2005 IEEE International Conference on Granular Computing*, (pp. 85 – 90). IEEE.

Yao, Y. Y. (2007). The art of granular computing. In *Proceedings of the International Conference on Rough Sets and Emerging Intelligent Systems Paradigms*, (pp. 101 – 112). IEEE.

Yao, Y. Y. (2008). A unified framework of granular computing. In *Handbook of granular computing* (pp. 401–410). Academic Press. doi:10.1002/9780470724163.ch17

Yao, Y. Y., & Yao, B. (2012). Covering based rough set approximations. *Information Sciences, 200*, 91–107. doi:10.1016/j.ins.2012.02.065

Zadeh, L. A. (1965). Fuzzy sets. *Information and Control, 8*(11), 338–353. doi:10.1016/S0019-9958(65)90241-X

Zakowski, W. (1983). Approximations in the space (U II). *Demonstration Mathematics, 16*, 761–769.

KEY TERMS AND DEFINITIONS

Algebraic Properties: The properties of objects in sets with or without giving emphasis on the properties of the set as a whole.

Classification: A decomposition of a universe into disjoint set of subsets such that their union is the whole universe.

Cover: A decomposition of a universe into subsets such that their union is the whole universe. It is a generalisation of the concept of classification.

Fuzzy Set: A model proposed by L.A.Zadeh in 1965 to capture imprecision in data through membership values.

Granule: The smallest addressable unit of knowledge in any application.

Hybrid Models: Models obtained by combining two or more models by imposing the structure of one on the other(s).

Intuitionistic Fuzzy Set: A model to capture imprecision in data proposed by Atanassov, which generalises the concept of Fuzzy set by allowing the non-membership value to be defined in such a way that it may not be the one's complement of the membership value but its sum with membership value must lie in [0, 1].

Multigranulation: The granulation of knowledge obtained by taking two or more granulations at a time.

Neighborhood: The set of elements close to a particular objet. The closeness is defined through some measure and parameter(s).

Rough Set: A model, proposed by Pawlak in 1982, to capture imprecision in data through boundary approach (proposed by Gottlob Freze, the father of modern logic).

Topological Properties: The properties of sets taken as a whole without considering the properties of individual objects into account.

Chapter 2
Pattern Recognition and Robotics

P. Geethanjali
VIT University, India

ABSTRACT

During the last few decades, there has been a considerable growth of interest in pattern recognition in the field of robotics. An application of pattern recognition in robotics includes mobile robots and service robots. Visual and signal recognition of patterns enables the robots to perform a variety of tasks such as object and target recognition, navigation, grasping, and manipulation, assisting physically challenged people. This chapter surveys trends in robotics with pattern recognition that focuses more on the interaction between robot assistive device and human with signal pattern recognition. This interaction helps to enhance the capability of people in rehabilitation and in the field of medicine. Finally, this chapter includes the application of pattern recognition in the development of a prosthetic hand.

INTRODUCTION

Pattern recognition has evolved in the field of robotics for rehabilitation of people, surgeons and natural human robot interaction. Signal pattern recognition finds application in prosthetic devices, orthotic devices, brain controlled wheelchair etc. in the field of rehabilitation to assist the disabled people resulted from accidents, peripheral vascular disease, diabetes etc. to improve their day-to-day activity. In rehabilitation engineering robots are employed to serve as an external assistants or artificial extensions of missing or impaired limbs known as prosthesis. Besides prostheses, the assistive robotic systems are also developed to help disabled people through physical interaction using interfaces such as joysticks and keyboards. Information to access hand-free, man-machine communication to help the disabled people can be obtained from various forms of human bio-signal including electroencephalogram (EEG), electrocardiogram (ECG), electrooculogram

DOI: 10.4018/978-1-4666-4940-8.ch002

(EOG), electromyogram (EMG) also referred as myoelectric signal (MES). Among them EMG signals pattern recognition has been widely used for the control of prosthetic devices. EEG signals pattern recognition has been widely used for the control of wheelchair for people who have disruptive communication path between brain and body due to spinal cord injury.

The most important advantage of hands-free EMG/EEG controlled robot systems over other types of control system, such as body-powered mechanical systems, assistive robotic systems, is in the capability to control from an intention of the user. An intention of the user can be detected either from EMG/EEG signals through pattern recognition. Decoding and extracting information contained in the EMG/EEG signals is a tempting task undertook by many engineers and physiologists in various fields of research such as man-machine communication channel to help people with/without disabilities, virtual-environment applications. The development of an intuitive and accurate man-machine communication opened the door for a life opportunity to the disabled people includes mobility impaired people and people who have lost their limbs. Enormous number of research papers exists in the area of man-machine communication in the development of robotic assistive devices using pattern recognition techniques.

In addition to signals, images also used in localization and mapping for navigation of mobile robots. Robots with new capability are available due to recent advances in pattern recognition algorithm and high speed processor. Visual pattern recognition can be used in human-robot interaction, security, surgical assistant etc. To achieve full autonomy, a robot must able to recognize visual images. For example robots are developed for the retail market which detects and recognizes the items placed in basket. This necessitates the use of pattern recognition technique from the images captured using camera.

This chapter will discuss the application of pattern recognition in robots for assisting the disabled people. This chapter will provide implementation of pattern recognition based motion control of a prosthetic drive, through continuous myoelectric signal acquisition, classification with and without principal component analysis using neural network classifier.

PATTERN RECOGNITON IN ROBOTS

The problem of pattern recognition involves decision making in most of the robotics applications. The process of preprocessing in pattern recognition of signal/image processing is required to remove noise and redundant data. In the decision making approach, the process consists of data segmentation, feature extraction and feature selection/reduction as shown in Figure 1.

After preprocessing of data, it is necessary to extract the features that will potentially help in decision making. Features contain information and the extraction of relevant features for decision making application depends upon the patterns and the number of decisions under consideration. Several approaches are available for extraction of features, selection of features and classification in different robotic applications.

Enormous number of research papers exists in the area of development of myoelectric controlled prosthetic hand. Pattern based-recognition for myoelectric control of prosthetic devices may be explained under feature extraction and/or feature dimensionality reduction, and classification of myoelectric data. Sardis, G.N. & Gootee, T.P. (1982) identified patterns of pre-specified motion from the feature space of variance (VAR) and zero crossing (ZC). Later, Lee, S., & Sardis, G.N. (1984) used integral absolute value (IAV) also known as mean absolute value (MAV) along with VAR, ZC for the myoelectric control of arm. Hudgins, B., Parker.P., & Scott, R.N. (1993) investigated the information content in the transient burst of

Figure 1. Illustration of pattern recognition based robot system

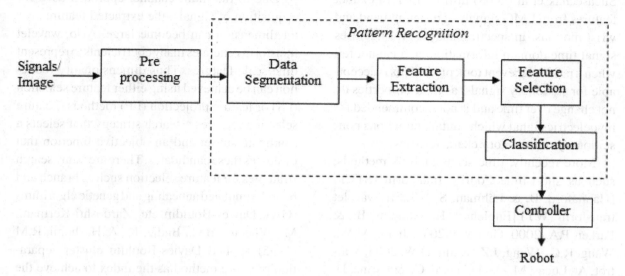

myoelectric activity using MAV, mean absolute value slope (MAVS), number of zero crossings (ZC), number of slope sign changes (SSC) and waveform length (WL). Because of the stochastic and non-linear nature of EMG signals, a considerable amount of research has been carried out using autoregressive (AR) models to describe feature sets. Graupe, D., Magnussen, J., & Beex, A.A. (1978), Karlik, B., Tokhi, M.O., & Alci, M. (2003), and Soares, A., Andrade, A., Lamounier, E., & Carrijo, R. (2003) made use of autoregressive (AR) model to represent non-stationary nature of EMG signals. The increase in accuracy is low and attains saturation for AR model of five and more. Kang et al (1995), Chang et al (1996) took advantage of cepstral coefficients (CC) of EMG signal as the control command of man-machine interface. Knox, R. & Brooks, D.H. (1994) compared the classification performance with the features based on time-series modeling such as Auto regressive coefficients (ARC), reflection coefficients (RC) and logarithmic area ratios (LAR) on steady state signals and found that all the feature types tested had approximately equivalent classification rates. Huang, Y.,Englehart, K., Hudgins, B., & Chan, A.D.C. (2005) compared three groups of feature set such as Hudgins' TD features, AR coefficients and root means square (RMS) using Gaussian mixture model (GMM) classifier. AR+RMS and AR+RMS+TD resulted in lower average error rate. But, results have shown that a combination of RMS with a six-order ARC, yields good performance compared to AR+RMS+TD. Feature vector in the later is too high, thus computation time is more. Hargrove, L., Englehart, K. & Hudgins, B. (2006) compared the performance of TD, AR+RMS and TD+AR features for EMG pattern recognition with the effect of electrode displacement.

Besides time domain features, the fast Fourier transform (FFT) has been applied to the EMG signals to verify model of EMG generation, for diagnosis of diseases affecting neuromuscular conduction and for determining the frequency spectrum of EMG signal. Uchida, N., Hiraiwa, A., Sonehara, N., & Shimohara, K. (1988) analyzed finger movements using FFT. Farry, K.A., Walker, I.D., & Baramiuk, R.G. (1996) used the FFT in tele-operation of prosthetic hand. Nishikawa, D., Wenwei Yu, Yokoi, H., & Kakazu, Y. (1999) obtained classification performance with Gabor transform and MAV applied to EMG.

Sueaseenak et al (2008) utilised FFT to extract features from EMG signals of different hand and wrist motions. In spectral analysis, a FFT loses signal time domain information, and cannot tell when a particular event took place. This is acceptable for stationary signals, as their properties do not change over time and is not recommended for myoelectric signal which contain numerous non-stationary or transitory characteristics.

More recently, time-scale analysis methods, such as short-time Fourier transform (STFT) [Hannaford, B. & Lehman, S. (1986)], wavelet transform (WT) [Englehart, K., Hudgins, B., & Parker, P.A. 2000, Guo et al 2004, Jiang, M.W., Wang, R.C., Wang, J.Z., & Jin, D.W. 2005, Maitrot, A., Lucas, M. –F., Doncarli, C., & Farina, D. 2005, Zhao et al 2006, Arvetti, M., Gini, G., & Folgheraiter, M. 2007, Kakoty, N.M., & Hazarika, S.M. 2009], and wavelet packet transform (WPT) [Englehart, K., Hudgins, B., & Parker, P.A. 2000, Li, D., Pedrycz, W., & Pizzi, N.J. 2005, Ren, X., Huang, H., & Deng, L. 2009] are widely used. Englehart, K., Hudgins, B., & Parker, P.A. (2001) compared the performance of TD features with time-scale features comprised of a STFT, WT and WPT using principal component analysis (PCA). The results indicated that classification performance improved in a progression from TD→STFT→WT→WPT indicating the relative efficacy of the feature set applied with principal component analysis (PCA). This was a significant improvement over Hudgin's TD features. Englehart, K. & Hudgins, B (2003) demonstrated that in steady state TD features outperformed the time-scale features using continuous classification.

In pattern recognition, reduction of feature dimensionality is mostly applied to cope with the curse of dimensionality that occurs when using time-scale features. A wavelet transform generates many coefficients to represent time-scale features. These higher dimensional feature space need to be mapped into a lower dimension, while preserving the most discriminative information in the signals.

Due to the multi-channel approach used for acquisition of signals, the extracted feature vector dimension can become large. Also, wavelet transform generates many coefficients to represent time-scale features. Thus dimensionality reduction can be achieved using either feature selection (FS) or feature projection (FP) methods. Feature selection requires a search strategy that selects a candidate subset and an objective function that evaluates these candidates. There are many search strategies for feature selection such as branch and bound, simulated annealing and genetic algorithms (GA), Davies-Bouldin etc. Zardoshti-Kermani, M., Wheeler, B.C., Badie, K., & Hashemi, R.M (1995) applied Davies-Bouldin cluster separation measure method as the index to achieve the feature selection task. Huang, H.-P., Liu, Y.-H., & Wong, C.-S. (2003) demonstrated reduction of feature space by Kohonen's self-organizing map. An important factor that limits the applicability of feature selection methods to EMG classification problems is caused by the large variance of the EMG signals [Chu et al (2007)]. Increased number features can also be reduced by channel selection as proposed by the researchers.

Pattern recognition (classification), maps the feature vectors into specific classes of motion. Many literatures highlight the success of neural networks (NN) and its ability to learn the distinction among different conditions in pattern recognition. The advantage of the neural network is, its ability to learn linear and non-linear relationships directly from data being modelled. As pioneers in developing real-time pattern recognition-based myoelectric control, Hudgins, B., Parker.P., & Scott, R.N. (1993), Tenore, F., & Ramos, A. (2007), Tsenov et al (2006) used a multi-layer perceptron (MLP) neural network to classify time-domain features. Wang et al (2005) applied back-propagation neural network (BPNN) with AR coefficients for classification. Zhao et al (2005) applied Levenberg-Marquardt based neural network with parametric AR model and integral of EMG to control five-fingered prosthetic hand.

Tsuji et al (2000) proposed a NN that combines a common BPNN with recurrent neural filter to classify from time-series of EMG signals, rather than features. Barrero et al (2001) discriminated EMG signals for externally controlled upper extremity prosthesis using artificial neural network (ANN). Del Boca, A. & Park, D.C. (1994) extracted MES features through Fourier analysis and clustered using Fuzzy C-Means algorithm. Data obtained by this unsupervised learning technique are then presented to MLP type NN. Jung et al (2007) proposed linear vector quantization (LVQ) neural network to classify spectral estimates from fourth order AR parameters of EMG signals obtained using Yule-Walker method. Guo et al (2006) used wavelet packet transform features of EMG signals to LVQ neural network. Ito, K., Tsukamoto, M. & Kondo,T. (2008) proposed a multiple NN to determine the movement intended by an amputee from EMG signals Ma, N., Kumar, D.K., & Pah, N. (2001) used NN to classify EMG signals resulting from the dynamic muscle contraction. Guo et al (2009) used Levenberg-Marquardt algorithm to advance the training speed and accuracy compared to back-propagation algorithm for pattern recognition of human motion from AR coefficients. Matsumura et al (2002) used NN to FFT spectra of EMG signals for recognition hand motion.

In the pattern-based recognition system, EMG signals are recognized into a number of classes. Most modern techniques have been applied for the classification of signals. These classifier performances depend on features vector. Choosing a feature set is not trivial. Extracting the usable information from EMG through the development of feature set is important. Larger features sets must be used in conjunction with dimensionality reduction to overcome the curse of dimensionality. But reducing the burden to the classifier introduces time delay and reduced analysis window size with a degradation of classification performance [Hargrove, L., Guangline, L. Englehart, K., & Hudgins, B. (2009)].

In pattern recognition-based controllers, the desired classes of functions are identified from signal patterns by classifiers, and the variety of functions depends directly on classification performance. The different stages of typical pattern recognition based-myoelectric control as shown in Figure 1 are discussed below. This chapter details the pattern recognition of continuous MES which contains both transient and steady state with time domain statistical feature due to ease of extraction compared to transform techniques. The extracted features are classified using neural network with and without feature dimensionality reduction.

Methodology

This chapter presents the recognition of six hand motion from the four-channel EMG data corresponding to six different limb motions are obtained by using surface electrodes. To acquire the EMG signals, disc electrodes (Ag/Agcl) are placed at flexor digitorum superficialis, supinator, extensor digitorum communis and extensor indicis with a conductive paste on the surface of the skin for able-bodied subject. The EMG signal is acquired by digitizing at a sample rate of 1000 Hz through DS1104 control board and dSPACE® software. The subject performed the following motions i.e.; hand open (HO), hand close (HC), wrist flexion (WF), wrist extension (WE), ulnar deviation (UD) and radial deviation (RD) for 8 trials. Each motion is continued for 5 seconds. Figure 2 shows the one of the channels signal pattern variations for different hand motion.

Data Segmentation and Windowing

Data segmentation comprises various techniques and methods to improve accuracy and response time. A time slot for acquiring stream of myoelectric data for feature extraction is regarded as data segment. A myoelectric data acquired for classification comprises of two states: (i) a transient state emanating from a burst of fibers, as a muscle

Figure 2. EMG signals for different hand motions

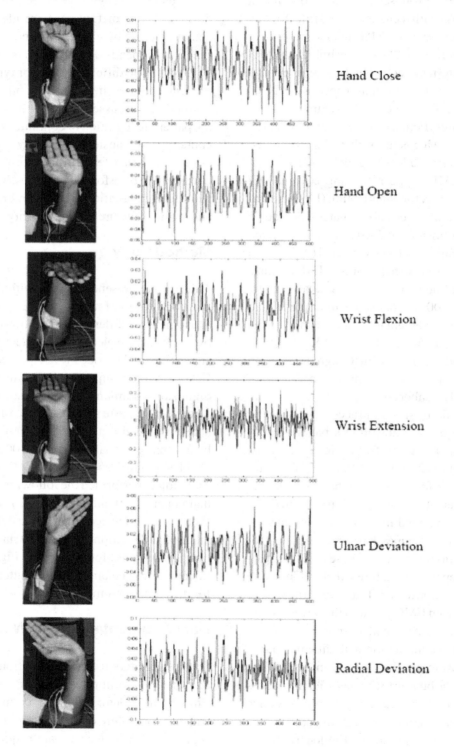

goes from rest to a voluntary contraction level and (ii) a steady state produced during constant contraction in a muscle. Hudgins, B., Parker.P., & Scott, R.N. (1993) were the first to investigate the information content of a transient data that comes with the onset of sudden muscular effort. Also Kondo, T., Amagi, O., & Nozawa, T. (2008), detected patterns of EMG from transient state. The main disadvantage in using a transient state in myoelectric control is that it requires initiating a contraction from rest. This prohibits switching from class to class in an effective or intuitive manner, and also impedes the coordination of complex tasks involving multiple degrees of freedom.

Englehart, K., Hudgins, B., & Parker, P.A. (2001) demonstrated that steady-state data classified more accurately than transient data and rate

of classification degrades more quickly as the segment length of transient data is decreased, than with steady-state data. A myoelectric signal has an undetermined state during transition between different levels of contractions. Therefore, most errors in classification occur when switching between classes. In addition, due to the intrinsic inertia, prosthetic devices would not be able to respond to transitory states. As a result, the detection and elimination of data segments belonging to a transition period, can improve accuracy of the controller. This can be most applicable when generating a reliable training data set. Huang, Y.,Englehart, K., Hudgins, B., & Chan, A.D.C. (2005) omitted transition data between motions to improve the quality of training data. However, Hargrove, L., Losier,L., Lock,B., Englehart,

Figure 3. EMG data segmentation

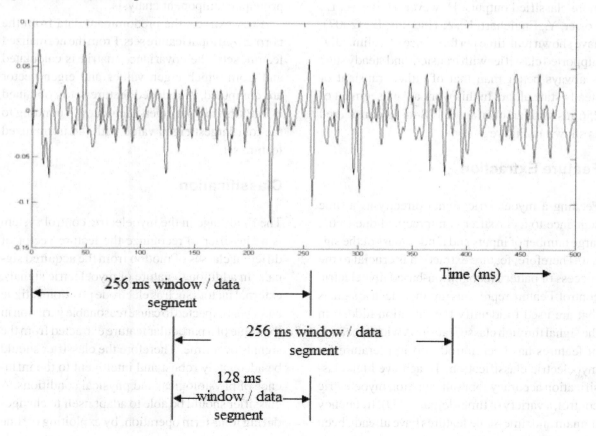

K.,& Hudgins, B. (2007) demonstrated that the effectiveness of the prosthetic devices improves by considering both transient and steady state myoelectric data. Therefore, it is attractive to consider the application of a steady-state and transient data in real time applications.

In data segmentation, after segment length and the state of data is the selection of data windowing technique. There are two major techniques in data windowing: adjacent windowing and overlapped windowing. In adjacent windowing, adjacent disjoint segments with a pre-defined length of data are used for feature extraction and classification of intended motion. Since processing time is a small portion of segment length, the processor is under utilised during the remaining time of the segment length. In the overlapped windowing technique, the new segment slides over the current segment, with an increment time less than the segment length to use the idle time of the processor to generate more classified outputs. However, Hargrove, L., Losier, Y., Englehart, K., & Hudgins, B., (2007), have shown real-time performance of a clinically-supported classifier with transient and steady state is always better than that of either transient or steady state alone. In this work a data segment of 256 ms with an overlap of 128 ms is considered as shown in Figure 3.

Feature Extraction

Feeding a myoelectric signal directly as a time sequence to a classifier is impractical due to the large number of inputs and randomness of the signal. Therefore, feature extraction is crucial to the success of pattern recognition-based myoelectric control. Feature represents raw myoelectric signals that are used to identify the intention hidden in the signal through classification. A wide spectrum of features has been introduced in literature for myoelectric classification. To achieve high classification accuracy for multifunction myoelectric control, a variety of time-domain (TD), frequency domain and time-scale features have already been

proposed by the researchers. Selection or extraction of highly effective features is one of the most critical stages in designing myoelectric controllers.

In this chapter four time domain statistical features such as mean absolute value (MAV), zero crossings (ZC), slope sign changes (SSC) and waveform length (WL) and fourth order auto regressive (AR) coefficients are extracted using a rectangular windowing technique.

Reduction of Feature Dimensionality

Generally, the high dimensionality of a feature vector overwhelms the classifier with increased learning parameters. Thus, it requires reduction of the feature vector dimension without much loss of classification accuracy. The common method in all signal classification method is to provide a feature set that improves classification performance. The reduction in feature dimension is achieved using principal component analysis.

PCA extracts the predominant data from the normalized input feature sets. From the normalized feature sets, the covariance matrix is calculated and from which eigen values and eigen vector are computed. A reduced feature set is obtained by multiplying the eigen vector corresponding to the four largest eigen value with the normalized feature set.

Classification

The final stage in the myoelectric control system is a classifier to recognize the feature vector of different classes of motion from the acquired signals. In addition to nature of myoelectric signals, external factors such as electrode position, fatigue and sweat expected to cause reasonable variation in the value of a particular feature extracted from the signals over time. Therefore the classifier should be adequately robust and intelligent to the influence of physiological and physical conditions. A classifier should be able to adapt itself to changes during long-term operation, by exploiting offline

Figure 4. Performance of NN classifier in identification of intended limb motion

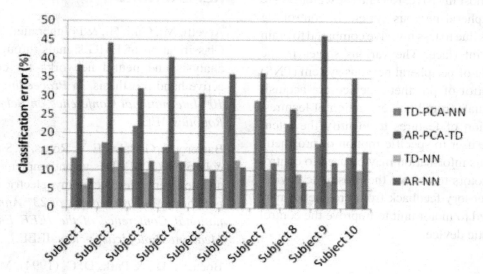

and or online training as well as adequately fast to meet real-time constraints. For the extracted feature vectors, the classification performance has been investigated using neural network classifier with and without reduction of features.

Different multilayer neural networks are built for TD statistical data and AR coefficients considering entire feature vector and reduced feature vector. Neural network is composed of 5 input neurons including threshold and six output neurons is built using WEKA software for reduced features and 17 input neurons for recognition of motion from entire feature vector. The classification was divided into two stages: the training stage and the testing stage. Three trials of all six motions out of 8 trials have been considered in training. During testing, the remaining five trials of six motions are used. The performance of the classifier is shown in Figure 4.

From Figure 4 the average percentage classification error is less for TD features. Further, NN classifier without reduction of time domain statistical performs better than NN classifier with reduced features. In the initial stage of development of prosthetic hand, the authors implemented the NN classifier for actuation of three DC motor to manifest six motions of hand.

Controller

To obtain desired output control commands based on signal patterns and control schemes, researchers worked on microprocessors, microcontrollers and DSP controllers. With the intent of maximizing classification accuracy and reduction of response time for a desired movement, the research often involves a variety of methods to identify and control the intended motions. The author implemented the offline actuation of drive using personal computer.

FUTURE RESEARCH DIRECTIONS

Researchers are attempting to emulate the biological features for the movement of human limb with multifunction and multi-channel actuation of a bio-mimetic artificial limb using EMG signals. Several significant problems, like response time, computational burden etc. with the present prosthetic devices have been reported. Researchers can attempt on pattern recognition technique that overcome above mentioned drawbacks.

Further, few researchers have shown that hand area of motor cortex stimulation enable movement of fingers to provide dexterity in prosthetics. But these are most invasive. Recently researchers are using peripheral nervous system in controlling prosthetics due to less invasive compared to brain computer interface. The various stages in the functioning of peripheral nervous system (PNS) based control of prosthetic device are acquisition of signals from PNS, extraction of features, classification of features to identify the intention of the user to specific motion of prosthetic device. This information may be used to control electric motors to actuate the prosthetic device. Further, sensory feedback from prosthetics may be provided to motor unit to improve the control of prosthetic device.

CONCLUSION

This chapter briefs about the application of pattern recognition in identification of intended motion from myoelectric signals in the application of robotics. Then, the various techniques used in the pattern recognition have been discussed in respect of myoelectric control of prosthetic hand. The pattern recognition techniques that have been used in identifying the intended limb motions of the subject is successfully implemented through the computer based actuation of the drive as well as digital signal controller based drive. Researchers are working towards increasing the dexterity of prosthetic with less processing time from multi-channel data in order to enable the user to use the prosthetic hand without delay. Further, EEG-based brain controlled robots are being developed which necessitate the application of pattern recognition in order to support for disabled people in daily activities.

REFERENCES

Arvetti, M., Gini, G., & Folgheraiter, M. (2007). Classification of EMG signals through wavelet analysis and neural networks for controlling active hand prosthesis. In *Proceedings of IEEE 10th International Conference on Rehabilitation Robotics*. IEEE.

Barrero, V., Grisales, E. V., Rosas, F., Sanchez, C., & Leon, J. (2001). Design and implementation of an intelligent interface for myoelectric controlled prosthesis. In *Proceedings of 23rd Annual International Conference of the IEEE Engineering Medicine Biological Society*. IEEE.

Boca, A. D., & Park, D. C. (1994). Myoelectric signal recognition using fuzzy clustering and artificial neural networks in real time. In *Proceedings of IEEE International Conference on Neural Networks,* (vol. 5, pp.3098-3103). IEEE.

Chang, G.-C., Kang, W.-J., Jer-Junn, L., Cheng, C.-K., Lai, J.-S., Chen, J.-J.J., & Kuo, T.-S. (1996). Real-time implementation of electromyogram pattern recognition as a control command of man-machine interface. *Journal of Medical Engineering and Physics, 18*(7), 529-537.

Chu, J.-U., Moon, I., Lee, Y.-J., Kim, S.-K., & Mun, M.-S. (2007). A supervised feature-projection-based-real-time EMG pattern recognition for multifunction myoelectric hand control. *IEEE Transaction on Mechatronics, 12*(3), 282–290. doi:10.1109/TMECH.2007.897262

Englehart, K., & Hudgins, B. (2003). A robust, real-time control scheme for multifunction myoelectric control. *IEEE Transactions on Bio-Medical Engineering, 50*(7), 848–854. doi:10.1109/TBME.2003.813539 PMID:12848352

Englehart, K., Hudgins, B., & Parker, P. A. (2000). Time-frequency based classification of the myoelectric signal: Static vs dynamic contractions. In *Proceedings of 22nd Annual International Conference of the IEEE Engineering Medicine Biological Society*. IEEE.

Englehart, K., Hudgins, B., & Parker, P. A. (2001). A wavelet-based continuous classification scheme for multifunction myoelectric control. *IEEE Transactions on Bio-Medical Engineering*, 48(3), 302–310. doi:10.1109/10.914793 PMID:11327498

Farry, K. A., Walker, I. D., & Baramiuk, R. G. (1996). Myoelectric teleoperation of a complex robotic hand. *IEEE Transactions on Robotics and Automation*, 12(5), 775–788. doi:10.1109/70.538982

Geethanjali, P., & Ray, K. K. (2011). Identification of motion from multi-channel EMG signals for control of prosthetic hand. *Australasian Physical & Engineering Sciences in Medicine*, 34, 419–427. doi:10.1007/s13246-011-0079-z PMID:21667211

Graupe, D., Magnussen, J., & Beex, A. A. (1978). A microprocessor system for multifunctional control of upper-limb prostheses via myoelectric signal identification. *IEEE Transactions on Automatic Control*, 23(4), 538–544. doi:10.1109/TAC.1978.1101783

Guo, X. Yang., P., Chen, L., Wang, X. & Li, L. (2006). Study of the control mechanism of robot-prosthesis based-on the EMG processed. In *Proceedings of 6th World Congress on Intelligent Control and Automation*. IEEE.

Guo, X., Yu, H., Zhen, G., Liu, Y., Zhang, Y., & Zhang, Y. (2009). Artificial intelligent based human motion pattern recognition and prediction for the surface electromyographic signals. In *Proceedings of International Conference on Information Technology and Computer Science*, (pp.289-292). IEEE.

Hannaford, B., & Lehman, S. (1986). Short time Fourier analysis of the electromyogram: Fast movements and constant contraction. *IEEE Transactions on Bio-Medical Engineering*, 33(12), 1173–1181. doi:10.1109/TBME.1986.325697 PMID:3817851

Hargrove, L., Englehart, K., & Hudgins, B. (2006). The effect of electrode displacements on pattern recognition based myoelectric control. In *Proceedings 28th Annual International Conference of the IEEE Engineering Medicine Biological Society*. IEEE.

Hargrove, L., Guangline, L., Englehart, K., & Hudgins, B. (2009). Principal components analysis preprocessing for improved classification accuracies in pattern-recognition-based myoelectric control. *IEEE Transactions on Bio-Medical Engineering*, 56(5), 1407–1414. doi:10.1109/TBME.2008.2008171 PMID:19473932

Hargrove, L., Losier, L., Lock, B., Englehart, K., & Hudgins, B. (2007). A real-time pattern recognition based myoelectric control usability study implemented in a virtual environement. In *Proceedings of 29th Annual International Conference of the IEEE Engineering Medicine Biological Society*. IEEE.

Huang, H.-P., Liu, Y.-H., & Wong, C.-S. (2003). Automatic EMG feature evaluation for controlling a prosthetic hand using supervised feature mining method: An intelligent approach. In *Proceedings of IEEE International Conference on Robotics and Automation*. IEEE.

Huang, Y., Englehart, K., Hudgins, B., & Chan, A. D. C. (2005). A gaussian mixture model based classification scheme for myoelectric control of powered upper limb prostheses. *IEEE Transactions on Bio-Medical Engineering*, 52(11), 1801–1901. doi:10.1109/TBME.2005.856295 PMID:16285383

Hudgins, B., Parker, P., & Scott, R. N. (1993). A new strategy for multifunction myoelectric control. *IEEE Transactions on Bio-Medical Engineering, 40*(1), 82–94. doi:10.1109/10.204774 PMID:8468080

Ito, K., Tsukamoto, M., & Kondo, T. (2008). Discrimination of intended movements based on nonstationary EMG for a prosthetic hand control. In *Proceedings of 3ʳᵈ International Symposium on Communications, Control and Signal Processing.* IEEE.

Jiang, M. W., Wang, R. C., Wang, J. Z., & Jin, D. W. (2005). A method of recognizing finger motion using wavelet transform of surface EMG signal. In *Proceedings of. 27ᵗʰ Annual International Conference of the IEEE Engineering Medicine Biological Society.* IEEE.

Jung, K. K., Kim, J. W., Lee, H. K., Chung, S. B., & Eom, K. H. (2007). EMG pattern classification using spectral estimation and neural network. In *Proceedings of Annual Conference on Society of Instrumentation and Control Engineers.* IEEE.

Kakoty, N. M., & Hazarika, S. M. (2009). Classification of grasp types through wavelet decomposition of EMG signals. In *Proceedingsof 2ⁿᵈ International Conference on Biomedical Engineering and Informatics.* IEEE.

Kang, W.-J., Shiu, J.-R., Cheng, C.-K., Lai, J.-S., Tsao, H.-W., & Kuo, T.-S. (1995). The application of cepstral coefficients and maximum likelihood method in EMG pattern recognition. *IEEE Transactions on Bio-Medical Engineering, 42*(8), 777–785. doi:10.1109/10.398638 PMID:7642191

Karlik, B., Tokhi, M. O., & Alci, M. (2003). A fuzzy clustering neural network architecture for multifunction upper-limb prosthesis. *IEEE Transactions on Bio-Medical Engineering, 50*(11), 1255–1261. doi:10.1109/TBME.2003.818469 PMID:14619995

Knox, R., & Brooks, D. H. (1994). Classification of multifunction surface EMG using advanced AR model representations. In *Proceedings of Bioengineering Conference.* IEEE.

Kondo, T., Amagi, O., & Nozawa, T. (2008). Proposal of anticipatory pattern recognition for EMG prosthetic hand control. In *Proceedings of IEEE International Conference on Systems, Man and Cybernetics.* IEEE.

Lee, S., & Sardis, G. N. (1984). The control of a prosthetic arm by EMG pattern recognition. *IEEE Transactions on Automatic Control, 29*(4), 290–302. doi:10.1109/TAC.1984.1103521

Ma, N., Kumar, D. K., & Pah, N. (2001). Classification of hand direction using multi-channel electromyography by neural network. In *Proceedings of 7ᵗʰ Australian and New Zealand Intelligent Information Systems Conference.* IEEE.

Maitrot, A., Lucas, M.-F., Doncarli, C., & Farina, D. (2005). Signal-dependent wavelets for electromyogram classification. *Journal of Medical and Biological Engineering and Computing, 43*(4), 487–492. doi:10.1007/BF02344730 PMID:16255431

Matsumura, Y., Mitsukura, Y., Fukumi, M., & Akamatsu, N. (2002). Recognition of EMG signal patterns by neural networks. In *Proceedings of 9ᵗʰ International. Conference on Neural Information Processing,* (vol. 2, pp. 750-754). Singapore: IEEE.

Nishikawa, D., Yu, W., Yokoi, H., & Kakazu, Y. (1999). EMG prosthetic hand controller using real-time learning method. In *Proceedings of IEEE Systems Man and Cybernetics.* IEEE.

Ren, X., Huang, H., & Deng, L. (2009). MUAP classification based on wavelet packet and fuzzy clustering technique. In *Proceedings of 3ʳᵈ International Conference on Bioinformatics and Biomedical Engineering.* IEEE.

Sardis, G. N., & Gootee, T. P. (1982). EMG pattern analysis and classification for a prosthetic arm. *IEEE Transactions on Bio-Medical Engineering, 29*(6), 403–412. doi:10.1109/TBME.1982.324954 PMID:7106790

Soares, A., Andrade, A., Lamounier, E., & Carrijo, R. (2003). The development of a virtual myoelectric prosthesis controlled by an EMG pattern recognition system based on neural networks. *Journal of Intelligent Information Systems, 21*(2), 127–141. doi:10.1023/A:1024758415877

Sueaseenak, D., Wibirama, S., Chanwimalueang, T., Pintavirooj, C., & Sangworasil, M. (2008). Comparison study of muscular-contraction classification between independent component analysis and artificial neural network. In *Proceedings of International Symposium on Communications and Information Technologies*. IEEE.

Tenore, F., & Ramos, A. (2007). Towards the control of individual fingers of a prosthetic hand using surface EMG signals. In *Proceedings of 29th Annual International Conference of the IEEE Engineering Medicine Biological Society*. IEEE.

Tsenov, G., Zeghbib, A. H., Palis, F., Shoylev, N., & Mladenov, V. (2006). Neural networks for online classification of hand and finger movements using surface EMG signals. In *Proceedings of 8th Seminar on Neural Network Applications in Electrical Engineering*. IEEE.

Tsuji, T., Fukuda, O., Kaneko, M., & Koji, I. (2000). Pattern classification of time-series EMG signals using neural networks. *International Journal of Adaptive Control and Signal Processing, 14*(8), 829–848. doi:10.1002/1099-1115(200012)14:8<829::AID-ACS623>3.0.CO;2-L

Uchida, N., Hiraiwa, A., Sonehara, N., & Shimohara, K. (1988). EMG pattern recognition by neural networks for multi fingers control. In *Proceedings of Annual International Conference of the IEEE Engineering Medicine Biological Society*. IEEE.

Wang, J. Z., Wang, R. C., Li, F., Jiang, M. W., & Jin, D. W. (2005). EMG signal classification for myoelectric teleoperating a dexterous robot hand. In *Proceedings of. 27th Annual International Conference of the IEEE Engineering Medicine Biological Society*. IEEE.

Zardoshti-Kermani, M., Wheeler, B. C., Badie, K., & Hashemi, R. M. (1995). EMG feature evaluation for movement control of upper extremity prosthesis. *IEEE Transactions on Rehabilitation Engineering, 3*(4), 324–333. doi:10.1109/86.481972

Zhao, J. Xie, Z., Jiang, L., Cai, H., Liu, H., & Hirzinger, G. (2005). Levenberg-Marquardt based neural network control for a five-fingered prosthetic hand. In *Proceedings of IEEE International Conference on Robotics and Automation*. IEEE.

Zhao, J., Jiang, L., Cai, H., Liu, H., & Hirzinger, G. (2006). A novel EMG motion pattern classifier based on wavelet transform and nonlinearity analysis method. In *Proceedings of IEEE International Conference on Robotics and Biomimetics*. IEEE.

ADDITIONAL READING

Acharaya, S., Tenore, F., Aggarwal, V., Ettienne-Cummings, R., Schiber, M. H., & Thakor, N. (2008). Decoding individuated finger movments using volume-constrained neuronal ensembles in the M1 hand area. *IEEE Transactions on Neural Systems and Rehabilitation Engineering, 16*(1), 15–23. doi:10.1109/TNSRE.2007.916269 PMID:18303801

Baker, J. J., Bishop, W., Kellis, S., Levy, T., House, P., & Greger, B. (2009). Multi-scale recordings for neuroprosthetic control of finger movements, *Proceedings of IEEE International Conference on Engineering Medicine Biological Society* (pp.4573-4577).

Dowden, B. R., Wilder, R. M., Hiatt, S. D., Normann, R. A., Brown, N. A. T., & Clark, G. A. (2009). Selective and graded recruitment of cat hamstring muscles with infrafascicular stimulation. *IEEE Transactions on Neural Systems and Rehabilitation Engineering*, *17*(6), 545–552. doi:10.1109/TNSRE.2008.2011988 PMID:19696002

Geethanjali, P., & Ray, K. K. (2013). Statistical Pattern Recognition Technique for Improved Real-Time Myoelectric Signal Classification. *Biomedical Engineering: Applications, Basis and communications, 25*(2).

Heasman, J. M., Scott, T. R. D., Kirkup, L., Flynn, R. Y., Vare, V. A., & Gschwind, C. R. (2002). Control of a hand grasp neuroprosthess using an electroencephalogram-triggered switch: demonstration of improvements in performance using wavepacket analysis. *Medical & Biological Engineering & Computing*, *40*(5), 588–593. doi:10.1007/BF02345459 PMID:12452421

Lauer, R. T., Peckham, P. H., & Kilgore, K. (1999). EEG based control of hand grasp neuroprosthetics. *Neuroreport*, *10*(8), 1767–1771. doi:10.1097/00001756-199906030-00026 PMID:10501572

Schieber, M. H. (1991). Indivuated finger movements of rhesus monkeys: a means of quantifying the independence of the digits. *Journal of Neurophysiology*, *65*(6), 1381–1391. PMID:1875247

Schieber, M. H. (1995). Muscular production of individuated finger movements: the roles of extrinsic finger muscles. *The Journal of Neuroscience*, *15*(1), 284–297. PMID:7823134

Schieber, M. H. (2001). Constraints on somatotopic organizaton in the primary motor cortex. *Journal of Neurophysiology*, *86*(5), 2125–2141. PMID:11698506

Schmidt, E. M. (1980). Single neuron recording from motor cortex as a possible source of signals for control of external devices. *Annals of Biomedical Engineering*, *8*(4-6), 339–349. doi:10.1007/BF02363437 PMID:6794389

Weir, R., Troyk, P. R., DeMichele, G. A., Kerns, D. A., Schorsch, J. F., & Mass, H. (2009). Implantable myoelectric sensors for intramuscular electromyogram recording. *IEEE Transactions on Bio-Medical Engineering*, *56*(1), 159–171. doi:10.1109/TBME.2008.2005942 PMID:19224729

KEY TERMS AND DEFINITIONS

Classification: Identification of a category/class from the input feature vector.

Electromyogram (EMG): A record of the electrical activity of the muscle.

Feature Extraction: The process of defining meaningful and efficient information from the raw data.

Feature Reduction: The process of reducing number of extracted features to optimal numbers to identify a category/class of data.

Neural Network: A computing system made up of a number of simple, highly interconnected processing elements which process information by their dynamic state response to external inputs.

Pattern Recognition: The process of identification of category/class of the pattern from the raw data.

Prosthetic Hand: An artificial hand that replaces the missing hand.

Chapter 3
Privacy Preservation in Information System

D. P. Acharjya
VIT University, India

Geetha Mary A.
VIT University, India

ABSTRACT

The information technology revolution has brought drastic change in the way data is collected or generated for decision mining. The accumulated data has no relevance unless it provides certain useful information pertaining to the interest of an organization. The real challenge lies in converting high dimensional data into knowledge and to use this knowledge for the development of the organization. On the other hand, hiding an organization's sensitive information is a major concern. Much research has been carried out in this direction. This chapter discusses various privacy preservation techniques that can be employed in an information system to safeguard the sensitive information of an organization. This chapter also highlights sensitive fuzzy association rules that can be generated from an information system. The authors provide illustrations wherever necessary to give a clear idea of the concepts developed.

INTRODUCTION

Across the world, quintillions and trillions of bytes of data are produced and stored. The majority of the data are generated from social networks, email, blogs, sms etc. But most of these are unstructured and becomes hectic to generate knowledge from it. Business intelligence software's focuses on business point of view and it is not of much help. It is

because the data collected from multiple sources may not be relevant for an organization. It leads to big data analysis which reacts to all the customer queries with an analysis. These analysis used for customer satisfaction like products a customer may like or a place a customer most likely to visit etc. Many of the institutions after generating the data go for publishing the data in World Wide Web for research purposes. According to Health Insurance

DOI: 10.4018/978-1-4666-4940-8.ch003

Portability and Accountability Act, signed by President of United States, security rule updated on 2006, specifically states about technical safe guard of patient details. Patient safety rule of the Patient Safety and Quality Improvement Act of 2005 specifies about confidentiality of data but allows minimum disclosure. During March and April of 2011, 8.3 and 10 million people were affected by security breaches. Almost 3 months once, privacy attacks happen and personal health information gets stolen. Nowadays patient details like transcription information are outsourced from USA to many of the countries like India, while doing so patient details need to be safeguarded. Therefore there is a need of privacy algorithms in order to adhere the privacy laws enforced at each country like USA, Italy, and India. Since a lot of projects are outsourced from USA, the data given outside the country should undergo privacy methods. In India, there is no specific act of privacy for patients regarding their health record disclosure, but the individual could file a petition in human rights law for privacy disclosure (Shrikant, 2010).

While publishing the data, institutions take enough measures to publish the data in a format that doesn't lead to identification of an individual person which in turn reveals the sensitive information of a person such as salary drawn by an employee or diseases a person is suffering from. Though personal identifiers like name, social security number, employee id, voters id, hospital id are removed from the published data, an individual can be identified if the hacker has some back ground information or any other supplementary materials by using data linkage techniques (Peter, 2012). The above said problems can be avoided by using privacy preserving data mining techniques. Usually data is either distorted or generalized in privacy preserving data mining, but the main decisive factor is the level to which the data is to be distorted or generalized so that there is no extensive change in exactness of data or the knowledge developed from it.

INFORMATION SYSTEM

The basic objective of inductive learning and data mining is to learn the knowledge for classification. However, in real world problems, we may not be faced with simply classification. One such problem is the ordering of objects. On the contrary, we are interested in hiding sensitive associations that is present in an information system. Before we discuss, various privacy preservation techniques to hide sensitive associations, one must know about an information system. An information system contains a finite set of objects typically represented by their values on a finite set of attributes. Such information system may be conveniently described in a tabular form in which each row represents an object whereas each column represents an attribute. Each cell of the information system contains an attribute value. Now, we define formally an information system as below.

An information system is defined as a quadruple $I = (U, A, V_a, f_a)$ where U is a finite nonempty set of objects called the universe, A is a finite nonempty set of attributes, V_a is a nonempty set of values for $a \in A$, $f_a : U \rightarrow V_a$ is an information function. For example, consider a sample information system as presented in Table 1 in which $U = \{o_1, o_2, o_3, o_4, o_5\}$ represents a nonempty finite set of objects; and $A = \{$Humidity, Windy, Temperature$\}$ be a finite set of attributes. The information system presented in Table 1 is a qualitative system, where all the attribute values are discrete and categorical (qualitative).

In the information system shown in Table 2, $U = \{o_1, o_2, o_3, o_4, o_5\}$ represents a set of patients and $A = \{$Temperature, Blood Pressure, Cholesterol$\}$ represents a finite set of attributes. This information system is a quantitative system, since all the attribute values are non categorical.

The information system presented in Table 3 is a good example of hybrid information system, in which the attribute values are either qualitative

Table 1. Qualitative information system

Objects	Humidity	Windy	Temperature
o_1	High	Yes	Hot
o_2	Low	No	Cool
o_3	Normal	No	Mild
o_4	Low	Yes	Cool
o_5	High	No	Hot

Table 2. Quantitative information system

Object	Temperature (F)	Blood Pressure	Cholesterol
o_1	98.7	112	180
o_2	102.3	143	184
o_3	99	125	197
o_4	98.9	106	193
o_5	100.3	134	205

Table 3. Hybrid information system

Object	CGPA	Programme	Year of joining	Year of passing	IQ
o_1	8.6	B. Tech.	2004	2008	High
o_2	7.8	M. Tech.	2006	2008	Low
o_3	8.2	M. Tech.	2005	2007	Average
o_4	9.3	B. Tech.	2005	2009	Average
o_5	6.9	B. Tech.	2003	2007	High

or quantitative. Here, we have

$U = \{o_1, o_2, o_3, o_4, o_5\}$; and $A = \{$CGPA, Programme, Year of joining, Year of passing, $IQ\}$.

An erroneous information system is presented in Table 4, in which an attribute IQ has both quantitative and qualitative values. Though the information system is understandable for a user, it is unreadable for a system. It is because; the system is designed to process the attribute values to be either quantitative or qualitative but not both. So, this information system becomes non-usable.

In many real life situations, it is observed that attribute values are missing in an information system. It is because the attribute may not be ap-

plicable to the information system or due to loss of data. Table 5 portrays an information system with missing values. In the information system, some of the attribute values are missing due to loss of data. Some of the attribute values of the attribute *Previous Degree* are specified as missing since the data is not applicable for the course. Here, we use the notation '?' to specify missing attribute values in an information system. Words like 'do not know', 'NA' etc. can also be used to denote missing values.

The information system presented in Table 3, becomes an ordered information system after imposing the following ordering relations:

Table 4. Erroneous information system

Object	CGPA	Programme	Year of joining	Year of passing	IQ
o_1	8.6	B. Tech.	2004	2008	High
o_2	7.8	M. Tech.	2006	2008	Low
o_3	8.2	M. Tech.	2005	2007	65
o_4	9.3	B. Tech.	2005	2009	Average
o_5	6.9	B. Tech.	2003	2007	High

Table 5. Missing values in information system

Object	CGPA	Programme	Year of joining	Year of passing	IQ	Previous Degree
o_1	8.6	B. Tech.	2004	2008	High	?
o_2	7.8	M. Tech.	2006	2008	Low	MCA
o_3	8.2	M. Tech.	?	2007	Low	B. Tech
o_4	9.3	B. Tech.	2005	2009	?	?
o_5	6.9	B. Tech.	2003	2007	High	?

$\prec_{CGPA}: 9.3 \prec 8.6 \prec 8.2 \prec 7.8 \prec 6.9$

$\prec_{Programme}: M.Tech. \prec B.Tech.$

$\prec_{Year\ of\ joining}: 2006 \prec 2005 \prec 2004 \prec 2003$

$\prec_{Year\ of\ passing}: 2009 \prec 2008 \prec 2007$

$\prec_{IQ}: High \prec Average \prec Low$

DISCRETIZATION OF ATTRIBUTE VALUES

Data mining algorithms such as naïve Bayesian classification; Apriori algorithm; frequent pattern mining algorithms works well on qualitative datasets. But, in many real life situations we come across quantitative datasets. Thus to obtain knowledge from it, quantitative datasets has to be converted to qualitative datasets. The process of conversion from quantitative to qualitative datasets is known as discretization. The various techniques used for this purpose are partitioning the values by intervals (Ramakrishnan and Rakesh, 1996; Nitin et al, 2006; Yiping et al, 2008), fuzzy membership functions (Shragai and Schneider, 2001; Berberoglu and Kaya, 2008; Vijay and Radha, 2008) and statistical methods (Yonatan and Yehuda, 2003). On employing interval partitioning over the attribute CGPA, the hybrid information system, Table 3, reduces to modified hybrid information system as presented in Table

6. It is observed that, after employing interval partitioning, the information system suffers from skew ness. From Table 6, it is clearly identified that, objects o_1, o_2, o_3, o_4 are grouped in the category 7-10 whereas o_5 in the category 6-7. Out of 5 objects, 4 are under one category, which leads to bottle neck problem while considering large dataset for computation. In addition, there is loss of information because the value 7.8 and also 9.3 comes under the same category 7-10. The problem with using fuzzy membership function for discretization of numerical values is with defining the membership function. The membership function has to be defined according to the application and domain of the values which requires expertise.

Rough set on fuzzy approximation with ordering (Acharjya and Tripathy (2008, 2010)) and rough set on intuitionistic fuzzy approximation space with ordering (Acharjya and Tripathy (2009, 2011); Acharjya and Ezhilarasi (2011); Saleem et al (2012)) are the two different approaches to discretize the quantitative data. In such cases, the classification of objects is carried out by employing either fuzzy proximity relation or by intuitionistic fuzzy proximity relation. It identifies the almost indiscernibility among the objects. The following example provides insight on the process of discretization. Consider the information system presented in Table 7. Let us define a fuzzy prox-

Table 6. Interval partitioned information system

Object	CGPA	Programme	Year of joining	Year of passing	IQ
o_1	7-10	B. Tech.	2004	2008	High
o_2	7-10	M. Tech.	2006	2008	Low
o_3	7-10	M. Tech.	2005	2007	Average
o_4	7-10	B. Tech.	2005	2009	Average
o_5	6-7	B. Tech.	2003	2007	High

Table 7. Information system

Employee	o_1	o_2	o_3	o_4	o_5
Hours of work	6	12	7	10	8

Table 8. Fuzzy proximity relation for the attribute hours of work

R	o_1	o_2	o_3	o_4	o_5
o_1	1	0.5	0.917	0.667	0.833
o_2	0.5	1	0.583	0.833	0.667
o_3	0.917	0.583	1	0.75	0.917
o_4	0.667	0.833	0.75	1	0.833
o_5	0.833	0.667	0.917	0.833	1

Table 9. Ordered information system

Employee	o_1	o_2	o_3	o_4	o_5
Hours of work	Low	High	Low	Average	Low

imity relation between objects o_i and o_j as $R(o_i, o_j) = 1 - \dfrac{|V_{o_i} - V_{o_j}|}{12}$. The fuzzy proximity relation for the attribute 'hours of work' is presented in Table 8.

On considering the almost indiscernibility of 90%, it is clear that the employees o_1, o_3 and o_5 belongs to one category whereas employees o_2 and o_4 belongs to independent categories. Let us assume the three categories as high, average and low. On imposing the ordering relation, the ordered information system is presented in Table 9.

ATTRIBUTE REDUCTION

In today's scenario, since most of the applications are web based, learning from the data should be fast and efficient. Though the present technologies helps in taking decisions by using huge databases, most of the information may not be relevant and it leads to increase in run time. Therefore, attribute reduction becomes an important aspect while attaining the same accuracy. It can be achieved by employing various methods such as principal component analysis (PCA) (Hwang et al, 2002; Gilmour et al, 2002; Chen and Zhu, 2004), independent component analysis (ICA) (Cheung and Xu (2001); Wakako, 2002), and linear discriminant analysis (LDA). Weaknesses of these methods are requirement of complex computation and features constructed do not have any true meaning (Tsang et al, 2003). On the contrary, rough set (Pawlak, 1982, 1991) attribute reduction is applied in many applications. In practical applications it can be observed that reduct attributes can remove the superfluous attributes with respect to a specific classification generated by attributes and give the decision maker simple and easy information.

PRIVACY PRESERVATION

Privacy preserving data mining (PPDM) is broadly classified into two categories such as input privacy and output privacy (Wang and Jafari (2005)). It is based on the level the analyst wants to hide the data. In input privacy the dataset is initially distorted whereas in output privacy a specific rule is distorted or generalized. One of the output privacy methods is association rule hiding. Some of the input privacy methods are perturbation (Rakesh and Ramakrishnan, 2000; Agrawal and Aggarwal, 2001); Kargupta et al, 2003), anonymization (Sweeney, 1997, 2001, 2002), multi party computation (Lindell and Benny, 2009), blocking (Verykios et al, 2004), swapping (Moore, 1996) etc. Perturbation and multi party computation are generally used for quantitative data whereas anonymization and association rule hiding works well over both qualitative and quantitative data.

ANONYMIZATION

Anonymization, a term explicated in oxford dictionary as 'unknown'. Anonymization makes an object indifferent from other objects. In this technique, distortion and generalization are used to achieve anonymized dataset. For example, consider a hospital information system as presented in Table 10. According to anonymization, identifiers are removed from the information system while publishing the information system. Anonymized information system is presented in Table 11.

The data presented in Table 11 is not fully anonymized since individual person could be re-identified from the table. If a person know the area (ZIP) in which the patient resides, the gender of the person and age of the person, then the individual patient disease could be identified. Using background knowledge of a patient a user can extract knowledge from the information system by linking the attribute values. For example, from Table 11 it is clear that the female residing in area 02139 is suffering from chest pain. Likewise if the patient age is around 27, gender is male and from area 02138 then the patient has visited hospital for having a painful eye. It indicates that, the information system that has been published without applying efficient algorithms is prone to identification. To avoid such limitation, generalization of attribute values in a distorted way is introduced and we call it as suppression. For example, Table 12 presented below is a generalization of ZIP code. There are three major methods generally employed to achieve anonymization are k-anonymization, l-diversity and t-closeness. We provide a brief idea about these concepts in the following section.

K-ANONYMIZATION

The level of generalization is set based upon the user requirement of threshold of anonymity. The threshold is set up by a constant k, where the value of 'k' depends upon the minimum level of anonymization required by the user. Let k be an integer. After considering the value k, the attribute values are generalized in such a way that at least k number of attribute values will remain identical. As a result, the probability of identifying an object will be less as compared to simple anonymization. Table 12 presented earlier is a 2-anonymization of the hospital information system. K-Anonymization (Sweeney, 1997, 2001, 2002) is done using dif-

Table 10. Hospital information system

ID	Name	Birth Date	Gender	ZIP	Disease
O_1	Tim	20/9/1965	Male	02141	Short of breath
O_2	John	14/2/1965	Male	02142	Wheezing
O_3	Sam	10/3/1984	Male	02138	Painful eye
O_4	Jane	24/8/1965	Female	02139	Chest pain
O_5	Lincoln	11/7/1984	Male	02139	Obesity
O_6	Angelina	12/1/1965	Female	02138	Fever

Table 11. Anonymized information system

Birth Date	Gender	ZIP	Disease
1965	male	02141	Short of breath
1965	male	02142	Wheezing
1984	male	02138	Painful eye
1965	female	02139	Chest pain
1984	male	02139	Obesity
1965	female	02138	Fever

Table 12. Suppression of attribute values ZIP

Birth Date	Gender	ZIP	Disease
1965	Male	0214*	Short of breath
1965	Male	0214*	Wheezing
1984	Male	0213*	Painful eye
1965	Female	0213*	Chest pain
1984	Male	0213*	Obesity
1965	Female	0213*	Fever

ferent algorithms like datafly, μ-argus, MinGen. However, it has some limitations as it is vulnerable to some of the attacks like homogeneity attack and background knowledge attack. Consider a k-anonymization information system of some information system presented in Table 13.

Consider the first two objects of the information system presented in Table 13. It is clear that, the first two objects are anonymous, since the disease values in the first two objects are same. If the user knows that the object (patient) is less than 30 years of age, then the user is 100% sure

Table 13. K-Anonymized information system

ID	Zip code	Age	Nationality	Disease
o_1	63201*	<30	*	Arthritis
o_2	63201*	<30	*	Arthritis
o_3	64028*	>30	*	Tonsillitis
o_4	64028*	>30	*	Bronchitis
o_5	6503**	4*	*	Tonsillitis
o_6	6503**	4*	*	Heart Pain

that the patient has Arthritis. Such type of attacks is known as homogeneity attack. Similarly, consider the 5th and 6th objects of the information system presented in Table 13. From Table 13, it is clear that object o_5 is indiscernible with the object o_6 though the information system is two anonymous. Consider, the user knows that the patient is around 40 years of age and is Japanese. Since, Japanese are mostly not affected by Heart pain, the user can conclude that the object (patient) is affected by Tonsillitis. In such cases, attacker uses his back ground knowledge to get the information. We call such type of attack as background knowledge attack.

L-DIVERSITY

Since *k*-anonymization is susceptible to homogeneity and background knowledge attacks, the next level of anonymization is l-diversity proposed by Ashwin et al (2007). An information system is l-diverse, if no two objects have same attribute values. However, it is susceptible to similarity and skew-ness attack. Consider the information system as shown in Table 14. It is 2-diverse and does not suffer from homogeneity attack. However, if the

attacker knows that the object (patient) is from zip code 63201, then the attacker knows that the object (patient) suffers from some bone related disease. Since Osteoporosis and Osteoarthritis are some form of bone related diseases. Consider another instance of an information system as shown in Table 15. It is clear that, the Table 15 is 2-diverse, but the possibility of finding out an object (person) suffering from Osteoporosis is 75%. So, even l-diversity has some privacy issues.

T-CLOSENESS

Since l-diversity suffers from similarity attack, Ninghui et al (2007) proposed t-closeness where the distribution of sensitive attribute in this class and the distribution of the attribute in the information system is not more than the threshold value *t*. So, the sensitive attribute value is distributed perfectly among the objects and protects from similarity attack. It uses Earth Mover's distance to uphold the threshold value *t*.

Table 14. 2-diverse information system

ID	Zip code	Age	Nationality	Disease
o_1	63201*	<30	*	Osteoporosis
o_2	63201*	<30	*	Osteoarthritis
o_3	64028*	>30	*	Sinusitis
o_4	64028*	>30	*	Bronchitis
o_5	6503**	4*	*	Flu
o_6	6503**	4*	*	Sinusitis

Table 15. Another instance of 2-diverse information system

ID	Zip code	Age	Nationality	Disease
o_1	63201*	<30	*	Osteoporosis
o_2	63201*	<30	*	Osteoarthritis
o_3	63201*	<30	*	Osteoporosis
o_4	63201*	<30	*	Osteoporosis
o_5	6503**	4*	*	Bronchitis
o_6	6503**	4*	*	Bronchitis
o_7	6503**	4*	*	Flu
o_8	6503**	4*	*	Sinusitis

PERTURBATION

Perturbation is also a major technique followed in privacy preserving data mining, introduced by Agarwal and Aggrawal (2001). In this technique, random noise is added to the information system and then the information system is given to the data miner, who reconstructs the data for analysis.

In such cases, reconstruction algorithm should be effective in such a way that loss of accuracy is as low as possible. Perturbation is of two types such as additive data perturbation and multiplicative data perturbation (Kun et al, 2006). In additive data perturbation, random data are introduced in the quantitative information system whereas in multiplicative data perturbation we multiply the quantitative information system by a random noise matrix. Perturbation are mostly implemented in two phase (Rakesh and Ramakrishnan, 2000); Agrawal and Aggarwal, 2001; Kargupta et al, 2003). In the first phase, we inject noise to original data, whereas second phase check for distribution, *i.e.*, maintaining mean of zero and allowed variance.

Secure Multi Party Computation

Secure multi party computation (Lindell and Benny, 2009) has roots from cryptography. These methods facilitate to do computations among many parties without having to disclose the data to each other or to an external third party. In such cases, user compute their results locally and the result is summed up later to form a global result of all parties. Some of the techniques to implement multiparty computation are secure sum, secure set union, secure size of set intersection, scalar product etc. A very simple example is party 1 sends the sum of salary of all employees along with the number of employees to party 2, party 2 then adds the sum of salary of all employees and number of employees and then sends to party 3. Now party 3 add his employees total salary and number of employees, calculates the overall results. The final result is then transmitted to party 2 and then to party 1.

Association Rule Mining

The universe can be considered as a large collection of objects. There is some information associated with each object. To find knowledge about the universe we need to elicit some information about these objects. Therefore, it is essential to know the relationship between the attributes and these values to gain knowledge. Association rule is a type of relationship among attribute values of the objects of the universe. Let $S = (U, A)$ be an information system. Let C and D be a set of attribute values of the objects of the universe U. $C \Rightarrow D$ is called an association rule if it satisfies

certain criteria. We define these criteria in terms of two factors called support and confidentiality of $C \Rightarrow D$ as follows:

$$Sup(C) = \frac{\text{Number of objects containing } C}{\text{Total Number of Objects in the Universe}}$$

$$Conf(C \Rightarrow D) = \frac{Support \; of \; (C \cup D)}{Support(C)}$$

In this chapter, we use notation $Sup(C)$ for support of C and notation $Conf(C \Rightarrow D)$ for confidentiality of $C \Rightarrow D$. If support of C is greater than or equal to minimum support and confidentiality of $C \Rightarrow D$ is greater than or equal to minimum confidentiality, then $C \Rightarrow D$ is a strong association rule, otherwise it is not a strong association rule (Agrawal et al, 1993; Hipp et al, 2000).

Fuzzy Association Rule Mining

Association rules generated from a fuzzy information system is termed as fuzzy association rules. Support and confidences are calculated as specified below,

$$Sup \; (C \Rightarrow D) = \frac{\Sigma_{(x \in U)}(C \cap D)(x)}{\text{Total number of objects in the universe}}$$

$$Conf \; (C \Rightarrow D) = \frac{Sup \; (C \Rightarrow D)}{Sup \; (C)}$$

An association rule is frequent if its support and confidentiality are more than the specified level of minimum support and minimum confidentiality. But, the objective of privacy preservation in information system is to hide certain sensitive information so that the sensitive information cannot be discovered through data mining technique. The frequent rule which is having sensitive information and not suppose to be disclosed is termed as sensitive rule. It indicates that all sensitive rules are frequent rule whereas the converse is not true.

Association Rule Hiding

Association rule mining finds interesting association among a large set of data items. Many organizations are acquiring interest in mining association rules from their databases. The discovery of interesting association relationship among huge amount of data can help in many decision making process. Therefore, it is essential to hide sensitive association rules and fuzzy sensitive association rules in an information system. Association rule hiding technique is broadly classified into two categories such as distortion based technique and blocking based technique. In blocking based technique, uncertainty is introduced in the input data to hide sensitive rules. In distortion based technique, the input data is distorted so that the support and confidentiality go below the specified threshold value. In order to achieve this, association rule hiding technique uses either Increase Support of Left hand side (ISL) or Decrease Support of Right hand side (DSR) (Wang et al, 2004). In this chapter, we discuss a fuzzy association rule hiding algorithm (Geetha et al) that hides sensitive fuzzy association rules in an information system.

Fuzzy Association Rule Hiding algorithm

Geetha et al (2013) proposed a sensitive rule hiding algorithm that hides all the sensitive fuzzified association rules by decreasing the support value of right hand side from the dataset. The following steps are used in order to hide the sensitive fuzzified association rules. The following abbreviations are used in Algorithm 1.

Min_Sup: Minimum support value
Min_Conf: Minimum confidentiality value
SC: Support count
AR: Attribute region

SC_AR: Support count of the attribute region
S: Attribute region set
SR: Set of sensitive rules
$C \Rightarrow D$: Rule generated from the attribute region set *S*.
$F_{AR}(x_i)$: Fuzzified value of the attribute region for object x_i

AN EMPIRICAL STUDY ON MARKETING STRATEGIES

This section demonstrates how sensitive fuzzy association rules can be hided in a quantitative information system by considering a real life problem. The case study consists of different cosmetic company's business strategies in a country. In Table 16 given below, we consider a few parameters for business strategies to get maximum sales, their possible range of values and a fuzzy proximity relation as defined below which characterizes the relationship between parameters.

$$R(x_i, x_j) = 1 - \frac{\left| V_{x_i} - V_{x_j} \right|}{2(V_{x_i} + V_{x_j})}$$

The companies, having high expenditure in marketing, advertisement, distribution, miscellaneous, and research and development, are the ideal cases for getting maximum sales. But such a blend of cases is rare in practice. So, a company may not excel in all the parameters in order to get maximum sales. However, out of these parameters, some parameters may have greater influence on others. But, the attribute values on these parameters obtained are almost indiscernible and hence can be classified by using rough set on fuzzy approximation space and ordering rules. The companies are judged by the sales output that is produced. The amount of sales is judged by the different parameters of the companies. These parameters form the attribute set for our analysis. Here the marketing expenditure means, all expen-

Algorithm 1.

Input: Reduced OIS, *Min_Sup*, *Min_Conf*
Output: A transformed information system from which sensitive fuzzy association rules can not be mined.
1.   Reduced OIS
2.   Fuzzification of reduced OIS
3.   Compute *SC* for each *AR* in the fuzzified information system.
4. $S = \phi, SR = \phi$
5.   If $(SC\_AR > Min\_Sup)$
6. $S = S \cup \{AR\}$
7.   Else exit
8.   For *S*, generate all the rules
9.   Compute the *Conf* of each rule.
10.   For each rule $C \Rightarrow D$, if $(Conf(C \Rightarrow D) > Min\_Conf)$ and is sensitive
11. $SR = SR \cup \{C \Rightarrow D\}$
12.   Else go to step 27
13.   For each rule $(C \Rightarrow D)$ in *SR*
14.   For each object $x_i \in U$
15.   If $F_D(x_i) > 0.5$; $F_D(x_i) > F_C(x_i)$ and $F_D(x_i) \neq 1$
16. $F_D(x_i) = 1 - F_D(x_i)$
17.   Recalculate $Conf(C \Rightarrow D)$
18.   If $(Conf(C \Rightarrow D) > Min\_Conf)$
19.   For each object $x_i \in U$
20.   If $F_D(x_i) = 1$
21. $F_D(x_i) = 0.5$
22.   Recalculate $Conf(C \Rightarrow D)$
23.   If $(Conf(C \Rightarrow D) > Min\_Conf)$
24.   For each object $x_i \in U$
25.   If $F_D(x_i) > 0.25$
26. $F_D(x_i) = F_D(x_i) - 0.25$
27.   Output the transformed information system from which the sensitive rules can not be mined.
28.   End

diture incurred for corporate promotion, which includes event marketing, sales promotion, direct marketing etc. which comes to around 6%. The advertising expenditure includes promotional activities using various medium like television, newspaper, internet etc. which comes around 36%. The miscellaneous expenditure is mainly incurred through activities like corporate social responsibility and it leads to maximum of 28%. The distribution cost includes expense on logistic,

Table 16. Notation representation table

Parameter	Attribute	Possible range	Parameter	Attribute	Possible range
Expenditure on marketing	Mkt	[1 – 150]	Expenditure on miscellaneous	Misc	[1 – 700]
Expenditure on advertisement	Advt	[1 – 900]	Expenditure on research and development	R&D	[1 – 150]
Expenditure on distribution	Dist	[1 – 600]	Sales	Sales	[1– 12000]

supply chain etc. and it comes around 24%. The investment made on new product development and other research activities are taken on research and development activities and it takes around 6%. The last one, the sales which basically deals with the sales that a company can produce after investing the expenditure in different fields mentioned above. The company can observe the profit by subtracting the value of the total expen-

diture from the value of the total sales. The data collected from ten different companies is considered to be the representative figure and tabulated below in Table 17. Here we use the notation o_i, $i = 1, 2, 3, \cdots, 10$, for different companies for the purpose of our study to demonstrate the proposed sensitive rule hiding algorithm. It is to be noted

Table 17. Marketing information system

Comp	Mkt	Advt	Dist	Misc	R&D	Sales
o_1	18.276	162.236	30.236	72.146	9.156	1220.586
o_2	2.076	5.393	6.793	8.290	0.383	215.767
o_3	0.496	1.330	0.433	2.733	0.393	42.593
o_4	0.940	0.060	0.666	5.890	1.243	166.41
o_5	27.333	38.660	16.496	24.343	1.523	561.697
o_6	7.033	866.916	508.676	637.530	38.963	11449.56
o_7	4.323	4.173	1.753	3.176	0.003	60.89
o_8	38.516	40.046	3.126	8.026	0.056	303.57
o_9	0.466	0.460	0.993	3.803	0.053	62.836
o_{10}	0.603	0.036	0.393	0.613	0.016	20.523

that, in the information system all non-ratio figures shown in the Table 17 are ten million INR.

A target dataset for analysis as shown in Table 17 is considered. We have designed fuzzy proximity relations based on the attributes and computed the almost similarity between them. The fuzzy proximity relation identifies the almost indiscernibility among the objects. This result induces the equivalence classes. The fuzzy proximity relation $R_i, i = 1, 2, 3, 4, 5, 6$ corresponding to the attributes Mkt., Advt., Dist., Misc., R&D and sales are calculated. We present the fuzzy proximity relation for the attribute Mkt in Table 18. Keeping in view the length of the chapter, the computation of the other fuzzy proximity relations for the attribute Advt., Dist., Misc., R&D, and Sales are omitted.

Now on considering the almost similarity of 90% *i.e.*, $\alpha \geq 0.90$ it is observed from Table 18 that $R_1(o_1, o_1) = 1$; $R_1(o_1, o_5) = 0.901$; $R_1(o_2, o_2) = 1$; $R_1(o_3, o_3) = 1$; $R_1(o_3, o_9) = 0.984$; $R_1(o_3, o_{10}) = 0.951$; $R_1(o_4, o_4) = 1$; $R_1(o_5, o_5) = 1$; $R_1(o_5, o_8) = 0.915$; $R_1(o_6, o_6) = 1$; $R_1(o_6, o_7) = 0.881$. Thus, the companies o_1, o_5, o_8 are α-identical. Similarly, o_3, o_9, o_{10} are α-identical; o_2 is α-identical; o_4 is α-identical; o_6 is α-identical and o_7 is α-identical. Therefore, we get

$$U/R_1^{\alpha} = \{\{o_1, o_5, o_8\}, \{o_2\}, \{o_3, o_9, o_{10}\}, \{o_4\}, \{o_6\}, \{o_7\}\}$$

Therefore, the values of the attribute expenditure on marketing are classified into six categories namely low, average, medium, high, very high, and outstanding. Thus, it can be ordered. Similarly, the different equivalence classes obtained for the

Table 18. Fuzzy proximity relation for the attribute marketing

R_1	o_1	o_2	o_3	o_4	o_5	o_6	o_7	o_8	o_9	o_{10}
o_1	1.000	0.602	0.526	0.549	0.901	0.778	0.691	0.822	0.525	0.532
o_2	0.602	1.000	0.693	0.812	0.571	0.728	0.824	0.551	0.683	0.725
o_3	0.526	0.693	1.000	0.845	0.518	0.566	0.603	0.513	0.984	0.951
o_4	0.549	0.812	0.845	1.000	0.533	0.618	0.679	0.524	0.831	0.891
o_5	0.901	0.571	0.518	0.533	1.000	0.705	0.637	0.915	0.517	0.522
o_6	0.778	0.728	0.566	0.618	0.705	1.000	0.881	0.654	0.562	0.579
o_7	0.691	0.824	0.603	0.679	0.637	0.881	1.000	0.601	0.597	0.622
o_8	0.822	0.551	0.513	0.524	0.915	0.654	0.601	1.000	0.512	0.515
o_9	0.525	0.683	0.984	0.831	0.517	0.562	0.597	0.512	1.000	0.936
o_{10}	0.532	0.725	0.951	0.891	0.522	0.579	0.622	0.515	0.936	1.000

attributes Advt., Dist., Misc., R&D, and Sales are given below.

$$U/R_2^\alpha = \{\{o_1\},\{o_2,o_7\},\{o_3\},\{o_4\},\{o_5,o_8\},\{o_6\},\{o_9\},\{o_{10}\}\}$$

$$U/R_3^\alpha = \{\{o_1\},\{o_2\},\{o_3,o_{10}\},\{o_4,o_9,\},\{o_5\},\{o_6\},\{o_7\},\{o_8\}\}$$

$$U/R_4^\alpha = \{\{o_1\},\{o_2,o_4,o_8\},\{o_3,o_7,o_9,\},\{o_5\},\{o_6\},\{o_{10}\}\}$$
$$U/R_5^\alpha = \{\{o_1\},\{o_2,o_3\},\{o_4,o_5\},\{o_6\},\{o_7\},\{o_8,o_9\},\{o_{10}\}\}$$
$$U/R_6^\alpha = \{\{o_1\},\{o_2,o_4,o_8\},\{o_3,o_7,o_9\},\{o_5\},\{o_6\},\{o_{10}\}\}$$

From the above classification, it is clear that the values of the attribute expenditure on advertisement and distribution are classified into eight categories namely poor, very low, low, average, medium, high, very high and outstanding. The values of the attribute expenditure on miscellaneous are classified into six categories namely low, average, medium, high, very high and out-standing. The values of the attribute expenditure on research and development are classified into seven categories namely very low, low, average, medium, high, very high and outstanding. Finally, the values of the attribute sales are classified into six categories namely low, average, medium, high, very high and outstanding. The ordered information system of the business strategies of different cosmetic companies of Table 17 is given below in Table 19. On considering the weights of outstanding, very high, high, medium, average, low, very low and poor as 8, 7, 6, 5, 4, 3, 2 and 1 respectively, the OIS is given below in Table 19.

$\prec_{Mkt}$: Outstanding $\prec$ Very high $\prec$ high $\prec$ Medium $\prec$ Average $\prec$ Low

$\prec_{Adv}$: Outstanding $\prec$ Very high $\prec$ High $\prec$ Medium $\prec$ Average $\prec$ Low $\prec$ Very low $\prec$ Poor

Table 19. Ordered information system

Comp	Mkt	Advt	Dist	Misc	R&D	Sales
o_1	Outstanding (8)	Very high (7)	Very high (7)	Very high (7)	Very high (7)	Very high (7)
o_2	Medium (5)	Medium (5)	Medium (5)	Medium (5)	Medium (5)	Medium (5)
o_3	Low (3)	Average (4)	Poor (1)	Average (4)	Medium (5)	Average (4)
o_4	Average (4)	Very low (2)	Very low (2)	Medium (5)	High (6)	Medium (5)
o_5	Outstanding (8)	High (6)	High (6)	High (6)	High (6)	High (6)
o_6	Very high (7)	Outstanding (8)	Outstanding (8)	Outstanding (8)	Outstanding (8)	Outstanding (8)
o_7	High (6)	Medium (5)	Low (3)	Average (4)	Very Low (2)	Average (4)
o_8	Outstanding (8)	High (6)	Average (4)	Medium (5)	Average (4)	Medium (5)
o_9	Low (3)	Low (3)	Very low (2)	Average (4)	Average (4)	Average (4)
o_{10}	Low (3)	Poor (1)	Poor (1)	Low (3)	Low (3)	Low (3)

$\prec_{Dist}$: Outstanding $\prec$ Very high $\prec$ High $\prec$ Medium $\prec$ Average $\prec$ Low $\prec$ Very low $\prec$ Poor

$\prec_{Misc}$: Outstanding $\prec$ Very high $\prec$ high $\prec$ Medium $\prec$ Average $\prec$ Low

$\prec_{R\&D}$: Outstanding $\prec$ Very high $\prec$ High $\prec$ Medium $\prec$ Average $\prec$ Low $\prec$ Very low

$\prec_{Sales}$: Outstanding $\prec$ Very high $\prec$ High $\prec$ Medium $\prec$ Average $\prec$ Low

In order to hide a fuzzy association rule, either we decrease the support of right hand side of the rule (DSR) or we increase the support of left hand side of the rule (ISL). We hide critical

fuzzy association rules from the reduced ordered information system by using DSR method. The data obtained from the ordered information system is then fuzzified by using triangular and trapezoidal membership functions. The triangular membership function is defined below by using three parameters p, q and r, where p is considered as the left end of the triangle, r is considered as the right end of the triangle and q is considered as the peak of the triangle.

$$\mu = Max \left(Min \left(\frac{x-p}{q-p}, \frac{r-x}{r-q} \right), 0 \right)$$

The second, trapezoidal membership function is defined below by using two parameters s

Table 20. Fuzzified information system

Comp	Mkt		Advt		Dist		Misc		R&D		Sales	
	Mkt_A	Mkt_B	$Advt_A$	$Advt_B$	$Dist_A$	$Dist_B$	$Misc_A$	$Misc_B$	$R\&D_A$	$R\&D_B$	$Sales_A$	$Sales_B$
o_1	0	1	0.25	0.75	0.25	0.75	0.25	0.75	0.25	0.75	0.25	0.75
o_2	0.75	0.25	0.75	0.25	0.75	0.25	0.75	0.25	0.75	0.25	0.75	0.25
o_3	0.75	0	1	0	0.25	0	1	0	0.75	0.25	1	0
o_4	1	0	0.5	0	0.5	0	0.75	0.25	0.5	0.5	0.75	0.25
o_5	0	1	0.5	0.5	0.5	0.5	0.5	0.5	0.5	0.5	0.5	0.5
o_6	0.25	0.75	0	1	0	1	0	1	0	1	0	1
o_7	0.5	0.5	0.75	0.25	0.75	0	1	0	0.5	0	1	0
o_8	0	1	0.5	0.5	1	0	0.75	0.25	1	0	0.75	0.25
o_9	0.75	0	0.75	0	0.5	0	1	0	1	0	1	0
o_{10}	0.75	0	0.25	0	0.25	0	0.75	0	0.75	0	0.75	0
S	4.75	4.5	5.25	3.25	4.75	2.5	6.75	3	6	3.25	6.75	3

and t, where s is considered as the left end of the trapezium and t is the left peak of the trapezium.

$$\mu = Max\left[Min\left(\frac{x-s}{t-s},1\right),0\right]$$

The memberships functions are defined above are depicted in the following Figure 1, where x represents the attribute values in the ordered information system.

The fuzzified information system is generated from ordered information system using the above membership function is presented in Table 20.

On considering the minimum support 3.5 and minimum confidentiality value 80%, the regions Mkt_A, Mkt_B, $Advt_A$, $Dist_A$, $Misc_A$, $R\&D_A$ and

$Sales_A$ have their support values greater than the minimum support. These attribute regions are considered in forming the rules and finding the corresponding confidentiality values. The two frequent item sets generated are $\{Mkt_A, Advt_A\}$, $\{Mkt_A, Dist_A\}$, $\{Mkt_A, Misc_A\}$, $\{Mkt_A, R\&D_A\}$, $\{Mkt_A, Sales_A\}$, $\{Mkt_B, Advt_A\}$, $\{Mkt_B, Dist_A\}$, $\{Mkt_B, Misc_A\}$, $\{Mkt_B, R\&D_A\}$, $\{Mkt_B, Sales_A\}$, $\{Advt_A, Dist_A\}$, $\{Advt_A, Misc_A\}$, $\{Advt_A, R\&D_A\}$, $\{Advt_A, Sales_A\}$, $\{Dist_A, Misc_A\}$, $\{Dist_A, R\&D_A\}$, $\{Dist_A, Sales_A\}$, $\{Misc_A, Sales_A\}$, $\{Misc_A, R\&D_A\}$, $\{R\&D_A, Sales_A\}$. These two frequent item sets generate many fuzzy association rules. Some of theseare $Mkt_A \Rightarrow Advt_A$, $Mkt_A \Rightarrow Misc_A$, $Dist_A \Rightarrow Mkt_A$, $Misc_A \Rightarrow Mkt_A$, $Advt_A \Rightarrow Dist_A$, $Advt_A \Rightarrow Misc_A$, $Dist_A \Rightarrow Advt_A$, $Advt_A \Rightarrow$

Table 21. Computation of support and support count of $Dist_A \Rightarrow Misc_A$

Comp	DistA	MiscA	Support of ($Dist_A \Rightarrow Misc_A$)
o_1	0.25	0.25	0.25
o_2	0.75	0.75	0.75
o_3	0.25	1	0.25
o_4	0.5	0.75	0.5
o_5	0.5	0.5	0.5
o_6	0	0	0
o_7	0.75	1	0.75
o_8	1	0.75	0.75
o_9	0.5	1	0.5
o_{10}	0.25	0.75	0.25
S	4.75	6.75	4.5

Figure 1. Membership function

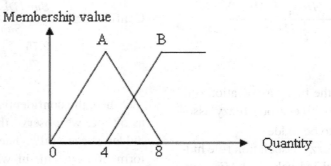

$R \& D_A$ and $Dist_A \Rightarrow Misc_A$. To illustrate the algorithm, we consider the fuzzy association rule $Dist_A \Rightarrow Misc_A$. In order to compute the confidentiality of the fuzzy association rule, we present the fuzzy values of $Dist_A, Misc_A$ and the

support of $Dist_A \Rightarrow Misc_A$ in Table 21. From the table it is clear that:

Support count ($Dist_A \Rightarrow Misc_A$) = 4.5

Table 22. Modified computation of support and support count of $Dist_A \Rightarrow Misc_A$

Comp	$Dist_A$	$Misc_A$	Support of ($Dist_A \Rightarrow Misc_A$)
o_1	0.25	0.25	0.25
o_2	0.75	0.5	0.5
o_3	0.25	0.25	0.25
o_4	0.5	0.25	0.25
o_5	0.5	0.25	0.25
o_6	0	0	0
o_7	0.75	0.25	0.25
o_8	1	0.5	0.5
o_9	0.5	0.25	0.25
o_{10}	0.25	0.25	0.25
S	4.75	2.75	2.75

Confidentiality

$$(Dist_A \Rightarrow Misc_A) = \frac{Sup\ (Dist_A \Rightarrow Misc_A)}{Sup\ (Dist_A)}$$

$$= \frac{4.5}{4.75} = 94.7\%$$

This indicates that the fuzzy association rule $Dist_A \Rightarrow Misc_A$ is a sensitive strong fuzzy association rule and it has to be hidden.

On employing the fuzzy association rule hiding algorithm, the fuzzified values of $Misc_A$ are altered. The modified computation of support and support count of the related sensitive fuzzy association rule are presented in Table 22.

Confidentiality $(Dist_A \Rightarrow Misc_A) = \frac{Sup\ (Dist_A \Rightarrow Misc_A)}{Sup\ (Dist_A)} = \frac{2.75}{4.75} = 57.8\%$

Since, the confidentiality of the rule is found as 57.8%, we observe that the sensitive rule is hidden successfully. The modified fuzzified information system, in which the sensitive rule $Dist_A \Rightarrow Misc_A$ is hidden, is presented in the Table 23 whereas after defuzzification, the ordered information system, in which the sensitive rule $Dist_A \Rightarrow Misc_A$ is hidden, is presented in Table 24.

Table 23. Modified fuzzified information system

Comp.	Mkt		Advt		Dist		Misc		R&D		Sales	
	Mkt_A	Mkt_B	$Advt_A$	$Advt_B$	$Dist_A$	$Dist_B$	$Misc_A$	$Misc_B$	$R\&D_A$	$R\&D_B$	$Sales_A$	$Sales_B$
o_1	0	1	0.25	0.75	0.25	0.75	0.25	0.75	0.25	0.75	0.25	0.75
o_2	0.75	0.25	0.75	0.25	0.75	0.25	0.5	0.25	0.75	0.25	0.75	0.25
o_3	0.75	0	1	0	0.25	0	0.25	0	0.75	0.25	1	0
o_4	1	0	0.5	0	0.5	0	0.25	0.25	0.5	0.5	0.75	0.25
o_5	0	1	0.5	0.5	0.5	0.5	0.25	0.5	0.5	0.5	0.5	0.5
o_6	0.25	0.75	0	1	0	1	0	1	0	1	0	1
o_7	0.5	0.5	0.75	0.25	0.75	0	0.25	0	0.5	0	1	0
o_8	0	1	0.5	0.5	1	0	0.5	0.25	1	0	0.75	0.25
o_9	0.75	0	0.75	0	0.5	0	0.25	0	1	0	1	0
o_{10}	0.75	0	0.25	0	0.25	0	0.25	0	0.75	0	0.75	0
S	4.75	4.5	5.25	3.25	4.75	2.5	2.75	3	6	3.25	6.75	3

Table 24. *Ordered information system in which the sensitive rule* $Dist_A \Rightarrow Misc_A$ *is hidden*

Comp	Mkt	Advt	Dist	Misc	R&D	Sales
O_1	Outstanding (8)	Very high (7)	Very high (7)	Very high (7)	Very high (7)	Very high (7)
O_2	Medium (5)	Medium (5)	Medium (5)	Medium (5)	Medium (5)	Medium (5)
O_3	Low (3)	Average (4)	Poor (1)	Poor (1)	Medium (5)	Average (4)
O_4	Average (4)	Very low (2)	Very low (2)	Medium (5)	High (6)	Medium (5)
O_5	Outstanding (8)	High (6)	High (6)	High 6)	High (6)	High (6)
O_6	Very high (7)	Outstanding (8)	Outstanding (8)	Outstanding (8)	Outstanding (8)	Outstanding (8)
O_7	High (6)	Medium (5)	Low (3)	Poor (1)	Very Low (2)	Average (4)
O_8	Outstanding (8)	High (6)	Average (4)	Medium (5)	Average (4)	Medium (5)
O_9	Low (3)	Low (3)	Very low (2)	Poor (1)	Average (4)	Average (4)
O_{10}	Low (3)	Poor (1)	Poor (1)	Poor (1)	Low (3)	Low (3)

CONCLUSION

In this chapter, we have discussed various privacy preservation techniques that are generally employed in an information system. We have also discussed an algorithm to hide sensitive fuzzy association rules in a quantitative information system after reducing superfluous attributes from the information system. For this it uses rough set on fuzzy approximation space and ordering rules to reduce the superfluous attributes and DSR technique to hide the sensitive fuzzy association rules. The chapter also presents a case study to illustrate the fuzzy association rule hiding algorithm. The proposed algorithm is validated over Prowess-CMIE database to demonstrate the viability of the proposed research (Geetha et al).

REFERENCES

Acharjya, D. P., & Ezhilarasi, L. (2011). A knowledge mining model for ranking institutions using rough computing with ordering rules and formal concept analysis. *International Journal of Computer Science Issues*, 8(2), 417–425.

Acharjya, D. P., & Tripathy, B. K. (2008). Rough sets on fuzzy approximation spaces and applications to distributed knowledge systems. *International Journal of Artificial Intelligence and Soft Computing*, 1(1), 1–14. doi:10.1504/IJAISC.2008.021260

Acharjya, D. P., & Tripathy, B. K. (2009). Rough sets on intuitionistic fuzzy approximation spaces and knowledge representation. *International Journal of Artificial Intelligence and Computational Research*, 1(1), 29–36.

Agrawal, D., & Aggarwal, C. (2001). On the design and quantification of privacy preserving data mining algorithms. In *Proceedings of the Twentieth ACM SIGACT-SIGMOD-SIGART Symposium on Principles of Database Systems* (pp. 247-255). New York, NY: ACM.

Agrawal, R., Marlins, T., & Swami, A. (1993). Mining association rules between sets of items in large databases. In *Proceedings of International Conference on Management of Data* (pp. 207-216). Washington, DC: ACM.

Ashwin, M., Johannes, G., & Daniel, K. (2007). l-Diversity: Privacy beyond k-anonymity. *ACM Transactions on Knowledge Discovery from Data*, *1*(1), 1–52.

Berberoglu, T., & Kaya, M. (2008). Hiding fuzzy association rules in quantitative data. In *Proceedings of International Conference on Grid and Pervasive Computing* (pp. 387-392). Kunming, China: IEEE Computer Society.

Chen, S., & Zhu, Y. (2004). Subpattern-based principle component analysis. *Pattern Recognition*, *37*(5), 1081–1083. doi:10.1016/j.patcog.2003.09.004

Cheung, Y., & Xu, L. (2001). Independent component ordering in ICA time series analysis. *Neurocomputing*, *41*, 145–152. doi:10.1016/S0925-2312(00)00358-1

Geetha, M. A., Acharjya, D. P., & Iyengar, N. C. S. N. (2014). *Privacy preservation in fuzzy association rules using rough computing and DSR*. Cybernetics and Information Technologies.

Gilmour, J., & Wang, L. (2002). Detection of process abnormality in food extruder using principle component analysis. *Chemical Engineering Science*, *57*(7), 1091–1098. doi:10.1016/S0009-2509(01)00432-8

Hipp, J., Guntzer, U., & Nakhaeizadeh, G. (2000). Algorithms for association rule mining-A general survey and comparison. *SIGKDD Explorations*, *2*(2), 1–58.

Hwang, K. F., & Chang, C. C. (2002). A fast pixel mapping algorithm using principal component analysis. *Pattern Recognition Letters*, *23*(14), 1747–1753. doi:10.1016/S0167-8655(02)00148-4

Kargupta, H., Datta, S., Wang, Q., & Krishnamoorthy, S. (2003). On the privacy preserving properties of random data perturbation techniques. In *Proceedings of the ICDM 2003- 3rd IEEE International Conference on Data Mining* (pp. 99-106). Los Alamitos, CA: IEEE Computer Society.

Kun, L., Hillol, K., & Jessica, R. (2006). Random projection-based multiplicative data perturbation for privacy preserving distributed data mining. *IEEE Transactions on Knowledge and Data Engineering*, *18*(1), 92–106. doi:10.1109/TKDE.2006.14

Lindell, Y., & Benny, P. (2009). Secure multiparty computation for privacy preserving data mining. *The Journal of Privacy and Confidentiality*, *1*(1), 59–98.

Moore, R. A. Jr. (1996). *Controlled data-swapping techniques for masking public use microdata sets. Statistical Research Division Report Series RR 96-04*. Washington, DC: US Bureau of the Census.

Ninghui, L., Tiancheng, L., & Venkatasubramanian, S. (2007). t-Closeness: Privacy beyond k-anonymity and l-diversity. In *Proceeding of ICDE 2007 IEEE 23rd International Conference on Data Engineering* (pp. 106-115). Istanbul, Turkey: IEEE.

Nitin, G., Nitin, M., Kamal, T., & Pabitra, M. (2006). Mining quantitative association rules in protein sequences. *Lecture Notes in Computer Science*, *3755*, 273–281. doi:10.1007/11677437_21

Pawlak, Z. (1982). Rough sets. *International Journal of Computer Information Science, 11,* 341–356. doi:10.1007/BF01001956

Pawlak, Z. (1991). *Rough sets: Theoretical aspects of reasoning about data.* Dordrecht, The Netherlands: Kluwer Academic Publishers.

Peter, C. (2012). A survey of indexing techniques for scalable record linkage and deduplication. *IEEE Transactions on Knowledge and Data Engineering, 24*(9), 1537–1555. doi:10.1109/TKDE.2011.127

Rakesh, A., & Ramakrishnan, S. (2000). Privacy-preserving data mining. In *Proceedings of the 2000 ACM SIGMOD International Conference on Management of Data* (pp. 439-450). New York: ACM.

Ramakrishnan, S., & Rakesh, A. (1996). Mining quantitative association rules in large relational table. *SIGMOD Record, 25*(2), 1–12. doi:10.1145/235968.233311

Saleem, D. M. A., Acharjya, D. P., Kannan, A., & Iyengar, N. C. S. N. (2012). An intelligent knowledge mining model for kidney cancer using rough set theory. *International Journal of Bioinformatics Research and Applications, 8*(5/6), 417–435. doi:10.1504/IJBRA.2012.049625 PMID:23060419

Shragai, A., & Schneider, M. (2001). Discovering quantitative associations in databases. In *Proceedings of IFSA World Congress and 20th NAFIPS International Conference* (pp. 423-428). Vancouver, Canada: IEEE.

Shrikant, A., Tanu, S., Swati, S., Vijay, C., & Abhishek, V. (2010). Privacy and data protection in cyberspace in Indian environment. *International Journal of Engineering Science and Technology, 2*(5), 942–951.

Sweeney, L. (1997). Guaranteeing anonymity when sharing medical data the Datafly system. In *Proceedings Journal of the American Medical Informatics Association* (pp. 51–55). Washington, DC: AMIA.

Sweeney, L. (2001). *Computational disclosure control: A primer on data privacy protection.* (Ph.D. Thesis). Massachusetts Institute of Technology. Cambridge, MA.

Sweeney, L. (2002). Achieving k-anonymity privacy protection using generalization and suppression. *International Journal on Uncertainty. Fuzziness and Knowledge-Based Systems, 10*(5), 571–588. doi:10.1142/S021848850200165X

Tripathy, B. K., & Acharjya, D. P. (2010). Knowledge mining using ordering rules and rough sets on fuzzy approximation spaces. *International Journal of Advances in Science and Technology, 1*(3), 41–50.

Tripathy, B. K., & Acharjya, D. P. (2011). Association rule granulation using rough sets on intuitionistic fuzzy approximation spaces and granular computing. *Annals Computer Science Series, 9*(1), 125–144.

Tsang, E. C. C., Yeung, D. S., & Wang, X. Z. (2003). OFFSS: Optimal fuzzy-valued feature subset selection. *IEEE Transactions on Fuzzy Systems, 11*(2), 202–213. doi:10.1109/TFUZZ.2003.809895

Verykios, V. S., Bertino, E., Fovino, I. N., Provenza, L. P., Saygin, Y., & Theodoridis, Y. (2004). State-of-the-art in privacy preserving data mining. *SIGMOD Record, 33*(1), 50–57. doi:10.1145/974121.974131

Vijay, K. G., & Radha, K. P. (2008). A novel approach for statistical and fuzzy association rule mining on quantitative data. *Journal of Scientific and Industrial Research, 67,* 512–517.

Wakako, H. (2002). Separation of independent components from data mixed by several mixing matrices. *Signal Processing*, *82*(12), 1949–1961. doi:10.1016/S0165-1684(02)00197-4

Wang, S. L., & Jafari, A. (2005). Hiding sensitive predictive association rules. In *Proceedings of IEEE International Conference on Systems, Man and Cybernetics*, (pp. 164-169). IEEE.

Wang, S. L., Lee, Y. H., Billis, S., & Jafari, A. (2004). Hiding sensitive items in privacy preserving association rule mining. In *Proceedings of International Conference on Systems, Man and Cybernetics*. IEEE.

Yiping, K., James, C., & Wilfred, N. (2008). An information-theoretic approach to quantitative association rule mining. *Knowledge and Information Systems*, *16*(2), 213–244. doi:10.1007/s10115-007-0104-4

Yonatan, A., & Yehuda, L. (2003). A statistical theory for quantitative association rules. *Journal of Intelligent Information Systems*, *20*(3), 255–283. doi:10.1023/A:1022812808206

KEY TERMS AND DEFINITIONS

Additive Perturbation: Additive perturbation randomly introduces data in the quantitative information system.

Almost Indiscernibility: Attribute values that are not exactly identical but almost identical are termed as almost indiscernible.

Anonymization: Anonymization makes an object indifferent from other objects.

Association Rule: Association rule is a type of relationship between attribute values of the objects of the universe.

Discretization: The process of conversion from quantitative dataset to qualitative dataset is termed as Discretization.

Frequent Rule: An association rules whose support and confidentiality are greater than the minimum Support and minimum confidentiality is termed as frequent rule.

Fuzzy Proximity Relation: A fuzzy relation which is reflexive and symmetric is termed as fuzzy proximity relation.

Information System: An information system contains a finite set of objects typically represented by their values on a finite set of attributes.

Input Privacy: Input privacy initially distorted the dataset before publication of the dataset.

Multiplicative Perturbation: Multiplicative perturbation simply multiplies the quantitative information system by a random noise matrix.

Output Privacy: In output privacy specially a specific rule is distorted or generalized.

Sensitive Rule: A frequent rule which contains sensitive information of an information system is termed as sensitive rule.

Chapter 4
Predictive Analytics and Data Mining:
A Framework for Optimizing Decisions with R Tool

Ritu Chauhan
Amity University, India

Harleen Kaur
Hamdard University, India

ABSTRACT

High dimensional databases are proving to be a major concern among the researches to extract relevant information for futuristic decision making. Real world data is high dimensional in nature and comprises of irrelevant features, missing values, and redundancy, which requires serious concerns. Utilizing all such features can mislead the results for emergent prediction. Therefore, such databases are critical in nature to determine optimal solutions. To deal with such issues, the authors have developed and implemented a Cluster Analysis Study Behavior of School Children from Large Databases (CABS) framework to retrieve effective and efficient clusters from high dimensional human behavior datasets for school children in US. They have applied feature selection technique and hierarchical agglomerative clustering technique to discover clusters of vivid shape and size to retrieve knowledge from large databases. This study was conducted for Health Behavior in School-Aged Children (HBSC) using Correlation-Based Feature Selection (CFS) technique to reduce the inconsistent data records and select relevant features that will eventually extract the appropriate data to merge similar data and retrieve clusters. However, predictive analytics can facilitate a more thorough extraction of knowledge to facilitate better quality and faster decisions. The authors have implemented the current framework in R language where the clustering was emphasized using pvclust package. The proposed framework is highly efficient in discovering hidden and implicit knowledge from large databases due to its accessibility to handling and discovering clusters of variant shapes.

DOI: 10.4018/978-1-4666-4940-8.ch004

INTRODUCTION

In past decades there has being explosive growth in raw data from various sources. There are vibrant ranges of existing data resources from distinct background such as medical technology, business oriented organization, market based analysis, social analysis, science exploration, geographical information studies, and several other computerization, technologies for retrieval of information and storage of data. Numerous efforts are accomplished by researchers to retrieve effective and efficient patterns to discover knowledge from such large databases (Agrawal et al., 1998). But it's not possible by human capabilities all alone to retrieve patterns from such terabytes of data, to overcome such problem data analysis technique such as pattern detection, rules generation and decision making are widely appreciated around the globe for retrieval of relevant information from large databases. In recent review of literature we have found that statistical analysis tools involve series of flaws while handling large amount of complex and high dimensional databases. The method involves generation of several hypotheses testing on data sets for analysis and retrieval of knowledge; hence it was difficult to retrieve effective and efficient patterns for decision making. These techniques prove to be expensive, complex and time consuming for users. Therefore, Statistical tools were proven to be an irrelevant tool utilized for retrieval of information for knowledge discovery (Miller and Han, 2001; Mannila, 2002).

To overcome such flaws of statistical technique analyses among large databases, industry has developed several functionalities for databases such as: collection of data, creation of database, management of data, and finally analysis of data for better perceptive which tends to be relevant key factors for future discoveries of data (Han and Kamber, 2000). The last process involved in this development is defined as Knowledge Discovery in Database (KDD) (Branchmann and Anand, 1996). There are several definitions discussed in past for KDD, but most famous studied by Fayyad et al., 1996a. Several definitions for KDD are discussed below:

Definition 1. *It is defined as a non-trivial process for retrieval of valid, novel, potentially useful and ultimately understandable patterns in data and describing them in a definite, concise and meaningful way (Fayyad et al., 1996b).*

Data mining can be termed as most important step in KDD for retrieval of information or knowledge from raw data. Several KDD processes are followed by data mining techniques for extraction of patterns which are useful to discover hidden knowledge from large databases (Smyth, 2001). Therefore, without these valid additional steps there exists high risk of uninteresting and non valid patterns (Chen et al., 1996). Therefore, Data mining tasks can be defined as a process to extract hidden implicit interesting patterns from large databases for knowledge discovery process. It can be vitally defined as learning process to generate patterns from raw data automatically by building a computer based environment for complex datasets. There are several definitions discussed in past by researchers for data mining techniques such as:

Definition 2. *The goal of Data mining focuses on retrieval of deep hidden information which can be utilized for knowledge discovery process for strategic decision making and equating fundamental research problems (Miller and Han, 2001).*

Data mining techniques involves several of statistical techniques as well as sophisticated data analysis technique to retrieve effective and efficient patterns from large and complex databases (Afifi and Azen, 1972). The real world datasets usually consists of inconsistent data records, missing values and irrelevant data features; the major concern among the researchers is to retrieve efficient patterns and knowledge from such databases. To deal with such databases feature selection techniques are used as pre processing to remove inconsistent features from large and complex databases (Almuallim and Dietterich, 1991). In this chapter we have designed and implemented a CABS (Cluster Analysis to Study Behavior of School Children from Large Databases) framework for retrieval of effective and efficient clusters from high dimensional human behavior datasets for school children in US.

This study was conducted for Health Behavior in School-Aged Children (HBSC) using CFS (correlation based Feature selection) technique to reduce the inconsistent data records and select relevant features for clustering of data. The next step involves the clustering of data where we have utilized Hierarchical based clustering technique which will eventually extract the appropriate data to merge similar data and retrieve clusters of variant shapes and size (Kaur et al. 2012a). We have implemented the current framework in R language where the clustering was emphasized using pvclust package. The focus of chapter is to retrieve effective and efficient patterns from high dimensional databases using R language and discover patterns which can be fruitfully applied for decision making process.

The rest of the chapter is organized as follows. Section 2 briefly discusses literature survey of several data mining techniques for detecting clusters. In Section 3, we discuss the proposed CABS (Cluster Analysis to Study Behavior of School Children from Large Databases) framework for detecting clusters in R language. Section 4 describes the overall CABS (Cluster Analysis to Study Behavior of School Children from Large Databases) framework with its implementation details. In Section 5 experimentation results were conducted on Health Behavior in School-Aged Children (HBSC) for retrieval of clusters and finally conclusion is referred in last Section.

RELATED WORKS

Data mining has evolved as an emerging field which is currently used in medical database, marketing, Surveillance fraud detection, human factor related issue and scientific discovery (Fayyad et al., 1996b; Dunham, 2003; Abraham et al., 2007; Kaur et al., 2010; Piatetsky- Shapiro et al., 1996). Over the last decade, data mining technology has made serious impact many different domains to discover knowledge from raw data. It is not only used by business organization to collect the business information but is used in the science and technology to extract information from the enormous data set generated by modern computation and research methods. It is estimated that digital universe is expanding at unlimited speed and consumes approximately 281 exabytes in 2007, and projected size tends to be 10 times by 2011, Gantz, 2008 (One exabyte is ~1018 bytes or 1,000,000 terabytes).

Recently many commercial data mining techniques have evolved and their usage is increasing tremendously. Researchers are putting their best efforts to achieve the fast and efficient algorithm for abstraction of data. Data mining techniques find efficient patterns with the limitation of time and hardware requirements. In traditional systems Data mining is also known as knowledge extraction, information discovery, information harvesting, exploratory data analysis, data archeology, data pattern processing, and functional dependency analysis. There exist two types of Data mining techniques such as Predictive and Descriptive (Witten and Frank, 2005; Han and Kamber, 2000).

Predictive data mining the name itself suggest the prediction of data about future theories. It involves statistical and artificial intelligence techniques to analyze data for futuristic prediction. However, Predictive data mining techniques has been used as essential tool for making strategic decision making among the organizations. These techniques are further categorized into: Classification and Regression (Breiman et al., 1984; Arabie et al., 1996). There are several Predictive data analytics tools utilized by researchers, industrialist, healthcare practioners and others who are seeking means of making smarter decisions and getting better results by utilizing their data assets (Kaur et al., 2012b). Hence, several advances are made in computational power and software to find optimization techniques for new emerging class of scientists to discover knowledge and information available from the vast amounts of data. There are past works referred by recent publication where the focus was to discover knowledge for future prediction and decision making (Miller et al., 2006; Davenport and Harris, 2010).

However, descriptive data mining techniques aims to determine the interesting patterns and. data is categorized to create meaningful subgroups. These techniques are broadly divided into Clustering, Association and Sequential analysis. It can be used as analysis process by several organizations to discover knowledge from databases. There existing users from different application domain can access data mining techniques (Abraham et al., 2007; Benoit, 2002; Arabie and Hubert, 1996; Kaur et al., 2010). The benefit of data mining techniques is to process large amount of complex data for different application areas. But high dimensionality of data can cause several problems for analysis methods (Dash and Liu, 1997). As data consists of irrelevant or noisy attributes which can drastically change the variation of results. Hence real world data consists of inconsistent data records and missing values which need further pre processing to discover knowledge from raw data. To overcome these flaws of high dimensionality feature selection techniques are involved to reduce irrelevant features from large databases (Yu and Liu, 2003; Kaur et al., 2012).

Earlier feature selection techniques were more subjective to retrieve subset of features among supervised learning algorithms. Recently the research area has being driven their scope to unsupervised learning algorithm to select subset of features or to gather the optimal set of features for searching clusters (Mitra et al., 2002; Dy and Brodley, 2000; Dy and Brodley, 2004; Fisher et al., 1991). These technique works according to specific clustering method such as K means or expectation maximization (EM) (Bradley et al., 1998). However the process should not completely rely on specific clustering algorithms for retrieval of feature subsets. As K means clustering technique is not able to generate clusters of variant size and shape hence only circular shaped clusters are formed. The major challenge is dealing with high dimensionality of data and very large size to determine clusters of variant shape and sizes (Yu and Liu, 2003).

Clustering is a process of grouping the objects according to similarity among data objects. Clustering can be defined for two dimensional or more dimensional, as compared to traditional data clustering algorithms. The objective of the clustering algorithm is to maximize intra cluster similarity and minimize inter cluster similarity (Everitt et al., 2001; Hand et al., 2001). The objects within data sets are close to each other if they belong to the same cluster. Euclidean, Manhattan, Mehalanobis, Minkowski distance formula are applied to measure distance among the data objects inside a cluster; several other statistical techniques can also be synthesize to measure similarity among data objects. In clustering the datasets are usually placed inside the cluster, if the distance calculated is less among the data objects as well data is similar in nature. The adjacencies of data objects are determined and clustering algorithm are applied according to the data elements present around the neighbors (Han and Kamber, 2000). The main focus of clustering algorithm is to group the similar data together into similar cluster. The similarity should be maximum within the cluster, whereas distinct clusters can have different objects (Hinneburg and Keim, 1998; Leuski, 2001; Yu et al., 1998; Kaur et al 2010). There are different types of pre existing data types, so different statistical techniques are taken into account to measure similarity of objects. There are certain dissimilarity measures adopted for real world datasets to cluster data. The major approach is to retrieve effective and efficient clusters to discover knowledge from large and complex high dimensional databases.

CABS: CLUSTER ANALYSIS TO STUDY BEHAVIOR OF SCHOOL CHILDREN FROM LARGE DATABASES

The enlarged databases have created furious interests among the researchers to develop new technologies to process databases for futuristic prediction. Whereas the challenge is to design frameworks which can effectively and efficiently handle large databases and discover knowledge for decision making. To discover such an environment which has integrated approach is challenging task? In our proposed approach we have designed a framework which deals with problem of large databases and discover clusters of variant shapes. Figure 1 represents the framework in which integrated data mining techniques are used to retrieve clusters of variant shapes. The database D contains data collected from Health Behavior in School-Aged Children (HBSC). The data was studied for United States whereas the collaboration work was performed with Health Behavior in School-Aged Children (HBSC) and World Health Organization (WHO-Euro). This study was performed for year 2002 where the children of 11+, 13+, and 15+ year-old were closely interviewed and experiences concerning their health behavior with certain features were closely studied. There was wide range of differences in their actual behavior was studied from early- to mid-adolescent age group across the majority was analyzed.

The data was analyzed over specific time $t < t_0$, $t_1, t_2...t_n >$, each technique involves certain spe-cific time and finally total time is calculated for entire framework. The proposed framework retrieves effective and efficient clusters to discover knowledge from large databases.

The current framework is utilized to retrieve clusters of variant shapes from large scale databases. However, framework can be interesting to end users if it can retrieve hidden clusters which can be utilized for futuristic prediction which can deal with complexity of databases and finally retrieved clusters which can benefit end users

Preprocessing of Data

Preprocessing of data is essential as real world databases consists of missing values which can lead to inconsistency among the results. There are assured data mining algorithms which cannot evaluate databases when the nature of data is inconsistent. The data is usually cleaned irrespective to type of data mining technique. The preprocessing usually comprise of removal of missing values, duplicate and redundant data values. The raw data is transformed so mining process can be performed on databases. In this approach we have utilized database of Health Behavior in School-aged Children (HBSC) and finally preprocessing of data is performed using R language.

The data is retrieved from database and missing values were deleted with help of R language where new dataset is evaluated from omit function.

Newdata <– na.omit (D)

There are other functions available in R such as mitools which can easily deal with missing values. Furthermore we have utilized feature selection technique to reduce the irrelevant features

Figure 1. CABS framework: Cluster analysis to study behavior of school children from large databases

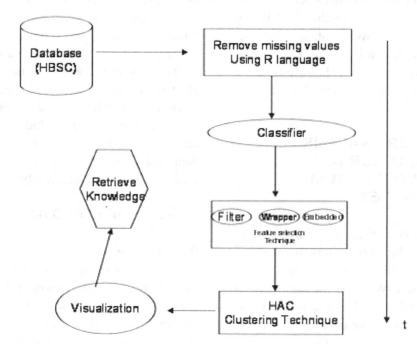

Feature Selection

The dimensionality of data plays the major role for retrieval of efficient patterns from large databases. Hence finding an optimal set of features subset is challenging task in high dimensional databases. Feature selection technique has an objective to retrieve subset of features from database and remove irrelevant features which are of no predictive information (John et al., 1994; Langley, 1994; Chauhan et al., 2010; Dash et al., 2000). Feature selection techniques are widely applied in research areas such as pattern recognition, machine learning, statistics and several data mining approaches (Aha and Bankert, 1995; Langley, 1994; Blum, 1997; Kaur et al., 2010; Duch, 2006). They have proved to be really efficient technique for several data mining algorithms by improving the complexity and enhancing the learning efficiency of algorithms. The main objective of feature selection techniques can be stated as:

- It improves the performance of algorithms in data mining by improvising the prediction such as in case of classification and cluster retrieval in clustering technique
- The complexity of algorithm is improved with cost efficiency
- It clearly gets insight of data and deeper knowledge is retrieved with much efficiency

The feature selection technique can be defined as:

Definition 3. *Feature selection retrieves optimal feature subsets that define the entire databases $F(f_{0, ...,} F_n) \subset F'(f_0, f_1, f_2, ..., f_m)$. Where F represents the 'n' subset of features retrieved from original dataset F' where 'm' defines number of features.*

The feature selection technique comprise of four basic steps such as subset generation, subset evaluation, stopping criterion and finally validation process. The subset generation step generates features subsets with help of search process for further evaluation. The next step comprise of evaluation where the comparison is made among the evaluate subsets according to certain evaluation criterion. The replacement process is carried when new subset tends to be better than the earlier subset. The process is repeated until the stopping criterion is matched.

After the feature selection, we will validate the result on other clustering algorithms, such as Hierarchical clustering technique. With the selected features, these algorithms retrieve clusters of variant shape and sizes.

Clustering

Clustering can be defined as a standalone tool for analysis of data and may be further utilized as pre processing step in other data mining algorithms. It is unsupervised learning technique in which predefined classes are not defined in beginning. Clustering methods are generally classified into different types widely discussed by Hand et al., 2001. The clustering process utilizes several similarity measures such as Euclidian, Manhattan and other distance measures to retrieve clusters of variant shapes.

The application of clustering techniques can be used in wide domains areas such as medical databases, marketing, education sector, galaxy clustering, remote sensing, micro array data and several other research areas (Arabie and Hubert, 1994; Arabie et al., 1996; Anderberg, 1973; Devaney and Ram, 1997). There have been several clustering approaches applied to micro array data for functional group of genes by Eisen et al., 1998. According to Hand et al., 2001 the clustering algorithms can be divided into four general categories: partitioning based method, hierarchical method, density-based method and grid-based method (Han and Kamber, 2000).

The cluster analysis generally consists of seven steps (Everitt et al., 2001):

- **Extraction of Data:** The attributes are carefully extracted from the defined source; basically data preparation is performed in this step
- **Selection of Data:** The relevant selected variables are ready and shall be included for clustering procedure. The irrelevant and missing variables should not be included if possible
- **Similarity or Proximity Measure:** A similarity measure should be adopted for preparation of data for clustering. The basic characteristic and dimensionality of data are examined at this stage
- **Clustering Tendency:** It checks whether data should be clustered or not, usually this step is ignored in case of large databases
- **Clustering Algorithm:** This step utilizes the relevant clustering algorithm and number of clusters to be formed
- **Cluster Validation:** Validation of each cluster is usually performed with manual and visualization techniques. The results are usually compared with other clustering algorithms for its validation
- **Interpretation:** The results can be further utilized with other data mining techniques for retrieval of knowledge discovery from large databases

Clustering has being associated with several fields of studies. It has being applied in field of statistics for long time (Arabie et al., 1996, relative studies has being conducted in field of bioinformatics, (Kasturi and Acharya, 2004; Guo, 2004), information retrieval, Leuski, 2001, marketing (Agrawal et al., 1998), and many others related works in field of clustering. In this chapter we have applied Hierarchical clustering algorithm to measure the similarity among the data elements.

Hierarchical Algorithms

It is the clustering approach in which the data are grouped together in form of trees which is known as dendogram. The grouping of data usually occurs in form of nested sequence and finally dendogram is formed (Fisher, 1995). The hierarchical clustering technique are generally classified into two types of approach such as agglomerative approach and divisive approach it's also known as Agglomerative nesting (AGNES) and Divisive Analysis (DIANA) (Zhao and Karypis, 2002).

- In Agglomerative approach bottom up strategy is involved to cluster data objects. It merges the atomic clusters into larger and larger until all the objects are merged into single cluster.
- Divisive approach is the clustering technique in which top down strategy is implemented to cluster the data objects. In this method the larger clusters are divided into smaller clusters until each object forms cluster of its own.

The algorithms existing under hierarchy are Balanced iterative Reducing and Clustering using Hierarchies (BIRCH) (Zhang et al., 1996, Clustering Using Representatives (CURE) (Guha, et al., 1998), and CHAMELEON (Karypis et al., 1999).

Visualization and Knowledge Discovery

Visualization process enables user to present the data mining results in better way. In data mining tools they are generally present in form of patterns and results are visualized in generalized view. The concept of visualization came into view when two major problems were faced by researchers such as firstly it is not easy to understand the complex structure of data as it contains numerous features which are outputted in the result. Secondly the knowledge discovery from such databases was becoming more difficult. Visualization has become an important tool to understand the data and finally retrieve patterns for knowledge discovery process (Fayyad et al., 2002).

There are wide ranges of study performed on Visualization techniques to represent the data mining results (Keim and Kreigel, 1996; Klosgen, 1996). For example, multidimensional visualization techniques have being utilized to have a view of C4.5 decision tree outcomes (Lee and K.L, 1996). He has organized a system as WinViz which finally visualizes discovered results with conventional graphs, plots, bar charts, slider bars and parallel coordinate plot (PCP). They are other studies which have more focused on Graphical models as representation tool for representing probabilistic knowledge to grasp the process of understanding, reasoning, and knowledge from databases (Buntine, 1996).

Visualization techniques can assist human to develop better understanding of data by using several visualization tools such as tables, graph, charts, scatter plot and histogram which can finally lead to discover knowledge for futuristic prediction (Harris, 1999).

IMPLEMENTATION

The proposed framework CABS is implemented on high dimensional datasets for Health Behavior in School-aged Children (HBSC) for determination of relevant clusters. As discussed earlier firstly we have utilized preprocessing technique to remove the missing values from data then secondly naïve bayes classifier is used with CFS (Correlation Based Filter method) feature selection technique to reduced the irrelevant features from the data set and finally apply hierarchical clustering approach where the data is clustered with help of similarity measures using *R* language.

Correlation-Based Filter Method (CFS) for Feature Selection

Correlation-based filter method (CFS) is technique which gives high scores to subsets of features which have high association among the features (Hall and Lloyd, 1997). CFS also correlates with the Symmetrical uncertainties to measure the degree of association between discrete features or between features and classes.

The association of variables among the data can be measured with help of contingency table in two dimensional space where a feature is set as target attribute and other as predictor.

$$A \in \{a_1, \ldots a_l \ldots a_L\}, B \in \{b_1, \ldots b_k \ldots b_K\}$$

Such A and B are two features and association is calculated between them for retrieval of feature subsets.

The various frequencies are computed between them using following statistical equations:

$$p_{kl} = \frac{n_{kl}}{n}; p_{k.} = \frac{n_{k.}}{n}; p_{.l} = \frac{n_{l.}}{n}$$

The mutual information can be used to measure the mutual dependency between the two variables. It minimizes the dependency among the selected features, and entropy is used to measure the discretized data. The mutual information is specified as I (M;N) between two random variables with set of feature values M and the set of classes N. I (M;N) measures the interdependence between two random variables M and N. It can be computed as follows:

$$I(A,B) = \sum_k \sum_l p_{kl} \times \log_2 \frac{p_{kl}}{p_{k.} \times p_{.l}}$$

The entropy H (A) measures the degree of uncertainty entailed by the set of classes N, and can be computed as

$$H(A) = n\sum_k p_k \log_2 p_{k.}$$

Finally the symmetrical uncertainty among the data can be calculated as:

$$P_{(A,B)} = 2 \times \left[\frac{I(A,B)}{H(A) + H(B)} \right]$$

After feature selection technique retrieves the feature subsets the data is clustered with help of hierarchical agglomerative clustering (HAC) technique to discover clusters of variant shape.

Hierarchical Agglomerative Clustering (HAC)

The HAC clustering algorithm is evaluated using pvclust package in R language. The first step involved was installing of pvclust package and then data was evaluated with help of dendogram. The pvclust package calculates p-values for hierarchical clustering via utilizing multiscale bootstrap resampling. Hierarchical clustering is applied for each data sample and p-values are computed for each clusters formed. We have utilized agglomerative clustering technique in which we have used average as default parameter for hclust and correlation based technique to measure the distance among the data members and finally 1000 number of bootstrap replications are conducted. The pvclust package utilizes the data element in form of frame or matrix. The code for retrieval of clusters in form of dendogram is written in Box 1.

Box 1.

```
## Import a sample data set
## Download dataset from Health Behavior in School-Aged Children (HBSC), 2005-
2006 in TXT format. The direct link to the download is:
## http://dx.doi.org/10.3886/ICPSR28241.v1
## Uncompress the downloaded file.
## the txt data set was then converted into .csv format with usage of XL
sipinia because R language easily access this format
## Import the data set into R

ab <- read.table("d:/ab.csv", header=T)
print(ab)
cat(ab[-grep("^!|^\"$", ab)], file="ab.csv", sep="\n");
mydata <- read.table("ab.csv ", header=T, sep="\t") # cleanup step to get rid
of unnecessary annotation lines and corrupted return signs
newdata <-na.omit (mydata) # missing values were deleted with help of omit
function

## Hierarchical clustering routine by pvclust bootstrap analysis
library(pvclust) # Loads the required pvclust package.
Y <- newdata
result <- pvclust(Y, method.hclust = "average", method.dist=
"correlation", use.cor = "pairwise.complete.obs", nboot=1000)
# set the number of bootstrap resampling and perform hierarchical clustering
algorithm
plot(result, hang=-1)
pvrect(result)#results are plotted with help of dendogram where significant
clusters are visible
```

EXPERIMENTATION

The proposed framework is implemented using public domain datasets available from Health Behavior in School-Aged Children (HBSC). The study involves data from year 2001-2002 in United States, where the numerous variables dealing with health behavior of school children were evaluated with frequency of drug usage and components of their personal as well as school behavior activities. Some of these features can be illustrated as their eating habits, body image, health problems, family make-up, personal injuries, bullying, fight-

ing, and bringing weapons to school. The results reveal data that data mining technique tends to be effective to discover interesting facts which can't be computed by human capabilities

Experiment 1

The objective of the first experiment is to show the effectiveness of the approach in reducing the number of features. The numbers of discovered subsets are interesting in nature as it reduces the irrelevant features. We experimented with CFS technique using naïve bayes classifier. The Naïve

Table 1. Result for correlation feature selection (CFS)

Calculations details

INPUT selection			
Before filtering	48		
After filtering	10		

Selected attribute	MERIT(S)	Selected attribute	MERIT(S)
d_eqW_Q4_1	0.496055	d_eqW_Q14_1	0.509685
d_eqW_AGE_1	0.509645	d_eqW_Q15A1_1	0.509695
d_eqW_Q12_1	0.508445	d_eqW_Q15A2_1	0.509696
d_eqW_Q13A_1	0.509655	d_eqW_Q15A3_1	0.509697
d_eqW_Q13B_1	0.509675	d_eqW_Q15A4_1	0.509699

Bayes technique evaluates the data in relation with famous Bayesian approach following a simple, clear and fast classifier (Witten and Frank, 2005). 'Naïve' signifies mutually independent attributes is preprocessed to find the most dependent categories. The classifier is utilized in several research areas to learn the probabilistic knowledge and determine significant results in machine learning. The naïve Bayesian technique input the variable values with relevance to class attribute by recording dependencies between them. Table 1 observes the results of CFS with Naïve Bayes classifier to remove the irrelevant features.

The results from Table 1 retrieve attributes with high correlation factor among the attributes and determine the relevant attributes which tends to be correlated and further processed as well as other subjected features were ignored.

Figure 2. Representation of dendogram with three major clusters

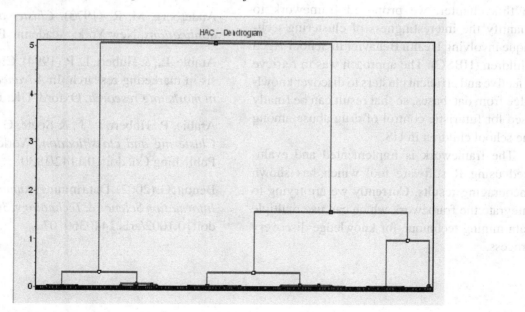

Experiment 2

The second experiment was conducted using subset of features evaluated from feature selection technique. The experiment calculates similarity between subsequent levels of tree and correlation techniques was associated to measure the similarity among different clusters when examined independently. The goal of our research is to retrieve clusters for knowledge discovery process. Figure 2 Depicts a cross-section view of dendogram which subsequently reveals three major clusters which are formed using similarity measure.

The three significant clusters indicate the high level usage of alcohol among the students in school whose parents were unemployed due to certain cause. We observed the children in between the age group of 11-14 years in United States are high risk of getting prone to abusive substance usage. The output is generated using R language software tool. The purpose of this research is to retrieve effective and efficient clusters for enhanced decision making in knowledge discovery process.

CONCLUSION AND FUTURE WORK

In this chapter, we proposed framework to quantify the interestingness of clustering technique involving Health Behavior in School-Aged Children (HBSC). The approach was to retrieve effective and efficient clusters to discover knowledge from databases, so that result can be finally used for futuristic control of drug abuse among the school children in US.

The framework is implemented and evaluated using R software tool which has shown encouraging results. Currently we are trying to integrate the framework which can use multiple data mining technique for knowledge discovery process.

REFERENCES

Abraham, R., Simha, J. B., & Iyengar, S. S. (2007). Medical data mining with a new algorithm for feature selection and naïve Bayesian classifier. In *Proceedings of IEEE International Conference on Information Technology*, (pp. 44-49). IEEE.

Afifi, A. A., & Azen, S. P. (1972). *Statistical analysis: A computer oriented approach*. New York: Academic Press Inc.

Agrawal, R., Gehrke, J., Gunopulos, D., & Raghavan, P. (1998). Automatic subspace clustering of high dimensional data for data mining applications. In *Proceedings of ACM SIGMOD International Conference on Management of Data*. Seattle, WA: ACM.

Aha, D. W., & Bankert, R. L. (1995). A comparative evaluation of sequential feature selection algorithms. In *Proceedings of Fifth International Workshop on Artificial Intelligence and Statistics*. IEEE.

Almuallim, H., & Dietterich, T. G. (1991). Learning with many irrelevant features. In *Proceedings of the Ninth National Conference*. Cambridge, MA: MIT Press.

Anderberg, M. R. (1973). *Cluster analysis for applications*. New York: Academic Press.

Arabie, L., & Hubert, L. P. (1994). Cluster analysis in marketing research. In *Advanced methods in marketing research*. Oxford, UK: Blackwell.

Arabie, P., Hubert, L. J., & Soete, G. D. (1996). *Clustering and classification*. World Scientific Publishing Co. doi:10.1142/1930

Benoit, G. (2002). Data mining. *Annual Review of Information Science & Technology*, *36*, 265–310. doi:10.1002/aris.1440360107

Blum, A. L., & Langley, P. (1997). Selection of relevant features and examples in machine learning. *Artificial Intelligence, 97*, 245–271. doi:10.1016/S0004-3702(97)00063-5

Brachmann, R., & Anand, T. (1996). The process of knowledge discovery in databases: A human centered approach. In *Advances in knowledge discovery and data mining*. Menlo Park, CA: AAAI Press.

Bradley, P. S., Fayyad, U. M., & Reina, C. A. (1998). *Scaling EM clustering to large databases*. Microsoft Research.

Breiman, L., Friedman, J. H., Olshen, R. A., & Stone, C. J. (1984). *Classification and regression trees*. Wadsworth.

Buntine, W. (1996). Graphical models for discovering knowledge. In U. Fayyad, G. Piatetsky-Shapiro, P. Smyth, & R. Uthurusay (Eds.), *Advances in knowledge discovery* (pp. 59–82). Cambridge, MA: AAAI Press/The MIT Press.

Chauhan, R., Kaur, H., & Alam, M. A. (2010). Data clustering method for discovering clusters in spatial cancer databases. *International Journal of Computers and Applications, 10*(6), 24–28.

Chen, M. S., Han, J., & Yu, P. S. (1996). Data mining: An overview from database perspective. *IEEE Transactions on Knowledge and Data Engineering, 8*, 866–883. doi:10.1109/69.553155

Dash, M., & Liu, H. (1997). Feature selection methods for classifications. *Intelligent Data Analysis, 1*, 131–156. doi:10.1016/S1088-467X(97)00008-5

Dash, M., Liu, H., & Motoda, H. (2000). Consistency based feature selection. In *Proceedings of Pacific-Asia Conference on Knowledge Discovery and Data Mining* (PAKDD), (pp. 98–109). PAKDD.

Davenport, T. H., & Harris, J. (2010). *Analytics at work: Smarter decisions, better results*. Cambridge, MA: Harvard Business Press.

Devaney, M., & Ram, A. (1997). Efficient feature selection in conceptual clustering. In *Proceedings of the Fourteen International Conference on Machine Learning*. San Francisco, CA: Morgan Kaufmann.

Duch, H. (2006). Filter methods. In I. Guyon, S. Gunn, M. Nikravesh, & L. Zadeh (Eds.), *Feature extraction, foundations and applications: Studies in fuzziness and soft computing* (pp. 89–118). Berlin: Springer Verlag.

Dunham, M. H. (2003). *Data mining introductory and advanced topics*. Upper Saddle River, NJ: Pearson Education, Inc.

Dy, J. G., & Brodley, C. E. (2000). Feature subset selection and order identification for unsupervised learning. In *Proceedings of Seventeenth International Conference on Machine Learning*. Palo Alto, CA: Stanford University.

Dy, J. G., & Brodley, C. E. (2004). Feature selection for unsupervised learning. *Journal of Machine Learning Research, 5*, 845–889.

Eisen, M., Spellman, P. T., Brown, P. O., & Botstein, D. (1998). Cluster analysis and display of genome-wide expression patterns. *Proceedings of the National Academy of Sciences of the United States of America, 95*, 14863–14868. doi:10.1073/pnas.95.25.14863 PMID:9843981

Everitt, B. S., Landau, S., & Leese, M. (2001). *Cluster analysis*. New York: Oxford University Press.

Fayyad, U., Grinstein, G. G., & Wierse, A. (2002). *Information visualization in data mining and knowledge discovery*. San Francisco: Morgan Kaufmann Publishers.

Fayyad, U., Piatetsky-Shapiro, G., & Smyth, P. (1996b). Data mining to knowledge discovery-A review. In *Advances in knowledge discovery.* AAAI Press/The MIT Press.

Fayyad, U. M., Haussler, D., & Stolorz, Z. (1996a). KDD for science data analysis: Issues and examples. In *Proceedings of Second International Conference on Knowledge Discovery and Data Mining.* AAAI Press.

Fisher, D. H. (1995). Iterative optimization and simplification of hierarchical clustering. In *Proceedings of the First International Conference on Knowledge Discovery & Data Mining.* AAAI Press.

Fisher, D. H., Pazzani, M. J., & Langley, P. (1991). *Concept formation: Knowledge and experience in unsupervised learning.* San Mateo, CA: Morgan Kaufmann Publishers.

Gantz, J. F. (2008). *The diverse and exploding digital universe.* Retrieved from http://www.emc.com/collateral/analyst-reports/diverse-exploding-digital-universe.pdf

Guha, S., Rastogi, R., & Shim, K. (1998). CURE: An efficient clustering algorithm for large databases. In *Proceedings of ACM SIGMOD International Conference on Management of Data,* (pp. 73 – 84). ACM.

Guo, A. (2004). A new framework for clustering algorithm evaluation in the domain of functional genomics. In *Proceedings of ACM Symposium on Applied Computing,* (pp. 143–146). ACM.

Hall, M., & Lloyd, S. (1997). Feature subset selection: A correlation based filter approach. In *Neural information processing and intelligent information systems.* Berlin: Springer.

Han, J., & Kamber, M. (2000). *Data mining: Concepts and techniques.* San Francisco: Morgan Kaufmann Publisher.

Hand, D. J., Mannila, H., & Smyth, P. (2001). *Principles of data mining.* Cambridge, MA: MIT Press.

Harris, R. L. (1999). *Information graphics: A comprehensive illustrated reference.* Oxford, UK: Oxford Press.

Health Behavior in School-Aged Children (HBSC). (n.d.). Retrieved from http://www.hbsc.org

Hinneburg, A., & Keim, D. A. (1998). An efficient approach to clustering in large multimedia databases with noise. *Knowledge Discovery and Data Mining,* 58–65.

John, G. H., Kohavi, R., & Pfleger, K. (1994). Irrelevant features and the subset selection problem. In *Proceedings of the Eleventh International Conference on Machine Learning,* (pp. 121-129). IEEE.

Karypis, G., Eui-Hong, H., & Kumar, V. (1999). CHAMELEON: A hierarchical clustering algorithm using dynamic modeling. *IEEE Computer, 32*(8), 68–75. doi:10.1109/2.781637

Kasturi, J., & Acharya, R. (2004). Clustering of diverse genomic data using information fusion. In *Proceedings of the 2004 ACM Symposium on Applied Computing,* (pp. 116–120). ACM.

Kaur, H. (2005). Actionable rules: Issues and directions. *World Academy of Science. Engineering and Technology, 5,* 61–64.

Kaur, H., Chauhan, R., & Ahmed, Z. (2012b). Role of data mining in establishing strategic policies for the efficient management of healthcare system–A case study from Washington DC area using retrospective discharge data. *BMC Health Services Research, 12*(Suppl. 1), 12. doi:10.1186/1472-6963-12-S1-P12 PMID:22236336

Kaur, H., Chauhan, R., & Alam, M. A. (2010). An optimal categorization of feature selection methods for knowledge discovery. In Visual analytics and interactive technologies: Data, text and web mining applications. Hershey, PA: IGI Global Publishing.

Kaur, H., Chauhan, R., Alam, M. A., Aljunid, S., & Salleh, M. (2012). SpaGRID: A spatial grid framework for high dimensional medical databases. In *Proceedings of International Conference on Hybrid Artificial Intelligence Systems* (LNCS), (vol. 7208, pp. 690-704). Berlin: Springer.

Kaur, H., Chauhan, R., & Aljunid, S. (2012a). Data mining cluster analysis on the influence of health factors in Casemix data. *BMC Health Services Research, 12*(1), O3. doi:10.1186/1472-6963-12-S1-O3

Keim, D. A., & Kreigel, H. P. (1996). Visualization techniques for mining large databases: A comparison. *IEEE Transactions on Knowledge and Data Engineering, 8.*

Klosgen, W. (1996). Explora: A multipattern and multistategy discovery assistant. In U. Fayyad, G. Piatetsky-Shapiro, P. Smyth, & R. Uthurusay (Eds.), *Advances in knowledge discovery* (pp. 249–272). Cambridge, MA: AAAI Press/The MIT Press.

Langley, P. (1994). Selection of relevant features in machine learning. In *Proceedings of the AAAI Fall Symposium on Relevance.* New Orleans, LA: AAAI Press.

Lee, H. Y., & Ong, K.-L. (1996). Visualization support for data mining. *IEEE Intelligent Systems, 11*(5), 69–75.

Leuski, A. (2001). Evaluating document clustering for interactive information retrieval. In *Proceedings of Tenth International Conference on Information and Knowledge Management,* (pp. 33–40). IEEE.

Mannila, H. (2002). Local and global methods in data mining: Basic techniques and open problems. In *Proceedings of Twenty-Ninth International Colloquium on Automata, Languages and Programming* (LNCS), (pp. 57-68). Berlin: Springer-Verlag.

Miller, G. J., Bräutigan, D., & Gerlach, S. V. (2006). *Business intelligence competency centres: A team approach to maximising competitive advantage.* New York: Wiley and Sons.

Miller, H. J., & Han, J. (2001). *Geographic data mining and knowledge discovery.* San Francisco: Taylor and Francis. doi:10.4324/9780203468029

Mitra, P., Murthy, P. A., & Pal, S. K. (2002). Unsupervised feature selection using feature similarity. *IEEE Transactions on Pattern Analysis and Machine Intelligence, 24*(3), 301–312. doi:10.1109/34.990133

Piatetsky-Shapiro, G., Brachman, R., Khabaza, T., Kloesgen, W., & Simoudis, E. (1996). An overview of issues in developing industrial data mining and knowledge discovery application. In *Proceedings of Second International Conference on Knowledge Discovery and Data Mining.* Portland, OR: AAAI Press.

R Package. (n.d.). Retrieved from http://www.r-project.org

Smyth, P. (2001). Breaking out of the black-box: Research challenges in data mining. In *Proceedings of ACM SIGMOD International Workshop on Research Issues in Data Mining and Knowledge Discovery* (DMKD'01). ACM.

Witten, I. H., & Frank, E. (2005). *Data mining: Practical machine learning tools and techniques* (2nd ed.). San Francisco: Morgan Kaufmann.

Yu, D., Chatterjee, S., Sheikholeslami, G., & Zhang, A. (1998). *Efficiently detecting arbitrary shaped clusters in very large datasets with high dimensions*. Buffalo, NY: State University of New York at Buffalo.

Yu, L., & Liu, H. (2003). Feature selection for high-dimensional data: A fast correlation-based filter solution. In *Proceedings of Twelfth International Conference on Machine Learning*. San Francisco: Morgan Kaufmann.

Zhang, T., Ramakrishnan, R., & Livny, M. (1996). BIRCH: An efficient data clustering method for very large databases. In *Proceedings of SIGMOD International Conference*, (pp. 103–114). ACM.

Zhao, Y., & Karypis, G. (2002). Evaluation of hierarchical clustering algorithms for document datasets. In *Proceedings of Information and Knowledge Management*. McLean, VA: Academic Press.

KEY TERMS AND DEFINITIONS

Clustering: The grouping of objects in context with the similarity among the data is called clustering.

Correlation based Feature Selection (CFS): CFS is a feature selection technique to reduce irrelevant and redundant features using correlation to determine the correlation among the attributes.

Data Mining: Data mining can be defined as an efficient tool to determine relevant patterns for knowledge discovery process.

Feature Selection: Feature selection generates the features subsets by removing the redundant and irrelevant features from databases.

Hierarchical Clustering: The clustering in which data are clustered in form of tree is known as hierarchical clustering.

Knowledge Discovery in Databases (KDD): The knowledge discovery in databases can be defined as process to discover meaningful, novel and hidden patterns from large and complex database.

Visualization: Visualization is used to retrieve results in form of graphs, pie charts etc to get generalized view of data in epigrammatic structure.

Chapter 5
Characterizing Intelligent Intrusion Detection and Prevention Systems Using Data Mining

Mrutyunjaya Panda
GITA, India

Manas Ranjan Patra
Berhampur University, India

ABSTRACT

Intrusion Detection and Prevention Systems (IDPS) are being widely implemented to prevent suspicious threats in computer networks. Intrusion detection and prevention systems are security systems that are used to detect and prevent security threats to computer networks. In order to understand the security risks and IDPS, in this chapter, the authors make a quick review on classification of the IDPSs and categorize them in certain groups. Further, in order to improve accuracy and security, data mining techniques have been used to analyze audit data and extract features that can distinguish normal activities from intrusions. Experiments have been conducted for building efficient intrusion detection and prevention systems by combining online detection and offline data mining. During online data examination, real-time data are captured and are passed through a detection engine that uses a set of rules and parameters for analysis. During offline data mining, necessary knowledge is extracted about the process of intrusion.

INTRODUCTION

Computer network security and their resource protection is one of the major concerns in today's IT activities, as complete removal of security breaches at present, found to be unrealistic (John,

2006, p.84-87). In the present scenario, one can use either Firewall in order to strengthen the implementation of executing rules and policy being silent on insider security violations or can think of deploying antivirus software which is ineffective in detecting new viruses. Alternatively, one can go for intrusion detection systems which can only detect intrusions and send alerts to the

DOI: 10.4018/978-1-4666-4940-8.ch005

network administrator for appropriate action, but cannot prevent any intrusions to occur further in the network. Thus, what is required in such a scenario is an Intrusion Prevention System (IPS) which combines both the requirements, viz., ability to detect intrusions and try to stop the detected intrusion attempts.

Intrusion Prevention System

The main functions of intrusion prevention systems are to identify malicious activity, log information about this activity, attempt to block/stop it, and report it. Intrusion prevention systems (IPS) were developed to resolve ambiguities in passive network monitoring by placing detection systems in-line. With improved firewall technologies, IPS can make access control decisions based on application content, rather than IP address or ports as traditional firewalls had done. As IPS systems were originally a literal extension of intrusion detection systems, they continue to be related. Intrusion prevention systems may also serve secondarily at the host level to stop potentially malicious activity. An Intrusion Prevention system must also be enabling a low rate of false positives and false negative errors in detection alerts. Some IPS systems can also prevent yet to be discovered attacks, such as those caused by a Buffer overflow. There are three common detection and prevention methodologies: misuse detection, novel or anomaly detection, and stateful protocol analysis with regards to the former. We can make another distinction in terms of the residency of the IPS. In this respect, IPS is usually divided into host-based, Network Behavior Analysis (NBA) and network-based systems technologies, which are differentiated, primarily by the types of events that they can recognize and the methodologies that they use to identify possible incidents (Scarfone & Mell, 2007, p.457-471). Host-based systems are present on each host that requires monitoring, and collect data concerning the operation of this host for suspicious activity. While Network Behavior

Analysis examines network traffic to identify threats that generate unusual traffic flows, such as detect denies of service attacks, scanning, and certain forms of malware (Choo, 2011, p.719-731). In contrast, network-based IPSs monitor the network traffic on the network containing the hosts to be protected. Hybrid systems, which include host and network-based elements, can offer the best prevention and protective capabilities, and systems to protect against attacks from multiple sources have been developed (Shabtai, Fledel, Kanonov, Elovici, Dolev & Glezer, 2010, p. 35-44). To achieve secure and multi defense capability of network security system, the hybrid technology has been applied in the proposed approach. Intrusion prevention is a new approach system to defense networking systems, which combine the technique firewall with the Intrusion detection properly, which is proactive technique. Prevent the attacks from entering the network by examining various data record and prevention demeanor of pattern recognition sensor. When an attack is identified, intrusion prevention blocks and logs the offending data. The primary IPS uses signature to identify activity in network traffic and host perform detection on inbound-outbound packets and would be to block that activity before the damage and access network resources. A general architecture of IDPS consisting of four functional blocks is shown in Figure 1.

The Event block captures events from the environment and passes them to the database block

Figure 1. General architecture for IDPS systems

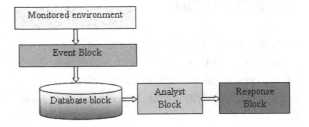

where they are maintained for further processing. The analyst block extracts the events from the database block and analyses them for possible intrusion. In case some intrusive behavior is detected alerts are raised. The alerts are then passed on to the Response block in order to initiate suitable action to deal with the intrusion.

RELATED RESEARCH

The authors (Koller, Rangaswami, Marrero, Hernandez, Smith, Barsilai, Necula, Sadjadi, Li, & Merrill, 2008, p.151-160) have proposed a holistic approach to obtain a real-time intrusion prevention system that combines the merits of misbehavior based and anomaly-based detection. In this, they provided four design principles that can help towards making IDPS an accurate, effective, and practical intrusion prevention solution. A survey on intrusion detection and prevention system is provided in (Sandhu, Haider,Naseer,& Obaid Ullah, 2011, p.66-71). In (Hu, Wang, & Zhao, 2011, p.55-62), the authors declared IPS has correlation between intrusion detection and firewall, with an aim to design and implement trusted communication protocol based on XML. In (Wasniowski, 2006, p.392-396), authors have proposed data mining based intrusion detection and prevention techniques and have examined how multiple intrusion detection sensors are integrated in order to minimize the number of incorrect-alarms. The recent network security challenges can be taken care of successfully with an early detection and response mechanism, as proposed by many a researchers (Debar, Thomas, Cuppens, & Cuppens-Boulahia, 2008, p. 129-170; Stakhanova, Babu & Wong, 2007, p. 169-184; Manikopoulos, 2003, p. 53-59; Sahah & Kahtani, 2010, p.6-15). A data mining based intrusion prevention in depth system model to manage the huge amounts of unreliable and uncontrollable security events, which are generated by the extensive utilization of heterogeneous security devices in computer networks is proposed by the researchers in (Jie, Xiao, Yabin & Chenghui, 2009,p.22). In (Chalak, Harale & Bhosale, 2011, p.200-203), the authors present data mining techniques for intrusion detection and prevention system that can identify which type of attack on database occurs. Analysis of contemporary information security systems using some novel intrusion prevention and detection methods are provided in (Jotsov, 2008,p.14-20), in which the author claims that all of the presented methods may be used independently or can improve traditional data mining based information security systems. In (Patil & Meshram, 2012,p.1-4), the authors illustrate the idea of detecting DOS attacks as a step towards designing an IDPS. An intelligent collaborative IDPS for smart grid environment is proposed in (Patel, Juir, & Pedersen, 2013, in-Press) to provide maximum protection for future smart grids with a fully distributed management structure supporting network. The authors (Patel, Taghavi, Bakhtiyari, & Juier, 2013,p.25-41) provide a systematic review on how to use cloud computing for IDPS with a list of germane requirements and then leverage the concepts of automatic computing, ontology and fuzzy logic to meet these requirements.

Evolution of Intrusion Detection and Intrusion Prevention Techniques

Intrusion detection system (IDS) considers being passive, watchful of data packets that are traversed in the network monitoring port, configures the rules from the network traffic and then sets an alarm if it detects any intrusion. On the other hand, Intrusion prevention system (IPS) contains all the good features of IDS, sits inline with the traffic flows on an active wired network, thereby shutting down any attempted attacks occurred by blocking either access from the user account, IP address or all access to the targeted host, service, application etc. Response to a detected intrusion is done by reconfiguring firewalls or routers for blocking the attack or by applying patches if some specific vulnerability is found in a host.

Emerging Need for Intrusion Detection and Prevention

Over the years, the number of information security related computer crime due to intrusion incidents and the losses incurred have increased significantly (Birdi & Jansen, 2006, p.1-5). Further, the following issues trigger enterprises to pay close attention to their network intrusion detection and prevention.

- **Strategic Business Changes:** Initiative has been taken by many organizations to enhance their competitiveness in the market through increased "web presence, e-commerce, integration with business partners, mergers and acquisitions, etc".
- **Legal and Regulatory Requirements:** Many regulations have been introduced such as: Sarbanes-Oxley and Bill 198 (accounting regulations), the Health Insurance Portability & Accountability Act and the Personal Information Protection and Electronic Documents Act (privacy legislations) as a possible measure.

- **Public and Stakeholder Expectations:** In order to safeguard the expectations of public and stakeholder, from the possible computer incidents that could have resulted in exposure of "confidential information, unavailability of systems and unreliable information".
- **Sophistication of Network Intrusions:** Network-based intrusions that include "viruses, hacking, Trojan horses, unauthorized system changes, denial of service, brute force, social engineering, spyware and spam have increased significantly due to system vulnerabilities or human errors."

IDS vs. IPS

At the first instance, IDS or IPS both looks for atomic pattern and composite pattern matching in a signature based system, as discussed below. (see Table 1)

- **Atomic Pattern Matching:** With this kind of pattern matching, an attempt is made to access a specific port on a specific host, where malicious content is contained in a single packet. While an IDS allows the malicious single packets into the network until

Table 1. Steps of IDS and IPS

Steps of IDS	Steps of IPS
Step 1. An attack is launched on a network that has a sensor deployed in IDS mode.	Step 1. An attack is launched on a network that has a sensor deployed in IPS.
Step 2. The switch sends copies of all packets to the IDS sensor to analyze the packets. At the same time, the target machine experiences the malicious attack.	Step 2. The IPS sensor analyzes the packets as soon as they come into the IPS sensor interface. The IPS sensor, using signatures, matches the malicious traffic to the signature and the attack is stopped immediately. Traffic in violation of policy can be dropped by an IPS sensor.
Step 3. The IDS sensor, using a signature, matches the malicious traffic to the signature.	Step 3. The IPS sensor can send an alarm to a management console for logging and other management purposes.
Step 4. The IDS sensor sends the switch a command to deny access to the malicious traffic.	
Step 5. The IDS sends an alarm to a management console for logging and other management purposes.	

it confirms the attack, an IPS prevents these packets from entering at all on the other hand.

- **Composite Pattern Matching:** In this case, a sequence of operations distributed across multiple hosts over an arbitrary period of time is chosen. The following are some of the steps in order to illustrate how IDS and IPS works differently when attack is launched on the network.

There are different kinds of sensors available depending upon the detection capabilities with their own Pros and Cons as: Signature based, anomaly based, policy based and honey pot based sensors. However, choosing the best one among them is quite a difficult task, we may summarize some framework as a guidelines in this regard, as in Table 2.

Further, a critical analysis to understand IPS in a better way is provided in Table 3.

DATA MINING IN IPS

Data mining is the process of extracting patterns from large dataset by combining methods from statistics, artificial intelligence and database management. Following are something considered while using data mining for intrusion detection and prevention system (IPS).

- Remove activity from alarm data.
- Identify false alarm generators and attack sensor signatures.
- Identify long, ongoing IP packets.
- Find bad activity.

The first step is to capture the packets in order to detect the attacks or malicious traffic on the network in two modes. One is Normal capturing mode, in which the packets intended to the system are only captured by the system, where the other is Promiscuous mode where the system captures every packet those are going through the interface. So, we have to use the promiscuous packet capturing mode to monitor the network traffic.

The overall architecture of NIPS contains the following attributes.

Table 2. Guidelines in choosing an IDPS (Beigh & Peer, 2012, p.661-675)

Type	The type of tool, or category to which a tool belongs, e.g., "Web Application Scanning"
Operating System	The operating system(s) on which the tool runs. If the tool is an appliance, this field will contain a "not applicable" symbol (N/A) because the operating system is embedded in the tool.
Hardware	The third-party hardware platform(s) on which the tool runs, plus any significant additional hardware requirements, such as minimum amount of random-access memory or free disk space. If the tool is an appliance, this field will contain a "not applicable "symbol (N/A) because the hardware is incorporated into the tool.
License	The type of license under which the tool is distributed, e.g., Commercial, Freeware, GNU Public License
NIAP Validated	An indication of whether the product has received validation by the National Information Assurance Partnership (NIAP) under the Common Criteria, Federal Information Processing Standard 140, or another certification standard for which NIAP performs validations. If no such validation has been performed, this field will be blank or put N/A
Common Criteria	If the tool has received a Common Criteria certification, the Evaluation Assurance Level and date of that certification. If no such certification has-been performed, this field will be blanker N/A
Developer	The individual or organization responsible for creating and/or distributing the tool
URL	The Uniform Resource Locator (URL) of the Webpage from which the tool can be obtained (downloaded or purchased), or in some cases, the Web page at which the supplier can be notified withal request to obtain the tool

Table 3. Some critical analysis of IDPS (Sandhu, Haider, Naseer & Ateeb, 2011,p.426-431)

System	Category	Type or Approach	Signature Detection	Signature Prevention	Anomaly Detection	Anomaly Prevention	Technique	Advantages	Disadvantages
IDPS	HIDPS and NIDPS	Operating system and Application level approach	Yes	Yes	Yes	Yes	Signature based and anomaly based	Automatic response, reduce human effort	Cost ineffective, Implementation, updating, monitoring issues
IDPS (SNORT)	NIDPS	OS and Application level approach	Yes	Yes	No	No	Signature based	Flexibility of self configuration	Cannot detect anomaly behavior of intrusion
IDPS	HIDPS	Secure mobile agent	Yes	Yes	Yes	Yes	Signature based and anomaly based	Real time response, reduce human effort	Security of mobile agent, needs to adopt some other techniques

Table 4. Comparison of IDS and IPS (Zhang & Li, 2004,p.386-390)

	IDS	IPS
Advantages	1. it can detect external hackers and internal network-based attacks; 2. it scales easily to provide protection for the entire network; 3. it offers centralized management for correlation of distributed attacks; 4. it gives systems administrators the ability to quantify attacks.	1. it protect at the application layer; 2. it prevent attacks rather than simply reacting to them; 3. it uses a behavioral approach; 4. it permits real-time event correlation; 5. it permits real-time event correlation.
Disadvantages	1. it generates false positives and negatives; 2. it reacts to attacks rather than preventing them; 3. it requires full-time monitoring; 4. it requires a complex incident-response process; 5. it cannot monitor traffic at higher transmission rates; 6. it generates an enormous amount of data to be analyzed; 7. it is susceptible to low and slow attacks; 8. it requires highly skilled staff dedicated to interpreting the data; 9. it cannot deal with encrypted network traffic; 10. it is expensive.	1. it generate false positives that can create serious problems if automated responses are used; 2. it create network bottlenecks; 3. IPS is a new technology and is expensive.

1. Packet Sniffer unit, which captures the packet from the interface either in promiscuous mode or in normal mode.

2. Intrusion Detection or Preprocessing engine, which uses the different approaches to detect the attack depending on flow based analysis or protocol based analysis.

3. Countermeasures, in order to observe the packet flow for any malicious code within it. If any abnormal flow of packets is observed, then the particular action is selected to avoid the intruder to enter in to the network.

How to Implement IDPS and Mapping of IDPS

Before we think of how to implement IPS, we should understand their advantages and disadvantages with IDS, as in Table 4.

As IPS and IDS have different advantages and disadvantages, an entity should use both systems so that they would complement each other such as detecting some events that the others cannot, or detecting with significantly greater accuracy than the other technologies. Further, one can think of using multiple types of both IPS and IDS, so as to achieve more comprehensive and accurate detection and prevention of malicious activity, with lower false positives and false negatives rates (Le, AL-Shaer, & Boutaba, 2008,1-6).

MAPPING PROBLEM OF IPS

Profiles of user behavior can be generated from the user activity log which needs to be updated periodically in order to include the most recent changes; otherwise it will be counterproductive to information security.

In general, as inside users have privilege of authenticated and authorized access to resources, inside intrusions are easy to happen than from outside ones. At the same time, outside intruders can become insiders through a proxy of a current insider. Thus, filtering, screening, blocking, authentication, authorization, and accounting are standard mechanism to get rid of such types of inside and outside intrusions.

Sensor deployment is an important part of IPSs with which network monitoring can be done with ease. This can smoothen the process of alert incident response, notify administrator, or block traffic immediately and finally change control if necessary. The mapping of IPS is provided in Figure 2.

1. **Placement:** There are two factor that will affect the placement: First, the sensor placement, and Second, the number of sensor. The purpose of deploying sensors is to recognize and identify suspicious data and then provide the alarm if suspicious activity is identified. Furthermore, the situation trigger of alarm (valid or invalid but feasible) from sensor to event response.
2. **Accuracy:** As evident, a positive alarm is considered to be an attack data, while a negative is considered to be a normal data in intrusion detection and prevention system. Furthermore, evaluation accuracy and speed

has been proposed by (Oh & Lee, 2003,596-612), they were measured in terms of FP and FN with timelines activity approaches. Additionally, more appropriately accurate mechanism keeps the number of false negative and false positive low. The main problem in sensor are accuracy and timeliness performance that identifies threat, and sensitivity, as to how effective a particular filter was in blocking knowing and unknown threat response. It was measured in term of FPR and FNR.

3. **Precision:** As network IPS sensor identifies potentially malicious traffic; it must response to the stream traffic by performing some type of action such as: block, allow, report, logging,(Carter & Hoque, 2006,p.1-316).
4. **Techniques:** In this, many research efforts have been focused on how to effectively and accurately construct Intrusion detection models followed by to prevent them. Combination of expert system and statistical approach was very popular (Panda, Abraham, Das & Patra, 2011, p.347-356; Panda, Abraham & Patra, 2012).

RESEARCH METHODOLOGY AND DISCUSSIONS

This research considers packet sniffer tool to capture the online packet and Snort to have rule based classification of the IDPS. Here, false positives and false negatives are basically used as performance measures to evaluate the IDPS, which is described below:

False Positives or False Alarms

The term false positive describes a situation in which an IDS device generates an alarm when there is intrusive activity. Other common terms used to describe this condition are "false alarms" and "benign trigger". False alarms can be subdi-

Figure 2. Mapping problem of IPS

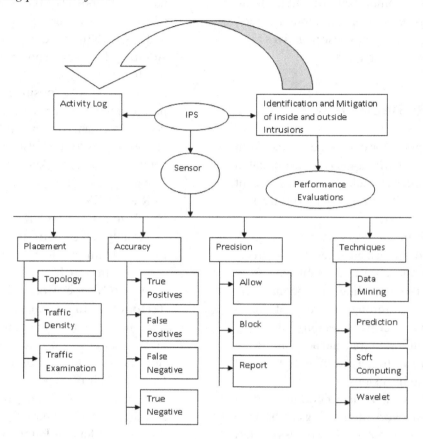

vided into several more meaningful and specific categories. Common categories into which false alarms can be divided include:

- **Reactionary Traffic Alarms:** This alarm is generated when traffic that is caused by another network event, often non malicious. An example of this would be a NIDS device triggering an ICMP flood alarm when it is really several destination unreachable packets caused by equipment failure somewhere in the Internet cloud.
- **Equipment-Related Alarms:** This alarm is generated as alerts to the intrusions that are triggered by odd, unrecognized packets generated by certain network equipment. Load balancers often generate these types of alarms.

- **Protocol Violations:** Alarms are generated when there is a protocol violation occurs. Intrusion alerts that are caused by unrecognized network traffic often caused by poorly or oddly written client software fall under this category.
- **True False Positives:** Alarms that are generated by an IDS for no apparent reason. Example includes alerts generated by IDS software bugs.
- **Non Malicious Alarms:** This alarm is generated through some real occurrence that is non malicious in nature.

A normal IDS sensor without any customization may have only 10% of its alarms associated with a true security event depending on network traffic and the IDS design that is deployed. The remaining 90% of noise is not an acceptable percentage. While it may be debatable what can be considered an acceptable percentage of false alarms, an average real alarm rate of 60-70% or better is possible under normal conditions.

False Negatives

False negative is the inability to detect true security events under certain circumstances. In other words, Intrusive activity is not detected and alerted. Hence, we should take necessary steps to reduce the chance of false negative conditions without increasing the number of false positives. Some causes for false negatives are as discussed hereunder.

- **Network Design Issues:** Here, Network design flaws such as improper port spanning on switches and traffic exceeding the ability of a switch or hub contribute to these problems. Other problems include multiple entry point networks where the NIDS device cannot see all incoming and outgoing traffic.
- **Encrypted Traffic Design Flaws:** False negative arises because the IDS are unable to understand encrypted traffic. Placing the NIDS behind VPN termination points and use of SSL accelerators are some possible ways to ensure the NIDS.
- **Lack of Change Control:** It has been observed many a times that false negative created by a lack of communication between IS departments, networking, and security staff and is in the form of network or server changes that are not properly communicated to network administrator.
- **Improperly Written Signatures:** As signatures have not been written properly, it can not properly catch the attack or mutations of the attack even though the attack is known and the signature is developed.

- **Unpublicized Attack:** This type of attack is not publicly known, unseen before, therefore network administrators have no prior knowledge about it and no signature is developed.

Firewall Rules

A firewall security policy is a list of ordered filtering rules that define the actions performed on packets that satisfy specific conditions (Ahmed, Zolkipli & Abdalla, 2009,p.721-725). Before developing filtering rules using packet filter, enough consideration is to be made beforehand on how far demarcation will be applied, as more and more demarcation applied increases the search time and space requirements of the packet filtering process and consequences to make downhill performance progressively (Al-Shaer & Hamed, 2004,p.2605-2616; P-pale,2007, p.685-690). It is well understood that every incoming and outgoing network packet are checked beforehand by rules alternately until matching rule found in firewall. Firewall rules can limit to access the connection of pursuant to parameter: source IP, destination IP, source port, destination port, protocol and others (Suehring & Ziegler, 2006,p.1-552). An example of firewall rules is shown in Figure 3.

The above Firewall rule explains to enhance the order by the end of chain (A) for the incoming traffic to firewall (INPUT) by source IP address (-s) 203.130.201.6 with the type protocol (-p) icmp to destination IP address (-d) 10.10.15.7 and destination port (--dport) 80. Finally, action taken (-j) dropped (DROP) by firewall.

Log Files

Log files can give an idea about what the different parts of system are doing. Logs can show what is going right and what is going wrong. Log files can provide a useful profile activity. From a security standpoint, it is crucial to be able to distinguish normal activity from the activity of someone to

Figure 3. Firewall rules

```
-A INPUT –s 203.130.201.6 –p icmp –d 10.10.15.7 --dport 80 –j DROP
```

Figure 4. Snort log files

```
[**] INFO - Possible Squid Scan [**] 02/20-14:16:23.953376
192.170.0.33:1022 -> 192.170.0.1:2212 TCP TTL:128 TOS:0x0 ID:393 IpLen:20 DgmLen:48
DF ******S* Seq: 0x60591B9 Ack: 0x0 Win: 0x4000 TcpLen: 28 TCP Options (4) => MSS:
1460 NOP NOP SackOK
```

Figure 5. Syslog files

```
Jan 1 21:02:13 (none) sshd[14938]: Failed password for mitu from 172.15.64.26 port 3419
ssh2
```

attack server or network (Terpstra, Love, Reck & Scanlon, 2004,p.504).

Log files are useful for the following three reasons (Abbes, Bouhoula & Rasinowitch, 2004,p.404):

- Troubleshooting system problems and understanding what is happening on the system
- Logs serve as an early warning for both system and security events
- They can be indispensable in reconstructing events, whether determined an intrusion has occurred and performing the follow-up forensic investigation or just profiling normal activity.

Figures 4 and 5 are some of the examples from log files shown.

The example in Figure 4 using Snort log files (/var/log/snort), there is effort for the scan of existence of Squid proxy server at 192.170.0.1

port 2212 from workstation 192.170.0.33 port 1022. TCP Synchronized package delivery can be seen from ******S* Workstation 192.170.0.33.

The example in Figure 3 using syslog files (/var/log/syslog), says that there is someone trying mitu user login and the failed password from the IP address 172.15.64.26 port 3419 passing ssh service (port 22 protocol tcp).

Decision Tree of Data Mining

Decision tree is a popular technique in classification based data mining for learning patterns from data and using these patterns for classification (Ahmed, Zolkipli, & Abdalla, 2009, p.721-725). Each decision tree represents a rule, which categorizes data according to these attributes]. Where each node (non-leaf node) denotes a test on an attribute, each branch represents an outcome of the test and each leaf node or terminal node holds a class label. The topmost node in a tree is the root node.

MATERIALS AND METHODS

In this section, we explain the background of proposed methodology used to design intrusion detection and prevention system. In general, IDPS performs analysis to discover hostile traffic in a monitored environment. We use SNORT, to perform various tasks that include: data decoding, preprocessing, rule checking, and action implementation.

This research discusses the usefulness of ID3 decision tree as a data mining technique to find the characteristics of possible intrusions. Network traffic logs that describe the human behavior in network traffics characterized as either intrusive or normal activities used as training data. The results obtained after training of decision tree represents the rules of intrusion characteristics and then these rules are used in the firewall rules as prevention. Determining occurrence of intrusion or normal activities at network traffic log can be determined in either of the following way:

- Observe manually about the activities of the network traffic in log files. Example application software of log files includes syslog, syslog_ng, tcpdump and others. Through these log files, Pattern obtained are used to see if intrusion occurs, for example there are some times trying to access using login or password failed, trying port scan, abundant ping, delivery of abundant package by repeat etc.

- Using snort software as Network Intrusion Detection System (NIDS) make it possible to determine intrusion activities or normal activities.

Solutions and Recommendations

Table 5 provides some sample collection of network traffics and extraction of log files of intrusive and normal activities consisting of five parameters as attributes that includes: source IP address, destination IP address, source port, destination port and protocol. The class label whether intrusion occurs, represented as yes or no.

Considering IPS as a combination of first detection of intrusions followed by preventing those using firewalls, the research process is shown in Figure 6.

From the above process as in Table 4, by taking intrusion as source node, we got Intrusion=Yes for 2 times and Intrusion=No for 3 times, the probability of getting intrusive activities=2/5=0-4 and the probability for Normal activities=3/5=0.6.

Now, entropy: H (Intrusion) = $-p^+ \log_2(p^+) - p^- \log_2(p^-)$, where p^+ denotes intrusions and p^- as Normal. So, H (Intrusion) = $-0.4 \log_2 0.4 - 0.6 \log_2 0.6 = 0.971$.

Similarly, considering Source IP address as root node, we can see from Table 4 that source IP address 191.302.13.102 having all normal activities, while other two addresses 122.306.13.100 and 203.306.14.20 are intrusive.

Table 5. Sample network traffics

Instance No	Protocol	Source IP Address	Destination IP Address	Source Port	Destination Port	Whether Intrusion
1	TCP	191.302.13.102	12.12.1.1	1239	80	No
2	UDP	122.306.13.100	10.10.1.2	1421	23	Yes
3	ICMP	191.302.13.102	10.10.1.5	1559	21	Yes
4	TCP	191.302.13.102	12.12.1.5	1624	80	No
5	TCP	191.302.13.102	12.12.1.3	1597	22	No

Figure 6. Research process for constructing an IPS

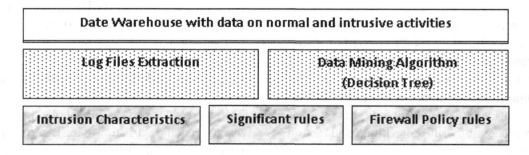

Now, Entropy H (Intrusion, Source IP) = 4/5(1/4 log$_2$ 1/4–3/4 log$_2$3/4) + 1/5(1/1 log$_2$ 1/1–0/1log$_2$0/1) =0.4

Similarly, by considering protocol and intrusion, we can obtain H (Intrusion, Protocol). In the same way, H (Intrusion, Destination Port), H (Intrusion, Source Port), H (Intrusion, Destination IP) can be calculated.

We can consider Gain Information as a tool to obtain the super attributes that have a highest value.

So, Gain (Intrusion, Source IP) = E (Intrusion) - E (Intrusion, Source IP) =0.971-0.4=0.571 and so on.

The training data is evaluated by Shannon entropy, as above. We remove the alerts associated to true attacks, which called as Intrusion Alert. The remainders are called as False Alert. Then, re-evaluate the Noise Alert in the training data set. The Shannon entropies are relatively smooth when no attack occurs; otherwise, one or some of the values would change abruptly.

This process continues until all data are classified correctly and the complete tree is formed. From the decision tree, one can obtain the rule from the root to a leaf node using IF-THEN rules. Then these rules will be applied to the firewall policy rules in order to make necessary preventions to network intrusions.

CONCLUSION AND FUTURE DIRECTIONS

When a computer is connected to a network, there has to be more security provided to it. Now-a-days tools are available using which one can attack computer networks. As such incidents are increasing day by day, it is required to detect the attacks and take necessary counter measures to protect against such attacks. Snort is the De-facto standard for IDS which comes as open source software which has been used in our research. Implementing an IPS can be risky because it has the potential to slow down network traffic or to set up a self-imposed denial of service attack by blocking legitimate traffic. IPS system presents additional performance challenges because of its in-line nature. Both algorithms based on misuse detection and anomaly detection has advantages and drawbacks. Major drawback of any IPS or IDS is that a computer system becomes slow after their installation. Even if it protects the computer from internal, external threats and attacks, it is required to train the IPS and IDS system and continuously update attack signatures or profiles. If the profiles/signatures are not updated regularly then any IDS or IPS cannot protect the system from new threats and attacks. Decision tree technique is good for the intrusion characteristic of the network traffic logs for IDS and implemented in the firewall as prevention.

REFERENCES

Abbes, T. O., Bouhoula, A., & Rasinowitch, M. (2004). Protocol analysis in intrusion detection using decision tree. In *Proc. of Intl. Conf. on Information Technology*. IEEE.

Ahmed, S. N., Zolkipli, M. F., & Abdalla, A. N. (2009). Intrusion prevention system using IDS decision tree data mining. *Amrican Journal of Engg., & Applied sciences, 2*(4), 721-725.

Al-Shaer, & Hamed, H. H. (2004). Discovery of policy anomalies in distributed firewalls. In *Proc. of the 23rd Annual Joint Conf. on Computer and Communication Societies* (pp.2605-2616). IEEE.

Beigh, B. M., & Peer, M. A. (2012). Intrusion detection and prevention system: Classification and quick review. *ARPN Journal of Science and Technology, 2*(7), 661–675.

Birdi, T., & Jansen, K. (2006). Network intrusion detection: Know what you do (not) need. *Information System Control Journal, 1*, 1–5.

Carter, E., & Hogue, J. (2006). *Intrusion prevention fundamentals*. CISCO Press.

Chalak, A., Harale, N. D., & Bhosale, R. (2011). Data mining techniques for intrusion detection and prevention system. *Intl. Journal of Computer Science and Network Security, 11*(8), 200–203.

Choo, K. K. R. (2011). The cyber thread landscape: Challenges and future research directions. *Computers & Security, 30*, 719–731. doi:10.1016/j.cose.2011.08.004

Debar, H., Thomas, Y., Cuppens, F., & Cuppens-Boulahia, N. (2008). Response: Bridging the link between intrusion detection alerts and security policies. *Intrusion Detection Systems, 38*, 129–170.

Hu, V., Wang, W., & Zhao, K. (2011). The design and implementation of trusted communication protocol for intrusion prevention system. *Journal of Convergence Information Technology, 6*, 55–62. doi:10.4156/jcit.vol6.issue3.7

Jie, V., Xiao, Z., Yabin, L., & Chenghui, S. (2009). Intrusion prevention in depth system research based on data mining. *International Journal of Distributed Sensor Networks, 5*(22).

John, S. (2006). Adapting an enterprise software security framework. *IEEE Security and privacy Journal, 4*(2), 84-87.

Jotsov, V. S. (2008). Novel Intrusion prevention and detection methods IS2008. In *Proceedings of IEEE Intl. Conference on Intelligent Systems*. IEEE Press.

Koller, R., Rangaswami, R., Marrero, J., Hernandez, I., Smith, G., & Barsilai, M. ... Merrill, K. (2008). Anatomy of real time intrusion prevention system. In *Proceedings of International Conference on Autonomic Computing* (pp.151-160). IEEE Press.

Le, A. AL-Shaer, E., & Boutaba, R. (2008). On optimizing load balancing of IDPS. In *Proceedings of IEEE Infocom Workshop* (pp.1-6). IEEE Press.

Manikopoulos, C. (2003). Early statistical anomaly intrusion detection of DOS attacks using MIB traffic parameters. In *Proceedings of IEEE Systems, Man and Cybernetics Society* (pp. 53-59). IEEE.

Oh, S. H., & Lee, W. K. (2003). An anomaly intrusion detection method by clustering normal user behavior. *Computers & Security, 22*, 596–612. doi:10.1016/S0167-4048(03)00710-7

P-pale. T.K. (2007). Optimization of firewall rules. In *Proc. of ITI 29th Intl. Conf. on Information Technology Interfaces*, (pp. 685-690). IEEE.

Panda, M., Abraham, A., Das, S., & Patra, M. R. (2011). Network intrusion detection system: A machine learning approach. *Intelligent Decision Technologies Journal, 5*(4), 347–356.

Panda, M., Abraham, A., & Patra, M. R. (2012). *Hybrid intelligent systems for detecting network intrusions*. Wiley Security and Communication Network Journal. doi:10.1002/sec.592

Patel, A., Juir, J. C., & Pedersen, J. M. (2013). *An intelligent collaborative IDPS for smart grid environments*. Computer Standards and Interface Journal.

Patel, A., Taghavi, M., Bakhtiyari, K., & Juier, J. C. (2013). An IDPS in cloud computing: A systematic review. *Journal of Network and Computer Applications, 36*, 25–41. doi:10.1016/j.jnca.2012.08.007

Patil, S., & Meshram, B. B. (2012). Network intrusion detection and prevention technique for DOS attack. *Intl. Journal of Scientific and Research Publications, 2*(7), 1–4.

Sahah, K., & Kahtani, A. (2010). Performance evaluation comparison of snort NIDS under LINUX and windows server. *Journal of Network and Computer Applications, 33*, 6–15. doi:10.1016/j.jnca.2009.07.005

Sandhu, U. A., Haider, S., Naseer, S., & Ateeb, O. U. (2011). A survey of Intrusion detection and prevention technology. In *Proceedings of Intl. Conf. on Information Communication and Management*. IACSIT Press.

Sandhu, U. S., Haider, S., Naseer, S., & Ateeb, O. U. (2011). A study of novel approaches used in intrusion detection and prevention system. *Intl. Journal of Information and Education Technology, 1*(5), 426–431. doi:10.7763/IJIET.2011.V1.70

Scarfone, K., & Mell, P. (2007). *Guide to Intrusion detection and prevention system (IDPS)*. Retrieved from http://csrc.nist.gov/publications/nistpubs/800-94/sp 800-94.pdf

Shabtai, A., Fledel, Y., Kanonov, V., Elovici, Y., Dolev, S., & Glezer, C. (2010). Google Android: A comprehensive security assessment. *IEEE Security and Privacy, 8*, 35–44. doi:10.1109/MSP.2010.2

Stakhanova, N., Babu, S., & Wong, J. (2007). A taxonomy of intrusion response system. *International Journal of Computer Security, 1*, 169–184. doi:10.1504/IJICS.2007.012248

Suehring, S., & Ziegler, R. L. (2006). *LINUX firewalls* (3rd ed.). Pearson Education Inc.

Terpstra, J. H., Love, P., Reck, R. P., & Scanlon, T. (2004). *Hardening LINUX*. New York: McGraw-Hill.

Wasniowski, R. (2006). Data mining support for intrusion detection and prevention. In *Proc. of the 6th WSEAS Intl. Conf. on Applied Computer Science* (pp. 392-396). Tenerife, Spain: WSEAS.

Xinyou Zhang, W. Z., & Li, C. (2004). Intrusion prevention system design. In *Proceedings of Computer and Information Technology* (pp. 386–390). CIT.

KEY TERMS AND DEFINITIONS

Classification: Grouping of items into different classes according to some established criteria.

Data Mining: Process of extracting hidden patterns in a large volume of data.

Intrusion Detection: Detecting attempts of illegal access to resources of a computer network.

Intrusion Prevention: Preventing unauthorized access to a computer network.

Network Traffic: Volume of activities (sending & receiving of data) in a computer network.

Section 2
Project and Knowledge Management Infrastructure

Chapter 6
The Role of Knowledge Management on Job Satisfaction:
A Systematic Framework

Kijpokin Kasemsap
Suan Sunandha Rajabhat University, Thailand

ABSTRACT

This chapter introduces the framework and causal model of organizational culture, organizational learning, knowledge management, and job satisfaction. It argues that dimensions of organizational culture, organizational learning, and knowledge management have mediated positive effect on job satisfaction. Knowledge management positively mediates the relationships between organizational culture and job satisfaction and between organizational learning and job satisfaction. Organizational culture is positively related to organizational learning. Furthermore, the author hopes that understanding the theoretical constructs of organizational culture, organizational learning, knowledge management, and job satisfaction through the use of the framework and causal model will not only inform researchers of a better design for studying organizational culture, organizational learning, knowledge management, and job satisfaction, but also assist in the understanding of intricate relationships among different factors.

INTRODUCTION

Knowledge management has become one of the most important trends in modern businesses across the globe (Pandey & Dutta, 2013). A general goal of knowledge management is to

DOI: 10.4018/978-1-4666-4940-8.ch006

improve the systematic handling of knowledge and potential knowledge within the organization (Heisig, 2009). Knowledge must be refreshed by the organization, and therefore, knowledge networks are needed to ensure employees have opportunities to share knowledge (McGurk & Baron, 2012). This requires certain processes to capture organizational learning (McGurk & Baron, 2012). Labedz, Cavaleri, and Berry (2011) stated that knowledge management processes that have been integrated into work processes can be used to correct dysfunctional organizational behavior. Organizations adapt from their experiences when they have integrated processes to support what they have learned (Labedz et al., 2011). The need for techniques and management models for regional knowledge-based management remains topical and it is on the increase (Sotarauta, Horlings, & Liddle, 2012; Uotila, Melkas, & Harmaakorpi, 2005; Zhao & Ordóñez de Pablos, 2011). The role of knowledge has been studied from the managerial perspective in several streams of academic literature and no common title for the wide knowledge-related research field exists (Lönnqvist & Laihonen, 2013). Knowledge has been used as an effective tool to improve the firm's functioning (Perez-Lopez & Alegre, 2012; Zaim, Ekrem, & Selim, 2007).

Organizational knowledge from learning process will help members in organization discern competitive opportunities (Tuan, 2013). Knowledge management has been shown to be a powerful ingredient in the success of organizations (Davenport & Prusak, 1998; Desouza & Awazu, 2006). Knowledge management is aimed at getting people to innovate, collaborate, and make correct decisions efficiently; it is aimed at getting people to act by focusing on high-quality knowledge (Plessis, 2005). Knowledge is considered the most important resource in organizations (Choe, 2004). Knowledge management is a systematic and integrative process of coordinating organization-wide activities of acquiring, creating, storing, sharing, diffusing, developing, and deploying knowledge by individuals and groups in the pursuit of major organizational goals (Rastogi, 2000). It is necessary for the existence of organizational culture to support the organizational learning so that it is available to obtain, improve, and transfer the required knowledge with ease (Hall, 2001; Pool, 2000). Organizational learning is the development of knowledge related to the relationships among actions, consequences, and work environment.

Learning is the power of growth, and individual is also the resource of business growth (Duncan & Weiss, 1979). The capability of controlling information means a learning achievement (Hong, 2001).

Organizational learning means a procedure through which knowledge is obtained and created to improve behavioral modes (Chou, 2003). Organizational learning is a type of experience conclusion and process to explore and create new knowledge, together with the systematic infusion of knowledge of organizational input (Van der Heijden, 2004). Both public and private sector organizations of advanced and developing countries are susceptible to the contextual implications which substantially change the level of job satisfaction or otherwise (Sattar & Nawaz, 2011). A huge community is concerned about the quality of job satisfaction including managers, employees and general public (Sattar, Khan, Nawaz, & Qureshi, 2010). Furthermore, job satisfaction is one of the most researched concepts (Dormann & Zapf, 2001). Job satisfaction serves as central to work and organizational psychology (Dormann & Zapf, 2001). Job satisfaction serves as a mediator for creating relationship between work conditions, on the one hand, and individual/organizational outcomes on the other (Dormann & Zapf, 2001). This chapter introduces the framework and causal model of organizational culture, organizational learning, knowledge management, and job satisfaction.

BACKGROUND

The details of constructs such as organizational culture, organizational learning, knowledge management, and job satisfaction related to this chapter are shown as follows.

Organizational Culture

Culture is being investigated to impact the miscellany of organizational process (Shahzad, Luqman, Khan, & Shabbir, 2012). Organizational culture has a deep impact on the performance of employees that can cause to improve in the productivity and enhance the organizational performance (Shahzad et al., 2012). The adoption of culture of the organization is helpful for the employees to efficiently do their work (Shahzad et al., 2012). Organizational culture helps in internalizing joint relationship that leads to manage effective organization (Awadh & Saad, 2013). Strong culture enables the effective and efficient management of work force employees (Awadh & Saad, 2013). The complete knowledge and awareness of organizational culture should help to improve the ability to examine the behavior of organization which assists to manage and lead (Brooks, 2006). Culture is a system of common values which can be estimated that people describe the similar organizational culture even with different background at different levels within the organization (Robbins & Sanghi, 2007). According to Ravasi and Schultz (2006), organizational culture is a set of shared mental assumptions that guide interpretation and action in organizations by defining appropriate behavior for various situations. Organizational culture is the most difficult organizational attribute to change, outlasting organizational products, services, founders and leadership and all other physical attributes of the organization (Schein, 1992).

Denison (1990) defined cultural artifacts as the tangible aspects of culture shared by members of an organization. According to Schein (1992), the two main reasons why cultures develop in organizations are due to external adaptation and internal integration. External adaptation reflects an evolutionary approach to organizational culture (Schein, 1992). Cultures develop and persist because they help an organization to survive and flourish (Schein, 1992). If the culture is valuable, then it holds the potential for generating sustained competitive advantages (Schein, 1992). The role of culture plays an important role in the effectiveness of an organization regardless of the structure, hierarchy, industry and goals (Jones, 2010). Internal integration is an important function since social structures are required for organizations to exist (Schein, 1992). Organizational practices are learned through socialization at the workplace (Schein, 1992). Work environments reinforce organizational culture on a daily basis by encouraging employees to exercise organizational culture values (Schein, 1992). Furthermore, innovativeness, productivity through people, and the other cultural factors have positive economic consequences (Peters & Waterman, 1982). According to Denison, Haaland, and Goelzer (2004), organizational culture contributes to the success of the organization, but not all dimensions contribute the same. The study on organizational culture can take on a multitude of aspects including levels (visible, expressed values, and underlying assumptions), strength (strong or weak), and adaptiveness (adaptive or unadaptive).

Organizational cultures can be assessed in many dimensions resulting in the conceptually different models and theories (Denison et al., 2004). Organizational culture can be categorized as adaptability, achievement, clan, and bureaucratic system (Daft, 2005). Furthermore, organizational culture can be categorized as clan, adhocracy, hierarchy, and market (Cameron & Freeman, 1991; Quinn & Cameron, 1983). Wallach's (1983) framework is adapted for the purpose of this study. Wallach (1983) stated that the Organizational Culture Index (OCI) profiles the culture on the three stereotypical dimensions, and the flavor of an organization can be derived from the combination of these three dimensions (i.e., bureaucratic, innovative and supportive cultures) A bureaucratic culture is hierarchical, compartmentalized, organized, systematic, and has clear lines of responsibility and authority (Wallach, 1983). An innovative culture refers to a creative, results-oriented, challenging work environment (Wallach, 1983). A supportive culture exhibits teamwork and a people-oriented, encouraging, trusting work environment (Wallach, 1983). An employee can be more effective in his or her current job, and realize his or her best potentials, when there is a match between the individual's motivation and the organizational culture. This has significant implications in recruitment, management, motivation, development and retention of employees (Shadur, Kienzle, & Rodwell, 1999).

Organizational culture is a critical factor that influences knowledge management or the effectiveness of knowledge sharing (Gold, Malhora, & Segars, 2001). Organizational culture consists of some combination of artifacts (also called practices, expressive symbols or forms), values and beliefs and underlying assumptions that organizational members share about appropriate behavior (Gordon & DiTomaso, 1992; Schein, 1992). Organizational culture has been viewed as holistic, historically determined, and socially constructed. Organizational culture involves beliefs and behavior, exists at a various level, and manifests itself in a wide range of features of organizational life (Hofstede, Neuijen, Ohayv, & Sanders, 1990). As such, organizational culture refers to a set of shared values, belief, assumptions, and practices that shape and guide members' attitudes and behavior in the organization (O'Reilly & Chatman, 1996; Wilson, 2001). Long (1997) suggested that organizational culture provides the value of knowledge and the existence of the advantage of knowledge innovation in an organization. This kind of advantage further affects the willingness of employees to share and be involved (Long, 1997). Alavi and Leidner (1999) stated that the knowledge-sharing experience in an organization is mostly related to organizational culture. Therefore, a successful knowledge management depends on the cooperation of domains of culture, management, and organization (Alavi & Leidner, 1999). Davenport, De Long, and Beers (1998) introduced eight factors of successful knowledge management projects, and most of them are influenced by organizational culture. Furthermore,

Davenport and Prusak (1998) indicated that the components of an organizational culture are also the key elements for successful knowledge control and transference. Furthermore, culture of knowledge sharing in an organization is a criterion for successful knowledge management (Davenport et al., 1998; Hauschild, Licht, & Stein, 2001).

Organizational Learning

Neilson (1997) defined organizational learning as a continuous process of knowledge creation, acquisition, and transformation. Organizational learning is defined as a process that increases the actionable knowledge of the organization and by which the members of the organization can conduct activities for interpretation, comprehension and assimilation of tacit and explicit information (Ruiz-Mercader, Merono-Cerdan, & Sabater-Sanchez, 2006). According to Duncan and Weiss (1979), organizational learning is concerned with developing knowledge related to the relationships among actions, consequences, and environment. Kang, Morris, and Snell (2007) demonstrated that firms need to not only develop strategies based on core knowledge and capabilities but also must work toward acquiring, transferring, and integrating new knowledge, facilitating the process of organizational learning in order to create the valuable human capital. Organizational learning is routine-based, history-dependent, and target-oriented (Levitt & March, 1988). Ju, Li, and Lee (2006) indicated that organizational learning is difficult to achieve, especially for the sharing of tacit knowledge, and the major elements to enable an organizational learning are channels of communication. The learning employees are the valuable asset in any organization as they make the effort to continuously improve their competencies that can benefit the organization (Pantouvakis & Bouranta, 2013). In order to benefit from individual learning, organizations should create an environment that promotes and supports learning (Pantouvakis & Bouranta, 2013).

According to Thompson and Cavaleri (2010), managers use systematic thinking about causal relationships when formal learning processes are in place within the organization. Many researchers proposed some distinct measurement dimensions for organizational learning, such as the work of Huber (1991) and Pace, Regan, Miller, and Dunn (1998) based on Levitt and March's (1988) research to develop organizational learning profiles (OLP). Hanvanich, Sivakumar, Tomas, and Hult (2006) focused on learning orientation and organizational memory to provide a complete view of firms' learning characteristics. Crossan, Lane, and White (1999) proposed an organizational learning framework with four processes – intuiting, interpreting, integrating and institutionalizing; these processes link the individual, group and organizational levels. Organizational learning is a dynamic process which occurs over time and across levels, but it also creates tension between assimilating new learning and exploiting what has learned (Crossan et al., 1999). Organizational learning means a procedure through which knowledge is obtained and created to improve behavioral modes (Chou, 2003). Organizational learning is a type of experience conclusion and process to explore and create new knowledge, together with the systematic infusion of knowledge of organizational input (Van der Heijden, 2004). Organizational learning incorporates the system, mechanism and process improving the competency and capability of employees (Sabir & Kalyar, 2013).

Management team can pay attention to, in order to manage the job satisfaction of employees engaged in knowledge work (Narang & Dwivedi, 2010). Santos-Vijande, Lopez-Sanchez, and Trespalacios (2012) stated that organizational learning is a crucial tool in modern markets to enhance organizational performance by means of competitive strategy design and flexible adaptation to fast market evolution. A crucial factor behind a company's competency for unremitting change and renewal is organizational learning (Flores, Zheng, Rau, & Thomas, 2012). Furthermore,

organizational learning is pivotal to both individual and organization-level innovative performance (Wang & Ellinger, 2011). Employees develop appropriate learning strategies to bridge the gap between their perceived and experienced quality of work life (Yeo & Li, 2013). Accordingly, employees will be more willing to connect to their tasks through collaboration with others to increase organizational learning capabilities (Cohen, Chang, & Ledford, 2006; Nykodym, Longenecker, & Ruud, 2008). Organizational learning refers to the process of developing new knowledge and insights derived from the common experiences of people within the organization (Senge, 1990; Slater & Narver, 1995). Organizational learning has the potential to influence behaviors and improve a firm's capabilities (Senge, 1990; Slater & Narver, 1995). This process includes the acquisition of information and existing knowledge from both internal and external environment of organization, distribution within the company, interpretation and storing for future use in organizational memory (Senge, 1990; Slater & Narver, 1995). The result of this process will be the development of organizational knowledge, which will be reflected in theories in use, shared mental models, information databases, formalized procedures and routines, and formal cultural models that guide behavior (Slater & Narver, 1995).

Knowledge Management

Knowledge is widely recognized as a strategic asset in improving organizational performance (Sharma & Djiaw, 2011). Knowledge management provides the processes and structures to create, capture, analyze, and act on information which helps organizations to manage continuous change in a highly dynamic environment (Lim & Klobas, 2000). Knowledge management is crucial for maintaining and gaining competitive advantage, as it supports more effective knowledge acquisition and transfer (Bollinger & Smith, 2001; McKinlay, 2005; Offsey, 1997). Knowledge management practice is the most effective aspect when it is considered strategically, and aligned with business objectives (Davenport et al., 1998; Greiner, Bohmann, & Krcmar, 2007). Knowledge management practice is available for improving the performance of the creative, non-routine activities (Bettiol, Di Maria, & Grandinetti, 2012). Current literature in the field of knowledge management is focusing on certain sectors or industries: the public sector (Chong, Salleh, Ahmad, & Sharifuddin, 2011; Ferguson, Burford, & Kennedy, 2013; Salleh, Chong, Syed Ahmad, & Syed Ikhsan, 2012), non-governmental organizations (Corfield, Paton, & Little, 2013), the banking industry (Bidmeshgipour, Ismail, & Omar, 2012; Dutt, Qamar, & Jha, 2011; Oluikpe, 2012), small to medium-sized enterprises (Durst & Edvardsson, 2012), manufacturing organizations (Birasnav & Rangnekar, 2010), and human service and professional services firms (Austin, Ciaassen, Vu, & Mizrahi, 2008; Palte, Hertlein, Smolnik, & Riempp, 2011). Knowledge management has been considered to be an important resource in competitive advantage (Nahapiet & Ghoshal, 1998).

Knowledge management can be defined as a systematic approach that provides efficient disciplines and procedures to enable knowledge to grow and create value for organizations (Rao, 2002; Sajeva, 2010). As knowledge is the core element of knowledge management, organizational competitiveness will depend on how knowledge is applied, exploited and integrated (Sajeva, 2010). Knowledge management is the fundamental approach for organizational competitive advantage (Fugate, Stank, & Mentzer, 2009; Huang & Lai, 2012; Kiessling, Richey, Meng, & Dabic, 2009; Massa & Testa, 2009). Furthermore, Marques and Simon (2006) have studied the importance of knowledge management as a source of sustainable competitive advantage for firms and they have found a strong and positive relationship between the adoption of knowledge management process and firm performance. Accordingly, Chadha and Kapoor (2010) stated that knowledge transferred

and shared effectively within an organization can considerably affect its competitive ability and business performance. Knowledge management is considered to be effective if it contributes to increase in productivity by making the right information to the right people (Gunasekaran & Ngai, 2007). Singh, Shankar, Narain, and Kumar (2006) explained that the cornerstone to the long-term survival of a firm is recognizing the value of the knowledge that is a key to the innovative thinking and investment. Tang (1999) mentioned that knowledge and skills affect organizational innovation research capability.

When knowledge is delivered and distributed in an organization, its potential values will appear eventually (Davenport & Prusak, 1998). If knowledge can be applied appropriately or new knowledge can be created substantially, it does not only improve productivity, but it also inspires creativity (Davenport & Prusak, 1998). Furthermore, Johannessen, Olsen, and Olaisen (1999) combined organizational vision with knowledge management. Johannessen et al. (1999) indicated that organizational vision leads to knowledge creation, and knowledge creation leads to organizational creation and integrates knowledge utilization. Once the knowledge is efficiently integrated and utilized, it can therefore improve organizational innovation and strengthen visions (Johannessen et al., 1999). Likewise, new product development is deemed as a knowledge management concept (Arora, 2002). Knowledge management system can improve a firm's operational processes (Arora, 2002). Therefore, the performance indices include the frequency of solving operational obstacles (Arora, 2002). Knowledge management efforts typically focus on organizational objectives such as improved performance, competitive advantage innovation, the sharing of lessons learned, integration and continuous improvement of the organization (Sanchez, 1996). Knowledge management efforts overlap with organizational learning and may be distinguished from that by a greater focus on the management of knowledge as a strategic asset and a focus on encouraging the sharing of knowledge (Sanchez, 1996).

Knowledge management is seen as an enabler of organizational learning (Sanchez, 1996). Knowledge is easily stored because it may be codified, while the relational perspective recognizes the contextual and relational aspects of knowledge which can make knowledge difficult to share outside the specific location where the knowledge is developed (Hayes & Walsham, 2003). Knowledge management systems can be categorized as falling into one or more of the following groups: groupware, document management systems, expert systems, semantic networks, relational and object oriented databases, simulation tools, and artificial intelligence (Gupta & Sharma, 2004). Furthermore, Bogner and Bansal (2007) stated that there are three components of knowledge management systems that influence firm performance: the firm's ability to produce new knowledge. A successful knowledge management effort needs to convert internalized tacit knowledge into explicit knowledge in order to share it, but the same effort must also permit individuals to internalize and make personally meaningful any codified knowledge retrieved from the knowledge management effort (Serenko & Bontis, 2004). Subsequent research into knowledge management suggested that a distinction between tacit knowledge and explicit knowledge represents an over-simplification and that the notion of explicit knowledge is self-contradictory (Serenko & Bontis, 2004). Specifically, for knowledge to be made explicit, it must be translated into information (Serenko & Bontis, 2004).

Job Satisfaction

Job satisfaction is defined as a person's evaluation of his or her job and work context (McShane, 2004) and as a global feeling about the job or as a related constellation of attitudes about various aspects or facets of the job (Spector, 1997). Job satisfaction has two major components of intrinsic job satisfaction (level of satisfaction with features associated with the job itself) and extrinsic job satisfaction (level of satisfaction with various features associated with the environment) (Valez, 1972). Job satisfaction is a pleasurable or positive emotional state resulting from the appraisal of one's job or job experiences (Locke, 1976). Job satisfaction has been identified as a major requirement for organizations which aim to achieve excellence in their organizations (Chiboiwa, Samuel, & Chipunza, 2011). Job satisfaction is generally recognized as a multifaceted construct that includes employee feelings about a variety of both intrinsic and extrinsic job factors. Job satisfaction encompasses specific aspects of satisfaction related to pay, benefits, promotion, work conditions, supervision, organizational practices, and relationships with co-workers (Misener, Haddock, Gleaton, & Ajamieh, 1996). Job satisfaction is associated with aspects of work environment and would develop more quickly than organizational commitment, which would require a worker to make a global assessment of his or her relationship to the organization (Williams & Hazer, 1986). Job satisfaction influences both customer satisfaction and service quality in general (Gu & Siu, 2009).

Job satisfaction is an immediate antecedent of intention to leave the workplace and turnover. Unsatisfied workers will leave their jobs more than their satisfied colleagues (Martin, 1990). Job satisfaction is a function of the perceived relationship between what person wants from his or her job and what person perceives the offers (Locke, 1969). Job satisfaction refers to the extent to which employees gain enjoyment from their efforts in the workplace (Fogarty, 1994). Job satisfaction is an attitude that people have about their jobs and the organizations in which they perform these jobs (Mosadeghrad, 2003). Job satisfaction is a positive feeling about one's job resulting from an evaluation of its characteristics (Robbins & Judge, 2009). Satisfaction can be considered as either positive or negative evaluative judgments made by people about their job or work situation (Weiss, 2002). Job satisfaction has been associated with organizational commitment (Boles, Madupalli, Rutherford, & Wood, 2007; Cohen, 2006; Cooper-Hakim & Viswesvaran, 2005; Pool & Pool, 2007). Job satisfaction is an emotional reaction and behavioral expression to a job that results from individual assessment of his or her work achievement, office environment, and work life (Golbasi, Kelleci, & Dogan, 2008). Job satisfaction includes several related attitudes. For example, people can experience emotional responses to remuneration, promotion opportunities, relations with superiors and colleagues, and the work itself (McKenna, 2006). Furthermore, job satisfaction affects productivity of employees in a diversified environment (Randeree & Chaudhry, 2007).

Relationship Among Variables

Knowledge management is a systematic and integrative process of coordinating organization-wide activities of acquiring, creating, storing, sharing, diffusing, developing, and deploying knowledge by individuals and groups in the pursuit of major organizational goals (Rastogi, 2000). Organizational learning is the development of knowledge related to relationships among actions, consequences, and work environment (Duncan & Weiss, 1979). Organizational culture is generally seen as a set of key values, assumptions, understandings, and norms shared by members of an organization and taught to new members as correct (Daft, 2005; Wallach, 1983). Organizations aimed at achieving knowledge management objectives should align them to organizational culture (De Long & Fahey, 2000; Lopez, Peon, & Ordas, 2004). Knowledge management initiatives will not take hold unless they are supported by an organizational culture (Holowetzki, 2002). Knowledge management initiatives may be more effective to align the knowledge management system with the organizational culture than to attempt to change its organizational culture (Park, Ribiere, & Schulte,

2004). Organizations should build their knowledge management approach to fit their organizational culture (McDermott & O'Dell, 2001). If the general organizations are required to develop learning organizations, the administrators shall cultivate the learning capability of individuals and working teams (Garrate, 1990). In addition, it is more necessary to create the organizational climate and organizational culture of organizational learning (Hall, 2001; Pool, 2000).

Furthermore, there is an increasing consensus on the idea that organizations, making the effort to introduce an organizational culture which encourages communication among their members, experimentation and risk taking, and motivates employees to question fundamental beliefs and work patterns, will achieve a favorable working atmosphere for the development of their capacity to learn (Lopez et al., 2004). Cultural values of respect for people, innovation, stability, and aggressiveness have strong association with affective commitment, job satisfaction, and information sharing (McKinnon, Harrison, Chow, & Wu, 2003). Job satisfaction of the employees is affected by the culture of the organization (Arnold, 2006; Chang & Lee, 2007; Mansoor & Tayib, 2010). Whenever the individual demand is congruent with organizational culture, it will result in the highest job satisfaction (Robbins & Judge, 2009). Organizational culture is the core of the human resource management and organizational culture will influence the job satisfaction (Harris & Mossholder, 1996). Establishing organizational structure which promotes active learning and information sharing is the critical issue that should be the focus of all organizations (Wickramasinghe, 2007). Currie and Kerrin (2003) adopted an organizational learning perspective to reflect upon the problems of knowledge management.

Ju et al. (2006) stated that level of organizational learning has a significant impact on knowledge integration, knowledge management capability, and firm innovation ability. The interaction effects of human-oriented knowledge management strategies, organizational learning, system-oriented knowledge management strategies and knowledge integration significantly impact the knowledge management capability (Ju et al., 2006). Zellmer-Bruhn and Gibson (2006) found that organizational contexts emphasizing global integration reduce team learning, but those emphasizing responsiveness and knowledge management increase team learning. Team learning positively influences both task performance and the quality of interpersonal relations (Zellmer-Bruhn & Gibson, 2006). There is a positive impact of interactive internal service quality characteristics and learning organization dimensions, namely, empowerment and continuous learning, on job satisfaction in hospital care services (Pantouvakis & Mpogiatzidis, 2013). Hanvanich et al. (2006) demonstrated how learning orientation and organizational memory are related to the important organizational outcomes, not only when organizations have different levels of environmental turbulence but also when organizations have the same level of environmental turbulence. Ruiz-Mercader et al. (2006) stated that individual learning and organizational learning explain significant and positive effects on organizational performance and that information technology has a significant impact on organizational learning outcomes only when a proper context of organizational learning is in place. Lee and Lee (2007) indicated that there are the statistically significant relationships among knowledge management capabilities, processes, and organizational performance. Lin and Tseng (2005) stated that corporate performance is significantly influenced by these management gaps in knowledge management activities.

MAIN FOCUS OF THE CHAPTER

This chapter focuses on building a systematic framework and a causal model of organizational culture, organizational learning, knowledge management, and job satisfaction of pharmaceutical company employees in Thailand.

Material and Methods

Data of this study was collected from 583 operational employees out of 8,607 operational employees working in the 39 pharmaceutical companies in Thailand by using the formula of Yamane (Yamane, 1970) for a 96% confidence level with a 4% margin of error by the proportional random sampling method. All the constructs were operationalized based on a five-point Likert scale ranging from 1 (strongly disagree) to 5 (strongly agree). Data were analyzed with descriptive statistics using SPSS (version 20) and assessed with confirmatory factor analysis (CFA) to confirm the heterogeneity of all constructs and path analysis (Joreskog & Sorborn, 1993) to detect the cause-effect relationships among various dimensions of main constructs of the study using LISREL (version 8.8) on a structured questionnaire containing standard scales of organizational culture, organizational learning, knowledge management, and job satisfaction, besides some demographic details like age, education, and tenure with the organization.

Organizational culture was measured using the 24-item Organizational Culture Questionnaire (OCQ) developed by Wallach (1983) to assess three cultural facets of bureaucratic, innovative, and supportive cultures. The major factors for evaluating organizational learning were revised to create the organizational learning profile (Huber, 1991). Based on other recent studies (Pace et al., 1998), four factors have been analyzed and extracted, and consequently used in the present study to measure organizational learning with 15 items of four elements of information-sharing patterns, inquiry climate, learning practices, and achievement mindset. Knowledge management was measured using questionnaire developed by Darroch (2003) comprising three elements of knowledge acquisition, knowledge dissemination, and responsive to knowledge. Job satisfaction was measured using the Minnesota Satisfaction Questionnaire (MSQ) developed by Weiss, Dawis, England, and Lofquist (1967) comprising 20 items of intrinsic job satisfaction and extrinsic job satisfaction.

Solutions and Recommendations

A framework and a causal model are built shown in Figure 1. Research findings indicate that dimensions of organizational culture, organizational learning, and knowledge management have mediated positive effect on job satisfaction. Knowledge management positively mediates the relationships between organizational culture and job satisfaction and between organizational learning and job satisfaction. Furthermore, organizational culture is positively related to organizational learning. Regarding the systematic framework and causal model, there are lots of researchers studying about the relationships of organizational culture, organizational learning, knowledge management, and job satisfaction in a wide variety of fields. The systematic framework is positively compatible with the following research findings. Organizational culture, organizational learning, and knowledge management are positively linked to job satisfaction. Therefore, firms should take consideration of their organizational culture and organizational learning in the transition process of knowledge management to increase job satisfaction.

According to the result, organizational learning and knowledge management act as intervening variables between organizational culture and job satisfaction. When firms adopt knowledge management activities to promote job satisfaction, the role of organization culture and organizational learning becomes more evident and critical. Therefore, the strength of knowledge management affecting job satisfaction will be influenced by what kinds of organization culture and organizational learning that firms adopted. If firms possess a higher degree of organizational learning, the

degrees of knowledge management would be more enhanced. These finding show that organizational learning can promote a higher degree of knowledge creation and sharing within firms. In addition, the present results are also quite instructive in helping to explain the effects of organizatioal culture and organizational learning on knowledge management and job satisfaction. In general, if the characteristics of organizational culture are less centralized, less formalized, and more integrated, the levels of knowledge management would be more enhanced.

In addition, firms should carefully design and nurture appropriate organizational contexts to facilitate knowledge management. Firms need to cultivate an innovative and supportive atmosphere to enhance knowledge creation and sharing. In addition, firms need to design their culture as less formalized, more centralized, and more integrated to provide employees more autonomy and make them feel honored to participate in their work. The appropriate organizational contexts would result in a more satisfied level of knowledge management within firms. It is important that the other organizations implementing large-scale manufacturing reformations need to pay great attention to organizational culture, organizational learning, knowledge management, and job satisfaction in order to effectively achieve business success.

FUTURE RESEARCH DIRECTIONS

The author indicates some limitations in this study and suggests possible directions for future research. This study is based on self-report data that may have the possibility of common method variance. Future research is suggested to benefit from using objective measures for job satisfaction that can be independently verified. The low return rate of the survey is still noted as a potential limitation in this study. Future research can benefit from a larger sample to bring more statistical power and a higher degree of representation.

Figure 1. Systematic framework and causal model
Key: OC = Organizational Culture, BC = Bureaucratic Culture, IC = Innovative Culture, SC = Supportive Culture, OL = Organizational Learning, IP = Information-Sharing Patterns, IQ = Inquiry Climate, LP = Learning Practices, AM = Achievement Mindset, KM = Knowledge Management, JS = Job Satisfaction, IJS = Intrinsic Job Satisfaction, EJS = Extrinsic Job Satisfaction

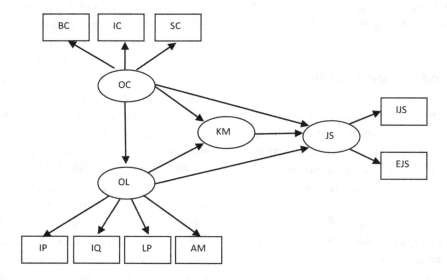

This study was done by empirically investigating Thai firms. Potential cultural limitation should be noted and it is suggested that future research be done in different cultural contexts to generalize or modify the concepts. Furthermore, this study mainly concerns the effects of organizational culture and organizational learning on knowledge management and job satisfaction. Future research may work on examining other variables (i.e., team climate, proactive personality, leadership behavior, leader-member exchange, knowledge-sharing behavior, and strategic orientation) on knowledge management and job satisfaction.

CONCLUSION

The purpose of this study was to build a framework and a causal model of organizational culture, organizational learning, knowledge management, and job satisfaction for pharmaceutical company employees in Thailand. The findings show that the organizational culture, organizational learn-

ing, and knowledge management have strengths to mediate positive effects on job satisfaction. In relation to the systematic framework and causal model, that is the extent to which organizational culture, organizational learning, and knowledge management have mediated positive effect on job satisfaction. Given the need for knowledge management and job satisfaction as a solution to the complex challenges, firms need to be aware of the implications of organizational contexts that may affect knowledge management and job satisfaction. Firms should recognize the importance of knowledge management and need to put more efforts in building up the effective knowledge creation and sharing mechanisms to promote their job satisfaction. Firms should pay special attentions to organization contexts in which knowledge creation and sharing are most likely to enhance job satisfaction, and those in which such enhancement is less likely to occur. Firms may create a positively organizational learning to encourage employees not only behave in interactive ways, but are also stimulated to create and share their different perspectives and opinions and to manifest creative and innovative behaviors.

In addition, firms should recognize and shape organizational culture and organizational learning favorable to knowledge management and job satisfaction. Managers in firms also need to emphasize the development of an open climate to permit tacit knowledge sharing (Seidler-de Alwis & Hartmann, 2008) and informally to encourage creativity through knowledge sharing (Taminiau, Smit, & De Lange, 2009). Managers need to promote frequent interaction among employees to enhance the creation of team-based knowledge (Donnelly, 2008) and the sharing of tacit knowledge (Cavusgil, Calantone, & Zhao, 2003). When organizations tolerate mistakes in the knowledge development process, the barriers to knowledge creation and sharing diminish (McLaughlin, Paton, & Macbeth, 2008). Frequent interaction among employees promotes the sharing of knowledge (Cavusgil et al., 2003) and supports team-based knowledge creation (Donnelly, 2008). Organizations aiming to increase job satisfaction and achieve business goals should focus on developing organizational culture, organizational learning, and knowledge management. In terms of managerial implications, the results suggest that managers desiring to enhance their business performance should consider creating organizational culture and organizational learning, and thereby creating an effective cycle of knowledge management and job satisfaction. Organizational culture and organizational learning can be developed in various ways.

For example, by encouraging employees to try out new approaches, and recognizing and rewarding those that work well; practicing transparent and honest communication between the managers and employees about what is happening and about changes that could be important for employees; striving for cohesion through a clearly enunciated vision, by building commitment to organizational goals, fostering cooperation and collaboration, and allowing employees to participate in formulating strategy; and building warm interpersonal relationships by expressing concern for employees'

well-being, helping employees to set and achieve individual goals, caring about their opinions, and making an effort to show kindness to them. Organizations are realizing that corporate knowledge is a valuable asset that can be managed as a physical asset in order to improve knowledge management and job satisfaction. The focus of knowledge management along with both organizational culture and organizational learning is connecting people, processes, and technology for the purpose of leveraging corporate knowledge to achieve the business goal and better job satisfaction.

REFERENCES

Alavi, M., & Leidner, D. E. (1999). Knowledge management system: Issues, challenges, and benefits. *Communications of the AIS, 1*(7), 1–37.

Arnold, T., & Spell, S. C. (2006). The relationship between justice and benefits satisfaction. *Journal of Business and Psychology, 20*(4), 599–620. doi:10.1007/s10869-005-9006-1

Arora, R. (2002). Implementing KM – A balanced scorecard approach. *Journal of Knowledge Management, 6*(3), 240–249. doi:10.1108/13673270210434340

Austin, M. J., Ciaassen, J., Vu, C., & Mizrahi, P. (2008). Knowledge management: Implications for human service organizations. *Journal of Evidence-Based Social Work, 5*(1-2), 361–389. doi:10.1300/J394v05n01_13 PMID:19064454

Awadh, A. M., & Saad, A. M. (2013). Impact of organizational culture on employee performance. *International Review of Management and Business Research, 2*(1), 168–175.

Bettiol, M., Di Maria, E., & Grandinetti, R. (2012). Codification and creativity: Knowledge management strategies in KIBS. *Journal of Knowledge Management, 16*(4), 550–562. doi:10.1108/13673271211246130

Bidmeshgipour, M., Ismail, W. K. W., & Omar, R. (2012). Knowledge management and organizational innovativeness in Iranian banking industry. *Knowledge Management and E-Learning*, *4*(4), 481–499.

Birasnav, M., & Rangnekar, S. (2010). Knowledge management structure and human capital development in Indian manufacturing industries. *Business Process Management Journal*, *16*(1), 57–75. doi:10.1108/14637151011017949

Bogner, W. C., & Bansal, P. (2007). Knowledge management as the basis of sustained high performance. *Journal of Management Studies*, *44*(1), 165–188. doi:10.1111/j.1467-6486.2007.00667.x

Boles, J., Madupalli, R., Rutherford, B., & Wood, J. (2007). The relationship of facet of salesperson job satisfaction with affective organization commitment. *Journal of Business and Industrial Marketing*, *22*(5), 311–321. doi:10.1108/08858620710773440

Bollinger, A. S., & Smith, R. D. (2001). Managing organizational knowledge as a strategic asset. *Journal of Knowledge Management*, *5*(1), 8–18. doi:10.1108/13673270110384365

Brooks, I. (2006). *Organizational behavior: Individuals, groups and organization*. Essex, UK: Pearson Education.

Cameron, K. S., & Freeman, S. J. (1991). Cultural congruence, strength, and type: Relationships to effectiveness. *Research in Organizational Change and Development*, *5*(2), 23–58.

Cavusgil, S. T., Calantone, R. J., & Zhao, Y. (2003). Tacit knowledge transfer and firm innovation capability. *Journal of Business and Industrial Marketing*, *18*(1), 6–21. doi:10.1108/08858620310458615

Chadha, S. K., & Kapoor, D. (2010). A study on knowledge management practices of auto component manufacturing companies in Ludhiana city. *The IUP Journal of Knowledge Management*, *8*(1-2), 68–76.

Chang, S., & Lee, M. S. (2007). A study on the relationship among leadership, organizational culture, the operation of learning organization and employees' job satisfaction. *The Learning Organization*, *14*(2), 155–185. doi:10.1108/09696470710727014

Chiboiwa, M., Samuel, M., & Chipunza, C. (2011). Evaluation of job satisfaction and organizational citizenship behavior: Case study of selected organizations in Zimbabwe. *African Journal of Business Management*, *5*(7), 2910–2918.

Choe, J. M. (2004). The consideration of cultural differences in the design of information systems. *Information & Management*, *41*(5), 669–688. doi:10.1016/j.im.2003.08.003

Chong, S. C., Salleh, K., Ahmad, S. N. S., & Sharifuddin, S. I. (2011). Knowledge management implementation in a public sector accounting organization: An empirical investigation. *Journal of Knowledge Management*, *15*(3), 497–512. doi:10.1108/13673271111137457

Chou, S. W. (2003). Computer systems to facilitating organizational learning: IT and organizational context. *Expert Systems with Applications*, *24*(3), 273–280. doi:10.1016/S0957-4174(02)00155-0

Cohen, A. (2006). The relationship between multiple commitments and organizational citizenship behavior in Arab and Jewish culture. *Journal of Vocational Behavior*, *69*(1), 105–118. doi:10.1016/j.jvb.2005.12.004

Cohen, S. G., Chang, L., & Ledford, G. E. (2006). A hierarchical construct of self-management leadership and its relationship to quality of work life and perceived work group effectiveness. *Personnel Psychology*, *50*(2), 275–308. doi:10.1111/j.1744-6570.1997.tb00909.x

Cooper-Hakim, A., & Viswesvaran, C. (2005). The construct of work commitment: Testing an integrative framework. *Psychological Bulletin*, *131*(2), 241–259. doi:10.1037/0033-2909.131.2.241 PMID:15740421

Corfield, A., Paton, R., & Little, S. (2013). Does knowledge management work in NGOs? A longitudinal study. *International Journal of Public Administration, 36*(3), 179–188. doi:10.1080/01900692.2012.749281

Crossan, M., Lane, H., & White, R. (1999). An organizational learning framework: From intuition to institution. *Academy of Management Review, 34*(3), 523–537.

Currie, G., & Kerrin, M. (2003). Human resource management and knowledge management: Enhancing knowledge sharing in a pharmaceutical company. *International Journal of Human Resource Management, 14*(6), 1027–1045. doi:10.1080/0958519032000124641

Daft, R. L. (2005). *The leadership experience*. Vancouver, Canada: Thomson-Southwestern.

Darroch, J. (2003). Developing a measure of knowledge management behaviors and practices. *Journal of Knowledge Management, 7*(5), 41–54. doi:10.1108/13673270310505377

Davenport, T. H., De Long, D. W., & Beers, M. C. (1998). Successful knowledge management projects. *Sloan Management Review, 39*(2), 43–57.

Davenport, T. H., & Prusak, L. (1998). *Working knowledge: Managing what your organization knows*. Boston, MA: Harvard Business School Press.

De Long, D. W., & Fahey, L. (2000). Diagnosing cultural barriers to knowledge management. *The Academy of Management Executive, 14*(4), 113–128.

Denison, D. R. (1990). *Corporate culture and organizational effectiveness*. New York, NY: John Wiley & Sons.

Denison, D. R., Haaland, S., & Goelzer, P. (2004). Corporate culture and organizational effectiveness: Is Asia different from the rest of the world? *Organizational Dynamics, 33*(1), 98–109. doi:10.1016/j.orgdyn.2003.11.008

Desouza, K. C., & Awazu, Y. (2006). Knowledge management at SMEs: Five peculiarities. *Journal of Knowledge Management, 10*(1), 32–43. doi:10.1108/13673270610650085

Donnelly, R. (2008). The management of consultancy knowledge: An internationally comparative analysis. *Journal of Knowledge Management, 12*(6), 71–83. doi:10.1108/13673270810875877

Dormann, C., & Zapf, D. (2001). Job satisfaction: A meta-analysis of stabilities. *Journal of Organizational Behavior, 22*(5), 483–504. doi:10.1002/job.98

Duncan, R., & Weiss, A. (1979). Organizational learning: Implications for organizational design. *Research in Organizational Behavior, 1*, 75–123.

Durst, S., & Edvardsson, I. R. (2012). Knowledge management in SMEs: A literature review. *Journal of Knowledge Management, 16*(6), 879–903. doi:10.1108/13673271211276173

Dutt, H., Qamar, F., & Jha, V. S. (2011). A research to identify knowledge orientation in Indian commercial banks. *International Journal of Knowledge Management Studies, 4*(4), 389–418. doi:10.1504/IJKMS.2011.048435

Ferguson, S., Burford, S., & Kennedy, M. (2013). Divergent approaches to knowledge and innovation in the public sector. *International Journal of Public Administration, 36*(3), 168–178. doi:10.1080/01900692.2012.749278

Flores, L. G., Zheng, W., Rau, D., & Thomas, C. H. (2012). Organizational learning subprocess identification, construct validation, and an empirical test of cultural antecedents. *Journal of Management, 38*(2), 640–667. doi:10.1177/0149206310384631

Fogarty, T. (1994). Public accounting experience: The influence of demographic and organizational attributes. *Managerial Auditing Journal, 9*(7), 12–20. doi:10.1108/02686909410067552

Fugate, B. S., Stank, T. P., & Mentzer, J. T. (2009). Linking improved knowledge management to operational and organizational performance. *Journal of Operations Management*, 27(3), 247–264. doi:10.1016/j.jom.2008.09.003

Garrate, B. (1990). An old idea that has come of age. *People Management*, 1(19), 25–28.

Golbasi, Z., Kelleci, M., & Dogan, S. (2008). Relationships between coping strategies, individual characteristics and job satisfaction in a sample of hospital nurses: Cross-sectional questionnaire survey. *International Journal of Nursing Studies*, 45(12), 1800–1806. doi:10.1016/j.ijnurstu.2008.06.009 PMID:18703192

Gold, A. H., Malhora, A., & Segars, A. H. (2001). Knowledge management: An organizational capabilities perspective. *Journal of Management Information Systems*, 18(1), 185–214.

Gordon, G. G., & DiTomaso, N. (1992). Predicting corporate performance from organizational culture. *Journal of Management Studies*, 29(6), 783–798. doi:10.1111/j.1467-6486.1992.tb00689.x

Greiner, M. E., Bohmann, T., & Krcmar, H. (2007). A strategy for knowledge management. *Journal of Knowledge Management*, 11(6), 3–15. doi:10.1108/13673270710832127

Gu, Z., & Siu, R. C. S. (2009). Drivers of job satisfaction as related to work performance in Macao casino hotels: An investigation based on employee survey. *International Journal of Contemporary Hospitality Management*, 21(5), 561–578. doi:10.1108/09596110910967809

Gunasekaran, A., & Ngai, E. W. (2007). Knowledge management in 21st century manufacturing. *International Journal of Production Research*, 45(11), 2391–2418. doi:10.1080/00207540601020429

Gupta, J., & Sharma, S. (2004). *Creating knowledge based organization*. Boston, MA: Idea Group Publishing.

Hall, B. P. (2001). Values development and learning organizations. *Journal of Knowledge Management*, 5(1), 19–32. doi:10.1108/13673270110384374

Hanvanich, S., Sivakumar, K., Tomas, G., & Hult, M. (2006). The relationship of learning and memory with organizational performance: The moderating role of turbulence. *Journal of the Academy of Marketing Science*, 34(4), 600–612. doi:10.1177/0092070306287327

Harris, S. G., & Mossholder, K. W. (1996). The affective implications of perceived congruence with culture dimensions during organizational transformation. *Journal of Management*, 22(4), 527–547. doi:10.1177/014920639602200401

Hauschild, S., Licht, T., & Stein, W. (2001). Creating a knowledge culture. *The McKinsey Quarterly*, 74(1), 74–82.

Hayes, M., & Walsham, G. (2003). Knowledge sharing and ICTs: A relational perspective. In M. Easterby-Smith, & M. A. Lyles (Eds.), *The Blackwell handbook of organizational learning and knowledge management* (pp. 54–57). Malden, MA: Blackwell.

Heisig, P. (2009). Harmonisation of knowledge management: Comparing 160 KM frameworks around the globe. *Journal of Knowledge Management*, 13(4), 4–31. doi:10.1108/13673270910971798

Hofstede, G., Neuijen, B., Ohayv, D. D., & Sanders, G. (1990). Measuring organizational cultures: A qualitative and quantitative study across twenty cases. *Administrative Science Quarterly*, 35(2), 286–316. doi:10.2307/2393392

Holowetzki, A. (2002). *The relationship between knowledge management and organizational culture: An examination of cultural factors that support the flow and management of knowledge within an organization*. Eugene, OR: Applied Information Management Program.

Hong, J. (2001). *Knowledge innovation and organization learning*. Taipei: Wu-Nan Publisher.

Huang, L. S., & Lai, C. P. (2012). An investigation on critical success factors for knowledge management using structural equation modeling. *Technology Management, 40*, 24–30.

Huber, G. P. (1991). Organizational learning: The contributing processes and the literatures. *Organization Science, 2*(1), 88–115. doi:10.1287/orsc.2.1.88

Johannessen, J. A., Olsen, B., & Olaisen, J. (1999). Aspects of innovation theory based knowledge management. *Journal of International Management, 19*(2), 121–139.

Jones, G. R. (2010). *Organizational theory, design, and change*. Upper Saddle River, NJ: Prentice Hall.

Joreskog, K. G., & Sorbom, D. (1993). *LISREL 8: User's reference guide*. Chicago, IL: Scientific Software International.

Ju, T. L., Li, C. Y., & Lee, T. S. (2006). A contingency model for knowledge management capability and innovation. *Industrial Management & Data Systems, 106*(5/6), 855–877. doi:10.1108/02635570610671524

Kang, S. C., Morris, S. S., & Snell, S. A. (2007). Relational archetypes, organizational learning, and value creation: Extending the human resource architecture. *Academy of Management Review, 32*(1), 236–256. doi:10.5465/AMR.2007.23464060

Kiessling, T. S., Richey, R. G., Meng, J., & Dabic, M. (2009). Exploring knowledge management to organizational performance outcomes in a transitional economy. *Journal of World Business, 44*(4), 421–433. doi:10.1016/j.jwb.2008.11.006

Labedz, C., Cavaleri, S., & Berry, G. (2011). Interactive knowledge management: Putting pragmatic policy planning in place. *Journal of Knowledge Management, 15*(4), 551–567. doi:10.1108/13673271111151956

Lee, Y. C., & Lee, S. K. (2007). Capability, processes, and performance of knowledge management: A structural approach. *Human Factors and Ergonomics in Manufacturing, 17*(1), 21–41. doi:10.1002/hfm.20065

Levitt, B., & March, J. (1988). Organizational learning. *Annual Review of Sociology, 14*(3), 319–340. doi:10.1146/annurev.so.14.080188.001535

Lim, D., & Klobas, J. (2000). Knowledge management in small enterprises. *The Electronic Library, 18*(6), 420–432. doi:10.1108/02640470010361178

Lin, C. H., & Tseng, S. E. (2005). The implementation gaps for the knowledge management system. *Industrial Management & Data Systems, 105*(2), 208–222. doi:10.1108/02635570510583334

Locke, E. A. (1969). What is job satisfaction? *Organizational Behavior and Human Performance, 4*(4), 309–336. doi:10.1016/0030-5073(69)90013-0

Locke, E. A. (1976). The nature and causes of job satisfaction. In M. P. Dunnette (Ed.), *Handbook of industrial and organizational psychology* (pp. 1297–1359). Chicago, IL: Rand McNally.

Long, D. D. (1997). *Building the knowledge-based organizations: How culture drives knowledge behaviors*. Cambridge, MA: Center for Business Innovation, Ernst & Young LLP.

Lönnqvist, A., & Laihonen, H. (2013). Managing regional development: A knowledge perspective. *International Journal of Knowledge-Based Development, 4*(1), 50–63. doi:10.1504/IJKBD.2013.052493

Lopez, S. P., Peon, J. M. M., & Ordas, C. J. V. (2004). Managing knowledge: The link between culture and organizational learning. *Journal of Knowledge Management, 8*(6), 93–104. doi:10.1108/13673270410567657

Mansoor, M., & Tayib, M. (2010). An empirical examination of organizational culture, job stress, job satisfaction within the indirect tax administration in Malaysia. *International journal of Business and Social Sciences, 1*(1), 81-95.

Marques, D. P., & Simon, F. J. G. (2006). The effect of knowledge management practices on firm performance. *Journal of Knowledge Management, 10*(3), 143–156. doi:10.1108/13673270610670911

Martin, B. J. (1990). A successful approach to absenteeism. *Nursing Management, 21*(8), 45–48. doi:10.1097/00006247-199008000-00019 PMID:2381601

Massa, S., & Testa, S. (2009). A knowledge management approach to organizational competitive advantage: Evidence from the food sector. *European Management Journal, 27*(2), 129–141. doi:10.1016/j.emj.2008.06.005

McDermott, R., & O'Dell, C. (2001). Overcoming cultural barriers to sharing knowledge. *Journal of Knowledge Management, 5*(1), 76–85. doi:10.1108/13673270110384428

McGurk, J., & Baron, A. (2012). Knowledge management: Time to focus on purpose and motivation. *Strategic HR Review, 11*(6), 316–321. doi:10.1108/14754391211264776

McKenna, E. (2006). *Business psychology and organisational behaviour*. New York, NY: Psychology Press.

McKinlay, A. (2005). Knowledge management. In S. Ackroyd, R. Batt, & P. Thompson (Eds.), *The Oxford handbook of work and organization* (pp. 242–262). Oxford, UK: Oxford University Press.

McKinnon, J., Harrison, G., Chow, C., & Wu, A. (2003). Organizational culture: Association with commitment, job satisfaction, propensity to remain, and information sharing in Taiwan. *International Journal of Business Studies, 11*(1), 25–44.

McLaughlin, S., Paton, R. A., & Macbeth, D. K. (2008). Barrier impact on organizational learning within complex organizations. *Journal of Knowledge Management, 12*(2), 107–123. doi:10.1108/13673270810859550

McShane, S. (2004). *Canadian organizational behavior*. Toronto, Canada: McGraw-Hill Ryerson.

Misener, T. R., Haddock, K. S., Gleaton, J. U., & Ajamieh, A. R. A. (1996). Toward an international measure of job satisfaction. *Nursing Research, 45*(2), 87–91. doi:10.1097/00006199-199603000-00006 PMID:8604370

Mosadeghrad, A. M. (2003). The role of participative management (suggestion system) in hospital effectiveness and efficiency. *Research in Medical Sciences, 8*(3), 85–89.

Nahapiet, J., & Ghoshal, S. (1998). Social capital, intellectual capital, and organizational advantage. *Academy of Management Review, 23*(2), 242–266.

Narang, R., & Dwivedi, A. (2010). Managing the job satisfaction of knowledge workers: An empirical investigation. *Asia Pacific Journal of Business and Management, 1*(1), 1–14.

Neilson, R. (1997). *Collaborative technologies & organizational learning*. Hershey, PA: Idea Group Publishing.

Nykodym, N., Longenecker, C., & Ruud, W. (2008). Improving quality of work life with transactional analysis as an intervention change strategy. *Applied Psychology, 40*(4), 395–404. doi:10.1111/j.1464-0597.1991.tb00999.x

O'Reilly, C. A., & Chatman, J. A. (1996). Culture as social control: Corporation, cults, and commitment. In B. M. Staw, & L. L. Cummings (Eds.), *Research in organizational behavior* (pp. 157–200). Greenwich, CT: JAI Press.

Offsey, S. (1997). Knowledge management: Linking people to knowledge for bottom line results. *Journal of Knowledge Management, 1*(2), 113–122. doi:10.1108/EUM0000000004586

Oluikpe, P. (2012). Developing a corporate knowledge management strategy. *Journal of Knowledge Management, 16*(6), 862–878. doi:10.1108/13673271211276164

Pace, R. W., Regan, L., Miller, P., & Dunn, L. (1998). Natural growth goals and short-term training: A boomerang effect. *International Journal of Training and Development, 2*(2), 128–140. doi:10.1111/1468-2419.00041

Palte, R., Hertlein, M., Smolnik, S., & Riempp, G. (2011). The effects of a knowledge management strategy on KM performance in professional services firms. *International Journal of Knowledge Management, 7*(1), 16–34. doi:10.4018/jkm.2011010102

Pandey, S. C., & Dutta, A. (2013). Role of knowledge infrastructure capabilities in knowledge management. *Journal of Knowledge Management, 17*(3), 435–453. doi:10.1108/JKM-11-2012-0365

Pantouvakis, A., & Bouranta, N. (2013). The link between organizational learning culture and customer satisfaction: Confirming relationship and exploring moderating effect. *The Learning Organization, 20*(1), 48–64. doi:10.1108/09696471311288528

Pantouvakis, A., & Mpogiatzidis, P. (2013). The impact of internal service quality and learning organization on clinical leaders' job satisfaction in hospital care services. *Leadership in Health Services, 26*(1), 34–49. doi:10.1108/17511871311291714

Park, H., Ribiere, V., & Schulte, W. D. (2004). Critical attributes of organizational culture that promote knowledge management technology implementation success. *Journal of Knowledge Management, 8*(3), 106–117. doi:10.1108/13673270410541079

Perez-Lopez, S., & Alegre, J. (2012). Information technology competency, knowledge processes and firm performance. *Industrial Management & Data Systems, 112*(4), 644–662. doi:10.1108/02635571211225521

Peters, T. J., & Waterman, R. H. (1982). *In search of excellence: Lessons from America's best run company.* New York, NY: Harper & Row.

Plessis, M. D. (2005). Drivers of knowledge management in the corporate environment. *International Journal of Information Management, 25*(3), 193–202. doi:10.1016/j.ijinfomgt.2004.12.001

Pool, S. (2000). The learning organization: Motivating employees by integrating TQM philosophy in a supportive organizational culture. *Leadership and Organization Development Journal, 21*(8), 373–378. doi:10.1108/01437730010379276

Pool, S., & Pool, B. (2007). A management development model: Measurement organizational commitment and its impact on job satisfaction among executives in a learning organization. *Journal of Management Development, 26*(4), 353–369. doi:10.1108/02621710710740101

Quinn, R. E., & Cameron, K. (1983). Organizational life cycles and sifting criteria of effectiveness: Some preliminary evidence. *Management Science, 29*(1), 33–51. doi:10.1287/mnsc.29.1.33

Randeree, K., & Chaudhry, A. (2007). Leadership in project managed environments: Employee perceptions of leadership styles within infrastructure development in Dubai. *International Review of Business Research Papers, 3*(4), 220–232.

Rao, M. (2002). *Knowledge management tools and techniques: Practitioners and experts evaluate KM solutions.* Amsterdam, The Netherlands: Elsevier.

Rastogi, P. (2000). Knowledge management and intellectual capital: The new virtuous reality of competitiveness. *Human Systems Management, 19*(1), 39–49.

Ravasi, D., & Schultz, M. (2006). Responding to organizational identity threats: Exploring the role of organizational culture. *Academy of Management Journal*, *49*(3), 433–458. doi:10.5465/AMJ.2006.21794663

Robbins, S. P., & Judge, T. (2009). *Organizational behavior*. Upper Saddle River, NJ: Pearson Prentice Hall.

Robbins, S. P., & Sanghi, S. (2007). *Organizational behavior*. New Delhi, India: Pearson Education.

Ruiz-Mercader, J., Merono-Cerdan, A. L., & Sabater-Sanchez, R. (2006). Information technology and learning: Their relationship and impact on organizational performance in small business. *International Journal of Information Management*, *26*(1), 16–29. doi:10.1016/j.ijinfomgt.2005.10.003

Sabir, H. M., & Kalyar, M. N. (2013). Firm's innovativeness and employee job satisfaction: The role of organizational learning culture. *Interdisciplinary Journal of Contemporary Research in Business*, *4*(9), 670–686.

Sajeva, S. (2010). The analysis of key elements of socio-technical knowledge management system. *Economics and Management*, *15*, 765–774.

Salleh, K., Chong, S. C., Syed Ahmad, S. N., & Syed Ikhsan, S. O. (2012). Learning and knowledge transfer performance among public sector accountants: An empirical survey. *Knowledge Management Research and Practice*, *10*(2), 164–174. doi:10.1057/kmrp.2011.46

Sanchez, R. (1996). *Strategic learning and knowledge management*. Chichester, UK: John Wiley & Sons.

Santos-Vijande, M. L., Lopez-Sanchez, J. A., & Trespalacios, J. A. (2012). How organizational learning affects a firm's flexibility, competitive strategy, and performance. *Journal of Business Research*, *65*(8), 1079–1089. doi:10.1016/j.jbusres.2011.09.002

Sattar, A., Khan, S., Nawaz, A., & Qureshi, Q. (2010). Theories of job satisfaction: Global applications and limitation. *Gomal University Journal of Research*, *26*(2), 45–62.

Sattar, A., & Nawaz, A. (2011). Investigating the demographic impacts on the job satisfaction of district officers in the province of KPK, Pakistan. *International Research Journal of Management and Business Studies*, *1*(2), 68–75.

Schein, E. H. (1992). *Organizational culture and leadership: A dynamic view*. San Francisco, CA: Jossey-Bass.

Seidler-de Alwis, R., & Hartmann, E. (2008). The use of tacit knowledge within innovative companies: Knowledge management in innovative enterprises. *Journal of Knowledge Management*, *12*(1), 133–147. doi:10.1108/13673270810852449

Senge, P. M. (1990). *The fifth discipline: The art & practice of the learning organization*. London, UK: Random House.

Serenko, A., & Bontis, N. (2004). Meta-review of knowledge management and intellectual capital literature: Citation impact and research productivity rankings. *Knowledge and Process Management*, *11*(3), 185–198. doi:10.1002/kpm.203

Shadur, M. A., Kienzle, R., & Rodwell, J. J. (1999). The relationship between organizational climate and employee perceptions of involvement. *Group & Organization Management*, *24*(4), 479–503. doi:10.1177/1059601199244005

Shahzad, F., Luqman, R. A., Khan, A. R., & Shabbir, L. (2012). Impact of organizational culture on organizational performance: An overview. *Interdisciplinary Journal of Contemporary Research in Business*, *3*(9), 975–985.

Sharma, R. S., & Djiaw, V. (2011). Realising the strategic impact of business intelligence tools. *Vine*, *41*(2), 113–131. doi:10.1108/03055721111134772

Singh, M. D., Shankar, R., Narain, R., & Kumar, A. (2006). Survey of knowledge management practices in Indian manufacturing industries. *Journal of Knowledge Management, 10*(6), 110–128. doi:10.1108/13673270610709251

Slater, S. F., & Narver, J. C. (1995). Market orientation and the learning organization. *Journal of Marketing, 59*(3), 63–74. doi:10.2307/1252120

Sotarauta, M., Horlings, L., & Liddle, J. (2012). *Leadership and change in sustainable regional development.* London, UK: Routledge.

Spector, P. (1997). *Job satisfaction: Application, sssessment, sauses, and consequences.* Thousand Oaks, CA: Sage Publications.

Taminiau, Y., Smit, W., & De Lange, A. (2009). Innovation in management consulting firms through informal knowledge sharing. *Journal of Knowledge Management, 43*(1), 42–55. doi:10.1108/13673270910931152

Tang, H. K. (1999). An inventory of organizational innovativeness. *Technovation, 19*(1), 41–51. doi:10.1016/S0166-4972(98)00077-7

Thompson, J., & Cavaleri, S. (2010). Dynamic knowledge, organizational growth, and sustainability: The case of Prestwick memory devices. *International Studies in Management and Organization, 40*(3), 50–60. doi:10.2753/IMO0020-8825400303

Tuan, L. T. (2013). Leading to learning and competitive intelligence. *The Learning Organization, 20*(3), 216–239. doi:10.1108/09696471311328460

Uotila, T., Melkas, H., & Harmaakorpi, V. (2005). Incorporating futures research into regional knowledge creation and management. *Futures, 37*(8), 308–317. doi:10.1016/j.futures.2005.01.001

Valez, G. V. (1972). A study of faculty satisfaction and dissatisfaction with the intrinsic and extrinsic job factors in Columbia University. *Dissertation Abstracts International, 33*(3), 997-A.

Van der Heijden, K. (2004). Can internally generated futures accelerate organizational learning? *Futures, 36*(2), 145–159. doi:10.1016/S0016-3287(03)00143-5

Wallach, E. (1983). Individuals and organizations: The cultural match. *Training and Development Journal, 37*(2), 29–36.

Wang, Y. L., & Ellinger, A. D. (2011). Organizational learning: Perception of external environment and innovation performance. *International Journal of Manpower, 32*(5-6), 512–536. doi:10.1108/01437721111158189

Weiss, D., Dawis, R., England, G., & Lofquist, L. (1967). *Manual for the Minnesota satisfaction questionnaire.* Minneapolis, MN: University of Minnesota Industrial Relations Center.

Weiss, H. (2002). Deconstructing job satisfaction: Separating evaluations, beliefs and affective experiences. *Human Resource Management Review, 12*(2), 173–194. doi:10.1016/S1053-4822(02)00045-1

Wickramasinghe, N. (2007). Fostering knowledge assets in health with the KMI model. *International Journal of Management and Enterprise Development, 4*(1), 52–65. doi:10.1504/IJMED.2007.011455

Williams, L. J., & Hazer, J. T. (1986). Antecedents and consequences of satisfaction and commitment in turnover models: A reanalysis using latent variable structural equation methods. *The Journal of Applied Psychology, 71*(2), 219–231. doi:10.1037/0021-9010.71.2.219

Wilson, A. M. (2001). Understanding organizational culture and the implication for corporate marketing. *European Journal of Marketing, 35*(3-4), 353–367. doi:10.1108/03090560110382066

Yamane, T. (1970). *Statistics – An introductory analysis.* Tokyo, Japan: John Weatherhill.

Yeo, R. K., & Li, J. (2013). In pursuit of learning: Sensemaking the quality of work life. *European Journal of Training and Development*, *37*(2), 136–160. doi:10.1108/03090591311301662

Zaim, H., Ekrem, T., & Selim, Z. (2007). Performance of knowledge management practices: A casual analysis. *Journal of Knowledge Management*, *11*(6), 54–67. doi:10.1108/13673270710832163

Zellmer-Bruhn, M., & Gibson, C. (2006). Multinational organization context: Implications for team learning and performance. *Academy of Management Journal*, *49*(3), 501–518. doi:10.5465/AMJ.2006.21794668

Zhao, J., & Ordóñez de Pablos, P. (2011). Regional knowledge management: The perspective of management theory. *Behaviour & Information Technology*, *30*(1), 39–49. doi:10.1080/0144929X.2010.492240

ADDITIONAL READING

Abdulla, J., Djebarni, R., & Mellahi, K. (2011). Determinants of job satisfaction in the UAE: A case study of the Dubai police. *Personnel Review*, *40*(1), 126–146. doi:10.1108/00483481111095555

Argote, L. (2011). Organizational learning research: Past, present, and future. *Management Learning*, *42*(4), 439–446. doi:10.1177/1350507611408217

Argote, L. (2013). *Organizational learning: Creating, retaining, and transferring knowledge*. New York, NY: Springer.

Argote, L., & Miron-Spektor, E. (2011). Organizational learning: From experience to knowledge. *Organization Science*, *22*, 1123–1137. doi:10.1287/orsc.1100.0621

Bogers, M., & Lhuillery, S. (2011). A functional perspective on learning and innovation: Investigating the organization of absorptive capacity. *Industry and Innovation*, *18*(6), 581–610. doi:10.1080/13662716.2011.591972

Borges, R. (2013). Tacit knowledge sharing between IT workers: The role of organizational culture, personality, and social environment. *Management Research Review*, *36*(1), 89–108. doi:10.1108/01409171311284602

Chai, S., & Kim, M. (2012). A socio-technical approach to knowledge contribution behavior: An empirical investigation of social networking sites users. *International Journal of Information Management*, *32*(2), 118–126. doi:10.1016/j.ijinfomgt.2011.07.004

Chiva, R., Grandio, A., & Alegre, J. (2010). Adaptive and generative learning: Implications from complexity theories. *International Journal of Management Reviews*, *12*(2), 114–129. doi:10.1111/j.1468-2370.2008.00255.x

Cohen, A., Rosenblatt, Z., & Buhadana, T. (2011). Organizational learning and individual values: The case of Israeli civil service employees. *Administration & Society*, *43*(4), 446–473. doi:10.1177/0095399711413080

Connell, J., & Voola, R. (2013). Knowledge integration and competitiveness: A longitudinal study of an industry cluster. *Journal of Knowledge Management*, *17*(2), 208–225. doi:10.1108/13673271311315178

Dalal, R. S., Bashshur, M. R., & Crede, M. (2011). The forgotten facet: Employee satisfaction with management above the level of immediate supervision. *Applied Psychology*, *60*(2), 183–209. doi:10.1111/j.1464-0597.2010.00431.x

Denford, J. S. (2013). Building knowledge: Developing a knowledge-based dynamic capabilities typology. *Journal of Knowledge Management*, *17*(2), 175–194. doi:10.1108/13673271311315150

Donate, M. J., & Guadamillas, F. (2011). Organizational factors to support knowledge management and innovation. *Journal of Knowledge Management*, *15*(6), 890–914. doi:10.1108/13673271111179271

Easterby-Smith, M., & Lyles, M. A. (2011). *Handbook of organizational learning and knowledge management*. Oxford, UK: Blackwell.

Ellis, S., Margalit, D., & Segev, E. (2012). Effects of organizational learning mechanisms on organizational performance and shared mental models during planned change. *Knowledge and Process Management, 19*(2), 91–102. doi:10.1002/kpm.1384

Froese, F. J., & Peltokorpi, V. (2011). Cultural distance and expatriate job satisfaction. *International Journal of Intercultural Relations, 35*(1), 49–60. doi:10.1016/j.ijintrel.2010.10.002

Garcia-Morales, V. J., Matias-Reche, F., & Verdu-Jover, A. J. (2011). Influence of internal communication on technological proactivity, organizational learning, and organizational innovation in the pharmaceutical sector. *The Journal of Communication, 61*(1), 150–177. doi:10.1111/j.1460-2466.2010.01530.x

Hoe, S. L., & McShane, S. (2010). Structural and informal knowledge acquisition and dissemination in organizational learning: An exploratory analysis. *The Learning Organization, 17*(4), 364–386. doi:10.1108/09696471011043117

Huang, J., & Kim, H. J. (2011). Conceptualizing the processes, benefits, and challenges of organizational lifelong learning at Yuhan-Kimberly, Korea: The notion of anticipative affordance. *International Journal of Human Resource Management, 22*(7), 1423–1441. doi:10.1080/09585192.2011.561958

Jakonis, A. (2010). Organisational culture in multicultural organizations – Mexico. *Journal of Intercultural Management, 2*(2), 83–96.

Jimenez-Jimenez, D., & Sanz-Valle, R. (2011). Innovation, organizational learning, and performance. *Journal of Business Research, 64*(4), 408–417. doi:10.1016/j.jbusres.2010.09.010

Jo, S. J., & Joo, B. K. (2011). Knowledge sharing: The influences of learning organization culture, organizational commitment, and organizational citizenship behaviors. *Journal of Leadership & Organizational Studies, 18*(3), 353–364. doi:10.1177/1548051811405208

Käpylä, J. (2012). Towards a critical societal knowledge management. *Journal of Intellectual Capital, 13*(3), 288–304. doi:10.1108/14691931211248873

Kim, C., Song, J., & Nerkar, A. (2011). Learning and innovation: Exploitation and exploration trade-offs. *Journal of Business Research, 65*(8), 1189–1194. doi:10.1016/j.jbusres.2011.07.006

Korte, R. (2012). Exploring the social foundations of human resource development: A theoretical framework for research and practice. *Human Resource Development Review, 11*(1), 6–30. doi:10.1177/1534484311430629

Lee, J., & Fink, D. (2013). Knowledge mapping: Encouragements and impediments to adoption. *Journal of Knowledge Management, 17*(1), 16–28. doi:10.1108/13673271311300714

Lee, M. R., & Lan, Y. (2011). Toward a unified knowledge management model for SMEs. *Expert Systems with Applications, 38*(1), 729–735. doi:10.1016/j.eswa.2010.07.025

Lerro, A., Iacobone, A. F., & Schiuma, G. (2012). Knowledge assets assessment strategies: Organizational value, processes, approaches and evaluation architectures. *Journal of Knowledge Management, 16*(4), 563–575. doi:10.1108/13673271211246149

Liao, S. H., & Wu, C. C. (2010). System perspective of knowledge management, organizational learning, and organizational innovation. *Expert Systems with Applications, 37*(2), 1096–1103. doi:10.1016/j.eswa.2009.06.109

Luu, T. T. (2011). Organisational culture and trust as organisational factors for corporate governance. *International Journal of Management and Enterprise Development, 11*(2-4), 142–162.

Matayong, S., & Mahmood, A. K. (2013). The review of approaches to knowledge management system studies. *Journal of Knowledge Management, 17*(3), 472–490. doi:10.1108/JKM-10-2012-0316

Mills, A. M., & Smith, T. A. (2011). Knowledge management and organizational performance: A decomposed view. *Journal of Knowledge Management, 15*(1), 156–171. doi:10.1108/13673271111108756

Myers, P. S. (2012). *Knowledge management and organizational design*. London, UK: Routledge.

Parvin, M. M., & Kabir, M. M. N. (2011). Factors affecting employee job satisfaction of pharmaceutical sector. *Australian Journal of Business and Management Research, 1*(9), 113–123.

Purcarea, I., Espinosa, M., & Apetrei, A. (2013). Innovation and knowledge creation: Perspectives on the SMEs sector. *Management Decision, 51*(5), 1096–1107. doi:10.1108/MD-08-2012-0590

Rabeh, H. A. D., Jimenéz-Jimenéz, D., & Martínez-Costa, M. (2013). Managing knowledge for a successful competence exploration. *Journal of Knowledge Management, 17*(2), 195–207. doi:10.1108/13673271311315169

Rebelo, T. M., & Gomes, A. M. (2011). Conditioning factors of an organizational learning culture. *Journal of Workplace Learning, 23*(3), 173–194. doi:10.1108/13665621111117215

Ruiz-Jiménez, J. M., & Fuentes-Fuentes, M. (2013). Knowledge combination, innovation, organizational performance in technology firms. *Industrial Management & Data Systems, 113*(4), 523–540. doi:10.1108/02635571311322775

Sanchez, J. A. L., Vijande, M. L. S., & Gutierrez, J. A. T. (2011). The effects of manufacturer's organizational learning on distributor satisfaction and loyalty in industrial markets. *Industrial Marketing Management, 40*(4), 624–635. doi:10.1016/j.indmarman.2010.12.003

Schiuma, G. (2012). Managing knowledge for business performance improvement. *Journal of Knowledge Management, 16*(4), 515–522. doi:10.1108/13673271211246103

Scott-Kennel, J., & Von Batenburg, Z. (2012). The role of knowledge and learning in internationalization of professional service firms. *The Service Industries Journal, 32*(10), 1667–1678. doi:10.1080/02642069.2012.665897

Serenko, A., Bontis, N., & Hull, E. (2011). Practical relevance of knowledge management and intellectual capital scholarly research: Books as knowledge translation agents. *Knowledge and Process Management, 18*(1), 1–9. doi:10.1002/kpm.363

Siong, C. C., Salleh, K., Syed, N. S., & Syed-Ikhsan, S. O. (2011). KM implementation in a public sector accounting organization: An empirical investigation. *Journal of Knowledge Management, 15*(3), 497–512. doi:10.1108/13673271111137457

Skerlavaj, M., Song, J. H., & Lee, Y. (2010). Organizational learning culture, innovative culture and innovations in South Korean firms. *Expert Systems with Applications, 37*(9), 6390–6403. doi:10.1016/j.eswa.2010.02.080

Song, J. H., Jeung, C. W., & Cho, S. H. (2011). The impact of the learning organization environment on the organizational learning process in the Korean business context. *The Learning Organization, 18*(6), 468–485. doi:10.1108/09696471111171312

Swart, J., & Kinnie, N. (2010). Organizational learning, knowledge assets and HR practices in professional service firms. *Human Resource Management Journal*, 20(1), 64–78. doi:10.1111/j.1748-8583.2009.00115.x

Wallace, D. P., Fleet, C. V., & Downs, L. J. (2011). The research core of the knowledge management literature. *International Journal of Information Management*, *31*(1), 14–20. doi:10.1016/j.ijinfomgt.2010.10.002

Zheng, S., Zhang, W., Wu, X., & Du, J. (2011). Knowledge- based dynamic capabilities an innovation in networked environments. *Journal of Knowledge Management*, *15*(8), 1035–1051. doi:10.1108/13673271111179352

KEY TERMS AND DEFINITIONS

Framework: Broad overview, outline, or skeleton of interlinked items which support a particular approach to a specific objective of the study.

Job Satisfaction: Contentment arising out of interplay of employee's positive and negative feelings towards his or her work.

Knowledge Acquisition: An activity through which knowledge is obtained among employees in an organization.

Knowledge Dissemination: An activity through which knowledge is circulated among employees in an organization.

Knowledge Management: Strategies and processes designed to identify, capture, structure, value, leverage, and share an organization's intellectual assets to enhance its performance and competitiveness.

Organizational Culture: The values and behaviors that contribute to the unique social and psychological environment of an organization.

Organizational Learning: Organization-wide continuous process that enhances its collective ability to accept, make sense of, and respond to internal and external change.

Responsiveness to Knowledge: A perception of knowledge received from employees in an organization.

Chapter 7
Assessment of Technical Efficiency of Indian B-Schools:
A Comparison between the Cross-Sectional and Time-Series Analysis

Sreekumar
Rourkela Institute of Management Studies, India

Gokulananda Patel
Birla Institute of Management Technology, India

ABSTRACT

In the present economy, both at national and international front service sector, is playing a pivotal role as a major contributor towards the GDP. The importance of service sector necessitates the efficiency measurement of various service units. The opening of Indian economy (Liberalisation – Privitisation – Globalisation) has affected every segment of Indian industry and service sector, education being no exception. Today, management education is one of the most sought after higher education options for Indian students. Management education in India has also undergone many changes in the last decade or so, meeting the need of industries. Meeting this growing demand has lead to proliferation of management institutions, and in many a cases the quality of education is compromised. Some popular Indian magazines and journals started ranking the Indian B-Schools intending to give information to all the stake holders involved. All these methods either use weighted average or clustering method to rank the institutes. This chapter proposes an alternative method based on efficiency analysis using Data Envelopment Analysis to rank the Indian B-Schools. The B-schools are observed over multiple periods of time, and the variations of efficiency are used to draw a conclusion about the performance of B-schools. Window analysis is used to compare the performance of B-schools over the period of time.

DOI: 10.4018/978-1-4666-4940-8.ch007

INTRODUCTION

The development of management education in terms of Post Graduate program in India dates back to 1960's. The growth of management education has become very much prominent in 1990s particularly after the initiation of New Economic Policy (NEP) in the year 1991. The main feature of NEP like Liberalization, Privatization and Globalization (LPG) marked an end to protectionism and saw the expansion and diversification of private sectors resulting in improved industrial growth in the country as compared to the pre reformed era. But at the same time it exposed the Indian industries to competition not only from within but also from multinational companies (MNCs) and foreign companies. In this scenario it becomes expedient to manage the companies in a more scientific way to face the challenge of competition.

These factors necessitated the development of business professionals to manage business in a more scientific way, thus creating a huge demand for business professionals. This resulted in mushrooming growth of B-Schools in post liberalized period in India.

The growth of B-Schools in an increasing number is a recent phenomenon and there are more than 1400 B-Schools approved by All India Council for Technical Education (AICTE) at present. But what we find is that there is a wide divergence in the standards of B-Schools in terms parameters like placement records, infrastructure availability, quality of the faculty, number of companies visiting the campus, average salary of the students recruited from the B-Schools etc. When the B-Schools are so much in number and there are wide differences among them on the basis of various parameters, it becomes necessary to rank them in a more judicious and scientific way so that the ranking exercises rightly informs all groups of stakeholders linked with management education like current students, prospective candidates, employers, programme administrators. The ranking helps all stakeholders involved in

the management education- it helps the students in choice of institution in which to pursue the academic programme, university administrator for defending their budgets, obtaining government assistance, justifying new faculty and students etc., Faculty for job and inter-institution mobility, Parents in deciding where to send their children to maximize return on investment (ROI), Employers in deciding from where to recruit, and Government in deciding the funding (Natarajan, 2003).

Since last decade various Indian magazines & journals publishes the ranking of top B-schools in India, the leading being Outlook –Cfore survey, survey done by All India Management Association (AIMA) through Indian Marketing Research Bureau (IMRB), Business World survey etc. This ranking of B-Schools can be useful in knowing where one stands. The results of these ranking are all the more important in building popular perception about the institutes and provide a basis to the aspiring students to choose the school, affect the undergoing students by influencing their salaries and Corporate can use these to decide which schools shall be chosen for campus recruitments. Thus, the ranking helps all the stakeholders involved in the management education.

The ranking method attempts to measure a number of factors that they think are important, and then assigns weightage to these factors and emerges with a single number that depicts the overall quality of the school (Martin, 1993). The major criticisms about the media effort lie in the subjective methodology and the apparent 'profit and publicity' driven motive. To correct these two flaws, academics can offer a reliable methodology and the merits of both the approaches can be combined (Stella and Woodhouse, 2006). Another area of concern is weightages assigned to each parameter. As per Van Dyke (Van Dyke, 2005), the choice of weights is subjective and arbitrary, with little or no theoretical or empirical basis. The difficulty, of course, is how to report results without assigning weights, since the various measures cannot then be combined into any overall ranking or clustering. One more point which seems to be important in the existing ranking system is, favouring the highly reputed B-school which again is based on the previous ranking. So the rankings themselves play a prominent role in affecting reputation, the circular nature of these endeavours makes them a particularly strong self-perpetuating force (Guarino et al., 2005).

The above discussion shows the need for a ranking methodology that is mathematically right and will take care of the problems in the existing ranking methodology. In the following section we review some of the techniques, which can be used for ranking Indian B-Schools. This paper uses Data Envelopment Analysis a non-parametric method based on the application of a mathematical technique called linear programming to rank B-Schools. It has been successfully employed for assessing the relative importance of set of firms, which use a variety of identical inputs to produce a variety of identical outputs. Unlike statistical methods of performance analysis, DEA is non-parametric in the sense that it does not require an assumption of functional form relating inputs to outputs.

QUALITY IN MANAGEMENT EDUCATION

The word 'quality' stands for various things based on the context of use and perception. Quality stands for 'Excellence' (Peter and Waterman,1982), 'fitness for use' (Juran, 1988), 'Meeting and/or exceeding customers' exceptions' (Parasuraman et al, 1985) etc.Due to the variation in the definition of the quality, so also the indicators used to describeeducation quality also differ.The quality of management education is a multidimensional concept and cannot be easily accessed by only one indicator. Furthermore, theexpectations of different stakeholders on management education may also differ. It isoften very difficult for a B-School to meet all the expectations or needs at the

same time. So the ability of B-Schools to convert the inputs into outputs becomes very important.

Quality of a management programme can be judged by- Quality of intake, Intellectual Capital and its development, Infrastructure, Pedagogy, and Placement. Quality of students taken for management programmes are very important and is in line with the concept that if the raw material is good then the product will be good. The students interested for management programme shall be selected through a common entrance test. Due weightage shall be given to the work experience, academic ability, personal characteristics, and leadership qualities etc.(Sreekumar and Patel, 2007)

LITERATURE REVIEW

In the recent years, several studies have undertaken analysis of efficiency in education sector using Data Envelopment Analysis (DEA) methodology. Each study differs in its scope, meaning, and definition of decision making units (DMUs) i.e. unit under study. Rodhes and Southwick (*1986*) used DEA to compare the efficiency of some private universities with the public universities in USA. Johnes and Johnes investigated the use of Data Envelopment analysis in the assessment of performance of university departments of the UK over the period 1984-1988.McMullen (1997) has applied DEA to assess the relative desirability of AACSB accredited MBA programs. In this study they incorporated several attributes of these MBA programs into model to find which programs are most desirable in terms of these attributes. The research finds that of 188 AACSB-accredited MBA programs studied, several possess characteristics that are dominant over others. Mcmillan and Datta (1998) reported the results of using Data Envelopment Analysis (DEA) to assess the relative efficiency of 45 Canadian universities. Outcomes are obtained from nine different specifications of inputs and outputs. The relative efficiencies are quite consistent across the alternative specifications. A subset of universities — including universities from each of three categories (comprehensive with medical school, comprehensive without medical school, and primarily undergraduate) — are regularly found efficient and a subset quite inefficient but, overall and for most universities, the efficiency scores are relatively high. Regression analysis is used in an effort to identify further determinants of efficiency. Ramanathan (2001) has compared the performance of selected schools in the Netherlands using DEA. They found that the DEA efficiencies of the schools are in line with their performance. They also observed the effect of several non – discretionary input variables which can influence the efficiency scores but which are not in direct control of management of the school. Lopes and Lanzer (2002) address the issue of performance evaluation – productivity and quality – of academic departments at a University. A DEA model was used to simulate a process of cross-evaluation between departments. The results of DEA in the dimensions of teaching, research, service and quality were modeled as fuzzy numbers and then aggregated through a weighted ordered aggregator. A single index of performance for each department was generated. The model applied to a set of fifty-eight departments of a Brazilian University. Fifteen of them showed low performance. Zero correlation between department teaching, research and service were observed. Weak correlation was detected between research productivity and quality. Weak scale effects were detected. Calhoun (2003) employs two methods of Data Envelopment Analysis (DEA) to compare relative efficiencies of institutions of higher learning (IHLs). In addition to comparing private and public IHLs, the paper introduces a new way to group institutions. IHLs are separated by the percent of unrestricted revenue; those with unrestricted revenue above a certain threshold are grouped together and those with unrestricted revenue below that threshold are grouped together, regardless of their private or public affiliation. The research has taken the sample of 1,323 four-year institutions for the study. Johnes (1993) applied Data envelopment analysis (DEA) to 2568 graduates from UK universities in 1993 in order to assess teaching efficiency. Each individual's efficiency is decomposed into two components: one attributable to the university at which the student studied, and the other attributable to the student himself. From the former component, a measure of each institution's teaching efficiency is derived and compared to efficiency scores derived from a conventional DEA applied using each institution as a decision making unit (DMU). The results suggest that efficiencies derived from DEA performed at an aggregate level include both institution and individual components, and are therefore misleading. Thus the unit of analysis in a DEA is highly important. Moreover, an analysis at the individual level can give institutions insight into whether it is the student's own efforts or the institution's efficiency which are a constraint on increased efficiency. Ray and Yongil (2003) in their study, employed a measure of Pareto-Koopmans global efficiency to evaluate the efficiency levels of the MBA programs in Business Week's top-rated list. They computed input- and output oriented radial and non-radial efficiency measures for comparison. Among three tier groups, the schools from a higher tier group on average are more efficient than those from lower tiers, although variations in efficiency levels do occur within the same tier, which exist over different measures of efficiency.

Objective of the Study

The management education is characterized by presence of multiple input and multiple output. The technical efficiency score of the B-schools can give aggregate picture of performance of a school which in turn can be helpful to them re-position themselves in the market-place. The inefficient institutions can pursue continuous improvement strategies by adjusting the slack and target values. To address these issues, the objectives of present study focuses on ranking of some B-schools of India based on their efficiency scores, find out bench marking institutions and discusses improvement areas for inefficient institutions. The study is also extended by considering the performance of the B-schools across the year. A sensitivity analysis is done to know the robustness of the model.

Data Set

For our study we have considered the surveys conducted by one of the popular Indian magazine Outlook. The data is collected for three consecutive years i.e. year-1(Y1), year-2(Y2) and Year3 (Y3). The performance of the B-Schools is assessed for first two years then the time series analysis is done taking all the three years data. The data is compiled from various sources (outlook; Bschool Directory, Business School Directory, www.bschools.com). We have considered top twenty eight Indian B-schools for analysis over these periods.

DATA ENVELOPMENT ANALYSIS (DEA)

The discussion and application of Data Envelopment Analysis (DEA) was initiated after the work of Charnes et al (1978) and subsequent evidence can be found in (Banker et al, 1984; Ramanathan 2001). DEA is a linear programming based technique for measuring the relative performance of organizational units where the presence of multiple inputs and outputs makes the comparison difficult.

To develop the DEA model, we use the following parameters and variables:

n = Number of DMU $\{j = 1, 2, ..., n\}$

s = Number of outputs $\{r = 1, 2, ..., s\}$

m = Number of inputs $\{i = 1, 2, ..., m\}$

y_{rj} = Quantity of rth output of jth DMU

x_{ij} = Quantity of ith input of jth DMU

u_r = weight of rth output

v_i = weight of ith input

DEA Model

The relative efficiency score of j_0 DMU is given by

Maximise the efficiency of unit j_0, subject to the efficiency (output / input) of all units being ≤ 1 or, output - input ≤ 0.

Algebraically the model can be written as

$$\max h_{j_0}(u, v) = \frac{\sum_{r=1}^{s} u_r y_{rj_0}}{\sum_{i=1}^{m} v_i x_{ij_0}} \qquad (1)$$

$$subject \quad to \quad \sum_{r=1}^{s} u_r y_{rj} - \sum_{i=1}^{m} v_i x_{ij} \leq 0 \qquad j = 1, 2, ..., n$$

$$u_r, v_i \geq 0 \ \forall \ r, i$$

The variables of the above problem are the weights and the solution produces the weights most favourable to unit j_0 and also produces a measure of efficiency. The decision variables are the input and output weights.

The DEA model shown in equation (1) assumes a Constant Return to Scale (CRS). The CCR model compares DMUs only based on overall efficiency assuming constant returns to scale. It ignores the fact that different DMUs could be operating at different scales. To overcome this drawback, Banker, Charnes and Cooper developed a model which considers variable returns to scale and compares DMUs purely on the basis of technical efficiency (Banker et al.,1984).

$$\min \theta$$

$$subject\ to\ \sum_{i=1}^{n} \lambda_i x_{ji} - \theta x_{jj_0} \leq 0\ \forall\ j$$

$$\sum_{i=1}^{n} \lambda_i y_{rj} - y_{jj_0} \geq 0\ \forall\ r \qquad (2)$$

$$\lambda_i = 1\ \forall\ i$$

The difference between the CRS model (1) and the VRS model (2) is that the λ_i is restricted to one. This has the effect of removing the constraint in the CRS model that DMUs must be scale efficient. Consequently, the VRS model allows variable returns to scale and measures only technical efficiency for each DMU. Thus, a DMU to be considered as CRS efficient, it must be both scale and technical efficient. For a DMU to be considered VRS efficient, it only needs to be technically efficient.

DATA CLASSIFICATION AND REVERSAL FOR DEA APPLICATIONS

For our DEA analysis the data is classified into two categories viz. inputs and outputs. The criteria of selection of inputs and outputs are quite subjective; there is no specific rule for determining the procedure for selection of inputs and outputs (Ramanathan, 2001). The parameters used for the analysis is shown below:

- **ECA:** extracurricular activities
- **FEE:** fee collected from the students
- **FS:** faculty satisfaction score
- **IC:** intellectual capitals
- **IF:** infrastructure & facilities
- **II:** industry interface
- **IL:** international linkages
- **PP:** placement performance
- **RS:** recruiters satisfaction score
- **SAL:** initial salary at which graduating students are placed

- **SS:** students satisfaction score

The data is classified as inputs and outputs as follows (Sreekumar and Patel, 2005).

- *Inputs*
  - Y_1: *IC*
  - Y_2: *IF*
  - Y_3: *FEE*
- *Outputs*
  - X_1: *II*
  - X_2: *PP*
  - X_3: *IL*
  - X_4: *RS*
  - X_5: *SS*
  - X_6: *FS*
  - X_7: *ECA*
  - X_8: *SAL*

For applying the DEA we have reversed two of the inputs "IC" and "IF". The scores on IC and IF are not directly taken for DEA analysis as higher score of IC and IF means they have developed more infrastructure, facilities and intellectual capital, which is desirable. If we directly use the score in the model higher value will be reflected as usage of more input for producing the desired output, which is contradictory. So for the DEA analysis the complement of the score from the total is used.

ANALYSIS AND RESULTS

The general output oriented BCC DEA model is used to solve the problem and get the efficiency score. We have used DEA Solver to solve the model. The result of DEA analysis is shown in Table 1. The 1st column of the table-I shows the rank as assigned by the Magazine, the 2nd column shows the efficiency score as calculated from BCC model for the year Y1 and 3rd column for the year Y2. The 4th column is new rank assigned to the B-Schools based on the efficiency score for

Table 1. Results of BCC -output orientated DEA model

DMU/ Rank (I)	Efficiency Y1	Efficiency Y2	New Rank(II)Y1	New Rank(III) Y2	D_1 (I-II)	D_2 (I-III)
1	1	1	1	1	0	0
2	1	1	1	1	1	1
3	1	1	1	1	2	2
4	1	1	1	1	3	3
5	1	1	1	1	4	4
6	0.918367	1	13	1	-7	5
7	0.902937	0.933465	19	21	-12	-14
8	0.918367	0.913751	13	27	-5	-19
9	0.884011	0.977761	22	16	-13	-7
10	0.869822	1	26	1	-16	9
11	0.79845	0.952867	28	19	-17	-8
12	1	1	1	1	11	11
13	0.94808	0.972128	11	18	2	-5
14	1	1	1	1	13	13
15	0.897959	0.99376	20	13	-5	2
16	0.973211	1	8	1	8	15
17	0.912843	0.919431	15	25	2	-8
18	0.877607	0.983258	24	15	-6	3
19	0.909846	0.926927	17	23	2	-4
20	0.872909	0.92611	25	24	-5	-4
21	0.959184	0.8083	9	28	12	-7
22	0.906798	0.933034	18	22	4	0
23	0.89258	1	21	1	2	22
24	0.95352	0.988082	10	14	14	10
25	0.910084	0.947667	16	20	9	5
26	0.931626	0.916263	12	26	14	0
27	0.882043	1	23	1	4	26
28	0.815822	0.976355	27	17	1	11

Mean Efficiency (2004) = 0.926288, Mean Efficiency (2005) = 0.966756

Y1 and 5th column for the new rank for the year Y2. The 6th and 7th column shows the deviation in conventional ranking and the DEA ranking for Y1 and Y2 respectively.

The results show that top six Indian B-schools are retaining their positions. There is a improvement in the mean efficiency score of the institute over the year. The high value of efficiency score is obtained as only very top B-schools are considered for the analysis. It is also interesting to see the last two columns that the position of top five schools is not changing over the year. DMU-$_1$which is one of the top B-School in India (IIM-Ahmedabad) is retaining its position in all rankings. The highest loser in the year Y1 on technical efficiency score is DMU_{11} which lost

Table 2. Sensitivity analysis report (Output Oriented DEA, Scale Assumption: VRS)

DMU/ Rank (I)	Efficiency Y1	Efficiency Y2	Dropping IC Y1	Dropping IC Y2	Dropping FEE Y1	Dropping FEE Y2	Dropping DMU 1, Y1	Dropping DMU 1, Y2	Dropping DMU 12, Y1	Dropping DMU 12, Y2
1	1	1	1	1	1	1	---	---	1	1
2	1	1	1	1	1	1	1	1	1	1
3	1	1	1	1	1	1	1	1	1	1
4	1	1	1	1	1	1	1	1	1	1
5	1	1	1	1	**0.902**	1	1	1	1	1
6	0.918	1	0.918	1	0.918	1	0.918	1	0.918	1
7	0.902	0.933	0.902	0.933	0.902	0.933	0.902	0.933	0.902	0.933
8	0.918	0.913	0.918	0.913	0.918	0.901	0.918	0.930	0.918	0.913
9	0.884	0.977	0.884	0.977	0.883	0.977	0.888	0.977	0.884	0.977
10	0.869	1	0.869	1	0.869	1	0.869	1	0.869	1
11	0.798	0.952	0.798	0.952	0.798	0.952	0.814	0.952	0.798	0.952
12	1	1	1	1	0.834	0.879	1	1	---	---
13	0.948	0.972	0.948	0.972	0.897	0.936	0.948	0.979	0.986	0.972
14	1	1	1	1	**0.918**	**0.922**	1	1	1	1
15	0.897	0.993	0.897	0.993	0.897	0.978	0.897	0.995	0.897	0.993
16	0.973	1	0.973	1	0.834	0.957	0.973	1	1	1
17	0.912	0.919	0.912	0.919	0.846	0.871	0.912	0.919	1	0.919
18	0.877	0.983	0.877	0.983	0.828	0.936	0.877	0.987	0.899	0.984
19	0.909	0.926	0.909	0.926	0.857	0.879	0.909	0.938	0.925	0.928
20	0.872	0.926	0.872	0.926	0.822	0.886	0.872	0.930	0.886	0.926
21	0.959	0.808	0.959	0.808	0.959	0.797	0.959	0.836	0.959	0.808
22	0.906	0.933	0.906	0.933	0.869	0.884	0.906	0.946	0.913	0.936
23	0.892	1	0.892	1	0.836	0.948	0.892	1	0.919	1
24	0.953	0.988	0.953	0.988	0.857	0.914	0.953	1	0.974	1
25	0.910	0.947	0.910	0.947	0.834	0.914	0.910	0.954	0.941	0.947
26	0.931	0.916	0.931	0.916	0.846	0.855	0.931	0.916	0.949	0.932
27	0.882	1	0.882	1	0.852	0.980	0.882	1	0.889	1
28	0.815	0.976	0.815	0.976	0.804	0.957	0.815	0.976	0.817	0.976

seventeen position and highest gainer being DMU_{24} and DMU_{26} which gained fourteen positions. Similarly the last column of the Table-I shows the lose and gain of the B-Schools for the year Y2.

Sensitivity Analysis

DEA is an extreme point technique because the efficiency frontier is formed by the actual performance of best-performing DMUs. A direct consequence of this aspect is that errors in measurement can affect the DEA result significantly. So according to DEA technique, it is possible for a B-School to become efficient if it achieves exceptionally better results in terms of one output but performs below average in other outputs.

The sensitivity of DEA efficiency can be verified by checking whether the efficiency of a DMU is affected appreciably:

Table 3. Window analysis report

DMU	Period-1	Period-2	Period-3
1	1.000	1.000	1.000
2	1.000	1.000	1.000
3	1.000	1.000	1.000
4	1.000	0.974	1.000
5	1.000	1.000	1.000
6	1.000	0.926	1.000
7	0.906	0.866	0.950
8	0.895	1.000	1.000
9	0.970	0.880	1.000
10	0.959	0.864	0.992
11	0.941	0.784	0.958
12	1.000	1.000	0.933
13	0.964	1.000	0.962
14	1.000	1.000	0.972
15	0.939	0.898	0.970
16	1.000	1.000	0.973
17	0.919	0.901	0.888
18	0.954	0.869	0.948
19	0.913	0.902	0.899
20	0.922	0.864	0.905
21	0.786	0.959	0.799
22	0.905	0.901	0.898
23	1.000	0.883	0.976
24	0.967	0.940	0.934
25	0.918	0.897	0.910
26	0.914	0.917	0.877
27	0.993	0.877	0.998
28	0.922	0.814	0.950

- If only one input or output is omitted from DEA analysis.
- Dropping one efficient DMU at a time from DEA analysis.

The result of the sensitivity analysis is shown in the Table 2

It is observed from the table above that when the input IC is dropped from the analysis there is no change in the technical score. When the input "Fee" is dropped from the analysis then there is change in efficiency scores two DMUs viz. DMU_5 and DMU_{14} is becoming inefficient. Dropping the efficient DMUs from the analysis is not making the efficient units inefficient one. The analysis shows the robustness of the model used.

Time-Series Analysis

A time series are the values of a function sampled at different points in time. In the previous sections we have considered the cross-sectional analysis of data where, each DMU was observed only once. In this section we have observed the DMUs over multiple time periods to find the changes in efficiency over time. In such a setting, it is possible to perform DEA over time by using a moving average analogue, where a DMU in each different period is treated as if it were a "different" DMU. Specifically, a DMU's performance in a particular period is contrasted with its performance in other periods in addition to the performance of the other DMUs (Cooper et al.). For analysis purposes we used a software called Win4DEAP version 1.1.0 written by Tim Coelli.

Table 3 reflects the stability of technical efficiency score over a period of time. It is observed that the technical efficiency score of inefficient units has decreased in period -2, but is maximum in period -3. The performance of DMU_{14} and DMU_{16} has come down over the period and is becoming relatively inefficient over the period.

CONCLUSION

As the management education characterizes multi-input and multi-output system, Data Envelopment Analysis (DEA), with its ability to handle multiple inputs and multiple outputs has been used in this paper to rank the Indian B-Schools based on their technical efficiency score. The ranking is done using BCC model and the results are compared with conventional ranking done by popular Indian magazines. The comparison shows that ranking using DEA-VRS model differs significantly from the conventional ranking. The sensitivity analysis done shows that there is no significant change in the efficiency score of DMUs when an input or output is dropped from the DEA analysis in both the models. The dropping of efficient DMUs

from the analysis also shows the same fact. This shows the robustness of the model. The time series analysis done over three periods of time shows the stability of technical efficiency score over a period of time. It is observed that the technical efficiency score of inefficient units has decreased in period -2. The analysis has shown the performance of schools has improved over period of time. The methodology suggested in the paper can provide useful information by identifying clusters of DMUs performing better in certain contexts. This technique allows the researcher to investigate why and how they are able to perform better. The proposed method has many advantages over the other available methods. It can handle multiple inputs and multiple outputs and doesn't require relating inputs to outputs. The comparisons are directly made against peers. The Inputs and outputs can have very different units.

FUTURE RESEARCH DIRECTIONS

The present study can still be extended to other types of Institutions/Institutes of higher learning or any other organisations whose objective is not only profit maximisation. With the data used and the results obtained in the study an Artificial Neural Network (ANN) can be developed. This network can be trained to calculate the efficiency score with the given input and output values. Using this ANN B-School can directly feed the expected scores on various inputs and outputs to the network and get the expected efficiency score. The school can then make necessary variations in the score to make it efficient.

REFERENCES

B – School Directory. (2005). Largest listing of b-schools. *Business India*.

Banker, R. D., Charnes, A., & Cooper, W. W. (1984). Some models for estimating technical & scale efficiencies in data envelopment analysis. *Management Science, 30,* 1078–1092. doi:10.1287/mnsc.30.9.1078

Business School Directory. (2005). *Dalal street.* Author.

Calhoun, J. (2003). *Relative efficiencies of institutions of higher learning.* University of Georgia. Retrieved from http://www.arches.uga.edu/~calhounj/personal/deadisagg.pdf

Charnes, A., Cooper, W. W., & Rhodes, E. (1978). Measuring efficiency of decision making units. *European Journal of Operational Research, 2,* 429–444. doi:10.1016/0377-2217(78)90138-8

Guarino, C. G. R., Chun, M., & Buddin, R. (2005). Latent variable analysis: A new approach to university ranking. *Higher Education in Europe, 30*(2). doi:10.1080/03797720500260033

Johnes, G., & Johnes, J. (n.d.). Measuring the research performance of UK economics departments: An application of data envelopment analysis. *Oxford Economics Papers, 4*(2), 332-347.

Johnes, J. (1993). *Measuring teaching efficiency in higher education: an application of data envelopment analysis to graduates from UK universities* (Working Paper 2003/007). JEL Classification: I21, C14.

Juran, J. M., & Gryna, F. M. (1988). *Juran's quality control handbook* (4th ed.). New York: McGraw-Hill.

Lopes, A., Lúcia, M., & Lanzer, E. A. (2002). Data envelopment analysis – DEA and fuzzy sets to assess the performance of academic departments: A case study at Federal University of Santa Catarina – UFSC. *PesquisaOperacional, 22*(2), 217–230.

Martin, S. (1993). What's wrong with MBA ranking surveys? *Management Research News, 16*(7), 15–18. doi:10.1108/eb028322

Mcmillan, L. M., & Datta, D. (1998). The relative efficiencies of Canadian universities: A DEA perspective. *Canadian Public Policy – Analyse De Politiques, 24*(4), 485-511.

McMullen, P. R. (1997). Assessment of MBA programs via data envelopment analysis. *Journal of Business and Management, 5*(1), 77–91.

Natarajan, R. (2003). Quality and accreditation in technical & management education. *Productivity, 44*(2), 165–172.

Parasuraman, A., Zeithaml, V. A., & Berry, L. L. (1985). A conceptual model of service quality and its implication for future research. *Journal of Marketing, 49,* 41–50. doi:10.2307/1251430

Peters, T. J., & Waterman, R. H. (1982). *In search of excellence.* New York: Harper and Row.

Ramanathan, R. (2001). A data envelopment analysis of comparative performance of schools in Netherland. *Opsearch, 38*(2), 160–182.

Ray, C. S., & Yongil, J. (2003). *Reputation and efficiency: A nonparametric assessment of America's top-rated MBA programs* (Working Paper 2003-13). Retrieved from http://www.econ.uconn.edu/

Rhodes, E. Y., & Southwick, L. (1986). *Determinants of efficiency in public and private universities.* Department of Economics, University of South Carolina.

Sreekumar, & Patel, G. (2007). Comparative analysis of b-school rankings and an alternate ranking method. *International Journal of Operations and Quantitative Management, 13*(1), 33-46.

Sreekumar, & Patel, G.N. (2005). Measuring the relative efficiency of some Indian MBA programmes- A DEA approach. *Business Perspective, 7*(2), 47-59.

Stella, A., & Woodhouse, D. (2006). Australian universities quality agency. *Occasional Publications*, *6*, 1446–4268.

Van Dyke, N. (2005). Twenty years of university report cards. *Higher Education in Europe*, *30*(2), 103–124. doi:10.1080/03797720500260173

William, W., Cooper, L., Seiford, M., & Zhu, J. (2011). Data envelopment analysis history, models and interpretations. *International Series in Operations Research & Management Science*, *16*(4), 1–39.

KEY TERMS AND DEFINITIONS

B-education: Management education.

Data Envelopment Analysis: A non parametric approach for efficiency measurement.

Efficiency: weighted ratio of output to input

Rank: relative position of B-School.

Chapter 8
Detection of
Non–Technical Losses:
The Project MIDAS

Juan I. Guerrero
Universidad de Sevilla, Spain

Jesús Biscarri
Universidad de Sevilla, Spain

Íñigo Monedero
Universidad de Sevilla, Spain

Rocío Millán
Universidad de Sevilla, Spain

Félix Biscarri
Universidad de Sevilla, Spain

Carlos León
Universidad de Sevilla, Spain

ABSTRACT

The MIDAS project began in 2006 as collaboration between Endesa, Sadiel, and the University of Seville. The objective of the MIDAS project is the detection of Non-Technical Losses (NTLs) on power utilities. The NTLs represent the non-billed energy due to faults or illegal manipulations in clients' facilities. Initially, research lines study the application of techniques of data mining and neural networks. After several researches, the studies are expanded to other research fields: expert systems, text mining, statistical techniques, pattern recognition, etc. These techniques have provided an automated system for detection of NTLs on company databases. This system is in the test phase, and it is applied in real cases in company databases.

INTRODUCTION

The main objective of data mining techniques is the evaluation of data sets to discover relationships in information. These relationships may identify anomalous patterns or patterns of frauds. Fraud detection is a very important problem in telecommunication, financial and utility companies. Currently data mining is one of the most important techniques which are applied to solve these types of problems, joined with: rough sets, neural networks, time series, support vector machines, etc. There are a lot of references about the detection of abnormalities or frauds in a set of data.

The increase of storage capacity and the process capacity allow one to manage large databases. Data mining provides a set of techniques of artificial

DOI: 10.4018/978-1-4666-4940-8.ch008

intelligence which can be used to increase the efficiency of data mining methods.

The utility companies have large databases which support the management processes. In addition, these companies invest their effort in maintenance of infrastructure and anomaly detection. These anomalies are frauds in telecommunication and financial sectors; breakdown or fraud in power, water or gas sectors; etc.

The non-technical losses (NTLs) in power utilities are defined as any consumed energy or service which is not billed because of measurement equipment failure or ill-intentioned and fraudulent manipulation of said equipment. This paper describes advances developed for the MIDAS project. The paper proposes a framework to analyze all information available about customers. This framework uses: data mining, text mining, expert systems, statistical techniques, regression techniques, etc. The proposed framework is actually in the testing phase. It is the main result of the MIDAS Project a collaborative project between the Endesa Company, Ayesa and the University of Seville.

In this paper, a description of the framework is made, following these steps:

- Review of current state about the anomaly detection and NTLs detection. Additionally, the Endesa utility company is described.
- The MIDAS project is explained.
- Each module is described.
- Finally, the conclusions are presented.

REVIEW OF THE CURRENT STATE

Bibliographical Review

The Non-Technical Losses (NTLs) were increasingly regarded as a cause of concern in distribution utility companies. There exists several causes of NTLs and they can affect quality of supply, electrical load on the generating station and tariff imposed on electricity consumed by genuine customers. (Depuru, Lingfeng Wang, Devabhaktuni, & Gudi, 2010) discusses various factors those influence the consumer to make an attempt to steal electricity. There are a lot of methods for detection NTL. The distribution utility companies are interested in analysis of NTLs for detection, location and classification of NTLs, with the objective of reducing them. There are many ways to perform these processes, and can be taken as reference similar methods used for fraud detection in telecommunications, finance, etc. (Yufeng Kou, Chang-Tien Lu, Sirwongwattana, & Yo-Ping Huang, 2004) and (Weatherford, 2002) show different techniques related with data mining for fraud detection, including the most interesting parameters for using with them.

Financial Sector

In the financial sector there are a lot of references with the use of data mining and computational intelligence in the fraud detection. Noteworthy is the use of these techniques in credit card fraud detection. In the nineties, (Ghosh & Reilly, 1994), (Fanning, Cogger, & Srivastava, 1995), (Aleskerov, Freisleben, & Rao, 1997) and (Dorronsoro, Ginel, Sgnchez, & Cruz, 1997) used neural networks to detect ones. Some authors publish researches with other techniques: intelligent hybrid system (Hambaba, 1996), neural networks compared to statistical techniques (Richardson, 1997), neural data mining (Brause, Langsdorf, & Hepp, 1999), distributed data mining (Chan, Fan, Prodromidis, & Stolfo, 1999), etc. In addition, other techniques are used latter, for example: Genetic Algorithm (Özçelik, Işik, Duman, & Çevik, 2010), neural networks and logistic regression (Y. Sahin & Duman, 2011), time series (Seyedhossein & Hashemi, 2010), decision trees (Yusuf Sahin, Bulkan, & Duman, 2013), etc.

In financial sector, there are other areas of interest, for example, based in the theory of Rough Sets (Yezheng Liu, Yuanchun Jiang, & Wenlong

Lin, 2006), (Qian Liu, Tong Li, & Wei Xu, 2009). However, the most often used techniques are neural networks and data mining (Dianmin Yue, Xiaodan Wu, Yunfeng Wang, Yue Li, & Chao-Hsien Chu, 2007).

Communication Sector

In the communication or telecommunication sector, there is a growing interest in fraud detection. In this sector, several techniques are used, from basic data mining techniques, as feature extraction (Wang Dong, Wang Quan-yu, Zhan Shou-yi, Li Feng-xia, & Wang Da-zhen, 2004), or neural networks (Mohamed et al., 2009) and probabilistic methods (Taniguchi, Haft, Hollmen, & Tresp, 1998), to fuzzy rough sets (Wei Xu et al., 2008) or knowledge-based management (Davis & Goyal, 1992). In fact, this interest has been extended to VoIP (Rebahi, Nassar, Magedanz, & Festor, 2011) and (Seo, Lee, & Nuwere, 2013).

Intrusion Detection

In this subject, there are a lot of techniques which is used as a part of an Intrusion Detection System. Noteworthy is the use of feature analysis (Shuyuan Jin, Daniel So Yeung, Xizhao Wang, & Tsang, 2005), Support Vector Machines or SVM (Liu Wu, Ren Ping, Liu Ke, & Duan Hai-xin, 2011), neural networks (Raghunath & Mahadeo, 2008) and (Lei & Ghorbani, 2012) and several data mining techniques (Ming Xue & Changjun Zhu, 2009) and (Li Han, 2010). This new field of research becomes important due to the proliferation of computer networks and Internet. These facts are important in other research fields, for example Smart Grids. The security of Smart Grids is a very interesting problem and is very related with intrusion detection, because Smart Grids are based in the mix of telecommunication with utility network.

Non-Technical Losses

There are some references about NTLs detection, but wide scope of techniques is used. There are several references about computational intelligence based solutions, but, sometimes, initially the companies start with a strategic plan (Gonzalez & Figueroa, 2006) or implant new follow-up and control mechanisms (Iglesias, 2006), (Mwaura, 2012) of NTL reduction. This paper is oriented in the use of computational intelligence. In this sense, a lot of references can be found, and they will be showed below.

(Nizar, Zhao Yang Dong, & Pei Zhang, 2008) uses detection rules for non-technical analysis, the technique compounds a series of data mining tasks, including feature selection, clustering and classification techniques. (Cabral, Pinto, Martins, & Pinto, 2008) and (Cabral, Pinto, & Pinto, 2009) propose a methodology based on a non-supervised artificial neural network called SOM (Self-Organizing Maps) which is robust on several cases. (Nizar, Dong, Zhao, & Zhang, 2007) proposes two popular classification algorithms, Naïve Bayesian an Decision Tree, extracting the patterns of customers' consumption behavior from historical data and arranging the data in various ways by averaging them yearly, monthly, weekly, and daily. Both techniques are used and compared. Various authors use the Support Vector Machines (SVM) method related with non-technical losses detection. For example: (Aranha Neto & Coelho, 2013), (Depuru, Lingfeng Wang, & Devabhaktuni, 2011), (Nagi, Yap, Sieh Kiong Tiong, Ahmed, & Mohamad, 2010) and (Nagi, Mohammad, Yap, Tiong, & Ahmed, 2008). Each one proposes different ways to make analysis or detection of non-technical losses. In addition, this technique can be combined with any other computational intelligence, for example, with fuzzy inference system (FIS) (Nagi, Keem Siah Yap, Sieh Kiong Tiong, Ahmed, & Nagi, 2011) or with genetic algorithm (GA) (Nagi, Yap, Tiong, Ahmed, & Mohammad,

2008). The use of these mixed methods improves the efficiency of SVM technique.

(Brun, Pinto, Pinto, Sauer, & Colman, 2009) proposes the use of deferential evolution algorithm to find the parameters of a data mining system used to pre-select electrical energy consumers with suspect of fraud, building a pattern recognition system for suspicious behavior detection. The parameter of the pattern recognition system must be well tuned, and that can be modeled as an optimization problem using the available training data.

(Markoc, Hlupic, & Basch, 2011) proposes a new approach based on neural network trained by generated samples.

(Cabral & Gontijo, 2004) describes an application of rough sets in the fraud detection of electrical energy consumers. Rough set is an emergent technique of soft computing that have been used in many knowledge discovery in database applications. From an information system, rough sets concept of reduce was used to reduce the number of conditional attributes and the minimal decision algorithm was used to reduce some values of conditional attributes. The reduced information system derives a set of rules that reaches consumers behavior, allowing the classification rule system to predict many fraud consumer profiles.

(Caio C. O Ramos, Papa, Souza, Chiachia, & Falcao, 2011) shows the importance of using feature selection in non-technical losses detection, in fact, there are several authors which use this technique (Nizar, Jun Hua Zhao, & Zhao Yang Dong, 2006). Also in [44], a characterization of customer using evolutionary-based feature selection method.

(de Oliveira, Boson, & Padilha-Feltrin, 2008) proposes a statistical analysis of relationship between load factor and loss factor using the curves of a sampling of consumers in a specific company, these curves are summarized in different bands of coefficient k. Then, it is possible determine where each group of consumer has its major concentration of points.

Even, there exist computational techniques specifically developed for NTL detection, for example, (dos Angelos, Saavedra, Cortés, & de Souza, 2011) proposes a computational technique for the classification of electricity consumption profiles based on fuzzy clustering and Euclidean distance.

Other references are based on load profiling calculation. These are additional point of view, they use remote management systems and smart metering. These systems provide more information about client consumption. (Nizar, Dong, & Zhao, 2006) and (Nizar, Dong, Jalaluddin, & Raffles, 2006) propose a study for detection the best load profiling methods and data mining techniques to classify, detect and predict NTLs in the distribution sector, due to faulty metering and billing errors, as well as to gather knowledge on customer behavior and preferences so as to gain a competitive advantage in the deregulated market. (Nizar & Dong, 2009) and (Nizar, Dong, & Wang, 2008) propose Extreme Learning Machine (ELM) and online sequential-ELM (OS-ELM) algorithms which are used to achieve an improved classification performance and to increase accuracy of results. A comparison of this approach with other classification techniques, such as the SVM algorithm, is also showed. (C. C.O Ramos, Souza, Papa, & Falcao, 2009) and (C. C.O Ramos, de Sousa, Papa, & Falcão, 2011) propose Optimum Path Forest (OPF) classifier for a fast non-technical losses recognition, they show a comparison with neural networks and SVM, getting best results with OPF than neural networks and similar results than SVM. However, (Depuru, Lingfeng Wang, Devabhaktuni, & Nelapati, 2011) proposes a hybrid neural network, which implements a neural network model and suggests a hierarchical model for enhanced estimation of the classification efficiency. In addition, this paper proposes and encoding a new technique that can identify illegal consumers. (Yi Zhang, Weiwei Chen, & Black, 2011) presents a method to accurately identify anomalous days for individual premises so that they can be removed from the premise data.

The new technologies related with Smart Grids, provides more information and control over the consumption and demand. Smart Grids provides new technologies to improve the reduction of NTL (Abaide, Canha, Barin, & Cassel, 2010). For example, smart metering (Openshaw, 2008) or Hall Effect based electrical energy metering devices (Wilks, 1990). In this sense, there are some references which are based on increasing of metering infrastructure capabilities. (Alves, Casanova, Quirogas, Ravelo, & Gimenez, 2006), (Kerk, 2005) and (Nagi, Yap, Nagi, et al., 2010) propose an Advanced Metering Infrastructure based on remote management of equipment, provides more information about consumption and events which could happen in consumer installation. These new information compounds: more information about consumption (quarter-hourly), information about events (illegal manipulation, inspector operations, alarms, etc.), etc. Some references also use this information with computational intelligence techniques, for example, (Depuru, Lingfeng Wang, & Devabhaktuni, 2011) proposes a SVM which take information from smart metering infrastructure.

Normally, works that use more information have best results. The references which use load profiling or data from smart metering have more information about consumer and optimal pattern consumption can be established. Currently, the companies have a lot of clients. Smart Metering provides a new research field, but it is necessary to establish the methods and techniques of NTL detection in scenarios when limited information in consumption are available. For example, there exist a lot of clients with monthly measurements, because they don't have smart meters. Although there exists smart metering infrastructure, the company databases have a lot of additional information about client, which could be used for NTL detection. It is necessary to determine methods for analysis of present and future situations (Gemignani, Tahan, Oliveira, & Zamora, 2009), which compounds monthly and quarter-hourly periods, taking advantage of the rest of company databases information. A complete framework for NTL detection is proposed in this paper. This framework is based on data mining, statistical techniques, text mining, neural network and expert system, which gather all information about client to get a classification of the client, according to the problem which the client's facility shows. Most references specified above are based on consumption, contracted power, tariff, economic sector and geographic location. In the corporate databases much more information exists, for example, results of inspections, inspectors' feedback information, etc. The proposed framework takes advantage of all information stored in corporate databases.

Do Companies Fight Against NTLs

The system proposed in this paper is actually operating in the testing phase in the Endesa Company. Endesa is the most important Spanish energy distribution company with more than 12 million clients in Spain, and more than 73 million clients in European and South American markets.

Traditionally, companies identify two different types of losses: non-technical losses (NTLs) and technical losses. The NTLs are caused by breakdown or illegal manipulation in customer facilities. These types of losses are very difficult to predict. Normally, utility companies use massive inspection to reduce NTLs. These inspections are performed on the customer who carries out a series of conditions, as example: customers who have measure equipment without transformers and it is located in a limited geographic zone. These conditions reduce the volume of number of customers to inspect. Utility companies are very interested in the detection of NTLs.

The Technical Losses represents the rest of the losses which is produced by distribution problems (Joule effect). The Technical Losses can be forecasted because they are approximate constants, but the NTLs are very irregular and very difficult to forecast. The technical losses are caused by faults in distribution lines. These faults are predictable with a low rate of error.

When the inspector finds an NTL, the company has to be notified. The inspector stores all information about the problem when it is detected until it is solved. This information is named proceeding.

THE PROJECT MIDAS

The objective of the MIDAS Project is the detection of Non-Technical Losses (NTLs) using computational intelligence over Endesa databases. This project is the collaboration between Endesa, Ayesa Tecnología and Electronic Technology Department of University of Seville. This project began at 2006 with the study of a little set of customers, and getting good results.

In this project a lot of lines are researched: data mining, statistical techniques, neural networks, expert systems, text mining, pattern recognition, etc.

Traditionally, the utility companies used massive inspections to avoid the NTLs, but this method is very expensive both in time and in money. Currently the utility companies use more advanced systems that allow the selection of clients who carry out some simple conditions. This type of system allows one to reduce the economic and time cost, increasing the efficiency. But these simple conditions aren't automatically selected and, normally, they only detect some type of NTLs.

As it is said, the prototype developed is in test stage and is tested with Endesa databases. This system has provided better results than the traditional system of inspection.

SYSTEM ARCHITECTURE

The proposed system architecture contains several modules. Each module is implemented with different techniques. Each module can increase their capabilities with each new prototype, using the previous results to make better modules. Each prototype is tested with real data of Endesa databases and it is validated with inspections made by Endesa staff.

The system architecture is shown in Figure 1. In this architecture the different steps of the process are applied in an ordered way. In the first place, a sample of customers is selected using the data stored in utility company databases. In the second place, several artificial intelligence and statistical techniques are applied. The regression analysis techniques and data mining modules provide a set of customers whose have some anomalies regarding customer's own consumption or the other customers' consumption. Mainly, these modules work with some parameters: consumption, contracted power, economic activity. In the last place, the integrated expert system analyzes the rest of information about the customer. The integrated expert system provides the results on databases and reports that they can be both used by inspectors as an additional source of information. In the following sections each of these modules is described.

SELECT SAMPLE

The sample selection uses several data sources. Each data source provides information about different aspects about the customers:

- **Period of time of recorded invoices:** We use monthly and bimonthly invoices belonging to the sample of customers. Hourly or daily data are not available.
- **Geographic localization**
- **Economic Activity:** Some economic sectors historically present a high rate of NTLs.
- **Consumption range:** Sometimes, the consumption range can be used to restrict the quantity of customers.
- **Electricity charges**

These parameters allow restricting the quantity of customers to analyze. The information of each customer compounds information about: contract,

Figure 1. System architecture

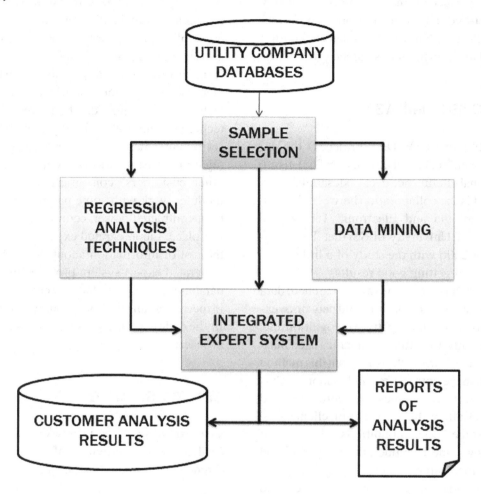

installed equipment, results of inspections realized over the facilities, etc.

The information about consumption is analyzed in different ways by each module. Additionally the rest of information is analyzed by integrated expert system.

DATA MINING

First of all, and as previous step to the data mining, two processes from which taken the data all the detection methods was carried out:

- **Data Selection:** In this step, a set of the sample to process was selected by the proposed data mining techniques.
- **Data Preprocessing:** A pre-processing of the data, during which data was carried out sets were prepared (generating new tables, filtering wrong data, etc) for the mining process.

Mainly, the objective of these processes was to normalize and to discrete the sample set for the set of data mining models developed in the project.

Initially, the first techniques developed for the data mining process were the outliers' analysis and inherent data variability. These techniques are described in (Biscarri et al., 2008). For this process a sample of homogeneous data which have utility customers with similar characteristics were selected. The temporary and the local components of the individual consumption of customer were removed by means of normalization. After this step, the probability distribution of the transformed sample, for the normal operating condition, as Gaussian is considered. The threshold of the sample variance is calculated and adjusted. Finally, the detected outliers are used to guide the inspections. This process would be fired in the first step in the framework of data mining. The resulting customers (not detected by this process) would be those processed by the other data mining techniques.

Thus, after the development of these methods, the inclusion of other techniques of data mining was carried out. In this way, the framework of MIDAS integrates several methods related to different data mining techniques. These methods were classified in different modules depending on the type of technique used for detection, in purely statistical or evolved models (referring to association and segmentation). All of them allow increasing the efficiency of detection process by means of complementary detections using the same information.

Statistical Methods Based on Comparison with Similar Customers

These three statistical techniques are used in this module: one based on the variability of customer consumption, another based on the consumption trend and a third one that summarizes other feature contributions of NTL detection. This module was described in (Biscarri, Monedero, León, Guerrero, & Biscarri, 2009).

The variability analysis provides an algorithm that emphasizes customers with a high variability of monthly consumption in comparison to other customers of similar characteristics. The classic approach to the study of variability classifies data in 'normal data' and outliers. The proposed variability analysis uses the standard deviation estimation (STD) to associate to each customer a new feature that will be used as an input for a supervised detection method, showed in the Predictive data mining section.

The consumption trend uses a streak-based algorithm. Streaks of past outcomes (or measurements) are one source of information for a decision maker trying to predict the next outcome (or measurement) in the series.

This set of techniques is strongly dependent of the cluster of customers considered and highly changeable amongst different clusters. The study of the individual trend consumption and also the comparative among trends of customer with similar characteristics is very interesting and it contributed to detect NTLs relative to customers with a different behavior to their similar environment.

Statistical Methods Based on an Individual Analysis of the Customers

This method is used to identify the customers with pattern of drastic drop of consumption. It is because according to the Endesa inspectors and the studies of consumption, the main symptom of a NTL is a drop in billed energy of the customers. The detection methods referring to this module are described in (Hutchison et al., 2010).

This method compounds several algorithms: based on regression analysis, based on the Pearson correlation coefficient and based on a windowed linear regression analysis. These algorithms are based on a regression analysis on the evolution of the consumption of the customer. The aim is to search for a strong correlation between the time (in monthly periods) and the consumption of the customer. The regression analysis makes it possible to adjust the consumption pattern of the customer by means of a line with a slope. This slope must be indicative of the speed of the drop of the consumption and, therefore, the degree of correlation. These algorithms identify with a high grade of accuracy two types of suspicious (and typically corresponding to NTL) drops.

Thus, this module provided a set of effective and robust techniques to detect cases with a particular manifestation of the NTLs (consumption drops).

Evolved Models Based on Clustering and Decision Trees

In this type of detections, as well as those ones with association rules, the objective was to find new NTLs searching for customers with similar behavior to those NTL detected in the past. For it, first of all, we featured the type of contract and consumption pattern of the customer. After featuring the customers, the different techniques search for similar customers in the sample set. The feature vector included the following patterns:

- Number of hours of maximum power consumption.
- Standard deviation of the monthly or bi-monthly consumption.
- Maximum and minimum value of the monthly or bimonthly consumptions.
- Reactive/Active energy coefficient.
- The number of valid consumption lectures. Usually, when there is not a valid lecture value and the company is sure that consumption existed, the consumption is estimated and billed.

In addition, two parameters are added to this set. These parameters were those ones based on the concept of streak (and generated in the work described in [63]).

Concretely, the use of these two techniques (clustering and decision trees) is described in (Monedero et al., 2009). Thus, this work included a process of generation of clusters by means of the K-Means algorithm and, in parallel, an algorithm that generates decision trees.

Both algorithms carry out a clustering of the customers (one by clusters and other by branches) and those clusters with a higher rate of NTLs identified by Endesa Company in the past were studied. Two techniques with the objective of that both ones searched the same thing by two complementary ways were used.

Evolved Models Based on Association Rules

The module uses an inference of a rule set to characterize each of two following classes: 'normal' or 'anomalous' customer (depending if there was been detected as NTL in the past by Endesa Company in its inspections). Each customer is characterized by means of the attributes previously described. The association uses supervised learning that by means of a set of input attributes search of NTLs. This module is described in (Biscarri et al., 2009).

In particular, the algorithm uses the Generalize Rule Induction (GRI) model. It discovers association rules in the data.

The test of the set of rules generated four values, according to the following classifications (Cabral et al., 2008):

- **True positives (TP):** Quantity of test registers correctly classified as fraudulent.
- **False positives (FP):** Quantity of test registers falsely classified as fraudulent.
- **True negatives (TN):** Quantity of test registers correctly classified as non-fraudulent.
- **False negatives (FN):** Quantity of test registers falsely classified as correct.

A decision tree algorithm GRI extracts rules with the highest information content based on an index that takes both the generality (support) and accuracy (confidence) of rules into account. GRI can handle numeric and categorical inputs, but the target must be categorical.

The objective that we searched with association rules was the same one that with clustering and decision trees: Detecting new NTLs identifying a similar pattern to those ones detected in the past. In contrast, the advantage is that the association rule algorithm over the more standard decision tree algorithms is that associations can exist between any of the attributes. This made it possible to detect different customers to those ones detected with the methods of previous sections and therefore, to do new complementary detections.

The detections carried out by each of these modules were later analyzed by the Integrated Expert System (it is described in C section) in order to perform a deeper study (with other parameters not only related to consumption pattern).

Summarizing the overall data mining process, Figure 2 shows the framework of this process.

INTEGRATED EXPERT SYSTEM

The Integrated Expert System has a core based on a Rule Based Expert System (RBES). Although this RBES was described in (León et al., 2011), this paper presents new advances in some modules and it is used as part of a complete framework. This system uses the information extracted from Endesa staff and inspectors. The RBES has several additional modules which provide dynamic knowledge using rules. The expert system has additional modules which uses different techniques: data warehousing (it is used as a preprocessing step), text mining, statistical techniques and neural networks.

In the proposed framework, the RBES may be used as additional methods to analyze the rest of information about the customer. The company

Figure 2. Flow chart of the data mining process

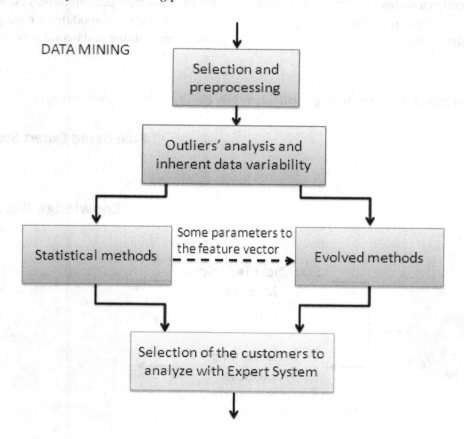

databases store a lot of information, including: contract, customers' facilities, inspectors' commentaries, customers, etc. All of them are analyzed by RBES using the rules extracted from Endesa staff, inspectors and rules from the statistical techniques and text mining modules. This information is not analyzed by the previously described modules. The system provides the point of view of the Endesa staff and inspectors.

Integrated Expert System Architecture and Application

The integrated expert system is compounds of several modules; each module has an information type as objective:

- **Statistical techniques module.** This module is used to make patterns of correct range and trend of consumption. This module generates a series of values which they are used in dynamic rules of a dynamic knowledge base.

- **Text mining and neural network module.** This module is used to treat the information provided by inspectors' commentaries. This module generates a series of dictionaries with characterized concepts which they are used in dynamic rules of a dynamic knowledge base.

- **Integrated expert system.** This module uses the rules (extracted from inspectors and staff of Endesa, generated by statistical techniques module and generated by text mining and neural network module) for analyzing the clients.

The integrated expert system is applied in two steps. The first step or learning step the modules of statistical techniques and text mining and neural network are applied in a database of clients as large as possible. This fact allows make a reference for dynamic knowledge base. In Figure 3, this step is shown. This step is performed only once per month in case of statistical module or once per year in case of text mining and neural network module.

Figure 3. First step or learning step of application process of integrated expert system

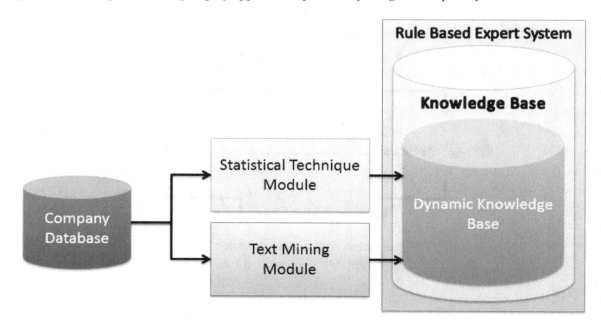

In the second step or analysis step, the integrated expert system uses the results of the first step or learning step to make the analysis of the information about the clients. In Figure 4 this step is shown. The analysis is applied over sample selection; this sample may compound the clients selected by other type of analysis methods that they showed in previous sections.

The statistical techniques and text mining and neural network modules are described in the following sections.

Figure 4. Second step or analysis step of application process of integrated expert system

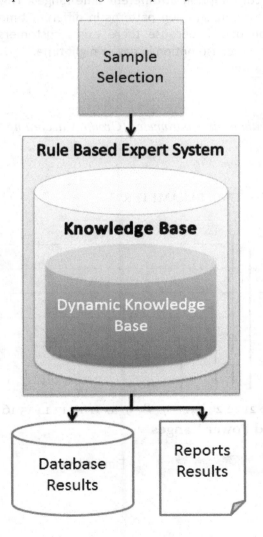

Statistical Technique Module

The statistical techniques are based in basic consumption indicators such as: maximum, minimum, average and standard deviation of consumption. These indicators are used as patterns to detect correct consumption. Additionally, the slope of regression line is used to detect the regular consumption trend. Each of these techniques is made for different sets of characteristics. These characteristics are: time, contracted power, measure frequency, geographical location, postal code, economic activity and time discrimination band. Using these characteristics it is possible to determine the patterns of correct consumption of a customer with a certain contracted power, geographic location and economic activity. These groups are described in Table 1.

It is necessary a learning step in which a lot of clients are used to apply all statistical calculations. In this study all customers are not used because the anomalous consumption of the customers with an NTL is filtered. This idea allows the elimination the anomalous consumption getting better results. This step is made before the client analysis, because this process provides the correct reference of consumption which it is stored in dynamic knowledge base.

Several tables of data are generated as a result of this study. These data are used to create rules which implement the detected patterns. If a customer carries out the pattern, this means that the customer is correct. But if a customer does not carry out the pattern, this does not mean that the customer could be correct.

In Figure 5 only contracted power, zone and measurement frequency are used, this case there are several intervals, in 23 and 24 ranges, in which the correct consumption limits are defined. Each of these ranges represents identifiers of intervals, for example, the 24 range represents the customers with the interval of contracted power between 366 kW to 455 kW. These intervals can be obtained for others contracted power ranges if more

Table 1. Groups of consumption characteristics

Consumption Characteristics	Description
Basis Group (A)	This group provides consumption patterns by general geographical location: north, south, etc.
Basis Group and Postal Code (B)	This group provides patterns useful for cities with coastal and interior zones.
Basis Group and Economic activity (C)	The granularity of geographical location is decreased, in this way, the economic activity takes more importance, but the geographical location cannot be eliminated, because, as for example, a bar has not the same consumption whether is in interior location or coastline location.
Basis Group and time discrimination band (D)	There are several time discrimination bands each band register the consumption at different time ranges. This group provides consumption patterns in different time discrimination bands, because there exists customers who makes their consumption in day or night time.

Figure 5. Ranges of correct consumption for a group without time parameter (Group A according to Table 1)

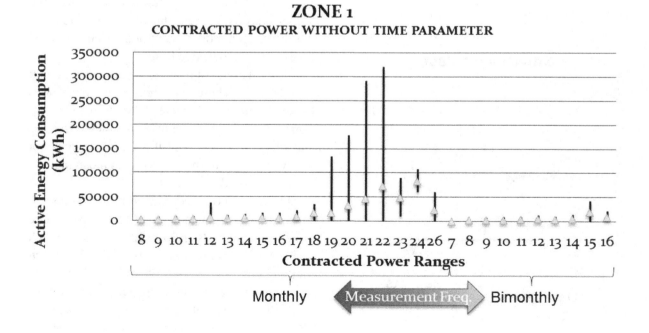

characteristics are added, for example, in Figure 6, the intervals are more specific and provide patterns for correct consumption. Additionally, in Figure 7, the intervals are more specific if the year characteristic is added.

This module is applied in samples as large as possible, because it is necessary to get a better statistical reference. This learning process only is made monthly or bimonthly.

The information generated by statistical techniques module is stored in a database and it is automatically translated to dynamic knowledge base of the integrated expert system, using several classes according to the group of consumption characteristics.

Text Mining and Neural Network Module

The text mining method is based on Natural Language Processing (NLP). The neural network is based on a multi-layer neural network. This method is used to provide a method to analyze the inspectors' commentaries. When an inspection in customer's location is made, the inspector has to register their observations and commentaries. This data is stored in company databases.

This information is not commonly analyzed, because the traditional models are based on consumption study. This module uses the rest of important information, because the inspectors' commentaries provide real information about the client facilities, which may be different from the stored in database.

The process begins with the application of text mining method. This technique uses NLP and fuzzy algorithms to extract concepts from inspectors' commentaries. Concept is a word or group of words which has own meaning. In addition, the fuzzy algorithms and the utilization of synonyms' dictionaries allow the interpretation of different language and dialects. These concepts are classified initially according to their frequency of appearance. The more frequent concepts are classified manually according to their meaning. Additionally, consumption indicators, date of commentary, number of measures (estimated and real), number of proceedings, source of commentary, frequency of appearance, time discrimination band and some others are associated to each concept. This data is used in a neural network, which is trained with data of the more frequent concepts and is tested with the concepts which were not classified manually. In the test process, the correct classification of concepts was verified manually. This neural network can be used to classify the new concepts which could appear.

The neural network is trained by means of a multiple method. This method creates several neural networks of different topologies. At the end of training, the model with the lowest Root Mean Square or RMS error is presented as the final neural network. The trained neural network assigns an importance value to each feature. SoftMax transfer function was used as a punctuation method. The trained neural network has two hidden layers and its structure is 22-28-26-4, due to the quantity of inputs. The first and last layers are the input and output layers, respectively.

Initially, the utilization of neural networks in non-structured language learning could seem very complex, not only the synonyms' dictionaries and the concepts' characterization make easy the process, but the inspectors have to make a lot of inspections in a day, and they must to store all information and commentaries in the company database. Due to this they use a very brief and concrete language.

This process generates dictionaries with characterized concepts. These dictionaries are stored in a database and it is automatically translated to dynamic knowledge base of the integrated expert system, using a class which allows to analysis the commentaries.

The first version of text proposed text mining and neural network module is described in (Guerrero et al., 2010).

Figure 6. Ranges of correct consumption for zone 2, several contracted power range, measurement frequency (monthly) and service sector. The grasfts show the limits of consumption for different contracted power ranges without the influence of time parameter (Group C according to Table 1)

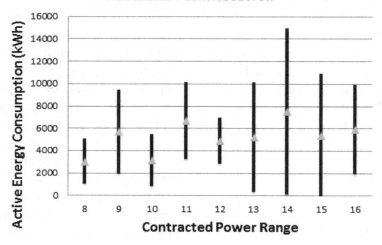

Figure 7. Ranges of correct consumption for zone 2, several contracted power range, measurement frequency (monthly) and service sector. The grasfts show the limits of consumption for different contracted power ranges with the influence of time parameter (Group C according to Table 1)

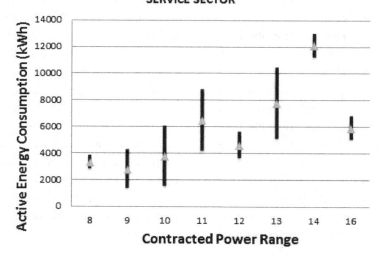

EXPERIMENTAL RESULTS

Several studies are made over several real cases, testing the efficiency and accuracy of the proposed framework. In this paper, only the last study is showed, because is the only one in which the framework is completely tested.

The sample compounds clients which carried out the following conditions:

- Contracted Power greater than 15 kW.
- Clients of north of Spain.

Although, the study compounds consumers with several economic sectors, the inspectors' experience and the results of other studies showed that the service sector is the one which have greater number of NTL cases.

The experimental results are described using architecture described in Figure 1. The first step of the process was Select Sample. In this step 540 consumers was selected, using different consumers' characteristics. In this step, only two possible groups are considered, the customers getting by data mining and regression analysis techniques. 119 customers were selected by the system and were inspected. Henceforth this group was referred as Group S1. Really, in these methods is possible to add some factors which determine probability of NTL. The quantity of selected customers was defined by utility company according to this factor.

The Expert System module can be used alone or joined with other methods. In case of the use of Expert System alone, the select sample step can include more customers, in this case, 81385 customers were selected for analysis in expert system. After analysis of customers, the number of selected customers with any detected problem was 3215. Henceforth, this group was referred as Group S2. At the same time, the Expert System determined that 63411 customers were not presented any NTL. The rest of customers, 14759, did not have enough information, because:

- They did not have enough information.
- They had few measurements.
- They were recently inspected.

The Group S1 is included in Group S2. Finally, Group S1 was selected by company and was send to inspectors. There are cases in which the expert system rule selected customers by the methods of data mining and regression analysis techniques, in this case, it is discarded if the customer is classified as correct by the text mining rules of the Integrated Expert System.

After inspections, the following results are obtained:

- Inspections could not be performed: 28 customers. These inspections could not be performed for various reasons, usually because it is indoors or with customers whose refuse, therefore, cannot ensure the existence of an NTL.
- Without NTL: 54 customers.
- With NTL: 37 customers.

In this way, the correctness was 40,66%. This result is better than massive inspections campaigns carried out by companies. Furthermore, the time spent in the analysis is 90% lower than traditional techniques.

The framework provided reports about analysis about each customer, in which it is possible to check:

- Problems or incidents found in the facilities or consumption of customer. These problems can mask an NTL.
- The method and rules used in analysis of each client.
- The conclusions of analysis.
- Statistical information about analysis process.

Highlight Cases

The proposed framework has been more efficient in analysis. There are some cases which traditionally were very difficult to detect. Concretely, two cases are treated in this section.

The first case is a client with an irrigation activity. The consumption of this type of client is strongly influenced by climate. The consumption of this client is very irregular, and difficult to analyze. These clients decrease their consumption when rainfalls increase. In this system, data about climate are not available, and only use the information about client. Sometimes, variations of climate conditions make that the data mining or regression analysis techniques select this type of clients. This client is analyzed by expert system, and normally it is dismissed according to the elapsed time since the last inspection.

The second case is the client with seasonal consumption. This type of clients is very difficult to detect with traditionally methods. The consumption of these clients shows one or two great peaks, which can be classified as a fraud. This type of clients can be hotels in coast line, which only has consumption in month with a good climate or in holiday periods. The using of descriptive data mining and expert system allows detecting these cases.

FUTURE RESEARCH DIRECTIONS

Future research fields are addressed to improve the knowledge about non-technical losses and extract knowledge from companies' databases. These objectives are translated in different research areas:

- Researching on the knowledge of other inspectors, and trying to extend the possibilities of detection.
- Application of the techniques and models developed in other utility companies, not only power distribution but also gas and water distribution.
- Adaptation to new technologies, such as smart metering or smart grids environments.
- Researching on the optimization of inspection routes.
- Improving these results with other techniques of data mining, computational intelligence and statistical inference.
- Testing with larger sample size and greater number of supplies to inspect.
- Researching on clients of medium and low voltage. This area is very similar to the fraud detection with smart metering facilities, because these clients used to have advanced measurement equipment.

CONCLUSION

The MIDAS project proposes an integrated framework which provides several methods to obtain better results in NTL detection. This framework is being used in Endesa company to make campaigns of massive inspections which includes computational intelligence in the analysis process. The process includes computational intelligence based on statistical techniques and data mining. Additionally, it includes an expert system based on knowledge of the inspectors of the company. This variety of modules provides different detection spectrum, i.e. regression analysis and data mining modules, provide NTL detection methods which are traditionally not detected, enriched by the knowledge of inspectors. Moreover, the expert system provides an automated method for traditional NTL detection.

The developed framework shows better results than traditional techniques of massive inspection campaigns. These methods provide additional intelligence to customer selection for inspection. These ones take advantage of all the stored information to make a decision about the customer. By automating this framework is achieved by making available to inexperienced staff of Endesa, with the possibility of their use in training.

Additionally, the contribution of this work with respect to previous work is the integration into a single framework of the knowledge of inspectors with knowledge extracted from information. Thus, this framework is able to detect non-technical losses obtained by supervised learning techniques and provides new information about non-technical losses previously not easy to detect. This framework not only classifies the different types of consumers suspected of having a non-technical loss but also classifies consumers without non-technical losses.

This framework is used by Endesa and it is in the testing process. Furthermore, it is researching the use of this framework in other utilities.

REFERENCES

Abaide, A. R., Canha, L. N., Barin, A., & Cassel, G. (2010). *Assessment of the smart grids applied in reducing the cost of distribution system losses.* Paper presented at the Energy Market (EEM). London, UK. doi:10.1109/EEM.2010.5558678

Aleskerov, E., Freisleben, B., & Rao, B. (1997). CARDWATCH: A neural network based database mining system for credit card fraud detection. In *Proceedings of the IEEE/IAFE 1997*. IEEE. doi:10.1109/CIFER.1997.618940

Alves, R., Casanova, P., Quirogas, E., Ravelo, O., & Gimenez, W. (2006). *Reduction of non-technical losses by modernization and updating of measurement systems.* Paper presented at the Transmission & Distribution Conference and Exposition: Latin America, 2006. doi:10.1109/TDCLA.2006.311590

Aranha Neto, E. A. C., & Coelho, J. (2013). Probabilistic methodology for technical and non-technical losses estimation in distribution system. *Electric Power Systems Research*, *97*, 93–99. doi:10.1016/j.epsr.2012.12.008

Biscarri, F., Monedero, Í., León, C., Guerrero, J. I., & Biscarri, J. (2009). A mining framework to detect non-technical losses in power utilities. In J. Cordeiro & J. Filipe (Eds.), *Proceedings of the 11th International Conference on Enterprise Information Systems* (pp. 96–101). IEEE.

Biscarri, F., Monedero, I., León, C., Guerrero, J. I., Biscarri, J., & Millán, R. (2008). A data mining method based on the variability of the customer consumption - A special application on electric utility companies. In J. Cordeiro & J. Filipe (Eds.), *Proceedings of the Tenth International Conference on Enterprise Information Systems* (pp. 370–374). Academic Press.

Brause, R., Langsdorf, T., & Hepp, M. (1999). Neural data mining for credit card fraud detection. In *Proceedings of the 11th IEEE International Conference on Tools with Artificial Intelligence*. IEEE. doi:10.1109/TAI.1999.809773

Brun, A. D., Pinto, J. O., Pinto, A. M. A., Sauer, L., & Colman, E. (2009). Fraud detection in electric energy using differential evolution. In *Proceedings of the 15th International Conference on Intelligent System Applications to Power Systems*. IEEE. doi:10.1109/ISAP.2009.5352917

Cabral, J. E., & Gontijo, E. M. (2004). Fraud detection in electrical energy consumers using rough sets. In *Proceedings of the 2004 IEEE International Conference on Systems, Man and Cybernetics*. IEEE. doi:10.1109/ICSMC.2004.1400905

Cabral, J. E., Pinto, J. O., Martins, E. M., & Pinto, A. M. (2008). Fraud detection in high voltage electricity consumers using data mining. In *Proceedings of the Transmission and Distribution Conference and Exposition. IEEE/PES.* doi:10.1109/TDC.2008.4517232

Cabral, J. E., Pinto, J. O., & Pinto, A. M. A. (2009). Fraud detection system for high and low voltage electricity consumers based on data mining. In *Proceedings of the IEEE Power & Energy Society General Meeting.* IEEE. doi:10.1109/PES.2009.5275809

Chan, P. K., Fan, W., Prodromidis, A. L., & Stolfo, S. J. (1999). Distributed data mining in credit card fraud detection. *IEEE Intelligent Systems and their Applications, 14*(6), 67–74. doi:10.1109/5254.809570

Davis, A. B., & Goyal, S. K. (1992). Knowledge-based management of cellular clone fraud. In *Proceedings of the Third IEEE International Symposium on Personal, Indoor and Mobile Radio Communications.* IEEE. doi:10.1109/PIMRC.1992.279930

De Oliveira, M. E., Boson, D. F., & Padilha-Feltrin, A. (2008). A statistical analysis of loss factor to determine the energy losses. In *Proceedings of the Transmission and Distribution Conference and Exposition: Latin America.* IEEE/PES. doi:10.1109/TDC-LA.2008.4641691

Depuru, S. S. S., Wang, L., & Devabhaktuni, V. (2011). Support vector machine based data classification for detection of electricity theft. In *Proceedings of the Power Systems Conference and Exposition* (PSCE). IEEE/PES. doi:10.1109/PSCE.2011.5772466

Depuru, S. S. S., Wang, L., Devabhaktuni, V., & Gudi, N. (2010). Measures and setbacks for controlling electricity theft. In *Proceedings of the North American Power Symposium* (NAPS). IEEE. doi:10.1109/NAPS.2010.5619966

Depuru, S. S. S., Wang, L., Devabhaktuni, V., & Nelapati, P. (2011). A hybrid neural network model and encoding technique for enhanced classification of energy consumption data. In *Proceedings of the 2011 IEEE Power and Energy Society General Meeting.* IEEE. doi:10.1109/PES.2011.6039050

Dong, W., Quan-yu, W., Shou-yi, Z., Feng-xia, L., & Da-zhen, W. (2004). A feature extraction method for fraud detection in mobile communication networks. In *Proceedings of the Fifth World Congress on Intelligent Control and Automation, 2004.* IEEE. doi:10.1109/WCICA.2004.1340996

Dorronsoro, J. R., Ginel, F., Sgnchez, C., & Cruz, C. S. (1997). Neural fraud detection in credit card operations. *IEEE Transactions on Neural Networks, 8*(4), 827–834. doi:10.1109/72.595879 PMID:18255686

Dos Angelos, E. W., Saavedra, O. R., Cortés, O. A., & de Souza, A. N. (2011). Detection and identification of abnormalities in customer consumptions in power distribution systems. *IEEE Transactions on Power Delivery, 26*(4), 2436–2442. doi:10.1109/TPWRD.2011.2161621

Fanning, K., Cogger, K. O., & Srivastava, R. (1995). Detection of management fraud: A neural network approach. In *Proceedings of the 11th Conference on Artificial Intelligence for Applications.* IEEE. doi:10.1109/CAIA.1995.378820

Gemignani, M., Tahan, C., Oliveira, C., & Zamora, F. (2009). Commercial losses estimations through consumers' behavior analysis. In *Proceedings of the 20th International Conference and Exhibition on Electricity Distribution - Part 1.* IET.

Ghosh, S., & Reilly, D. L. (1994). Credit card fraud detection with a neural-network. In *Proceedings of the Twenty-Seventh Hawaii International Conference on System Sciences.* IEEE. doi:10.1109/HICSS.1994.323314

Gonzalez, G., & Figueroa, L. (2006). Strategic plan for the control and reduction of non-technical losses applied in C.A. Energia ElÃƒÂ©ctrica de Valencia. In *Proceedings of the Transmission & Distribution Conference and Exposition: Latin America, 2006*. IEEE/PES. doi:10.1109/TDCLA.2006.311491

Guerrero, J. I., León, C., Biscarri, F., Monedero, I., Biscarri, J., & Millán, R. (2010). Increasing the efficiency in non-technical losses detection in utility companies. In *Proceedings of the ME-LECON 2010 - 2010 15th IEEE Mediterranean Electrotechnical Conference*. IEEE. doi:10.1109/MELCON.2010.5476320

Hambaba, M. L. (1996). Intelligent hybrid system for data mining. In *Proceedings of the IEEE/IAFE 1996 Conference on Computational Intelligence for Financial Engineering, 1996*. IEEE. doi:10.1109/CIFER.1996.501832

Han, L. (2010). Research and implementation of an anomaly detection model based on clustering analysis. In *Proceedings of the 2010 International Symposium on Intelligence Information Processing and Trusted Computing* (IPTC). IEEE. doi:10.1109/IPTC.2010.94

Hutchison, D., Kanade, T., Kittler, J., Kleinberg, J. M., Mattern, F., & Mitchell, J. C. … Millán, R. (2010). Using regression analysis to identify patterns of non-technical losses on power utilities. In R. Setchi, I. Jordanov, R. J. Howlett, & L. C. Jain (Eds.), *Knowledge-based and intelligent information and engineering systems* (Vol. 6276, pp. 410–419). Berlin, Germany: Springer. Retrieved from http://www.springerlink.com/content/43m1340538478854/

Iglesias, J. M. (2006). Follow-up and preventive control of non-technical losses of energy in C.A. Electricidad de Valencia. In *Proceedings of the Transmission & Distribution Conference and Exposition: Latin America, 2006*. IEEE. doi:10.1109/TDCLA.2006.311381

Jin, S., So Yeung, D., Wang, X., & Tsang, E. C. (2005). A feature space analysis for anomaly detection. In *Proceedings of the 2005 IEEE International Conference on Systems, Man and Cybernetics*. IEEE. doi:10.1109/ICSMC.2005.1571706

Kerk, S. G. (2005). An AMR study in an Indian utility. In *Proceedings of the Power Engineering Conference, 2005*. IEEE. doi:10.1109/IPEC.2005.206894

Kou, Y., Lu, C.-T., Sirwongwattana, S., & Huang, Y.-P. (2004). Survey of fraud detection techniques. In *Proceedings of the 2004 IEEE International Conference on Networking, Sensing and Control*. IEEE. doi:10.1109/ICNSC.2004.1297040

Lei, J. Z., & Ghorbani, A. A. (2012). Improved competitive learning neural networks for network intrusion and fraud detection. *Neurocomputing*, *75*(1), 135–145. doi:10.1016/j.neucom.2011.02.021

León, C., Biscarri, F., Monedero, I., Guerrero, J. I., Biscarri, J., & Millán, R. (2011). Integrated expert system applied to the analysis of non-technical losses in power utilities. *Expert Systems with Applications*, *38*(8), 10274–10285. doi:10.1016/j.eswa.2011.02.062

Liu, Q., Li, T., & Xu, W. (2009). A subjective and objective integrated method for fraud detection in financial systems. In *Proceedings of the 2009 International Conference on Machine Learning and Cybernetics*. IEEE. doi:10.1109/ICMLC.2009.5212307

Liu, Y., Jiang, Y., & Lin, W. (2006). A rough set and evidence theory based method for fraud detection. In *Proceedings of the Sixth World Congress on Intelligent Control and Automation, 2006*. IEEE. doi:10.1109/WCICA.2006.1712608

Markoc, Z., Hlupic, N., & Basch, D. (2011). Detection of suspicious patterns of energy consumption using neural network trained by generated samples. In *Proceedings of the ITI 2011 33rd International Conference on Information Technology Interfaces (ITI)*. IEEE.

Mohamed, A., Bandi, A. F., Tamrin, A. R., Jaafar, M. D., Hasan, S., & Jusof, F. (2009). Telecommunication fraud prediction using backpropagation neural network. In *Proceedings of the International Conference of Soft Computing and Pattern Recognition, 2009*. IEEE. doi:10.1109/SoCPaR.2009.60

Monedero, Í., Biscarri, F., León, C., Guerrero, J. I., Biscarri, J., & Millán, R. (2009). *New methods to detect non-technical losses on power utilities*. Paper presented at the IASTED - Artificial Intelligence and Soft Computing. Palma de Mallorca, Spain.

Mwaura, F. M. (2012). Adopting electricity prepayment billing system to reduce non-technical energy losses in Uganda: Lesson from Rwanda. *Utilities Policy*, *23*, 72–79. doi:10.1016/j.jup.2012.05.004

Nagi, J., Mohammad, A. M., Yap, K. S., Tiong, S. K., & Ahmed, S. K. (2008). Non-technical loss analysis for detection of electricity theft using support vector machines. In *Proceedings of the Power and Energy Conference, 2008*. IEEE. doi:10.1109/PECON.2008.4762604

Nagi, J., Siah Yap, K., Kiong Tiong, S., Ahmed, S. K., & Nagi, F. (2011). Improving SVM-based nontechnical loss detection in power utility using the fuzzy inference system. *IEEE Transactions on Power Delivery*, *26*(2), 1284–1285. doi:10.1109/TPWRD.2010.2055670

Nagi, J., Yap, K. S., Kiong Tiong, S., Ahmed, S. K., & Mohamad, M. (2010). Nontechnical loss detection for metered customers in power utility using support vector machines. *IEEE Transactions on Power Delivery*, *25*(2), 1162–1171. doi:10.1109/TPWRD.2009.2030890

Nagi, J., Yap, K. S., Nagi, F., Tiong, S. K., Koh, S. P., & Ahmed, S. K. (2010). NTL detection of electricity theft and abnormalities for large power consumers. In *Proceedings of the 2010 IEEE Student Conference on Research and Development (SCOReD)*. IEEE. doi:10.1109/SCORED.2010.5704002

Nagi, J., Yap, K. S., Tiong, S. K., Ahmed, S. K., & Mohammad, A. M. (2008). Detection of abnormalities and electricity theft using genetic support vector machines. In *Proceedings of the TENCON 2008 - 2008 IEEE Region 10 Conference*. IEEE. doi:10.1109/TENCON.2008.4766403

Nizar, A. H., & Dong, Z. Y. (2009). Identification and detection of electricity customer behaviour irregularities. In *Proceedings of the Power Systems Conference and Exposition, 2009*. IEEE. doi:10.1109/PSCE.2009.4840253

Nizar, A. H., Dong, Z. Y., Jalaluddin, M., & Raffles, M. J. (2006). Load profiling method in detecting non-technical loss activities in a power utility. In *Proceedings of the Power and Energy Conference, 2006*. IEEE. doi:10.1109/PECON.2006.346624

Nizar, A. H., Dong, Z. Y., & Wang, Y. (2008). Power utility nontechnical loss analysis with extreme learning machine method. *IEEE Transactions on Power Systems*, *23*(3), 946–955. doi:10.1109/TPWRS.2008.926431

Nizar, A. H., Dong, Z. Y., & Zhao, J. H. (2006). Load profiling and data mining techniques in electricity deregulated market. In *Proceedings of the IEEE Power Engineering Society General Meeting, 2006*. IEEE. doi:10.1109/PES.2006.1709335

Nizar, A. H., Dong, Z. Y., Zhao, J. H., & Zhang, P. (2007). A data mining based NTL analysis method. In *Proceedings of the IEEE Power Engineering Society General Meeting, 2007.* IEEE. doi:10.1109/PES.2007.385883

Nizar, A. H., Hua Zhao, J., & Yang Dong, Z. (2006). Customer information system data preprocessing with feature selection techniques for non-technical losses prediction in an electricity market. In *Proceedings of the International Conference on Power System Technology, 2006.* IEEE. doi:10.1109/ICPST.2006.321964

Nizar, A. H., Yang Dong, Z., & Zhang, P. (2008). Detection rules for non technical losses analysis in power utilities. In *Proceedings of the 2008 IEEE Power and Energy Society General Meeting - Conversion and Delivery of Electrical Energy in the 21st Century.* IEEE. doi:10.1109/PES.2008.4596300

Openshaw, D. (2008). Smart metering an energy networks perspective. In *Proceedings of the 2008 IET Seminar on Smart Metering - Gizmo or Revolutionary Technology.* IET.

Özçelik, M. H., Işik, M., Duman, E., & Çevik, T. (2010). Improving a credit card fraud detection system using genetic algorithm. In *Proceedings of the 2010 International Conference on Networking and Information Technology* (ICNIT). IEEE. doi:10.1109/ICNIT.2010.5508478

Raghunath, B. R., & Mahadeo, S. N. (2008). Network intrusion detection system (NIDS). In *Proceedings of the First International Conference on Emerging Trends in Engineering and Technology, 2008.* IEEE. doi:10.1109/ICETET.2008.252

Ramos, C. C. O., de Sousa, A. N., Papa, J. P., & Falcão, A. X. (2011). A new approach for nontechnical losses detection based on optimum-path forest. *IEEE Transactions on Power Systems, 26*(1), 181–189. doi:10.1109/TPWRS.2010.2051823

Ramos, C. C. O., Papa, J. P., Souza, A. N., Chiachia, G., & Falcao, A. X. (2011). What is the importance of selecting features for non-technical losses identification? In *Proceedings of the 2011 IEEE International Symposium on Circuits and Systems* (ISCAS). IEEE. doi:10.1109/ISCAS.2011.5937748

Ramos, C. C. O., Souza, A. N., Papa, J. P., & Falcao, A. X. (2009). Fast non-technical losses identification through optimum-path forest. In *Proceedings of the 15th International Conference on Intelligent System Applications to Power Systems, 2009.* IEEE. doi:10.1109/ISAP.2009.5352910

Rebahi, Y., Nassar, M., Magedanz, T., & Festor, O. (2011). A survey on fraud and service misuse in voice over IP (VoIP) networks. *Information Security Technical Report, 16*(1), 12–19. doi:10.1016/j.istr.2010.10.012

Richardson, R. (1997). Neural networks compared to statistical techniques. In *Proceedings of the Computational Intelligence for Financial Engineering (CIFEr).* IEEE.

Sahin, Y., Bulkan, S., & Duman, E. (2013). A cost-sensitive decision tree approach for fraud detection. *Expert Systems with Applications, 40*(15), 5916–5923. doi:10.1016/j.eswa.2013.05.021

Sahin, Y., & Duman, E. (2011). Detecting credit card fraud by ANN and logistic regression. In *Proceedings of the 2011 International Symposium on Innovations in Intelligent Systems and Applications* (INISTA). IEEE. doi:10.1109/INISTA.2011.5946108

Seo, D., Lee, H., & Nuwere, E. (2013). SIPAD: SIP–VoIP anomaly detection using a stateful rule tree. *Computer Communications, 36*(5), 562–574. doi:10.1016/j.comcom.2012.12.004

Seyedhossein, L., & Hashemi, M. R. (2010). Mining information from credit card time series for timelier fraud detection. In *Proceedings of the 2010 5th International Symposium on Telecommunications* (IST). IEEE. doi:10.1109/ISTEL.2010.5734099

Taniguchi, M., Haft, M., Hollmen, J., & Tresp, V. (1998). Fraud detection in communication networks using neural and probabilistic methods. In *Proceedings of the 1998 IEEE International Conference on Acoustics, Speech and Signal Processing.* IEEE. doi:10.1109/ICASSP.1998.675496

Weatherford, M. (2002). Mining for fraud. *IEEE Intelligent Systems*, *17*(4), 4–6. doi:10.1109/MIS.2002.1024744

Wilks, A. J. (1990). Hall effect based electrical energy metering device with fraud detection and instantaneous voltage, current and power outputs. In *Proceedings of the Sixth International Conference on Metering Apparatus and Tariffs for Electricity Supply*. IET.

Wu, L., Ping, R., Ke, L., & Hai-xin, D. (2011). Intrusion detection using SVM. In *Proceedings of the 2011 7th International Conference on Wireless Communications, Networking and Mobile Computing* (WiCOM). IEEE. doi:10.1109/wicom.2011.6040153

Xu, W., Pang, Y., Ma, J., Wang, S.-Y., Hao, G., Zeng, S., & Qian, Y.-H. (2008). Fraud detection in telecommunication: A rough fuzzy set based approach. In *Proceedings of the 2008 International Conference on Machine Learning and Cybernetics*. IEEE. doi:10.1109/ICMLC.2008.4620596

Xue, M., & Zhu, C. (2009). Applied research on data mining algorithm in network intrusion detection. In *Proceedings of the International Joint Conference on Artificial Intelligence, 2009*. IEEE. doi:10.1109/JCAI.2009.25

Yue, D., Wu, X., Wang, Y., Li, Y., & Chu, C.-H. (2007). A review of data mining-based financial fraud detection research. In *Proceedings of the International Conference on Wireless Communications, Networking and Mobile Computing*. IEEE. doi:10.1109/WICOM.2007.1352

Zhang, Y., Chen, W., & Black, J. (2011). Anomaly detection in premise energy consumption data. In *Proceedings of the 2011 IEEE Power and Energy Society General Meeting*. IEEE. doi:10.1109/PES.2011.6039858

ADDITIONAL READING

Aggarwal, C. C., & Zhai, C. (2012). *Mining Text Data*. Springer. doi:10.1007/978-1-4614-3223-4

Banchs, R. E. (2013). *Text Mining with MATLAB*. Springer. doi:10.1007/978-1-4614-4151-9

Berry, M. W. (2004). *Survey of Text Mining I: Clustering, Classification, and Retrieval*. Springer.

Berry, M. W., & Castellanos, M. (2008). *Survey of Text Mining II: Clustering, Classification, and Retrieval*. Springer.

Berry, M. W., & Kogan, J. (2010). *Text Mining: Applications and Theory*. John Wiley & Sons.

Dawid, P., Lauritzen, S. L., & Spiegelhalter, D. J. (2007). *Probabilistic Networks and Expert Systems: Exact Computational Methods for Bayesian Networks*. Springer.

Eberhart, R. C., & Shi, Y. (2011). *Computational Intelligence: Concepts to Implementations*. Elsevier.

Elder, J., Hill, T., Delen, D., & Fast, A. (2012). *Practical Text Mining and Statistical Analysis for Non-Structured Text Data Applications*. Academic Press.

Feldman, R., & Sanger, J. (2007). *The Text Mining Handbook: Advanced Approaches in Analyzing Unstructured Data.* Cambridge University Press.

Gallant, S. I. (1993). *Neutral network learning and expert systems.* MIT Press.

Gibbons, J. D., & Chakraborti, S. (2003). Nonparametric Statistical Inference, Fourth Ed.: Revised and Expanded. CRC Press.

Giudici, P., & Figini, S. (2009). *Applied Data Mining for Business and Industry.* John Wiley & Sons. doi:10.1002/9780470745830

Gorunescu, F. (2011). *Data Mining: Concepts, Models and Techniques.* Springer. doi:10.1007/978-3-642-19721-5

Gottlob, G., & Nejdl, W. (1990). *Expert Systems in Engineering: Principles and Applications.* Springer. doi:10.1007/3-540-53104-1

Hand, D. J., Mannila, H., & Smyth, P. (2001). *Principles of Data Mining.* MIT Press.

Hayes-Roth, F., & Lenat, D. B. (1983). *Building expert systems.* Addison-Wesley Pub. Co.

Ibrahim, M., Küng, J., & Revell, N. (2000). *Database and Expert Systems Applications: 11th International Conference, DEXA 2000 London, UK, September 4-8, 2000 Proceedings.* Springer.

Kao, A., & Poteet, S. R. (2007). *Natural Language Processing and Text Mining.* Springer. doi:10.1007/978-1-84628-754-1

Klahr, P., & Waterman, D. A. (1986). *Expert systems: techniques, tools, and applications.* Addison-Wesley Pub. Co.

Konar, A. (2005). *Computational Intelligence: Principles, Techniques and Applications.* Springer.

Krishnamoorthy, C. S., & Rajeev, S. (1996). *Artificial Intelligence and Expert Systems for Engineers.* CRC PressINC.

Liebowitz, J. (1988). *Introduction to Expert Systems.* Mitchell Publishing.

Liebowitz, J. (1998). *The Handbook of Applied Expert Systems.* CRC PressINC.

Lucas, P., & Gaag, L. V. D. (1991). *Principles of Expert Systems.* Addison-Wesley.

Marik, V., Retschitzegger, W., & Stepankova, O. (2003). *Database and Expert Systems Applications: 14th International Conference, DEXA 2003, Prague, Czech Republic, September 1-5, 2003, Proceedings.* Springer.

Olson, D. L., & Delen, D. (2008). *Advanced data mining techniques* [electronic resource]. Springer.

Pace, L., & Salvan, A. (1997). *Principles of Statistical Inference: From a Neo-Fisherian Perspective.* World Scientific.

Parthasarathy, S. (2010). *Enterprise Information Systems and Implementing IT Infrastructures: Challenges and Issues.* IGI Global Snippet. doi:10.4018/978-1-61520-625-4

Rohatgi, V. K. (2003). *Statistical Inference.* Courier Dover Publications.

Rutkowski, L. (2008). *Computational Intelligence: Methods and Techniques.* Springer.

Segura, J. M., & Reiter, A. C. (2011). *Expert System Software: Engineering, Advantages and Applications.* Nova Science Publisher's, Incorporated.

Shafer, G. (1996). *Probabilistic Expert Systems.* SIAM. doi:10.1137/1.9781611970043

Shapiro, A. D. (1987). *Structured Induction in Expert Systems.* Turing Inst. Press.

Slatter, P. E. (1987). *Building expert systems: cognitive emulation.* Ellis Horwood.

Sol, H. G., Takkenberg, C. A. T., & Robbé, P. F. de V. (1987). Expert Systems and Artificial Intelligence in Decision Support Systems. Springer.

Srivastava, A., & Sahami, M. (2010). *Text Mining: Classification, Clustering, and Applications*. CRC Press.

Tommelein, I. D. (1997). *Expert Systems for Civil Engineers: Integration Issues*. ASCE Publications.

Turban, E., & Frenzel, L. E. (1992). *Expert Systems and Applied Artificial Intelligence*. Macmillan Publishing Company.

Turban, E., & Watkins, P. R. (1988). *Applied expert systems*. North-Holland.

Weiss, S. M., Indurkhya, N., & Zhang, T. (2010). *Fundamentals of Predictive Text Mining*. Springer. doi:10.1007/978-1-84996-226-1

Williams, G. J., & Simoff, S. J. (2006). *Data Mining: Theory, Methodology, Techniques, and Applications*. Springer.

Witten, I. H., Frank, E., & Hall, M. A. (2011). *Data Mining: Practical Machine Learning Tools and Techniques: Practical Machine Learning Tools and Techniques*. Elsevier.

KEY TERMS AND DEFINITIONS

Data Mining: Data mining is the discovery of interesting, unexpected or valuable structures in large datasets.

Neural Network: Neural networks imitate the brain's ability to sort out patterns and learn from trial and error, discerning and extracting the relationships that underlie the data with which it is presented.

Non-Technical Losses: The non-technical losses (NTLs) in power utilities are defined as any consumed energy or service which is not billed because of measurement equipment failure or ill-intentioned and fraudulent manipulation of said equipment.

Power Utility: Industry dedicated to the power distribution.

Rule-Based Expert Systems: An expert system based on a set of rules that a human expert would follow in diagnosing or analysis problems.

Statistical Inference: Statistical inference is the process of drawing conclusions from data that is subject to random variation.

Text Mining: Text mining deals with the machine supported analysis of text, it uses techniques from information retrieval, information extraction as well as natural language processing (NLP) and connects them with the algorithms and methods of Knowledge Discovery in Databases (KDD), data mining, machine learning and statistics.

Chapter 9
Graphical Evaluation and Review Technique (GERT):
The Panorama in the Computation and Visualization of Network-Based Project Management

Ramesh Kannan
VIT Chennai, India

ABSTRACT

This chapter focuses primarily on Graphical Evaluation and Review Technique (GERT), one of the intriguing techniques used for network-based management. It is a stochastic network technique and has many advantages over the conventional Critical Path Method (CPM) and Programme Evaluation and Review Techniques used for project management. The formulation of the GERT network for linear situation can be development by analytical techniques (such as signal flow graph theory); thus for a non-linear and other complex conditions, the Q-GERT (included Queueing Concepts) is used. To reinforce the importance of GERT and Q-GERT, a firm study is carried out on the limitations of the CPM and PERT. Thus, a solid comparison of GERT network with the CPM and PERT network is done not only to emphasize the applicability of the network but also to validate of the network. The scheduling of concrete formwork systems are considered for the comparison.

DOI: 10.4018/978-1-4666-4940-8.ch009

INTRODUCTION

The representation of activities in a project in the form of network is one of the most important and simplest techniques adapted in the project management. The reasons for the adaptation of network-based project management are

- it can be used to model complex project by fragmenting into simpler network of inter-related activities of the entire systems,
- the computation of the project attributes requires minimum time and are highly reliable,
- it serves as a better communication aid among different project associates involved in the project,
- above all it is the best method of data visualisation and specifying data requirement for the modelling, analysis and design of multifarious projects.

The network-based project management has wide range of applications includes Industrial Engineering, production and manufacturing, contract management, construction project management, operation research, software project management and so on (Pristker, 1977). The most popular and commonly used techniques in the network-based project management are Critical Path Method (CPM) and Programme Evaluation and Review Technique (PERT). However these techniques have inherent drawbacks that the results obtained are not highly reliable and thus an intriguing technique which incorporates the human-factor (Pristker, 1977) into consideration is needed. One such network technique is the Graphical Evaluation and Review Technique (GERT). This chapter illustrates the advantages of GERT over CPM and PERT. The GERT technique is applied to the scheduling of concrete formwork systems to reinforce the importance of GERT over other project network techniques.

PROJECT NETWORK TECHNIQUES

Critical Path Method (CPM)

The Critical Path Method (CPM) was first developed by Morgan R. Walker of the Engineering Services Division of DuPont and James E. Kelly Jr. of Remington Rand in 1957 (Baboulene, 1970). Later was developed considering not only the logical dependencies between the activities but also the inclusion of resource related to each activity. CPM is generally regarded as the activity oriented networks.

The CPM includes categorization of all activities in the project known as work breakdown structure by a technique called arrow diagramming (Martino, 1970), determination of duration of the activities, determination of critical activities (activities having maximum duration) and the formulation of Critical Path (path associated with the critical activities) in otherwords the path associated with the longer duration as shown in Figure 1. Ultimately the network is modeled as a linear relationship between cost and time.

The most important thing to be considered in the CPM is that it is can be applied only to the activities associated with the deterministic durations (Baboulene, 1970). The CPM can be used to obtain feasible solution for the Least-cost scheduling. However, CPM accounts only for the determination of the earliest completion time but not probable completion time of the project.

Activity-on-arrow technique used to compute CPM was still in use however the Activity-on-node is mostly preferred as shown in Figure 2.

The CPM is very effective but suffers seriously on the fact that it requires deterministic time, however the project durations cannot be altered or incase of any delay in the project, it is highly difficult to resolve or retrieve the activities and sometimes it would even lead to the collapse of entire network.

Figure 1. Typical CPM network diagram (Single-time estimate)

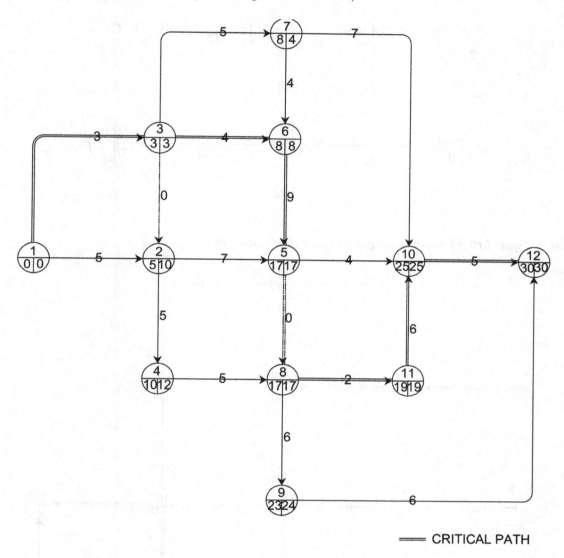

=== CRITICAL PATH

Programme Evaluation and Review Technique (PERT)

The PERT was developed later in 1958 by the Special Project Office of the U.S. Navy Bureau of Ordnance in association with the management consulting firm of Booz-Allen and Hamilton for managing the Polaris Missile program. PERT is generally a statistical network technique that has three important components such as time, resources and technical performance specifications (Miller, 1963).

The time assumed for the analysis is probabilistic time (Optimistic Time, Most-likely time, Pessimistic Time) than the deterministic time as in the case of CPM as in Figure 3. Thus the PERT is known as three time estimate and it is advantageous over CPM since it not incorporates the duration of any network with some degree of uncertainty but also provides the information

Figure 2. Graphical representation of the (a) Activity-on-arrow diagram, (b) Activity-on-node diagram

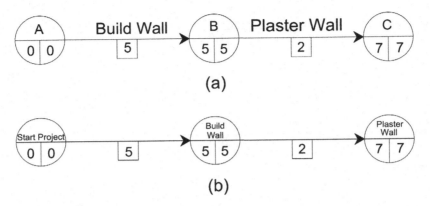

Figure 3. Typical PERT network diagram (Three-time estimate)

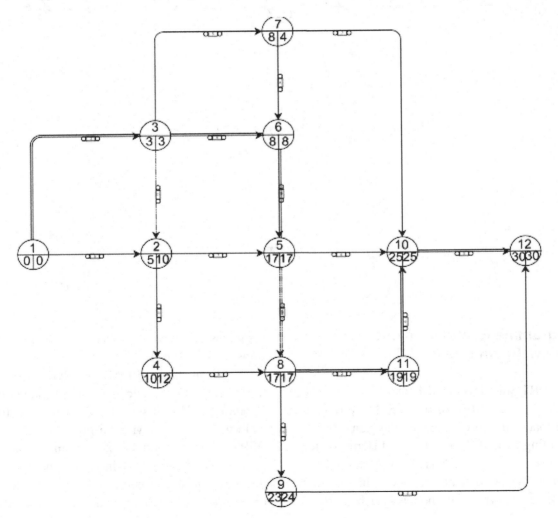

Figure 4. Conceptual diagram of looping error in CPM/PERT network

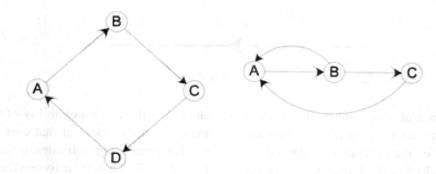

regarding the probable completion time of the project (Miller, 1963).

Although CPM and PERT were developed independently and from different origins, the methods adopted for computation are quite similar. In current practice, the words PERT and CPM are sometimes used interchangeably. However PERT was originally developed for control and reporting of complex research and development projects but both the methods computes the critical path in the similar fashion. PERT calculates the expected value of activity duration as a weighted average of the three estimates. The optimistic and pessimistic activity times, t_o and t_p are about equally likely to occur as in eqn.1. The probability of completion of the projects is calculated using Eqn.2.

$$t_e = \frac{t_0 + 4t_m + t_p}{6} \qquad (1)$$

$$Z = \frac{T_s - T_E}{\tilde{A}} \qquad (2)$$

where, t_e, t_o, t_m, t_p = expected, optimistic, most likely and pessimistic activity times; Ts, T_E = scheduled completion and earliest expected time, Z = probability factor, A. standard deviation.

Limitations of CPM and PERT

Both PERT and CPM has an inherent drawback that the network must be acyclic that is no cycles or loops can occur as in Figure 4. Though the looping of activities eliminates the discrepancies in the early stage of the project however it is considered as an error (Moder et al., 1967).

The CPM network is determinate in nature, and PERT network incorporates the concept of probability in the project duration. However there are other areas of uncertainty in project networks (Moder et al., 1967). Thus an intriguing method which incorporates not only the looping of activities but also the provision for uncertainty in the project network is required. Once such method which has these characteristics was first described in 1966 by Dr.A.A.B.Pritsker of Purdue University and W.W.Happ known as Graphical Evaluation Review Technique (GERT) during the development of procedures for automatic checkout equipment for the Apollo Program.

GRAPHICAL EVALUATION AND REVIEW TECHNIQUE (GERT)

GERT is a stochastic network analysis technique that allows for conditional and the probabilistic treatment of the logical relationships between the project's activities following randomly de-

Figure 5. Symbolic representation of directed branch (without the nodes) in GERT network

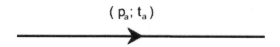

termined sequence of observations. The logical relationships between the project's activities are primarily based on the dependency between the two project activities or the dependency between a project activity and milestone.

The key objective of the GERT is to evaluate on the basis of the network logic and estimated duration of the activity and derive inference about some activities that may not be performed.

GERT Network Representation

The components of stochastic networks are branches (arcs, edges, transmittances) and logical nodes (vertices). A directed branch has associated with it one node from which it emanates and one node at which it terminates.

Two parameters are associated with a branch: (1) the probability that a branch is taken, P_a, given that the node from which it emanated is realized; and (2) a time, t_a, required, if the branch is taken, to accomplish the activity which the branch represents.

The t_a can be a random variable. If the branch is not a part of the realization of the network then the time for the activity represented by the branch is zero. The visual representation of a directed branch (without the nodes) is shown in Figure 5.

A node in a stochastic network consists of an input function (receiving, contributive) and an output function (emitting, distributive). These nodes are called Probabilistic Nodes. These nodes differ from the nodes used in the ordinary project network (i.e., events). The significance of these nodes is that certain nodes may be released when one or more (but necessary all) activities leading into them are completed. These networks also show that there is a possibility of probabilistic exists from the node; in that case only one of several proceeding activities is actually taken (Wiest, 2008). Thus, the activities themselves may be probabilistic, occurring with some probability which may be less than 1.

In GERT, the most extensively developed and widely studied system employing probabilistic networks, nodes are considered to have an input and output function, each characterized by certain logical relations with respect to connecting activities (Wiest, 2008). GERT considers three logical input functions and two logical output functions are shown in Tables 1 and 2.

These input and output functions can be combined to form six different types of nodes as shown in Figure 6.

Topology of GERT Network

Before we describe the GERT network, let us consider a simple GERT network representing a Cricket match involving the scoring of runs by two batsmen (Striker and Runner) after the ball being hit by the striker as in Figure 7. In the act of scoring both batsmen must complete a run. Even if one gets out which would result in no scoring.

For the node S to be realized, both branches leading into it must be realized (AND node). Node F will be realized if either branch incident to it is realized (INCLUSIVE-OR). This represents a simple model. However the node S can be branched into many nodes as in Figure 8.

Thus from the above extended GERT network, the node R1 is deterministic since for all the branches emanating from S will be realized. That is once a run is completed by the batsmen, the

Table 1. Logical input functions in GERT network

S.No.	Symbol	Name	Characteristics
1.		AND	The node is realized when all branches leading into it is realized.
2.		INCLUSIVE-OR	The node is realized when any branches leading into it is realized.
3.		EXCLUSIVE-OR	The node is realized when any branches leading into it is realized, under the condition that only one branch can be realized at a given time.

Table 2. Logical output functions in GERT network

S.No.	Symbol	Name	Characteristics
1.		DETERMINSTIC	All the branches emanating from the node are taken if the node is realized.
2.		PROBABILISTIC	Exactly one branch emanating from the node is taken if the node is realized.

Figure 6. Graphical representation of different types of nodes in GERT network

Figure 7. Sample GERT network representing an activity in a Cricket match

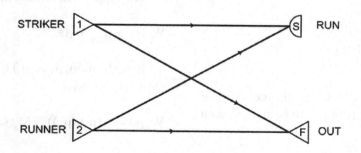

Figure 8. Sample GERT network representing an activity in a Cricket match (with an extension)

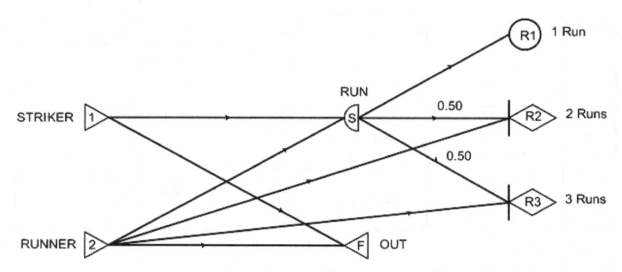

default score will be one. In case of additional runs, a probability of say 0.5 each is associated with the nodes R2 and R3.

The input function of R2 can be further considered from other parameters such as speed of the bastmen, no fielders in the spot or even poor fielding. Such factors are generally taken when we consider the entire match in the GERT network. However this is a generic example illustrates the basic concept in modeling of the GERT networks.

() Consider a network G = (N,A) with only GERT nodes in the set N. Let the random variable Y_{ij} be the duration and f_{ij} be the conditional probability (incase of discrete function) or density function (incase of continuous function) of the activity (i,j) as in Figure 9.

The conditional moment generating function of the random variable Y_{ij} is defined as M_{ij}.

$$M_{ij}(s) = \begin{cases} \int e^{sy_{ij}} f(y_{ij}) dy_{ij} \\ \sum e^{sy_{ij}} f(y_{ij}) \end{cases} \qquad (3)$$

Now let us consider p_{ij} be the conditional probability that activity (i,j) will be under-taken

given that node i is realized. The W-function of the random variable is defined as

$$W_{ij}(s) = p_{ij \, x} \, M_{ij}(s) \qquad (4)$$

Branches in Series

Consider the simple network as shown in Figure 10. This network consists of two branches in series. These two branches can be substituted by an equivalent branch as indicated. The original branches have W-transformations as follows.

$$W_{ij}(s) = p_{ij \, x} \, M_{ij}(s) \qquad (5)$$

$$W_{jk}(s) = p_{jk \, x} \, M_{jk}(s) \qquad (6)$$

The equivalent branch (i,k) has w-function is

$$W_{ik}(s) = p_{ik \, x} \, M_{ik}(s)$$

By definition, $p_{ik} = (p_{ij}).(p_{jk})$ and $M_{ik}=[M_{ij}(s)].[Mjk(s)]$, we have

$$W_{ik}(s) = [((p_{ij}).(p_{jk}))_x (M_{ij}(s).Mjk(s))]$$

Figure 9. Generalized GERT network

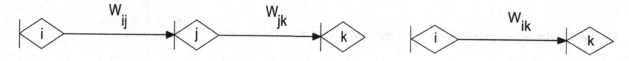

Figure 10. Branches in series and their equivalent representation

$$W_{ik}(s) = [(p_{ij}. M_{ij}(s))_x (p_{jk}.Mjk(s))]$$

Therefore, $W_{ik}(s) = W_{ij}(s).W_{jk}(s)$ \quad (7)

The equivalent branch has a W-function equal to the product of the W-functions of the branches in series.

Branches in Parallel

Consider the simple network as shown in Figure 11. This network consists of two branches in parallel. These two branches can be substituted by an equivalent branch as indicated. The original branches have W-transformations as follows.

$$W_{ij}(s) = p_{ij\,x} M_{ij}(s)$$

By definition, $p_{ij} = [(p_a)+(p_b)]$ and

$$M_{ij}(s) = \left[\frac{p_a M_a(s) + p_b M_b(s)}{p_a + p_b}\right]$$

$$W_{ij}(s) = [((p_a)+(p_b)).(\frac{p_a M_a(s) + p_b M_b(s)}{p_a + p_b})]$$

$$W_{ij}(s) = p_a M_a(s)+p_b M_b(s)$$

$$W_{ij}(s) = W_a(s)+W_b(s) \quad (8)$$

The equivalent branch has a W-function equal to the sum of the W-functions of the branches in parallel.

Branches in Loops

A Loop is a connected sequence directed branches with every node being common to exactly two branches (Pristker, 1966). A loop is usually referred to as a first-order loop to indicate that it does not contain another loop and that each node can be reached from every other node. The loops can be of single-loop or multiple loops system (Phillips et al., 1981).

1. Self-Loop

A self-loop can be viewed as a degenerate first-order loop (Pristker, 1966). Consider the simple network as shown in Figure 12. This network consists of one self-loop and one arc and can also be reduced to an equivalent one-arc network.

$$W_{ij}(s) = p_{ij\,x} M_{ij}(s)$$

By definition, $p_{ii} = [(p_a)+(p_b)]$, $p_{ij} = [(p_b)]$,
$M_{ii}(s) = \left[(M_a(s).M_b(s))\right]$,
$M_{ij}(s) = \left[(M_b(s))\right]$

Figure 11. Branches in parallel and their equivalent representation

Figure 12. Branches in parallel and their equivalent representation

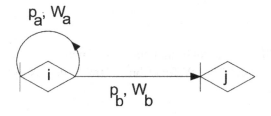

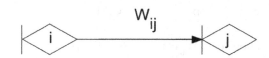

$W_{ij}(s) = [(p_{ij\,x}\,M_{ij}(s)) + (p_{ii\,x}\,M_{ii}(s))]$

$W_{ij}(s) = [(p_{b\,x}\,M_b(s)) + ((p_{a\,x}\,M_a(s) \cdot p_{b\,x}\,M_b(s))]$

$$W_{ij}(s) = W_b + W_a W_b \qquad (9)$$

The above result can be used to generate equivalent branch of a loop in the GERT network and as follows.

$$W_{ij}(s) = W_b + W_a W_b + \cdots = W_b[1 + \sum_{m=1}^{\infty} W_a^m]$$

The above equation can be simplified using binomial series as follows.

$$(1-W_a(s))^{-1} = 1 + W_a(s) + W_a^2 + W_a^3 + \ldots =$$
$$1 + \sum_{m=1}^{\infty} W_a^m$$

$$W_{ij}(s) = W_b(s)[1-W_a(s)]^{-1}$$

$$W_{ij}(s) = \frac{W_b(s)}{\left[1 - W_a(s)\right]} \qquad (10)$$

If a looping involves multiple nodes can be reduced to a self-loop using the equation and can be analyzed as before.

2. Multiple-Loops

In many situations we may encounter a GERT network with multiple loops. Consider the simple network as shown in Figure 13. This network consists of multiple loops and can also be reduced to an equivalent one-arc network (Pristker, 1966).

FORMULATION OF GERT NETWORK

The following is the detailed methodology adopted for the formulation of GERT networks.

1. Representation of the system as a stochastic network with GERT nodes,

Figure 13. Branches in parallel and their equivalent representation

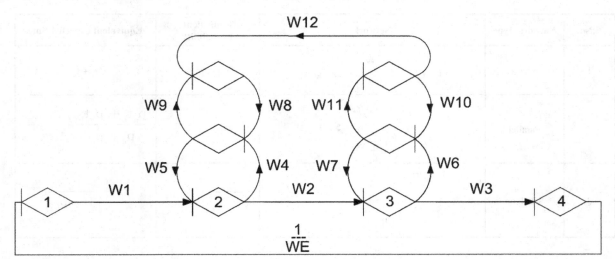

2. Determination conditional probabilities and moment generating functions for all branches of the network,
3. Computation of W-function for all the branches of the network,
4. Reduction of network to an equivalent one-branch network.
5. Conversion of the equivalent function into the following performance measures of the network:
   ○ The probability that a specific node is realized and
   ○ The Moment Generating Function (M.G.F) of the time associated with an equivalent network.
6. Make inferences concerning the system under study from the information obtained from the performance measure of the network.

GERT network in series and parallel are already discussed. The equivalent probability and the equivalent expected time and expected moment generating functions using basic network analysis, topological equations and random variables respectively for the network reductions (Phillips et al., 1981) are tabulated in Tables 3, 4, and 5.

Q-GERT

Analytical techniques were used to formulate the GERT network models of linear system through flow graph-theory. However for the non-linear systems involving complex logic and Queueing systems, Queueing Graphical Evaluation and Review Technique (Q-GERT) was developed later, allowing the user to consider queueing within the system and the simulation of the network is performed inorder obtain statistical estimates of the measure of interest.

Application of GERT and Q-GERT

To reinforce the importance of GERT network over CPM and PERT, the scheduling of concrete formwork systems is considered. The scheduling of formwork system is the complicated process in the reinforced concrete construction. It includes repeated activities; the complexity gets increases when the number of stories gets also increased. Generally CPM schedule is employed for the concrete formwork construction (Horowitz, 1963) and is shown in Figure 14. The GERT network schedule is shown in Figures 15 and 16.

Table 3. Equivalence Calculation of Basic GERT network

S.No.	Network Type	Network	Equivalent Probability	Equivalent expected time
1	Series	$\overset{W_{ik}}{i \longrightarrow k}$	$p_a \cdot p_b$	$t_a + t_b$
2	Parallel	$i \overset{p_a, W_a}{\underset{p_b, W_b}{\rightleftarrows}} j$	$p_a + p_b$	$\dfrac{p_a t_a + p_b t_b}{p_a + p_b}$
3	Self-loop	$i \overset{p_a, W_a}{\underset{p_b, W_b}{\circlearrowleft \longrightarrow}} j$	$\dfrac{p_a}{1 - p_b}$	$ta + \dfrac{p_a}{1 - p_b} t_b$

Table 4. Network reduction employing the topological equations

S.No.	Network Type	Paths	Loops	Equivalent Function W_E	Equivalent M.G.F, ME(s)
1	Series	$W_a W_b$	-	$W_a \cdot W_b$	$e^{s(t_a + t_b)}$
2	Parallel	$W_a ; W_b$	-	$W_a + W_b$	$[p_a + p_b] [pa\, e^{st_a} + p_b e^{st_b}]$
3	Self-loop	W_a	W_b	$\dfrac{W_a}{1 - W_b}$	$(1 - p_b)\, e^{st_a} [1 - p_b e^{st_b}]^{-1}$

Table 5. Network reduction using stochastic time interval

S.No.	Network Type	Equivalent function	Equivalent MGF
1	Series	$p_a p_b M_a(s) M_b(s)$	$M_a(s) M_b(s)$
2	Parallel	$p_a \cdot M_a(s) + p_b \cdot M_b(s)$	$[p_a + p_b]^{-1} \cdot [p_a \cdot M_a(s) + p_b \cdot M_b(s)]$
3	Self-loop	$p_a \cdot M_a(s) [1 - p_b \cdot M_b(s)]^{-1}$	$(1 - p_b) M_a(s) [1 - p_b \cdot M_b(s)]^{-1}$

From the above networks, it is clear that the GERT & Q-GERT has additional information that could be used to track, update the network during the course of the project. Unlike CPM schedule the GERT schedule are flexible (Pristker, 1977) and hence it could be used for fragmenting the whole network into cluster of important activities. Thus the crashing of the network for the cost-time control is effective when using GERT network.

Figure 14. CPM schedule for concrete formwork construction

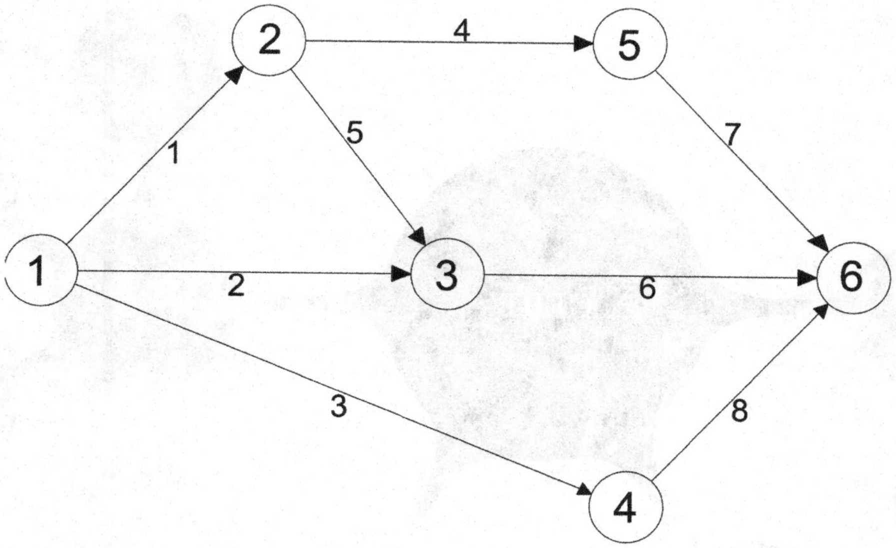

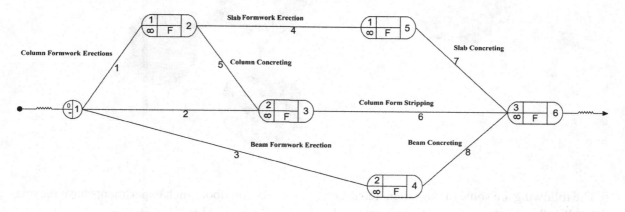

Figure 15. Q-GERT network for concrete formwork construction

FUTURE RESEARCH DIRECTIONS

The GERT network described in this chapter are generic however for advanced and complex systems more sophisticated GERT network should be generated. The following mind map illustrates the possible applications of GERT in the other disciplines as shown in Figure 16.

CONCLUSION

Compared to other project network techniques, GERT is only rarely used in complex systems. Nevertheless, the GERT approach addresses the majority of limitations associated with both CPM and PERT techniques. GERT allows loops between tasks and incorporate probabilistic nodes and thus considers the degree of uncertainty in the projects.

Figure 16. Conceptual mindmap of GERT networks

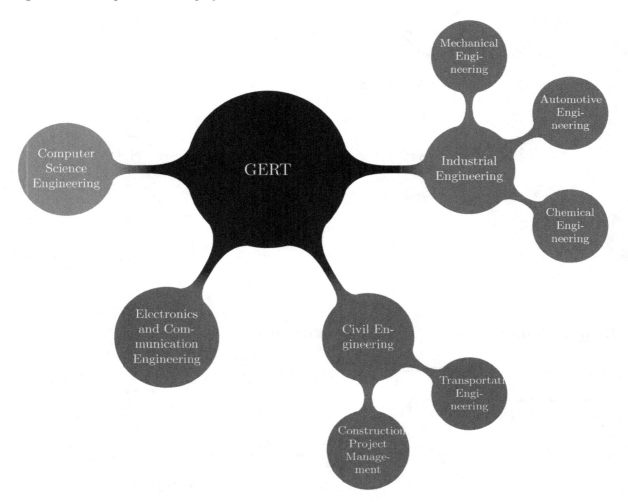

The following are some of the salient features of the GERT network over other techniques used in the network based project management.

- It could also be quite useful in speeding up action at each branching node in network, since the requirements and implications of each alternative decision are quite clear.
- Another potential use of GERT networks is in the planning and scheduling of the activities that are associated with the extremely expensive programs carried out in the hostile environments of space or on the

ocean floor. Such experiments have recycle loops and branching nodes.

- They play a key role in the data visualization of complex networks, incorporating the feedback loops and uncertainty in the operations. For example, incase of communication industry. The network congestion can be resolved using GERT network if incorporated.

Thus GERT is an intriguing technique for visualization and computation of network based project management.

REFERENCES

Baboulene, B. (1970). *Critical path made easy.* London: Gerald Duckworth & Company Limited.

Horowitz, J. (1967). *Critical path scheduling management control through CPM and PERT.* New York: The Ronald Press Company.

Martino, R. L. (1970). *Finding the critical path, project management and control.* New York: American Management Association.

Miller, R. W. (1963). *Schedule, cost, and profit control with PERT a comprehensive guide for program management.* New York: McGraw-Hill Book Company.

Moder, J. J., & Phillips, C. R. (1967). *Project management with CPM and PERT.* New York: Reinhold Publishing Corporation.

Phillips, D. T., & Garcia-Diaz, A. (1981). *Fundamentals of network analysis.* Upper Saddle River, NJ: Prentice Hall Inc.

Pritsker, A.A.B. (1966). *GERT: Graphical evaluation and review technique, memorandum.* RM-4973-NASA.

Pritsker, A. A. B. (1968). *GERT networks.* New York: The Projection Engineer.

Pritsker, A. A. B. (1977). *Modeling and analysis using Q-GERT networks.* New York: John Wiley & Sons.

Wiest, J. D., & Levy, F. K. (2008). *A management guide to CPM/PERT with GERT/PDM/DCPM and other networks.* New Delhi, India: Prentice-Hall of India.

KEY TERMS AND DEFINITIONS

CPM: The abbreviation CPM stands for Critical Path Method is a method to formulate the project network with deterministic time.

Formwork: Formwork is a mould which is used to cast concrete and to give definite structural shape and texture.

GERT: The acronym GERT stand for Graphical Evaluation and Review Technique is a method to formulate the project network with stochastic time.

PERT: The acronym PERT stand for Programme Evaluation and Review Technique is a method to formulate the project network with three times i.e., optimistic time, most likely time and pessimistic time.

Queueing Theory: It is the mathematical study of queueing theory and the waiting lines phenomenon.

Scheduling: Scheduling is the process of listing the entire activities of the project, its dependencies and start and finish time of the activities.

Stochastic: Stochastic mean randomness or non-deterministic. In GERT, the time is not constant, i.e., it follows stochastic time characteristics.

Section 3
Distributed Computing and Network Management

Chapter 10
Heuristic Resource Allocation Algorithms for Dynamic Load Balancing in Heterogeneous Distributed Computing System

Bibhudatta Sahoo
NIT Rourkela, India

Sanjay Kumar Jena
NIT Rourkela, India

Sudipta Mahapatra
IIT Karagpur, India

ABSTRACT

Distributed heterogeneous computing is being widely applied to a variety of large-size computational problems. These computational environments consist of multiple heterogeneous computing modules; these modules interact with each other to solve the problem. The load balancing problem in the Heterogeneous Distributed Computing System (HDCS) deals with allocation of tasks to computing nodes, so that computing nodes are evenly loaded. The complexity of dynamic load balancing increases with the size of HDCS and becomes difficult to solve effectively. Due to the complexity of the dynamic load balancing problem, the majority of researchers use a heuristic algorithm to obtain near optimal solutions. The authors use three different type of resource allocation heuristic techniques, namely greedy heuristic, simulated annealing, and genetic algorithm, for dynamic load balancing on HDCS. A new codification suitable to simulated annealing and the genetic algorithm has been introduced for dynamic load balancing on HDCS. This chapter demonstrates the use of the common coding scheme and iterative structure by simulated annealing and genetic algorithms for allocating the tasks among the computing nodes to minimize the makespan. The resource allocation algorithm uses sliding window techniques to select the tasks to be allocated to computing nodes in each iteration. A suitable codification for simulated annealing and genetic algorithm for dynamic load balancing strategy are explained along with implementation details. Consistent Expected Time to Compute (ETC) matrix is used to simulate the effect of the genetic algorithm-based dynamic load balancing scheme compared with first-fit, randomized heuristic, and simulated annealing.

DOI: 10.4018/978-1-4666-4940-8.ch010

1. INTRODUCTION

Distributed heterogeneous computing is being widely applied to a variety of large size computational problems. The large scale computing problems requires more computing time, which can be meat by utilizing the ideal computing time of the vast computing resources distributed over the globe. These computational environments are consists of multiple heterogeneous computing modules, these modules interact with each other to solve the problem. In a Heterogeneous distributed computing system (HDCS), processing loads arrive from many users at random time instants. A proper scheduling policy attempts to assign these loads to available computing nodes so as to complete the processing of all loads in the shortest possible time. Modern distributed computing technology includes clusters, the grid, service-oriented architecture, massively parallel processors, pear-to-peer networking, and cloud computing (Hwang 2012). The central *or serial scheduler* schedules the processes in a distributed system to make use of the system resources in such a manner that resource usage, response time, network congestion, and scheduling overhead are optimized. There are number of techniques and methodologies for scheduling processes of a distributed system. These are *task assignment, load-balancing, load-sharing* approaches (Wu 1999, Watts 1998). Due to heterogeneity of computing nodes, jobs encounter different execution times on different processors. Therefore, research should address scheduling in heterogeneous environment. Genetic algorithm have been proposed over the years for solving static and dynamic load balancing problems on distributed system.

In task assignment approach, each process submitted by a user for processing is viewed as a collection of related tasks and these tasks are scheduled to suitable nodes so as to improve performance. In load sharing approach simply attempts to conserve the ability of the system to perform work by assuring that no node is idle while processes wait for being processed. In load balancing approach, processes submitted by the users are distributed among the nodes of the system so as to equalize the workload among the nodes at any point of time. Processes might have to be migrated from one machine to another even in the middle of execution to ensure equal workload. Load balancing strategies may be static or dynamic (Grosu 2002, Ucar 2006, Wu 1999, Zomaya 20011). To improve the utilization of the processors, parallel computations require that processes be distributed to processors in such a way that the computational load is spread among the processors. Dynamic load distribution (also called load balancing, load sharing, or load migration) can be applied to restore balance (Spies 1996). In general, load-balancing algorithms can be broadly categorized as centralized or decentralized, dynamic or static, periodic or non-periodic, and those with thresholds or without thresholds (Casavant 1988, Dandamudi 1998, Wu 1999). Central scheduler or serial scheduler or load balancing service should be able to effectively control the computing resource for dynamic allocation to the tasks (Ghosh 2010). We have used a centralized load-balancing algorithm framework as it imposes fewer overheads on the system than the decentralized algorithm (Zomaya 2001).

The load-balancing problem aims to compute the assignment with smallest possible makespan (i.e. the completion time at the maximum loaded computing node). The load distribution problem is known to be NP-hard (Garey 1979) in most cases and therefore intractable with number of tasks and/or the computing node exceeds few units. Here, the load balancing is a job scheduling policy which takes a job as a whole and assign it to a computing node (Ahmad 1991, Braun 2008, Tseng 2009). The exponential solution space for the load balancing problem can searched using heuristic techniques(GA, Tabu search, SA) to obtained suboptimal solution in the acceptable time (Maheswaran 1999, Munetomo 1994, Lee 2006, Zomaya 2001). These Artificial intelligence techniques have been used by researchers and proven to be effective in solving many optimization problems. Simulated Annealing (SA), proposed by Kirkpatrick et al. (Kirkpatrick 1983), has been used as a popular heuristic to solve optimization problems. Genetic Algorithms are used as one the popular technique to search the solution space to obtain sub-optimal solution. The version of the heuristic used to design genetic algorithm was adapted from (Zomaya 2001) for load balancing on HDCS.

This chapter considers the problem of finding an optimal solution for load balancing in heterogeneous distributed system using Heuristic Resource Allocation Algorithms. The rest of the paper is organized as follows. *Section 2* highlights the contribution of various researchers in the related area of load balancing on distributed computing system and solving dynamic load balancing problem with simulated annealing and genetic algorithm.. *Section 3* discusses Heterogeneous distributed computing system (HDCS) structure and the linear programming formulation of load-balancing problem. *Section 4* describes the task model and stochastic iterative dynamic load balancing techniques for dynamic load distribution. *Section 5 and 6* outlines the design details of load balancing algorithm using simulated annealing and genetic algorithm respectively. Finally, conclusions and directions for future research are discussed in *Section 7*.

2. RELATED WORKS

Load balancing for distributed computing system is a problem that has been deeply studied for a long time. Different heuristic algorithms are used by researcher to find suboptimal solutions for homogeneous and heterogeneous distributed system. Dandamudi (1998) addressed dynamic load sharing in distributed systems and established that load sharing improves performance by moving work from heavily loaded nodes to lightly loaded nodes. An algorithmic approach to load balancing problem is presented in (Kafil 1998). Different form of linear programming formulation of the load balancing problem has been discussed along with greedy, randomized and approximation algorithm to produce sub-optimal solutions to the problem. The solution to this intractable problem was discussed under different algorithm paradigm. Modeling of optimal load balancing strategy using queuing theory was proposed by Francois Spies (Spies 1996). This is one of the pioneer works reported in the literature that presents an analytical model of dynamic load balancing techniques as M/M/k queue and simulate with fundamental parameters like load, number of nodes, transfer speed and overload rate (Spies 1996). Queuing-Theoretic models for parallel and distributed system can be found in (Boxma 1994, Caffrey 1995). General Job scheduling problem of n tasks with m machines, is presented as an optimization problem in (Kleinberg 2006) to minimize the makespan. Bora Ucar and *et al.* have considered the assignment of communicating tasks to heterogeneous processors(Ucar 2006), that uses a task clustering method based upon execution time to allocate the task though the heuristic techniques. A classification of iterative dynamic load balancing technique is discussed in (Xu 1997). An impact of heterogeneity using greedy algorithms with consistent ETC on HDCS can be found in (Sahoo 2013)

SA is a heuristic method that has been implemented to obtain good solutions of an objective function defined on a number of discrete optimization problems. Simulated Annealing (SA), proposed by Kirkpatrick et al. (Kirkpatrick 1983, Kalyanmoy 2004), has been used as a popular heuristic to solve several optimization problems to obtain sub-optimal solution. A heuristic algorithm based on simulated annealing is discussed (Liu 2007), which guarantees good load balancing on grid environment. A comparative study of the three algorithms (Hill-climbing, simulated annealing and genetic algorithms) is then carried out in (Tong 2009) considering performance criteria as the amount of search time. Makespan minimization of scheduling problem on identical parallel machines using simulated annealing has been presented by Lee and et al. in (Lee 2006). Grid Computing is one of heterogeneous distributed computing system geographically dispersed among several entities. Fidanova used simulated annealing to obtain near optimal solutions for scheduling problem in large grid (Fidanova 2006). Rahmani and Rezvani presented a genetic algorithm for static scheduling, which is again improved by simulated annealing to obtain an improvised solution (Rahmani 2009). They have also established that running time depends on the number of task.

Genetic algorithms(GAs) are used for searching exponential solutions space to find sub-optimal solution. A genetic algorithm operates with an appropriate mix of exploration and exploitation with the use of three operators: (i) selection, (ii) crossover, and (iii) mutation. Zomaya and Teh proposed a dynamic load balancing framework on genetic algorithm that uses central scheduler approach to handle all load balancing decisions (Zomaya 2001). Effectiveness of central server in load-balancing has been demonstrated for homogeneous distributed computing system. A batch-mode genetic scheduler has been used by Page and Naughton (Page 2005a, Page 2005b) to compare the performance with *batch-mode schedules* and *immediate-mode schedulers,* for heterogeneous task on HDCS. Researchers have examined, 11 different heuristics(Opportunistic Load Balancing, Minimum Execution Time, Minimum Completion Time, Min–min, Max–min, Duplex, Genetic Algorithm, Simulated Annealing, Genetic Simulated Annealing, Tabu, and A*) on Mixed-machine heterogeneous computing (HC) environments to minimize the total execution time of the metatask (Theys 2001). A GA based task allocation method has been proposed for multiple disjoint tasks in HDCS. Maximizing reliability of distributed computing system with task al-

location using genetic algorithm was discussed in (Vidyarthi 2001) with the task represented as task graph. This comparison on different heuristic through simulations proves the effectiveness of genetic algorithms on HDCS. Simulated annealing has been used to solve unconstrained and bound-constrained optimization problems. Greene presented a dynamic load-balancing genetic algorithm with three variations i.e. number of processor, number of task to be schedule, and distribution duration of task, to minimize makespan on multiple machines (Greene 2001). Several researchers used SA and GA for load balancing on distributed computing system; however majority of the papers have no specific representation for simulated annealing and genetic algorithm. This chapter presents detail frame work for the simulated annealing algorithm to solve dynamic load balancing problem using ETC matrix for n number of tasks on m computing nodes.

3. HETEROGENEOUS DISTRIBUTED COMPUTING SYSTEM MODEL

Heterogeneous Distributed Computing System

Heterogeneous distributed computing system (HDCS) utilizes a distributed suite of different high-performance nodes, interconnected with high-speed links, to perform different computationally intensive applications that have diverse computational requirements (Maheswaran 1998, Liu 2007, Lin 1992, Siegel 2000, Zeng 2006). Distributed computing provides the capability for the utilization of remote computing resources and allows for increased levels of flexibility, reliability, and modularity (Choi 2003, Attiya 2006, Xu 1994). In heterogeneous distributed computing system the computational power of the computing entities are possibly different for each processor as shown in Figure 1. A large heterogeneous distributed computing system (HDCS) consists of

Figure 1. Heterogeneous distributed computing system with central scheduler

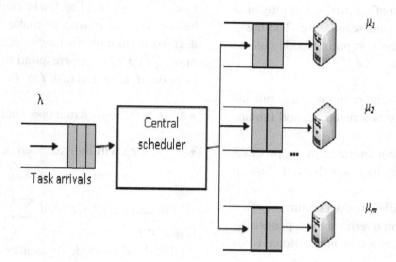

potentially millions of heterogeneous computing nodes connected by the global Internet.

The applicability and strength of HDCS are derived from their ability to meet computing needs to appropriate resources (Kang 2011, Theys 2001, Wu 20 1999, Zomaya 2001). Heterogeneity in DCS can be expressed by considering three systems attributes *(i) Processor with computing node*, (ii) *memory*, and *(iii) networking* (Attiya 2004). The metrics used to quantify the processor or node processing power by means of processing speed and represented with FLOPS (Floating point Operations per Second) and can be measured through LINPACK (Bunch 1979. Memory attributes are measured as the available memory capacity to support the process. The networking attributes are the link capacity associated with transmission medium, propagation delay and available communication resources (Karatza 2000).

We have carried out the simulation only considering processing power of the node, which can be represented as Markovian service time distribution (Fidanova 2006, Gopal 1996, Greene 2001). In general, load-balancing algorithms can

be broadly categorized as centralized or decentralized, dynamic or static, periodic or non-periodic, and those with thresholds or without thresholds (Casavant 1988, Wu 1999). We have used a centralized load-balancing algorithm framework as it imposes fewer overheads on the system than the decentralized algorithm. Centralized load balancing algorithms requires the global information on computing nodes at a single location and the load balancing policy is initiated from the central location. Heterogeneity of architecture and configuration complicates the load balancing problem (Wu 1999). Heterogeneity can arise due to the difference in task arrival rate at homogeneous processors or processors having different task processing rates. We have assumed that all computational tasks are capable of executed on any computing nodes of DCS. A single computing node that acts as a central scheduler or resource manager of the DCS collects the global load information of other computing nodes. Resource management sub systems of the HDCS are designated to schedule the execution of the tasks dynamically as that arrives for the service. HDCS environments are well suited to meet the computational demands of large, diverse groups of tasks. The problem of optimally mapping also defined as matching and scheduling. The basic assumptions about the computing node can be summarized as follows:

- Each node M_j is autonomous, has full information on its own resource, and it manages its work load.
- Each node is characterized by its processing rate and only its true value only known to M_j.
- Each node handles its own communication and computation overheads independently.
- Each node incurs a cost proportional to its utilization.
- Each computing node is always available for processing.

Load Balancing Problem in Heterogeneous Distributed Computing System

We have used the characterization model proposed by Shoukat Ali and et al as the basic framework to study the impact of system heterogeneity against different heuristic resource allocation algorithms (Ali 2000). We consider a heterogeneous distributed computing system (HDCS) consists of a set of M = $\{M_1, M_2, \dots M_m\}$, m independent heterogeneous, uniquely addressable computing entity (computing nodes). Let there are T = $\{t_1, t_2, \dots, t_n\}$ n number of tasks with each task t_i has an expected time to compute t_{ij} on node M_j. The entire task has expected time to compute on m nodes of HDCS. Hence the generalized load-balancing problem is to assign each task to one of the node M_j so that the loads placed on all nodes are as "balanced" as possible (Hamidzadeh 1995). Let A(j) be the set of jobs assigned to node M_j; and T_j be the total time machine M_j have to work to finish all the task in A(j). Hence $T_j = \sum_{t_i \in A(j)} t_{ij}$; for all task in A(j).

This is otherwise denoted as L_j and defined as load on node M_j. The basic objective of load balancing is to minimize make span, which is defined as maximum loads on any node (T = $\max_{j:1:m} (T_j)$. Let x_{ij} correspond to each pair (i, j) of node $M_j \in M$ and task $t_i \in T$.

- $x_{ij} = 0$; implies that task i not assign to node j.
- $x_{ij} = t_{ij}$; will indicate load of task i on node j.

For each task t_i we need $\sum_{j=1}^{m} x_{ij} = t_{ij}$; for all task $t_i \in T$.

The load on node M_j can be represented as $Lj = \sum_{i=1}^{n} x_{ij}$, where $x_{ij} = 0$ whenever task $t_i \notin A(j)$. The load balancing problem aims to find an assignment that minimizes the maximum load. Let L be the load of a HDCS with m nodes. Hence the generalized load balancing problem on HDCS can be formulated as

Minimize L = $\sum_{j=1}^{m} x_{ij} = t_{ij}$, for all $t_i \in T$

$$(1)$$

Subjected to condition

$\sum_{i=1}^{n} x_{ij} \leq L$,
for all $M_j \in M$ $x_{ij} \in \{0, t_{ij}\}$,
for all $t_i \in T$ and $M_j \in M$ $x_{ij} = 0$,
for all $t_i \notin A(j)$

$$(2)$$

Feasible assignments are one-to-one correspondence with x satisfying the above constraints (4). Hence an optimal solution to this problem is the load L_i on a machine (corresponding assignment). The problem of finding an assignment of minimum makespan is NP-hard (Hochbaum 2003, Horowitz 200319). The problem is therefore untractable with number tasks or computing nodes (processors) exceeds a few units. The solutions to load balancing problem can be obtained using a dynamic programming algorithm with time complexity $O(n\ L^m)$, where L is the minimum makespan(Kleinberg 2006) The load balancing problem has been evenly treated, in both the fields of computer science and operation research. The algorithm approaches used for load balancing problem are roughly classified as (i) exact algorithms and (ii) heuristic algorithms (Attiya 2004, Karatza 2002) Queuing models are used as the key model for performance analysis and optimization of parallel and distributed system (Lin 1992, Penmatsa 2007, Spies 1996, Zeng 2006). The HDCS can be modeled as M/M/m/n (Markovian arrivals, Markovian distributed service times, m computing nodes as server, and space for n ≥ m tasks in the system) multi-server queuing system with m servers as computing nodes. However, the heterogeneous multi-server queuing systems are not adequately addressed in research with respect to certain quality of service (Rykov 2008).

The HDCS is modeled as M/M/m/n queuing system with node M_1 is the fastest computing node and M_m is the slowest computing node. Assume that service time of the computing nodes follow exponential distribution with service rate so that $\mu_1 > \mu_2 > \ldots \mu_m$, where μ_i is the service rate of node M_i. The arrivals of the tasks at the central server or resource manager are modeled as Poisson with arrival rate λ. Each computing nodes can be modeled as shown in Figure 2. The tasks that are to be executed at a node are under the control of local scheduler and the scheduling policy of the node is responsible for the execution of the assigned task. We have assumed FCFS policy is being used at computing nodes, which can be modeled as M/M/1 queuing system (Page 2005b, Trivedi 2001). A node in HDCS has three components that involved in task. The *local scheduler* is responsible for scheduling of tasks that arrives to the computing node. The *dispatcher* invokes the next task to be executed on the node following a scheduling policy. The *global scheduler interacts* with the scheduler of other nodes in order to perform load distribution among other nodes in HDCS.

Figure 2.

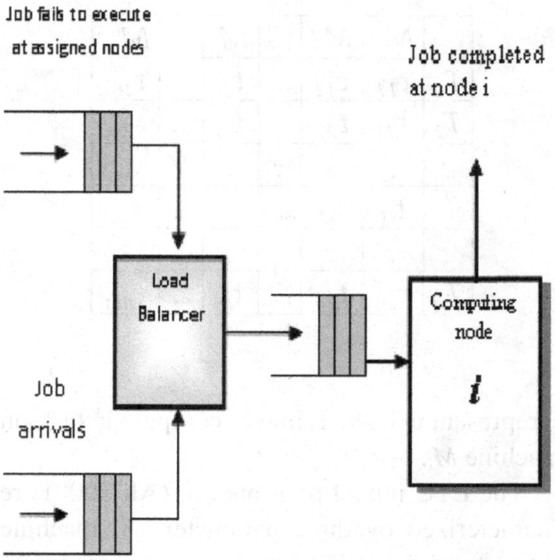

4. TASK MODEL AND ITERATIVE LOAD BALANCING TECHNIQUES

Task Model on HDCS

In literature of distributed computing researchers have used two different task models as (i) Task graph(TG) or Task interaction graph(TIG), (ii) expected time to compute(ETC) matrix. The task graphs are both directed and undirected weighted graph that represents process or task to be executed, however majority of the models are not representing any mathematical model for quantifying task heterogeneity. In this chapter we have use ETC matrix representation of task (Ali 2000) that represents task heterogeneity and machine heterogeneity. The tasks are arriving from the different users or nodes to the central scheduler or or serial scheduler have the probability to be allocated to any of the m computing nodes. Hence the tasks are characterized by expected time to compute (ETC) on all *m* computing nodes, can be represented as follows, In ETC matrix, the elements along a row indicate the execution time of a given task on different nodes, in particular

Table 1. Expected time to compute (ETC) matrix

	M_1	M_2	...	M_j	...	M_m
T_1	t_{11}	t_{12}	...	t_{1j}	...	t_{1m}
T_2	t_{21}	t_{22}	...	t_{2j}	...	t_{2m}
.	.	.	.	.	.	.
T_i	t_{i1}	t_{i2}	...	t_{ij}	...	t_{im}
.	.	.	.	.	.	.
T_n	t_{1n}	t_{2n}	...	t_{nj}	...	t_{nm}

Table 2 Example of consistent etc matrix for 10 tasks on five machines

Node→ Task ↓	M1	M2	M3	M4	M5
t1	22	21	6	16	15
t2	7	46	5	28	45
t3	64	83	45	23	58
t4	53	56	26	42	53
t5	11	12	14	7	8
t6	33	31	46	25	23
t7	24	11	17	14	25
t8	20	17	23	4	3
t9	13	28	14	7	34
t10	2	5	7	7	6

t_{ij} represent expected time to compute i[th] task on machine M_j.

The ETC model presented in (Ali 2000) are characterized by three parameters (i) machine heterogeneity, task heterogeneity and consistency. The task heterogeneity can be represented with two categories (i) *consistent* and (ii) *inconsistent*, here a consistent ETC matrix the computing nodes are arranged in the order of their processing capability or may be arranged as decreasing order of FLOPS. In particular a node M_i has a lower execution time than node M_j for task t_k, then $t_{ki} < t_{kj}$. Inconsistent ETC matrix is resulted in practice, when HDCS includes different type of machine architectures.(HPC clusters, Multi-core processor based workstations, parallel computers, work station with GPU units). In literature most of the task execution times are uniformly distributed (Ali 2000, Karatza 2002). A consistent ETC matrix for ten tasks on five machines is shown on Table 2, which is taken from (Ali 2000).

To generate ETC matrix, we have used range base ETC generation technique discussed in (Ali 2000) and added one component as arrival time of task. The arrival pattern of the task is based on Poisson distribution. For the analysis of the simulation results through the graph we have used expected completion time of task uniformly distributed {1, 500} time unit or seconds.

Iterative Centralized Algorithms

A dynamic load distribution algorithm must be general, adaptive, stable, fault tolerant and transparent to applications. Load balancing algorithms can be classified as (i) global vs. local, (ii) centralized vs. decentralized, (iii) Non-cooperative vs. cooperative, and (iv) adaptive vs. non-adaptive(Wu 1999, Siegel 2000). Tasks are assigned to the computing nodes with centralized load balancing algorithm; a central node collects the load information from the other computing nodes in HDCS. Central node communicates the assimilated information to all individual computing nodes, so that the nodes get updated about the system state. This updated information enables the nodes to decide whether to send the task to other nodes or accept new task for computation. The computing nodes depend on the information available with central node for all allocation decision. The three heuristic based resource allocation used to balance the load on computing nodes of HDCS are *First Come First serve (FF), genetic algorithm* and *Simulated Annealing (SA)*. A randomized resource allocation algorithm is selected along with the heuristic algorithms because the randomness can (probabilistically) guarantee average case behavior as well as it produces an efficient approximate solution to intractable problems. The FF algorithm follows the order of arrival time of the task with central scheduler. The *random task allocation algorithm* selects the node randomly from m nodes to allocate task t_j. SA and GA based load balancing algorithm uses an iterative structure with stopping criteria as maximum number of iteration.

We have also assumed that tasks are independent and can be processed by any computing node in distributed environment. For stability it is also assumed that tasks must not be generated faster than the HDCS can process i.e. $\lambda \leq \mu_1 + \mu_2 + \mu_3 \cdots + \mu_m$.

Coding Structure

Genetic algorithm and simulated annealing algorithm require a suitable representation and evaluation mechanism for solution. In this case we have use a window structure of fixed length say k, with integer value assigned to individual element of the array of size k. That on each step k no of task to be allocated to the computing node through simulated annealing with a minimized value of makespan. Task is assigned dynamically to the computing nodes on the fly. At the time of allocation there may be a large number of tasks are with central scheduler. A sliding window technique is used to select those tasks only that are in the window. The number of elements in the window is fixed is equal to the size of window. Figure 3, represents 10 tasks and their respective allocation to five computing node and corresponding structure of allocation list, and indicates the computing node. We have assumed that, current work load as dedicated tasks for each own node, so that the calculation of makespan is carried out from the time point when sliding window is selected.

SA and GA requires an appropriate representation to find the solution, we have used the

Figure 3. Allocation list (Chromosome structure)

t_1	t_2	t_3	t_4	t_5	t_6	t_7	t_8	t_9	t_{10}
M_5	M_3	M_5	M_3	M_2	M_2	M_4	M_4	M_1	M_1

Allocation list of task to computing node

5	3	5	3	2	2	4	4	1	1

Allocation list (Chromosome structure)

window structure as shown in Figure 3, the length of an array is the maximum number of task in the widow . The use of linear array helps to use the index as task number in the window so that a one dimensional list representation is selected. The individual element on window indicates the machine on which the corresponding task to be executed. Each window shows a possible allocation of computing nodes for which the makespan can be calculated from the ETC matrix. Each iteration of the algorithm GA and SA selects number of task through the window and allocated to the computing node to meet the objective. To prevent the nodes from overloading, before the task to be assigned to the node queue, a threshold is used. The percentage of acceptable queue for each node is calculated using formula:

number of acceptable node queues / Total number of nodes in the system

The higher the percentage leads to minimization of makespan(Zomaya 2001). Each computing nodes are modeled as M/M/1/k queue with maximum capacity to have k tasks in the system, so that it can also be a constraint on assignment.

Performance Metric

The performance analysis of allocation algorithms are based on three performance metric (i) makespan, (ii) average utilization, and (iii) acceptable queue size. The average utilization for a computing node can be calculated as the ration (makespan/L_i). To prevent the nodes from overloading, before the task to be assigned to the node queue, a threshold is used. The percentage of acceptable queue for each node is calculated using formula:

number of acceptable node queues / Total number of nodes in the system

The higher the percentage leads to minimization of makespan. Each computing nodes are modeled as M/M/1/k queue with maximum capacity to have k tasks in the system, so that it can also be a constraint on assignment.

Tables 3 shows two makespan value (i) assuming the initial load of the computing node as zero, (ii) the computing nodes are with some arbitrary load. The makespan is computed to be 73 for the chromosome in Figure 3 with corresponding average utilization (AU) without any initial load with the corresponding computing nodes.

When the computing nodes are with an initial load as shown in Table 3, the corresponding makespan value computed is 78 for the chromosome in Figure 3 with corresponding average

utilization(AU) on five computing nodes. The genetic algorithm uses fitness function to evaluate the quality of the task assignment for the chromosome is based on the (Zomaya 2001) by Zomaya and The, defined by following equation:

$$fitness = \frac{1}{makespan} \times AU \times \frac{\#\,acceptable\,queues}{\#\,computing\,nodes}$$

where AU is average utilization .

5. LOAD BALANCING USING SIMULATED ANNEALING

SA is a heuristic method that has been implemented to obtain good solutions of an objective functions defined on a number of discrete optimization problem (Theys 2001, Ucar 2006). The simulated annealing method mimics the physical process of heating a material and then slowly lowering the temperature (cooling) to decrease defects so as to minimize the system energy (Suman 2005, Kalyanmoy 2004). SA is implemented using iterative algorithm that only considers one possible solution for each task window at a time. The solution uses representation as the fixed window size for *k* number of task from the list of *n* tasks. The SA approaches randomly generates initial solution representing an allocation of tasks with a fixed window size. A new solution is generated based upon the neighborhood structure. Temperature is used as a control parameter in SA and decreases gradually with each iteration. This decides the probability of accepting a worst solution at any step and commonly used a stopping criterion. The initial temperature is used as an integer value and decreased by a rate called annealing schedule.

At each iteration Scheduling of tasks from a task set to different processors such that the loads of the assigned computing nodes is balanced, is a well-known instance of combinatorial optimization, which is tackled using the SA technique in the

Table 3. Makespan of the system

Node	A(i)		L_i	AU
1	t(9,1)=13	t(10,1)=2	15	0.2054
2	t(5,2)=12	t(6,2)=31	43	0.5890
3	t(2,3)=5	t(4,3)=26	31	0.4246
4	t(7,4)=14	t(8,4)=4	28	0.3835
5	t(1,5)=15	t(3,5)=58	73	1.0000

(a)   Makespan of the system

Node	Initial Load	A(i)		L_i	AU
1	9	t(9,1)=13	t(10,1)=2	24	0.3076
2	11	t(5,2)=12	t(6,2)=31	54	0.6923
3	7	t(2,3)=5	t(4,3)=26	38	0.4871
4	15	t(7,4)=14	t(8,4)=4	43	0.5512
5	5	t(1,5)=15	t(3,5)=58	78	1.0000

(b) Makespan with initial load

Algorithm 1. INVERSION (TS, WIN_SIZE)

```
Input: TS = (ts1, ts2, ts3, …, ts10)  Task Schedule
WIN_SIZE = Size of the Task Schedule TS
Output:      TS*=(ts1, ts2ⱼ, ts3, …, ts10) Task Schedule
1. Generate a random number S₁ to represent the starting point and another
     random number L₁ for the length of the substring.
2. Let SS = StringReverse (SubString (TS, S₁, L₁));
3. For i = 1 to WIN_SIZE repeat,
     a.  if i < S₁ or (i > S₁ and i >= S₁ + L₁),
          S = concat (S, TS (i));
     b.  if i == S₁, S = concat (S, SS);
     (End of for loop)
4. Return (TS);
```

following steps. Task schedule (TS) is the linear representation of nodes on which the tasks are to be executed in order. We have use the similar structure as Figure 3 to represent the task schedule $TS = (ts1, ts2_j, ts3, …, tsWIN\_SIZE)$. With n task to be scheduled on m computing nodes, simulated annealing based algorithm selects asset of k tasks from the task pool of n tasks, and generated an allocation for those tasks randomly on m machine. In next iteration the new allocated is based upon the move set representation. We are presenting three move sets representations *(i) inversion*, *(ii) translation*, and *(iii) switching* for SA. The details of these algorithms are presented with illustration as follows.

Inversion

Inversion process can be expressed by the following algorithm which operates on a task list (say) *TS* that includes the machine numbers to which tasks are allocated for a fixed number of task = *WIN_SIZE*.

In the process of inversion, we select four randomly chosen consecutive nodes and replace it by the reverse order of the same node number. Figure 4 illustrates the process of 10 tasks on 5 nodes.

Figure 4. Allocation list on inversion

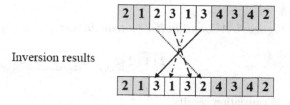

Inversion results

Translation

Translation process uses following algorithm for the list *TS*.

Translation is transformation functions that remove two or more consecutive nodes from the schedule and place it in between any two randomly selected consecutive nodes as shown in Figure 5.

Switching

Move set can be constructed for the schedules using a switching function, which randomly select two nodes and switch them in a schedule. Generally speaking, the switching move set tends to rupture the original schedule and results in an allocation that has a makespan significantly different from that of the original allocation. Comparisons be-

Algorithm 2. TRANSLATION (TS, WIN_SIZE)

```
Input:        TS = (ts1, ts2, ts3, …, ts10)  Task Schedule
WIN_SIZE  =  Size of the Task Schedule TS
Output:       TS*=(ts1, ts2₃, ts3, …, ts10) Task Schedule
1.  Generate a random number S₁ to represent the starting point and another
        random number L₁ for the length of the substring.
2.  Generate a random number I₁ for the insertion point.
3.  Let SS = SubString (TS, S₁, L₁);
4.  For i = 1 to WIN_SIZE repeat,
        a.  if i <= I₁ and (i < S₁ or (i > S₁ and
              i >= S₁ + L₁)), S= concat (S, TS (i));
        b.  if i == I₁, TS = concat (TS, SS);
        c.  if i > I₁ and (i < S₁ or (i > S₁ and
              i >= S₁ + L₁)), S= concat (S, TS (i));
    (End of for loop)
5.  Return (TS);
```

Figure 5. Allocation list on translation

Figure 6. Outcome of switching operation

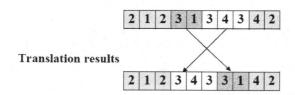

Translation results

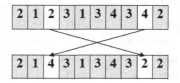

tween inversion and switching move set can be found in (Krikpatrick 1983). Example of switching function is shown in Figure 6.

In our model, simulated annealing algorithm starts with generating initial schedule **TS** randomly for 10 tasks. Following that move set is created for an initial schedule, by any one of the three different methods *(i) Inversion, (ii) Translation* and *(iii) Switching* by selecting a random number between 1 to 3. A final allocation list for the tasks is obtained after the 25 iteration. Tasks are allocated to the nodes and average utilization is calculated for those 10 tasks before selecting a next 10 tasks from the set of waiting tasks. The simulated annealing algorithm for dynamic load balancing outlined as algorithm *SA_DLB*. The algorithm *SA_DLB* called for maximum (n/

WIN_SIZE) times to allocate n tasks to the computing nodes.

Common approaches used as the stopping criteria in simulated annealing algorithm (SA) are, (i) one may use a given number of iteration, or (ii) a time limit, or (iii) a given number of iteration without an improvement of the objective function value, (iv) value of the objective function limit as set by the user(25). We have used a fixed number of iteration proportional to number of task to be schedule on computing nodes. The simulation experiment was conducted with n=1000 tasks on m=60 computing nodes. The simulation results are compared with two heuristic algorithms: first fit and randomized (17, 40). Randomized algorithms are known for efficient approximate solutions to intractable problems

Algorithm 3. SWITCHING (TS, WIN_SIZE)

```
Input:     TS = (ts1, ts2, ts3, …, ts10) Task Schedule
WIN_SIZE = Size of the Task Schedule TS
Output:    TS*=(ts1, ts2ⱼ, ts3, …, ts10) Task Schedule
1.  Generate a random number i to represent the task 1 and another random
       number j to represent task 2.
2.  swap (TS(i), TS(j));
3.  Return (TS);
```

Algorithm 4. SA_DLB (TS, WIN_SIZE)

```
Input: TS = (ts1, ts2, ts3, …, ts10) Task Schedule
WIN_SIZE = Size of the Task Schedule TS
Output:        TS*= (ts1, ts2ⱼ, ts3, …, ts10)  and  AU(TS*)
1.  Calculate makespan for  TS = ms
2.  For i = 1 to 25 repeat,
3.  Generate a random integer  m from {1,2,3}
4.  if  m = 1,  call INVERSION (TS, WIN_SIZE) to create move set
5.  if  m = 2,  call TRANSLATION (TS, WIN_SIZE) to create move set
6.  if  m = 3,  call SWITCHING (TS, WIN_SIZE) to create move set
7.  calculate the makespan  for the new move set  TS* as ms*
8.  if ms* < ms  then  TS = TS*
    (End of for loop)
9.  Allocate the tasks to Nodes using TS and calculate  average utilization(AU)
10.  Return (TS*, AU);
```

with better complexity bounds. Moreover randomized algorithm is selected for performance comparison as it is simple to describe and implement than the deterministic algorithm. We executed several simulations on proposed simulated annealing algorithm for dynamic load balancing on HDCS, to compare with conventional first fit (FF), and randomized algorithm. The simulation results are presented in Figure 7 and 8 with completion time and processor utilization respectively. The Fast come first serve (FF) and randomized algorithms for resource allocation can make an instantaneous decision to allocation of the task to computing nodes, which results a shorter makespan. The SA-based load balancing algorithm shows very much similar performance to that of FF in

both average *processor utilization* and completion time or *makespan*.

6. GENETICS BASED LOAD BALANCING ALGORITHMS

The genetic algorithm (GA) is a computational intelligence optimization and search technique based on the principles of genetics and natural selection (Goldberg 1988). A simple genetic algorithm consists of four main steps initialization, evaluation, exploitation, and exploration (Goldberg 2013, Haupt 2004, Rahmani 2009, Vidyarthi). At each step (iteration) the genetic algorithm selects individuals at random from the

Figure 7. Completion time of 1000 tasks using SA, RAND, and FF

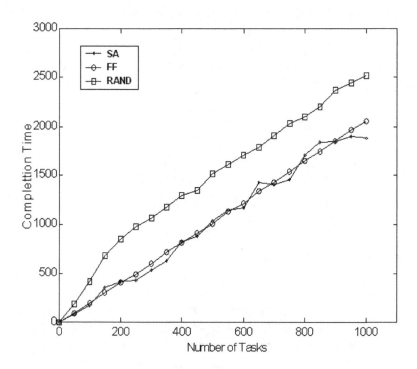

Figure 8. Average processor utilization of 1000 tasks using SA, RAND, and FF

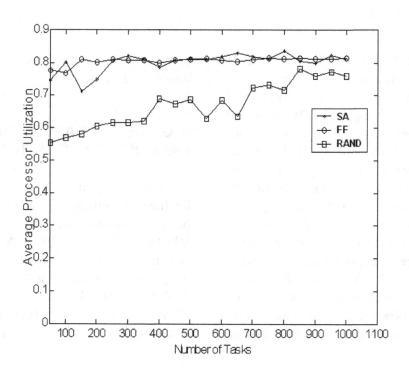

current population to be parents, and use them to produce the children for the next generation. Over successive generation this process evolves toward an optimal solution. The next generation from the current population can be created using three main types of rules:

- *Selection rules* sect the individuals, called parents from the mating pool or current population.
- *Crossover rules* combine two individuals otherwise called parents to form the children for the next generation
- *Mutation rules* makes random changes to the genes of individual parent to form children

The number of genes and their values in each chromosome are specific to the problem. We have use the chromosomes of length equal to the size of window (i.e. number of task) and the values are the node numbers on which respective tasks are to be executed. The initial solution or initial population generated randomly. The GA operates on the fixed number of tasks and each task is characterized by the task model as ETC matrix. In this section we have discussed the genetic algorithm framework for resource allocation to heterogeneous tasks on heterogeneous computing resources with the fitness function as objective function to minimize the make span L. The construction of genetic algorithm for load balancing problem can be divided into parts: the representation of individuals in the population (also termed as chromosome structure), the determination of fitness function, the design of genetic operators and the fixing of probabilities to control genetic operators.

Chromosome Structure

Genetic algorithms require a suitable representation and evaluation mechanism. In this case we have use a chromosome structure of fixed length, with integer value assigned to individual genes

as the node number. GA requires an appropriate chromosome (individual) representation to find the solution, we have used the chromosome structure as shown in Figure 3, the length of a chromosome is the maximum number of task in the widow(window size)(Zomaya 2001). The use of linear array helps to use the index as task number in the window so that a one dimensional chromosome representation is selected. The individual gene on chromosome indicates the machine on which the corresponding task to be executed. Each chromosome shows a possible allocation of computing nodes for which the *makespan* can be calculated from the ETC matrix. The *makespan* for individual in Figure 3 is computed to 73 as shown in Table 3 along with corresponding average utilization. We have simulated the proposed genetic algorithm with individual of size = 10, however an analysis is present to study the performance of proposed genetic scheme by varying length of individual that corresponds to window size.

Fitness Function

In genetic algorithm literature, the term evaluation and fitness are sometimes used interchangeably. In this chapter, the evaluation function, or objective function provides the measure of makespan with respect to dynamic load balancing problem as define as in problem statement. The fitness function transforms that measure of performance into an allocation of reproductive opportunities. The evaluation of an individual representing a set of parameters is independent of the evaluation of any other individual. The fitness of that individual, however, is always defined with respect to other members of the current population. The fitness function used is based on three performance metric (i) makespan, (ii) average utilization, and (iii) acceptable queue size . This parameter has been defined in third Section of this chapter . The genetic algorithm uses fitness function to evaluate the quality of the task assignment for the chromosome by calculating corresponding makespan for the window.

Genetic Operators

The basic implementation of genetic algorithm follows the Simple Genetic Algorithm(SGA) frame work suggested by Goldberg (Goldberg 2013). The execution of genetic algorithm is a two stage process. The process begins with the randomly generated initial population or current population . The selection process is applied to the initial population to create a mating pool or intermediate population . Then the members of intermediate population are subjected to recombination and mutation to create the next population. This process of transforming current population to next population constitutes one generation. Genetic algorithms are blind search techniques and hence require problem-specific genetic operators to get the good solutions. The genetic operator used by us to design genetic algorithm for load balancing are explained in details.

Selection for Reproduction

The reproduction process is used to create a new population of individuals from old population by selecting individuals from old population based on their fitness values. The most common selection schemes used in Genetic Algorithms are (i) rank selection, and (ii) roulette wheel selection (Goldberg 2013, Haput 2004). The reproduction process forms new population, (in every iteration) by selecting individuals from the old population based upon their fitness value that optimizes the objective function. From the initial population, individuals are selected to form a mating pool or intermediate population via proportional selection process, also termed as "roulette wheel selection" (Kalyanmoy 2004). This process can view the population as mapping onto a roulette wheel, where each individual is represented by a space that proportionally corresponds to its fitness. By repeatedly spinning the roulette wheel, individuals are chosen using " using stochastic sampling with replacement to fill the intermediate population (Whitley 1994). The Table 4 shows the application

Table 4. The Process of designing mating pool from initial population

Sl. No	Initial Population	Load on machine	Max load: makespan	$L_i/\Sigma L$	L_i/L	Mating pool	Parent Id
1	2123134342	(18,109,95,21,0)	109	0.114	0.919	2123134342	P1
2	4141553132	(80,5,31,39,31)	80	0.084	0.674	4141553132	P2
3	3322122524	(11,209,11,7,3)	209	0.220	1.762	4141553132	P3
4	3435423531	(2,31,82,35,56)	82	0.086	0.691	3435423531	P4
5	5522423311	(15,170,40,7,60)	170	0.179	1.433	3435423531	P5
6	2234421355	(24,98,68,49,40)	98	0.103	0.826	2234421355	P6
7	4323142254	(11,111,31,48,34)	111	0.116	0.935	4323142254	P7
8	4345331554	(24,0,65,46,90)	90	0.094	0.758	4345331554	P8
		Sum	949	0.996	7.998		
		Minimum	80	0.084	0.691		
		Average	118.6≈119	0.124	0.999≈1		

roulette wheel selection to replace two individuals of higher makespan (3rd and 5th) and replace them with individual having lower makespan (2nd and 4th) to design the mating pool.

Crossover

On completion of the construction of intermediate population also termed as mating pool are subjected to recombination to create the next population . The recombination can occur with the application of crossover to randomly paired individuals with a probability namely cross over probability denoted as p_c . Crossover operation selects a pair of individual from the mating pool, then randomly selects two points to apply standard two-point-cross over, and produces two offspring. In this chapter we have used cross over probability $p_c = 0.7$. Example in Figure 9 crossover depicts two point crossover processes with P1 and P2 as parent.

In this example two parents P1 and P2 are selected randomly with makespan value as 109 and 80 respectively based on ETC matrix in Table 2 . Two cross over points are randomly selected

Figure 9. Crossover operation

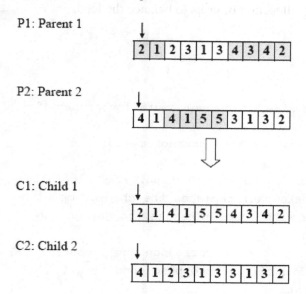

Figure 10. Results of mutation on chromosome

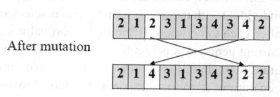

After mutation

(say 2, 6) to produce upspring C1 and C2 with makespan 60 and 103 respectively. Two individuals with higher makespan are discarded and a constant population size is maintained throughout the solution finding process.

Mutation

In the process of mutation, the individual is changed by swapping two genes position randomly with a small probability. After crossover, we can apply a mutation operator. For each bit in the individual mutate with some probability known as mutation probability and denoted as p_m . Typically the mutation rate is applied with less than 0.15 probability (Whitley 1994). The mutation probability is used to select the individual that is subjected to mutation process. The Figure 10 shows the mutation process: first two random positions are selected to exchange their values that designate the node or processor number. This mutation process produces a chromosome with makespan 95 from the chromosome with makespan 109 as depicted in Figure 10. In a single generation the process of selection, crossover and mutation are applied to the initial population to create the next population.

Stopping Conditions

Each iterative step goes through the process of evaluation, selection, recombination and mutation forms one generation in the execution of a genetic algorithm. Task is to be assigned on the fly, and the search on the solution space is carried out in random, hence we have to accept the suboptimal solution which can be found at the earliest. The individual with the smallest makespan is selected after each generation. If the makespan value of current generation is less than the previous generation, the iteration continues till the maximum generation. If the makespan value found to be higher the GA stops evolving. The stopping criteria used by us in this algorithm is the maximum number of generation = 40.

Genetic Algorithm Framework

The genetic algorithm framework considering the operators discussed above can be given in Algorithm 5.

In general a genetic algorithm operates on the finite population of chromosomes. The initial population in this problem is based upon the chromosome structure depicted in Figure 3. A population size of 20 is used for the fixed window size= 10 for maximum number of 40 generation. In particular the genetic algorithm for load balancing uses the following parameters as listed:

- Number of task = 1000
- Number of node = 60
- Max. generation = 40
- Population size = 20
- Multi point Crossover Rate = 0.7
- Mutation Rate = 0.05

- Window size = 10

Let us assume that expected completion time of task uniformly distributed in the interval of (mintime, maxtime). Window size represents maximum number of task or genes in the individual. The *inipopsize* is the size of initial population representing chromosomes of equal length. We have used fixed population size for all the iteration with maximum number of generation as stopping criteria. Initial population (IP) can be generated as an array of size = inipopsize using the following formula: IP = mintime + (maxtime - mintime) *rand(inipopsize,windowsize)

The procedure to create mating pool from a initial population for the proposed genetic algorithm is presented as a small example in Table 4, where an initial population of size 8 is created using above Equation. The makespan for each member of initial population are computed using ETC matrix from Table 2. Roulette wheel selection procedure is used to weight the individuals. As load balancing problem is a minimization problem i.e. to minimize makespan, third and fifth individual are replaced with second and fourth individual to create mating pool. Through the above process initial population are evaluated to select that chromosome that represents better allocation of tasks to balance the load.

Algorithm 5. Genetic algorithm for load balancing

```
Step 1.  Initialize parameters: Population size, crossover, mutation probability
Step 2.  Random generation of initial population
Step 3.  Evaluation of fitness (i.e. makespan of each chromosome) of the
         current population.
Step 4.  Select the new population using roulette wheel method, {The algorithm
         keeps chromosome with smaller makespan; replaces the chromosome with
         higher make span  by Chromosome with lower makespan, to design the
         mating pool for next generation}
Step 5.  Apply two point crossover and mutation with corresponding probability.
Step 6.  Repeat Step 3, Step 4, and Step 5 until the stopping condition is
         reached.(maximum number of iteration)
```

Figure 11. Completion time of 1000 tasks using GA, SA, RAND, and FF

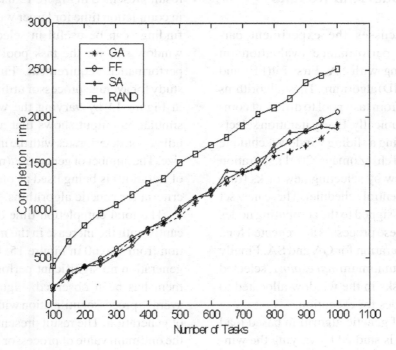

Figure 12. Average processor utilization of 1000 tasks using SA, RAND, and FF

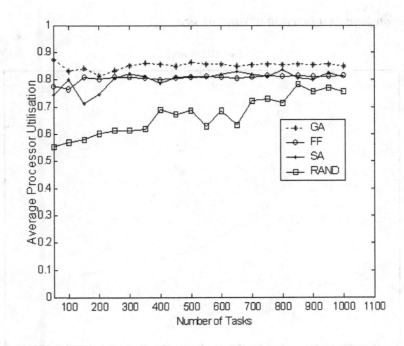

Simulation Model And Results

This section discusses the experiment carried out for the performance evaluation on proposed GA along with SA, First Fit(FF) and Randomized(RAND) algorithm. These algorithms allocate the tasks from task pool to different computing nodes dynamically. Every iteration selects a set of 10 tasks using a sliding window technique by Zomaya and Teh (Zomaya 2001). Iteration updates the window by selecting new tasks from the task queue of central scheduler. These new set of tasks are to be assigned to the computing nodes in the iteration. These processes are repeated for a fixed number of iteration for GA and SA. Finally an individual with minimum *makespan* is selected as solution and tasks in the window allocated to the computing nodes for execution.

Performance of genetic algorithm based load balancing scheme is studied by varying the window size from 10 to 50 on fixed number of computing nodes m = 60 for 100 task. The simulation result presented in Figure 13 indicates a decrease in completion time for larger window size. These findings can be useful in selecting appropriate window size for the task pool to meet specific performance requirement. Further simulation study for average processor utilization is depicted in Figure 14 by varying the window size. The simulation output shows that average processor utilization deteriorates with the increase in window size. The number of generation(maximum number of iteration) is being used as one of the stopping criteria for genetic algorithms.

The total completion time decreases significantly with the increase in the number of generation from 5 to 60 in Figure 15. However after 30 generation no significant performance improvement has been observed. Figure 16 shows the average processor utilization with varying number of generation. The result presented also indicates the optimum value of processor utilization for the generation.

Figure 13. Completion time as a function of window size

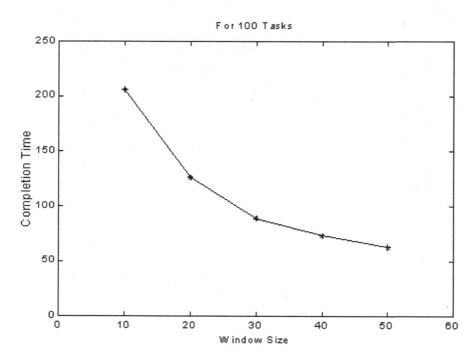

Figure 14. Average processor utilization as a function of window size

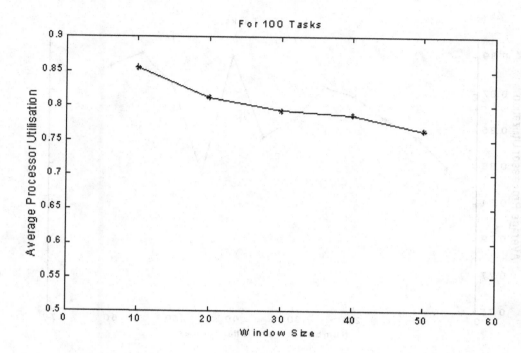

Figure 15. Task completion time as function of generation

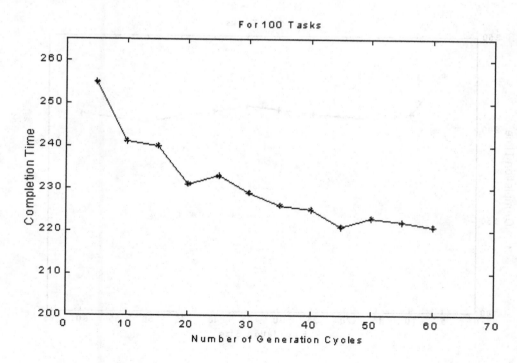

Figure 16. Average processor utilization as a function of generation

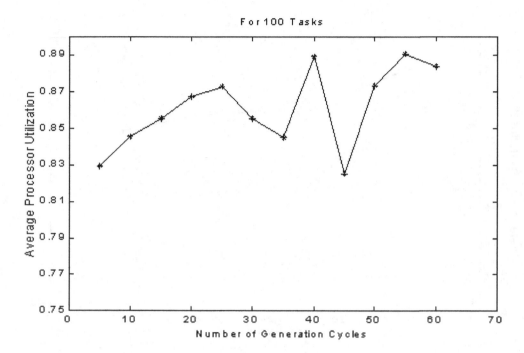

Figure 17. Completion time as a function of population size

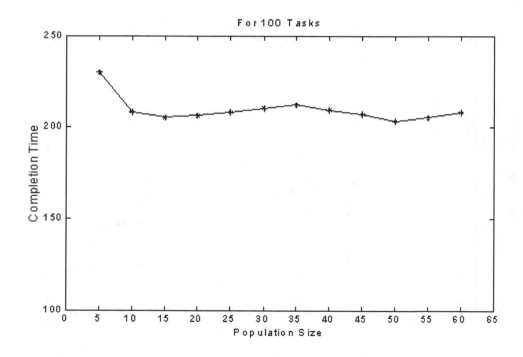

Figure 18. Average processor utilization as a function of population size

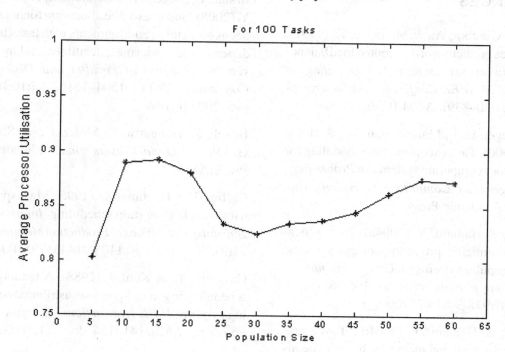

Different population size has been selected to study the performance of genetic algorithm for load balancing. The Figure 17 indicates a decrease in completion time for the tasks with the increase in population size. This study may be use to fine tune the genetic algorithm for a desired performance. The average processor utilization with changing population size is shown in Figure 18. The results show the optimum processor utilization, but the performance decreases with increase in population size.

The simulation results presented here are for the randomly generated ETC matrix with expected time to compute uniformly distributed. So every time the simulation is performed on a different task pool, hence running the more generation does not have scope to include the same population. So the results obtained may be slightly different for the same problem specification.

7. CONCLUSION

Load balancing is being performed during runtime at various stages to keep the workload balance on different computing nodes of a HDCS. This chapter presents a performance comparison of two iterative heuristic and two greedy heuristic load balancing strategy using central scheduler. The Fast come first serve (FF) and randomized algorithms for resource allocation can make an instantaneous decision to allocation of the task to computing nodes, which results a shorter makespan. Simulated annealing and genetic algorithm based resource allocation algorithm uses sliding widow techniques to select the tasks to be allocated to computing nodes. The proposed dynamic load-balancing mechanism developed using genetic algorithms has been very effective, especially in the case of a large number of tasks. The GA-based algorithm worked rather well in terms of achieving the goals of minimum total completion time and maximum processor utilization.

REFERENCES

Ahmad, I., Ghafoor, A., & Mehrotra, K. (1991). Performance prediction of distributed load balancing on multicomputer systems. In *Proceedings of the 1991 ACM/ IEEE Conference on Supercomputing* (pp. 830–839). ACM/IEEE.

Ali, S., Siegel, H. J., Maheswaran, M., & Hensgen, D. (2000). Task execution time modeling for heterogeneous computing systems. In *Proceedings of Heterogeneous Computing Workshop,* (pp. 185–199). Academic Press.

Attiya, G., & Hamam, Y. (2004a). Task allocation for minimizing programs completion time in multicomputer systems. In *Computational science and its applications* (pp. 97–106). Springer. doi:10.1007/978-3-540-24709-8_11

Attiya, G., & Hamam, Y. (2004b). Two phase algorithm for load balancing in heterogeneous distributed systems. In Proceedings of Parallel, Distributed and Network-Based Processing, (pp. 434–439). Academic Press.

Attiya, G., & Hamam, Y. (2006). Task allocation for maximizing reliability of distributed systems: A simulated annealing approach. *Journal of Parallel and Distributed Computing*, *66*(10), 1259–1266. doi:10.1016/j.jpdc.2006.06.006

Boxma, O., Koole, G., & Liu, Z. (1994). *Queueing-theoretic solution methods for models of parallel and distributed systems. Centrum voor Wiskunde en Informatica.* Department of Operations Research, Statistics, and System Theory.

Braun, T., Siegel, H., Beck, N., Bˇolˇoni, L., Maheswaran, M., & Reuther, A. et al. (2001). A comparison of eleven static heuristics for mapping a class of independent tasks onto heterogeneous distributed computing systems. *Journal of Parallel and Distributed Computing*, *61*(6), 810–837. doi:10.1006/jpdc.2000.1714

Braun, T., Siegel, H., Maciejewski, A., & Hong, Y. (2008). Static resource allocation for heterogeneous computing environments with tasks having dependencies, priorities, deadlines, and multiple versions. *Journal of Parallel and Distributed Computing*, *68*(11), 1504–1516. doi:10.1016/j.jpdc.2008.06.006

Bunch, J., Dongarra, J., Moler, C., & Stewart, G. (1979). *Linpack users guide*. Philadelphia, PA: SIAM.

Caffrey, J., & Hitchings, G. (1995). Makespan distributions in flow shop scheduling. *International Journal of Operations & Production Management*, *15*(3), 50–58. doi:10.1108/01443579510080553

Casavant, T., & Kuhl, J. (1988). A taxonomy of scheduling in general-purpose distributed computing systems. *IEEE Transactions on Software Engineering*, *14*(2), 141–154. doi:10.1109/32.4634

Choi, M., Yu, J., Kim, H., & Maeng, S. (2003). Improving performance of a dynamic load balancing system by using number of effective tasks. [IEEE.]. *Proceedings of Cluster Computing*, *2003*, 436–441.

Dandamudi, S. (1998). Sensitivity evaluation of dynamic load sharing in distributed systems. *IEEE Concurrency*, *6*(3), 62–72. doi:10.1109/4434.708257

Fidanova, S. (2006). Simulated annealing for grid scheduling problem. In *Proceedings of Modern Computing, 2006*. IEEE.

Garey, M., & Johnson, D. (1979). *Computing and intractability, a guide to the theory of NP-completeness*. New York: W.H. Freeman and Company.

Ghosh, S. (2010). *Distributed systems: An algorithmic approach*. Boca Raton, FL: CRC Press.

Goldberg, D. E. (2013). *Genetic algorithms in search, optimization, and machine learning*. Upper Saddle River, NJ: Pearson Education.

Goldberg, D. E., & Holland, J. H. (1988). Genetic algorithms and machine learning. *Machine Learning, 3*(2), 95–99. doi:10.1023/A:1022602019183

Gopal, T., Nataraj, N., Ramamurthy, C., & Sankaranarayanan, V. (1996). Load balancing in heterogenous distributed systems. *Microelectronics and Reliability, 36*(9), 1279–1286. doi:10.1016/0026-2714(95)00133-6

Greene, W. (2001). Dynamic load-balancing via a genetic algorithm. In *Proceedings of Tools with Artificial Intelligence* (pp. 121–128). Academic Press.

Grosu, D., & Chronopoulos, A. (2004). Algorithmic mechanism design for load balancing in distributed systems. *IEEE Transactions on Systems, Man, and Cybernetics. Part B, Cybernetics, 34*(1), 77–84. doi:10.1109/TSMCB.2002.805812 PMID:15369053

Grosu, D., Chronopoulos, A., & Leung, M. (2002). Load balancing in distributed systems: An approach using cooperative games. In *Proceedings of Parallel and Distributed Processing Symposium* (pp. 52–61). Academic Press.

Hamidzadeh, B., Atif, Y., & Lilja, D. (1995). Dynamic scheduling techniques for heterogeneous computing systems. *Concurrency (Chichester, England), 7*(7), 633–652. doi:10.1002/cpe.4330070705

Haupt, R. L., & Haupt, S. E. (2004). *Practical genetic algorithms.* New York: John Wiley & Sons.

Hochbaum, D. S. (2003). *Approximation algorithms for NP-hard problems.* Thomson Asia Pte Ltd.

Horowitz, E., Sahni, S., & Rajasekaran, S. (2003). *Fundamentals of computer algorithms.* New Delhi: Galgotia Publications.

Hwang, K., Fox, G., & Dongarra, J. (2012). *Distributed and cloud computing: From parallel processing to the internet of things.* San Francisco: Morgan Kaufmann.

Kafil, M., & Ahmad, I. (1998). Optimal task assignment in heterogeneous distributed computing systems. *IEEE Concurrency, 6*(3), 42–50. doi:10.1109/4434.708255

Kalyanmoy, D. (2004). *Optimization for engineering design: Algorithms and examples.* PHI Learning Pvt. Ltd.

Kang, Q., He, H., & Song, H. (2011). Task assignment in heterogeneous computing systems using an effective iterated greedy algorithm. *Journal of Systems and Software, 84*(6), 985–992. doi:10.1016/j.jss.2011.01.051

Karatza, H. (2000). A comparative analysis of scheduling policies in a distributed system using simulation. *International Journal of Simulation Systems, Science & Technology,* 1–2.

Karatza, H., & Hilzer, R. (2002). Load sharing in heterogeneous distributed systems. In *Proceedings of Simulation Conference,* (Vol. 1, pp. 489–496). Academic Press.

Kim, J.-U., & Kim, Y.-D. (1996). Simulated annealing and genetic algorithms for scheduling products with multi-level product structure. *Computers & Operations Research, 23*(9), 857–868. doi:10.1016/0305-0548(95)00079-8

Kirkpatrick, S., Jr, D. G., & Vecchi, M. P. (1983). Optimization by simmulated annealing. *Science, 220*(4598), 671–680. doi:10.1126/science.220.4598.671 PMID:17813860

Kleinberg, J., & Tardos, E. (2006). *Algorithm design.* Upper Saddle River, NJ: Pearson Education Inc.

Kumar Tripathi, A., Kumer Sarker, B., Kumar, N., & Vidyarthi, D. P. (2000). A GA based multiple task allocation considering load. *International Journal of High Speed Computing, 11*(4), 203–214. doi:10.1142/S0129053300000187

Lee, W.-C., Wu, C.-C., & Chen, P. (2006). A simulated annealing approach to makespan minimization on identical parallel machines. *International Journal of Advanced Manufacturing Technology, 31*(3), 328–334. doi:10.1007/s00170-005-0188-5

Lin, H., & Raghavendra, C. (1992). A dynamic load-balancing policy with a central job dispatcher (lbc). *IEEE Transactions on Software Engineering, 18*(2), 148–158. doi:10.1109/32.121756

Liu, G., Poh, K., & Xie, M. (2005). Iterative list scheduling for heterogeneous computing. *Journal of Parallel and Distributed Computing, 65*(5), 654–665. doi:10.1016/j.jpdc.2005.01.002

Liu, K., Subrata, R., & Zomaya, A. (2007). On the performance-driven load distribution for heterogeneous computational grids. *Journal of Computer and System Sciences, 73*(8), 1191–1206. doi:10.1016/j.jcss.2007.02.007

Maheswaran, M., Ali, S., Siegal, H., Hensgen, D., & Freund, R. (1999). Dynamic matching and scheduling of a class of independent tasks onto heterogeneous computing systems. In *Proceedings of Heterogeneous Computing Workshop, 1999.* Academic Press.

Maheswaran, M., & Siegel, H. (1998). A dynamic matching and scheduling algorithm for heterogeneous computing systems. In *Proceedings of Heterogeneous Computing Workshop, 1998.* Academic Press.

Munetomo, M., Takai, Y., & Sato, Y. (1994). A genetic approach to dynamic load balancing in a distributed computing system. [IEEE.]. *Proceedings of Evolutionary Computation, 1994,* 418–421.

Page, A., & Naughton, T. (2005a). Dynamic task scheduling using genetic algorithms for heterogeneous distributed computing. In *Proceedings of Parallel and Distributed Processing Symposium, 2005.* IEEE.

Page, A., & Naughton, T. (2005b). Framework for task scheduling in heterogeneous distributed computing using genetic algorithms. *Artificial Intelligence Review, 24*(3), 415–429. doi:10.1007/s10462-005-9002-x

Penmatsa, S., & Chronopoulos, A. (2007). Dynamic multi-user load balancing in distributed systems. In *Proceedings of Parallel and Distributed Processing Symposium, 2007.* IEEE.

Rahmani, A. M., & Rezvani, M. (2009). A novel genetic algorithm for static task scheduling in distributed systems. *International Journal of Computer Theory and Engineering, 1*(1), 1793–8201.

Sahoo, B., Kumar, D., & Jena, S. K. (2013). Analysing the impact of heterogeneity with greedy resource allocation algorithms for dynamic load balancing in heterogeneous distributed computing system. *International Journal of Computers and Applications, 62*(19), 25–34. doi:10.5120/10190-5070

Siegel, H. J., & Ali, S. (2000). Techniques for mapping tasks to machines in heterogeneous computing systems. *Journal of Systems Architecture, 46*(8), 627–639. doi:10.1016/S1383-7621(99)00033-8

Spies, F. (1996). Modeling of optimal load balancing strategy using queueing theory. *Microprocessing and Microprogramming, 41*(8), 555–570. doi:10.1016/0165-6074(95)00006-2

Suman, B., & Kumar, P. (2005). A survey of simulated annealing as a tool for single and multiobjective optimization. *The Journal of the Operational Research Society, 57*(10), 1143–1160. doi:10.1057/palgrave.jors.2602068

Theys, M. D., Braun, T. D., Siegal, H., Maciejewski, A. A., & Kwok, Y. (2001). Mapping tasks onto distributed heterogeneous computing systems using a genetic algorithm approach. In *Solutions to parallel and distributed computing problems: Lessons from biological sciences* (pp. 135–178). Academic Press.

Tong, X., & Shu, W. (2009). An efficient dynamic load balancing scheme for heterogenous processing system. []. Academic Press.]. *Proceedings of Computational Intelligence and Natural Computing, 2,* 319–322.

Trivedi, K. S. (2001). *Probability and statistics with reliability, queuing and computer science applications*. Upper Saddle River, NJ: Prentice Hall.

Tseng, L., Chin, Y., & Wang, S. (2009). A minimized makespan scheduler with multiple factors for grid computing systems. *Expert Systems with Applications, 36*(8), 11118–11130. doi:10.1016/j.eswa.2009.02.071

Ucar, B., Aykanat, C., Kaya, K., & Ikinci, M. (2006). Task assignment in heterogeneous computing systems. *Journal of Parallel and Distributed Computing, 66*(1), 32–46. doi:10.1016/j.jpdc.2005.06.014

Vidyarthi, D. P., & Tripathi, A. K. (2001). Maximizing reliability of distributed computing system with task allocation using simple genetic algorithm. *Journal of Systems Architecture, 47*(6), 549–554. doi:10.1016/S1383-7621(01)00013-3

Watts, J., & Taylor, S. (1998). A practical approach to dynamic load balancing. *IEEE Transactions on Parallel and Distributed Systems, 9*(3), 235–248. doi:10.1109/71.674316

Whitley, D. (1994). A genetic algorithm tutorial. *Statistics and Computing, 4*(2), 65–85. doi:10.1007/BF00175354

Wu, J. (1999). *Distributed system design*. Boca Raton, FL: CRC Press.

Xu, C., & Lau, F. (1994). Iterative dynamic load balancing in multicomputers. *The Journal of the Operational Research Society*, 786–796.

Zeng, Z., & Veeravalli, B. (2006). Design and performance evaluation of queue-and-rate-adjustment dynamic load balancing policies for distributed networks. *IEEE Transactions on Computers, 55*(11), 1410–1422. doi:10.1109/TC.2006.180

Zomaya, A., & Teh, Y. (2001). Observations on using genetic algorithms for dynamic load-balancing. *IEEE Transactions on Parallel and Distributed Systems, 12*(9), 899–911. doi:10.1109/71.954620

ADDITIONAL READING

Aguilar, J., & Gelenbe, E. (1997). Task assignment and transaction clustering heuristics for distributed systems. *Information Sciences, 97*(1), 199–219. doi:10.1016/S0020-0255(96)00178-8

Allen, A. O. (2005). *Probability, statistics, and queuing theory with computer science applications* (2nd ed.). Academic Press.

Attiya, H., & Welch, J. (2000). *Distributed computing: Fundamentals, simulations, and advanced topics*. John Wiley and Sons Inc.

Chen, H., Marden, J., & Wierman, A. (2008). The effect of local scheduling in load balancing designs. *ACM SIGMETRICS Performance Evaluation Review, 36*(2), 110–112. doi:10.1145/1453175.1453200

Dong, F., & Akl, S. G. (2006). *Scheduling algorithms for grid computing: State of the art and open problems*. Kingston, Ontario: School of Computing, Queens University.

Garg, V. K. (2006). *Elements of distributed computing*. Wiley-Interscience: John Wiley and Sons, Inc. Publication.

George Coulouris, J. D., & Kindberg, T. (2000). *Distributed operating system-concepts and design* (2nd ed.). Addison Wesley.

Grosu, D., & Chronopoulos, A. (2003). A truthful mechanism for fair load balancing in distributed systems. In *Network computing and applications, 2003. NCA 2003. second IEEE international symposium on* (pp. 289–296).

Jayasinghe, M., Tari, Z., Zeephongsekul, P., & Zomaya, A. (2011). Task assignment in multiple server farms using preemptive migration and flow control. *Journal of Parallel and Distributed Computing, 71*(12), 1608–1621. doi:10.1016/j.jpdc.2011.07.001

Kabalan, K., Smari, W., & Hakimian, J. (2002). Adaptive load sharing in heterogeneous systems: Policies, modifications, and simulation. *International Journal of Simulation, Systems. Science and Technology, 3*(1-2), 89–100.

Kołodziej, J., & Khan, S. U. (2012). Multi-level hierarchic genetic-based scheduling of independent jobs in dynamic heterogeneous grid environment. *Information Sciences, 214*, 1–19. doi:10.1016/j.ins.2012.05.016

Kremien, O., & Kramer, J. (1992). Methodical analysis of adaptive load sharing algorithms. *Parallel and Distributed Systems. IEEE Transactions on, 3*(6), 747–760.

Kumar, B. K., Madheswari, S. P., & Venkatakrishnan, K. (2007). Transient solution of an m/m/2 queue with heterogeneous servers subject to catastrophes. *International journal of information and management sciences, 18* (1), 63.

Li, J., & Kameda, H. (1998). Load balancing problems for multiclass jobs in distributed/parallel computer systems. *Computers. IEEE Transactions on, 47*(3), 322–332.

Li, Y., Yang, Y., Ma, M., & Zhou, L. (2009). A hybrid load balancing strategy of sequential tasks for grid computing environments. *Future Generation Computer Systems, 25*(8), 819–828. doi:10.1016/j.future.2009.02.001

Maheswaran, M., Braun, T., & Siegel, H. (1999). *Heterogeneous distributed computing*. Wiley Encyclopedia of Electrical and Electronics Engineering.

Michalewicz, Z. (1994). *Genetic Algorithms + Data Structures = Evolution Programs* (2nd ed.). Berlin: Springer-Verlag. doi:10.1007/978-3-662-07418-3

Mitzenmacher, M. (2001). The power of two choices in randomized load balancing. *Parallel and Distributed Systems. IEEE Transactions on, 12*(10), 1094–1104.

Motwani, R. (1995). *Randomized algorithms*. Cambridge university press. doi:10.1017/CBO9780511814075

Salleh, S., & Zomaya, A. Y. (1999). *Scheduling in Parallel Computing Systems, Fuzzy and Annealing Techniques*. Kluwer Academic. doi:10.1007/978-1-4615-5065-5

Shivaratri, N., Krueger, P., & Singhal, M. (1992). Load distributing for locally distributed systems. *Computer, 25*(12), 33–44. doi:10.1109/2.179115

Subrata, R., Zomaya, A., & Landfeldt, B. (2007). Artificial life techniques for load balancing in computational grids. *Journal of Computer and System Sciences, 73*(8), 1176–1190. doi:10.1016/j.jcss.2007.02.006

Talbi, E.-G., & Muntean, T. (1993). Hill-climbing, simulated annealing and genetic algorithms: a comparative study and application to the mapping problem. In *System sciences, 1993, proceeding of the twenty-sixth hawaii international conference on,* Vol. 2, 565–573.

Wang, T. Y., Ke, J. C., Wang, K. H., & Ho, S. C. (2006). Maximum likelihood estimates and confidence intervals of an m/m/r queue with heterogeneous servers. *Mathematical Methods of Operations Research*, 63(2), 371–384. doi:10.1007/s00186-005-0047-z

Xu, C., & Lau, F. (1997). *Load Balancing in Parallel Computers-Theory and Practice*. Kluwer Academic.

Yu, K., & Chen, C. (2008). An evolution-based dynamic scheduling algorithm in grid computing environment. In *Intelligent systems design and applications, 2008. ISDA'08. eighth international conference on,* Vol. 1, 450–455.

KEY TERMS AND DEFINITIONS

Heterogeneous Distributed Computing System (HDCS): HDCS is a distributed suite of different high-performance nodes each having its own private memory, interconnected with high-speed links to perform different computationally intensive applications that have diverse computational requirements.

Load Balancing: Load-balancing problem is to assign each task to one of the computing node so that the loads placed on all nodes of the system are as "balanced" as possible.

Load: The load of a computing node is the sum of the weights of the task assigned to it, and measured as sum of the expected time to compute of the individual task.

Makespan: The completion time at the maximum loaded computing node.

Solution Space: The space of all feasible solutions of a problem is called solution space (also search space or state space).

Task: A task is a scheduling entity and its execution cannot be preempted.

Chapter 11
Design Issues of 4G–Network Mobility Management

D. H. Manjaiah
Mangalore University, India

P. Payaswini
Mangalore University, India

ABSTRACT

Fourth Generation wireless networking (4G network) is expected to provide global roaming across different types of wireless and mobile networks. In this environment, roaming is seamless and users are always connected to the best network. Moreover, 4G networks will be packet switched systems entirely based on the IPv6 protocol. The essentiality of Quality of Service (QoS) and the heterogeneous nature of 4G pose high demands onto the mobility management technology. Due to this, one of the most challenging research areas for the 4G network is the design of intelligent mobility management techniques that take advantage of IP-based technologies to achieve global roaming among various access technologies. In order to address the issue of heterogeneity of the networks, IEEE 802.21 working group proposed Media Independent Handover (MIH). The scope of the IEEE 802.21 MIH standard is to develop a specification that provides link layer intelligence and other related network information to upper layers to optimize handovers between heterogeneous media. The IEEE 802.21 group defines the media independent handover function that will help mobile devices to roam across heterogeneous networks and stationary devices to switch over to any of the available heterogeneous networks around it.

INTRODUCTION

The explosive growth of the Internet and the increasing demand for all sorts of IP-based services like voice & data, multimedia has led the wireless industry to evolve its core network towards the IP technology. It is expected that in future, IP connectivity will penetrate the access network as well, resulting in an all-IP network concept (Akan, & Edemen, September 2010). A 4G system is expected to provide a comprehensive and secure all-IP based solution where users are allowed to roam

DOI: 10.4018/978-1-4666-4940-8.ch011

between different types of access networks. The International Telecommunications Union (ITU) has specified that the peak speed requirements for the 4G standard are to be 100Mbps for a mobile connection and 1Gbps for stationary connections (Akyildiz, Gutierrez-Estevez, & Reyes, 2010).

The future 4G infrastructures will consist of a set of various networks using IP as a common protocol. It will have broader bandwidth, higher data rate, and smoother and quicker handoff. The focus of 4G will be ensuring seamless service across a multitude of wireless systems and networks such as cellular networks, WiFi, WiMAX, satellite, Digital Video Broadcasting - Handheld (DVB-H) (Cerqueira, Zeadally, Leszczuk, Curado & Mauthe, 2011). After successful implementation, 4G - technology is likely to enable ubiquitous computing, that will simultaneously connects to numerous high date speed networks offers faultless handoffs all over the geographical regions.

4G will be a convergence platform providing clear advantages in terms of coverage, bandwidth and power consumption. 4G services will be end-to-end QoS (Belhoul, 2007), high security (Aiash, Mapp, Lasebae, & Phan, May 2010), available at anytime, anywhere with seamless mobility, affordable cost, one billing, and fully personalized. It is about convergence, convergence of networks, of technologies, of applications and of services, to offer a personalized and pervasive network to the users. The 4G network will be an umbrella of multitude of technologies. The glue is likely to be seamless mobility over heterogeneous wireless networks.

4G network systems require higher reliability and high spectral efficiency. To achieve this Orthogonal Frequency Division Multiplexing (OFDM) is considered to be the best modulation technique for 4G- networks (John, October 2011). OFDM can provide large data rates with sufficient robustness to radio channel impairments. Orthogonal FDM's spread spectrum technique spreads the data over a lot of carriers that are spaced apart at precise frequencies. This spacing provides the

"orthogonality", which prevents the receivers/demodulators from seeing frequencies other than their own specific one. The main benefit of OFDM is high spectral efficiency. 4G networks will also use smart antenna technology, which is used to aim the radio signal in the direction of the receiver in the terminal from the base station. When teamed up with adaptive techniques, multiple antennas can cancel out more interference while enhancing the signal.

Although 4G wireless technology offers higher data rates and the ability to roam across multiple heterogeneous wireless networks, several issues require further research and development. Since 4G is still in the cloud of the sensible standards creation, ITU and IEEE form several task forces to work on the possible completion for the 4G mobile standards as well. 3GPP LTE (Bai et al., 2012) is an evolution standard from UMTS, and WiMAX is another candidate from IEEE. These technologies have different characteristics and try to meet 4G characteristics to become a leading technology in the future market. The advantage of 4G wireless systems has created many research opportunities. The expectations from 4G are high in terms of data rates, spectral efficiency, mobility and integration. Figure 1 gives the scenario of 4G network.

KEY COMPONENTS OF 4G NETWORK

The key components of 4G Network are access scheme, Mobile IPv6, Multi-Antenna Systems, Software Defined Radio (SDR). The brief overview of key components is given below.

Access Schemes

As the wireless standards evolved, the access techniques used also exhibited increase in efficiency, capacity and scalability. There are various numbers of multiple access techniques which are

Figure 1. An illustration of a wireless roaming scenario in 4G

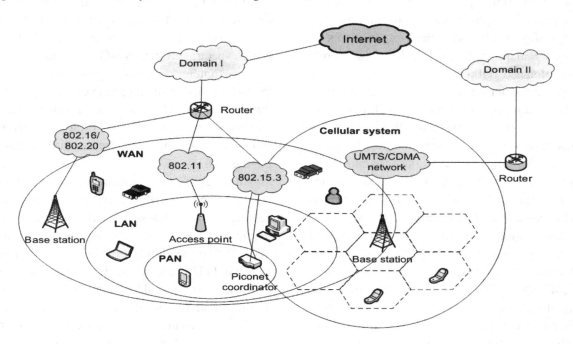

proposed for 4G system named as Direct Spread-Code Division Multiple Access (DS-CDMA), Multicarrier-CDMA (MC-CDMA), Orthogonal FDMA (OFDMA), Interleave Division Multiple Access (IDMA) etc., (Sehgal & Agrawal, 2010). WiMAX is using OFDMA in the downlink and in the uplink. The advantage of the above mentioned access techniques are that they require less complexity for equalization at the receiver. This is an added advantage especially in the Multi Input Multi Output (MIMO) (Louta, & Bellavista, 2013) environments since the spatial multiplexing transmission of MIMO systems inherently requires high complexity equalization at the receiver.

Mobile IPv6

4G network is pure packet switched network. This will require low-latency data transmission. IP is considered a unified protocol layer that connects applications to network infrastructure and serves as the common connectivity layer that simultaneously handle circuit-switched and packet-switched traffic (Belhoul, 2007). An all IP-based 4G wireless network has inherent advantages over its predecessors. It is compatible with, and independent of the underlying radio access technology. Although IPv6 is considered as key integrating technology, there has been almost universal recognition that IPv6 needs to be enhanced to meet the need for future 4G cellular environments. In particular, the absence of a location management hierarchy leads to concerns about the signalling scalability and handoff latency. This is especially significant when we consider that 4G aims at providing mobility support to potentially billions of mobile devices, within the stringent performance bounds associated with real time multimedia traffic.

Multi-Antenna Systems

The performance of radio communications depends on an antenna system. Recently, multiple antenna technologies are emerging to achieve the goal of 4G systems such as high rate, high reliability, and long range communications. To increase the reliability of the communication systems, multiple antennas can be installed at the transmitter or/and at the receiver. It offers significant increases in data throughput and link range without additional bandwidth or increased transmit power. It achieves this goal by spreading the same total transmit power over the antennas to achieve an array gain that improves the spectral efficiency or to achieve a diversity gain that improves the link reliability. MIMO (Louta, & Bellavista, 2013), a smart-antenna, shows promise in 4G system, particularly since the antenna systems at both transmitter and receiver are usually a limiting factor when attempting to support increased data rates. Because of these properties, MIMO is an important part of 4G network.

Software-Defined Radio (SDR)

4G network is based on Software Defined radio (SDR) (Zhang, Ariyavisitakul & Tao, 2012). SDR is a radio communication system where components that have been implemented in hardware are instead implemented using software on a personal computer or other embedded computing devices. SDR removes the requirement of expensive hardware and allows with an antenna and receiver hardware to receive signals and use their computer to do the decoding. The key point is that SDRs have the ability to go beyond simple single-channel, single-mode transceiver technology with the ability to change modes arbitrarily because the channel bandwidth, rate, and modulation are all flexibly determined through software.

CHARACTERISTICS OF 4G NETWORKS

The 4G networks have the following characteristics:

- **IP Connectivity:** 4G is entirely packet switched network, with IP as backbone.
- **Fully Converged Services:** A wide range of services will be available to the mobile user conveniently and securely via the 4G Core Network. Personal communications, information systems and entertainment will seem to be merged into a seamless pool of content.
- **Enhanced WLANs:** To provide low-cost, high bandwidth coverage over campus-sized networks with support for the real-time hand-over of time-sensitive services such as voice and video.
- **A Potentially Open Business Model:** Whereby users are billed customers of a service provider and can gain access to services from any access network.
- **A Flexible and Dynamic IP Service-Creation Platform:** To allow the rapid creation of services, potentially by third parties, for delivery, suitably adapted, to an authenticated user with any terminal on any IP connected network.
- **Vertical Handover Support:** Allowing users to move from, one technology to another without re-starting a session and having the underlying service respond to the change of bandwidth and delay, etc.
- **Ubiquitous Mobile Access:** Mobile handsets used in 4G network will be intelligent and software-reconfigurable on the fly to allow them to interface with different types of networks on the move. Also, there will be full cross compatibility on a world-wide scale since each type of network has a gateway to the IP backbone.
- **Software Dependency:** Advanced software systems are employed for all purposes - network operation, service provision, interfacing and integration, etc. Not only the Core Network but the mobile devices will be highly intelligent as well as re-configurable via software.

- **Diverse User Devices:** 4G network supports vast array of devices that are capable of accessing the 4G backbone. Not only personal devices like phones, PDAs, laptops, etc. but also sensors, embedded controllers and other specialized equipment can also access 4G to allow them to autonomously communicate with each other. By building in sophisticated software, they will be able to automatically initiate timely actions.
- **Autonomous Networks:** While user devices are highly intelligent, the core network will also be very sophisticated. It will be capable of managing itself and dynamically adapting to changing network conditions and user preferences for seamless communication. Apart from evolved mobility management, connection control, handover mechanisms, etc, dynamic bandwidth allocation will make far more efficient use of the available radio spectrum.

BACKGROUND

Cellular communications has experienced explosive growth in the past two decades. As the technology evolved, the first operational cellular communication system was deployed in the Norway in 1981 and was followed by similar systems in the US and UK. These first generation systems provided voice transmissions by using frequencies around 900 MHz and analogue modulation. As the number of cellular subscribers grew and there was a need for increased network capacity, digital systems were invented. These included Global System for Mobile communication (GSM) and Code Division Multiple Access (CDMA). The second generation (2G) of the wireless mobile network was based on low-band digital data signaling. The first GSM systems used a 25MHz frequency spectrum in the 900MHz band. With digital technologies, digitized voice can be coded and encrypted. Therefore, the 2G cellular network is also more secure (Akan, & Edemen, September 2010).

2.5G is an intermediary phase, uses the GPRS standard, which delivers packet-switched data capabilities to existing GSM networks (Akyildiz et al., 2010). It allows users to send graphics-rich data as packets. 2.5G use circuit switching for voice and packet switching for data transmission. Circuit switched technology requires that the user be billed by airtime rather than the amount of data transmitted. This is because of bandwidth is reserved for the user. In Packet switched technology bandwidth is utilized much more efficiently, so it allows each user's packets to compete for available bandwidth, and billing users for the amount of data transmitted. Thus a move towards using packet-switched, and therefore IP networks, is natural.

The third generation (3G) integrates cellular phones into the Internet world by providing high-speed packet-switching data transmission in addition to circuit-switching voice transmission (Correia, 2010). The 3G revolution allowed mobile telephone customers to use audio, graphics and video applications. Over 3G it is possible to watch streaming video and engage in video telephony. 3G phone speeds deliver up to 2 Mbps, but only under the best conditions and in stationary mode (Correia, 2010). Moving at a high speed can drop 3G bandwidth to a mere 145 Kbps.

The 4G has been developing with the aim of providing transmission rates up to 20 Mbps while simultaneously accommodating Quality of Service (QoS) features. The goal of 4G will be to replace the entire core of cellular networks with a single worldwide cellular network completely standardized based on the IP for video, packet data utilizing Voice over IP (VoIP) and multimedia services. The newly standardized networks would provide uniform video, voice, and data services to the cellular handset or handheld Internet appliance, based entirely on IP (Marsch, 2012). In a fourth-generation wireless system, cellular providers have the opportunity to provide data access to a wide variety of devices. The cellular network would become a data network on which cellular phones could operate as well as any other data device (Martin, Amin, Eltawil, & Hussien, June 2011). Table 1 shows the history of generation of networks and its comparison.

RECENT TECHNOLOGIES

WiFi

The term WiFi is an abbreviation of 'wireless fidelity' and it uses the 802.11 standard. WiFi is a mechanism for wirelessly connecting electronic devices (Correia, 2010). A device enabled with Wi-Fi, such as a personal computer, video game console, Smartphone, or digital audio player, can connect to the Internet via a wireless network access point. An access point (or hotspot) has a range of about 20 meters indoors and a greater range outdoors. Multiple overlapping access points can cover large areas. There are three versions of WiFi radios currently available - the ones that work with 802.11b, 802.11g and 802.11a standards. While the first two- 802.11b and 802.11g - transmit 2.4 GHz, the radios operating at 802.11a standard can transmit at 5GHz. The 802.11a and 802.11g standard radios use Orthogonal Frequency-Division Multiplexing (OFDM) technique while the 802.11b uses Complementary Code Keying (CCK) technique. Due to the higher frequencies and the encoding techniques, WiFi radios can transmit a very high amount of data per second. The 802.11a and 802.11g standard radios transfer between 30-54 megabits per second and the 802.11b standard typically conveys 7-11 megabits per second (Malekian, November 2008).

WiMAX

WiMAX is designed to accommodate both fixed and mobile broadband applications. WiMax stands for Worldwide Interoperability for Microwave Access based on the IEEE 802.16 standard (Malekian, November 2008). It is a telecommunications technology that offers transmission of wireless data via a number of transmission methods; such as portable or fully mobile internet access via point to multipoint links. The WiMAX technology offers around 72Mbps without any need for the cable infrastructure. It is developed by an industry consortium, overseen by a group called the WiMAX Forum. The WiMAX Forum certifies WiMAX equipment to ensure it meets the technology standards.

Table 1. Generation of networks

Technology	1G	2G	2.5G	3G	4G
Design Began	1970	1980	1985	1990	2000
Implementation	1984	1991	1999	2002	-
Service	Analog voice, Synchronous data to 9.6kbps	Digital Voice, Short messages	Higher capacity, Packetized data	Higher capacity, broadband data up to 2Mbps	Higher capacity, completely IP oriented, Multimedia, data to hundreds of mega bites
Standards	AMPS, TACS, NMT, etc	TDMA, CDMA, GSM, PDC	GPRS, EDGE, 1xRTT	WCDMA, CDMA 2000	Single standard
Data Bandwidth	1.9kbps	14.4 kbps	384kbps	2 Mbps	200 Mbps
Multiplexing	FDMA	TDMA, CDMA	TDMA, CDMA	CDMA	CDMA
Core Network	PSTN	PSTN	PSTN, Packet network	Packet network	Internet

The IEEE 802.16e standard, also known as Mobile WiMAX, was initially designed to allow vehicular mobility applications. It was completed in December 2005 and was published formally as IEEE 802.16e-2005. It uses Scalable Orthogonal Frequency Division Multiple Access (SOFDMA), a multi-carrier modulation technique that uses sub-channelization, where channel bandwidths are selectable, ranging between 1.25MHz and 20MHz. The key attribute of IEEE 802.16e is the introduction of the handover capability for users moving between cells. In October 2007, the Radio Communication Sector of the International Telecommunication Union (ITU-R) included WiMAX technology in the IMT-2000 set of standards, also known as 3G (Martin et al., June 2011).

UMTS

Universal Mobile Telecommunications Service (UMTS) is a third-generation broadband, packet-based transmission of text, digitized voice, video, and multimedia at data rates up to 2Mbps. UMTS offers a consistent set of services to mobile computer and phone users, no matter where they are located in the world. UMTS is based on the Global System for Mobile (GSM) communication standard (Martin et al., June 2011). It is also endorsed by major standards bodies and manufacturers as the planned standard for mobile users around the world. Once UMTS is fully available, computer and phone users can be constantly attached to the Internet wherever they travel and, as they roam, will have the same set of capabilities. Users will have access through a combination of terrestrial wireless and satellite transmissions.

LTE

LTE (Long Term Evolution) is a wireless broadband technology designed to support roaming Internet access via cell phones and handheld devices (Bai et al., 2012). Because LTE offers significant improvements over older cellular communication standards, some refer to it as a 4G (fourth generation) technology along with WiMAX. LTE is an update to the UMTS technology that will enable it to provide significantly faster data rates for both uploading and downloading (Bikos, & Sklavos, 2013). LTE or the E-UTRAN (Evolved Universal Terrestrial Access Network) is the access part of the Evolved Packet System (EPS). The main requirements for the new access network are high spectral efficiency, high peak data rates, short round trip time and frequency flexibility.

PROBLEMS IN EXISTING NETWORK

Bandwidth will always be the limiting factor in the development of applications and devices whether it is wired or wireless. The short fall of 3G networks is because of limited bandwidth. It doesn't meet the requirements of what the end user has come to expect these days. There are a number of trends which are already visible today which will increase bandwidth requirements in the future (Conti et al., 2011):

- **Rising Use:** As prices get more attractive, more and more people will use wireless networks for data applications. Consequently, bandwidth demand will rise.
- **Multimedia Content:** Due to recent advancement of mobile devices, they are capable of handling multimedia contents like video, images, and music files. Such multimedia downloads are also starting to become popular which again increase bandwidth requirements.
- **Mobile Social Networks:** Similar to the fixed line Internet, a different breed of applications is changing the way people are using the net. Blogs as well as podcasts, picture- and video sharing, sharing sites are reshaping the internet as users suddenly do not only simply consume content

anymore but also create their own content which they want to share with others.

- **Voice Over IP:** The fixed line world is rapidly moving towards Voice over IP these days. VoIP requires much more air interface bandwidth than the super slim voice codecs which are currently used for circuit switched voice calls over wireless networks. The air interface has been optimized on all layers of the protocol stack for circuit switched voice. The same is not possible for VoIP as the IP stack is a general data transmission stack and thus it cannot be optimized for voice. The only solution is to increase the available bandwidth.

- **Fixed Line Internet Replacement:** Voice revenue in both the fixed line and the wireless market are on the decline. In many countries, operators are trying to compensate by offering Internet access for PCs, notebooks, etc. over their UMTS/HSDPA or CDMA networks.

- **Competition from Alternative Wireless Internet Providers:** In some countries, alternative operators are already offering wireless broadband Internet access with WiFi or (pre-) WiMAX 802.16d networks.

RESEARCH CHALLENGES

In the 4G networks, various types of wireless networks are expected to be interconnected to support ubiquitous high speed data services. These wireless systems were designed independently and targeting different service types, data rates, and users, and thus require an intelligent interworking approach to be effective. Providing service continuity and service quality in a heterogeneous network environment would create several research challenges in the 4G Networks and these challenges are listed below (Stevens-Navarro & Wong, May 2006) (Yang, Gondal, Qiu, & Dooley, November 2007):

- **Multimode User Terminals:** In order to access different kinds of services and technologies, the user terminals should be able to configure themselves in different modes. This eliminates the need of multiple terminals. Adaptive techniques like smart antennas and software radio have been proposed for achieving terminal mobility.

- **Network Discovery:** 4G network devices will be multi-mode, multi-access and re-configurable. Which means each terminal can be using more than one type of network and possibly can access multiple networks simultaneously for different applications. In such an environment, a terminal must be able to discover what networks are available for use.

- **Access Technologies:** 4G- network is a heterogeneous wireless environment consist of number of radio technologies and may have overlapped radio coverage. A mobile user needs to switch between access networks to maintain service continuity and optimize service quality. Dealing with heterogeneous access technologies is a challenge to the design of 4G network. The greatest challenge is to select the network that will satisfy the QoS requirements of the current service and that will be the most economical.

- **Terminal Mobility:** This is one of the biggest issues the researchers are facing. Terminal mobility allows the user to roam across different geographical areas that uses different technologies. There are two important issues related to terminal mobility. One is location management where the system has to locate the position of the mobile for providing service. Another important issue is hand off management. In the traditional mobile systems only horizontal hand off has to be performed where as in 4G systems both horizontal and vertical hand off should be performed. Horizontal hand off is performed when a mobile movies from one cell to another and vertical handoff is performed when a mobile moves between two wireless systems.

- **Personal Mobility:** Personal mobility deals with the mobility of the user rather than the user terminals. The idea behind this is, no matter where the user is located and what device he is using, he should be able to access his messages.
- **Network Architectures:** 4G is an integration of heterogeneous wireless networks. Moreover these networks rely on different network architectures and protocols for transport, routing, mobility management and so forth. The interconnection of these networks in an integral manner to facilitate the cooperation between them is another research challenge.
- **Network Conditions:** Network conditions such as bandwidth, delay, jitter and so forth may vary across wireless networks, and result in different service quality to be provided. How does a mobile user deal with the variation in network conditions, and maintain service quality when crossing heterogeneous wireless networks is needs to be addressed.

OVERVIEW OF MOBILITY MANAGEMENT IN 4G NETWORK

Mobility management is used to trace physical user and subscriber locations to provide mobile phone services, like calls and Short Message Service (SMS). In general, mobility management includes location management, handoff management. Location management is a two-stage process that enables the network to discover current attachment point of the mobile user for call delivery. The first stage is location update or registration. In this stage, the MT periodically notifies the network of its new access point, allowing the network to authenticate the user and revise the user's location profile. The second stage is call delivery. Here the network is queried for the user location profile and the current position of the mobile terminal is found. Handoff management deals with communication connections with a mobile node (MN) when the MN moves from current serving area to a new serving area in a same system. It is classified into two types, namely Make-before-break and break-before-make handover. In make-before-break handover, the connection with the new target access node is established before releasing the connection with the old one. Make before break handover also called as soft handover. Conversely, in break-before-make handover, the old connection is terminated before the new one with the new target access node is established. It is also known as hard handover.

Mobility management in 4G networks can take place in different layers of the OSI model including network layer (L3), link layer (L2) and cross-layer (L3 + L2) (Xie & Akyildiz, 2002) (Belhoul, 2007). The layer-2 (L2) mobility refers to the case where the MN roams among different access nodes while the point of attachment to IP network remains the same. The layer-3 (L3) mobility involves the change of IP addresses. For efficient delivery of services to the mobile users, the 4G networks require new mechanisms of mobility management where the location of every user is proactively determined before the service is delivered. Moreover, for designing an adaptive communication protocol, various existing mobility management schemes are to be seamlessly integrated.

Location Management

Current techniques for location management involve database architecture design and the transmission of signaling messages between various components of a signaling network. As the number of mobile subscriber increases, new or improved schemes are needed to effectively support a continuously increasing subscriber's population (Taniuchi et al., 2009).

The design of a location management scheme must address the following issues:

- Minimization of signaling overhead and latency in the service delivery,
- Meeting the guaranteed quality of service (QoS) of applications,
- In a fully overlapping area where several wireless networks co-exist, an efficient and robust algorithm must be designed to select the best network. The selected network through which a mobile device should perform registration, deciding on where and how frequently the location information should be stored, and how to determine the exact location of a mobile device within a specific time frame.

Handoff Management

In 4G system handoff management is more complex to deal with since it covers both horizontal handoff and vertical handoff. Handoff between two base stations (BSs) of the same system is called Horizontal handoff and deals with the intra-system handoff. It involves a terminal device to change cells within the same type of to maintain service continuity (Akyildiz, Xie & Mohanty, 2004). Vertical handoff refers to a network node changing the type of connectivity it uses to access a supporting infrastructure. Vertical handoff handles the inter-system handoff and usually to support node mobility (Stevens-Navarro & Wong, May 2006). For example, handover from WiFi to WiMAX is termed as vertical handoff. It is difficult to realize the vertical handoff among different wireless communication systems while meeting the various Quality of Service (QoS) requirements. If handoff latency is too long, packets may get lost or disconnections may occur during the handoff. Therefore, fast and seamless handover is a big challenge for 4G networks. The Figure 2 shows the pictorial of horizontal and vertical handoff.

For achieving seamlessness mobility, the handover must be seamless. It means that the service must be continued even after performing handover to new network and transition to the new network is transparent to the user. Seamless handover requires, fast handover (minimal handover latency) and a smooth hand-over (minimal packet loss) (Makaya & Pierre, 2011). Regardless of handover types, the handover process control or the handover decision mechanism can be located in a network entity or in the MT itself. The handover decision involves some sort of measurements and information collection of handoff trigger and where to perform handover. This information obtained from mobile and network entity. Based on this, in Net work-Controlled Hand-Over (NCHO), the network entity has the primary control over the handover. Where as in Mobile-Controlled Hand-Over (MCHO), the MT must take its own measurement and make the handover decision on its own. When information and measurement s from the MT are used by the network to decide, it is referred to a Mobile-Assisted Hand-Over (MAHO). GSM uses MAHO technology. When the network collects information that can be used by the MT in a handover decision, it is a Network-Assisted Hand-Over (NAHO).

In order to support real-time high speed multimedia applications 4G requires small handoff delay and high data-rate transmission. The design of handoff management techniques in 4G networks must address the following issues (Stevens-Navarro & Wong, May 2006):

- Signaling overhead and power requirement for processing handoff messages should be minimized,
- QoS guarantees must be made,
- Network resources should be efficiently used,

Figure 2. Horizontal and vertical handoff

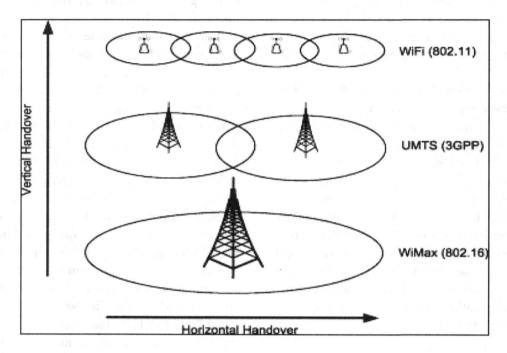

The handoff mechanism should be scalable, reliable and robust.

In vertical handover, there may be many IP address, many network interfaces, and many network connections and needs to develop a mechanism based on make before break. So handover latency time can be decreased or eliminating permanently. Efficiency of vertical handover depends on movement diction and capability of detecting that the current access network is going to become unusable before it actually does. The Mobility Manager (MM) can be used to provide mobility support to any kind of application for example VoIP application. In legacy applications, the MM delivers event notifications to an application mobility interface in charge of completing adaptation at the session layer and issuing adaptation commands for the legacy application.

HANDOVER PROCEDURE

The handover procedure can be divided into three phases namely, neighboring cell discovery and measurement, network selection and handover decision, and handover execution (Akyildiz, et al., 2004) (Fernandes & Karmouch, 2012).

Cell Discovery and Measurement

The cell discovery and measurement phase is to identify the need for handover which involves the following steps:

- **Neighboring Cell Discovery:** The Mobile Node can learn about its neighbors by scanning different channels or via the provisioning information from its current Base Station. It is a preliminary step to be considered before carrying out the signal strength measurement.

- **Signal Strength Measurement:** In order to measure the radio link quality of Neighboring cell, the MS should synchronize in frequency and in time with its neighboring cells. The signal strength is averaged over time so that fluctuations due to radio propagation can be eliminated. The network also makes itself the measurements such as the uplink quality, Bit Error Rate (BER) of the received data, etc.

- **Reporting of Measurement Result:** After the measurement, the Mobile Node sends measurement results to the network periodically or based on trigger events.

- **Information Gathering:** In 4G network, the Mobile Node is required to collect other information like the terminal capabilities, service experiences status, context information, etc. In order to assist the vertical handover decision.

Network Selection and Handover Decision

This phase is responsible for determining when and how to perform the handover and involves different steps:

- **Network Selection Triggering:** Network selection is triggered taking as input the measurement results.

- **Network Selection:** Network selection is the process of choosing the best access network among the multiple available ones. In 4G network, the network selection is done based on many criteria such as bandwidth, user preference, cost, QoS etc.

- **Handover Initiation:** If the network selection results in change of access node, the handover initiation must follow. If the access technology of the selected access node is different from the serving access technology, a vertical handover is executed.

- **Pre-Notification to All Recommended Target Base Stations:** The network selection gives a list of recommended target networks in the preferred order of networks. In this case, the network may query the recommended target network to check whether they can support the imminent handover. During this phase, certain pre-registration information of the Mobile Node will be relayed to the recommended target network for handover preparation purpose. At the end of this phase, the network can decide which target access network to select and send its decision to the Mobile Node.

Handover Execution

The handover execution includes the connection establishment, the resources release and the invocation of proper security services.

- **(Re-)Authentication:** Once the target access network is selected and the handover decision is launched, the MS must use appropriate user credentials to authenticate with the target network.

- **Execution:** Once the best access network is selected, and the re-authentication is successfully achieved, the communication session will be continued on the new radio interface through a new routing path. The change of routing path must be notified to the Corresponding Node (CN) or the content provider.

Several aspects can be considered in the handoff decision making to optimize the handoff performance. One is to find rules for when and how to trigger vertical handoff. For this various mobility metrics can be considered (Zahran & Liang, May 2005). The decision about when and how this handoff is executed is aided by handoff policy. For example, the priority can be set to provide the fastest network connection to the

Figure 3. Handover management concept

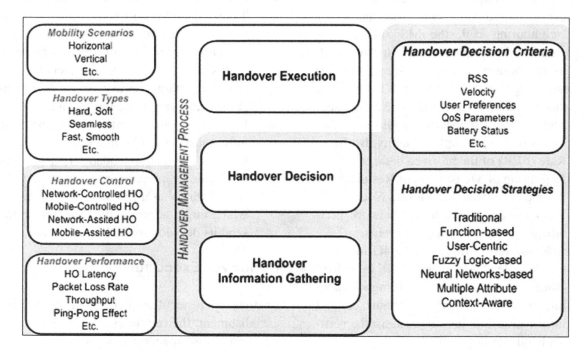

mobile user, or the cheapest. Policy parameters can be weighted as a set of tuples (factor, weight). For example, WLAN can be set as high priority, so that is used always when available, or alternatively handoff is made only when no latency or communication break sensitive application is active. Thus different mobility and application scenarios require different optimization aspects. (see Figure 3)

MOBILITY MANAGEMENT AT DIFFERENT LAYERS

Mobility management occurs in different layers of TCP/IP protocol suit due to the heterogeneity nature of the network. Several mobility management protocols have been proposed in the literature for mobility management in 4G networks. From the literature it is found that mobility management can be mainly classified into levels – link layer, networks layer and the cross-layer and it also

includes transport layer and application layer as well (Fernandes & Karmouch, 2012).

Link Layer Mobility Management

Link layer mobility mechanisms (Chen & Lin, 2012) provide mobility-related features in the underlying radio systems. It is specific for each wireless access network. For UMTS, it supports handoffs from one cell to another, whereas in WLANs, it allows roaming between access points belonging to the same subnet. It handles the issues related to inter-system roaming between heterogeneous access networks with different radio technologies and network management protocols. The protocols for air interface and the mobile application part (MAP) are two major considerations for designing inter-system roaming standards. In situations where a mobile node enters one wireless access network from another that support the same air interface protocols and MAP, the services are seamlessly migrated. However, when the MAPs are different for the two networks, additional network entities need to be placed and signaling traffic are to be transmitted for interworking. Each network has its own mobility management protocols and due this the new interworking entities should not replace existing systems. Rather, the entities should coexist and interwork. Additional gateways are usually required to be deployed to handle the inter-operating issues when roaming across heterogeneous access networks. Additional interworking entities are required for enabling information exchange between different systems while designing link layer-based mobility management schemes. In link layer protocols, handoff signals are transmitted through wireless links, and therefore, these protocols are tightly-coupled with specific wireless technologies. Mobility supported at the link layer is also called access mobility or link layer mobility.

Network Layer Mobility Management

Mobility at Network layer (Fernandes & Karmouch, 2012) provides a uniform mobility management that makes handoffs and network changes invisible to upper layers. Network layer mobility protocols use messages at the IP layer, and are nonbeliever of the underlying wireless access technologies. Different mobility management frameworks can be broadly distinguished into two categories - device mobility management protocol for localized or micro-mobility and protocols for inter-domain or macro mobility. The movement of a mobile node (MN) between two subnets within one domain is referred to as micro-mobility. Macro-mobility refers to mobility among administrative domains such as an enterprise network having a number of subnetworks.

There are two advantages we can get from network layer mobility:

- Better performance with respect to solutions implemented at upper layers of protocol stack.

- A transparent mobility management to any application or higher level protocol. Network application just use one source address which is known as home address and are unaware of access network changes.

Cross-Layer Mobility Management

The use of L2 hints for L3 handover has been widely explored in the literature. It refers to a L2/L3 cross-layer mobility management approach (Chan, Yokota, Xie, Seite & Liu, 2011). This mechanisms use link layer information to make an efficient network layer handoff. The utilization of link layer information reduces the delay in movement detection of the Mobile Node so that the overall handoff delay is minimized. One can recognize that a single layer-specific mobility management protocol can hardly provide the advanced mobility support in heterogeneous networks. The intrinsic reason is that mobility brings about significant impacts on each layer, which in turn has its convenience to deal with different level mobility impacts. A multi-layer architecture that can make full use of each layer's contributions while still keeping the basic structure of the protocol stack is highly demanded.

The cross-layer protocols are more common for handoff management. These protocols aim to achieve network layer handoff with the help of communication and signaling from the link layer. By receiving and analyzing, in advance, the signal strength reports and the information regarding the direction of movement of the mobile node from the link layer, the system gets ready for a network layer handoff so that packet loss is minimized and latency is reduced.

Transport Layer

Mobility in this layer uses an extension to transport protocols, as in the case of mobile SCTP. The drawback of this mobility approach is that mobility is restricted to applications using a specific transport protocol. The performance is also usually worse than in the network case.

Application Layer

It is actually application specific. For real time application such as VOIP an interesting opportunity is to introduce mobility management in the SIP protocol, so that it becomes part of the signaling protocol with no extra cost. SIP is capable of handling session, terminal, personal and service mobility. The main remedies are performance and lack of mobility support for non SIP based applications. When wireless links are in errors the disruption time in SIP horizontal handoffs increases much more with respect to the MIPv6.

REQUIREMENTS FOR MOBILITY MANAGEMENT IN 4G

Besides the basic functions that implement the goal of mobility management, there are many other requirements on performance and scalability that should be carefully taken into account when trying to design or select a mobility management scheme, including (Akyildiz, et al., 2004):

- **Seamless Handoff:** The handoff operations should be quick enough so that handoff latency is very less in order to reduce the packet drop as much as possible.
- **Signaling Traffic Overhead:** The number of signaling packets or the number of accesses to the related databases should be minimized to avoid the load on the network.
- **Routing Efficiency:** The routing paths between the communication nodes to the mobile nodes should be optimized to exclude redundant transfer or bypass path.
- **Quality of Service (QoS):** The mobility management scheme should support the establishment of new QoS reservation in order to deliver a variety of traffic, while minimizing the disruptive effect during the establishment.

- **Fast Security:** The mobility scheme should support different levels of security requirements such as data encryption and user authentication, while limiting the traffic and time of security process e.g. key exchange.
- **Bandwidth**: Higher offered bandwidth ensures lower call dropping and call blocking probabilities. Hence bandwidth handling should be an integral part of the handoff technique.
- **Handoff Latency:** Handoff Latencies affect the service quality of many applications of mobile users. Therefore a good handoff decision model should consider Handoff latency factor and the handoff latency should be minimized.
- **Power Consumption:** In 4G networks, we need to find ways to improve energy efficiency. Power is not only consumed by user terminal but also attributed to base station equipments. Power is also consumed during mobile switching or handoffs. During handoff, frequent interface activation can cause considerable battery drainage. The issue of power saving also arises in network discovery because unnecessary interface activation can increase power consumption. It is also important to incorporate power consumption factor during handoff decision.
- **Network Cost:** A multi criteria algorithm for handoff should also consider the network cost factor. The cost is to be minimized during vertical handoff in wireless networks.
- **User Preferences:** When handover happens, the users have more options for heterogeneous networks according to their preferences and network performance

parameters. The user preferences could be preferred networks, user application requirements (real time, non-real time), service types (Voice, data, video), Quality of service (It is a set of technologies for managing network traffic in a cost effective manner to enhance user experiences for wireless environments) etc.

- **Network Throughput:** As network throughput is considered in dynamic metrics for making decision of VHO, it is one the important requirement to be considered for the VHO.
- **Network Load Balancing:** Network load is to be considered during effective handoff. It is important to balance the network load to avoid deterioration in quality of services.
- **Network Security:** The security features provided in some wireless products may be weaker; to attain the highest levels of integrity, authentication, and confidentiality, network security features should be embedded in the handoff policies.
- **Velocity:** Velocity of the host should also be considered during handoff decision. Because of the overlaid architecture of heterogeneous networks, handing off to an embedded network, having small cell area, when travelling at high speeds is discouraged since a handoff back to the original network would occur very shortly afterwards.

EXISTING SOLUTIONS

From the literature it is found that a lot of research work is going on mobility management in 4G – Network. There are number of methods proposed in the literature to support mobility management in 4G. The basic method is mobility management based on MIPv6.

Mobile IPv6

Mobile IPv6 (MIPv6) was developed by the Internet Engineering Task Force (IETF) to maintain connectivity while users roam through IPv6 networks. It allows a mobile node to transparently maintain connections while moving from one subnet to another. The Mobile IPv6 protocol provides a unique permanent identifier (an IPv6 address) to a mobile node (MN) independently of its network of attachment. The key component of Mobile IPv6 is the home agent (HA) located in the mobile node's home network. It is a dedicated IPv6 router that manages the home IPv6 prefix, as well as the binding between the identifier and the locator which, in the Mobile IPv6 terminology, are respectively referred as Home Address and Care-of Address. The Care-of Address is used by the mobile node to communicate with its home agent. Packets sent to the Home Address by correspondent nodes (CN) are routed to the home network and intercepted by the home agent and then forwards it to the current location of the mobile node, i.e. its Care-of Address. Similarly, packets sent from the mobile node to its correspondent node must go through the home agent prior to being delivered. Figure 4 shows the working of mobile IPv6 (Marsch, 2012).

Even though Mobile IPv6 is considered to be one of the key technologies for the convergence of various heterogeneous access technologies, it requires some enhancement in order to achieve goals of 4G-network. The original Mobile IPv6 fails to support fast vertical handover and seamless mobility. The major problem that faces 4G networks is vertical handoff management. The existing handoff management protocols are not sufficient to guarantee handoff support that is transparent to the applications in 4G-network. There are some main areas that have to be improved prior to use as the core networking protocol in 4 G networks (Chen & Lin, 2012).

Figure 4. Working of Mobile IPv6

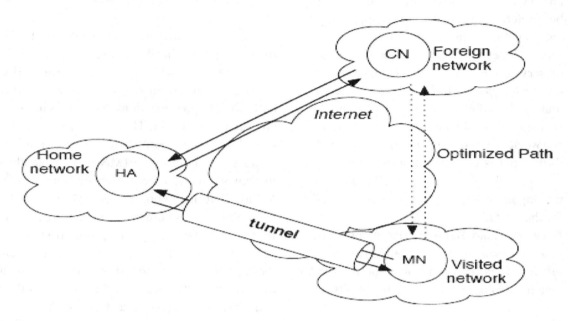

Paging Support

To preserve connectivity with the backbone communications, the MN needs to create location updates each time it changes its point of attachment. Massive signaling caused by regular action leads to a major wastage of the mobile node's battery power. So it is not appropriate to depend completely on location updates and it is require defining some sort of flexible paging support in the intra-domain mobility management.

Scalability

IPv6 support nodes to move within the internet topology while maintaining connections between mobile and CN. For this, a MN sends biding updates (BU) to it's HA and all CN s it communicates with every time it moves. Authenticating BU requires about 1.5 round trip times between the MN and CN. Additionally one round trip time (RTT) is needed to update the HA, this can be done while updating CNs. These RTT delays will disrupt active connections every time a handoff to

new radio technologies performed. So this delay needed to be eliminated. Additionally a mobile anchor point (MAP) has been suggested, that can be located anywhere in hierarchical routers. It is used to limit the signaling outside the local domain.

Hierarchical Mobile IPv6

Hierarchical Mobile IPv6 (HMIPv6) (Soliman, Bellier, Elmalki, & Castelluccia, 2008) is developed to reduce the amount of signaling traffic required, which affects handoff latency of MN's communications. HMIPv6 (Iqbal, Iqbal, Rasheed & Sandhu, October 2012) aims at reducing global signalization and providing improved local mobility management by introducing a hierarchical architecture. Hierarchical mobility management tends to reduce signalization overhead among the mobile node, its correspondent nodes, and its home agent. Unlike MIPv6, HMIPv6 addresses the issue of local mobility and global mobility separately, which means local handoffs are managed locally without notifying home agent, while global mobility is managed with the MIPv6 protocol. Indeed, by decomposing the network in several domains managed by a Mobility Anchor Point (MAP), a mobile node does not need to update its correspondent nodes when it moves or roams within the same domain.

MAP splits the management of the handover process into macro-mobility and micro-mobility and deals with them separately. Macro-mobility handover happens when MN moves globally from one MAP to another MAP that is located far away from each other. Micro-mobility handover happens when MN moves locally between access routers within one MAP domain. In HMIPv6, MN is assigned two addresses, regional care of address (RCoA) and on-link care of address (LCoA). These two addresses are very useful for managing macro-mobility and micro-mobility. Improvement of HMIPv6 over Mobile IPv6 is noticeable especially in the micro-mobility where the coverage area is small and the handover is frequent. HMIPv6 reduces the signaling over radio interface and supports more efficient handover. Moreover, by using MAPs, a network is likely to improve MIPv6 performances in terms of handover latency (Iqbal et al., October 2012).

Fast Handovers for Mobile IPv6

Due to the lengthy handoff procedure, MIPv6 is regarded as inappropriate for fast handover support in IPv6-based mobile networks. Under this circumstance, FMIPv6 (Soliman et al., 2008) is designed to enable a mobile node to configure a new Care-of-Address (CoA) before it changes subnetwork. Thus, the MN can use the CoA right after a connection with the new Access Router (NAR) is established. In this scheme the tunnel for a handover is established between the MAP and NAR, rather than between Previous AR (PAR) and NAR. For this purpose, the MN exchanges the signaling messages for the handover with MAP, not PAR. F-HMIPv6 utilizes the FMIPv6

messages for handover support without further defining any new messages.

The goal of FMIPv6 is to minimize handover latency since an MN can neither send nor receive packets until the hand-over completes. The principle is to create a new CoA before losing the connection with the PAR. Hence, when the mobile node finally connects to the NAR, it can continue its communications using a known address. If the early address registration failed, the MN can always resort to the traditional handover provided by MIPv6. The creation of the new CoA before the mobile node actually moves requires the protocol to anticipate the movement. This anticipation or prediction is based on messages exchanged by the physical layer or simply information gathered on layer 2. The goal here is to initiate a layer 3 handover (L3 handover) before the handover at Layer 2 (L2 handover) completes.

IEEE 802.21 MEDIA INDEPENDENT HANDOVER

In 4G networks, vertical handover (VHO) is a critical challenge to achieve always best connectivity (ABC) services. In order to address issue of VHO, the IEEE has proposed a new standard: 802.21 Media Independent Handover. It provides the necessary functionality by exchanging network information that helps MNs to determine the best available network to connect to. The core entity of its functionality is the Media Independent Handover Function (MIHF) which provides abstract services to higher layers through a unified interface (Griffith, Rouil & Golmie, 2010).

The IEEE Media Independent Handover protocol, also known as 802.21, defines an approach to facilitating service transition based on triggering and providing network detection and selection assistance. 802.21 support seamless handover between homogenous and heterogeneous networks. 802.21 does not in itself implement network

Figure 5. Overview of 802.21

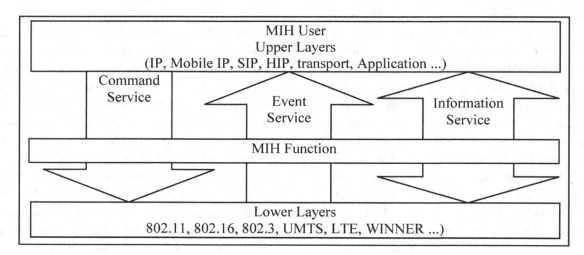

handover, rather it provides information to allow handover to and from a range of networks including cellular, GSM, GPRS, WiFi, Bluetooth. The network handover enabling function within the protocol is implemented through the MIH function. The MIH function provides new service access points (SAPs) and allows for information to be queried by the upper layers (Layer 3 and higher). Both mobile devices and network hardware must implement the standard to work, but everything should remain backward compatible for non-MIH aware devices. The Figure 5 gives overview of the standard IEEE 802.21 (Kumar, & Tyagi, July 2010).

In order to connect to the most appropriate network, the IEEE 802.21 standard uses the process of network discovery and selection to exchange network information, and it is based on certain mobile policies. The MIH in IEEE 802.21 uses two types of handovers: network controlled handovers and user controlled handovers. In case of network controlled handovers even though user battery consumption is less, it results in huge signaling overhead and high processing load in the network elements. Where in case of user controlled handovers the user initiates appropriate actions and there is high battery power consumption (Agarwal, Pramod & Jain, 2011).

The MIH function consists of three elements-the event service, command service and information service. The event service offers delivery of link status messages to the MIH users. The command service offers generic service primitives for controlling the handover. Both events and commands can be local or remote. The information service allows for information retrieval during handover preparation.

Media Independent Event Service

The Media Independent Event Service (MIES) includes all MIH actions that helps to detect and notify the events that are relevant to the selection and maintenance of the link over which the mobile terminal obtains network access. Which means the event service offers delivery of link status messages to the MIH users. Input events may affect the state of the MIH decision engine. State changes in the decision engine may generate output events. With respect to a given MIH instance, events may be either local or remote depending on whether they originate at the same network element/station or at a different one (Piri & Pentikousis, 2009).

The MIES [55] also provides event classification, event filtering and event reporting

Figure 6. Event, command and information services flow mode

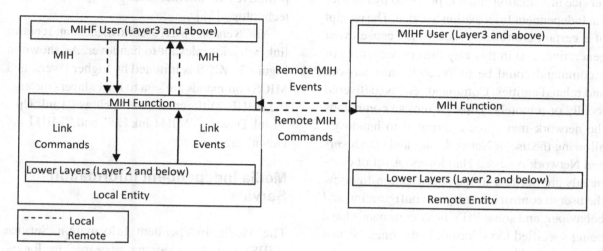

corresponding to dynamic changes in link characteristics, links status, and link quality. The MIH Function registers Link Event notifications with the interfaces. Any upper layers entities can register for an MIH Event notification, either in groups or with predetermined thresholds. These entities can be in a local or remote stack. Link Event generated by the lower layers is sent it to the MIH Function and which will report to any entity that has registered either an MIH Event or a Remote MIH Event. The information reported is meant to merely notify of an event occurrence. MIES can indicate or predict the changes in state and transmission behaviour of the physical, data link and logical link layers. This service can also be used to indicate management actions or command status on part of network or some such management entity. Some of the common events defined include "MIH Link Up", "MIH Link Down", "MIH Link Going Down", etc.

The Event Service may be broadly divided into two categories, Link Events and MIH Events. Both Link and MIH Events typically moves from a lower to higher layer. Link Events are those events that originate from event source entities below the MIH Function and typically terminate at the MIH Function. Entities generating Link

Events include various IEEE802-defined, 3GPP (Damnjanovic et al., 2011) defined and 3GPP2-defined interfaces but is not restricted to only those interfaces. Within the MIH Function, Link Events may be further propagated, with or without additional processing, to upper layer entities that have registered for the specific event. Events that are propagated by the MIH to the upper layers are defined as MIH Events.

Media Independent Command Service

The command service offers generic service primitives for controlling the handover. MICS refers to the commands sent from the higher layers to the lower layers in order to determine the status of links or control and configure the terminal to gain optimal performance or facilitate optimal handover policies. The mobility management protocols should combine dynamical information and static information to help in the decision making. The dynamic information includes regarding link status and parameters, and it is provided by the MICS (De La Oliva, Banchs, Soto, Melia & Vidal, 2008). The static information includes regarding network status, network operators or higher layer service information and it is provided by the Media Independent Information Service. The receipt of a certain command request may cause event generation, and in this way the consequences of a command could be followed by the network and related entities. Commands can be delivered locally or remotely. Through remote commands the network may force a terminal to handover, allowing the use of Network Initiated Handovers and Network Assisted Handovers. A set of commands are defined in the specification to allow the user to control lower layers configuration and behaviour, and some PHY layer commands have being specified too (Corujo, Guimaraes, Santos & Aguiar, 2011).

MIH commands are sent by the higher layers to the MIHF if the command is addressed to a remote MIHF, otherwise it will be sent to the local MIHF which will deliver the command to the appropriate destination through the MIHF transport protocol. To enable network initiated handovers as well as mobile initiated handovers, the command service provides a set of commands to help with network selection. Link commands are originated in the MIHF, on behalf of the MIH user, in order to configure and control the lower layers. Link commands are local only and should be implemented by technology dependant link

primitives to interact with the specific access technology [55].

MICS enables MIH users to manage and control link behavior relevant to handover. As shown in Figure 7, MICS is initiated by higher layers, and MICS commands are sent to lower layers through the MIHF. Different events such as ''Link Up'', ''Link Down'', ''MIH Link Up'', and ''MIH Link Down'' are defined.

Media Independent Information Service

The Media Independent Information Service (MIIS) provides a storage infrastructure for information that can be relevant to MIH decisions and a transport mechanism for requesting and distributing such information. It provides the capability for obtaining the necessary information for handovers including neighbor maps, link layer information, and availability of services. Basically, this service provides a two way street for all the layers to share information elements (IEs) to be used to make handover decisions (Corujo et al., 2011)

MIIS also provides a framework and corresponding schemes by which the MIHF entity can discover and obtain network information within geographic area. It provides a set of information

Figure 7. MICS and MIES models

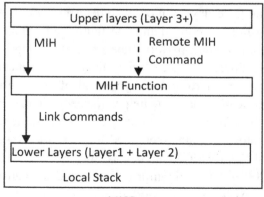

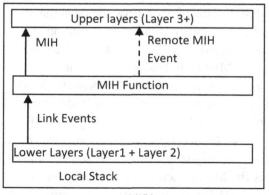

elements, the information structure and its representation and a query/reply type scheme. It also provides access to both static and dynamic information. The dynamic information such as channel information, MAC address and other information about higher layer services will help to make effective handover decisions. This information can be made available via both L2 and L3 layers.

The important component of MIIS is Information Elements (IEs). Information Elements provide necessary information that is essential for a handover module to make intelligent handover decision. The list of supported Information Elements can be very large and may vary from one application to another. The MIIS provides support for only those Information Elements that are necessary for mobility applications. The information service elements can be classified into three groups:

1. **General Network Information (GNI):** These information elements give a general overview of the network, such as location, name, network ID, Point of Attachment (POA) of the network, IP version, operator of the network.

2. **Link Layer Information (LLI):** These information elements include the information related to link layer layers such as, link layer parameters (channel, frequency, PHY types), data rates, neighbor information, security, QoS.

3. **Higher Layer Information (HLI):** These information elements include higher layer services or applications that are supported by the respective network. Some examples are support for Multimedia Message Service (MMS), Mobile IP (MIP), Virtual Private Network (VPN), types of applications supported (e.g. VoIP, e-mail, IPsec VPNs, streaming media, location based), pricing of access (e.g. "a fee is be required" versus "access to the network is free"), use of NAT, roaming partners.

FUTURE RESEARCH DIRECTIONS

Although 4G wireless technology offers higher bit rates and the ability to roam across multiple heterogeneous wireless networks, several issues require further research and development. It is not clear if existing 1G and 2G providers would upgrade to 3G or wait for it to evolve into 4G, completely bypassing 3G. The answer probably lies in the perceived demand for 3G and the ongoing improvement in 2G networks to meet user demands until 4G arrives. There are multiple research directions in the area of 4G network. Support for vertical handoff is a biggest challenge for research community. Even though there exists numerous vertical handoff algorithms in the literature, unfortunately the algorithms either lack a comprehensive consideration of various network parameters or the studies reporting these algorithms lack enough detail for implementation. Research into vertical handover decision algorithms in heterogeneous networks is still a challenging area. The main difficulty is devising an algorithm which is truly useful in a wide ranging conditions and user preferences. One possible solution would be, given that computational powers of handsets improve phenomenally every year, to implement several VHD algorithms in a handset and adopt adaptive methods that choose an algorithm intelligently based on conditions and user preferences. Apart from mobility management some other research areas are as mentioned below:

- **Charging and Billing:** The charge for accessing a network varies in different network. In the 4G network environment multiple service providers will be involved during a session, if the users roam from one service provider network to one or more other service provider networks. Thus, a single session may incur a number of charges. Moreover, different charging schemes maybe used for different types of services. One challenge is to keep track of charges per use per segment of a session that used their network, service or content. There will need to be more charging agreements between the service providers in order to allow roaming during a session in order to get a continued service as far as a customer is concerned.

- **Large Number of Operators:** A large number of network operators are expected to co-exist and collaborate in the 4G networks. In such circumstances, mobile users who are responsible for handover decision will require increased levels of control over how services can be secured in handover. This will be complicated by versatile trust relationships between network operators.

- **Fault Tolerance:** Fault tolerant systems are becoming more popular throughout the world. The existing wireless system structure has a tree like topology and hence if one of the components suffers damage the whole system goes down. This is not desirable in case of 4G.

- **Security:** The level of security provided in different networks is different. More interconnectivity and inter-working will make the vulnerability even greater. Monitoring, detecting, analyzing and preventing worms and viruses on networks is very difficult.

- **Integrating Non-IP-Based and IP-Based Devices:** It is known that devices that are not IP address based are generally used for services such as VoIP. On the other hand, devices that are IP address based are used for data delivery. 4G networks will serve both types of devices. Consequently, integrating the mechanisms of providing services to both non-IP-based as well as IP-based devices is one of key challenges 4G networks have to address.

- **Optimal Choice of Access Technology:** In other words how to be best connected (Kassar, Kervella & Pujolle, 2008). Given that a user may be offered connectivity

from more than one technology at any one time, one has to consider how the terminal and the network choose the technology suitable for services the user is accessing.

- **Design of a Mobility Enabled IP Networking Architecture:** Which contains the functionality to deal with mobility between access technologies. This includes fast, seamless handovers (IP micro-mobility), quality of service (QoS), security and accounting.

- **Adaptation of Multimedia Transmission Across 4G Networks:** Indeed multimedia will be a main service feature of 4G networks, and changing radio access networks may in particular result in drastic changes in the network condition. Thus the framework for multimedia transmission must be adaptive (Cerqueira et al., 2011).

CONCLUSION

In the next generation heterogeneous wireless networks, a user with a multi-interface terminal may have network access from different service providers using various technologies. As foreseen by many researchers and analysts, the 4G will be based on the heterogeneous underlying infrastructure integrating different wireless access technologies in a complementary manner. Before the dream of 4G becomes a reality several technical and business challenges need to be resolved. One of the major challenges in migration to 4G networks is to realize seamless handoffs among various communications systems with small handoff latency and packet loss. This switching is based on the discovered accesses, QoS constraints, operator policies, user preferences and available system capacity and utilization. Optimizing the vertical handoff process is an important issue of research, which leads to reduction of network signaling and mobile device power loss and on the other hand improves network quality of service (QoS) and grade of service (GoS).

IP mobility is a major issue since 4G networks are based on the IP protocol to glue the different radio networks together. Interactions between efficient IP mobility schemes and other functions, such as security and Quality of service, are required for 4G. Mobile IPv6 is considered to be key technology for migrating to 4G. However, original Mobile IPv6 has some limitations and it cannot provide fast handover. Mobile IPv6 needs some enhancements in the areas such as paging support, scalability, and integrating heterogeneous access technologies. Also to reduce the signaling and processing overhead induced by a large number a binding updates, intra-site mobility needs to be transparent to correspondent hosts and home agents. Hierarchical Mobile IPv6 is a scheme which exploits domain hierarchy. It handles local mobility and global mobility separately and reduces the amount of signaling traffic.

Another issue regarding mobility management is Vertical handover decision (VHD). To provide general solutions for the vertical handover in heterogeneous access networks, the IEEE 802.21 standards group is currently discussing the media independent handover function (MIHF). Media Independent Handover Services offers promise for the Next Generation of Internet connected devices and protocols. The services provided will allow mobile devices a seamless, standardized approach to enabled handover. For this MN must be capable of connecting to multiple access networks via multiple interfaces. The new IEEE 802.21 standard specifies link layer intelligence and other related network information to upper layers in order to optimize handovers between networks of different types. Thus IEEE 802.21 is an important step towards 4G network. It is expected that in the future it is widely deployed and there will be major works to be carried out to further amend and extend it in order to provide for even better services.

In summary we can say, the goal of 4G is to replace the current proliferation of core mobile networks with a single worldwide core network standard, based on IP for control, video, packet data, and voice. This will provide uniform video, voice, and data services to the mobile host, based entirely in IP. Although 4G wireless technology offers higher data rates and the ability to roam across multiple heterogeneous wireless networks, several issues require further research and development. Since 4G-network is integration of heterogeneous networks, mobility management in 4G-network is a complex problem comprising of a large number of challenging issues. Therefore mobility in 4G networks requires new level of mobility support as compared to traditional mobility. In this chapter we have presented issues related to mobility management in 4G networks.

REFERENCES

Agarwal, A., Pramod, P. J., & Jain, D. K. (2011). Implementation of IEEE 802.21 based media independent handover services. *Proceedings of the Asia-Pacific Advanced Network, 32*, 71–78. doi:10.7125/APAN.32.9

Aiash, M., Mapp, G., Lasebae, A., & Phan, R. (2010). Providing security in 4G systems: Unveiling the challenges. In *Proceedings of Telecommunications (AICT), 2010 Sixth Advanced International Conference on* (pp. 439-444). IEEE.

Akan, A., & Edemen, C. (2010). Path to 4G wireless networks. In *Proceedings of Personal, Indoor and Mobile Radio Communications Workshops (PIMRC Workshops), 2010 IEEE 21st International Symposium on* (pp. 405-407). IEEE.

Akyildiz, I. F., Gutierrez-Estevez, D. M., & Reyes, E. C. (2010). The evolution to 4G cellular systems: LTE-advanced. *Physical Communication, 3*(4), 217–244. doi:10.1016/j.phycom.2010.08.001

Akyildiz, I. F., Xie, J., & Mohanty, S. (2004). A survey of mobility management in next-generation all-IP-based wireless systems. *IEEE Wireless Communications*, *11*(4), 16–28. doi:10.1109/MWC.2004.1325888

Andersen, N. P. S. (2001). The third generation partnership project (3GPP). *GSM and UMTS, 247.*

Bai, D., Park, C., Lee, J., Nguyen, H., Singh, J., & Gupta, A. et al. (2012). LTE-advanced modem design: Challenges and perspectives. *IEEE Communications Magazine*, *50*(2), 178–186. doi:10.1109/MCOM.2012.6146497

Belhoul, A. (2007). Quality of service (QoS) provisioning mechanisms in fourth generation (4G) wireless all-IP networks. *Paper for the degree of Doctor of Philosophy.*

Bikos, A., & Sklavos, N. (2013). *LTE/SAE security issues on 4G wireless networks.*

Cerqueira, E., Zeadally, S., Leszczuk, M., Curado, M., & Mauthe, A. (2011). Recent advances in multimedia networking. *Multimedia Tools and Applications*, *54*(3), 635–647. doi:10.1007/s11042-010-0578-z

Céspedes, S., Shen, X., & Lazo, C. (2011). IP mobility management for vehicular communication networks: challenges and solutions. *IEEE Communications Magazine*, *49*(5), 187–194. doi:10.1109/MCOM.2011.5762817

Chan, H. A., Yokota, H., Xie, J., Seite, P., & Liu, D. (2011). Distributed and dynamic mobility management in mobile internet: current approaches and issues. *The Journal of Communication*, *6*(1), 4–15.

Chen, Y. S., & Lin, Y. W. (2012). *Protocols and applications of cross-layer in mobility management.*

Christakos, C. K., Izquierdo, A., Rouil, R., & Golmie, N. (2009). Using the media independent information service to support mobile authentication in fast mobile IPv6. In *Proceedings of Wireless Communications and Networking Conference, 2009.* IEEE.

Conti, M., Chong, S., Fdida, S., Jia, W., Karl, H., Lin, Y. D., & Zukerman, M. (2011). Research challenges towards the future internet. *Computer Communications*, *34*(18), 2115–2134. doi:10.1016/j.comcom.2011.09.001

Correia, L. M. (2010). *Mobile broadband multimedia networks: Techniques, models and tools for 4G.* Access Online via Elsevier.

Corujo, D., Guimaraes, C., Santos, B., & Aguiar, R. L. (2011). Using an open-source IEEE 802.21 implementation for network-based localized mobility management. *IEEE Communications Magazine*, *49*(9), 114–123. doi:10.1109/MCOM.2011.6011742

Damnjanovic, A., Montojo, J., Wei, Y., Ji, T., Luo, T., Vajapeyam, M., & Malladi, D. (2011). A survey on 3GPP heterogeneous networks. *IEEE Wireless Communications*, *18*(3), 10–21. doi:10.1109/MWC.2011.5876496

De La Oliva, A., Banchs, A., Soto, I., Melia, T., & Vidal, A. (2008). An overview of IEEE 802.21: Media-independent handover services. *IEEE Wireless Communications*, *15*(4), 96–103. doi:10.1109/MWC.2008.4599227

Fernandes, S., & Karmouch, A. (2012). Vertical mobility management architectures in wireless networks: A comprehensive survey and future directions. *IEEE Communications Surveys & Tutorials*, *14*(1), 45–63. doi:10.1109/SURV.2011.082010.00099

Gondara, M. K., & Kadam, S. (2011). Requirements of vertical handoff mechanism in 4G wireless networks. *arXiv preprint arXiv:1105.0043.*

Griffith, D., Rouil, R., & Golmie, N. (2010). Performance metrics for IEEE 802.21 media independent handover (MIH) signaling. *Wireless Personal Communications*, *52*(3), 537–567. doi:10.1007/s11277-008-9629-4

Iqbal, M. K., Iqbal, M. B., Rasheed, I., & Sandhu, A. (2012). 4G evolution and multiplexing techniques with solution to implementation challenges. In *Proceedings of Cyber-Enabled Distributed Computing and Knowledge Discovery (CyberC), 2012 International Conference on* (pp. 485-488). IEEE.

John, S. (2011). Research challenges in the migration to future mobile systems. In *Proceedings of Current Trends in Information Technology (CTIT), 2011 International Conference and Workshop on* (pp. 92-96). IEEE.

Kassar, M., Kervella, B., & Pujolle, G. (2008). An overview of vertical handover decision strategies in heterogeneous wireless networks. *Computer Communications, 31*(10), 2607–2620. doi:10.1016/j.comcom.2008.01.044

Kumar, V., & Tyagi, N. (2010). Media independent handover for seamless mobility in IEEE 802.11 and UMTS based on IEEE 802.21. In *Proceedings of Computer Science and Information Technology (ICCSIT), 2010 3rd IEEE International Conference on* (Vol. 4, pp. 474-479). IEEE.

Lee, W., Lee, I., Kwak, J. S., Ihm, B. C., & Han, S. (2012). Multi-BS MIMO cooperation: Challenges and practical solutions in 4G systems. *IEEE Wireless Communications, 19*(1), 89–96. doi:10.1109/MWC.2012.6155881

Louta, M., & Bellavista, P. (2013). Bringing always best connectivity vision a step closer: Challenges and perspectives. *IEEE Communications Magazine, 51*(2), 158–166. doi:10.1109/MCOM.2013.6461201

Makaya, C., & Pierre, S. (2011). *Emerging wireless networks: Concepts, techniques and applications.* Boca Raton, FL: CRC Press, Inc.

Malekian, R. (2008). The study of handover in mobile IP networks. In *Proceedings of Broadband Communications, Information Technology & Biomedical Applications, 2008 Third International Conference on* (pp. 181-185). IEEE.

Marsch, P., Raaf, B., Szufarska, A., Mogensen, P., Guan, H., Farber, M., & Kolding, T. (2012). Future mobile communication networks: Challenges in the design and operation. *IEEE Vehicular Technology Magazine, 7*(1), 16–23. doi:10.1109/MVT.2011.2179343

Martin, J., Amin, R., Eltawil, A., & Hussien, A. (2011). Limitations of 4G wireless systems. In *Proceedings of Virginia Tech Wireless Symposium.* Virginia Tech.

Paint, F., Engelstad, P., Vanem, E., Haslestad, T., Nordvik, A. M., Myksvoll, K., & Svaet, S. (2002). *Mobility aspects in 4G networks* (White Paper).

Piri, E., & Pentikousis, K. (2009). IEEE 802.21: Media independent handover services. *The Internet Protocol Journal, 12*(2), 7–27.

Ramraj, R., Ahmad, I., & Habibi, D. (2011). *Multiaccess environments in next generation networks.*

Rathore, A. K., Chaurasia, R. K., Mishra, R., & Kumar, H. (2012). Road map and challenges in 4G wireless system. *J Elec Electron, 1*(104), 2.

Ray, S. K., Pawlikowski, K., & Sirisena, H. (2010). Handover in mobile WiMAX networks: The state of art and research issues. *IEEE Communications Surveys & Tutorials, 12*(3), 376–399. doi:10.1109/SURV.2010.032210.00064

Ren, Y. S., Shang, F. J., & Lei, Y. (2008). Survey of mobility management and mobile IP technique. *Application Research of Computers, 12*, 9.

Saxena, N., Sengupta, S., Wong, K. K., & Roy, A. (2013). Special issue on advances in 4G wireless and beyond. *EURASIP Journal on Wireless Communications and Networking,* (1): 1–3.

Seddigh, N., Nandy, B., Makkar, R., & Beaumont, J. F. (2010). Security advances and challenges in 4G wireless networks. In *Proceedings of Privacy Security and Trust (PST), 2010 Eighth Annual International Conference on* (pp. 62-71). IEEE.

Sehgal, A., & Agrawal, R. (2010). QoS based network selection scheme for 4G systems. *IEEE Transactions on Consumer Electronics*, *56*(2), 560–565. doi:10.1109/TCE.2010.5505970

Shin, D. H. (2010). Challenges and drivers in the 4G evolution in Korea. *International Journal of Mobile Communications*, *8*(3), 297–312. doi:10.1504/IJMC.2010.032976

Snoeren, A. C., & Balakrishnan, H. (2000). An end-to-end approach to host mobility. In *Proceedings of the 6th Annual International Conference on Mobile Computing and Networking* (pp. 155-166). ACM.

Soliman, H., Bellier, L., Elmalki, K., & Castelluccia, C. (2008). *Hierarchical mobile IPv6 (HMIPv6) mobility management*.

Stevens-Navarro, E., & Wong, V. W. (2006). Comparison between vertical handoff decision algorithms for heterogeneous wireless networks. In *Proceedings of Vehicular Technology Conference, 2006* (Vol. 2, pp. 947-951). IEEE.

Suarez, A., & Macias, E. (2010). Video streaming based services over 4G networks: Challenges and solutions. In *Fourth-generation wireless networks: Applications and innovations* (pp. 494–525). Academic Press.

Taniuchi, K., Ohba, Y., Fajardo, V., Das, S., Tauil, M., Cheng, Y. H., & Famolari, D. (2009). IEEE 802.21: Media independent handover: Features, applicability, and realization. *IEEE Communications Magazine*, *47*(1), 112–120. doi:10.1109/MCOM.2009.4752687

Tian, J., Zheng, X., Hu, H., & You, X. (2011). A survey of next generation mobile communications research in China. *Chinese Science Bulletin*, *56*(27), 2875–2888. doi:10.1007/s11434-011-4658-x

Venmani, D. P., Gourhant, Y., Reynaud, L., Chemouil, P., & Zeghlache, D. (2013). Substitution networks based on software defined networking. In *Ad hoc networks* (pp. 242–259). Berlin: Springer. doi:10.1007/978-3-642-36958-2_17

Xie, J., & Akyildiz, R. (2002). An optimal location management scheme for minimizing signaling cost in mobile IP. In *Proceedings of Communications, 2002* (Vol. 5, pp. 3313–3317). IEEE.

Yang, K., Gondal, I., Qiu, B., & Dooley, L. S. (2007). Combined SINR based vertical handoff algorithm for next generation heterogeneous wireless networks. In *Proceedings of Global Telecommunications Conference, 2007* (pp. 4483-4487). IEEE.

Zahran, A. H., & Liang, B. (2005). Performance evaluation framework for vertical handoff algorithms in heterogeneous networks. In *Proceedings of Communications, 2005* (Vol. 1, pp. 173–178). IEEE. doi:10.1109/ICC.2005.1494342

Zhang, C., Ariyavisitakul, S. L., & Tao, M. (2012). LTE-advanced and 4G wireless communications. *IEEE Communications Magazine*, *50*(2), 102–103. doi:10.1109/MCOM.2012.6146488

ADDITIONAL READING

Glisic, S. G. (2011). *Advanced wireless communications and internet: future evolving technologies*. Wiley. com.

Hsieh, R., & Seneviratne, A. (2003, September). A comparison of mechanisms for improving mobile IP handoff latency for end-to-end TCP. In *Proceedings of the 9th annual international conference on Mobile computing and networking* (pp. 29-41). ACM.

Khan, R. A., & Shaikh, A. A. (2012). LTE Advanced: Necessities and Technological Challenges for 4th Generation Mobile Network. *International Journal of Engineering and Technology, 2*(8).

Kupetz, A. H., & Brown, K. T. (2003). *4G-A Look Into the Future of Wireless Communications*. Rollings Business Journal.

Lim, C., Yoo, T., Clerckx, B., Lee, B., & Shim, B. (2013). Recent trend of multiuser MIMO in LTE-advanced. *Communications Magazine, IEEE, 51*(3), 127–135. doi:10.1109/MCOM.2013.6476877

Makela, J., Ylianttila, M., & Pahlavan, K. (2000). Handoff decision in multi-service networks. In *Personal, Indoor and Mobile Radio Communications, 2000. PIMRC 2000. The 11th IEEE International Symposium on* (Vol. 1, pp. 655-659). IEEE.

Kellerer, W., Wagner, M., Hirschfeld, R., Noll, J., Svaet, S., Ferreira, J., & Fischer, C. (2002). *The operator's vision on systems beyond 3G*. Eurescom Technical Information.

Kassar, M., Kervella, B., & Pujolle, G. (2007, December). Architecture of an intelligent inter-system handover management scheme. In Future generation communication and networking (fgcn 2007) (Vol. 1, pp. 332–337). IEEE.

Maruyama, S., Tuexen, M., Stewart, R., Xie, Q., & Kozuka, M. (2007). *Stream Control Transmission Protocol (SCTP)*. Dynamic Address Reconfiguration.

McNair, J., & Zhu, F. (2004). Vertical handoffs in fourth-generation multinetwork environments. *Wireless Communications, IEEE, 11*(3), 8–15. doi:10.1109/MWC.2004.1308935

Oki, E., Rojas-Cessa, R., Tatipamula, M., & Vogt, C. (2012). *Advanced Internet Protocols, Services, and Applications*. Wiley. com.

Oki, E., Rojas-Cessa, R., Tatipamula, M., & Vogt, C. (2012). IP Version 6. In *Advanced Internet Protocols, Services, and Applications*. Hoboken, NJ, USA: John Wiley & Sons, Inc. doi:10.1002/9781118180822.ch11

Ren, Z., Tham, C. K., Foo, C. C., & Ko, C. C. (2001). Integration of mobile IP and multi-protocol label switching. In *Communications, 2001. ICC 2001. IEEE International Conference on* (Vol. 7, pp. 2123-2127). IEEE.

Rumney, M. (Ed.). (2013). LTE and the evolution to 4G wireless: Design and measurement challenges. Wiley. com.

Stevens-Navarro, E., Martínez-Morales, J. D., & Pineda-Rico, U. (2012). Multiple Attributes Decision Making Algorithms for Vertical Handover in Heterogeneous Wireless Networks. *Wireless Multi-access Environments and Quality of Service Provisioning: Solutions and Application, 52.*

Sun, J. Z., Tenhunen, J., & Sauvola, J. (2003, September). CME: a middleware architecture for network-aware adaptive applications. In *Personal, Indoor and Mobile Radio Communications, 2003. PIMRC 2003. 14th IEEE Proceedings on* (Vol. 1, pp. 839-843). IEEE.

Toskala, A., Holma, H., Pajukoski, K., & Tiirola, E. (2006, September). UTRAN long term evolution in 3GPP. In *Personal, Indoor and Mobile Radio Communications, 2006 IEEE 17th International Symposium on* (pp. 1-5). IEEE.

Vanem, E., Svaet, S., & Paint, F. (2003, March). Effects of multiple access alternatives in heterogeneous wireless networks. In Wireless Communications and Networking, 2003. WCNC 2003. 2003 IEEE (Vol. 3, pp. 1696-1700). IEEE.

Yan, X., Ahmet Şekercioğlu, Y., & Narayanan, S. (2010). A survey of vertical handover decision algorithms in Fourth Generation heterogeneous wireless networks. *Computer Networks*, *54*(11), 1848–1863. doi:10.1016/j.comnet.2010.02.006

Zhu, F., & McNair, J. (2004, March). Optimizations for vertical handoff decision algorithms. In *Wireless Communications and Networking Conference, 2004. WCNC. 2004 IEEE* (Vol. 2, pp. 867-872). IEEE.

KEY WORDS AND DEFINITIONS

4G Networks: In telecommunications, 4G is the fourth generation of mobile phone mobile communication technology standards.

Hierarchical Mobile IPv6: Hierarchical Mobile IPv6 (HMIPv6) is the proposed enhancement of Mobile Internet Protocol versions 6 (MIPv6) that is designed to reduce the amount of signaling required and to improve handoff speed for mobile connections.

Horizontal Handoff: handoff between base stations that are using the same type of wireless network.

IEEE 802.21 Media Independent Handover: Media Independent Handover (MIH) is a standard being developed by IEEE 802.21 to enable the handover of IP sessions from one layer 2 access technology to another, to achieve mobility of end user devices.

Mobile IPv6: Mobile IP is an Internet Engineering Task Force (IETF) standard communications protocol that is designed to allow mobile device users to move from one network to another while maintaining a permanent IP address.

Mobility Management: Mobility management is to track where the subscribers are, allowing calls, SMS and other mobile phone services to be delivered to them.

Vertical Handoff: handoff between different types of wireless network.

Chapter 12
Genetic Algorithms:
Application to Fault Diagnosis in Distributed Embedded Systems

Pabitra Mohan Khilar
NIT Rourkela, India

ABSTRACT

Genetic Algorithms are important techniques to solve many NP-Complete problems related to distributed computing and its application domains. Genetic algorithm-based fault diagnoses in distributed computing systems have been a feasible methodology to solve diagnosis problems recently. Distributed embedded systems consisting of sensors, actuators, processors/microcontrollers, and interconnection networks are one class of distributed computing systems that have long been used, staring from small-scale home appliances to large-scale satellite systems. Some of their applications are in safety-critical systems where occurrence of faults can result in catastrophic situations for which fault diagnosis in such systems are very important. In this chapter, different types of faults, which are likely to occur in distributed embedded systems and a GA-based methodology to solve these problems along with the performance analysis of fault diagnosis algorithm have been presented. Nevertheless, the diagnosis algorithm presented here is well suitable for general purpose distributed computing systems with appropriate modification over system and fault model. In fact, this book chapter will enable the reader not only to study various aspects of fault diagnosis techniques but will also provide insight to build robust systems to allow for continued normal service despite the occurrence of failures.

DOI: 10.4018/978-1-4666-4940-8.ch012

INTRODUCTION

Genetic Algorithms are important techniques used for searching large solution spaces for different problem domains in computer science and engineering field such as distributed computing systems (Khilar & Mahapatra, 2007, Barborak, Malek & Dahbura, 1993, Malek, M. 1980, Hakimi & Chwa, 1981, Maeng & Malek, 1981, Blough & Brown, 1999, Elhadef & Becher 2000, Elhadef & Becher 2001). The problem domains are usually consists of a number of metatasks based on different heuristics used to solve the fault diagnosis problems using GA fundamental operators. When the numbers of tasks are very large, the mapping of these tasks to underlying resources is an NP-Complete problem due to large solution space. In order to solve the meta task scheduling problem, different tasks are mapped to various nodes in a distributed computing system. Nodes are usually machines and the connection between nodes is the links.

Fault diagnosis is another important problem in distributed computing systems to locate the faulty node. This is required to identify a set of fault free nodes on which normal function of distributed systems can be successfully executed. As the results of applications are vital and some times safety critical, reliable results will assert in providing correct decision. Although, fault diagnosis tasks are observed as overheads at the initial stage of installation, subsequently they are essential due to deterioration of components of distributed systems. The cost overhead of the system can be very well evaluated and tested for the feasibility of the system in real environment. While considering the execution of normal tasks of a distributed system, the fault diagnosis tasks can be included and executed in an overlapped manner in order to successfully accomplish the normal functioning of the system despite the occurrence of fault.

Distributed embedded systems such as fly-by-wire (FBW), drive-by-wire (DBW) and break-by-wire (BBW) systems are becoming smarter by incorporation of higher computing and communication power along with the new generation automotive design. As the distributed embedded systems become smarter, the data traffic inside the in-house networks also increases dynamically. The total data traffic will be huge by adding up multiple video systems such as displays and cameras. Therefore, the new generation distributed embedded systems need to allow the effective and efficient communication among different subsystems. While the computation are implemented either using a set of processors or microcontrollers, the communication is implemented using multiple networks handling communication of data, varying in criticality as well as bandwidth requirement. The distributed embedded systems such as FBW, DBW and BBW use extensive electronics components in various subsystems such as power train, engine, chassis, body, in-house control for navigation system and equipments for connectivity to the external world. Advanced piloting or driving assistance systems (APDAS) are the innovations added to the traditional airplanes, aircrafts, rockets and vehicles. In fact, APDAS was originally considered under telematics due to the use of more and more new features. Moreover, APDAS systems may need to communicate with safety systems wherever some automatic takeover is required.

As the distributed embedded systems are smarter by including multiple electronic components, they become more complex. The complexity of these systems need to be analyzed by various algorithms which makes both the present and future generation distributed embedded systems the most bandwidth demanding and safety-critical systems. Therefore, the DESs have Quality of Service (QoS), security, and a higher degree of composability and extendibility requirements along with the high network bandwidth and flexibility requirements. When the components suffer from various faults, this may lead to error thereby leading to failure condition of the entire system. Faults, errors and failure conditions of these systems may affect the usability of the systems in many ways including catastrophic situations and degraded performance bottleneck. The communication network without low latency and high bandwidth cannot fulfill the safety critical requirements. Motivated by the need of fault tolerance in distributed embedded systems, my effort in this chapter is to present the design and implementation of fault diagnosis algorithms for distributed embedded systems.

This chapter will mainly emphasize on the requirement, design and implementation perspectives of fault diagnosis algorithms for detecting and diagnosing different faults in important components in safety critical distributed embedded systems such as fly-by-wire (FBW), Break-by-wire(BBW), Drive-by-wire(DBW) systems. Apart from fault diagnosis, it will also discuss computational time requirement. Also, we will discuss many important results of already established works in the field of fault diagnosis besides the author's noteworthy contribution in this area. We will also discuss basic fundamentals about fault diagnosis and distributed embedded system to avoid any difficulties in grasping the subject matter. The researchers and practicing engineers can use this chapter to design and implement more sophisticated future DESs. The readers can use this book for preparing the projects on microcontroller based distributed embedded system.

The chapter is organized as follows. In section 2, the use of genetic algorithms for fault diagnosis is discussed. The need of fault diagnosis is presented in section 3. Section 4 discussed the concept of distributed system such as distributed embedded system. The proposed intermittent fault diagnosis algorithm for k-connected distributed embedded system along with its evaluation using directed acyclic graph is presented in section 5. The future work in this direction is presented in section 6. Section 7 concludes the chapter.

GENETIC ALGORITHMS TO DIAGNOSE FAULTS IN DISTRIBUTED EMBEDDED SYSTEMS

A vast amount of diagnosis algorithms exist in the literature for fault diagnosis in distributed embedded systems. Many algorithms though look time efficient, the amount of traffic (i.e., the number of message exchanges) is high. The time needed to detect the faulty nodes from the set of nodes in a k-connected network using GA-based approach depends mainly upon the time taken for finding out the fitness of the chromosomes in the population at every generation. The time taken to perform repeated selection and supervised mutation is negligible as compared to the time taken to find the fitness of each chromosome. As all the nodes in the network are not participating to detect the faulty nodes in the network, the number of messages that is exchanged between nodes across the network is lesser than that of other fault diagnosis algorithms. The GA-based approach therefore leads to less traffic in the K-connected network due to which more bandwidth is available for application specific tasks. It is experimentally verified that the time taken to diagnose the faulty nodes using the GA-based approach varies within a certain range for a specific size network. Searching the accurate solution from a small solution pool of constant size is a better approach than the formation of huge network traffic by sending and receiving of diagnosis related information. It can be also noted that many small scale distributed networks exist where the nodes are energy or power constrained. In such type of distributed networks GA-Based approach consume less energy as compared to that of other fault diagnosis algorithms.

Fundamental GA Operators

The genetic algorithms generally include four fundamental operators such as selection, crossover, mutation, reproduction. However, sometimes three operators are enough to provide reasonable solutions particularly for fault diagnosis approaches. For example three operators such as selection, mutation and reproduction have been applied to diagnose intermittent faults in k-connected systems. The computational overhead in terms of CPU time is usually more for GA-based fault diagnosis algorithms in order to provide faster and accurate diagnosis solutions when solution space is large. On the other hand, the computational overhead is less to find diagnosis solutions for small and constant size of solution pool. When we consider the small and constant population size of the solution space for different size of K-connected networks, the GA-based fault diagnosis algorithms are usually faster.

FAULT DIAGNOSIS

Faults, errors and failure are three terms used interchangeably to refer to any kind of malfunctioning of distributed system. In its fundamental form, occurrence of a fault in system lead to error and error in a system causes failure which may lead to catastrophic failure. A fault is active when it produces an error otherwise it is dormant. Error is caused due to fault in the system and can propagate to other parts in the system. The error propagation can be either internal or external. Internal error propagation is due to an internal computational process whereas external propagation takes place from component to component. A service failure occurs when an error is propagated to the service interface and causes the service delivered by the system to deviate from correct service. A failure of a component causes either a permanent or transient fault in the system. We define the following terms with respect to fault diagnosis in a distributed system.

- **Fault Prevention/Avoidance:** This aims at reducing the creation or occurrence of fault in a distributed system.

- **Fault Tolerance:** This refers to the system which continues to provide the service despite the occurrence of faults in some or more components assuming a minimal number of fault free components. In fact, this is a compensation technique using structural redundancy (called masking). There are two types of hardware and software back up such as active or passive back up to mask the faults. Active back up allows executing the same function simultaneously in main and redundant component on the fly by which the moment actual component fails the redundant component can take over the function automatically without any delay. Whereas, in passive back up, the function in the redundant component is invoked after the main component fails which saves the power at the cost of switching time from main component to redundant one.

- **Fault Removal:** This aims at detecting and eliminating existing faults from the existing system components.

- **Fault Evasion:** This means to estimate the present faults, the future incidence and the likely consequences of faults using various generic metrics such as diagnostic latency, time complexity, cost overhead, false alarm rate, and message overhead.

Types of Faults

There are broadly four types of faults occur in a distributed system such as crash fault, transient faults, intermittent faults and byzantine faults. The occurrence of crash fault does not allow the system component to respond and also called as permanent fault. For example, a crash fault in a system component may be due to depletion of its battery energy or subjected to any kind of physical damage. A transient fault is nothing but a temporary fault in a system which lasts for a short span of time. Intermittent faults are the faults which affect any node of the system randomly and usually vital for sensor networks. Byzantine faults refer to an arbitrary fault in system component due to any cause in the system. In fact, byzantine fault is a superset of all the types of faults and difficult to diagnose.

The process of fault diagnosis consists of different phases such as fault detection, fault diagnosis, fault containment or fault isolation, fault masking, fault repair or fault recovery and fault compensation. Fault detection is identifying whether a fault is occurred in the system or not. Fault diagnosis is to locate the fault such as faulty node in a distributed system. Fault containment or fault isolation is to separate set of faulty nodes from the set of fault free nodes in a distributed system. Fault masking is overriding the presence of fault by using redundancy mechanism. Fault repair or recovery is to bring the correct state from the faulty state of the system either by replacing or repairing the faulty components. Fault compensation refers to the fact that the use of technique or device to override the fault in the system. Here, we shall concentrate on fault diagnosis i.e., identifying the faulty node in a distributed system. The so called traditional fault diagnosis technique known as system level diagnosis has been very much useful for diagnosing faulty components at the node level to avoid intrinsic details of the component which is usually taken care of by atomic component testing. This technique has been applied in the past to diagnose faulty components in multiprocessor and massively parallel processor systems to improve the yield rate. Recently, this technique works well with large class distributed systems such as distributed embedded system having a large number of nodes connected by an efficient and effective interconnection network such as field bus and controller area network. The traditional diagnosis algorithms are though efficient in diagnosing the faulty components the high message complexity leads to deplete the energy resources in distributed embedded system. In order to reduce message complexity without much compromise on com-

putational complexity, diagnosing of faulty nodes using genetic algorithm is a suitable approach. The stochastic search technique combined with system level fault diagnosis, overcomes various violent condition of the distributed system. The k-connected distributed systems are taken in to consideration, because in present time, most of the wired and wireless embedded systems are k-connected. As intermittent faults in safety critical k-connected systems such as distributed embedded system for Fly-by-wire and Steer-by-wire system are more likely, in this chapter we mainly focus on diagnosing intermittently faulty components in k-connected distributed embedded system which are safety critical in nature.

DISTRIBUTED EMBEDDED SYSTEMS

In order to diagnose the fault in a distributed embedded system (DES), we need to know about different components of the DES such as sensor, actuator, transceiver, memory, processor and the interconnection network that connects each of the components (Hakimi & Amin 1975, Dahbura, & Sengupta 1989, Dorf, Bishop & Cliffs 2001, Koptez & Gruensteidl 1993). The function of each of the component needs to be monitored based on their characteristics. For example, a sensor is usually a passive device whose function is to sense the parameter from the environment. Before reading the next values of the parameter, the previous values need to be stored in the memory otherwise the old values will be deleted because of less amount of memory available in a sensor node. The fault in the passive sensor circuit can be masked or avoided in order to get the accurate data. As each of the components functions are different, the behavior on occurrence of the fault will be different from components to components. This encompasses us to devise the techniques to detect the faulty components. Another component known as actuator used to provide appropriate signal to the device to perform the normal task. In fact, sensors and actuators are most often used in distributed embedded system in order to record the sensed values. The sensor, actuator, storage, processor and transceiver make a smart sensor node. The software and hardware of a distributed embedded system need to be designed by considering the fault tolerance as one of the design goal in order to use them in safety critical applications.

Sensors

Sensors are electronic devices that sense the physical environment, for example, there are sensors for temperature, pressure, light, metal, smoke, and proximity to an object. The sensor sends the signal to a computer or controllers. A sensor may be a CCD (charge-coupled device) camera to identify various objects or a microphone to recognize voices. Sensors in a mobile device facilitate interaction of the device with the surroundings. Some examples are as follows:

- Voice & Light Sensors.
- A sensor, for measuring the strength of the signal received, controls the applications of received signal.
- A microphone senses voice. It sends the voice signals to a speech processing system (SPS). The SPS authenticates the mobile owner.
- A sensor in fly-by-wire (FBW) system can sense the wind and wheel speed.

Smart sensors have computational, communication, and networking capabilities. They are deployed to communicate information to a network, a central computer, or a controller. A robotic system or an industrial automation system or an automobile system has multiple smart sensors embedded in it. The mobile robots need to find safe and reliable path while traveling from a source to destination. The computational intelligence techniques for path finding by mobile robots can

be classified into five types such as fuzzy systems, artificial neural network, evolutionary computing, swarm intelligence and hybrid approaches. Efficient path finding for a mobile robot depends various smart sensors and actuators. A smart sensor consists of the sensing device, processor, memory, analog-to-digital converter (ADC), signal processing element, wireless infrared receiver and transmitter, and performs communicational as well as computational functions under the control of an operating system and other system software. Smart sensors are generally programmed using assembly language or C including the micro functions at the underlying hardware level.

Actuators

A device which takes action after it receives signals from a controller or central computer and accordingly activates a physical device, appliances, or system. An actuator may or may not have computer embedded on it. An actuator receives the signals from a controller or central computer and accordingly activates a physical device, appliance or system.

Example of such physical devices are servomotor in a robotics hand, loud speaker, power transistor supply current to an oven, solenoid valve actuator, a transmitting device in a sensor network, etc. A smart actuator receives the commands or signals from a network, mobile device, computer, or controller and accordingly activates the physical device or system.

Sensor actuator pairs are used in control systems to monitor the system or environment. For example, a temperature sensor and current actuator pair controls the oven temperature, a light sensor and bulb current actuator pair controls the light levels, and a pressure sensor and valve actuator pair controls the pressure. Industrial plants have large numbers of pairs of sensors and actuators. A set of smart sensors and actuators are networked using a control area network bus (CAN bus), or field bus in a flight or automobile or industrial plant. Smart sensors can be programmed in assembly language or C using development tools.

Sensor and Actuator Programming

Sensors and actuators are connected to processors as well as memory devices which can be very well programmed using standard tools available for different applications. As far as the programming is concerned, assembly language of particular processor or language C is the best alternative to program smart sensors. Since these devices are programmed before the manufacturing time, whatever optimizations such as utilization of resources can be included at the design stage. For example, an automobile has a number of sensors, actuators and processors. Pressure sensors communicate to the display panel to provide warnings about tyre pressures. Sensors and actuators connect the embedded systems inside an automobile. The systems connect to the controller area network (CAN) bus a standard network meant for steer-by-wire (SBW) system.

Sensors and Actuators for Robotics Systems

Robotic systems incorporate a variety of overlapping technologies from the fields of artificial intelligence and mechanical engineering. Robotic systems are essentially programmable devices consisting of mechanical actuators and sensing organs that are linked to a computer embedded in them. The mechanical structure might involve manipulators, as in industrial robotics, or might concern the movement of the robot as a vehicle, as in mobile robotics. Some examples of sensors used in robotic systems are as follows:

- Acceleration and force sensors in the right and left feet.
- Infrared distance sensors at the head and hands.
- CCD camera in eyes.

- Angular sensor at the middle
- Microphones in ears
- Pinch detection at the belly.
- Thermo and touch sensors at shoulders, hands, and head.

Some of the actuators under the processor control used in a robot are:

- The mouth actuators such as a speaker can issue commands to other robots or relay sensed information via spoken messages in order to communicate orally.
- Actuators and motors at each moving joint-feet, hence, waist, neck, shoulder, hand and gripper palm to initiate physical actions.

The sensors transmit, through internal wires, the signals to the embedded processors at the central computer chip in the robot. The robot wirelessly communicates data to a central server when the actions of a group of robots need to be synchronized. Wirelessly communicating robots are mobile and are used in industrial plants for moving in areas not easily accessible by humans. Master-Slave systems of robots can be used for a variety of purposes. The master robot, in such a system, sends commands to the other (slave robots). The clocked master-slave flip-flop can used to allow master robot to control the slave robot. The following figure shows an arrangement of robots playing robo-soccer. The sensors, actuators, and transceivers in a robot allow the communication of robots for various applications. Robot servers can be programmed using either assembly language or C. The typical embedded processors are used for robots distributed system in a cost effective manner. The 68k architecture had dominated the embedded systems world since it was first invented, but the ARM architecture has emerged as today's most popular, 32-bit embedded processor. Also, ARM processors today outsell the Intel Pentium family by a 3 to 1 margin. The core is the naked, most basic portion of a microprocessor. When systems-on-silicon (systems-on-chips) are designed, one or more microprocessor cores are combined with peripheral components to create an entire system design on a single silicon die. Simpler forms of SOCs have been around for quite a while. In fact, these are known as microcontrollers. Intel and Motorola pioneered microcontroller innovations for various kind of distributed embedded systems.

Single and Multi-Rate Systems

Not only must operations be completed by deadlines, but many embedded computing systems have several real-time activities going on at the same time. They may simultaneously control some operations that run at slow rates and others that run at high rates. Multimedia applications are prime examples of multirate behavior. The audio and video portions of a multimedia stream run at very different rates, but they must remain closely synchronized. Failure to meet a deadline on either the audio or video portions spoils the perception of the entire presentation. Single rate systems are periodic systems whereas multi rate systems are aperiodic in nature.

GA-BASED INTERMITTENT FAULT DIAGNOSIS IN K-CONNECTED DISTRIBUTED SYSTEMS

Distributed Systems are being increasingly used in various applications like Steer-by-wire, fly-by-wire system, break-by-wire system, Smart home automation; Reliability of those systems is a vital factor to get exact performance within a particular time bound. Existance of some faulty nodes and faulty links cause catastrophic failure in the overall system if the faulty components are not diagnosed within a specific time period. Depending upon the behavior of the faults, Faults are categorized in to

different types in the literature. Here the intermittent type fault is introduced in the k-connected distributed system. An intermittently faulty node behaves faulty sometimes and faultfree sometimes. Diagnosing intermittent faults at system level or component level is cheaper and less complex than diagnosing faults at chip level.

The previous research has addressed the distributed diagnosis by assuming that nodes in the system test each other and transfer the test result among themselves to find the status of each node in the system (Khilar & Mahapatra 2007, Barborak, et. al.'s 1993). Since performing tests on each other is difficult in practice, comparison between the outcomes are done by assigning same task to pair of processors (Malek, M. 1980, Hakimi & Chwa 1981, Maeng & Malek 1981) in the systems. Broadcast Comparison model is introduced by authors Blough & Brown (1999), recently where two units being compared broadcast their status to all the processors in the system, which is an extended work of comparison based approach. System level fault diagnosis using various evolutionary technique has been proposed in the literature. An efficient stochastic search method with its extended work in identifying the set of all faulty units in t-diagnosable systems is described by (Elhadef & Becher 2000, Elhadef & Becher 2001). In their extended work, the stochastic search method is applied to comparison model, where the multiprocessor system is also assumed to be t-diagnosable. An artificial immune system based approach is proposed by authors in which the diagnosed system is originated from the concept of immune system (Elhadef, Das, & Nayak 2006). A comparison of evolutionary algorithms for system level diagnosis is proposed by authors in (Nassu, Duarte, & Pozo 2005). This paper develops a system level fault diagnosis algorithm using Genetic algorithm for k-connected distributed network which diagnose the nodes which are intermittent faulty.

System and Fault Model

In this section, the system and fault model for the proposed fault diagnosis algorithm for distributed embedded systems are provided.

System Model

A K-connected distributed system can be modeled as a collection of certain number of nodes connected with wire having minimum connectivity K. The connectivity K refers to the removal of K nodes lead to disconnect the network. Figure 1 shows a K-connected distributed system, where the minimum degree of node in the system is K which is also known as connectivity of the network. It is noted that most of the practical distributed embedded systems are satisfy as the K-connected system, Therefore, this is one of the most important property of interconnection network which is used for analyzing the performance of the system.

In the above figure, the network has five nodes. The nodes are assigned identification numbers which can be the IP address or the physical address for distinguishing the nodes from each other. The minimum degree of the network is 1.

Figure 1. K-connected distributed system having connectivity K=1

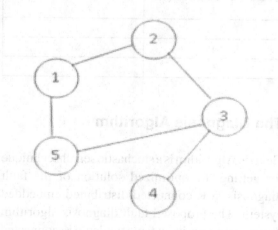

Fault Model

We consider the intermittent faulty nodes in a distributed system. The nodes which are subjected to intermittent faulty, may sometimes behave as fault free. However, we assume the links in the system are fault free. The assumption is valid in the sense that the link faults are usually considered as the node faults in many distributed systems. Therefore we assume that link faults are also node faults. The tests are executed to identify the status (fault free or faulty) of a node in the system and as per most traditional and popular PMC model. In this section, we define a t-diagnosable and Dt(n) distributed system for which the diagnosis algorithm has been developed.

t-Diagnosable Distributed Systems

In a system having n number of nodes, the problem of diagnosing all faults is a NP-hard problem, In literature, this problem is resolved by assuming the occurrence of maximum t number of faulty nodes in the system, where t is defined as floor((n-1)/2). So the system is said to be t-diagnosable, if maximum t number of faults can be diagnosed by the system.

$D_t(n)$ Design of K-Connected Distributed System

In literature, $D_t(n)$ design is proved to be t-diagnosable by authors in Hakimi & Amin (1975). For a test graph derived from the communication graph, the design of test graph is $D_t(n)$, if for all nodes in the system, the number of tester/comparator nodes is equal to t. For a K- connected system this design has a variation, In a K-connected system the number of tester nodes depends upon the connectivity. The connectivity is the number of nodes removal of which the system will be disconnected.

Figure 2. (a) Fault model of K-connected system, (b) Test syndrome

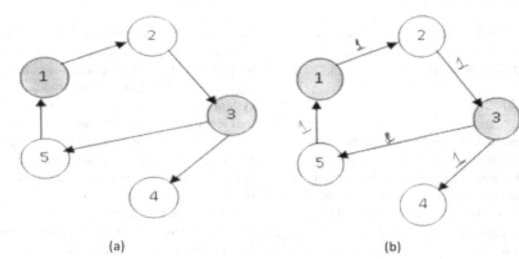

(a)   (b)

The tester nodes are the nearest connected nodes in the system depending on the access distance between tester and testee nodes.

The system is assumed to be t-diagnosable, so the maximum number of faulty nodes in Figure 2 is taken as 2, the faulty nodes in the system are 1 and 3, The idea of considering the t-diagnosable system is to isolate the set of faulty nodes from the total set of nodes to prevent the faulty nodes to participate in the normal functioning of the system irrespective of the types of faults (Pelc. A, 1992, Preparata, Metze, & Chien 1967, Sengupta, & Dahbura 1989, Tridandapani, Somani, & Reddy 1995, Walter, Lincoln, & Suri 1997, Yang, & Clarke 1999). They are the randomly generated faulty nodes assuming that every node is likely to be faulty after some period of time since their installation. If the system is to be renovated then also some of the obsolete components need to be replaced by fault free or upgraded components. The links represent test links by which tests are performed which are usually different from the physical link between nodes. This fault model follows the PMC model. Tables 1 and 2 represent the tester and tested nodes.

Table 1. Tester and tested nodes

Tester nodes	Tested nodes	Outcome
Faulty	Faulty	1
Faulty	Fault free	1
Fault free	Faulty	1
Fault free	Fault free	0

Table 2. Asymmetric PMC model

Tester nodes	Tested nodes
1	2
2	3
3	4,5
4	NIL
5	1

The Diagnosis Algorithm

Genetic Algorithm is a stochastic search technique for getting the optimized solution of the fault diagnosis in K-connected distributed embedded system. The proposed fault diagnosis algorithm diagnoses intermittent faulty nodes in K-connected distributed systems using GA based approaches to reduce the traffic. Due to its capability for handling stochastic situations, it can capture the intermittent faults efficiently for small scale systems i.e., smaller value of t and n. The factors such as number of test syndromes (collection of test results) as input and number of faulty nodes as the output are main goal in the proposed fault diagnosis algorithm

Representation of the Individuals in the Search Space

The solutions in the search space are represented by bit stings of length n, where '0' represents fault free units and '1' represents faulty units. The chromosome (bit string) representation of the given system in Figure 2 is represented by < 10100>,the length of bit string is 5. Illegal bit strings are the bit strings which violates the rule of t-diagnosability. The bit string represented by <0 0 0 0 0> for the given system is one illegal string, because at least 1 node is to be faulty in the system, as the fault condition is established in the distributed system. The bit string represented by <1 1 0 1 0 0> is an illegal string because as per the definition of t-diagnosable system the number of faulty nodes should not exceed the value t. The illegal strings need to be eliminated from the search space, so that the optimum solution is found easily.

Determination of Fitness Function

In genetic algorithm, fitness function determines the degree of survival of a chromosome in the solution space. Fitness function is the objective function that is optimized in the problem. In our proposed approach fitness function is the probability of correctness of diagnosis. The fitness function and meaning of other notations used in this work are as follows.

FT(a chromosome) = summation of fitness of each bit of chromosome of length n, n is the number of nodes in the K-connected system.

Fitness of each bit of a chromosome = Average(L);

L = L1+L2;
L1= mod (intersection (T*, T))/O
Mod = modulus operator
Intersection= Operator used in Set operation
/ = division operation
T^* = Test outcome obtained by the node in the real system, where node is a tester node.
T = Test outcome derived from randomly generated chromosome.
O = outdegree of the bit, that is the number of nodes tested by that node.
$L2 = mod(intersection(T^{*-1}, T^{-1})/I$
T^{*-1} = Test outcome obtained when the node is tested by other nodes in the real system.
T^{-1}= Test outcome derived from randomly generated chromosome.
I = in degree of the bit, that is the number of nodes, those test the particular node.

Design of the Genetic Operators and Determination of Probability of Controlling Genetic Operators

Genetic operators used in the proposed algorithm are:

1. **Mutation:** The process of alteration of bits in a chromosome is known as mutation. The frequency of applying mutation is controlled by mutation probability. Here the mutation probability is taken as .5 in the simulation. In the proposed approach, the mutation probability is compared with the fitness of each bit in the chromosome; the bit selected for mutation is having fitness less than mutation probability. The aim of mutation is to get diversified and different solutions that is equal to or nearly equal to optimal solution. During mutation process, the illegal bit strings are avoided by applying certain

trick, and the accurate result we can get in a less time.

2. **Crossover:** Crossover is the process of swaping substrings with one another in a pair, within the solution space. Frequency of crossover is controlled by crossover probability pc. Here one point crossover is applied.

Description of the Fault Diagnosis Algorithm

Input to the Algorithm

Fault model and the test syndrome S.

Output of the Algorithm

A fault set containing faulty units in the K-connected distributed system:

Step 1: Generate initial population
Step 2: For every chromosome v belongs to the initial population calculate FT(v)
Step 3: Sort the FT(v) in ascending order
Step 4: Repeat Step 5, 6, 7 till T(v)!=1 for all chromosome in the population
Step 5: Select parent chromosome having highest fitness value
Step 6: Create new population by the chromosomes having highest fitness values
Step 7: Perform Mutation on each chromosome of the generation obtained from Step 6, with mutation probability pm
Step 8: Perform crossover operation on the mutated chromosomes

While all the chromosomes have fitness value 1, the chromosomes represent the optimized solution, a collection of 0 and 1s. The bit value 1 represents faulty node and the bit value 0 represents fault free node of K-connected distributed system. The number of 0's and 1's in the chromosome indicate the set of fault free and faulty nodes in the system.

Tasks Mapping

Finding best possible node to schedule the tasks depends on various policies. In general, there are four types of policies such as transfer policy, selection policy, location policy and information policy. Transfer policy decides which node in the distributed system is a sender node. The node having maximum load is usually a sender node. The sender node distribute some of it's tasks to other receiver nodes. Selection policy decides which meta task is to be transferred to other nodes for execution. The location policy finds which node in the system is a receiver node based on a threshold mechanism. For example, if load in a system is below some threshold then that node is identified as a receiver node. A receiver node is identified which can execute the tasks from overloaded machines. Information policy decides the state information such as current load and number of opened files. All the distributed scheduling algorithms are designed based on these policies (Khilar & Mahapatra 2007, Khilar & Mahapatra 2009, Khilar & Punyotoya 2009, Punyotoya & Khilar 2009, Punyotoya & Khilar 2010, Mishra & Khilar 2011, Mahapatra & Khilar 2012).

The tasks are represented using a directed acyclic graph (DAG) based on the tasks characteristics and task dependencies. In fact, the normal functions of the system such as the processor controlled vehicle functions can consist of several tasks such as sensing, computing and actuating. The fault diagnosis tasks such as testing, computing chromosomes and then voting are followed by normal tasks constitute a single execution period. The entire task graphs are repeatedly executed in order to accomplish the task successfully. Advanced automotive control applications such as Steer-By-Wire (SBW) and Fly-By-Wire (FBW) system are typically implemented as real time distributed embedded system, which are basically K-connected distributed systems with connectivity K. Connectivity is the number of microcontrollers in the distributed embedded system removal of which will disconnect the controller area network. The dedicated and application specific microcontrollers are used for controlling sensors and actuators which are connected through controller area network to perform operations such as sensing, computing, actuating, monitoring, and voting in a designer specified deadline. Microcontrollers deviate from their actual behavior when fault occurs in them. They also work improperly if they will get the undesired input from their neighboring components. Fault causes error in the system and which subsequently leads catastrophic failures. So all the components of such real time distributed embedded system require high degree of safety as well as security.

Motivated by the need of robustness in the system, the proposed method is developed to achieve distributed failure diagnosis under deadline and resource constraints for safety critical K-connected distributed system. Microcontrollers are diagnosed in distributed fashion to provide a global diagnostic view of their fault status, where the communication medium is assumed to be fault-free. A software based approach is developed where multiple microcontrollers agree on the fault status of a specific microcontroller. In this approach the control and diagnosis tasks are executed concurrently to use the microcontrollers more efficiently. The scheme uses list-scheduling heuristic to schedule the normal control and diagnosis tasks in order to minimize the number of microcontrollers and accomplish their execution within designer specified deadline.

Graph partitioning is used to partition the task graphs and schedule the tasks into a fixed frame or slot. Different slots of the frame are allocated to tasks from different task graphs irrespective of their period. It should be noted that the tasks in the distributed embedded system are deterministic and follows a uniform distribution; the load balancing policies are implemented in scheduling the task graphs. We have considered a multi rate system that allows various types of applications such as multimedia video, fly-by-wire and steer-by-wire.

For example, in a fly-by-wire system we have the functionalities such as take-off, cruise control and landing of flight systems which are represented through different task graphs with different periods. Depending on the task execution time, the arrival time and departure time are set to schedule into the frame. The task graphs of different periods are executed in an overlapped fashion in order to finish the execution within a deadline with use of minimal number of microcontrollers in the k-connected distributed embedded system. The tasks are allowed to split into smaller units in order to schedule them in different frames when the current frame is fully allocated. In fact, demonstration of the practicality of the proposed diagnosis approach is done by applying it to a multi-rate fly-by-wire system example to identify faulty microcontroller in a timely fashion, where the type of fault occurs is assumed to be of intermittent type.

In literature, the diagnosis of intermittent faults is based on probabilistic analysis. The proposed fault diagnosis algorithms in this chapter provide accurate solutions for fault diagnosis in distributed embedded systems using GA-Based approaches. Though these fault diagnosis algorithms are most appropriate for the system having less number of devices such as microcontroller, sensors and actuators in a K-connected distributed embedded system, these algorithms are also useful for large class distributed embedded systems such as Fly-By-Wire system most often used in flight control system, satellite systems.

The comparison of time complexity between the non-GA based algorithm and GA-based algorithm have been made considering the non-GA based algorithm proposed by authors in (Becher Ayeb, 1999), where a new formal approach has been presented. The time complexity of the Non-GA-based algorithm proposed by authors has the time complexity $O(n2\sqrt{\tau}/\sqrt{\log n})$, $\tau < n/2$, where n is the total number of nodes and τ is the number of expected faulty nodes. The time complexity of GA based algorithm is $O(K \times p \times n \times ng)$, where K is the connectivity of the network, p is the size of population, n is the number of nodes in the system, and ng is the number of generation needed to diagnose faults. In the current work, the system is assumed to be t-diagnosable meaning that the system can tolerate maximum up to t faults where t is one less than connectivity K. The graph given in Figure 3 shows that the CPU time needed to diagnose the set of faulty nodes in GA based algorithm GAPFDA is lesser than that of existing non-GA based algorithm FIA. The message complexity of the fault diagnosis algorithm is O(nxKxr) where n is the number of nodes, K is the connectivity and r is the number of testing rounds. While n and K remains same for both traditional and proposed diagnosis algorithms, the number of testing rounds in the proposed GA based approach depend on number of generations and CPU time needed to diagnose faulty nodes which is lesser as compared to traditional algorithm. This leads reducing the message complexity of the proposed algorithm as compared to traditional algorithms. The result shows that the proposed approach not only outperform the non-GA based approach but also a good candidate approach to be useful for small to large scale distributed embedded systems available.

FUTURE WORKS

The fault diagnosis algorithms and approaches discussed in this chapter provide interesting concepts by considering the importance of its applications. When the distributed embedded system technology will become indispensable for the society, the design of robust embedded system can be mandatory. The fault diagnosis algorithms can be analyzed from various other aspects to tolerate any kind of failure at any point of time in order to produce robust embedded systems for general purpose and safety critical applications.

The proposed approach can be extended in various ways such as changing the system model, fault model and diagnosis model. In order to characterize the fault diagnosis algorithms some other metrics can be investigated. The simula-

Figure 3. Graph showing the CPU time needed for fault diagnosis

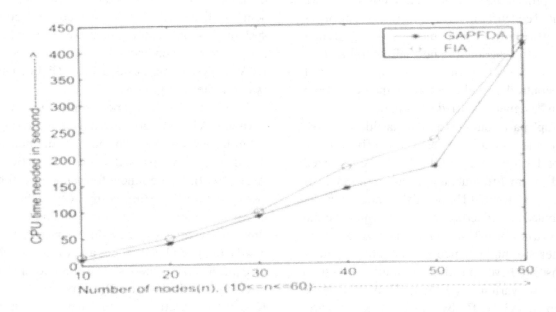

tion results before its implementation need to be analyzed. The developed model can be tested using prototype systems which can be built using commercial off the self-components.

The diagnosis latency or CPU time needed to diagnose faulty nodes increases by increasing the number of nodes, but at a particular point the diagnosis latency remains constant. In the future work, this diagnosis algorithm can be extended for larger classes distributed embedded systems. The classification of application areas of distributed embedded systems can also be made by reviewing an exhaustive list of articles in this area which will enable for finding various shortcomings of the existing techniques.

CONCLUSION

Fault diagnosis is an important problem in distributed embedded systems. Efficient and effective diagnoses of faults are needed to optimize the design cost and their feasibility in the safety critical applications such as FBW and SBW systems. Genetic based fault diagnosis algorithms are comparatively novel approaches to diagnose the fault with reducing the computational time requirement along with message traffic. Intermittent faults are more likely in safety critical systems. The proposed fault diagnosis approach is shown to be feasible for diagnosing fault in a K-connected distributed embedded system. It is applied in small scale distributed systems where number of nodes can be taken up to 100.

Nevertheless, the proposed algorithm can be also applicable to large class distributed embedded systems used in satellite and radar control system. The result shown are the outcomes of experimental model using Matlab.

REFERENCES

Barborak, M., Malek, M., & Dahbura, A. (1993). The consensus problem in fault-tolerant computing. *ACM Computing Surveys*, 25(2), 171–219. doi:10.1145/152610.152612

Becher, A. (1999). Fault identification algorithm: A new formal approach. In *Proceedings of 29th Annual International Symposium on Fault Tolerant Computing*. Academic Press.

Blough, D. M., & Brown, H. W. (1999). The broadcast comparison model for on-line fault diagnosis in multicomputer systems: Theory and implementation. *IEEE Transactions on Computers*, 48(5), 470–493. doi:10.1109/12.769431

Dahbura, A., Sabnani, K., & Henry, W. (1989). Spare capacity as a means of fault detection and diagnosis in multiprocessor systems. *IEEE Transactions on Computers*, 38(6), 881–891. doi:10.1109/12.24300

Dorf, R. C., Bishop, R. H., & Cliffs, N. J. (2001). *Modern control systems*. Upper Saddle River, NJ: Prentice-Hall.

Elhadef, M., & Becher, A. (2000). An evolutionary algorithm for identifying faults in t-diagnosable systems. In *Proc. of the 19th Symp. on Reliable Dist. Syst.*, (pp. 74–83). Academic Press.

Elhadef, M., & Becher, A. (2001). Efficient comparison-based fault diagnosis of multiprocessor systems using an evolutionary approach. In *Proceedings of Int. Symposium on Parallel and Distributed Processing*. Academic Press.

Elhadef, M., Das, S., & Nayak, A. (2006). A novel artificial immune based approach for system level fault diagnosis. In *Proc. of First International Conference on Availability, Reliability and Security*. Academic Press.

Hakimi, S. L., & Amin, A. T. (1975). Characterization of the connection assignment of diagnosable systems. *IEEE Transactions on Computers*, 1040–1042.

Hakimi., S., & Chwa, K. (1981). Schemes for fault tolerant computing: A comparison of modularly redundant and t-diagnosable systems. *Inform. Contr.*, 212–238.

Khilar, P. M., & Mahapatra, S. (2007). A distributed diagnosis approach to fault tolerant multi-rate real-time embedded systems. In *Proc. of 10th Intel Conf. on Information Technology,* (pp. 167–172). Academic Press.

Khilar, P. M., & Mahapatra, S. (2007). Two phase distributed diagnosis in dynamic fault environment. In *Proc. of International Conference on Advance Computing,* (pp. 120-124). Academic Press.

Khilar, P. M., & Mahapatra, S. (2009). Time-constrained fault tolerant x-by-wire systems. *International Journal of Computers and Applications*, *31*(4), 231–238. doi:10.2316/Journal.202.2009.4.202-2391

Khilar, P. M., & Punyotoya, S. (2009). A survey on system level diagnosis in distributed network. In *Proc. of International Conference on Information Technology*, (pp. 213-217). Academic Press.

Khilar, P. M., & Punyotoya, S. (2010). A novel fault diagnosis algorithm for k-connected distributed clusters. In *Proc. of IEEE International Conference on Industrial Electronics, Control and Robotics,* (pp. 101-105). IEEE.

Koptez, H., & Gruensteidl, G. (1993). TTP—A time-triggered protocol for fault-tolerant real-time systems. In *Proc. of IEEE Fault-Tolerant Computing Symp.,* (pp. 524-532). IEEE.

Maeng, J., & Malek, M. (1981). A comparison connection assignment for self-diagnosis of multiprocessor systems. In *Proc. of 11th Int. Symp. on Fault-Tolerant Comput.,* (pp. 173–175). Academic Press.

Mahapatra, A., & Khilar, P. M. (2012). On-line fault diagnosis of arbitrary connected networks. *International Journal on Network Security*, *3*(1), 10–13.

Mahapatra, A., & Khilar, P. M. (2012). An energy-efficient distributed approach for clustering-based fault detection and diagnosis in image sensor networks. *International Journal of Wireless Sensor Systems*, *2*(4).

Malek, M. (1980). A comparison connection assignment for diagnosis of multiprocessor systems. In *Proc. of 7th Int. Symp. on Comput. Architecture,* (pp. 31–35). Academic Press.

Mishra, S., & Khilar, P. M. (2011). Heartbeat based error diagnosis framework for distributed embedded systems. In *Proceedings of International Conference on Software and Computer Technology*. Academic Press.

Nassu, B. T., Duarte, E. P., Jr., & Pozo, A. T. (2005). A comparision of evolutionary algorithms for system level diagnosis. In *Proc. of Genetic and Evolutionary Computation Conference*. Academic Press.

Pelc, A. (1992). Optimal fault diagnosis in comparison models. *IEEE Transactions on Computers*, *41*(6), 779–786. doi:10.1109/12.144631

Preparata, M. G., & Chien, R. (1967). On the connection assignment problem of diagnosable systems. *IEEE Trans. Comps*, *16*(6), 848–854.

Punyotoya, S., & Khilar, P. M. (2009). Distributed micro-controller-based actuator fault diagnosis in multi-rate fly-by-wire system. In *Proc. of 12th International Conference on Information Technology*, (pp. 17-22). Academic Press.

Sengupta, A., & Dahbura, A. T. (1989). On self-diagnosable multiprocessor systems: Diagnosis by the comparison approach. In *Proc. IEEE Symp. on Fault-Tolerant Computing*, (pp. 54-61). IEEE.

Tridandapani, S., Somani, A. K., & Reddy, U. (1995). Low overhead multiprocessor allocation strategies exploiting system spare capacity for fault detection and location. *IEEE Transactions on Computers*, *44*(7), 865–877. doi:10.1109/12.392845

Walter, C. J., Lincoln, P., & Suri, N. (1997). Formally verified on-line diagnosis. *IEEE Transactions on Software Engineering*, *23*(11), 684–721. doi:10.1109/32.637385

Yang, J. C. Y., & Clarke, D. W. (1999). The self-validating actuator. *Control Engineering Practice*, *7*(3), 249–260. doi:10.1016/S0967-0661(98)00148-8

KEY TERMS AND DEFINITIONS

Diagnosis Algorithms: Algorithms those locate the set of fault-free and faulty nodes in a distributed embedded system.

Distributed Embedded System: A set of microcontrollers or processors with connectivity K are connected by a real time communication network.

Fault Diagnosis: It is the location of fault free or faulty status of each node in a distributed embedded system.

Genetic Algorithm: Genetic algorithm is a soft computing technique to solve complex problems when the solution space is large.

Genetic Operators: The set of operators those are used to generate population for search space.

K-Connected Networks: A network with connectivity K where K is defined as the number of nodes removal of which the network is disconnected.

Microcontrollers: Microprocessors for special purpose applications.

Performance Analysis: It is to measure the functional ability and feasibility of the algorithm or approach for different applications.

Section 4
Neural Network and Applications

Chapter 13
Conjugate Gradient Trained Neural Network for Intelligent Sensing of Manhole Gases to Avoid Human Fatality

Paramartha Dutta
Visva-Bharati University, India

Varun Kumar Ojha
Visva-Bharati University, India

ABSTRACT

Computational Intelligence offers solution to various real life problems. Artificial Neural Network (ANN) has the capability of solving highly complex and nonlinear problems. The present chapter demonstrates the application of these tools to provide solutions to the manhole gas detection problem. Manhole, the access point across sewer pipeline system, contains various toxic and explosive gases. Hence, predetermination of these gases before accessing manholes is becoming imperative. The problem is treated as a pattern recognition problem. ANN, devised for solving this problem, is trained using a supervised learning algorithm. The conjugate gradient method is used as an alternative of back propagation neural network learning algorithm for training of the ANN. The chapter offers comprehensive performance analysis of the learning algorithm used for the training of ANN followed by discussion on the methods of presenting the system result. The authors discuss different variants of Conjugate Gradient and propose two new variants of it.

DOI: 10.4018/978-1-4666-4940-8.ch013

INTRODUCTION

The study of Computational Intelligence (CI) enabled us to formulate and/or model real life problems, especially for those problems where statistical modeling is inefficient or infeasible. The first and the primary component of CI is the Artificial Neural Network (ANN). ANN leads the field of CI. Later, bio-inspired computational methods, fuzzy logic and swarm intelligence are contributing their significant role in the field of CI. ANN, a powerful mathematical model inspired by the natural neural network system, is still occupying the central stage in CI. To some extent ANN, like natural neural networks, is able to solve highly complex nonlinear problems. The ANN, as an alternative, may be used for modeling those problems whose statistical modeling may not be erected. Our goal in the course of this chapter is to show the application of ANN and its modeling for a real life problem. For such cases, we have identified manhole gas discrimination/detection problem to be modeled using ANN. The manhole gas detection problem is a critical problem in the sense that, the pattern of gases influencing sensor used for sensing of gases is not only random but also dependent on change in the environment, such as temperature, humidity and pressure. The former is a major concern. The latter one can be exerted by employing supreme quality of sensors for sensing gases. In this chapter, we mention a design of an intelligent sensory system for sensing manhole gases, the design of which is as follows. The proposed intelligent system is having three modules, the first module, viz, the input module comprises gas chamber, the sensor array and data acquisition unit is dedicated for sensing the presence of gases in the manholes. Second module, the intelligent module is the ANN model which receives input from the first module and provides its response to the output module after processing the inputs. In the whole exercise the major tasks are a collection of data sample used in the training of the ANN model and the training of the ANN

model itself. The ANN is trained in a supervised manner using the conjugate gradient method. Apart from the problem formulation, ANN training methodologies constitute the major subject to discuss through this chapter.

Chapter Organization

What else would be better to start, with, at first, we define the gas detection problem in section, *"the problem"*. The subsequent section *"survey"*, enriched this chapter with an exhaustive literature survey of the gas detection problem. With conclusive remarks on the survey, this section also include a brief note on *"our contribution"* of this chapter towards the mentioned problem. Subsequently, in section, *"the problem formulation"*, we discuss the mechanisms employed in formulating the problem as a pattern recognition problem using ANN technique. This section includes, discussion on various methods used, data collection procedures, ANN training prerequisites vide subsections, *"material and methods"*, *"collection and analysis of data samples"* and *"training prerequisites"* respectively. In section *"conjugate gradient"*, we explore the conjugate gradient method for the training of the ANN devised for gas detection problem. Subsequently, section *"performance study"*, offers a detailed performance evaluation of the conjugate gradient method used for ANN training (GCNN). This section is followed by sections *"discussion"* and *"conclusion"*.

THE PROBLEM

Health hazard is the primary concern nowadays. In every hazardous occupation, precautions are taken to avoid fatality. In this chapter, we address such a problem that may cause health hazard and potent to loss of human life. Such problem is detection of hazardous gases in closed space, especially in manholes, where persons have to work for its maintenance. The manholes are the access points

Table 1. Safety limits/LEL of the gases found in manholes

#	Gases	Cause of Formation	Safety Limits
1	Hydrogen Sulphide	Fermentation and Decomposition of stagnant Sewer.	50ppm
2	Carbon Monoxide	Oxidation of hydrocarbons in absence of oxygen.	40ppm
3	Methane	Decomposition of hydrocarbons.	5000ppm
4	Ammonia	Fermentation and Decomposition of biological waste.	25ppm
5	Carbon dioxide	Oxidation of hydrocarbons in presence of oxygen.	10000ppm

built across the sewer pipeline network or other similar underground networks. Especially, in sewer pipeline network, stagnant sewer decomposes into gases which are not only toxic but also explosive at times. Several manhole gas samples are tested and analyzed chemically establishing the presence of poisonous gases like Hydrogen Sulphide, Methane, Carbon Monoxide, Ammonia, Oxides of Nitrogen, Sulphur dioxide, etc. Together, the presence of an excessive proportion of these toxic gases and lack of adequate amount of Oxygen is among the primary factors of fatality of the persons, who have to get down into sewer pipeline through the manholes for maintenance work. To work with safety, the aforementioned factors should be minutely examined before accessing manholes. The solution is to use tools for predetermination of the proportion of the various toxic gases found in manholes including the proportion of Oxygen. Through this chapter, we offer a design of such tools for predetermination of toxic gases.

By exploring various commercially available gas detectors, we arrived at the conclusion that, seldom available in any gas detector specially designed for the detection of the gases found in manhole, though they do not encompass all the gases mentioned above. We want to draw the attention of the readers to the following issue. The sensors are sensitive to their target gases, but to some extent, they respond when exposed to non target gases. This results in cross sensitivity leading to misleading inference. The solution to this problem will be discussed in detail when we encounter *data collection and analysis* section. For

the time being, it is uncovered that the ANN and pattern classification techniques are introduced as remedy to cross sensitivity issue. Again, directing pointer to the toxic gases found in manhole, it is required to mention that the concentration/proportion of the gases are measured in ppm (parts per million) or percent. The labeling concentration in ppm plays important role in categorizing safe and unsafe concentration levels of the gases. The gases are not harmful, if their ppm value indicates concentration in safe zone. The margin of ppm value which separates safe and unsafe zone for a gas is known as threshold value/safety limit of that gas. The developed system should present their output in a manner such that, it can predict the ppm level of gases, so that alarm generator module generates alarm if concentration of any gas classified in unsafe zone. Table 1 indicates the safety limits of all the mentioned gases found in manholes. Please note that in case of explosive gases the term lower explosive limit (LEL) is used instead of the term, safety limits. The safety limits of the gases have identified over the past years are as follows Hydrogen Sulfide (USEPA, 1980), Methane (Fahey, 2002), Carbon Dioxide, Carbon Monoxide (Goldstein, 2008; OSHA, 2009), Ammonia (OSHA, 2009) and Nitrogen Oxides (Struttmann, et al., 1998).

SURVEY

The description of the gas detection problem in previous section uncovers all the issues in design of a gas detector or recognizer for detection of gases. To the research community, the subject of designing gas detector is formally known as electronic nose. The section presents an exhaustive literature survey on research work related to the gas detection, gas recognition, odour identification, electronic nose development and other related issues in developing a system that may be used for the detection of gases. Herein, a timeline provided may draw the attentions of the readers to the amount of research work performed in past decades related to aforementioned subjects. To the best of our knowledge and effort in the survey, we appreciate the initiation of the effort of the researcher towards the development of gas detector in the early 1990s the timeline described is as follows.

In (Li, 1993) author exhibits design of a mixed gases measurement system based on surface acoustic wave sensor array and neural network with continuous valued output style for detection of gas mixture of gases NO and CO. The Author presents the design of the sensor array and construction of neural network for the said purpose.

In (Srivastava, Srivastava, & Shukla, 2000) authors are demonstrating design of an intelligent electronic nose system for the identification of gas odours using sensor array and neural network pattern classification. The authors have shown two different learning approaches to train network. Where neural network receives input as the responses of surface acoustic wave sensors exposed to hazardous vapours like Diethyl Sulfide (DES) and Iso-Octane (ISO). Dimensionality of data set varied from 1 to 8 by taking different number of sensors. They have used backpropagation trained neural classification method and hybridized soft computing tools like neural network and genetic algorithm to provide design of better intelligent system.

In (Liu, Yong, Yonghuai, & Ming, 2001), techniques are demonstrated for cross sensitivity reduction of gas sensors using genetic algorithm based neural network. They use infrared sensors

absorption method in analyzing gas components, where cross sensitivity is due to the distribution of the absorption spectrum of a certain kind of gas intercrosses with another's. A Genetic neural network algorithm is used to recognize the patterns of the mixed gases.

In (Eduard, et.al, 2001), authors have presented multi-component gas mixture analysis using single tin oxide sensor and. They present a method based on the discrete wavelet transform for extracting important features from the response transients of tin oxide-based gas sensor. They show that two components in a mixture can be simultaneously and accurately quantified by processing the response dynamics of a single sensor operated in a temperature-modulated mode.

In (Chang, & Jeng, 2005) the authors are demonstrating the development of a system to detect a mixture of organic molecules. The Backpropagation Neural Network (BPN) is used to distinguish the species in the mixture organic molecules and multivariate linear regression analysis (MLR) are applied to compute the concentration of the species. Amine, carboxylic acid, alcohol and aromatic molecules can easily be distinguished by this system with a backpropagation neural network. Furthermore, the concentrations of the organic compounds were determined with an error of about 10 percent by multivariate linear regression analysis.

In (Kusmoputro et al., 2002) the authors demonstrate an application of fuzzy neural structure through a genetic algorithm in artificial odour recognition system.

In (Keller et al., 2003), the authors develop an electronic nose system for the automated detection and classification of odors, vapors, and gases. They mentioned that an electronic nose is generally composed of a chemical sensing system (e.g., sensor array or spectrometer) and a pattern recognition system (e.g., artificial neural network). They have developed electronic noses for the automated identification of volatile chemicals for environmental and medical applications.

In (Tsirigotis, Laure, & Maria, 2003), the author demonstrated a neural network based recognition, of CO and NH3 reducing gases, using metallic oxide gas sensor array. They present an analysis of gases using non-selective sensor elements which contain two steps. At first, the sensor is submitted in different gases (CO and NH3) of progressive increasing concentration and its characteristic responses are collected for each gas, each concentration and for each sensor element. In order to do the recognition, the signals of sensor output, are transformed into quantities independent of the gas concentration, but characteristic for its chemical compound. In the second step, after the realization of learning phase in a chosen neural network, using the collected characteristic signals, the unknown gases are submitted to the network for recognition.

In (Lee, D. S., Sang, W. B., Minho, L., & Duk, D. L, 2005), the authors reported the use of micro gas sensor array with neural network for recognizing combustible leakage gases. In their report a micro gas sensor array, consisting of four porous tin oxide thin films added with noble metal catalysts on a micro-hotplate, was designed and fabricated. The micro-hotplate was designed to obtain a uniform thermal distribution along with a low-power consumption and fast thermal response. The sensing properties of the sensors toward certain combustible gases, i.e., propane, butane, LPG, and carbon monoxide, were evaluated. A multilayer neural network was then used to classify the gas species. The results demonstrated that the proposed micro sensor array, plus multilayer neural network employing a backpropagation learning algorithm, has been found very effective in recognizing specific kinds and concentration levels of combustible gas below their respective threshold limit values.

In (Widyanto, et al., 2006), authors have proposed a fuzzy-similarity-based self-organized network inspired by immune algorithm to develop an artificial odor discrimination system for three mixture fragrance recognition. They reported that

their proposed system can deal with uncertainty in frequency measurements, which is inherent in odor acquisition devices, by employing a fuzzy similarity and mentioned that the use of the fuzzy similarity results on a higher dissimilarity between fragrance classes, therefore, the recognition accuracy is improved and the learning time is reduced.

In (Ambard, Guo, Martinez, & Bermak, 2008), the authors propose a bio-inspired signal processing method for odor discrimination of gases namely hydrogen, ethanol, carbon monoxide, methane. They have demonstrated a trained neural network successfully tested on a discrimination task between four gases.

In (Baha, & Dibi, 2009), the authors have demonstrated a novel neural network based technique for operating smart gas sensors in a dynamic environment. They have cited the common problems of metal oxide semiconductor sensors are lack of selectivity and environmental effects and suggested the use of neural network based technique to remedy these problems. Their idea was to create intelligent models with the first one, called corrector, can automatically linearize a sensor's response characteristic and eliminate its dependency on the environmental parameters. The corrector's responses are processed by the second intelligent model which has the role of discriminating exactly the detected gas (nature and concentration).

In (Pan, Ning, & Pandeng, 2009), authors have discussed the application of electronic nose for quantitative detection of gas mixture of gases carbon monoxide, methane and hydrogen. They propose a semiconductor based gas sensor array composed sensors of CO, CH_4, H_2, and an on-line data acquisition system combining with the pattern recognition techniques of back propagation neuron network to carry out the quantitative analysis of the partial gas concentration in a mixture.

In (Tao, & Wang, 2009), the authors developed a Micro-Electro- Mechanical Systems (MEMS) based technique to improve the sensitivity of the gas sensor which was sensitive to the special gas selected in the different application fields. Their sampling experiments showed that the gas sensors have the highest sensitivity and better repeatability and cross sensitivity and the pattern recognition algorithms based on a feedforward neural network based intelligent recognition system design system has a better identification effect and higher accuracy.

In (Won, S. et al., 2010) the authors propose a real-time monitoring and estimation technique for managing facilities that store hazardous materials. It relies on Gaussian dispersion model, optical sensor and backpropagation neural networks for the detection and analysis of hazardous (gas) releases.

In (Zhang, Haigang, & Zhongyu, 2010), authors have demonstrated the application of knowledge based genetic algorithms and data fusion technique for detection of mixed gas in the mine. They propose that the output signals of three sensors are trained by backpropagation neural network to get the mathematical model of information fusion for the analysis of a mixed gas of methane, hydrogen and carbon monoxide. The experiment shows that the information fusion could correct the crossed sensitivity error, and improve the accuracy of carbon monoxide, thereby achieving quantitative analysis mixed gas of a coal mine.

In (Wongchoosuka, et al., 2010), the authors have described a portable electronic nose based on hybrid carbon nanotube-SnO_2 gas sensors and its application for detection of methanol contamination in whiskeys. The hybrid gas sensors were fabricated using electron beam evaporation by means of powder mixing. Their instrument employs feature extraction techniques including integral and primary derivative, leading to higher classification performance as compared to the classical features (ΔR and $\Delta R/R0$). It was shown that doping of carbon nanotube (CNT) improves the sensitivity of hybrid gas sensors, while the quantity of CNT has a direct effect on the selectivity of volatile organic compounds, i.e., methanol and ethanol.

In (Sharma, 2010) the author is presenting a concept of developing an electronic nose system to implement backpropagation algorithm of the artificial neural network for odour identification of different tea samples. Chemical vapour identification is to build an array of sensors, where each sensor in the array is designed to respond to a specific chemical. The artificial neural network is trained for chemical vapour recognition. The operation consists of propagating the sensor data through the network to generate the output. Since the feedforward calculations are simply a series of vector-matrix multiplication, unknown chemical can be rapidly identified in the field.

In (Ojha, & Dutta, 2012a), the authors uncover the design issues in the development of an intelligent gas recognition system for detection of gases. In (Ojha, et. al. 2012b), the authors have presented a comprehensive comparison between different intelligent techniques applied to detecting proportion of different component in the manhole gas mixture. In (Ojha, & Dutta, 2012a) and (Ojha, et. al., 2012c), the authors have analyzed the performance of neurogenetic and neuroswarm algorithms applied for detecting proportion of component gases in the manhole gas mixture respectively. In (Ojha, et. al., 2012c), authors have demonstrated the backpropagation neural network based technique for detection of proportion of different gas components present in the manhole gas mixture. In (Ojha, et. al., 2012b), the authors have shown the application of the real valued neurogenetic algorithm for the detection of component gases present in the manhole gas mixture. In (Ojha, et. al., 2012f) and (Ojha, et. al., 2012e), the authors describe a novel neuro simulated annealing algorithm and neuro-swarm technique for detecting proportion of component gases in the manhole gas mixture respectively. In (Ojha, et. al., 2012d), a linear regression based statistical approach is offered for detecting proportion of component gases in the manhole gas mixture.

Our Contribution

The following conclusions may be drawn from the rigorous literature survey provided in section, *survey* above. It is derived that the majority of the article reported towards the design of a gas detection system are based on ANN technique. In all the cases, authors are favoring backpropagation neural network training algorithm and few of them are hybrid approach, such as the genetic algorithm for training of neural network. On the contrary, we resort to using the conjugate gradient method for the training of the ANN. Sensors used for sensing gases are sensitive to their target gases and due to poor selectivity, to some extent, these sensors are sensitive to non-target gases too. Few of the reportings are devoted to this vital issue. Of course few authors are showing their concern and in remedy they introduce additional circuitry padded with the sensor circuit. In our approach, we let the cross sensitivity effect to be propagated to the neural network and allow the ANN to be aware of the noise pattern induced on the sensors. This can be done by preparing training example for neural network with the knowledge of the noise pattern. In the remainder section of the chapter, we offer performance analysis of conjugate gradient trained neural network (CGNN) algorithm.

PROBLEM FORMULATION

In the scope of our research, the gas detection problem mentioned earlier is specifically targeted to provide a solution for manhole gas detection. Nevertheless, this specialization does not influence the basic design of gas detection system. However it compels us to stress towards specific study of manhole gases and their characteristics. Moreover, it influences the preparation of data samples, which is a prime concern to any pattern recognition problem solvable using neural network training. Let us talk about a basic design of a gas detection system. In detection of gases, the first step is to sense the presence of gases, and then it is the turn of intelligent unit comprising ANN to process the input and provide its prediction (processed output) to the user. A basic gas detection system is provided in Figure 1.

The block diagram illustrated in Figure 1 reveals the working principle of the gas detection system. It also exhibits the flow of information across the system. The gas detection system presented in block diagram vide Figure 1, may be modularized in three distinct parts namely, input module, intelligent module and output module. The input module, consisting of gas suction unit, sensor array, data acquisition system (DAS) and

Figure 1. Basic design of a gas detection system

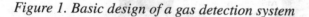

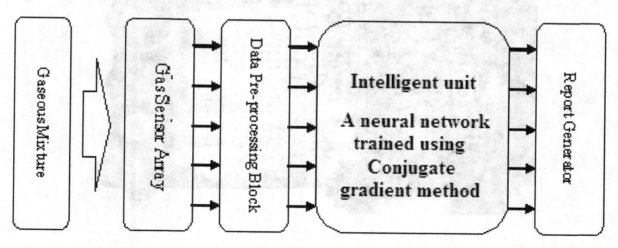

data preprocessing block, is responsible for sensing proportion of manhole gases. The intelligent module, comprising of ANN classifier, is responsible for filtering of noise by recognizing input patterns for classification anomalous and non-anomalous situation. The output module displays the system decision to the user. The materials and methods mentioned in the design of gas detection system are elaborated in the following subsection.

Materials and Methods

Input module, as discussed earlier, is consisting of gas suction chamber, sensor array, data acquisition system and data preprocessing block. The gas suction chamber is used to suck mixture of gases from the manholes and allow it to pass over the array of gas sensors. An array of sensors is an arrangement of sensors aligned to sense the proportion of their respective target gases present in the gas mixture blown over them. To constitute sensor array, we used various kinds of available

sensors, such as metal oxide semiconductor (MOS) gas sensors. A developed sensor array circuitry is shown in Figure 2. The MOS sensors are basically a resistance type electrical sensors. For change in the concentration of gases, the sensitivity of the respective MOS sensors is indicated by a change in their resistance value. The MOS sensors sensitivity is given by $\Delta R_s/R_0$ (ratio of change in sensor resistance and sensors base resistance) where the ΔR_s are the change in resistance of the MOS sensor and the R0 is the base resistance value (Ambard, Guo, Martinez, & Bermak, 2008; Chatchawal, et al., 2010; Tsirigotis, Laure, & Maria, 2003;). Semiconductor gas sensors are widely used for detecting inflammable gases and certain toxic gases in air. The adsorption or reaction of a gas on the surface of the semiconductor material induces a change in the density of the conducting electrons in the polycrystalline sensor element. This chemical reaction can be described by four steps as follows.

Figure 2. MOS sensor array circuitry

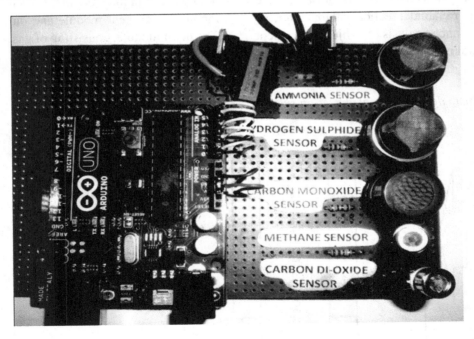

1. Pre-adsorption of oxygen on semiconductor material surface.
2. Adsorption of specific gas.
3. Reaction between oxygen and adsorbed gas.
4. Desorption of reacting gas on the surface.

The above process of delivering electrons between the gas and the semiconductor actually represents the sensitivity of the gas sensor (Kumar, Imam, & Khan, 2009).

DAS is used for acquiring response of the sensors, so that it may be used for further processing. Data preprocessing unit preprocessed the raw sensor response acquired by DAS in ANN manageable form. DAS plays vital role in collecting data for the training of the ANN. Data collection processes are discussed in the subsequent subsection followed by the discussion on ANN training prerequisites.

Analysis of Data Sample

As it is already mentioned, that the collection of data samples is one of the important tasks in the development of ANN based intelligent system. In the present section, we explore the methods adopted for the collection of data samples using which ANN will be trained. Together with the aforementioned materials, we need a gas mixture and analysis setup for preparing the data set. An established gas mixture and analysis setup in our laboratory is shown in Figure 3.

In Figure 3, front view of the setup is shown. By uncovering this setup, it is found that the setup contains three cylinders of toxic gases and one cylinder of a carrier gas. These gases are mixed in a mixture chamber in known proportion. The proportions of gases are regulated using a mass flow controller (MFC) of the respective gases. The gas mixture is then allowed to pass over an array of gas sensors (see Figure 2). A number of data samples produced by repeating this procedure several times. The following points are worth considering. (i) Safety limits of the gases take part in the mixture formation (ii) different combination of proportions of the component gases in each sample mixture. The safety limits of the gases are mentioned in Table 1. Now, we have arrived at a second point, where the gases are mixed in different combinations of their concentrations. We have identified five gases which are most toxic usually found in manholes.

Figure 3. Gas mixture and analysis setup

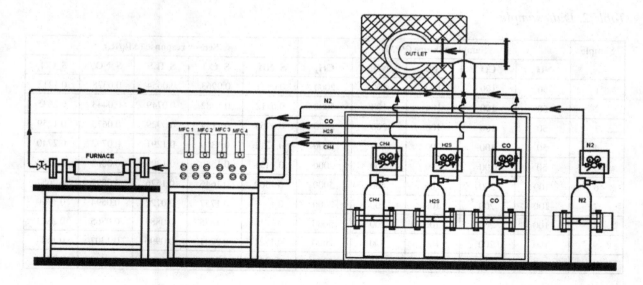

So the gas detection system is developed for these five gases. To prepare data samples, we take cylinders of these five gases and using mass flow controllers, we regulate their concentration level. Each time, a sample is to be prepared, all the five gases are mixed in specific concentrations. It is required to draw the attention to the question that what concentration levels should be taken for the gases. Safety limits of the gases play vital role in addressing this question. Sensor responses of each gas sensor are examined minutely. The observations are as follows. Sensors show minor changes in their response for the concentrations of the gases that are within certain range. In the present scope of research, we have identified three levels of concentration of each gases, one below their safety limits, their respective safety limits itself and above their safety limits. Hence, each of the five gases has three levels of concentration. As a result, two forty three different combinations are produced by mixing five gases by considering their three levels of concentrations. Following this procedure, a data sample may be produced as per Table 2.

Examining Table 2, it is observed that the change in concentration of any gas leads to change in responses of all the sensors in an array, of course the target sensor (sensor dedicated to the gas whose concentration is taken into account) response principally, whereas other non-target sensors are showing mild response. For example, in the second row of Table 2, the concentration of CH_4 is altered only. Due to changes in concentration of CH_4, the target sensor (sensor S_CH_4), respond principally, whereas non-target sensors (S_NH_3, S_CO, S_H_2S and S_NO_2) shows modest response. This is nothing but the cross sensitivity of non target sensors. Particularly for this reason, the sensors' responses are not used directly to report the concentration of gases in manholes. To report the concentration of the gases, a large lookup table is required to recognize the exact pattern/concentration of the gases. Nothing can be better than using ANN to mimic such large lookup table to recognize the pattern of the concentration of gases.

Training Prerequisites

The present section addresses three important issues, network configuration, data preprocessing, and training pattern that affects ANN training.

Table 2. Data sample

Sample	Sample mixture (PPM)					Sensor response ($\Delta R_s/R_0$)				
	NH_3	CO	H_2S	NO_2	CH_4	S_NH_3	S_CO	S_H_2S	S_NO_2	S_CH_4
1	50	100	100	100	2000	0.0531	0.0963	0.0654	0.0378	0.1212
2	50	100	100	100	5000	0.0812	0.1082	0.0749	0.0443	0.2635
3	50	100	100	200	2000	0.0963	0.1194	0.0929	0.0675	0.1259
4	50	100	200	200	5000	0.1212	0.1309	0.1291	0.0792	0.2740
5	50	100	200	400	2000	0.1451	0.1530	0.1399	0.0862	0.1238
6	100	200	200	400	5000	0.1569	0.1646	0.1526	0.0892	0.2687
7	100	200	100	200	2000	0.1693	0.1757	0.0722	0.0694	0.1310
8	100	200	100	200	5000	0.1715	0.1875	0.0883	0.0865	0.2821
9	100	200	100	400	2000	0.1821	0.2231	0.0996	0.1302	0.1544
10	100	200	200	400	5000	0.1924	0.2584	0.1869	0.1648	0.3124

Network Configuration

Configuration of ANN is specific to the problem for which it is devised. The ANN is configured according to the information available for gas detection. As per data sample mentioned in Table 1, each sample of a gas mixture is a combination of five distinct gases. Hence, the multilayer feedforward neural network used in this approach should have five input neurons and five output neurons. The neural network shown in Figure 4 is containing 5 input nodes, n hidden nodes each with m layers and 5 output nodes leading to a $5-n$ ... $n-5$ network configuration. The 5 nodes each in the input as well as in the output layer indicate that the system is used for detecting 5 gases from the gaseous mixture.

Data Preprocessing

Before feeding data into the neural network for its training, preprocessing of the raw data samples is essential to alleviate ANN from poor learning followed by poor forecasting. Normalization of the raw data samples serves the purpose. Where, by normalization, we mean to scale down the data values between 0 and 1. The processes adopted for normalization of data samples is as follows

$$processedValue = (rawValue - min)/(max - min), \qquad (1)$$

where, *processedValue* indicates the normalized value, *rawValue* indicates the targeted value to be normalized, *min* indicates the smallest value in data sample and *max* indicate the highest value

Figure 4. Network configuration

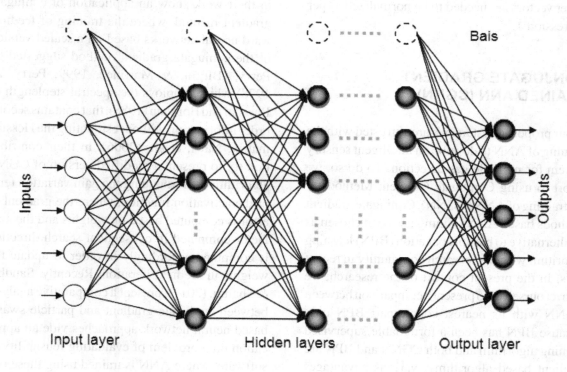

in data sample. Note that the sensor responses are already normalized, because it is a ratio of change in sensor resistance and base resistance. So only the concentration values are needed to be normalized.

ANN Training Pattern

The supervised mode of training is adopted for the training of the ANN. So the training pattern constitutes an input vector and target vector. It is required to mention that the proposed system receives sensor responses as input, which is fed to the ANN for further processing. As per data sample given in Table 2, input vector contains five elements, representing responses coming from five distinct senses. As per data sample given in Table 2, target vector is a five element entity, representing the concentration of five distinct gases in the sample gas mixture. Unlike input vector, target vectors are needed to be normalized as per expression 1.

CONJUGATE GRADIENT TRAINED ANN (CGNN)

In our proposed system, we are entrusted with the training of ANN to develop an intelligent sensory system for multiple gas detection. To do so, we resort to using Conjugate Gradient Method for the training of ANN (CGNN). Conjugate gradient methods based ANN training has been chosen as an alternative to backpropagation (BPN) learning algorithm with the research community in recent days. In the present context of the research, we restrict ourselves to present a comparison between CGNN with its nearest counterpart BPN only because BPN has been a formidable supervised training algorithm and both CGNN and BPN are gradient based algorithms. Various advantages of CGNN over BPN encourage us to explore this technique for the said purpose. In the following section we will first discuss the Conjugate Gradi-

ent Method for Neural Network Training (CGNN Algorithm) followed by performance analysis of the CGNN algorithm applied to the detection of manhole gas mixture. In the past few years research community is engaged in appreciating conjugate gradient method for the training of the ANN. Moller, (1993), in his scholarly contribution, "scaled conjugate gradient algorithm for fast supervised learning", introduces conjugate gradient method for supervised learning of ANN. In (Charalambous, 1992), the author demonstrates the application of conjugate gradient method for efficient training of the ANN. Skorin, & Wendy, (2001), in their contribution, compare and contrast backpropagation steepest decent and conjugate gradient methods. In (Zhang, Shira, & Patrick, 2002), the authors demonstrated an application of CGNN for solving the two-dimensional inverse scattering problem for ultrasound inverse imaging. Sotiropoulos, Kostopoulos, & Grapsa, (2002), in their work show an application of conjugate gradient method, where the training of feedforward neural networks based on a scaled version of the conjugate gradient method suggested by Perry, (Birgin, & Martinez, 1999; Perry, A. 1978) which employs the spectral steplength of Barzilai and Borwein (1988), that contains second order information without estimating the Hessian matrix. Nawi, et al., (2006), in their contribution try to present a modified version of CGNN algorithm by introducing the gain variation term of the activation function, where the gradient of error is computed based on weights and the gain factor computed in consequent search direction is computed accordingly in order to update the weights in the next iteration. Recently, Sandhu, & Shalini, (2011), present a comparative analysis between conjugate gradient and particle swarm based neural network approaches vide an application on a problem of evaluating reusability of software, where ANN is trained using these two approaches based on known as or reusability dataset. Livieris, & Panagiotis, (2011), in their contribution a conjugate gradient neural network training algorithm is proposed which achieves high-order accuracy in approximating the second-order curvature information on the error surface by utilizing the modified secant condition proposed by Li, Tang, & Wei, (2007). In the course of the present chapter, we contribute a demonstration of an application of CGNN algorithms for the detection of manhole gases.

The Conjugate Gradient for ANN Training

Among the several alternatives available to train a backpropagation neural network, the gradient descent (steepest decent) technique and the conjugate gradient technique are the most commonly used. The backpropagation algorithm uses first order gradient descent technique as learning algorithm. In steepest decent technique weights are modified in a direction corresponding to the negative gradient of the error surface. The choice of parameters such as learning rate and momentum rate are critical in gradient decent technique for the training of neural network. The classical backpropagation is quite sensitive to these parameters. If the learning rate is too small the learning will become very slow and if the learning rate is too large the learning will be zigzag and algorithm may not converge to the required degree of satisfaction. Hence the choice of learning rate is very critical. Apart from these the initial choices of synaptic weights also influence the convergence.

Unlike backpropagation, the gradient descent technique is a second-order minimization method. There are also other different second order minimization methods like Newton and quasi-Newton methods that can be directly applied to training neural networks. The conjugate gradient is the simplest and perhaps fastest among them and only because of this it is most commonly used second order minimization method for neural network training. Conjugate gradient descent does not proceed down the gradient; instead, it proceeds in a direction that is conjugate to the direction of

the previous step. In other words, the gradient corresponding to the current step stays perpendicular to the directions of all previous steps. Each step is at least as good as the steepest-descent from the same point. Such a series of steps are non-interfering, so that the minimization performed in one step will not be partially undone by the next.

We try to adjust synaptic weights of ANN, in order to minimize the difference between the actual output of the ANN and desired output for all training examples. Minimization of differences between actual and desired output of ANN may be expressed in terms of sum of squared error (SSE). SSE may be computed as follows

$$SSE = \frac{1}{2} \sum_p \sum_i (o_{pi} - t_{pi})^2, \qquad (2)$$

where, O_{pi} and t_{pi} are indicating actual and desired output of the ANN respectively. The variable 'p' indicates number of training examples and variable 'i' indicates number of output nodes at the output layer of ANN. In backpropagation algorithm the computed error is backpropagated to update the weights in anticipation to get reduced SSE in subsequent SSE computation. Similarly, conjugate gradient method is employed to do the same, by updating the weights. The conjugate gradient method is applied to perform this weight adjustment until the error come down below a tolerable range. The conjugate gradient trained neural network (CGNN) algorithm is sketched as shown in Algorithm 1.

Let $k = 0$ be a vector of initially chosen synaptic weights, W_k in which the elements (weights) are assigned randomly. It is now the responsibility of conjugate gradient method to update the weight vector iteratively in order to minimize SSE. In algorithm 1, step 3 is dedicated for this purpose. Weight vector W_k, updated iteratively, where in each iteration a steplength (analogous to learning rate) is chosen in such a manner that $SSE(W_{k+1}) < \text{SSE}(W_k)$, a line search mechanism

Algorithm 1. CGNN algorithm

```
Step 1: (Initialization)
        Randomly assign initial weight vector Wₖ, where k is epoch number,
        k = 0 initially.
Step 2: (Error Computation)
        Compute SSE(Wₖ) as per expression 2.
Step 3: (Weight vector Updation)
        Wₖ₊₁ = Wₖ + αₖdₖ,
        Where, learning rate αₖ is determined using line search algorithm such
        that SSE(Wₖ + αₖdₖ) < SSE(Wₖ)    dₖ is the search direction basically
        dₖ = -gₖ, where gₖ is gradient computed based on Wₖ. Note that,
```

$$d_k = \begin{cases} -g_k & k = 0 \\ -g_k + \beta_k d_{k-1} & Otherwise \end{cases}$$

```
        Where, βₖ is a factor which scales the influence previous gradient
        analogous to the momentum factor in backpropagation.
Step 4: (Stopping Criteria)
        If (SSE(Wₖ) < ε)           //ε is a predefine non negative integer
            Terminating criteria satisfied.
        Else
            k = k + 1 and go to step 2.
```

mentioned in algorithm 2, comes into play to achieve this objective. A line search technique is an effective mechanism to compute a search direction and then decide how far one can go in that direction. Equations 3 and 4 indicates such a line search method.

$$W_{k+1} = W_k + \alpha_k d_k, \qquad (3)$$

where, d_k is indicating the magnitude and the direction of the search, α_k is indicating the step-length that controls the magnitude of the search. In the present ANN training scheme, the search direction is computed as the gradient of error, and it is taken in the negative of the direction of the gradient. Now computation of step-length draws the entire attention. The computation of steplength, that controls the step size or in other words, the rate of learning, is critical and crucial. We have to strike a trade-off, where, we want to choose a steplength on one hand, such that SSE is

substantially minimized and at the same time, we do not want to spend a very long time in making this choice on the other. What typical approach can be adopted to serve this? The simplest approach, we could think of is to generate a sequence of α_k such that the inequality expressed in Equation 4 may be satisfied.

$$SSE(W_k + \alpha_k d_k) < SSE(W_k) \qquad (4)$$

We should catch hold of an important point from the discussion we had so far, that what should be the termination condition for a line search algorithm. Yes, of course expression of inequality given in Equation 4, is one that we thought off, but will it be enough to satisfy the essential issue of time consumption in search of the desired steplength. Various necessary modifications corresponding to inequality given in Equation 4, are reported, one of them is the Wolfe condition

(Wolfe, 1969, Wolfe, 1971). The Wolfe condition imposes on α_k as follows

$$SSE(W_k + \alpha_k d_k) \leq SSE(W_k) + c\,\alpha_k\,g_k^T d_k, \qquad (5)$$

where, c is a constant $0 < c < 1$, g_k^T, is derivative of SSE, i.e., basically the gradient of error, Apart from the Wolfe condition, Goldstein condition (Armijo, 1966; Goldstein, 1967) may also be imposed on steplength. Discussion on Goldstein condition is as follows.

$$SSE(W_k) + (1- c)\,\alpha_k\,g_k^T d_k \leq SSE(W_k + \alpha_k d_k) \leq SSE(W_k) + c\,\alpha_k\,g_k^T d_k \qquad (6)$$

where, c is a constant $0 < c < 1$. Putting things together, a backtracking line search algorithm is offered as algorithm 2.

Investigating step 3 of algorithm 1, it is found that the search direction for initial epoch (when $k = 0$) is the gradient of error, gradient computation procedure is available in Haykin, (2005), readers may explore (Haykin, 2005) to mitigate their interest. Search direction for epochs, k > 0, is having an influence of previous search direction as an additive term. However, the influence of the previous search direction is scaled down by a multiplicative factor β_k, where, β_k is a factor which scales the influence of the previous gradient analogous to the momentum factor in backpropagation. The simplest way of choosing βk is taking a small positive integer and keeping it fixed throughout the entire learning epochs, similar to the momentum rate in backpropagation (Rummelhart, Hinton, & Williams, 1986). Examining the literature, we found that various methods are suggested in literature. Moreover, the different methods employed in the computation of β_k lead to different versions of conjugate gradient methods. The methods of computing βk, are Hestenes-Stiefel (Hestenes, & Stiefel, 1952), Fletcher-Reeves (Fletcher, & Reeves, 1964), Polak-Ribi`ere (Polak, & Ribiere, 1969), Conjugate Descent (Fletcher, 1987), Liu-Storey (Liu, & Storey, 1991), Dai-Yuan (Dai, & Yuan, 2000) and Perry (Perry, 1978) are given as per expressions 6, 7, 8, 9, 10, 11 and 12.

$$\beta_k = \frac{g_k^T y_{k-1}}{y_{k-1}^T d_{k-1}} \qquad (6)$$

$$\beta_k = \frac{\|g_k\|^2}{\|g_{k-1}\|^2} \qquad (7)$$

Algorithm 2. Backtracking line search algorithm

```
Step 1: (Initialization)
        Choose α' > 0, ρ,c ← [0,1];
        Set α ← α';
Step 2: (Loop)
        While (true)
            If (SSE(Wk + α d) < SSE(W) + c α gᵀ d)
                Break Loop;
            Else
                α ← ρ α;
        End While
        Return α;
```

$$\beta_k = \frac{g_k^T y_{k-1}}{\left\| g_{k-1} \right\|^2} \qquad (8)$$

$$\beta_k = \frac{\left\| g_k^T \right\|}{d_{k-1}^T g_{k-1}} \qquad (9)$$

$$\beta_k = \frac{g_k^T y_{k-1}}{d_{k-1}^T g_{k-1}} \qquad (10)$$

$$\beta_k = \frac{\left\| g_k \right\|^2}{y_{k-1}^T d_{k-1}} \qquad (11)$$

$$\beta_k = \frac{g_k^T (y_{k-1} - S_{k-1})}{y_{k-1}^T d_{k-1}} \qquad (12)$$

where, $y_{k-1} = g_k - g_{k-1}$ and $S_k = W_k - W_{k-1}$. In Figure 5, we have summarized the entire discussion on the conjugate gradient algorithm in the form of a flow diagram. The best part of a flow diagram is that, it has ability to draw the entire picture of an algorithm in a single canvas.

PERFORMANCE STUDY

The CGNN algorithm is implemented in JAVA programming language and the performance of an algorithm applied to the said problem is observed accordingly. The neural network classifier is trained using the normalized data sample mentioned in Table 2. The performance of CGNN algorithm is demonstrated using Figures 6 and 7. The performance characteristic has been observed in terms of the quality of the sum of squared error

Figure 5. Schematic of CGNN algorithm

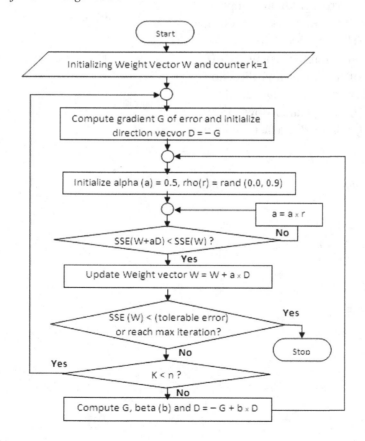

Figure 6. Average SSE vs. Number of Iterations

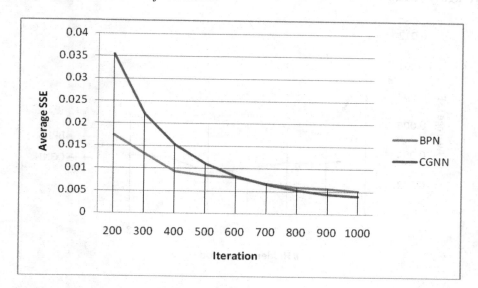

(SSE) induced on neural network. The data sample prepared according to Table 2 is fed as input to the neural network. In Figure 6, it is clearly indicated that the performance of CGNN algorithm excels in comparison to the backpropagation algorithm for the above mention data set and the problem. In Figure 6, the SSE minimizes to 0.005 in the case of classical backpropagation algorithm. In case of conjugate gradient method the SSE minimizes even lesser than the 0.005. And the convergence trajectory of CGNN algorithm is smoother than the backpropagation algorithm. It is because the property of CGNN algorithm ensures the minimization of SSE in consecutive steps, on the other hand backpropagation do not promise any such condition.

Figure 7 indicates the performance of CGNN algorithms in terms of network configuration. In Figure 7, we may appreciate the performance of the CGNN algorithm indicated by the red line (indicating performance of CGNN algorithm) below the blue line (indicating performance of backpropagation algorithm). It is indicated that, for choice of any network configuration CGNN excels backpropagation counterpart.

Figure 8, indicates the performance of a CGNN algorithm with respect to the initial choice of search space. In Figure 8, it may be observed that, the performance of the CGNN algorithm against various initializations is monotonically increasing function of search space initializations. It may be concluded that the algorithm performs better for the lower range of search space.

It is discussed earlier, that, in contrast to the backpropagation, the CGNN algorithm have an automatism for choosing optimum *alpha* (learning rate) and *beta* (momentum factor), the crucial parameters of learning. Earlier, we have discussed the methods that serve the purpose of such automation for the choice of *alpha* and *beta*. We have discussed the line search algorithm for the optimum choice learning parameter alpha. We have discussed various methods for calculation of the parameter *beta*. In our investigation, it is found that, the algorithm CGNN is very sensitive to these calculation methods. It found that the computation method Fletcher-Reeves (Fletcher, & Reeves, 1964) as given in Equation 6 produces best result with SSE 0.001, other than this, methods Polak-Ribi`ere (Polak, & Ribiere, 1969) (as per Equation 7) and Liu-Storey (Liu, & Storey,

Figure 7. Average SSE vs. network configuration

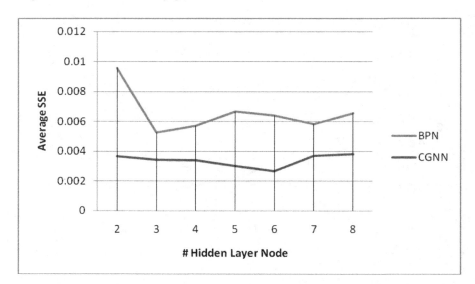

Figure 8. Average SSE vs. initial choice of population

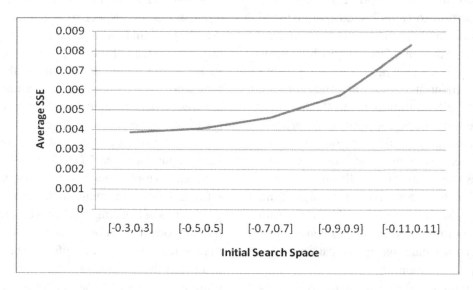

1991) (as per Equation 9) produces SSEs 0.004 and 0.006 respectively. Apart from this method -Stiefel (Hestenes, & Stiefel, 1952) (as per Equation 5) produces SSE 0.01 only better than the methods Conjugate Descent (Fletcher, 1987), Dai-Yuan (Dai, H. & Yuan, 2000) and Perry (Perry, 1978). Tables 3 and 4 illustrate the importance of the parameter beta of CGNN algorithm.

Table 3 is describing the performance of various forms of conjugate gradient methods. It may be observed that the method Fletcher, & Reeves, (1964) performs best among the methods discussed in section *"Conjugate Gradient Trained ANN"* above. It may be noted that, the time consumed by various methods enlisted in Table 3 are varied due to the time expended by the line search

Table 3. Various forms of conjugate gradient (beta computation)

#	beta computation methods	SSE (@1000 iteration)	Execution time (In millisecond)
1	Hestenes, & Stiefel, 1952	0.01583	1897 ms
2	Fletcher, & Reeves, 1964	0.00104	725 ms
3	Polak, & Ribiere, 1969	0.00501	200 ms
4	Conjugate Descent (Fletcher, 1987)	4.35200	840 ms
5	Liu, & Storey, 1991	0.00414	236 ms
6	Dai, & Yuan, 2000	0.06320	350 ms

Table 4. Taking fixed beta for each epoch

#	Fixing beta at	SSE (@1000 iteration)	CPU Execution time (In millisecond)
1	beta = 0.1	0.006	251 ms
2	beta = 0.3	0.003	201 ms
3	beta = 0.5	0.002	191 ms
4	beta = 0.7	0.002	204 ms
5	beta = 0.9	0.001	363 ms
6	beta = 1.1	not functioning above 1.0	

algorithm for searching out optimum value of parameter *alpha*. We researched to an interesting observation, while we are studying the performance of CGNN algorithm against various values of parameter beta fixed for entire epochs to be trained. It is similar to backpropagation momentum rate. Table 4 demonstrated the findings of such experiment. In Table 4, SSE induced on the neural network after thousand epoch of training is noted against different instances of parameter beta setting.

It may be observed that training is faster i.e., a satisfactory SSE is reached in a limited number of iterations by taking the large value of beta. A crucial observation says that the algorithm CGNN shows abnormal behavior for any value $\beta_k = 1.0$ and above. We may appreciate the speedy learning of CGNN algorithm for larger momentum rate ($\beta_k = 0.9$).

The results of Table 4 introduce the concept ceiling the value of the parameter $\beta_k = 0.9$. The Conjugate Descent (Fletcher, 1987) and Dai-Yuan (Dai, & Yuan, 2000) are poor in the sense that the algorithm shows abnormal behavior when these two methods are used. We modify these two methods as per Equations 13 and 14 respectively.

$$\beta_k = \frac{d_{k-1}^T g_{k-1}}{\left\| g_k^T \right\|} \tag{13}$$

$$\beta_k = \frac{y_{k-1}^T d_{k-1}}{\left\| g_k \right\|^2} \tag{14}$$

The methods given in Equations 13 and 14 performs better than the methods Conjugate Descent (Fletcher, 1987) and Dai-Yuan (Dai, & Yuan, 2000) given in Equations 9 and 11 respec-

Table 5. Sample output presentation

Testing I/P	Value (Sample 2)	N/W Actual O/P	System's O/P in PPM
1	0.260	0.016	0080
2	0.346	0.022	0110
3	0.240	0.023	0115
4	0.142	0.008	0040
5	0.843	0.993	4965

tively. The SSE and time of execution incurred by beta computation methods given in Equations 13 and 14 are 0.0039 in 195 ms and 0.003 in 188 ms respectively. It may be noted that the neural network is trained for giving training pattern in thousand epochs of training.

DISCUSSION

The output values of the neural network are denormalized so that system can report its output in terms of the amount of concentration of gas component present the in the given test mixture. From the prepared data samples we consider only 80% of the samples of the training of neural network and we are using 20% of the data sample for the testing purpose.

We provide a test result example for the input sample 2, which is given in Table 3. Where, the input vector is [0.260, 0.346, 0.240, 0.142, 0.843] and target vector is [0.01, 0.02, 0.02, 0.02, 1.0]. Now we are producing this input vector for testing of the neural network that has been trained using Backpropagation Algorithm. The sample test outcome is shown in Table 5.

The system output is nothing but the denormalization of the neural network actual output. The denormalization is simply performed using the Equation 15.

$$\text{System Output} = \text{Network Actual Output} * max, \quad (15)$$

where, the $max = 5000$ is the maximum gas concentration among all gases of all sample and recall the normalization process given in by the Equation 1.

CONCLUSION

Through present chapter, we are offering detail discussion on a Computational Intelligence approach for modeling manhole gas detection problem as a machine learning problem. The chapter provides discussion on a conjugate gradient based neural network training method. It also offers performance analysis of conjugate gradient trained neural network (CGNN) algorithm. The CGNN algorithm presented herein is used for training of the ANN, which is devised as intelligent system that may forecast hazardous satiation inside the manhole. We have talked about the intelligent systems proposes by other investigators in the past few years, sufficiently. In our survey, we have observed that, other authors prefer backpropagation based training, whereas we established the usefulness of CGNN algorithm. In the present chapter, we discussed the various methods reported in literature for computation of CGNN algorithm parameter *beta*. In the present chapter, we proposed two new methods for parameter *beta* computation for CGNN algorithm. We have empirically proven that our proposed modification lies only next to the Fletcher and Reeves (1964) method.

REFERENCES

Ambard, M., Guo, B., Martinez, D., & Bermak, A. (2008). A spiking neural network for gas discrimination using a tin oxide sensor array. In *Proceedings of 4th IEEE International Symposium on Electronic Design, Test and Applications* (pp. 394-397). IEEE. doi:10.1109/DELTA.2008.116

Armijo, L. (1966). Minimization of functions having Lipschitz continuous first partial derivatives. *Pacific Journal of Mathematics, 16*(1), 1–3. doi:10.2140/pjm.1966.16.1

Baha, H., & Dibi, Z. (2009). A novel neural network-based technique for smart gas sensors operating in a dynamic environment. *Sensors (Basel, Switzerland), 9*(11), 8944–8960. doi:10.3390/s91108944 PMID:22291547

Barzilai, J., & Borwein, J. M. (1988). Two point step size gradient methods. *IMA Journal of Numerical Analysis, 8*, 141–148. doi:10.1093/imanum/8.1.141

Birgin, E. G., & Martinez, J. M. (1999). A spectral conjugate gradient method for unconstrained optimization. *Applied Mathematics & Optimization, 43*, 117–128. doi:10.1007/s00245-001-0003-0

Chang, P., & Jeng, S. S. (2005). The application of backpropagation neural network of multi-channel piezoelectric quartz crystal sensor for mixed organic vapours. *Tamkang Journal of Science and Engineering, 5*, 209–217.

Charalambous, C. (1992). Conjugate gradient algorithm for efficient training of artificial neural networks. *IEE Proceedings-G, 139*.

Dai, Y. H., & Yuan, Y. X. (2000). A nonlinear conjugate gradient with a strong global convergence properties. *SIAM Journal on Optimization, 10*, 177–182. doi:10.1137/S1052623497318992

Eduard, L. et al. (2001). Multicomponent gas mixture analysis using a single tin oxide sensor and dynamic pattern recognition. *IEEE Sensors Journal, 1*(3), 207–213. doi:10.1109/JSEN.2001.954833

Fahey, D. W. (2002). *Twenty questions and answers about the ozone layer*. National Oceanic and Atmospheric Administration. Retrieved from http://www.esrl.noaa.gov/csd/assessments/ozone/2010/twentyquestions/

Fletcher, R. (1987). *Practical methods of optimization*. New York: John Wiley & Sons.

Fletcher, R., & Reeves, C. M. (1964). Function minimization by conjugate gradients. *The Computer Journal, 7*, 149–154. doi:10.1093/comjnl/7.2.149

Goldstein, A. A. (1967). *Constructive real analysis*. New York: Harper & Row Publishers.

Goldstein, M. (2008). Carbon monoxide poisoning. *Journal of Emergency Nursing: JEN*. doi:10.1016/j.jen.2007.11.014

Haykin, S. (2005). *Neural networks a comprehensive foundation*. Delhi, India: Pearson Prentice Hall.

Hestenes, M. R., & Stiefel, E. (1952). Methods for conjugate gradients for solving linear systems. *Journal of Research of the National Bureau of Standards, 49*, 409–436. doi:10.6028/jres.049.044

Kumar, R., Imam, S. A., & Khan, M. R. (2009). A critical review of taguchi gas sensor for the detection of VOC's. *MASAUM Journal of Reviews and Surveys, 1*(2), 177–183.

Lee, D. S., Sang, W. B., Minho, L., & Duk, D. L. (2005). Micro gas sensor array with neural network for recognizing combustible leakage gases. *IEEE Sensors Journal, 5*(3), 530–536. doi:10.1109/JSEN.2005.845186

Li, G., Tang, C., & Wei, Z. (2007). New conjugacy condition and related new conjugate gradient methods for unconstrained optimization. *Journal of Computational and Applied Mathematics, 202*(2), 523–539. doi:10.1016/j.cam.2006.03.005

Li, J. (1993). A mixed gas sensor system based on thin film saw sensor array and neural network. In *Proceedings of the Twelfth Southern Biomedical Engineering Conference*, (pp. 179-181). doi:10.1109/SBEC.1993.247403

Liu, J., Yong, Z., Yonghuai, Z., & Ming, C. (2001). Cross sensitivity reduction of gas sensors using genetic algorithm neural network. In Proc. SPIE 4201, Optical Methods for Industrial Processes. doi: doi:10.1117/12.417392

Liu, Y., & Storey, C. (1991). Efficient generalized conjugate gradient algorithms, part 1: Theory. *Journal of Optimization Theory and Applications, 69*, 129–137. doi:10.1007/BF00940464

Livieris, I. E., & Panagiotis, P. (2011). *An advanced conjugate gradient training algorithm based on a modified secant equation*. International Scholarly Research Network ISRN Artificial Intelligence.

Moller, M. F. (1993). A scaled conjugate gradient algorithm for fast supervised learning. *Neural Networks, 6*. doi:525-533.0893-6080/93

NIOSH. (2011). *Volunteer fire fighter dies during attempted rescue of utility worker from a confined space*. Retrieved from http://eww.cdc.gov/niosh/re/reports/face201031.html

Ojha, V. K., Datta, P., & Saha, H. (2012a). Performance analysis of neuro genetic algorithm applied on detecting proportion of components in manhole gas mixture. *International Journal of Artificial Intelligence and Application, 3*(4), 83–98. doi:10.5121/ijaia.2012.3406

Ojha, V. K., Datta, P., Saha, H., & Ghosh, S. (2012b). Application of real valued neuro genetic algorithm in detection of components present in manhole gas mixture. *Advances in Intelligent and Soft Computing, 166*, 333–340. doi:doi:10.1007/978-3-642-0157-5

Ojha, V. K., Datta, P., Saha, H., & Ghosh, S. (2012c). Detection of proportion of different gas components present in manhole gas mixture using backpropagation neural network. *International Proceedings of Computer Science and Information Technology, 1*, 11–15.

Ojha, V. K., Datta, P., Saha, H., & Ghosh, S. (2012d). Linear regression based statistical approach for detecting proportion of component gases in manhole gas mixture. In *Proceedings of International Symposium on Physics and Technology of Sensors*. IEEE. doi:10.1109/ISPTS.2012.6260865

Ojha, V. K., Datta, P., Saha, H., & Ghosh, S. (2012e). A neuro-swarm technique for the detection of proportion of components in manhole gas mixture. In *Proceedings of International Conference on Modeling, Optimization and Computing*. Kanyakumari, India: NI University.

Ojha, V. K., Datta, P., Saha, H., & Ghosh, S. (2012f). A novel neuro simulated annealing algorithm for detecting proportion of component gases in manhole gas mixture. In *Proceedings of International Conference on Advances in Computing and Communications*, (pp. 238-241). IEEE. Doi:10.1109/ICACC.2012.54

Ojha, V. K., & Dutta, P. (2012a). Performance comparison of different intelligent techniques applied on detecting proportion of different component in manhole gas mixture. In *Handbook of research on computational intelligence for engineering, science and business* (pp. 758–785). Academic Press. doi:10.4018/978-1-4666-2518-1.ch030

Ojha, V. K., & Dutta, P. (2012b). Performance analysis of neuro swarm optimization algorithm applied on detecting proportion of components in manhole gas mixture. *Artificial Intelligence Review, 1*(1), 31–46. doi: doi:10.5430/JNEP. V1N1PX

OSHA. (2009). *OSHA fact sheet: Carbon monoxide*. OSHA.

Pan, W., Ning, L., & Pandeng, L. (2009). Application of electronic nose in gas mixture quantitative detection. In *Proceedings of IC-NIDC*, (pp. 976-980). IEEE.

Perry, A. (1978). A modified conjugate gradient algorithm. *Operations Research, 26*, 1073–1078. doi:10.1287/opre.26.6.1073

Polak, E., & Ribiere, G. (1969). Note sur la convergence de methods de directions conjuguees. *Revue Francais d'Informatique et de Recherche Operationnelle, 16*, 35–43.

Rummelhart, D., Hinton, G., & Williams, R. (1986). Learning representations by back propagation errors. *Nature, 323*, 533–536. doi:10.1038/323533a0

Sandhu, P. S., & Shalini, C. (2011). A comparative analysis of conjugate gradient algorithms & PSO based neural network approaches for reusability evaluation of procedure based software systems. *Chiang Mai Journal of Science, 38*, 123–135.

Sharma, S. G. (2010). *Implementation of artificial neural network for odours identification using E-NOSE*. Paper presented at the National Conference on Computational Instrumentation CSIO. Chandigarh, India.

Skorin, K. J., & Wendy, K. T. (2001). Training artificial neural networks: Backpropagation via nonlinear optimization. *Journal of Computing and Information Technology, 9*, 1–14. doi:10.2498/cit.2001.01.01

Sotiropoulos, D. G., Kostopoulos, A. E., & Grapsa, T. N. (2002). A spectral version of perry's conjugate gradient method for neural network training. *Proceedings of 4th GRACM Congress on Computational Mechanics, 1*, 291-298.

Srivastava, A. K., Srivastava, S. K., & Shukla, K. K. (2000). *On the design issue of intelligent electronic nose system*. IEEE. doi:10.1109/ICIT.2000.854142

Struttmann, T. et al. (1998). Unintentional carbon monoxide poisoning from an unlikely source. *The Journal of the American Board of Family Practice, 11*(6), 481–484. doi:10.3122/jabfm.11.6.481 PMID:9876005

Tao, Z., & Wang, L. (2009). Mixed gases recognition based on feedforward neural network. In *Proceedings of Second International Symposium on Intelligent Information Technology and Security Information*. IEEE. DOI 10.1109/IITSI.2009.35

Tsirigotis, G., Laure, B., & Maria, G. (2003). Neural network based recognition, of CO and NH_3 reducing gases, using a metallic oxide gas sensor array. *Scientific Proceedings of RTU, Telecommunications and Electronics, 3*(7), 6-10.

USEPA. (1980). *Health and environmental effects problem for hydrogen sulfide*. USEPA.

Widyanto, M. R., Benyamin, K., Hajime, N., Kazuhiko, K., & Kaoru, H. (2006). A fuzzy-similarity-based self-organized network inspired by immune algorithm for three-mixture-fragrance recognition. *IEEE Transactions on Industrial Electronics, 53*(1), 313–321. doi:10.1109/TIE.2005.862212

Wolfe, P. (1969). Convergence conditions for ascent methods. *SIAM Review, 11*(2), 226–235. doi:10.1137/1011036. JSTOR 2028111

Wolfe, P. (1971). Convergence conditions for ascent methods: II: Some corrections. *SIAM Review, 13*(2), 185–188. doi:10.1137/1013035

Won, S., Dongil, S. Y., & Jamin, K. (2010). The estimation of hazardous gas release rate using optical sensor and neural network. In *Proceedings of European Symposium on Computer Aided Process Engineering, ESCAPE20*. Elsevier B.V.

Wongchoosuka, C., Wisitsoraatb, A., Tuantranontb, A., & Kerdcharoena, T. (2010). Portable Electronic nose based on carbon nanotube-sno$_2$ gas sensors and its application for detection of methanol contamination in whiskeys. *Sensors and Actuators. B, Chemical*. doi:10.1016/j.snb.2010.03.072

Zhang, Q., Haigang, L., & Zhongyu, T. (2010). *Knowledge-based genetic algorithms data fusion and its application in mine mixed-gas detection*. IEEE.

Zhang, X., Shira, L. B., & Patrick, J. F. (2002). A connjugate gradient neural network technique for ultrasound inverse imaging. *Journal of Computational Acoustics, 10*(2), 243–264.

ADDITIONAL READING

Bayati, A. Y., & Al, N. Sulaiman, A., & Gulnar W. S. (2009). A Modifed Conjugate Gradient Formula for Back Propagation Neural Network Algorithm. *Journal of Computer Science, 5*(11), 849-856. ISSN 1549-3636.

Dennis, J. E., & Schnabel, R. B. (1996). *Numerical Methods for Unconstrained Optimization and Nonlinear Equations*. Philadelphia: SIAM Publications. doi:10.1137/1.9781611971200

Nawi, N. M., Ransing, M. R., & Ransing, R. S. (2006). An Improved Learning Algorithm Based on the Conjugate Gradient Method for Back Propagation Neural Networks. *International Journal of Engineering and Applied Sciences, 2*(2), 8589.

Nocedal, J., & Wright, S. J. (1999). Numerical Optimization. New York, NY: Springer Verlag.

Plagianakos, V. P., Sotiropoulos, D. G., & Vrahatis, M. N. (1998), A Nonmonotone Backpropagation Training Method for Neural Networks, *Department. of Mathematics, University of Patras, Technical Report* No.98-04

Zakaria, Z., Nor, A. M. I., & Shahrel, A. S. (2010). A Study on Neural Network Training Algorithm for Multiface Detection in Static Images. *World Academy of Science. Engineering and Technology, 38*, 170–173.

KEY TERMS AND DEFINITIONS

Backpropagation: Error computed at output layer of neural network is back propagated to earlier layers for updating synaptic weights in order to minimize sum squared error induced on neural network.

Conjugate Gradient: Conjugate gradient descent does not proceed down the gradient; rather, it proceeds in a direction that is conjugate to the direction of the previous step.

Cross Sensitivity: The cross-sensitivity is the sensitivity of a gas sensor to any non target gas.

Manhole Gas: Gases accumulated in sewer pipelines due to decomposition of sewage.

Safety Limit: Maximum human tolerable concentration level limit towards any gas.

Sensor Array: Array of semiconductor based gas sensor.

Chapter 14
Artificial Neural Network Modeling for Electrical Discharge Machining Parameters

Raja Das
VIT University, India

M. K. Pradhan
Maulana Azad National Institute of Technology, India

ABSTRACT

The objective of the chapter is to present the application of Artificial Neural Network (ANN) modelling of the Electrical Discharge Machining (EDM) process. It establishes the best ANN model by comparing the prediction from different models under the effect of process parameters. In EDM, the motivation is frequently to get better Material Removal Rate (MRR) with fulfilling better surface quality of machined components. The vital requirements are as small a radial overcut with minimal tool wear rate. The quality of a machined surface is very important to fulfilling the growing demands of higher component performance, durability, and reliability. To improve the reliability of the machine component, it is necessary to have in depth knowledge of the effect of parameters on the aforesaid responses of the components. An extensive chain of experiments has been conducted over a wide range of input parameters, using the full factorial design. More than 150 experiments have been conducted on AISI D2 work piece materials using copper electrodes to get the data for training and testing. The additional experiments were obtained to validate the model predictions. The performance of three neural network models is discussed in the evaluation of the generalization ability of the trained neural network. It was observed that the artificial neural network models could predict the process performance with reasonable accuracy, under varying machining conditions.

DOI: 10.4018/978-1-4666-4940-8.ch014

INTRODUCTION

Owing to the growing trend to use light, slim and compact mechanical component in recent years, there has been an increased curiosity in advanced high hardness, temperature resistance, and high strength to weight ratio materials. However, these materials are mostly unable to process by traditional manufacturing process called "difficult to machine material. Electrical Discharge Machining (EDM) has been a mainstay of manufacturing for more than six decades, providing unique capabilities to machine difficult to machine" materials with desire shape, size, and required dimensional accuracy. It is the most widely and successfully applied machining high hardness, temperature resistance, and high strength to weight ratio materials, used in mould and die making industries, aerospace component, medical appliance, and automotive industries.

It is a thermal process of eroding electrically conductive materials with a series of successive electric sparks and the complex phenomenon involving several disciplines of science and branches of engineering. The formation of the plasma channel between the tool and the workpiece, thermodynamics of the repetitive spark causing melting and evaporating the electrodes, micro-structural changes, and metallurgical transformations of material, are still not clearly understood.

Since this process is complex and stochastic in nature there are several modelling attempts have been made to understand this process. But full prospective of the process is not exploited yet. However, the relationship between input process parameter and response may be established using mathematical, empirical, and statistical modelling. Several modeling attempts have been made to characterize the EDM process based on electrothermal theory since 1971. Many researchers have analyzed in terms of the temperature distribution, crater geometry, and material removal at the cathode Yeo et al. (2008); Dibitono et al. (1989); Patel et al. (1989); Eubank et al. (1989), semi-empirical

models Wang and Tsai (2001); Valentincic and Junkar (2004), mathematical analysis Kanagarajan et al. (2008); Kuppan et al. (2007); Puertas et al. (2004); Khan et al. (2009); Khan (2008); Karthikeyan et al. (1999), and statistical analysis Pradhan and Biswas (2011a, 2008a); Dhar et al. (2007); Dvivedi et al. (2008); Wang (2009); Kiyak and Cakir (2007); Jaharah et al. (2008); Caydas and Hascalik (2008); Keskin et al. (2006); Salonitis et al. (2009); Tsai and Wang (2001b)

The EDM process has some deficiencies, such as high specific energy consumption, lower machining performance (productivity) and accuracy of the dimensions. These are the some important aspects that constrict its applications. Researchers and Investigators are thus, mesmerized towards the process modelling and picking proper machining parameters. Traditionally, these are carried out by EDM operator's expertise or conventional technical data offered by the manufacturers that confines the machining performance. Modelling of the process is generally required for its better understanding of the impact of the machining parameters on the responses. An exact model will help the experimenter to trim down the experimental cost associated with it and optimize the process by setting the required objective.

Several modeling attempts have been made to characterize the EDM process based on electrothermal theory since 1971. Many researchers have analyzed in terms of the temperature distribution, crater geometry, and material removal at the cathode. Yeo et al.(2008);Dibitono et al. (1989);Patel et al. (1989);Eubank et al. (1989). For predicting the behavior of the EDM process, the conventional modelling techniques are found to be inadequate the artificial neural network (ANN) can be employed as a modelling tool, because the ANN can deliver justification to the wide variety of science and engineering problems with complex and uncertain data similar to EDM. Consequently, the use of ANN in modelling using responses obtained from experiments connecting different materials and machining conditions is gaining popularity.

There are numerous ANN applications in EDM, as it is an effective method to solve non-linear problem. Mandal et al. (2007) attempted to model the EDM process using ANN with back propagation as the learning algorithm. They modelled surface roughness, MRR and tool wear, with various input parameters and found suitable for predicting the responses. Panda and Bhoi (2005) developed an artificial feed forward neural network based on the Levenberg-Marquardt back propagation technique of logistic sigmoid activation function to predict MRR of AISI D2 steel. This model performs well under the stochastic environment of actual machining conditions without understanding the complex physical phenomena exhibited in EDM, and provides faster and more accurate results. They found that the 3-4-3-1 neural architecture has the highest correlation coefficient and used it for the analysis. Wang et al. (2003) combined the capabilities of ANN and a genetic algorithm to find an integrated solution to the existing problem of modeling and optimization of EDM processes. Gao et al. (2008) established machining process models based on different training algorithms of ANN, namely Levenberg-Marquardt algorithm, resilient algorithm, Scaled Conjugate Gradient algorithm and Quasi-Newton algorithm. All models have been trained by same experimental data, checked by another group data, their generalization performance is compared. Levenberg-Marquardt algorithm found to be the better generalization performance and convergence speed is faster. Pradhan (2009) offered a RSM and ANN predictive modelling using Ip, Ton, and dielectric flushing pressure (FP) to predict OC, MRR and TWR. A close agreement was observed among the actual experiment, RSM, and ANN predictive results.

Tsai and Wang (2001a) in their study compared six different ANN models and an ANFIS model on MRR in EDM. ANFIS shown to be more accurate and in their further investigations, [Tsai and Wang (2001c)] have applied the same method to predict the Ra. Results show that tangent sigmoid multi layered perceptron (TANMLP), radial basis function network (RBFN), Adaptive RBFN and ANFIS models have shown consistent results. The NF approach is becoming one of the major areas of interest because it gets the benefits of neural networks as well as of fuzzy logic systems, and it removes the individual disadvantages by combining them with the common features. Pradhan and Biswas (2010) in their study used two neuro-fuzzy models and a neural network model for predictions of MRR, tool wear rate, and radial overcut in die sinking EDM. The comparison results reveal that the artificial neural network and the Neuro-fuzzy models are comparable in terms of accuracy and speed. Further, A Neuro-fuzzy model and a regression model was developed to predict MRR, experiments were conducted with various levels of Ip, Ton and duty fraction. The model predictions were compared and found that the Neuro fuzzy model has better predictive capability than the regression model Pradhan and Biswas (2009, 2008b). These techniques have been used for modeling and optimization of various machining processes Pradhan et al. (2010); Pradhan and Biswas (2011b). Therefore, this chapter presents the applications of three different classes artificial neural network (ANN) models for the prediction of EDM parameters. (see Table 1)

Table 1. Chemical composition of AISI D2 (wt %)

Cr	Mo	V	C	Mn	Si	Ni	Fe
12	0.80	0.10	1.52	0.30	0.3	0.3	Balance

Table 2. Technical specifications of electro discharge machine

Machine Tool	PS50 ZNC
Work tank internal dimensions (W x D x H)	800 x500 x 350 mm
Work table dimensions	550 x 350 mm
Transverse(X,Y,Z)	300, 200, 250 mm
Maximum job weight	300 kg
Maximum electrode weight	100 kg
Maximum job height above the table	250 mm
Feed motor / servo system for Z axis	DC Servo
Position measuring system (X, Y, Z)	Incremental linear scale
Dielectric system	Integral with the machine tool
Dielectric capacity	400 liters
Filter element	10 *m* paper cartridge 2 nos.
Pulse Generator	S 50 ZNC
Pulse generator type	MOSFET
Current range, Ip	0-50 A
Pulse on time range Ton	0.5-4000 *ms*
Duty factor range, Tau	50-93%
Open circuit voltage, V	40-60 v
Power supply	3 phase, AC 415 V*, 50 Hz
Connected load	6KVA includes PF unit

Experimental Design and Parameter Selection

Full factorial design is the usually adopted for designing an experiment in which all possible combinations of factors and their levels are considered. However, if the levels are different, a mixed level factorial designs are generally implemented. In this work, the process parameters, *Ip* and Ton are assigned with five levels, whereas *Tau* and *V* are with three and two levels, respectively, yielding a total of 150 (= $5^2 \times 3^1 \times 2^1$) experiments. The experimental conditions are shown in Table 2. To eliminate the consequence of unaccounted factors on the responses the experiments were carried out in random order. The responses MRR, TWR and G have been observed for each experiment and the results obtained through a series of experiments for various sets of parametric combinations

as planned have been exhibited in Table 3. The outcomes of this factorial design facilitate to approximate all the main effects and their second order interactions in this research.

Experimental Environment

Processing machine:Machine Tool & PS50 ZNC, Pulse generator type &MOSFET Work piece material: AISI D2 workpiece electrode material: Electrolytic Copper Working Fluid: Commercial grade EDM oil was used as dielectric fluid polarity: reverse

Parameter Selection

Parameter selection is a very vital job in the EDM process. There are many parameters that influence the responses significantly. Since, the influence

Table 3. Experimental material removal rate and surface roughness for the EDM

Run	Ip (A)	Ton(μs)	Tau	V	MRR (mm3/min)	Ra (μm)
1	10	75	66.5	45	10.35	5.55
2	10	75	66.5	45	9.04	5.98
3	15	50	83	50	29.163	8.43
4	5	50	50	50	5.18	5.01
5	5	100	83	40	5.245	5.03
6	15	50	50	50	33.103	7.43
7	5	50	50	40	4.606	4.59
8	5	50	83	40	8.872	4.71
9	15	100	50	50	51.09	8.1
10	10	75	66.5	45	8.95	6.12
11	5	100	50	40	4.349	4.89
12	15	100	50	40	51.004	10.93
13	5	100	83	50	6.972	5.7
14	15	100	83	40	33.023	12.49
15	5	50	83	50	14.12	5.19
16	5	100	50	50	4.349	5.59
17	15	100	83	50	33.11	9.01
18	15	50	50	40	29.737	10.49
19	10	75	66.5	45	8.42	6.54
20	15	50	83	40	20.002	12.01
21	10	75	66.5	40	8.936	8.2
22	10	75	83	45	9.356	7.13
23	10	75	66.5	50	11.007	6.35
24	15	75	66.5	45	33.084	9.68
25	10	50	66.5	45	9.182	5.87
26	10	75	66.5	45	11.01	6.25
27	5	75	66.5	45	5.361	6.07
28	10	100	66.5	45	10.43	7.27
29	10	75	50	45	9.25	5.92
30	10	75	66.5	45	9.352	6.75

of EDM parameters is innumerable and complex, therefore it is neither scientific and nor easy to do with limited processing in the testing time to take account of all such factors. Extensive experiments were conducted, and the proposed models used the experimental data on EDMed AISI D2 tool steel.

Based on experience, literature's on EDM research and the working characteristics of the machine, the prime parameters chosen, in the present chapter, are discharge current, spark on-time, duty cycle and discharge voltage. The motivation, why these factors have been selected is that these are often

Table 4. Experimental tool wear rate and radial overcut for the EDM

Run	Ip	Ton	Tau	V	TWR (μm)	G(μm)
1	10	300	80	40	0.060	0.190
2	10	100	80	60	0.424	0.150
3	10	300	90	60	0.056	0.230
4	4	100	90	60	0.089	0.005
5	7	200	85	50	0.076	0.138
6	7	200	85	50	0.079	0.132
7	4	100	80	40	0.075	0.050
8	4	300	80	60	0.022	0.080
9	10	100	90	40	0.547	0.160
10	4	300	90	40	0.000	0.065
11	7	200	85	50	0.071	0.123
12	4	100	80	60	0.100	0.038
13	7	200	85	50	0.067	0.117
14	4	300	90	60	0.011	0.060
15	4	300	80	40	0.022	0.090
16	4	100	90	40	0.045	0.010
17	10	100	80	40	0.625	0.160
18	10	300	80	60	0.052	0.170
19	10	300	90	40	0.033	0.210
20	10	100	90	60	0.647	0.160
21	10	200	85	50	0.208	0.181
22	7	200	85	50	0.073	0.128
23	7	100	85	50	0.168	0.095
24	7	200	85	40	0.070	0.142
25	7	200	85	50	0.068	0.131
26	7	200	85	60	0.080	0.120
27	4	200	85	50	0.028	0.080
28	7	200	80	50	0.083	0.125
29	7	200	90	50	0.066	0.105
30	7	300	85	50	0.050	0.130

used among EDM researchers Dhar et al.(2007), Kung et al. (2009), Doniavi et al. (2008) and So-hani et al. (2009) for the said responses and are found significantly influencing them.

Experimental Scheme

Experiments were conducted on a CNC electrical discharge die sinking machine using a cylindrical pure copper (99.9% Cu) as a tool electrode with a diameter of 30 mm and AISID2 workpiece of diameter 100 mm and 10 mm thick. The specific factors with the levels were presented the table, and measurement of MRR, TWR, Ra and G are the responses. Commercial grade EDM oil was used as dielectric fluid, the power supply was linked with the tool electrode (Tool: positive polarity, workpiece: negative polarity). A lateral flushing system was employed for effective flushing of machining debr is from the working gap region with a pressure of 0.4 kg f /cm2. The partial experimental results are given in Table 3 and 4.

ARTIFICIAL NEURAL NETWORK

Artificial Neural Network (ANN), one application of Artificial Intelligence, has achieved considerable success in recent years and opened a new dimension for scientific research and industrial/business applications. Although the concept of ANN can be dated back to half a century ago, ANN application in EDM machining was only popular within the last decade. A number of authors have proposed the applications of ANNs to predict and optimize the machining process parameters . ANNs are built on the basis of the biological system of human nervous system. In fact, the human brain has a data processing system that appears to work like a parallel and nonlinear structure. ANNs are capable to learn from examples and to perform non-linear mappings. It consists of inputs, which are multiplied by weights, and then computed by a mathematical function which determines the activation of the neuron. Another function computes the output of the artificial neuron. ANNs combine artificial neurons in order to process information. Neural networks are characterized by their architecture, activation function and learning algorithms. Each type of neural networks has its own input-output characteristics; therefore it could be applied only on some specific processes. In this study three neural networks are employed for modeling the various responses in the EDM process. Three networks are discussed as follows.

Back-Propagation Neural Network

The back-propagation neural network (BPNN) architectural design consists of fully interconnected rows of processing units called nodes. In BPNN, nodes are organized into groups called layers. BPNN model contains an input layer, one or two hidden layers, and an output layer in a forward multi-layer neural network. Input layers receive input. Output layers produce outputs. Hidden layers provide the interconnections between input and output. A schematic diagram of a BPN with n inputs nodes, r outputs nodes and a single hidden layer of m nodes are shown in Figure 1. In the figure, the number of hidden layers is critical for the convergence rate during the training of parameters for a given number of nodes at inputs and outputs layers Pradhan et al. (2009). In addition, numerical experiments did not show any advantage of a double hidden layer over a single layer network Pradhan et al. (2009). All the connections have been multiplying weights associated with them. The input nodes have a transfer function of unity and the activation function of the hidden and output nodes are sigmoidal S (.) and linear, respectively.

$$y_j\left(x\right) = \sum_{i=1}^{n} W1_{ji} x_i + b1_j \tag{1}$$

where $W1ji$ is the weight between the ith input neuron and jth hidden neuron and $b1_j$ is the bias at jth hidden neuron.

The output of jth hidden neuron is described as

$$z_j = \frac{1}{1 + e^{-y_j(x)}} \tag{2}$$

The net output to kth output neuron is given by

$$o_k\left(x\right) = \sum_{j=1}^{m} w2_{kj} z_j + b2_k , \tag{3}$$

Figure 1. Schematic diagram of BPNN

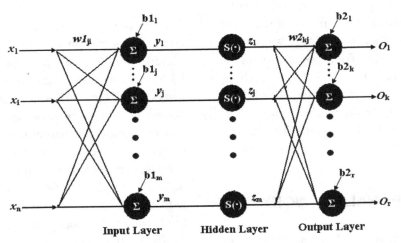

where $W2_{kj}$ is the weight between the jth hidden neuron and kth output neuron, and $b2_k$ is the bias at kth output neuron.

In the back propagation training, the weights are updated to reduce the output error. In the initial state, the network begins with a small random set of connection weights. In order for the network to learn, a set of inputs is presented to the system and a set of outputs is calculated. A difference between the actual outputs and desired outputs is calculated and the error is then back propagated through the network using the gradient descent rule to modify the weights and minimize the summed squared error. The weight changes are calculated to reduce the error for the case. The whole process is repeated for each of the example cases, then back to the first case again, and so on. The cycle is repeated until the overall error value drops below some predetermined threshold. At this point, we say that the network has learnt the problem.

Example

Design a back-propagation neural network with a single hidden layer for predicting Surface Rough-

ness in EDM machining using the experimental data as given in Table 3.

In this example, the process parameters Ip, Ton, τ and V are are taken as the inputs and surface roughness (Ra) is taken as the output. Thus, there are four input nodes and one output node. Initially, the number of neurons in each layer in the network is decided.

The size of the network becomes very large for a large number of training patterns. As such, the data for training are selected judiciously. Out of 30 experimental data, 18 training data sets are considered for both the networks to compare the performances. Besides, six validation sets outside the training data set are selected for validating the neural network and six testing sets outside the training data set are selected for testing the neural network. The ANNs was trained with the above data sets to reach the error goal (0.1). The performance of the neural network models is studied with the special attention to their generalization ability and the training time.

For the best performance of the BPN, the proper number of nodes in the hidden layer is selected through a trial and error method based on mean squared error (MSE) and mean percentile error (MPE) as shown in Figure 2 and Figure 3. It was

Figure 2. Mean square error surface roughness

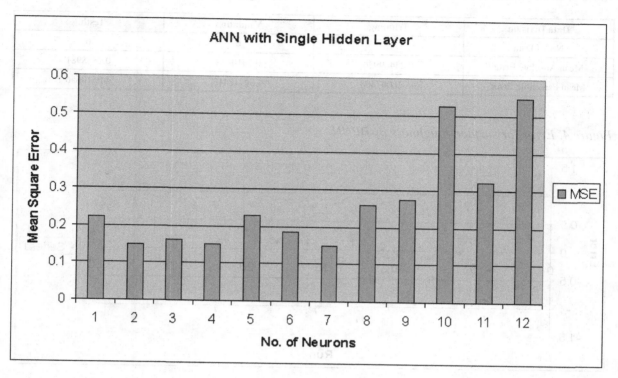

Figure 3. Mean percentile error surface roughness

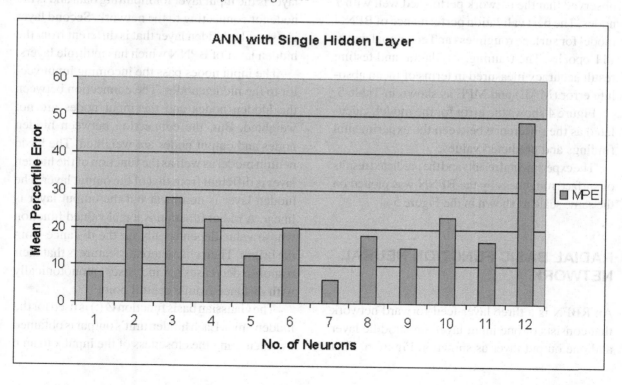

Table 5. Result accuracy in terms of mean absolute error and mean percentile error

Data Division	Training	Validation	Testing
No. of Data	18	6	6
Mean Absolute Error	0.23469936	0.3410133	0.2888981
Mean Percentile Error	4.026007408	4.60418415	4.0510656

Figure 4. Error for surface roughness by BPNN

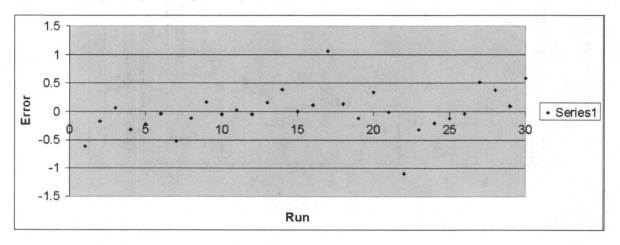

observed that the network performed well with 7 nodes. The best validation performance of BPNN model for surface roughness and error goal met at 111 epochs. The training, validation and testing result accuracy measured in terms of mean absolute error (MAE) and MPE as shown in Table 5.

Figure 4 shows the error for the model, calculated as the difference between the experimental findings and predicted values.

The experimental results and the predicted results of surface roughness by the BPNN was plotted on the same scale as shown in the Figure 5

RADIAL BASIC FUNCTION NEURAL NETWORK

An RBFN is a three layer feed-forward network that consists of one input layer, one middle layer and one output layer as shown in Figure 6. First layer is the input layer for inputting data and is the node for connecting to the network. Second layer is a singular hidden layer that is different from the hidden layer of BPNN which has multiple layers.

The input nodes pass the incoming input vector to the hidden nodes. The connection between the hidden nodes and the input nodes are not weighted. But, the connection between hidden nodes and output nodes are weighted. The basic neuron model as well as the function of the hidden layer is different from that of the output layer. The hidden layer is nonlinear but the output layer is linear. A radial function is a real valued function whose value depends only on the distance from the origin. Their characteristic feature is that their response decreases (or increases) monotonically with distance from a central point.

The Gaussian basis function Ø (.) is used for the hidden units. Each hidden unit's output is obtained by calculating the closeness of the input x to an n

Figure 5. Comparison between surface roughness experimental and surface roughness BPNN

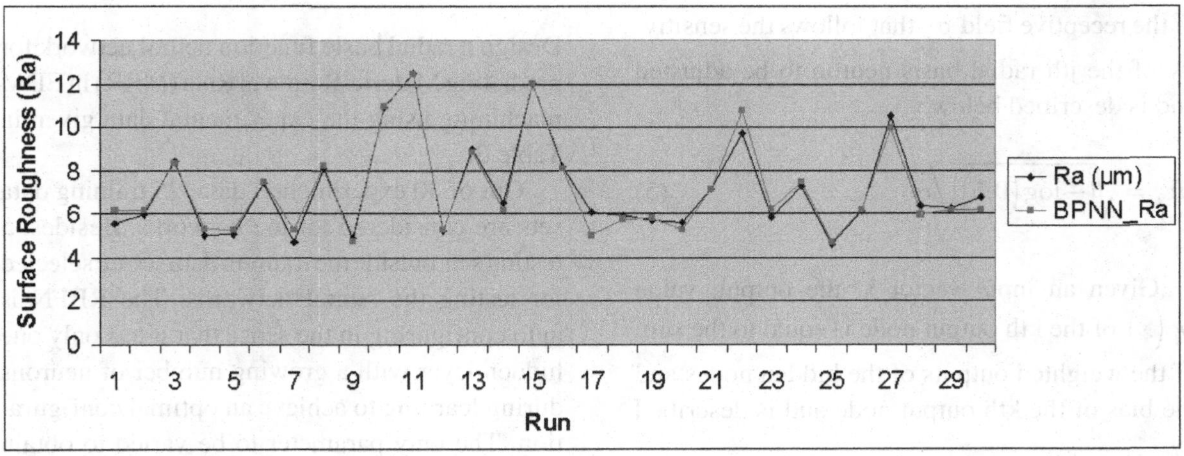

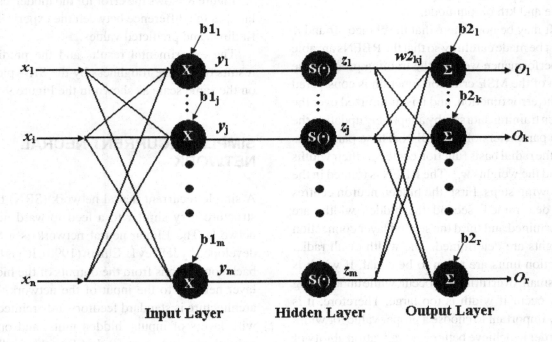

dimensional parameter vector μ_j associated with

Figure 6. Schematic Diagram of RBF

the jth hidden units.

Referring to Figure 6, the output of the jth radial basis neuron is described as:

$$z_j(x) = \exp\left(-\left(b1_j\left(\|x - \mu_j\|\right)\right)^2\right) \quad (4)$$

where the bias $b1_j$ is a fixed function of the width of the receptive field σ_j that follows the sensitivity of the jth radial basis neuron to be adjusted and is described below,

$$b1_j = \sqrt{\left(-\log\left(0.5\right)\right)}\Big/\sigma_j \tag{5}$$

Given an input vector x, the output, value $o_k\left(x\right)$ of the kth output node is equal to the sum of the weighted outputs of the hidden nodes and the bias of the kth output node and is described by.

$$o_k\left(x\right) = \sum_{j=1}^{m} w_{kj}z_j + b2_k \tag{6}$$

where w_{kj} is the weight between the jth hidden node and kth output node.

It may be noted here that the choice of σ and μ_j must be made carefully so that the RBFNs are able to performance well. In the training process, the sum of the MSE criterion function is considered as the error function, and it is minimized over the given training data sets by adaptively updating the free parameters of the RBFN. These parameters are the radial basis function centers μ_j, their widths σ and the weights w_{kj}. The RBFN is trained in the following steps. First, the hidden neuron centres are determined, second the hidden widths are determined and third the second layer connection weights are determined. The width of all radial function units are taken to be equal. If width is too small, overfitting can occur, while underfitting may occur if width is too large. Therefore, it is very important to choose a proper value for width in order to achieve better generalization ability of the RBFN. Finally, once the hidden units are synthesized, the second layer weights are computed by using the supervised least square rule.

Example

Design a radial basic function neural network for predicting Material Removal Rate (MRR) in EDM machining using the experimental data given in Table 3.

Out of 30 experimental data, 25 training data sets are considered for the networks. Besides, 5 testing sets outside the training data set are selected for testing the neural networks. The RBFN is auto configuring in the sense that it has only one hidden layer with a growing number of neurons during learning to achieve an optimal configuration. The only parameter to be varied to obtain the best generation ability is the spread factor. Computations are carried out for different values of the spread factor. It is observed that the best generalization ability of the network is achieved with a spread factor 0.9871 as shown in Figure 7.

Figure 8 shows the error for the model, calculated as the difference between the experimental findings and predicted values.

The experimental results and the predicted results of surface roughness by the SRN plotted on the same scale as shown in the Figure 9

SIMPLE RECURRENT NEURAL NETWORK

A simple recurrent neural network (SRN) has a structure very similar to a feed forward neural network. The Elman neural network is a SRN developed by Jeffrey L. Elman (1990). It has feedback connections from the outputs of the hidden layer neurons to the input of the network. This architecture is standard feedforward architecture with layers of inputs, hidden units, and output units shown in Figure 10. In SRN, the feedback connections send the output of the hidden nodes towards a set of additional nodes called "context units". The purpose of the context layer is to deal with input pattern dissonance. Pattern conflicts can possibly occur, resulting in multiple outputs

Figure 7. Spread for RBFN

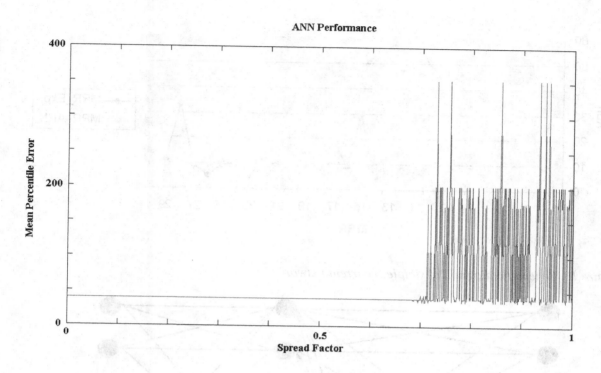

Figure 8. Error for MRR by RBFN

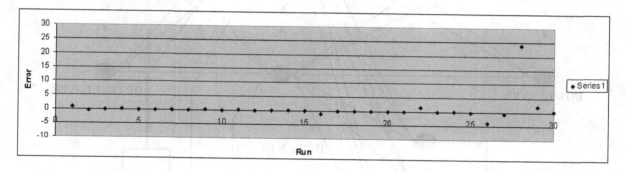

produced from a single input pattern. This could result in a perplexing situation for a standard backpropagation neural network. The SRN can be trained with gradient descent backpropagation methods, similar to regular feedforward neural networks. The SRN has a specific memory of one time lag. Therefore, when the input is fed to the network at time t, its output is computed also on the base of the hidden layer neuron activations at time t-1.

The structure of a SRN is exhibited in Figure 10. Here I, H, O and z^{-1} are input layer vector, hidden layer vector, context layer vector, output layer vector and unit delay element respectively. is the weight matrix between input layer and hidden layer, W2 is the weight matrix between context layer and hidden layer and W3 is the weight matrix between hidden layer and output layer. (see Figure 11)

At tth iteration,

Figure 9. Comparison between MRR Experimental and MRR (RBFN)

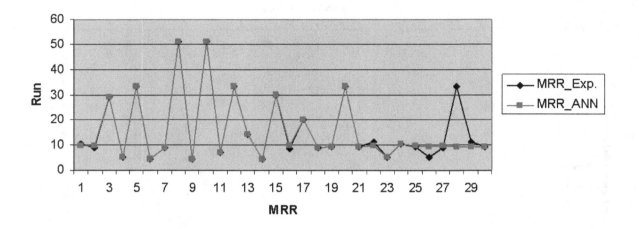

Figure 10. Schematic diagram of simple recurrent network

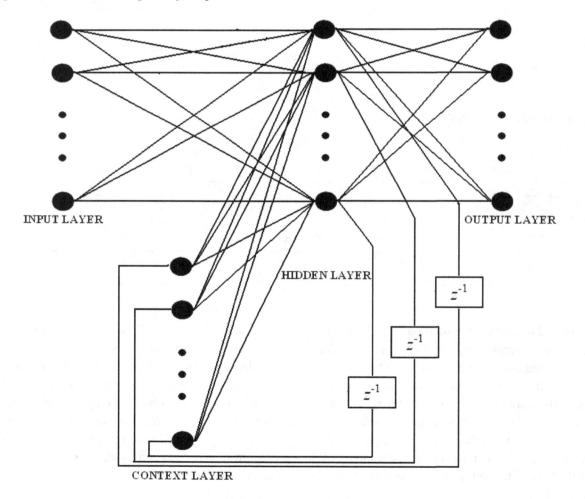

$$x_i(t) \in I, \quad i = 1, \cdots, n, \tag{7}$$

$$z_k(t) \in O, \quad k = 1, \cdots, l, \tag{8}$$

$$y_j(t) \in H, c_j(t) \in C, \quad j = 1, \cdots, m \tag{9}$$

where i and k are the number of nodes of input layer and output layer respectively and j is the number of nodes of hidden layer and context layer. Considering the activation function $f(.)$ for jth hidden node, the outputs of the neurons in the hidden layer and output layer for t th iteration are can be given by

$$y_j(t) = f\left(\sum_{i=1}^{n} w1_{ij} x_i(t) + \sum_{j=1}^{m} w2_{ij} y_j(t-1)\right), \tag{10}$$

$$c_j(t) = y_j(t-1) \text{ and } z_k(t) = f\left(\sum_{j=1}^{m} w3_{jk} y_j(t)\right) \tag{11}$$

where $w1_{ij} \in W1$, $w2_{ij} \in W2$ and $w3_{jk} \in W3$

For initial step, $y_j(0) = 0$. The context layer input at $t = 1$ leads to $c_i(1) = 0$.

The weights are updated to reduce the output error by back propagation training algorithm. In order for the network to learn, a set of inputs is presented to the system and a set of outputs is calculated. The error is then back propagated through the network using the gradient descent method to update the weights and optimize the summed squared error. The entire process is continued for each of the example cases, then back to the first case again, and so on. The cycle is repeated until the overall error value drops below some predetermined threshold. At this point, we say that the network has learnt the problem. (see Table 6)

However, finding the optimal configuration of SRN is a difficult task. There is no exact rule for how to find the number of neurons in the hidden layer to avoid overheating or underfitting and to make the learning phase convergent. For t he best performance of the SRN, the proper number of nodes in the hidden layer is selected through a trial and error method based on mean squared error (MSE) and mean percentile error (MPE) as shown in Figure 12 and Figure 13. It was observed that the network performed well with 6 nodes. The best validation performance of the SRN model for radial over cut met at 135 epochs as shown in the Figure 14. The training, validation and testing result accuracy measured in terms of mean absolute error (MAE) and MPE as shown in Table 7.

Figure 15 shows the error for the model, calculated as the difference between the experimental findings and predicted values.

The experimental results and the predicted results of surface roughness by the SRN plotted on the same scale as shown in the Figure 16

FUTURE RESEARCH DIRECTIONS

1. Construct BPNN and RBFNN to predict the surface roughness using the experimental data given in Table 3. Compare between their performances in the network.
2. Construct BPNN with two hidden layers to predict the MRR from the experimental data (Table 3).
3. Construct BPNN with a single hidden layer for predicting Surface Roughness and Material Removal Rate simultaneously.
4. Design a back-propagation neural network for predicting Material Removal Rate, Tool Wear Rate and Radial Overcut in EDM machining using the experimental Data.

Table 6. Result accuracy in terms of mean absolute error and mean percentile error

Data Division	Training	Testing
No. of Data	25	5
Mean Absolute Error	0.167296	6.101479998
Mean Percentile Error	1.737032199	34.89786091

Figure 11. Training performance

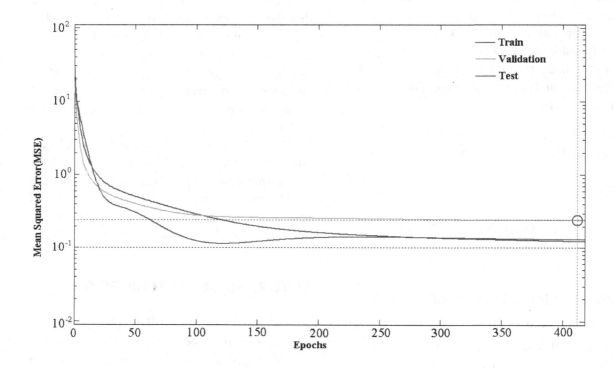

Figure 12. ANN single hidden layer

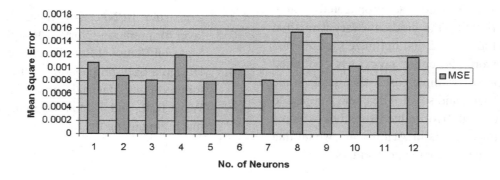

Figure 13. ANN with a single hidden layer

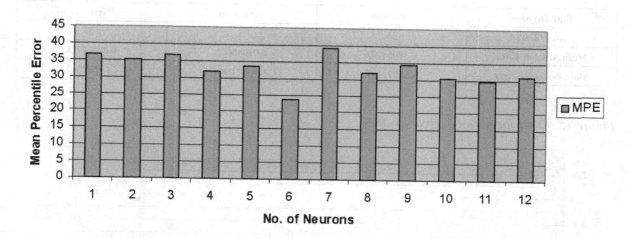

Figure 14. Training performance

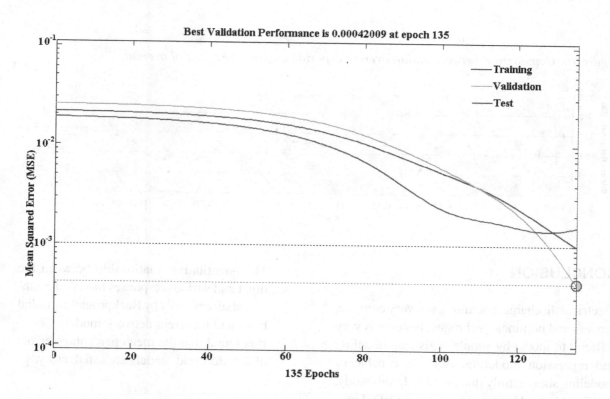

Table 7. Result accuracy in terms of mean absolute error and mean percentile error

Data Division	Training	Validation	Testing
No. of Data	18	6	6
Mean Absolute Error	0.38053905	0.01680672	0.02728728
Mean Percentile Error	23.3693347	4.98624385	28.3682062

Figure 15. Error for radial overcut by SRN

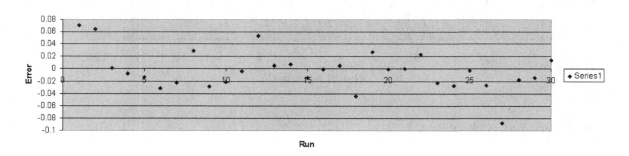

Figure 16. Comparison between radial overcut experimental and SRN radial overcut

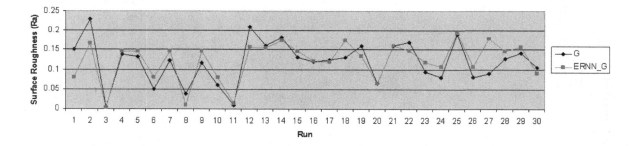

CONCLUSION

Electrical discharge machining is a very complex process and nonlinear technique, hence it is very difficult to model by simple statistical modeling and regression modeling. ANN is capable of modeling succcesfully this process. In this study, Artificial Neural Network modeling of EDM process was established for the best ANN model by comparing the prediction from different models under the effect of process parameters. The network was developed for the following conclusion can be drawn from this study:

1. The quantitative relationship between the input and various responses has been established successfully by Backprogation, radial basis and recurrent network models.

2. It is found that the mean percentage errors of the aforesaid models are satisfactory.

REFERENCES

Caydas, U., & Hascalik, A. (2008). Modeling and analysis of electrode wear and white layer thickness in die-sinking EDM process through response surface methodology. *International Journal of Advanced Manufacturing Technology*, *38*(11-12), 1148–1156. doi:10.1007/s00170-007-1162-1

Dhar, S., Purohit, R., Saini, N., Sharma, A., & Kumar, G. H. (2007). Mathematical modeling of electric - Discharge machining of cast Al-4Cu-6Si alloy-10 wt.% SiCP composites. *Journal of Materials Processing Technology*, *194*, 24–29. doi:10.1016/j.jmatprotec.2007.03.121

Dibitono, D. D., Eubank, P. T., Patel, M. R., & Barrufet, M. A. (1989). Theoretical model of the electrical discharge machining processes I: A simple cathode erosion model. *Journal of Applied Physics*, *66*, 4095–4103. doi:10.1063/1.343994

Doniavi, A., Eskandarzade, M., Abdi, A., & Totonchi, A. (2008). Empirical modeling of EDM parameters using grey relational analysis. *Asian Journal of Scietific Research*, *1*(5), 502–509. doi:10.3923/ajsr.2008.502.509

Dvivedi, A., Kumar, P., & Singh, I. (2008). Experimental investigation and optimisation in EDM of al 6063 SiCp metal matrix composite. *International Journal of Machining and Machinability of Materials*, *3*(3-4), 293–308. doi:10.1504/IJMMM.2008.020965

Elman, J. (1990). Finding structure in time. *Cognitive Science*, *14*, 179–211. doi:10.1207/s15516709cog1402_1

Eubank, P. T., Patel, M. R., Barrufet, M. A., & Bozkurt, B. (1989). Theoretical model of the electrical discharge machinings process I: A simple cathode erosion model. *Journal of Applied Physics*, *66*, 4095–4103. doi:10.1063/1.343994

Gao, Q., Zhang, Q., Su, S., Zhang, J., & Ge, R. (2008). Predictive models and generalization performance study in electrical discharge machining. *Applied Mechanics and Materials*, (10-12), 677–681.

Jaharah, A. G., Liang, Wahid, S. Z., Rahman, M. N. A., & Hassan, C. H. C. (2008). Performance of copper electrode in electrical discharge machining (EDM) of AISI H13 harden steel. *International Journal of Mechanical and Materials Engineering*, *3*(1), 25–29.

Kanagarajan, D., Karthikeyan, R., Palanikumar, K., & Sivaraj, P. (2008). Influence of process parameters on electric - Discharge machining of WC/30%Co composites. *Proceedings of the Institution of Mechanical Engineers. Part B, Journal of Engineering Manufacture*, *222*(7), 807–815. doi:10.1243/09544054JEM925

Karthikeyan, R., Lakshmi Narayanan, P. R., & Naagarazan, R. S. (1999). Mathematical modelling for electric - Discharge machining of aluminium-silicon carbide particulate composites. *Journal of Materials Processing Technology*, *87*, 59–63. doi:10.1016/S0924-0136(98)00332-X

Keskin, Y., Halkaci, H., & Kizil, M. (2006). An experimental study for determination of the effects of machining parameters on surface roughness in electrical discharge machinings (EDM). *International Journal of Advanced Manufacturing Technology*, *28*(11-12), 1118–1121. doi:10.1007/s00170-004-2478-8

Khan, A. (2008). Electrode wear and material removal rate during EDM of aluminum and mild steel using copper and brass electrodes. *International Journal of Advanced Manufacturing Technology*, *39*(5-6), 482–487. doi:10.1007/s00170-007-1241-3

Khan, A., Ali, M., & Haque, M. (2009). A study of electrode shape configuration on the performance of die sinking EDM. *International Journal of Mechanical and Materials Engineering*, *4*(1), 19–23.

Kiyak, M., & Cakir, O. (2007). Examination of machining parameters on surface roughness in EDM of tool steel. *Journal of Materials Processing Technology*, *191*, 141–144. doi:10.1016/j. jmatprotec.2007.03.008

Kung, K. Y., Horng, J. T., & Chiang, K. T. (2009). Material removal rate and electrode wear ratio study on the powder mixed electrical discharge machinings of cobalt-bonded tungsten carbide. *International Journal of Advanced Manufacturing Technology*, *40*(1-2), 95–104. doi:10.1007/ s00170-007-1307-2

Kuppan, P., Rajadurai, A., & Narayanan, S. (2007). Influence of EDM process parameters in deep hole drilling of inconel 718. *International Journal of Advanced Manufacturing Technology*, *38*, 74–84. doi:10.1007/s00170-007-1084-y

Mandal, D., Pal, S. K., & Saha, P. (2007). Modeling of electrical discharge machinings process using back propagation neural network and multi-objective optimization using non-dominating sorting genetic algorithm-II. *Journal of Materials Processing Technology*, *186*, 154–162. doi:10.1016/j. jmatprotec.2006.12.030

Panda, D. K., & Bhoi, R. K. (2005). Artificial neural network prediction of material removal rate in electro - discharge machining. *Materials and Manufacturing Processes*, *20*, 645–672. doi:10.1081/AMP-200055033

Patel, M. R., Maria, B. A., Eubank, P. T., & DiBitonto, D. (1989). Theoretical models of the electrical discharge machining process II - The anode erosion model. *Journal of Applied Physics*, *66*(9), 4104. doi:10.1063/1.343995

Pradhan, B. B., & Bhattacharyya, B. (2009). Modelling of micro-electrodischarge machining during machining of titanium alloy Ti-6Al-4V using response surface methodology and artificial neural network algorithm. *Proceedings of the Institution of Mechanical Engineers. Part B, Journal of Engineering Manufacture*, *223*(6), 683–693. doi:10.1243/09544054JEM1343

Pradhan, M., & Biswas, C. (2010). Neuro-fuzzy and neural network-based prediction of various responses in electrical discharge machining of AISI D2 steel - NF and NN based prediction of responses in EDM of D2 steel. *International Journal of Advanced Manufacturing Technology*, *50*, 591–610. doi:10.1007/s00170-010-2531-8

Pradhan, M. K., & Biswas, C. K. (2008a). Modeling of machining parameters for MRR in EDM using response surface methodology. In *Proceedings of the National Conference on Mechanism Science and Technology: From Theory to Application*, (vol. 1, pp. 535–542). Hamirpur, India: NIT.

Pradhan, M. K., & Biswas, C. K. (2008b). Neuro-fuzzy model on material removal rate in electrical discharge machining in AISI D2 steel. In *Proceedings of the 2nd International & 23rd All India Manufacturing Technology, Design and Research Conference (AIMTDR) Conference*, (vol. 1, pp. 469–474). Chennai, India: IIT Madras.

Pradhan, M. K., & Biswas, C. K. (2009). Neuro-fuzzy model and regression model a comparison study of MRR in electrical discharge machining of D2 tool steel. *International Journal of Mathematical. Physical and Engineering Sciences*, *3*, 48–53.

Pradhan, M. K., & Biswas, C. K. (2011a). Investigation into the effect of process parameters on surface roughness in EDM of AISID2 steel by response surface methodology. *International Journal of Precision Technology*, *2*(1), 64–80. doi:10.1504/IJPTECH.2011.038110

Pradhan, M. K., & Biswas, C. K. (2011b). Multi-response optimisation of EDM AISID2 tool steel using response surface methodology. *International Journal of Machining and Machinability of Materials, 9*, 66–85. doi:10.1504/IJMMM.2011.038161

Pradhan, M. K., Das, R., & Biswas, C. K. (2009). Comparisons of neural network models on surface roughness in electrical discharge machining. *Proceedings of the Institution of Mechanical Engineers. Part B, Journal of Engineering Manufacture, 223*(7), 801–808. doi:10.1243/09544054JEM1367

Pradhan, M. K., Das, R., & Biswas, C. K. (2010). Prediction of material removal rate using recurrent Elman networks in electrical discharge machining of AISI D2 tool steel. *International Journal of Manufacturing Technology And Industrial Engineering, 1*, 29–37.

Puertas, I., Luis, C. J., & Alvarez, L. (2004). Analysis of the influence of EDM parameters of surface quality, MRR and awe of WC-Co. *Journal of Materials Processing Technology, 153-154*(1-3), 1026–1032. doi:10.1016/j.jmatprotec.2004.04.346

Salonitis, K., Stournaras, A., Stavropoulos, P., & Chryssolouris, G. (2009). Thermal modeling of the material removal rate and surface roughness for die-sinking EDM. *International Journal of Advanced Manufacturing Technology, 40*(3-4), 316–323. doi:10.1007/s00170-007-1327-y

Sohani, M., Gaitonde, V., Siddeswarappa, B., & Deshpande, A. (2009). Investigations into the effect of tool shapes with size factor consideration in sink electrical discharge machining (EDM) process. *International Journal of Advanced Manufacturing Technology*, 1–15.

Tsai, K.-M., & Wang, P.-J. (2001a). Comparisons of neural network models on material removal rate in electrical discharge machinings. *Journal of Materials Processing Technology, 117*, 111–124. doi:10.1016/S0924-0136(01)01146-3

Tsai, K.-M., & Wang, P.-J. (2001b). Predictions on surface finish in electrical discharge machinings based upon neural network models. *International Journal of Machine Tools & Manufacture, 41*, 1385–1403. doi:10.1016/S0890-6955(01)00028-1

Tsai, K.-M., & Wang, P.-J. (2001c). Semi-empirical model of surface finish on electrical discharge machining. *International Journal of Machine Tools & Manufacture, 41*, 1455–1477. doi:10.1016/S0890-6955(01)00015-3

Valentincic, J., & Junkar, M. (2004). A model for detection of the eroding surface based on discharge parameters. *International Journal of Machine Tools & Manufacture, 44*, 175–181. doi:10.1016/j.ijmachtools.2003.10.013

Wang, C. C., & Lin, Y. (2009). Feasibility study of electrical discharge machining for W/Cu composite. *International Journal of Refractory Metals and Hard Materials, 27*(5), 872–882. doi:10.1016/j.ijrmhm.2009.04.005

Wang, K., Gelgele, H. L., Wang, Y., Yuan, Q., & Fang, M. (2003). A hybrid intelligent method for modelling the EDM process. *International Journal of Machine Tools & Manufacture, 43*, 995–999. doi:10.1016/S0890-6955(03)00102-0

Wang, P.-J., & Tsai, K.-M. (2001). Semi-empirical model on work removal and tool wear in electrical discharge machining. *Journal of Materials Processing Technology, 114*(1), 1–17. doi:10.1016/S0924-0136(01)00733-6

Yeo, S. H., Kurnia, W., & Tan, P. C. (2008). Critical assessment and numerical comparison of electro-thermal models in EDM. *Journal of Materials Processing Technology, 203*(1-3), 491. doi:10.1016/j.jmatprotec.2007.10.026

KEY TERMS AND DEFINITIONS

Artificial Neural Network: It is an extremely simplified model of the brain and essentially a function approximator which transforms input into output to the best of its ability

Back-propagation Algorithm: Backpropagation (generalized gradient descent) is a generalization of the LMS algorithm

Electrical Discharge Machining: Electrical Discharge Machining (commonly known as "EDM Machining") makes it possible to work with difficult to machine materials for which traditional machining techniques. The key point to remember with EDM Machining is that it will only with electrically conductive materials.

Material Removal Rate: Material Removal Rate is calculated by using the volume loss from the workpiece divided by the time of machining. The calculated weight loss is converted to volumatric loss in mm^3/min.

Radial Basis Function Network: It is a feed-forward neural network that computes their output as weighted linear superpositions of Gaussian functions.

Radial Overcut: Radial Overcut is expressed as half the difference of the diameter of the hole produced to the tool diameter, that is *radial overcut* $= di - dt/2$, where *dt* is the diameter of the tool and *di* is the diameter of the impression or cavity produce by the tool on the workpiece.

Simple Recurrent Network: It is a single hidden-layer feedforward neural network. It has feedback connections from the outputs of the hidden-layer neurons to the input of the network.

Chapter 15
Neural Network Model to Estimate and Predict Cell Mass Concentration in Lipase Fermentation

David K. Daniel
VIT University, India

Vikramaditya Bhandari
Shasun Pharma Solutions Limited, UK

ABSTRACT

Lipase is an industrially important enzyme with major use in food industries. The demand of lipase is increasing every year. An online prediction of cell mass concentration is of great value in real time process involving the production of lipase. In the current work, the use of a back-propagation multilayer neural network to predict cell mass during lipase production by Rhizopus delemar NRRL 1472 is targeted. Network training data with respect to time is generated by carrying out experiments in laboratory. The fungus is grown in erlenmeyer flasks at initial pH of 5.6, temperature of 30°C, and at 150 rpm. During the experiments, readings for cell mass growth are collected in specific period of time. By the training data, an artificial neural network model programmed in MATLAB for Windows is trained and used for prediction of cell mass. The Levenberg-Marquardt algorithm with back-propagation is used in the network to get the optimized weights. The optimum network configuration with different activation function and the number of nodes in the hidden layer are identified by trial and error method. Sigmoid unipolar activation function is 2-5-1, whereas logarithmoid and sigmoid bipolar is 2-3-1. These are chosen according to the values of Sum of Square of Errors (SSE), Root Mean Square (RMS) training and testing. The sigmoid unipolar activation function gives a good fit for estimated value with network configuration 2-5-1, which could be used for generalization.

DOI: 10.4018/978-1-4666-4940-8.ch015

INTRODUCTION

Biological process are both time variant and non-linear in nature. The non-linearity of these processes may be due to a variety of factors including kinetics of cellular growth and product formation, thermodynamic limitations of the processes, mass transfer and heat transfer affects and the fluid mechanics inside the cultivation vessel. Within the area of processes engineering, process design and simulation, process supervision, control, estimation, process fault detection and diagnosis rely on the effective processing of unpredictable and imprecise information. Such tasks are currently tackled by approaches based on some model of the process in question. The fundamental behavior of these processes can be understood by modeling which prove useful for on-line process control and optimization and are a prerequisite for scale up of bioprocess.

LITERATURE SURVEY

The idea of using artificial neural network as a potential solution strategy for problems, which required complex data analysis, is not new. In the early 1940's scientists came up with the hypothesis that neurons, fundamental, active cells is all animal nervous systems might be regarded as devices for manipulating binary numbers. With the advent of modern electronics, it was only natural to try to harness this thinking process. The first step toward artificial neural networks came in 1943 when Warren McCulloch, a neurophysiologist, and a young mathematician, Walter Pitts, wrote a paper on how a neuron might work. They modeled a simple neural network with electrical circuits. Frank Rosenblatt invented the artificial neural network in 1958 called perceptron and demonstrated how the human brain processed visual data and learned to recognize objects. In 1958, Bernard Widrow and Marcian Hoff developed models, which they called ADALINE and MADALINE. These models

were named for their use of Multiple Adaptive Linear Elements. MADALINE was first the neuron network to be applied to a real world problem. It was an adaptive filter, which eliminated echoes on phone lines. From then on, many researchers from diverse disciplines had concentrated in the field of ANN, including modeling, system identification and control. Bhat and McAvoy (1990) applied a back-propagation neural network to model the dynamic response of pH in a continuous stirred tank reactor. They proved that back- propagation neural network was able to model the non-linear characteristics of the continuous stirred tank reactor better than an auto regressive moving average model. Bhat *et al.,* (1990) applied neural nets for modeling non-linear chemical systems. A back-propagation net was used successfully to model a steady-state reactor, a dynamic pH stirred tank system, and interpretation of biosensor data. They proved that back-propagation neural network was able to model the non-linear characteristics of the continuous stirred tank reactor better than auto regressive moving average model. Linko & Zhu (1992) applied both in real-time estimation and multi-step ahead prediction of enzyme activity and biomass dry matter in fungal *Aspergillus niger* fermentation. Back-propagation algorithm with a momentum term was used in the training of the neural network on the basis of varying input/output pair data sets. Freeman and Skapura (1992) discussed the different algorithms, applications and programming techniques associated with artificial neural networks, particularly the Levenberg- Marquardt optimization algorithm. Horiuchi *et al.,* (2001) proposed a simple modeling method for microbial dynamic behavior in a chemostat using a neural network. They proposed and applied the same to the pH response in continuous anaerobic acidogenesis. A three-layered neural network with a back-propagation algorithm was used to model the pH step response of the acid reactor. The simulation results revealed that the ANN system could successfully model the transient behavior in response to pH change in the acid reactor under various retention times. To simulate the entire range of pH response, only the experimental data during the steady-state and the pH shift were required. Pramanik (2004) discussed the production of ethanol from the grape waste using the using *Saccharomyces cerevisiae* yeast based on based on feed forward architecture and back propagation as training algorithm. The Levenberg- Marquardt optimization algorithm was used to upgrade the network by minimizing the sum square error (SSE).

From literature it was evident that neural networks were successfully used for non- linear biological process modeling. The prediction capability of neural networks can be utilized as a promising technique for modeling, estimating and predicting bio-processes which are non-linear in nature and whose dynamics are poorly known. Efficient online estimation and prediction of enzyme activity and biomass concentration have been of great value in the control of the extra cellular fermentation process by fungi (Linko & Zhu, 1992). In biotechnology, however the measurements of essential state variables such as substrate, product and biomass concentration are tedious online in real time. Further the optimization and modeling of bioprocess for control purposes is often difficult owing to uncertainties, non- linearities, complex mechanisms of the biochemical reactions involved, and noisy or unavailable data (Linko & Zhu, 1992). Processes based on microbial growth are difficult to model as they are subject to influence of many, very often unforeseen factors, and microorganisms internal control systems are only partially introduced. Modeling on a physical bioreactor level is also complicated owing to intricate mass transfer in stirred vessel with variable rheology of biomass suspensions. In industrial practice, biomass and substrate concentration and enzyme activity are conventionally monitored off-line. The direct information of the state variables in an enzyme production process may be obtained by measuring quantity related to the activity of

the enzyme. Information on application of neural networks in bioprocess systems for predicting and estimating cell mass production using *Rhizopus delemar* fermentation is scarce. The present investigation was carried out to predict cell mass during batch *Rhizopus delemar* fermentation for batch production of lipase. In the present work the main objective was to model the cell mass formation during the production of lipase which is a commercial enzyme having a wide variety of applications. Literature on cell mass formation, mathematical model available and mass transfer limitations due to cell mass was reviewed and a series of experiments involving lipase production at the laboratory scale were performed. Based on the inputs and outputs a multi-layered feed-forward neural network model was developed. This was followed by the coding for the neural network program and generation of a user friendly interface for the estimation and prediction of cell mass in fermentation.

MICROORGANISM AND INOCULUM DEVELOPMENT

Rhizopus delemar NRRL 1472 a strain that produced lipase was used throughout this study. The microorganism provided by the U.S. Department of Agriculture, Illinois, U.S.A. the organism was maintained on potato dextrose agar slants at 4°C and sub- cultured regularly every 15 days. The basal medium contained 1 l of distilled water: poly-peptone 70.0 gm; $NaNO_3$ 1.0 gm; KH_2PO_4 1.0 gm; $MgSO_4.7H_2O$ 0.5 gm; olive oil 30 gm. The initial pH was maintained at 5.6. Seed cells from the erlenmeyer flask were inoculated into another flask containing 100ml of basal medium. It was kept in a temperature controlled shaker which was maintained at 30°C and at 150 rpm. Sampling was done at regular intervals followed by filtration to separate the cell mass.

BIOMASS ESTIMATION

The cell mass was determined using filtration method. Seed cells were inoculated in the Erlenmeyer flask containing 100ml of the growth medium. The flasks were kept on rotary shaker for 72 hours. The samples were taken at regular interval of 6 hours. The samples were filtered through the filter paper and kept in an oven at 60°C for 20hours. The dry cell mass was determined from the difference in weights before and after drying.

NEURAL NETWORK GUI AND LANGUAGE

Language selection is one of the most important parts for development of a GUI. The selection of language is done on the basis of coder's compatibility with the language and user's comfort to use it. It also depends on the advantages, disadvantages and tools available in the particular coding language with respect to other languages. For the Neural network GUI, MATLAB was used as the coding language since it is widely used by the scientific and research community. It has built in functions which are available to make coding easy for the developer, functions like transpose of a matrix, random numbers and determinants along with an excellent feature for plotting graphs. Moreover, easy drag and drop feature rendered the development of GUI very easy.

WEIGHTING FACTORS

A neuron usually receives many simultaneous inputs. Each input has its own relative weight, which gives the input the impact that it needs on the processing element's summation function. These weights perform the same type of function, as do the varying synaptic strengths of biological neurons. In both cases, some inputs are made more important than others so that they have a greater effect on the processing element as they combine to produce a neural response. They are a measure of an input's connection strength. This strength can be modified in response to various training sets and according to a network's specific topology or through its learning rules.

SUMMATION FUNCTION

The first step in a processing element's operation is to compute the weighted sum of all of the inputs. Mathematically, the inputs and the corresponding weights are vectors which can be represented as $(i1, i2... in)$ and $(w1, w2... wn)$. The total input signal is a dot, or inner, product of these two vectors. This simple summation function is found by multiplying each component of the input vector by the corresponding component of weight vector and adding up all the products. The result is a single number, not a multi-element vector.

ERROR FUNCTION AND BACK-PROPAGATED VALUE

In most learning networks the difference between the current output and the desired output is calculated. This raw error is then transformed by the error function to match particular network architecture. The most basic architectures use this error directly. The artificial neuron's error is then typically propagated into the learning function of another processing element. This error term is sometimes called the current error. The current error is typically propagated backward to a previous layer. Normally, this back-propagated value, after being scaled by the learning function, is multiplied against each of the incoming connection weights to modify the before the next learning cycle.

LEARNING FUNCTION

The purpose of the learning function is modifying the variable connection weights on the inputs of each processing element according to some neural based algorithm. This process of changing the weights of the input connection to achieve some desired result could also be called the adaptation function, as well as the learning mode. There are two types of learning-supervised and unsupervised. Supervised learning requires a teacher. The teacher may be training set of data or an observer who grades the performance of a network results. Either way, having a teacher is learning by reinforcement. When there is no external teacher, the system must organize itself by some internal criteria designed into the network.

A developer must go through a period of trial and error in the design decisions before coming up with satisfactory design. Designing a neural network consists of: arranging neurons in various layers, deciding the type of connection among neurons for different layers as well as among neurons within a layer, deciding the way a neuron receives input and produces output and determining the strength of connection within the network by allowing the network learn the appropriate values of connection weights by using a training data set. Once a network has been structured for a particular application, the network has to be trained. To start this process the initial weights are chosen randomly. The aim of training is to generate a network that is good at classifying patterns similar to, but not identical to, patterns in the training set i.e. a network that has the ability to generalize. There are two approaches to training – supervised and unsupervised. Supervised training involves a mechanism of providing the network with desired output either by manually "grading" the network's performance or by providing the desired outputs with the inputs. Supervised learning or associative learning in which the network is trained by providing it with input and matching output patterns. Error calculated by comparing the resulting output and desired output are propagated back through the systems, causing the system to adjust the weights, which control the network. The set of data that enables the training is called the "training set". During the training of a network the same set of data is processed many times as the connection weights are ever refined.

Unsupervised training is where the network has to make sense of the inputs without outside help. Unsupervised learning or self-organisation in which an (output) unit is trained to respond to clusters of pattern within the input. The system itself must then decide what features it will use to group the input data. Currently, unsupervised learning is not well understood. The memorization of patterns and the subsequent response of the network can be categorized into associative mapping and regulatory detection. In associative mapping the network learns to produce a particular pattern on the set of input units whenever another particular pattern is applied on the set of input units. The associative mapping can generally be broken down into auto-association and hetro-association mechanisms. In auto-association input pattern is associated both itself and the states of input and output units coincide. This is used to provide pattern completion, i.e. to produce a pattern whenever a portion of it or a distorted pattern is presented. In the second case, the network actually stores pairs of patterns building an association between two sets of patterns. Hetro-association is related to two recall mechanism. The first one is the nearest-neighbour recall, where the output pattern produced corresponds to the input pattern stored, which is closest to the pattern presented. The second one is the interpolative recall, where the output pattern is a similarity dependent interpolation of the patterns stored corresponding to the pattern presented. In regulatory detection the units learn to respond to particular properties of the input pattern, whereas in associative mapping the network stores the relationships among patterns, in regularity detection the response of each unit has a particular 'meaning'.

NEURAL NETWORK MODEL

Many types of alternative neural network are available for solving various types of problems which can be selected based on the characteristic and complexity of the problem (Linko and Zhu, 1992). For modeling of the non-linear complex system in chemical engineering applications, the most suitable type is feed forward network with back-propagation algorithm due to its simplicity and faster convergence (Bhat and McAvoy, 1990). In the present work, a three layered FFNN with only one hidden layer and with Levenberg-Marquardt learning technique was used, and further increasing the hidden layer did not give better results for this particular system as well as it was increasing the complexity of the network which was taking more time and iterations for learning. Each connection between two neurons in adjacent layers had a weight associated with it, and the information was stored in terms of weights between neurons. The data was collected at regular intervals. Prediction of cell mass was done by training the network by set of experimental data. For the batch fermentation studies, cell mass at time (t) and time were used as the input vector and the final cell mass at time (t) was used as the output vector. All the data collected were normalized between [0, 1]. The data were divided into two major groups for batch fermentation, i.e. training data set and test data set. The activation functions used for hidden layer in FFNN architecture are shown in table. Optimum configuration of the network was found by trial and error. The number of nodes in the hidden layer was increased stepwise for all activation function and the training and test results compared for optimum configuration for each activation function. The trained network configuration for each activation functions was compared to find out the optimum activation function. The optimum network determined was used to predict the output for test data

PROGRAMMING ENVIRONMENT AND TRAINING ALGORITHM

The neural network program was written in MATLAB for Windows to incorporate the algorithm. For faster convergence of the weight to the closest local minimum and good result for the generalization a hybrid learning algorithm, which comprised of incremental back-propagation and conjugate gradient-based back-propagation and used. This hybrid algorithm was based on Levenberg-Marquardt optimization.

BATCH EXPERIMENTATION

Experiments were carried out with varying inoculum sizes for generating data to train and test the neural network. The inoculum sizes used were 1, 3, 4, 5, 7 and 10 ml. The growth medium was inoculated with the different inoculum sizes followed by which regular sampling at 6 hours was done to generate the cell mass data. Filtration was carried out and the filter cake (wet cell mass) was kept for drying for 20 hours. After 20 hours the dry weight was measured and the actual cell mass was obtained.

MODELING OF BATCH CULTURE

In the present work, during batch mode of operation, the effect of initial mass concentration on final cell mass was determined. A total of six experiments were conducted of which one third of the sets were used for training and remaining for testing and generalization of network. The data was normalized between [0, 1]. The input and output vectors are described earlier. A three layered feed- forward neural network with one hidden layer was found to yield satisfactory results during testing. Increasing the number of hidden layer beyond one made the model complex with increased learning time. The activation functions

Table 1. Different activation functions

Serial No.	Activation Function	Equation
1.	Sigmoid Unipolar	$\nu = \dfrac{1}{(1 + e^{-x})}$
2.	Logarithmoid	$\nu = \dfrac{(x * \ln(1 + |x|))}{|\nu|}$
3.	Linear	$y = x$
4.	Sigmoid Bipolar	$\nu = (-1 + \dfrac{2}{1 + e^{-x}}) = \tanh(\dfrac{x}{2})$

used were as described in Table 1. The network configuration corresponding to each activation function was found by trial and error. The sum of squares of the error for the training as well as testing were determined compared. Each optimum configuration after comparison was used to select the best activation function. After training and testing the network with this activation functions, the network was used for generalization with test data.

Figure 1 depicts the optimum network configuration based on the SSE. Here for sigmoid unipolar, SSE was decreasing steadily upto hidden neurons five. Further increase of neurons did not give significant change in the error.

Figure 2 shows the optimum number of nodes for logarithmoid activation function with respect to SSE.

From Figure 2, which depicts logarithmoid behavior, the values were found to be increasing and decreasing and a steady value was not achieved.

Similarly in Figure 3, which shows sigmoid bipolar behavior, the values were increasing and decreasing. Steady values were not achieved. The linear activation function could not give satisfactory fit of estimated values as the present system was non- linear in nature (Kurtanjek, 1994).

Figure 4 depicts the optimum network configuration based on RMS training. For sigmoid unipolar, RMS for training was decreasing steadily upto hidden neurons five. Further increase of neurons did not give significant change in the error. RMS for testing was increasing initially but showed a dip at node five. For logarithmoid and sigmoid bipolar RMS values for both training and testing were going to imaginary.

Figure 5 depicts the optimum network configuration based on RMS testing. RMS for testing using sigmoid unipolar as activation function was increasing initially but showed a dip at node five. For logarithmoid and sigmoid bipolar RMS values for both training and testing were going to imaginary. The optimum network configuration for sigmoid unipolar activation function was 2-5-1. For logarithmoid and sigmoid bipolar it was 2-3-1. These were chosen according to the values of SSE, RMS training and testing.

Figure 6 shows the comparison of different activation functions with the SSE, which indicates that sigmoid unipolar is the optimum activation function. The sigmoid unipolar activation function gave a good fit for estimated value with network configuration 2-5-1, which could be used for generalization.

Figure 1. Optimum number of nodes in hidden layer for activation function-I (Sigmoid unipolar) from SSE for FFNN

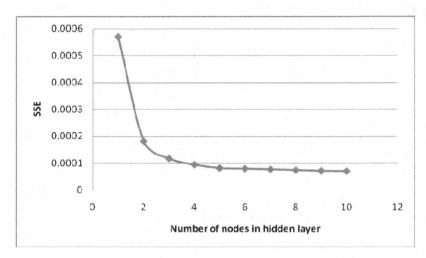

Figure 2. Optimum number of nodes in hidden layer for activation function-II (Logarithmoid) from SSE for FFNN

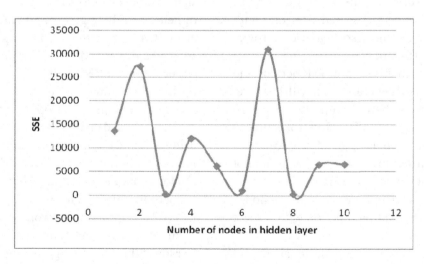

Data for inoculum size of 5ml was used for training the network and data for inoculum size of 3ml was used for testing the network. The remaining data with varying inoculum sizes were used for validation of the network. The experimental and the predicted data were compared, as shown in Figures 7, 8, 9, 10, and 11.

CONCLUSION

Prediction of cell mass during lipase production by *Rhizopus delemar* NRRL 1472 was done using neural network modeling. The artificial neural network models provided an ideal means of modeling the system considered. Data were generated by carrying out batch experiments for

Figure 3. Optimum number of nodes in hidden layer for activation function-IV (Sigmoid bipolar) from SSE for FFNN

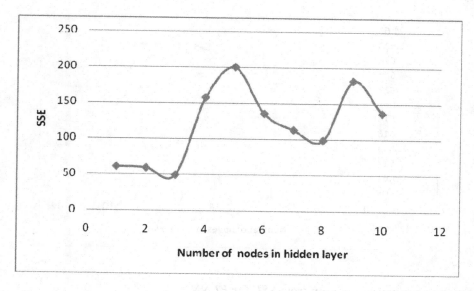

Figure 4. Optimum number of nodes in hidden layer for activation function-I (Sigmoid unipolar) from RMS training for FFNN

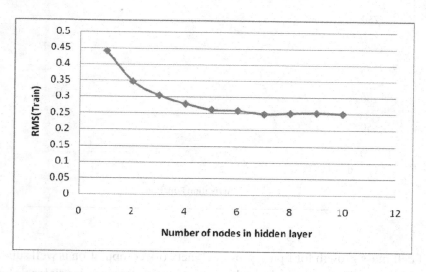

various initial concentrations in shake flasks. These data were used to construct an optimum neural network model as well as to train and test the network. Feed-forward neural network with three layers were used. Four activation functions were used to select best suitable activation function. The prediction of the neural network was compared by changing the hidden nodes for different activation functions. By trial and error method the optimized network with optimize nodes and activation function was identified. The optimized network for feed-forward neural network is 2-5-1 with sigmoid unipolar as activation function. The results obtained on application of neural network

Figure 5. Optimum number of nodes in hidden layer for activation function-I (Sigmoid unipolar) from RMS testing for FFNN

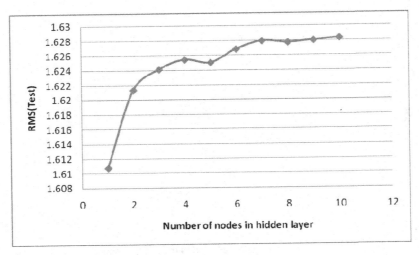

Figure 6. Optimum activation function from SSE for FFNN

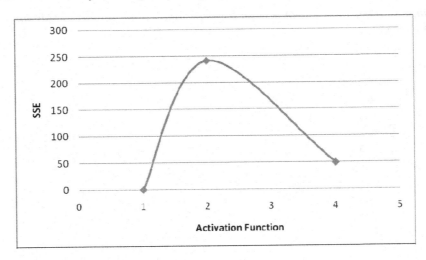

for prediction of cell mass growth for lipase production were encouraging. The success depends largely on good, representative data for training and statistical validation. There is still room for further improvement owing to relatively wide variations in the industrial fermentation data available for training and testing of the neural networks. The results clearly show that the neural network computation is well suited for prediction and estimation in industrial scale lipase production.

FUTURE WORK

The present work has shown the feasibility of the neural network modeling for the prediction of cell mass during the lipase fermentation by *Rhizopus*

Figure 7. Cell mass for initial volume 1ml

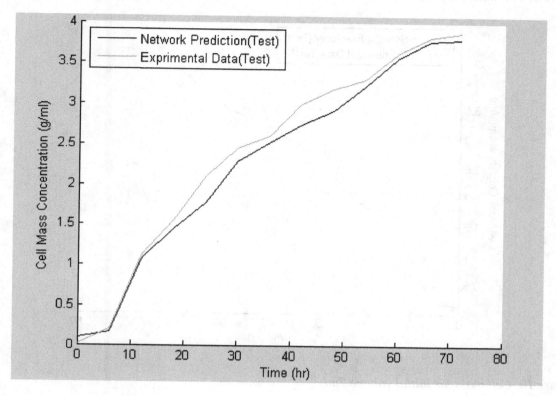

Figure 8. Cell mass for initial volume 3ml

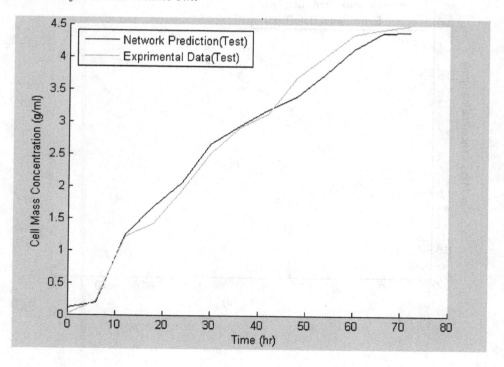

Figure 9. Cell mass for initial volume 4ml

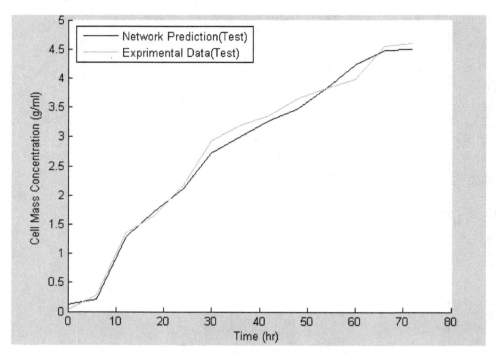

Figure 10. Cell mass for initial volume 7ml

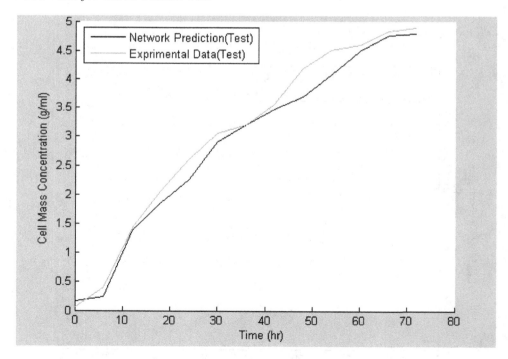

Figure 11 Cell mass for initial volume 10ml

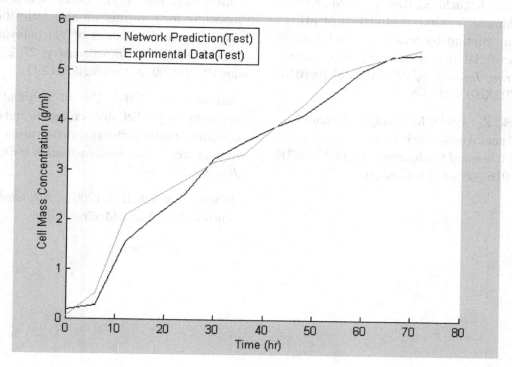

delemar NRRL1472. Future work in this aspect may be directed in the following three areas.

1. The other state variables such as substrate concentration, enzyme concentration can be incorporated for prediction and the results can be compared with complex kinetic models.
2. The physical variables such as pH, agitation, aeration and temperature can be incorporated for prediction.
3. The feasibility of a hybrid model which comprises of the neural network model with simple conventional models which may give better results than artificial neural networks alone can be checked.

REFERENCES

Bhat, N., & McAvoy, T. J. (1990). Use of neural nets for dynamic modeling and control of chemical process systems. *Computers & Chemical Engineering, 14*, 573–583. doi:10.1016/0098-1354(90)87028-N

Bhat, N., Minderman, P. A., McAvoy, T. J., & Wang, N. S. (1990). Modeling chemical process systems via neural computation. *IEEE Control Systems Magazine*, 24–29. doi:10.1109/37.55120

Freeman, J. A., & Skapura, D. M. (2003). *A neural network algorithms, applications and programming techniques*. Upper Saddle River, NJ: Pearson Education.

Horiuchi, J., Kikuchi, S., Kobayashi, M., Kanno, T., & Shimizu, T. (2001). Modeling of pH response in continuous anaerobic acidogenesis by an artificial neural network. *Biochemical Engineering Journal*, *9*, 199–204. doi:10.1016/S1369-703X(01)00153-X

Kurtanjek, Z. (1994). Modeling and control by artificial neural networks in biotechnology. *Computers & Chemical Engineering*, *18*, S627–S631. doi:10.1016/0098-1354(94)80102-9

Linko, P., & Zhu, Y. H. (1992). Neural network modeling for real-time variable estimation and prediction in the control of glucoamylase fermentation. *Process Biochemistry*, *27*, 275–283. doi:10.1016/0032-9592(92)85012-Q

Pramanik, K. (2004). Use of artificial neural networks for prediction of cell mass and ethanol concentration in batch fermentation using saccharomyces cerevisiae yeast. *Institution of Engineers Journal*, *85*, 31–35.

Robert, J., & Schalkof. (2001). *Artificial neural network*. New York: McGraw-Hill.

Chapter 16
Prediction of Structural and Functional Aspects of Protein:
In-Silico Approach

Arun G. Ingale
North Maharashtra University, India

ABSTRACT

To predict the structure of protein from a primary amino acid sequence is computationally difficult. An investigation of the methods and algorithms used to predict protein structure and a thorough knowledge of the function and structure of proteins are critical for the advancement of biology and the life sciences as well as the development of better drugs, higher-yield crops, and even synthetic bio-fuels. To that end, this chapter sheds light on the methods used for protein structure prediction. This chapter covers the applications of modeled protein structures and unravels the relationship between pure sequence information and three-dimensional structure, which continues to be one of the greatest challenges in molecular biology. With this resource, it presents an all-encompassing examination of the problems, methods, tools, servers, databases, and applications of protein structure prediction, giving unique insight into the future applications of the modeled protein structures. In this chapter, current protein structure prediction methods are reviewed for a milieu on structure prediction, the prediction of structural fundamentals, tertiary structure prediction, and functional imminent. The basic ideas and advances of these directions are discussed in detail.

DOI: 10.4018/978-1-4666-4940-8.ch016

INTRODUCTION

A protein is a sequence produced by combination of 20 amino acids. Amino acids are characterized by polar (hydrophilic) and non polar (hydrophobic) based on its residue. These amino acids are associated to each other with peptide bond to form a protein sequence (Laskowski*et al.,* 2003). The fabrication of a protein sequence is much effortless than the determination of a protein structure. However, the structure of a protein gives much more impending in the function of the protein than its sequence. Consequently, a number of methods for the computational prediction of protein structure from its sequence have been developed. Protein structure prediction is the prediction of the three-dimensional structure of a protein from its amino acid sequence that is, the prediction of its secondary, tertiary, and quaternary structure from its primary structure. The native structure is the 3D structure of the protein sequence. It necessitates knowing the native protein structure so that we can find out the function of that protein structure. There are numerous algorithms used to predict the native confirmation of a protein. Protein sequences are folded on lattice with non overlapping amino acid chain. These self circumventing conformations produced native structures which have smallest energy configuration. The protein sequence-structure gap is broadening speedily. The number of identified protein sequences (*Bairoch and Apweiler, 2000)* is blasting as a outcome of genome and other sequencing projects. The rising number of protein sequences is much bigger than the escalating number of known protein structures (Berman *et al.,* 2000). Hence, computational predictive tools for protein structures are badly needed to narrow the widening gap. Prediction of 3D protein structure from the amino acid sequence is one of the most exigent tribulations in theoretical structural biology (Montelione *et al.,* 1999; Skolnick *et al.,* 2000).Three-dimensional protein structures still cannot be correctly predicted straight from sequences. A transitional but helpful step is to predict the protein secondary structure, which is a way to simplify the prediction problem by projecting the very complicated 3D structure onto one dimension, i.e. onto a string of secondary structural coursework for each residue.

Fortitude of the exclusive tertiary (three-dimensional) structure of a protein from its amino acid sequence alone is one of the most significant and exigent problems in modern biology. The information on the tertiary structure of a protein is pretty decisive in accepting the function and biological responsibility of the protein. At present, genome-sequencing projects are producing an extraordinary amount of linear amino-acid sequences. An exponential growth of protein sequence database in current years by far outpaces the experimental determination of protein tertiary structures. Structure prediction is vitally dissimilar from the inverse problem of protein design. Protein structure prediction is one of the most key targets accomplished by bioinformatics and theoretical chemistry; it is extremely important in medicine and biotechnology for designing of the drug and novel enzymes.

This chapter begins with a thorough introduction to the protein structure prediction problem and is divided into four themes: a background on structure prediction, the prediction of structural elements, tertiary structure prediction, and functional insights.

The Protein Structure

Proteins are building blocks of life. It reveals more sequence and chemical complexity than DNA or RNA. It is a polymeric macromolecule fictitious of amino acid building blocks set in a linear chain and coupled jointly by peptide bonds. A protein sequence is a linear hetero polymer made up of one of the 20 different amino acids. Protein structures range in size from tens to several thousand residues (Brocchieri and Karlin, 1987). Protein structure is the bimolecular structure of a protein molecule that is a sequence formed from various residues. To be able to perform their biological function, proteins fold into one or more specific spatial conformations, driven by a number of non-covalent interactions such as hydrogen bonding, ionic interaction, Van der waals forces, and hydrophobic packing. The primary structure is usually symbolized by a sequence of letters above a 20-letter alphabet linked with the 20 naturally arising amino acids. Proteins are the foremost building blocks and useful molecules of the cell, pleasing up roughly twenty percent of a eukaryotic cells weight, the biggest involvement after water. They execute ample range of functions in the living organism, playing diverse catalytic, structural, regulatory and signaling roles essential for the cellular development, differentiation, replication and survival. The secondary structure is precised by a sequence classifying each amino acid into the consequent secondary structure constituents (e.g., alpha, beta, or gamma). The 3D structure of proteins can be solved by 1) Experimental methods, or 2) Structure prediction. It is incredibly inflexible to solve the structures experimentally. Solving through X-ray crystallography produces awfully excellent results but we require to have a very pure protein sample which should form crystals that are fairly perfect. Solving through NMR is restricted to tiny soluble proteins. The acquaintance of the 3D structure is helpful for rational drug design, protein engineering, exhaustive study of protein bimolecular interactions, study of evolutionary relationship between proteins or protein families etc. Structural features of proteins are frequently described at four levels of complexity. The primary structure of a protein can voluntarily be deduced from the nucleotide sequence of the analogous messenger RNA. Based on primary structure, various features of secondary structure can be predicted with the assist of computer programs. Conversely, predicting protein tertiary structure relics a very rough problem, although some progress has been made in this important area.

Primary Structure

The primary structure refers to linear arrangement of amino acids in a protein and the location of covalent linkages such as disulfide bonds between amino acids. The primary structure of a protein is determined by the gene corresponding to the protein. This structure is held together by covalent or peptide bonds, which are made during the process of protein biosynthesis or translation. The sequence of a protein can be determined by methods such as Edman degradation or tandem mass spectroscopy. Figure 1 A. Depicted a linear chain of amino acids.

Secondary Structure

Secondary structure is a confined frequently occurring structure in proteins and is mainly formed through hydrogen bonds between backbone atoms called random coils, loops or turns. There are two types of stable secondary structures: Alpha helices and beta-sheets (Figure.1B). Alpha-helices and beta-sheets are preferably located at the core of the protein, whereas loops prefer to reside in outer regions. Secondary structure prediction is a set of techniques in bioinformatics that aim to predict the local secondary structures of proteins . For proteins, a prediction consists of assigning regions of the amino acid sequence as likely alpha helices, beta strands, or turns. These secondary structures are defined by patterns of hydrogen bond between the main-chain peptide groups. They have a regular geometry, being constrained to specific values of the dihedral angles ψ and φ on the ramchandran plot (Chiang *et al.*, 2007). Specialized algorithms have been developed for the detection of specific well-defined patterns such as transmembrane helices and coiled coils in proteins, or canonical microRNA structures in RNA(Mount, 2004)

Figure 1. A) Primary Structure of protein, B) Secondary Structure C) Tertiary structure and D) Quaternary structure of Protein

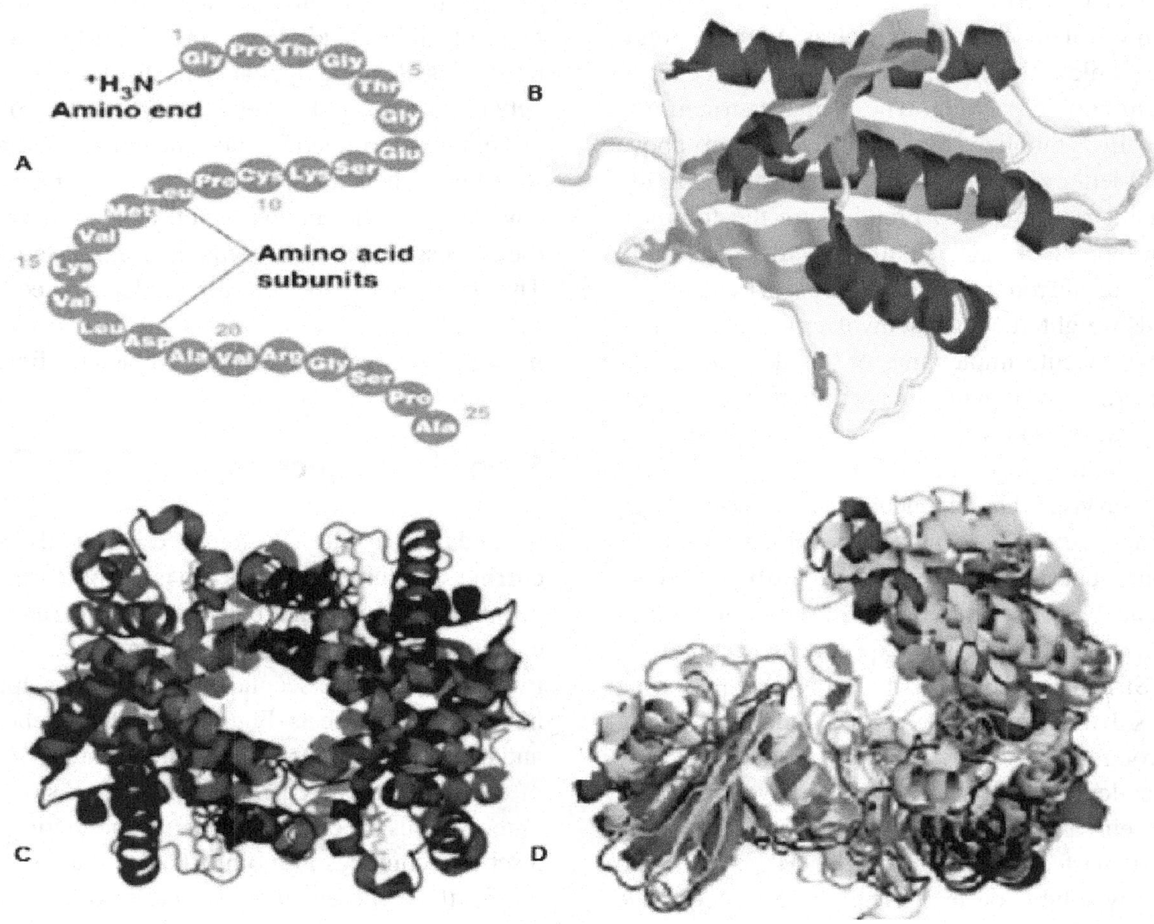

Tertiary Structure and Quaternary Structure

The three-dimensional structure of a protein that results from a large number of non-covalent interactions between amino acids (figure.1C). Quaternary structure is the 3D structure of a multi-subunit protein and how the subunits robust together. In this perspective, the quaternary structure is stabilized by the matching non-covalent connections and disulfide bonds as the tertiary structure. Complexes of two or more polypeptides are called multimers. Distinctively it would be called a dimer if it contains two subunits, a trimmer if it contains three subunits and a tetramer if it contains four subunits. The subunits are recurrently associated to one another by symmetry maneuver, such as a 2-fold axis in a dimer. The best example of quaternary structure is hemoglobin (Figure.1D).

Protein Structure Prediction and Modeling

Protein structure prediction is one of the largely imperative problems in modern computational biology. It is consequently becoming gradually more significant to predict protein structure from its amino acid sequence, using impending obtained from already known structures. Amino acid sequence analysis offers essential insight into the structure of proteins, which in turn deeply assisted the perceptive of its biochemical and cellular function. Endeavors to exploit computational techniques in predicting protein structure based only on sequence information started 40 years ago (Chou and Fasman, 1974). The tertiary structure of proteins involves the folding of the secondary structural elements. The physical properties that determine fold are the backbone rigidity, interaction between the amino acids which include the electrostatic interaction, the van der waals interaction, hydrogen and disulphide bonds and interaction with water. (Dunbrack *et al.*, 2000). The structure of an organized protein is indispensable for the understanding of its function. Even though the number of experimental accessible proteins is exponentially rising over the last several years, there are a large number of proteins with unidentified fold and devoid of a noticeable homology with any protein, which has been determined. Experimentally, protein structures possibly will be gritty *via* the X-ray crystallography or protein NMR (Chance *et al.*, 2002). Other experimental methods are currently of a lesser practical consequence. In practice, *abinitio* and molecular dynamics (MD) techniques are too sluggish or too imprecise. Thus, the best *de novo* prediction methods use mainly statistical information from known structures (Rohl et al., 2004). The most truthful prediction method so far is the template, or homology modeling approach, which predicts the structure by a comparison to a similar sequence. Understanding of a protein three-dimensional structure is an input to understanding the protein

biological function, to the rational drug design, protein engineering, etc. (Simons *et al.*, 2001).

Types of Protein Structure Predictions

There are assorted approaches and algorithms to predict the structure may be recapitulate as follows, 1) Prediction in 1D engross, Prediction of secondary structure, Prediction of solvent accessibility, Prediction of trans-membrane, helices. 2) Prediction in 2D engross, Prediction of the inter-residue and strand contacts. 3) Prediction in 3D engross, searching the database to locate a appropriate template for modeling. There are three methods for protein structure prediction namely, 1) homology modeling, 2) Fold recognition or threading, and 3) Ab-initio method. All these methods engage searching the database for a homologue to the target protein.

Homology Modeling

Homology modeling is sustained on the actuality that if two sequences have a high sequence similarity then they have similar 3D structure. But this is forever not the case. The free modeling technique has predicted some structures with very elevated precision; sometimes even exceeding the correctness of template/homology based approaches. The step in conventional homology modeling consists following possessions. Database search: Sequence similarity searching is a crucial step in analyzing newly determined protein sequences. A template for modeling desires to be recognized and sequence alignment between the template and target sequences has to be generated. Recurrently, template identification is executed by firm standard tools, such as PSI-BLAST, and the resulting alignment is consequently rectified by other tools and ultimately by physical professional corrections. The aligned fragments of templates are used to construct the corresponding fragments of the target structure. Multiple sequence alignment (MSA), main chain modeling, loop modeling, side chain modeling, energy refinement are the important parameters. The final, step of modeling is structure refinement which rivets repacking the side chains and energy minimization of the entire structure. The model obtained may be evaluated using PROVE, PROCHECK and what-if checks. There is some useful software routinely used for homology modeling like SwissPDB. TASSER, newer software also using the fragment approach, is very attractive because it is capable to predict the targets with similar precision while needing far less computing time (Zhou et al., 2007). Rosetta is also lucratively used for the homology modeling target as a refinement step.

Fold Recognition or Threading

Protein three-dimensional structure resolves protein function. But what resolves 3D structure is the question. The hypothesis that structure also referred to as 'the fold', is exclusively determined by the specificity of the sequence, has been confirm for many proteins (Kolinski and skolnick, 2004). Although it is now acknowledged that fussy proteins like chaperones frequently play a role in the folding pathway, and in correcting misfolds, it is still commonly implicit that the final structure is at the free-energy minimum (Sali, 1993,1995). The threading and sequence-structure alignment looms are stands on the observation that many protein structures in the PDB are incredibly analogous. The mainly exact prediction method so far is the template, or homology modeling approach, which predicts the structure by a contrast to a similar sequence. In favor of two thirds of sequences, a similar sequence can be establish and consequently the structure can be predicted by homology modeling with good exactitude for those with fewer than 300 residues. Nevertheless, it is expected that most of the remaining third also has identified folds. Homology modeling does not work for sequence disparity larger than 20% and thus *de novo* methods are desirable for those

(Zhou and Zhou, 2002). A cluster of methods, called "threading", were developed which used structural information from several less intimately related structures. Conversely, they are less truthful than modern fragment methods and are thus only used as a module in some software (Moult et al., 2005). The accomplishment of the prediction of protein three-dimensional structure from its amino acid sequence is inadequate by paucity in the conformational search procedures aimed at finding the global energy minimum and in the efficient impending used to evaluate the free energies of possible structures (Cymerman et al., 2004). The protein fold-recognition approach to structure prediction aims to recognize the known structural scaffold that accommodates the target protein sequence in the finest way. Classically, a fold-recognition plan encompasses four mechanism: (1) the illustration of the template structures (2) the evaluation of the compatibility between the target sequence and a template fold (3) the algorithm to compute the optimal alignment between the target sequence and the template structure, and (4) the way the ranking is computed and the statistical significance is estimated (Fischer and eisenberg, 1996). Homology modeling and fold recognition are the most steadfast structure-prediction practice is to identify its matching structural folds from offered known structures with or without significant sequence similarity. This approach is also referred as template based modeling. Template-based modeling becomes progressively more dominant because most popular structure folds are known (Daiet al., 2011). On the other hand, recognizing structurally similar folds in the absence of sequence similarity or fold recognition is exigent. New methods ORFeus (Observatories and Research Facilities for European Seismology) uses sequence profiles and ignore the experimental structural information from the template, and attempts to predict the structure de novo both for the target and the template families (Ginalskiand Rrychlewski, 2003). Protein fold recognition scheme endeavor to recognize the suitable template from a structure template library for a query protein and create an alignment between the query and the recognized template protein, from which the structure of query protein can be predicted. Protein fold recognition using the protein threading procedure has established enormous success (Moult et al., 2003).

Unusual techniques can be used in order to face the computational difficulty of protein fold recognition problem such as Molecular Dynamics, Monte Carlo, Genetic Algorithms and Neural Network. The GenTHREADER method uses a conventional sequence alignment algorithm to produce alignments which are then appraised by a method derived from threading techniques. All threaded model is evaluated by a neural network in order to produce a single gauge of assurance in the projected prediction (Jones, 1999).

Lin *et al*(2002) have developed a new program TUNE (Threading Using Neural network based on an artificial neural network model to predict compatibility of amino acid sequences with structural environment. Jiang *et al* (2005) anticipated a new fold recognition model with mixed environment-specific substitution mapping called MESSM. A support vector machine is engaged to measure the significance of the sequence-structure alignment. MESSM shows good performance on protein fold recognition. Support Vector Machine (SVM) regression approach to directly predict the alignment accuracy of a sequence template alignment has been implemented by (Xu, 2005). Threading or remote homologue design is a protein structure prediction technique carried when there is not enough sequence similarity between the target and template. The recognition of the template is a problem by itself and hence it is also called fold recognition.

AB-Initio Prediction

Proteins are among the foremost significant groups of biomolecules, with their biological functions ranging from structural elements to signal transducers between cells. Independently from their biological role, incident related to protein behavior in solutions and at solid interfaces can find an extensive range of engineering applications such as in biomedical implants, scaffolds for artificial tissues, bioseparations, biomineralization and biosensors. The functionality of a protein is directly related to its three-dimensional structure (i.e. conformation) for both biological and engineering applications. Process such as homology and threading that depend on a large database of accessible experimental data are the most popular means of predicting the conformation of proteins in their native environment. Ab-initio prediction is conceded out when there is no appropriate homologue found in the database. Prediction is done completely from the sequence that may be based on An finsen's hypothesis that the native state of the protein represents the global free energy minimum. Ab-initio method tries to find these global minima of the protein. *Ab initio* protein folding has regularly been an area of entirely academic interest characterized by relatively slow progress.

The purpose of ab initio structure prediction is effortless: Given a protein's amino acid sequence predict the structure of its native state. It is normally understood that a protein sequence folds to a native conformation or ensemble of conformations that is at or near the global free-energy minimum. Thus, the problem of finding native like conformations for a given sequence can be decomposed into two sub problems: (a) developing an accurate potential and (b) developing an efficient protocol for searching the resultant energy landscape. There are two mechanisms to *ab initio* prediction: devising a scoring (i.e, energy) function that can distinguish between correct (native or native-like) structures from incorrect ones, and a search method to investigate the conformational space. In various techniques, the two apparatus are coupled together such that a search function drives, and is driven by, the scoring function to find native-like structures. Unlike computational approaches to the problem fluctuate as to which assumptions are made. A promising approach, based on the discretization of the conformational space, is that of deriving a protein-centric lattice, by allowing the backbone torsion angles, phi, psi, and omega, to take only a distinct set of values for each different residue type. Under biological circumstances, the bond lengths and bond angles are fairly rigid. Consequently, the internal torsion angles along the protein backbone determine the main features of the final geometric shape of the folded protein. To predict protein structure *de novo* for larger proteins will necessitate superior algorithms and larger computational resources like those afforded by either influential super computers e.g. Blue Gene or MDGRAPE-3) or distributed computing. Even though these computational barriers are vast, the potential benefits of structural genomics make *ab initio* structure prediction an active research field. *Ab initio* prediction methods use just the sequence of the protein. Threading and Homology Modeling methods can build a 3D model for a protein of unknown structure from experimental structures of evolutionary related proteins (Zhang,2008). There are two kinds of model.

1. **Lattice Model:** This represents peptide chain as lattices. But fails to represent subtle geometric consideration like strand twist and its backbone prediction isnot all that accurate.

2. **Discrete State off-Lattice Model:** It improves upon the lattice modelby applying restraints like allowing only certain side chain structure and limiting the peptide bond rotation. In order to reduce the complexity, local structure biases are used. But the strength and multiplicity of the local structure prediction is highly sequence dependent. There are two type of scoring functions namely knowledge based scoring function and force field based function which are used. Currently there does not exist a reliable scoring function or search method. There is a new fully automated ab-intio prediction method in which

the Monte Carlo fragment insertion method (ROSETTA) of Baker and others has been merged with the Isite (library of sequences structure motifs) and the HMMSTR model for local structure in proteins.

Comparative Modeling

Comparative modeling predicts the 3D structure of a specified target protein sequence based principally on its alignment to one or more proteins of known structure i.e. templates. The prediction method consists of fold assignment, target–template alignment, model building, and model evaluation. The number of protein sequences that can be modeled and the accuracy of the predictions are growing progressively because of the growth in the number of known protein structures and because of the improvements in the modeling software. The aspire of comparative or homology protein structure modeling is to build a three-dimensional (3D) model for a protein of unknown structure on the basis of sequence similarity to proteins of known structure. Two situations must be met to build a useful model. First, the likeness between the target sequence and the template structure must be obvious. Second, a substantially correct alignment between the target sequence and the template structures must be calculated (Marti-Renom et al., 2002). Comparative modeling methods are useful for predicting the tertiary structure of the target protein if there is a template for a homologue with a comparatively high sequence similarity. During comparative modeling, the target sequence is aligned to templates, and then all atom structures of the target protein are formed ensuing to fulfilling in alignment gaps and correctly orienting side chains (Baker and Sali, 2001). Comparative modeling is presently the most habitually used approach to the theoretical prediction of protein structure (Holm and Sander, 1996).

Whereas a protein structure and function is evolutionary too much conserved than the protein sequence, similarity of sequence of a new protein to a protein of known structure entails their structural similarity (Clark, 1999).

A template protein probably will be identified by a sequence comparison method (Altschul *et al.*, 1997) or by a threading algorithm (Kihara and Skolnick, 2004).

The almost all conservative approach to the comparative modeling occasionally called homology modeling, although meticulously speaking homology is not required for the sequence and structure similarity. Comparative modeling ruins the most dependable and routinely used method for protein structure prediction (Eswar *et al.*, 2008, Ginalski, 2006). The unusual term of homology modeling is regularly used. That is because the identification of a structural template is classically based on the homology relation between the target protein and the templates, which is usually reflected by a certain level of sequence similarity. All existing comparative modeling methods consist of four sequential steps: fold assignment and template selection, template–target alignment, model building, and model evaluation. If the model is not satisfactory, template selection, alignment, and model building can be repeated until a satisfactory model is obtained.

Applications

Comparative modeling is an increasingly efficient way to obtain useful information about the proteins of interest. Comparative models can be helpful in designing mutants to test hypotheses about a protein's function

- Identifying active and binding sites,
- Identifying, designing and improving ligands for a given binding site,
- Modeling substrate specificity,
- Predicting antigenic epitopes,
- Simulating protein–protein docking,
- Inferring function from a calculated electrostatic potential around the protein,

- Facilitating molecular replacement in X-ray structure determination,
- Refining models based on NMR constraints,
- Testing and improving a sequence–structure alignment,
- Confirming a remote structural relationship and rationalizing known experimental observations.

Transmembrane Topology

Transmembrane protein topology prediction methods play significant roles in structural biology, since the structure determination of these types of proteins is enormously tricky by the common biophysical, biochemical and molecular biological methods. The need for accurate prediction methods is high, as the amount of known membrane protein structures plunge extreme behind the estimated number of these proteins in various genomes. The precision of these prediction methods emerges to be higher than most prediction methods applied on globular proteins, however it reduces vaguely with the increasing number of structures. A transmembrane protein is a protein that spans an entire biological membrane. These proteins go from one side of a membrane through to the other side of the membrane. Transmembrane proteins are aggregate and precipitate in water. They need nonpolar solvents for extraction, while some of beta-barrels can be also extracted using denaturing agents. Transmembrane proteins control the flow of information and substances into and out of the cell and are involved in a broad range of biological processes. All transmembrane proteins are integral membrane proteins, but not all integral membrane proteins are transmembrane proteins.

There are two fundamental types of transmembrane proteins: 1) Alpha-helix- This is the major category of transmembrane proteins present in the inner membranes of bacterial cells or the plasma membrane of eukaryotes. In humans, 27% of all proteins encompasses predictable to be alpha-helical membrane proteins. 2) Beta-plated sheets-These proteins are found only in outer membranes. Membrane proteins are crucial for survival. They constitute key components for cell–cell signaling, mediate the transport of ions and solutes across the membrane, and are crucial for recognition of self (Chen *et al.*, 2002). Most TM proteins are helical (TMH) proteins. Helices in membrane spanning regions are more tightly packed than the helices in soluble proteins. The topology of TMH proteins, includes, the membrane spanning regions and the amino-terminal orientations. The determination of the topology of a TMH protein is useful for the annotation of its biological function (Zhou, 2003). Many different methods have been developed to predict the topology of transmembrane protein TMH proteins. Transmembrane helices can be predicted based on the distinctive patterns of hydrophobic and polar regions within the sequence. Kyte and Doolittle developed one of the first methods that evaluated the hydrophilicity and hydrophobicity of a protein along the amino acid sequence (Kyte and Doolittle, 1982). The first HMM-based transmembrane protein topology predictors were introduced ten years ago: TMHMM and HMMTOP (Tusnady, 1998). TMpred is one of the methods using such statistical preferences to predict membrane helices taken from an expert-compiled data set of membrane proteins. The HMM Phobius was designed to combine the signal peptide model of Signal P-HMM [Nielsen and krogh, 1998] with the transmembrane topology model of TMHMM (Sonnhammer et al., 1998). Reynolds et al, 2008 described Philius, a DBN-based approach to transmembrane protein topology prediction. Hidden Markov models (HMMs) have been successfully applied to the tasks of transmembrane protein topology prediction and signal peptide prediction. Consensus methods based on multiple prediction algorithms were also developed (Drew et al., 2002).

Ligand-Binding Residue Prediction

In this section, we explore means for predicting protein residues that interact with small molecules. The accurate prediction of ligand binding residues from amino acid sequences is imperative for the programmed functional annotation of new proteins. The rationale of the ligand binding site residues in a protein is also vital, because substrate specificity of an enzyme is determined by the well information of the binding site residues, such as side chain orientation and physiochemical properties (Schwede, et al. 2009).

The conquering identification of ligand-binding sites on protein surfaces is usually the opening point for the annotation of protein function and drug discovery. The identification of ligand-binding sites is frequently the starting point for protein function annotation and structure based drug design. Many computational methods for the prediction of ligand-binding sites have been developed in latest decades. The protein surface can form pockets that are binding sites of small molecule ligands. Therefore, the identification of pocket sites on the protein surface is often the starting point for protein function annotation and structure-based drug design. The prediction of protein-ligand binding sites has great significance for protein function annotation and computer-aided drug design. Besides the binding site identification, the binding sites' ranking according to their likeliness to accept a molecule is also an important and challenging issue (Gao et al., 2012). Identifying ligand-binding residues reliably aids the overall understanding of the role and function of a protein by using them to subsequently predict the types of ligands to which they bind and, in the case of enzymes, the types of reactions that are catalyzed. Moreover, knowledge of the residues involved in protein-ligand interactions has broad applications in drug discovery and chemical genetics, as it may be used to better virtually screen large chemical compound libraries and to aid the process of lead optimization. In addition, the ligand-binding residues of a protein can be used to influence target-template sequence alignment in comparative protein modeling which has been shown to improve the quality of the 3D models produced for the target's binding site. These quality improvements in the binding site's 3D model are critical to docking-based approaches for virtual screening (Kauffman and Karypis, 2009).

The number of predictors that submitted new methods in this category was highly encouraging and suggests that current technology is at the level that experimental biochemists and structural biologists could benefit from what is clearly a growing field. Several different protein ligand binding site prediction methods have been developed, which mostly fall into two major categories: sequence-based methods and structure based methods. The sequence-based methods rely on identifying conserved residues that may be structurally or functionally important and include methods such as firestar, WSsas, FRcons, ConFunc, ConSurf, FPSD, Pand INTERPID. The structure based methods can be further subdivided into the geometric methods utilized by FINDSITE and Site Hunter; energetic methods utilized by SITEHOUND and Q-Site Finder. The FunFOLD software implements a competitive method for the prediction of protein binding site residues, which can also be used to determine the putative ligands interacting with a protein. The FunFOLD software is freely available as both a standalone package and a prediction server, providing competitive ligand binding site residue predictions for expert and non-expert users alike. The software provides a new fully automated approach for structure based function prediction using 3D models of proteins. Nevertheless, for the 3D models the LigandSite and Phyre server are frequently used. Similarly MAMMOTH used for structural superposition of similar templates with bound ligands (Roche et al., 2011).

To predict the potential binding site, several computational methods have been developed. In brief, these algorithms can be divided into three categories (1) purely geometry-based methods, which follow the assumption that the protein-ligand binding sites are generally located at crevices on the protein surface or cavities in the protein. Methods falling in this category include POCKET, LIGSITE, PASS, SURFNET, and Pocket Picker. (2) energetic-based methods, which coat the protein surface with a layer of probes to calculate van der Waals interaction energies between the protein and probes. As an example, Q-Site Finder is a classical tool falling in this category (3) knowledge based methods, which includes various statistical methods, machine learning methods and similarity comparison methods. Besides, a part of them predict protein-ligand binding sites by searching for clusters or patterns of the conserved residues. These methods include POCKET, LIGSITE, LIGSITEcs, SURFNET, CAST, PASS and Pocket Picker all of which use pure geometric characteristics and do not require any knowledge of the ligands (Roche et al.,2010). Identification of binding sites is of fundamental importance in SBDD and virtual ligand screening. Identifying sequence and structural similarity with proteins with known functional sites is an emerging area for identifying ligand binding sites. Energy-based methods of pocket detection include those of Meta Pocket and Q-Site Finder is online.

Loop Modeling

Loop modeling is conceivably the hardest step in comparative modeling process along with alignment. When target and template share above 35% sequence identity, errors in loops are the dominant problem in comparative modeling. *Loop modeling* is a crisis in protein structure predictions necessitating the prediction of the conformations of loop regions in protein with or without the use of a structural template. Computer programs that resolve these troubles have been used to research a extensive sort of scientific issues from ADP to breast cancer (Baloria et al., 2012). Since protein function is gritty by its shape and the physiochemical properties of its exposed surface, it is essential to build an accurate model for protein or ligand interaction studies (Fiser and Sali, 2003). The process for modeling a loop in a given situation is illustrated here by specifying its three main mechanisms: The depiction of a protein; the manacles that define the objective or energy function; and the scheme for optimizing the energy function. The modeling method is completely automated and is implemented in the program MODELLER-5. Whilst the mostly recurrent application of the technique is to predict single loops, it is also technically suitable for modeling any set of contiguous or noncontiguous residues or atoms e.g., several loops, a loop with a ligand, a huddle of side chains in the preset environment created by the respite of the protein. Consequently, ingenuous modeling of loops is indispensable for structure-based prediction of function from sequence. For example, a comparative model can occasionally be used with computational ligand docking to locate a putative ligand or determine preferences within a limited set of ligands (Xu et al., 1996). A somber complication is that the ligand may persuade conformational changes in loops with which it interacts. Loop modeling methods can be classified in two approaches: *Ab initio* methods and database searching or knowledge-based methods.

Ab Initio Methods

Ab initio loop prediction is based on a conformational search guided by a scoring or energy function -the later describing the physico-chemical properties of a protein and its environment. It is also called as non-template based technique. The non-template based looms employ a statistical model to seal in the gaps created by the unknown loop structure known as an *ab initio* method. Several of these programs include MODELLER, Loopy, and RAPPER; but each of these programs approaches the problem in a dissimilar way. Further programs exploit a de novo approach that samples sterically

feasible loop conformations and selects the best one. The determining a best model means that a scoring method must be fashioned to compare the diverse conformations (Adhikariet al., 2012)

Knowledge-Based Methods

Knowledge-based approaches, which are the most widely used also called as template based technique. It utilizes libraries of regular rotamers extracted from high resolution X-ray structures. This approach is executed in most automatic homology modeling events. The CORALL module of WHA-TIF and the SCWRL program important software using such approach. Sections of a structural model that are predicted by non-template-based loop modeling tend to be greatly less perfect than regions that are predicted using template-based techniques. Conversely, loops are commonly too short to present sufficient information about their local fold. Fragment of up to nine residues occasionally have totally unrelated conformations in different proteins (Cohen and Pressnell, 1993). It is furthermore referred as database searching approach. This is more precise and resourceful if it is precedent by a structural classification of the loops here in the database. This approach to loop prediction initiated by finding segments of main chain that fit the two stems of a loop. The stems are defined as the main chain atoms that herald and follow the loop but are not part of it. The search is carrying out through a database of many known protein structures, not only homologues of the modeled protein. The preferred segments are then superposed and annealed onto the stem regions. These initial crude models are often refined by optimization of some energy function. The database search ensue to loop modeling is truthful and proficient when a specific set of loops is created to tackle the modeling of that group of loops like b-hairpins and the hyper variable regions in immunoglobulins (Sibanda et al.,1989). There are many such methods, exploiting different protein representations, energy function terms, and optimization or enumeration algorithms. ModLoop is a web server for automated modeling of loops in protein structures. The server relies on the loop modeling usual in MODELLER that predicts the loop conformations by satisfaction of spatial restraints, without relying on a database of known protein structures (Fisher, 2009). FREAD is a database search loop modeling algorithm. Its principal use is to fill in the gaps in imperfect 3D models of protein structures. The input is a 3D model of a protein structure as well as the location and amino acid sequence of the loop region to be modeled (Choi et al.,2009). FALC-Loop is an internet server for protein loop modeling. The FALC-Loop server uses the protein loop modeling method that utilizes fragment assembly and analytical loop end developed in the Reference. The method shows a brilliant presentation when compared to earlier loop sampling methods (Lee et al., 2011).YASARA Structure features a loop modeler, that can swiftly retrieve loop conformations that overpass two sets of anchor residues from the Protein Data Bank. This knowledge-based approach profits extremely from the increasingly growing PDB, and has been shown to be a strong competition for ab-initio loop prediction (Michalsky et al., 2003).

CONCLUSION

The 3D structures of proteins are preset by a linear sequence of amino acid residues. To predict structure from sequence is an intricate job enough to have occupied a generation of researchers. Remarkable looms to predict the structure obtain into account unlike chemical and physical properties. Nonetheless these are not appreciably perfect or trust worthy adequate to predict all kinds of proteins. Ab-initio prediction methods even with their very low accuracy can give a reliable functional annotation.

REFERENCES

Adhikari, A. N., Peng, J., Wilde, M., Xu, J., Freed, K. F., & Sosnick, T. R. (2012). Modeling large regions in proteins: Applications to loops, termini, and folding. *Protein Science*, *21*(1), 107–121. doi:10.1002/pro.767 PMID:22095743

Altschul, S. F., Madden, T. L., Schaefer, A. A., Zhang, J., Zhang, Z., Miller, W., & Lipman, D. J. (1997). Gapped BLAST and PSIBLAST: A new generation of protein database search programs. *Nucleic Acids Research*, *25*, 3389–3402. doi:10.1093/nar/25.17.3389 PMID:9254694

Bairoch, A., & Apweiler, R. (2000). The SWISS-PROT protein sequence database and its supplement TrEMBL in 2000. *Nucleic Acids Research*, *28*, 45–48. doi:10.1093/nar/28.1.45 PMID:10592178

Baker, D., & Sali, A. (2001). Protein structure prediction and structural genomics. *Science*, *294*, 93–96. doi:10.1126/science.1065659 PMID:11588250

Baloria, U., Akhoon, B. A., Gupta, S. K., Sharma, S., & Verma, V. (2012). In silico proteomic characterization of human epidermal growth factor receptor 2 (HER-2) for the mapping of high affinity antigenic determinants against breast cancer. *Amino Acids*, *42*(4), 1349–1360. doi:10.1007/s00726-010-0830-x PMID:21229277

Berman, H. M., Westbrook, J., Feng, Z., Gilliland, G., Bhat, T. N., & Weissig, H. et al. (2000). The protein data bank. *Nucleic Acids Research*, *28*, 235–242. doi:10.1093/nar/28.1.235 PMID:10592235

Brocchieri, L., & Karlin. (1987). Prediction folding of short polypeptide segment by uniform conformational sampling. *Biopolymer*, *26*, 137–168. doi:10.1002/bip.360260114

Chance, M. R., Bresnick, A. R., Burley, S. K., Jiang, J. S., Lima, C. D., & Sali, A. et al. (2002). Structural genomics: A pipeline for providing structures for the biologist. *Protein Science, 11*, 723–738. doi:10.1110/ps.4570102 PMID:11910018

Chen, C. P., Kernytsky, A., & Rost, B. (2002). Transmembrane helix predictions revisited. *Protein Science, 11*, 2774–2791. doi:10.1110/ps.0214502 PMID:12441377

Chiang, Y. S., Gelfand, T. I., Kister, A. E., & Gelfand, I. M. (2007). New classification of supersecondary structures of sandwich-like proteins uncovers strict patterns of strand assemblage. *Proteins, 68*(4), 915–921. doi:10.1002/prot.21473 PMID:17557333

Choi, Y., & Charlotte, M. D. (2009). FREAD revisited: Accurate loop structure prediction using a database search algorithm. *Proteins, 78*(6), 1431–1440. PMID:20034110

Chou, P. Y., & Fasman, G. D. (1974). Prediction of protein conformation. *Biochemistry, 13*(2), 222–245. doi:10.1021/bi00699a002 PMID:4358940

Clark, M. S. (1999). Comparative genomics: the key to understand the human genome project. *BioEssays, 21*, 121–130. doi:10.1002/(SICI)1521-1878(199902)21:2<121::AID-BIES6>3.0.CO;2-O PMID:10193186

Cohen, F. E., & Presnell, S. R. (1996). The combinatorial approach. In *Protein structure prediction*. Oxford, UK: Oxford University Press.

Cymerman, I., Feder, M., Pawłowski, M.A., Kurowski, J.M., & Bujnicki. (Eds.). (2004). Practical bioinformatics. *Nucleic Acids and Molecular Biology, 15*.

Dai, T., Liu, Q., Gao, J., Cao, Z., & Zhu, R. (2011). A new protein-ligand binding sites prediction method based on the integration of protein sequence conservation information. *BMC Bioinformatics, 12*(Suppl 14), S9. doi:10.1186/1471-2105-12-S14-S9 PMID:22373099

Drew, D., Sjostrand, D., Nielsen, J., Urbig, T., Chin, C., de Gier, J., & von Heijne, G. (2002). Rapid topology mapping of escherichia coli inner-membrane proteins by prediction and PhoA/GFP fusion analysis. *Proceedings of the National Academy of Sciences of the United States of America, 99*, 2690–2695. doi:10.1073/pnas.052018199 PMID:11867724

Dunbrack, R. L. Jr, Dunker, K., & Godzik, A. (2000). Protein structure prediction in biology and medicine. *Pacific Symposium on Biocomputing. Pacific Symposium on Biocomputing, 12*, 93–94. PMID:10902159

Eswar, N., Eramian, D., Webb, B., Shen, M. Y., & Sali, A. (2008). Protein structure modeling with MODELLER. *Methods in Molecular Biology (Clifton, N.J.), 426*, 145–159. doi:10.1007/978-1-60327-058-8_8 PMID:18542861

Fischer, D. (2006). Servers for protein structure prediction. *Current Opinion in Structural Biology, 16*, 178–182. doi:10.1016/j.sbi.2006.03.004 PMID:16546376

Fiser, A., & Sali, A. (2003). ModLoop: Automated modeling of loops in protein structures. *Bioinformatics (Oxford, England), 19*(18), 2500–2601. doi:10.1093/bioinformatics/btg362 PMID:14668246

Fisher, D., & Eisenberg, D. (1996). Protein fold recognition using sequence-derived predictions. *Protein Science, 5*, 947–955. doi:10.1002/pro.5560050516 PMID:8732766

Gao, J., Xia, L., Lu, M., Zang, B., & Wang, I. (2012). TM7SF1 (GPR137B), a novel lysosome Integral membrane protein. *Molecular Biology Reports*, *39*(9), 8883–8889. doi:10.1007/s11033-012-1755-0 PMID:22729905

Ginalski, K. (2006). Comparative modeling for protein structure prediction. *Current Opinion in Structural Biology*, *16*, 172–177. doi:10.1016/j.sbi.2006.02.003 PMID:16510277

Ginalski, K., & Rychlewski, L. (2003). Protein structure prediction of CASP5 comparative modeling and fold recognition targets using consensus alignment approach and 3D assessment. *Proteins*, *53*(Suppl 6), 410–417. doi:10.1002/prot.10548 PMID:14579329

Holm, C., & Nad Sander, L. (1996). Mapping the protein universe. *Science*, *2*(273), 595–603. doi:10.1126/science.273.5275.595 PMID:8662544

Jiang, N., Wu, W. X., & Mitchell, I. (2005). Protein folds recognition using neural networks and support vector machines. In *Proceeding of the 6th International Conference on Intelligent Data Engineering and Automated Learning-IDEAL*. Springer-Verlag.

Jones, D. T. (1999). GenTHREADER: An efficient and reliable protein folds recognition method for genomic sequences. *Journal of Molecular Biology*, *287*, 797–815. doi:10.1006/jmbi.1999.2583 PMID:10191147

Kauffman, C., & Karypis, G. (2009). Librus: Combined machine learning and homology information for sequence-based ligand-binding residue prediction. *Bioinformatics (Oxford, England)*, *25*(23), 3099–3107. doi:10.1093/bioinformatics/btp561 PMID:19786483

Kihara, D., & Skolnick, J. (2004). Microbial genomes have over 72% structure assignment by the threading algorithm PROSPECTOR_Q. *Proteins*, *55*, 464–473. doi:10.1002/prot.20044 PMID:15048836

Ko, J., Lee, D., Park, H., Coutsias, E. A., Lee, J., & Seok, C. (2011). The FALC-loop web server for protein loop modeling. *Nucleic Acids Research*, *39*, W210–W214. doi:10.1093/nar/gkr352 PMID:21576220

Kolinski, A., & Skolnick, J. (2004). Reduced models of proteins and their applications. *Polymer*, *45*, 511–24S. doi:10.1016/j.polymer.2003.10.064

Kyte, J., & Doolittle, R. F. (1982). A simple method for displaying the hydropathic character of a protein. *Journal of Molecular Biology*, *157*, 105–132. doi:10.1016/0022-2836(82)90515-0 PMID:7108955

Laskowski, R. A., Watson, J. D., & Thornton, J. M. (2003). From protein structure to biochemical function? *Journal of Structural and Functional Genomics*, *4*, 167–177. doi:10.1023/A:1026127927612 PMID:14649301

Lin, K., May, A. C. W., & Taylor, W. R. (2002). Threading using neural network (TUNE), the measure of protein sequence-structure compatibility. *Bioinformatics (Oxford, England)*, *18*, 1350–1357. doi:10.1093/bioinformatics/18.10.1350 PMID:12376379

Marti-Renom, M. A., Madhusudhan, M. S., Fiser, A., Rost, B., & Sali, A. (2002). Reliability of assessment of protein structure prediction methods. *Structure (London, England)*, *10*, 435–440. doi:10.1016/S0969-2126(02)00731-1 PMID:12005441

Michalsky, E., Goede, A., & Preissner, R. (2003). Loops in proteins (LIP) - A comprehensive loop database for homology modeling. *Protein Engineering*, *16*, 979–985. doi:10.1093/protein/gzg119 PMID:14983078

Montelione, G. T., Zheng, D., Huang, Y. J., Gunsalus, K. C., & Szyperski, T. (2000). Protein NMR spectroscopy in structural genomics. *Nature Structural Biology*, *7*, 982–985. doi:10.1038/80768 PMID:11104006

Moult, J., Fidelis, K., Rost, B., Hubbard, T., & Tramontano, A. (2005). Critical assessment of methods of protein structure prediction (CASP)–Round 6. *Proteins*, *61*, 3–7. doi:10.1002/prot.20716 PMID:16187341

Moult, J., Fidelis, K., Zemla, A., & Hubbard, T. (2003). Critical assessment of methods of protein structure prediction (CASP)-Round V. *Proteins*, *53*, 334–339. doi:10.1002/prot.10556 PMID:14579322

Mount, D. M. (2004). *Bioinformatics: Sequence and genome analysis* (2nd ed.). New York: Cold Spring Harbor Laboratory Press.

Nielsen, H., & Krogh, A. (1998). Prediction of signal peptides and signal anchors by a hidden Markov model. *Proc ISMB, 6*, 122–30.

Pauling, L., Corey, R. B., & Branson, H. R. (1951). The structure of proteins, two hydrogen-bonded helical configurations of the polypeptide chain. *Proceedings of the National Academy of Sciences of the United States of America*, *37*(4), 205–211. doi:10.1073/pnas.37.4.205 PMID:14816373

Reynolds, S. M., Ka, L., Riffle, M. E., Bilmes, J. A., & Noble, W. S. (2008). Transmembrane topology and signal peptide prediction using dynamic bayesian networks. *PLoS Computational Biology*, *4*(11), e1000213. doi:10.1371/journal.pcbi.1000213 PMID:18989393

Roche, D. B., Buenavista, M. T., Tetchner, S. J., & McGuffin, L. J. (2011). The IntFOLD server: An integrated web resource for protein fold recognition, 3D model quality assessment, intrinsic disorder prediction, domain prediction and ligand binding site prediction. *Nucleic Acids Research*, *39*, W171-6. doi:10.1093/nar/gkr184 PMID:21459847

Roche, D. B., Tetchner, S. J., & McGuffin, L. J. (2010). The binding site distance test score: A robust method for the assessment of predicted protein binding sites. *Bioinformatics (Oxford, England)*, *26*(22), 2920–2921. doi:10.1093/bioinformatics/btq543 PMID:20861025

Rohl, C. A., Strauss, C. E. M., Misura, K. M. S., & Baker, D. (2004). Protein structure prediction using rosetta. *Methods in Enzymology*, *383*, 66–93. PMID:15063647

Sali, A. (1995). Comparative protein modeling by satisfaction of spatial restraints. *Molecular Medicine Today*, *1*, 270–277. doi:10.1016/S1357-4310(95)91170-7 PMID:9415161

Schwede, T., Sali, A., Honig, B., Levitt, M., Berman, H. M., & Jones, D. et al. (2009). Outcome of a workshop on applications of protein models in biomedical research. *Structure (London, England)*, *17*(2), 151–159. doi:10.1016/j.str.2008.12.014 PMID:19217386

Sibanda, B. L., Blundell, T. L., & Thornton, J. M. (1989). Conformation of hairpins in protein structures: A systematic classification with applications to modeling by homology, electron density fitting and protein engineering. *Journal of Molecular Biology*, *206*, 759–777. doi:10.1016/0022-2836(89)90583-4 PMID:2500530

Simons, K. T., Strauss, C., & Baker, D. (2001). Prospects for ab initio protein structural genomics. *Journal of Molecular Biology*, *306*, 1191–1199. doi:10.1006/jmbi.2000.4459 PMID:11237627

Skolnick, J., Fetrow, J. S., & Kolinski, A. (2000). Structural genomics and its importance for gene function analysis. *Nature Biotechnology*, *18*(3), 283–285. doi:10.1038/73723 PMID:10700142

Sonnhammer, E., von Heijne, G., & Krogh, A. (1998). A hidden Markov model for predicting transmembrane helices in protein sequences. *Proc ISMB, 6*, 175–182.

Tusnady, G., & Simon, I. (1998). Principles governing amino acid composition of integral membrane proteins: Application to topology prediction. *Journal of Molecular Biology*, *283*, 489–506. doi:10.1006/jmbi.1998.2107 PMID:9769220

Xu, J. (2005). Fold recognition by predicted alignment accuracy. *IEEE/ACM Transactions on Computational Biology and Bioinformatics*, *2*, 157–165. doi:10.1109/TCBB.2005.24 PMID:17044180

Xu, L. Z., S'anchez, R., Sali, A., & Heintz, N. (1996). Ligand specificity of brain lipid binding protein. *The Journal of Biological Chemistry*, *271*, 24711–24719. doi:10.1074/jbc.271.40.24711 PMID:8798739

Zhang, Y. (2008). Progress and challenges in protein structure. *Current Opinion in Structural Biology*, *18*(3), 342–348. doi:10.1016/j.sbi.2008.02.004 PMID:18436442

Zhou, H., Pandit, S. B., Lee, S. Y., Borreguero, J., Chen, H., Wroblewska, L., & Skolnick, J. (2007). Analysis of TASSER-based CASP7 protein structure prediction results. *Proteins*, *69*(8), 90–97. doi:10.1002/prot.21649 PMID:17705276

Zhou, H., & Zhou, Y. (2002). Distance-scaled, finite ideal-gas reference state improves structure-derived potentials of mean force for structure selection and stability prediction. *Protein Science*, *11*, 2714–2726. doi:10.1110/ps.0217002 PMID:12381853

KEY TERMS AND DEFINITIONS

Ab Initio Prediction: The ab initio structure prediction of proteins is to correctly characterize the 3D structure of a protein using only the amino acid sequence as input.

Insilico Analysis: The term 'in silico' is a modern word usually used to mean experimentation performed by computer and is related to the more commonly known biological terms in vivo and in vitro. These in silico methods include databases, quantitative structure-activity relationships, pharmacophores, homology models and other molecular modeling approaches, machine learning, data mining, network analysis tools and data analysis tools that use a computer.

Molecular Modeling: Molecular modeling is an application of computers to generate, manipulate, calculate and predict realistic molecular structures and associated properties. The techniques are mainly used in the fields of computational chemistry, drug design, computational biology and materials science for studying molecular systems.

Protein Structure: Proteins are single, unbranched chains of amino acid monomers. Protein structure is biological polymers composed of amino acids. Amino acids, linked together by peptide bonds, form a polypeptide chain. One or more polypeptide chains twisted into a 3-D shape form a protein. Proteins have complex shapes that include various folds, loops, and curves. Folding in proteins happens spontaneously.

Visualization Software: Visualization software is required to view the structure that is encoded by atomic coordinate PDB files and to be able to manipulate the images to view the molecule from various perspectives. Visualization typically takes the form of two dimensional displays, where interactive controls allow the user to explore and experience the three-dimensional structure of the protein under study.

Compilation of References

Abaide, A. R., Canha, L. N., Barin, A., & Cassel, G. (2010). *Assessment of the smart grids applied in reducing the cost of distribution system losses*. Paper presented at the Energy Market (EEM). London, UK. doi:10.1109/EEM.2010.5558678

Abbes, T. O., Bouhoula, A., & Rasinowitch, M. (2004). Protocol analysis in intrusion detection using decision tree. In *Proc. of Intl. Conf. on Information Technology*. IEEE.

Abraham, R., Simha, J. B., & Iyengar, S. S. (2007). Medical data mining with a new algorithm for feature selection and naïve Bayesian classifier. In *Proceedings of IEEE International Conference on Information Technology*, (pp. 44-49). IEEE.

Acharjya, D. P., & Ezhilarasi, L. (2011). A knowledge mining model for ranking institutions using rough computing with ordering rules and formal concept analysis. *International Journal of Computer Science Issues*, 8(2), 417–425.

Acharjya, D. P., & Tripathy, B. K. (2008). Rough sets on fuzzy approximation spaces and applications to distributed knowledge systems. *International Journal of Artificial Intelligence and Soft Computing*, 1(1), 1–14. doi:10.1504/IJAISC.2008.021260

Adhikari, A. N., Peng, J., Wilde, M., Xu, J., Freed, K. F., & Sosnick, T. R. (2012). Modeling large regions in proteins: Applications to loops, termini, and folding. *Protein Science*, 21(1), 107–121. doi:10.1002/pro.767 PMID:22095743

Afifi, A. A., & Azen, S. P. (1972). *Statistical analysis: A computer oriented approach*. New York: Academic Press Inc.

Agarwal, A., Pramod, P. J., & Jain, D. K. (2011). Implementation of IEEE 802.21 based media independent handover services. *Proceedings of the Asia-Pacific Advanced Network*, 32, 71–78. doi:10.7125/APAN.32.9

Agrawal, D., & Aggarwal, C. (2001). On the design and quantification of privacy preserving data mining algorithms. In *Proceedings of the Twentieth ACM SIGACT-SIGMOD-SIGART Symposium on Principles of Database Systems* (pp. 247-255). New York, NY: ACM.

Agrawal, R., Gehrke, J., Gunopulos, D., & Raghavan, P. (1998). Automatic subspace clustering of high dimensional data for data mining applications. In *Proceedings of ACM SIGMOD International Conference on Management of Data*. Seattle, WA: ACM.

Agrawal, R., Marlins, T., & Swami, A. (1993). Mining association rules between sets of items in large databases. In *Proceedings of International Conference on Management of Data* (pp. 207-216). Washington, DC: ACM.

Aha, D. W., & Bankert, R. L. (1995). A comparative evaluation of sequential feature selection algorithms. In *Proceedings of Fifth International Workshop on Artificial Intelligence and Statistics*. IEEE.

Ahmad, I., Ghafoor, A., & Mehrotra, K. (1991). Performance prediction of distributed load balancing on multicomputer systems. In *Proceedings of the 1991 ACM/IEEE Conference on Supercomputing* (pp. 830–839). ACM/IEEE.

Ahmed, S. N., Zolkipli, M. F., & Abdalla, A. N. (2009). Intrusion prevention system using IDS decision tree data mining. *Amrican Journal of Engg., & Applied sciences*, 2(4), 721-725.

Aiash, M., Mapp, G., Lasebae, A., & Phan, R. (2010). Providing security in 4G systems: Unveiling the challenges. In *Proceedings of Telecommunications (AICT), 2010 Sixth Advanced International Conference on* (pp. 439-444). IEEE.

Akan, A., & Edemen, C. (2010). Path to 4G wireless networks. In *Proceedings of Personal, Indoor and Mobile Radio Communications Workshops (PIMRC Workshops), 2010 IEEE 21st International Symposium on* (pp. 405-407). IEEE.

Akyildiz, I. F., Gutierrez-Estevez, D. M., & Reyes, E. C. (2010). The evolution to 4G cellular systems: LTE-advanced. *Physical Communication, 3*(4), 217–244. doi:10.1016/j.phycom.2010.08.001

Akyildiz, I. F., Xie, J., & Mohanty, S. (2004). A survey of mobility management in next-generation all-IP-based wireless systems. *IEEE Wireless Communications, 11*(4), 16–28. doi:10.1109/MWC.2004.1325888

Alavi, M., & Leidner, D. E. (1999). Knowledge management system: Issues, challenges, and benefits. *Communications of the AIS, 1*(7), 1–37.

Aleskerov, E., Freisleben, B., & Rao, B. (1997). CARD-WATCH: A neural network based database mining system for credit card fraud detection. In *Proceedings of the IEEE/IAFE 1997*. IEEE. doi:10.1109/CIFER.1997.618940

Ali, S., Siegel, H. J., Maheswaran, M., & Hensgen, D. (2000). Task execution time modeling for heterogeneous computing systems. In *Proceedings of Heterogeneous Computing Workshop*, (pp. 185–199). Academic Press.

Almuallim, H., & Dietterich, T. G. (1991). Learning with many irrelevant features. In *Proceedings of the Ninth National Conference*. Cambridge, MA: MIT Press.

Al-Shaer, & Hamed, H. H. (2004). Discovery of policy anomalies in distributed firewalls. In *Proc. of the 23rd Annual Joint Conf. on Computer and Communication Societies* (pp.2605-2616). IEEE.

Altschul, S. F., Madden, T. L., Schaefer, A. A., Zhang, J., Zhang, Z., Miller, W., & Lipman, D. J. (1997). Gapped BLAST and PSIBLAST: A new generation of protein database search programs. *Nucleic Acids Research, 25*, 3389–3402. doi:10.1093/nar/25.17.3389 PMID:9254694

Alves, R., Casanova, P., Quirogas, E., Ravelo, O., & Gimenez, W. (2006). *Reduction of non-technical losses by modernization and updating of measurement systems.* Paper presented at the Transmission & Distribution Conference and Exposition: Latin America, 2006. doi:10.1109/TDCLA.2006.311590

Ambard, M., Guo, B., Martinez, D., & Bermak, A. (2008). A spiking neural network for gas discrimination using a tin oxide sensor array. In *Proceedings of 4th IEEE International Symposium on Electronic Design, Test and Applications* (pp. 394-397). IEEE. doi:10.1109/DELTA.2008.116

Anderberg, M. R. (1973). *Cluster analysis for applications*. New York: Academic Press.

Andersen, N. P. S. (2001). The third generation partnership project (3GPP). *GSM and UMTS, 247*.

Arabie, L., & Hubert, L. P. (1994). Cluster analysis in marketing research. In *Advanced methods in marketing research*. Oxford, UK: Blackwell.

Arabie, P., Hubert, L. J., & Soete, G. D. (1996). *Clustering and classification*. World Scientific Publishing Co. doi:10.1142/1930

Aranha Neto, E. A. C., & Coelho, J. (2013). Probabilistic methodology for technical and non-technical losses estimation in distribution system. *Electric Power Systems Research, 97*, 93–99. doi:10.1016/j.epsr.2012.12.008

Armijo, L. (1966). Minimization of functions having Lipschitz continuous first partial derivatives. *Pacific Journal of Mathematics, 16*(1), 1–3. doi:10.2140/pjm.1966.16.1

Arnold, T., & Spell, S. C. (2006). The relationship between justice and benefits satisfaction. *Journal of Business and Psychology, 20*(4), 599–620. doi:10.1007/s10869-005-9006-1

Arora, R. (2002). Implementing KM – A balanced scorecard approach. *Journal of Knowledge Management, 6*(3), 240–249. doi:10.1108/13673270210434340

Arvetti, M., Gini, G., & Folgheraiter, M. (2007). Classification of EMG signals through wavelet analysis and neural networks for controlling active hand prosthesis. In *Proceedings of IEEE 10th International Conference on Rehabilitation Robotics*. IEEE.

Ashwin, M., Johannes, G., & Daniel, K. (2007). l-Diversity: Privacy beyond k-anonymity. *ACM Transactions on Knowledge Discovery from Data*, *1*(1), 1–52.

Atanassov, K. T. (1986). Intuitionistic fuzzy sets. *Fuzzy Sets and Systems*, *20*, 87–96. doi:10.1016/S0165-0114(86)80034-3

Attiya, G., & Hamam, Y. (2004). Two phase algorithm for load balancing in heterogeneous distributed systems. In Proceedings of Parallel, Distributed and Network-Based Processing, (pp. 434–439). Academic Press.

Attiya, G., & Hamam, Y. (2006). Task allocation for maximizing reliability of distributed systems: A simulated annealing approach. *Journal of Parallel and Distributed Computing*, *66*(10), 1259–1266. doi:10.1016/j.jpdc.2006.06.006

Austin, M. J., Ciaassen, J., Vu, C., & Mizrahi, P. (2008). Knowledge management: Implications for human service organizations. *Journal of Evidence-Based Social Work*, *5*(1-2), 361–389. doi:10.1300/J394v05n01_13 PMID:19064454

Awadh, A. M., & Saad, A. M. (2013). Impact of organizational culture on employee performance. *International Review of Management and Business Research*, *2*(1), 168–175.

B – School Directory. (2005). Largest listing of b-schools. *Business India*.

Baboulene, B. (1970). *Critical path made easy*. London: Gerald Duckworth & Company Limited.

Baha, H., & Dibi, Z. (2009). A novel neural network-based technique for smart gas sensors operating in a dynamic environment. *Sensors (Basel, Switzerland)*, *9*(11), 8944–8960. doi:10.3390/s91108944 PMID:22291547

Bai, D., Park, C., Lee, J., Nguyen, H., Singh, J., & Gupta, A. et al. (2012). LTE-advanced modem design: Challenges and perspectives. *IEEE Communications Magazine*, *50*(2), 178–186. doi:10.1109/MCOM.2012.6146497

Bairoch, A., & Apweiler, R. (2000). The SWISS-PROT protein sequence database and its supplement TrEMBL in 2000. *Nucleic Acids Research*, *28*, 45–48. doi:10.1093/nar/28.1.45 PMID:10592178

Baker, D., & Sali, A. (2001). Protein structure prediction and structural genomics. *Science*, *294*, 93–96. doi:10.1126/science.1065659 PMID:11588250

Baloria, U., Akhoon, B. A., Gupta, S. K., Sharma, S., & Verma, V. (2012). In silico proteomic characterization of human epidermal growth factor receptor 2 (HER-2) for the mapping of high affinity antigenic determinants against breast cancer. *Amino Acids*, *42*(4), 1349–1360. doi:10.1007/s00726-010-0830-x PMID:21229277

Banker, R. D., Charnes, A., & Cooper, W. W. (1984). Some models for estimating technical & scale efficiencies in data envelopment analysis. *Management Science*, *30*, 1078–1092. doi:10.1287/mnsc.30.9.1078

Barborak, M., Malek, M., & Dahbura, A. (1993). The consensus problem in fault-tolerant computing. *ACM Computing Surveys*, *25*(2), 171–219. doi:10.1145/152610.152612

Barrero, V., Grisales, E. V., Rosas, F., Sanchez, C., & Leon, J. (2001). Design and implementation of an intelligent interface for myoelectric controlled prosthesis. In *Proceedings of 23ʳᵈ Annual International Conference of the IEEE Engineering Medicine Biological Society*. IEEE.

Barzilai, J., & Borwein, J. M. (1988). Two point step size gradient methods. *IMA Journal of Numerical Analysis*, *8*, 141–148. doi:10.1093/imanum/8.1.141

Becher, A. (1999). Fault identification algorithm: A new formal approach. In *Proceedings of 29th Annual International Symposium on Fault Tolerant Computing*. Academic Press.

Beigh, B. M., & Peer, M. A. (2012). Intrusion detection and prevention system: Classification and quick review. *ARPN Journal of Science and Technology*, *2*(7), 661–675.

Belhoul, A. (2007). Quality of service (QoS) provisioning mechanisms in fourth generation (4G) wireless all-IP networks. *Paper for the degree of Doctor of Philosophy*.

Benoit, G. (2002). Data mining. *Annual Review of Information Science & Technology*, *36*, 265–310. doi:10.1002/aris.1440360107

Berberoglu, T., & Kaya, M. (2008). Hiding fuzzy association rules in quantitative data. In *Proceedings of International Conference on Grid and Pervasive Computing* (pp. 387-392). Kunming, China: IEEE Computer Society.

Berman, H. M., Westbrook, J., Feng, Z., Gilliland, G., Bhat, T. N., & Weissig, H. et al. (2000). The protein data bank. *Nucleic Acids Research*, *28*, 235–242. doi:10.1093/nar/28.1.235 PMID:10592235

Bettiol, M., Di Maria, E., & Grandinetti, R. (2012). Codification and creativity: Knowledge management strategies in KIBS. *Journal of Knowledge Management*, *16*(4), 550–562. doi:10.1108/13673271211246130

Bhat, N., & McAvoy, T. J. (1990). Use of neural nets for dynamic modeling and control of chemical process systems. *Computers & Chemical Engineering*, *14*, 573–583. doi:10.1016/0098-1354(90)87028-N

Bhat, N., Minderman, P. A., McAvoy, T. J., & Wang, N. S. (1990). Modeling chemical process systems via neural computation. *IEEE Control Systems Magazine*, 24–29. doi:10.1109/37.55120

Bidmeshgipour, M., Ismail, W. K. W., & Omar, R. (2012). Knowledge management and organizational innovativeness in Iranian banking industry. *Knowledge Management and E-Learning*, *4*(4), 481–499.

Bikos, A., & Sklavos, N. (2013). *LTE/SAE security issues on 4G wireless networks*.

Birasnav, M., & Rangnekar, S. (2010). Knowledge management structure and human capital development in Indian manufacturing industries. *Business Process Management Journal*, *16*(1), 57–75. doi:10.1108/14637151011017949

Birdi, T., & Jansen, K. (2006). Network intrusion detection: Know what you do (not) need. *Information System Control Journal*, *1*, 1–5.

Birgin, E. G., & Martinez, J. M. (1999). A spectral conjugate gradient method for unconstrained optimization. *Applied Mathematics & Optimization*, *43*, 117–128. doi:10.1007/s00245-001-0003-0

Biscarri, F., Monedero, Í., León, C., Guerrero, J. I., & Biscarri, J. (2009). A mining framework to detect non-technical losses in power utilities. In J. Cordeiro & J. Filipe (Eds.), *Proceedings of the 11th International Conference on Enterprise Information Systems* (pp. 96–101). IEEE.

Bloch, I. (2000). On links between mathematical morphology and rough sets. *The Journal of the Pattern Recognition Society*, 1487–1496.

Blough, D. M., & Brown, H. W. (1999). The broadcast comparison model for on-line fault diagnosis in multicomputer systems: Theory and implementation. *IEEE Transactions on Computers*, *48*(5), 470–493. doi:10.1109/12.769431

Blum, A. L., & Langley, P. (1997). Selection of relevant features and examples in machine learning. *Artificial Intelligence*, *97*, 245–271. doi:10.1016/S0004-3702(97)00063-5

Boca, A. D., & Park, D. C. (1994). Myoelectric signal recognition using fuzzy clustering and artificial neural networks in real time. In *Proceedings of IEEE International Conference on Neural Networks*, (vol. 5, pp. 3098-3103). IEEE.

Bogner, W. C., & Bansal, P. (2007). Knowledge management as the basis of sustained high performance. *Journal of Management Studies*, *44*(1), 165–188. doi:10.1111/j.1467-6486.2007.00667.x

Boles, J., Madupalli, R., Rutherford, B., & Wood, J. (2007). The relationship of facet of salesperson job satisfaction with affective organization commitment. *Journal of Business and Industrial Marketing*, *22*(5), 311–321. doi:10.1108/08858620710773440

Bollinger, A. S., & Smith, R. D. (2001). Managing organizational knowledge as a strategic asset. *Journal of Knowledge Management*, *5*(1), 8–18. doi:10.1108/13673270110384365

Boxma, O., Koole, G., & Liu, Z. (1994). *Queueing-theoretic solution methods for models of parallel and distributed systems. Centrum voor Wiskunde en Informatica*. Department of Operations Research, Statistics, and System Theory.

Brachmann, R., & Anand, T. (1996). The process of knowledge discovery in databases: A human centered approach. In *Advances in knowledge discovery and data mining*. Menlo Park, CA: AAAI Press.

Bradley, P. S., Fayyad, U. M., & Reina, C. A. (1998). *Scaling EM clustering to large databases*. Microsoft Research.

Braun, T., Siegel, H., Maciejewski, A., & Hong, Y. (2008). Static resource allocation for heterogeneous computing environments with tasks having dependencies, priorities, deadlines, and multiple versions. *Journal of Parallel and Distributed Computing*, *68*(11), 1504–1516. doi:10.1016/j.jpdc.2008.06.006

Brause, R., Langsdorf, T., & Hepp, M. (1999). Neural data mining for credit card fraud detection. In *Proceedings of the 11th IEEE International Conference on Tools with Artificial Intelligence*. IEEE. doi:10.1109/TAI.1999.809773

Breiman, L., Friedman, J. H., Olshen, R. A., & Stone, C. J. (1984). *Classification and regression trees*. Wadsworth.

Brocchieri, L., & Karlin. (1987). Prediction folding of short polypeptide segment by uniform conformational sampling. *Biopolymer, 26*, 137–168. doi:10.1002/bip.360260114

Brooks, I. (2006). *Organizational behavior: Individuals, groups and organization*. Essex, UK: Pearson Education.

Brun, A. D., Pinto, J. O., Pinto, A. M. A., Sauer, L., & Colman, E. (2009). Fraud detection in electric energy using differential evolution. In *Proceedings of the 15th International Conference on Intelligent System Applications to Power Systems*. IEEE. doi:10.1109/ISAP.2009.5352917

Bunch, J., Dongarra, J., Moler, C., & Stewart, G. (1979). *Linpack users guide*. Philadelphia, PA: SIAM.

Buntine, W. (1996). Graphical models for discovering knowledge. In U. Fayyad, G. Piatetsky-Shapiro, P. Smyth, & R. Uthurusay (Eds.), *Advances in knowledge discovery* (pp. 59–82). Cambridge, MA: AAAI Press/The MIT Press.

Business School Directory. (2005). *Dalal street*. Author.

Cabral, J. E., & Gontijo, E. M. (2004). Fraud detection in electrical energy consumers using rough sets. In *Proceedings of the 2004 IEEE International Conference on Systems, Man and Cybernetics*. IEEE. doi:10.1109/ICSMC.2004.1400905

Cabral, J. E., Pinto, J. O., & Pinto, A. M. A. (2009). Fraud detection system for high and low voltage electricity consumers based on data mining. In *Proceedings of the IEEE Power & Energy Society General Meeting*. IEEE. doi:10.1109/PES.2009.5275809

Cabral, J. E., Pinto, J. O., Martins, E. M., & Pinto, A. M. (2008). Fraud detection in high voltage electricity consumers using data mining. In *Proceedings of the Transmission and Distribution Conference and Exposition*. IEEE/PES. doi:10.1109/TDC.2008.4517232

Caffrey, J., & Hitchings, G. (1995). Makespan distributions in flow shop scheduling. *International Journal of Operations & Production Management, 15*(3), 50–58. doi:10.1108/01443579510080553

Calhoun, J. (2003). *Relative efficiencies of institutions of higher learning*. University of Georgia. Retrieved from http://www.arches.uga.edu/~calhounj/personal/deadisagg.pdf

Cameron, K. S., & Freeman, S. J. (1991). Cultural congruence, strength, and type: Relationships to effectiveness. *Research in Organizational Change and Development, 5*(2), 23–58.

Carter, E., & Hogue, J. (2006). *Intrusion prevention fundamentals*. CISCO Press.

Casavant, T., & Kuhl, J. (1988). A taxonomy of scheduling in general-purpose distributed computing systems. *IEEE Transactions on Software Engineering, 14*(2), 141–154. doi:10.1109/32.4634

Cavusgil, S. T., Calantone, R. J., & Zhao, Y. (2003). Tacit knowledge transfer and firm innovation capability. *Journal of Business and Industrial Marketing, 18*(1), 6–21. doi:10.1108/08858620310458615

Caydas, U., & Hascalik, A. (2008). Modeling and analysis of electrode wear and white layer thickness in die-sinking EDM process through response surface methodology. *International Journal of Advanced Manufacturing Technology, 38*(11-12), 1148–1156. doi:10.1007/s00170-007-1162-1

Cerqueira, E., Zeadally, S., Leszczuk, M., Curado, M., & Mauthe, A. (2011). Recent advances in multimedia networking. *Multimedia Tools and Applications, 54*(3), 635–647. doi:10.1007/s11042-010-0578-z

Céspedes, S., Shen, X., & Lazo, C. (2011). IP mobility management for vehicular communication networks: challenges and solutions. *IEEE Communications Magazine, 49*(5), 187–194. doi:10.1109/MCOM.2011.5762817

Chadha, S. K., & Kapoor, D. (2010). A study on knowledge management practices of auto component manufacturing companies in Ludhiana city. *The IUP Journal of Knowledge Management, 8*(1-2), 68–76.

Chalak, A., Harale, N. D., & Bhosale, R. (2011). Data mining techniques for intrusion detection and prevention system. *Intl. Journal of Computer Science and Network Security, 11*(8), 200–203.

Chan, C. C., & Grzymala Busse, J. (1989). Rough set boundaries as a tool for learning rules from examples. In *Proceedings of the ISMIS-89, 4th Int. Symposium on Methodologies for intelligent Systems*, (pp. 281 – 288). ISMIS.

Chan, P. K., Fan, W., Prodromidis, A. L., & Stolfo, S. J. (1999). Distributed data mining in credit card fraud detection. *IEEE Intelligent Systems and their Applications, 14*(6), 67–74. doi:10.1109/5254.809570

Chan, C. C., & Grzymala Busse, J. (1991). *On the attribute redundancy and the learning programs ID3, PRISM and LEM2*. Lawrence, KS: University of Kansas.

Chance, M. R., Bresnick, A. R., Burley, S. K., Jiang, J. S., Lima, C. D., & Sali, A. et al. (2002). Structural genomics: A pipeline for providing structures for the biologist. *Protein Science, 11*, 723–738. doi:10.1110/ps.4570102 PMID:11910018

Chang, G.-C., Kang, W.-J., Jer-Junn, L., Cheng, C.-K., Lai, J.-S., Chen, J.-J.J., & Kuo, T.-S. (1996). Real-time implementation of electromyogram pattern recognition as a control command of man-machine interface. *Journal of Medical Engineering and Physics, 18*(7), 529-537.

Chang, P., & Jeng, S. S. (2005). The application of back-propagation neural network of multi-channel piezoelectric quartz crystal sensor for mixed organic vapours. *Tamkang Journal of Science and Engineering, 5*, 209–217.

Chang, S., & Lee, M. S. (2007). A study on the relationship among leadership, organizational culture, the operation of learning organization and employees' job satisfaction. *The Learning Organization, 14*(2), 155–185. doi:10.1108/09696470710727014

Chan, H. A., Yokota, H., Xie, J., Seite, P., & Liu, D. (2011). Distributed and dynamic mobility management in mobile internet: current approaches and issues. *The Journal of Communication, 6*(1), 4–15.

Charalambous, C. (1992). Conjugate gradient algorithm for efficient training of artificial neural networks. *IEE Proceedings-G, 139*.

Charnes, A., Cooper, W. W., & Rhodes, E. (1978). Measuring efficiency of decision making units. *European Journal of Operational Research, 2*, 429–444. doi:10.1016/0377-2217(78)90138-8

Chauhan, R., Kaur, H., & Alam, M. A. (2010). Data clustering method for discovering clusters in spatial cancer databases. *International Journal of Computers and Applications, 10*(6), 24–28.

Chen, Y. S., & Lin, Y. W. (2012). *Protocols and applications of cross-layer in mobility management.*

Chen, C. P., Kernytsky, A., & Rost, B. (2002). Transmembrane helix predictions revisited. *Protein Science, 11*, 2774–2791. doi:10.1110/ps.0214502 PMID:12441377

Chen, M. S., Han, J., & Yu, P. S. (1996). Data mining: An overview from database perspective. *IEEE Transactions on Knowledge and Data Engineering, 8*, 866–883. doi:10.1109/69.553155

Chen, S., & Zhu, Y. (2004). Subpattern-based principle component analysis. *Pattern Recognition, 37*(5), 1081–1083. doi:10.1016/j.patcog.2003.09.004

Cheung, Y., & Xu, L. (2001). Independent component ordering in ICA time series analysis. *Neurocomputing, 41*, 145–152. doi:10.1016/S0925-2312(00)00358-1

Chiang, Y. S., Gelfand, T. I., Kister, A. E., & Gelfand, I. M. (2007). New classification of supersecondary structures of sandwich-like proteins uncovers strict patterns of strand assemblage. *Proteins, 68*(4), 915–921. doi:10.1002/prot.21473 PMID:17557333

Chiboiwa, M., Samuel, M., & Chipunza, C. (2011). Evaluation of job satisfaction and organizational citizenship behavior: Case study of selected organizations in Zimbabwe. *African Journal of Business Management, 5*(7), 2910–2918.

Choe, J. M. (2004). The consideration of cultural differences in the design of information systems. *Information & Management, 41*(5), 669–688. doi:10.1016/j.im.2003.08.003

Choi, M., Yu, J., Kim, H., & Maeng, S. (2003). Improving performance of a dynamic load balancing system by using number of effective tasks.[IEEE.]. *Proceedings of Cluster Computing, 2003*, 436–441.

Choi, Y., & Charlotte, M. D. (2009). FREAD revisited: Accurate loop structure prediction using a database search algorithm. *Proteins*, 78(6), 1431–1440. PMID:20034110

Chong, S. C., Salleh, K., Ahmad, S. N. S., & Sharifuddin, S. I. (2011). Knowledge management implementation in a public sector accounting organization: An empirical investigation. *Journal of Knowledge Management*, 15(3), 497–512. doi:10.1108/13673271111137457

Choo, K. K. R. (2011). The cyber thread landscape: Challenges and future research directions. *Computers & Security*, 30, 719–731. doi:10.1016/j.cose.2011.08.004

Chou, P. Y., & Fasman, G. D. (1974). Prediction of protein conformation. *Biochemistry*, 13(2), 222–245. doi:10.1021/bi00699a002 PMID:4358940

Chou, S. W. (2003). Computer systems to facilitating organizational learning: IT and organizational context. *Expert Systems with Applications*, 24(3), 273–280. doi:10.1016/S0957-4174(02)00155-0

Christakos, C. K., Izquierdo, A., Rouil, R., & Golmie, N. (2009). Using the media independent information service to support mobile authentication in fast mobile IPv6. In *Proceedings of Wireless Communications and Networking Conference, 2009*. IEEE.

Chu, J.-U., Moon, I., Lee, Y.-J., Kim, S.-K., & Mun, M.-S. (2007). A supervised feature-projection- based-real-time EMG pattern recognition for multifunction myoelectric hand control. *IEEE Transaction on Mechatronics*, 12(3), 282–290. doi:10.1109/TMECH.2007.897262

Clark, M. S. (1999). Comparative genomics: the key to understand the human genome project. *BioEssays*, 21, 121–130. doi:10.1002/(SICI)1521-1878(199902)21:2<121::AID-BIES6>3.0.CO;2-O PMID:10193186

Cohen, A. (2006). The relationship between multiple commitments and organizational citizenship behavior in Arab and Jewish culture. *Journal of Vocational Behavior*, 69(1), 105–118. doi:10.1016/j.jvb.2005.12.004

Cohen, F. E., & Presnell, S. R. (1996). The combinatorial approach. In *Protein structure prediction*. Oxford, UK: Oxford University Press.

Cohen, S. G., Chang, L., & Ledford, G. E. (2006). A hierarchical construct of self-management leadership and its relationship to quality of work life and perceived work group effectiveness. *Personnel Psychology*, 50(2), 275–308. doi:10.1111/j.1744-6570.1997.tb00909.x

Conti, M., Chong, S., Fdida, S., Jia, W., Karl, H., Lin, Y. D., & Zukerman, M. (2011). Research challenges towards the future internet. *Computer Communications*, 34(18), 2115–2134. doi:10.1016/j.comcom.2011.09.001

Cooper-Hakim, A., & Viswesvaran, C. (2005). The construct of work commitment: Testing an integrative framework. *Psychological Bulletin*, 131(2), 241–259. doi:10.1037/0033-2909.131.2.241 PMID:15740421

Corfield, A., Paton, R., & Little, S. (2013). Does knowledge management work in NGOs? A longitudinal study. *International Journal of Public Administration*, 36(3), 179–188. doi:10.1080/01900692.2012.749281

Correia, L. M. (2010). *Mobile broadband multimedia networks: Techniques, models and tools for 4G*. Access Online via Elsevier.

Corujo, D., Guimaraes, C., Santos, B., & Aguiar, R. L. (2011). Using an open-source IEEE 802.21 implementation for network-based localized mobility management. *IEEE Communications Magazine*, 49(9), 114–123. doi:10.1109/MCOM.2011.6011742

Crossan, M., Lane, H., & White, R. (1999). An organizational learning framework: From intuition to institution. *Academy of Management Review*, 34(3), 523–537.

Currie, G., & Kerrin, M. (2003). Human resource management and knowledge management: Enhancing knowledge sharing in a pharmaceutical company. *International Journal of Human Resource Management*, 14(6), 1027–1045. doi:10.1080/0958519032000124641

Cymerman, I., Feder, M., Pawłowski, M.A., Kurowski, J.M., & Bujnicki. (Eds.). (2004). Practical bioinformatics. *Nucleic Acids and Molecular Biology, 15*.

Daft, R. L. (2005). *The leadership experience*. Vancouver, Canada: Thomson-Southwestern.

Dahbura, A., Sabnani, K., & Henry, W. (1989). Spare capacity as a means of fault detection and diagnosis in multiprocessor systems. *IEEE Transactions on Computers, 38*(6), 881–891. doi:10.1109/12.24300

Dai, T., Liu, Q., Gao, J., Cao, Z., & Zhu, R. (2011). A new protein-ligand binding sites prediction method based on the integration of protein sequence conservation information. *BMC Bioinformatics, 12*(Suppl 14), S9. doi:10.1186/1471-2105-12-S14-S9 PMID:22373099

Dai, Y. H., & Yuan, Y. X. (2000). A nonlinear conjugate gradient with a strong global convergence properties. *SIAM Journal on Optimization, 10,* 177–182. doi:10.1137/S1052623497318992

Damnjanovic, A., Montojo, J., Wei, Y., Ji, T., Luo, T., Vajapeyam, M., & Malladi, D. (2011). A survey on 3GPP heterogeneous networks. *IEEE Wireless Communications, 18*(3), 10–21. doi:10.1109/MWC.2011.5876496

Dandamudi, S. (1998). Sensitivity evaluation of dynamic load sharing in distributed systems. *IEEE Concurrency, 6*(3), 62–72. doi:10.1109/4434.708257

Darroch, J. (2003). Developing a measure of knowledge management behaviors and practices. *Journal of Knowledge Management, 7*(5), 41–54. doi:10.1108/13673270310505377

Dash, M., Liu, H., & Motoda, H. (2000). Consistency based feature selection. In *Proceedings of Pacific-Asia Conference on Knowledge Discovery and Data Mining* (PAKDD), (pp. 98–109). PAKDD.

Dash, M., & Liu, H. (1997). Feature selection methods for classifications. *Intelligent Data Analysis, 1,* 131–156. doi:10.1016/S1088-467X(97)00008-5

Davenport, T. H., De Long, D. W., & Beers, M. C. (1998). Successful knowledge management projects. *Sloan Management Review, 39*(2), 43–57.

Davenport, T. H., & Harris, J. (2010). *Analytics at work: Smarter decisions, better results.* Cambridge, MA: Harvard Business Press.

Davenport, T. H., & Prusak, L. (1998). *Working knowledge: Managing what your organization knows.* Boston, MA: Harvard Business School Press.

Davis, A. B., & Goyal, S. K. (1992). Knowledge-based management of cellular clone fraud. In *Proceedings of the Third IEEE International Symposium on Personal, Indoor and Mobile Radio Communications.* IEEE. doi:10.1109/PIMRC.1992.279930

De La Oliva, A., Banchs, A., Soto, I., Melia, T., & Vidal, A. (2008). An overview of IEEE 802.21: Media-independent handover services. *IEEE Wireless Communications, 15*(4), 96–103. doi:10.1109/MWC.2008.4599227

De Long, D. W., & Fahey, L. (2000). Diagnosing cultural barriers to knowledge management. *The Academy of Management Executive, 14*(4), 113–128.

De Oliveira, M. E., Boson, D. F., & Padilha-Feltrin, A. (2008). A statistical analysis of loss factor to determine the energy losses. In *Proceedings of the Transmission and Distribution Conference and Exposition: Latin America.* IEEE/PES. doi:10.1109/TDC-LA.2008.4641691

Debar, H., Thomas, Y., Cuppens, F., & Cuppens-Boulahia, N. (2008). Response: Bridging the link between intrusion detection alerts and security policies. *Intrusion Detection Systems, 38,* 129–170.

Denison, D. R. (1990). *Corporate culture and organizational effectiveness.* New York, NY: John Wiley & Sons.

Denison, D. R., Haaland, S., & Goelzer, P. (2004). Corporate culture and organizational effectiveness: Is Asia different from the rest of the world? *Organizational Dynamics, 33*(1), 98–109. doi:10.1016/j.orgdyn.2003.11.008

Depuru, S. S. S., Wang, L., & Devabhaktuni, V. (2011). Support vector machine based data classification for detection of electricity theft. In *Proceedings of the Power Systems Conference and Exposition* (PSCE). IEEE/PES. doi:10.1109/PSCE.2011.5772466

Depuru, S. S. S., Wang, L., Devabhaktuni, V., & Gudi, N. (2010). Measures and setbacks for controlling electricity theft. In *Proceedings of the North American Power Symposium* (NAPS). IEEE. doi:10.1109/NAPS.2010.5619966

Depuru, S. S. S., Wang, L., Devabhaktuni, V., & Nelapati, P. (2011). A hybrid neural network model and encoding technique for enhanced classification of energy consumption data. In *Proceedings of the 2011 IEEE Power and Energy Society General Meeting.* IEEE. doi:10.1109/PES.2011.6039050

Desouza, K. C., & Awazu, Y. (2006). Knowledge management at SMEs: Five peculiarities. *Journal of Knowledge Management*, *10*(1), 32–43. doi:10.1108/13673270610650085

Devaney, M., & Ram, A. (1997). Efficient feature selection in conceptual clustering. In *Proceedings of the Fourteen International Conference on Machine Learning*. San Francisco, CA: Morgan Kaufmann.

Dhar, S., Purohit, R., Saini, N., Sharma, A., & Kumar, G. H. (2007). Mathematical modeling of electric - Discharge machining of cast Al-4Cu-6Si alloy-10 wt.% SiCP composites. *Journal of Materials Processing Technology*, *194*, 24–29. doi:10.1016/j.jmatprotec.2007.03.121

Dibitono, D. D., Eubank, P. T., Patel, M. R., & Barrufet, M. A. (1989). Theoretical model of the electrical discharge machining processes I: A simple cathode erosion model. *Journal of Applied Physics*, *66*, 4095–4103. doi:10.1063/1.343994

Dong, W., Quan-yu, W., Shou-yi, Z., Feng-xia, L., & Da-zhen, W. (2004). A feature extraction method for fraud detection in mobile communication networks. In *Proceedings of the Fifth World Congress on Intelligent Control and Automation, 2004*. IEEE. doi:10.1109/WCICA.2004.1340996

Doniavi, A., Eskandarzade, M., Abdi, A., & Totonchi, A. (2008). Empirical modeling of EDM parameters using grey relational analysis. *Asian Journal of Scietific Research*, *1*(5), 502–509. doi:10.3923/ajsr.2008.502.509

Donnelly, R. (2008). The management of consultancy knowledge: An internationally comparative analysis. *Journal of Knowledge Management*, *12*(6), 71–83. doi:10.1108/13673270810875877

Dorf, R. C., Bishop, R. H., & Cliffs, N. J. (2001). *Modern control systems*. Upper Saddle River, NJ: Prentice-Hall.

Dormann, C., & Zapf, D. (2001). Job satisfaction: A meta-analysis of stabilities. *Journal of Organizational Behavior*, *22*(5), 483–504. doi:10.1002/job.98

Dorronsoro, J. R., Ginel, F., Sgnchez, C., & Cruz, C. S. (1997). Neural fraud detection in credit card operations. *IEEE Transactions on Neural Networks*, *8*(4), 827–834. doi:10.1109/72.595879 PMID:18255686

Dos Angelos, E. W., Saavedra, O. R., Cortés, O. A., & de Souza, A. N. (2011). Detection and identification of abnormalities in customer consumptions in power distribution systems. *IEEE Transactions on Power Delivery*, *26*(4), 2436–2442. doi:10.1109/TPWRD.2011.2161621

Drew, D., Sjostrand, D., Nielsen, J., Urbig, T., Chin, C., de Gier, J., & von Heijne, G. (2002). Rapid topology mapping of escherichia coli inner-membrane proteins by prediction and PhoA/GFP fusion analysis. *Proceedings of the National Academy of Sciences of the United States of America*, *99*, 2690–2695. doi:10.1073/pnas.052018199 PMID:11867724

Dubois, D., & Prade, H. (1990). Rough fuzzy sets model. *International Journal of General Systems*, *46*(1), 191–208. doi:10.1080/03081079008935107

Duch, H. (2006). Filter methods. In I. Guyon, S. Gunn, M. Nikravesh, & L. Zadeh (Eds.), *Feature extraction, foundations and applications: Studies in fuzziness and soft computing* (pp. 89–118). Berlin: Springer Verlag.

Dunbrack, R. L. Jr, Dunker, K., & Godzik, A. (2000). Protein structure prediction in biology and medicine. *Pacific Symposium on Biocomputing. Pacific Symposium on Biocomputing*, *12*, 93–94. PMID:10902159

Duncan, R., & Weiss, A. (1979). Organizational learning: Implications for organizational design. *Research in Organizational Behavior*, *1*, 75–123.

Dunham, M. H. (2003). *Data mining introductory and advanced topics*. Upper Saddle River, NJ: Pearson Education, Inc.

Durst, S., & Edvardsson, I. R. (2012). Knowledge management in SMEs: A literature review. *Journal of Knowledge Management*, *16*(6), 879–903. doi:10.1108/13673271211276173

Dutt, H., Qamar, F., & Jha, V. S. (2011). A research to identify knowledge orientation in Indian commercial banks. *International Journal of Knowledge Management Studies*, *4*(4), 389–418. doi:10.1504/IJKMS.2011.048435

Dvivedi, A., Kumar, P., & Singh, I. (2008). Experimental investigation and optimisation in EDM of al 6063 SiCp metal matrix composite. *International Journal of Machining and Machinability of Materials*, *3*(3-4), 293–308. doi:10.1504/IJMMM.2008.020965

Dy, J. G., & Brodley, C. E. (2000). Feature subset selection and order identification for unsupervised learning. In *Proceedings of Seventeenth International Conference on Machine Learning*. Palo Alto, CA: Stanford University.

Dy, J. G., & Brodley, C. E. (2004). Feature selection for unsupervised learning. *Journal of Machine Learning Research, 5,* 845–889.

Eduard, L. et al. (2001). Multicomponent gas mixture analysis using a single tin oxide sensor and dynamic pattern recognition. *IEEE Sensors Journal, 1*(3), 207–213. doi:10.1109/JSEN.2001.954833

Eisen, M., Spellman, P. T., Brown, P. O., & Botstein, D. (1998). Cluster analysis and display of genome-wide expression patterns. *Proceedings of the National Academy of Sciences of the United States of America, 95,* 14863–14868. doi:10.1073/pnas.95.25.14863 PMID:9843981

Elhadef, M., & Becher, A. (2000). An evolutionary algorithm for identifying faults in t-diagnosable systems. In *Proc. of the 19th Symp. on Reliable Dist. Syst.,* (pp. 74–83). Academic Press.

Elhadef, M., & Becher, A. (2001). Efficient comparison-based fault diagnosis of multiprocessor systems using an evolutionary approach. In *Proceedings of Int. Symposium on Parallel and Distributed Processing*. Academic Press.

Elhadef, M., Das, S., & Nayak, A. (2006). A novel artificial immune based approach for system level fault diagnosis. In *Proc. of First International Conference on Availability, Reliability and Security*. Academic Press.

Elman, J. (1990). Finding structure in time. *Cognitive Science, 14,* 179–211. doi:10.1207/s15516709cog1402_1

Englehart, K., Hudgins, B., & Parker, P. A. (2000). Time-frequency based classification of the myoelectric signal: Static vs dynamic contractions. In *Proceedings of 22ⁿᵈ Annual International Conference of the IEEE Engineering Medicine Biological Society*. IEEE.

Englehart, K., & Hudgins, B. (2003). A robust, real-time control scheme for multifunction myoelectric control. *IEEE Transactions on Bio-Medical Engineering, 50*(7), 848–854. doi:10.1109/TBME.2003.813539 PMID:12848352

Englehart, K., Hudgins, B., & Parker, P. A. (2001). A wavelet-based continuous classification scheme for multifunction myoelectric control. *IEEE Transactions on Bio-Medical Engineering, 48*(3), 302–310. doi:10.1109/10.914793 PMID:11327498

Eswar, N., Eramian, D., Webb, B., Shen, M. Y., & Sali, A. (2008). Protein structure modeling with MODELLER. *Methods in Molecular Biology (Clifton, N.J.), 426,* 145–159. doi:10.1007/978-1-60327-058-8_8 PMID:18542861

Everitt, B. S., Landau, S., & Leese, M. (2001). *Cluster analysis*. New York: Oxford University Press.

Fahey, D. W. (2002). *Twenty questions and answers about the ozone layer*. National Oceanic and Atmospheric Administration. Retrieved from http://www.esrl.noaa.gov/csd/assessments/ozone/2010/twentyquestions/

Fanning, K., Cogger, K. O., & Srivastava, R. (1995). Detection of management fraud: A neural network approach. In *Proceedings of the 11th Conference on Artificial Intelligence for Applications*. IEEE. doi:10.1109/CAIA.1995.378820

Farry, K. A., Walker, I. D., & Baramiuk, R. G. (1996). Myoelectric teleoperation of a complex robotic hand. *IEEE Transactions on Robotics and Automation, 12*(5), 775–788. doi:10.1109/70.538982

Fayyad, U. M., Haussler, D., & Stolorz, Z. (1996a). KDD for science data analysis: Issues and examples. In *Proceedings of Second International Conference on Knowledge Discovery and Data Mining*. AAAI Press.

Fayyad, U. M., Shapiro, G. P., Smyth, P., & Uthurusamy, R. (Eds.). (1996). *Advances in knowledge discovery and data mining*. Cambridge, MA: MIT Press.

Fayyad, U., Grinstein, G. G., & Wierse, A. (2002). *Information visualization in data mining and knowledge discovery*. San Francisco: Morgan Kaufmann Publishers.

Fayyad, U., Piatetsky-Shapiro, G., & Smyth, P. (1996). Data mining to knowledge discovery-A review. In *Advances in knowledge discovery*. AAAI Press/The MIT Press.

Ferguson, S., Burford, S., & Kennedy, M. (2013). Divergent approaches to knowledge and innovation in the public sector. *International Journal of Public Administration, 36*(3), 168–178. doi:10.1080/01900692.2012.749278

Fernandes, S., & Karmouch, A. (2012). Vertical mobility management architectures in wireless networks: A comprehensive survey and future directions. *IEEE Communications Surveys & Tutorials, 14*(1), 45–63. doi:10.1109/SURV.2011.082010.00099

Fidanova, S. (2006). Simulated annealing for grid scheduling problem. In *Proceedings of Modern Computing, 2006*. IEEE.

Fischer, D. (2006). Servers for protein structure prediction. *Current Opinion in Structural Biology, 16*, 178–182. doi:10.1016/j.sbi.2006.03.004 PMID:16546376

Fiser, A., & Sali, A. (2003). ModLoop: Automated modeling of loops in protein structures. *Bioinformatics (Oxford, England), 19*(18), 2500–2601. doi:10.1093/bioinformatics/btg362 PMID:14668246

Fisher, D. H. (1995). Iterative optimization and simplification of hierarchical clustering. In *Proceedings of the First International Conference on Knowledge Discovery & Data Mining*. AAAI Press.

Fisher, D. H., Pazzani, M. J., & Langley, P. (1991). *Concept formation: Knowledge and experience in unsupervised learning*. San Mateo, CA: Morgan Kaufmann Publishers.

Fisher, D., & Eisenberg, D. (1996). Protein fold recognition using sequence-derived predictions. *Protein Science, 5*, 947–955. doi:10.1002/pro.5560050516 PMID:8732766

Fletcher, R. (1987). *Practical methods of optimization*. New York: John Wiley & Sons.

Fletcher, R., & Reeves, C. M. (1964). Function minimization by conjugate gradients. *The Computer Journal, 7*, 149–154. doi:10.1093/comjnl/7.2.149

Flores, L. G., Zheng, W., Rau, D., & Thomas, C. H. (2012). Organizational learning subprocess identification, construct validation, and an empirical test of cultural antecedents. *Journal of Management, 38*(2), 640–667. doi:10.1177/0149206310384631

Fogarty, T. (1994). Public accounting experience: The influence of demographic and organizational attributes. *Managerial Auditing Journal, 9*(7), 12–20. doi:10.1108/02686909410067552

Freeman, J. A., & Skapura, D. M. (2003). *A neural network algorithms, applications and programming techniques*. Upper Saddle River, NJ: Pearson Education.

Fugate, B. S., Stank, T. P., & Mentzer, J. T. (2009). Linking improved knowledge management to operational and organizational performance. *Journal of Operations Management, 27*(3), 247–264. doi:10.1016/j.jom.2008.09.003

Gantz, J. F. (2008). *The diverse and exploding digital universe*. Retrieved from http://www.emc.com/collateral/analyst-reports/diverse-exploding-digital-universe.pdf

Gao, Q., Zhang, Q., Su, S., Zhang, J., & Ge, R. (2008). Predictive models and generalization performance study in electrical discharge machining. *Applied Mechanics and Materials*, (10-12), 677–681.

Gao, J., Xia, L., Lu, M., Zang, B., & Wang, I. (2012). TM7SF1 (GPR137B), a novel lysosome Integral membrane protein. *Molecular Biology Reports, 39*(9), 8883–8889. doi:10.1007/s11033-012-1755-0 PMID:22729905

Garey, M., & Johnson, D. (1979). *Computing and intractability, a guide to the theory of NP-completeness*. New York: W.H. Freeman and Company.

Garrate, B. (1990). An old idea that has come of age. *People Management, 1*(19), 25–28.

Geetha, M. A., Acharjya, D. P., & Iyengar, N. C. S. N. (2014). *Privacy preservation in fuzzy association rules using rough computing and DSR*. Cybernetics and Information Technologies.

Geethanjali, P., & Ray, K. K. (2011). Identification of motion from multi-channel EMG signals for control of prosthetic hand. *Australasian Physical & Engineering Sciences in Medicine, 34*, 419–427. doi:10.1007/s13246-011-0079-z PMID:21667211

Gemignani, M., Tahan, C., Oliveira, C., & Zamora, F. (2009). Commercial losses estimations through consumers' behavior analysis. In *Proceedings of the 20th International Conference and Exhibition on Electricity Distribution - Part 1*. IET.

Ghosh, S., & Reilly, D. L. (1994). Credit card fraud detection with a neural-network. In *Proceedings of the Twenty-Seventh Hawaii International Conference on System Sciences*. IEEE. doi:10.1109/HICSS.1994.323314

Ghosh, S. (2010). *Distributed systems: An algorithmic approach.* Boca Raton, FL: CRC Press.

Gilmour, J., & Wang, L. (2002). Detection of process abnormality in food extruder using principle component analysis. *Chemical Engineering Science, 57*(7), 1091–1098. doi:10.1016/S0009-2509(01)00432-8

Ginalski, K. (2006). Comparative modeling for protein structure prediction. *Current Opinion in Structural Biology, 16*, 172–177. doi:10.1016/j.sbi.2006.02.003 PMID:16510277

Ginalski, K., & Rychlewski, L. (2003). Protein structure prediction of CASP5 comparative modeling and fold recognition targets using consensus alignment approach and 3D assessment. *Proteins, 53*(Suppl 6), 410–417. doi:10.1002/prot.10548 PMID:14579329

Golbasi, Z., Kelleci, M., & Dogan, S. (2008). Relationships between coping strategies, individual characteristics and job satisfaction in a sample of hospital nurses: Cross-sectional questionnaire survey. *International Journal of Nursing Studies, 45*(12), 1800–1806. doi:10.1016/j.ijnurstu.2008.06.009 PMID:18703192

Gold, A. H., Malhora, A., & Segars, A. H. (2001). Knowledge management: An organizational capabilities perspective. *Journal of Management Information Systems, 18*(1), 185–214.

Goldberg, D. E. (2013). *Genetic algorithms in search, optimization, and machine learning.* Upper Saddle River, NJ: Pearson Education.

Goldberg, D. E., & Holland, J. H. (1988). Genetic algorithms and machine learning. *Machine Learning, 3*(2), 95–99. doi:10.1023/A:1022602019183

Goldstein, A. A. (1967). *Constructive real analysis.* New York: Harper & Row Publishers.

Goldstein, M. (2008). Carbon monoxide poisoning. *Journal of Emergency Nursing: JEN.* doi:10.1016/j.jen.2007.11.014

Gondara, M. K., & Kadam, S. (2011). Requirements of vertical handoff mechanism in 4G wireless networks. *arXiv preprint arXiv:1105.0043.*

Gonzalez, G., & Figueroa, L. (2006). Strategic plan for the control and reduction of non-technical losses applied in C.A. Energia ElÃƒÂ©ctrica de Valencia. In *Proceedings of the Transmission & Distribution Conference and Exposition: Latin America, 2006.* IEEE/PES. doi:10.1109/TDCLA.2006.311491

Gopal, T., Nataraj, N., Ramamurthy, C., & Sankaranarayanan, V. (1996). Load balancing in heterogenous distributed systems. *Microelectronics and Reliability, 36*(9), 1279–1286. doi:10.1016/0026-2714(95)00133-6

Gordon, G. G., & DiTomaso, N. (1992). Predicting corporate performance from organizational culture. *Journal of Management Studies, 29*(6), 783–798. doi:10.1111/j.1467-6486.1992.tb00689.x

Graupe, D., Magnussen, J., & Beex, A. A. (1978). A microprocessor system for multifunctional control of upper-limb prostheses via myoelectric signal identification. *IEEE Transactions on Automatic Control, 23*(4), 538–544. doi:10.1109/TAC.1978.1101783

Greene, W. (2001). Dynamic load-balancing via a genetic algorithm. In *Proceedings of Tools with Artificial Intelligence* (pp. 121–128). Academic Press.

Greiner, M. E., Bohmann, T., & Krcmar, H. (2007). A strategy for knowledge management. *Journal of Knowledge Management, 11*(6), 3–15. doi:10.1108/13673270710832127

Griffith, D., Rouil, R., & Golmie, N. (2010). Performance metrics for IEEE 802.21 media independent handover (MIH) signaling. *Wireless Personal Communications, 52*(3), 537–567. doi:10.1007/s11277-008-9629-4

Grosu, D., Chronopoulos, A., & Leung, M. (2002). Load balancing in distributed systems: An approach using cooperative games. In *Proceedings of Parallel and Distributed Processing Symposium* (pp. 52–61). Academic Press.

Grosu, D., & Chronopoulos, A. (2004). Algorithmic mechanism design for load balancing in distributed systems. *IEEE Transactions on Systems, Man, and Cybernetics. Part B, Cybernetics, 34*(1), 77–84. doi:10.1109/TSMCB.2002.805812 PMID:15369053

Grzymala Busse, J. (1988). Knowledge acquisition under uncertainty- a rough set approach. *Journal of Intelligent & Robotic Systems, 1*, 3–16. doi:10.1007/BF00437317

Guarino, C. G. R., Chun, M., & Buddin, R. (2005). Latent variable analysis: A new approach to university ranking. *Higher Education in Europe, 30*(2). doi:10.1080/03797720500260033

Guerrero, J. I., León, C., Biscarri, F., Monedero, I., Biscarri, J., & Millán, R. (2010). Increasing the efficiency in non-technical losses detection in utility companies. In *Proceedings of the MELECON 2010 - 2010 15th IEEE Mediterranean. Electrotechnical Conference*. IEEE. doi:10.1109/MELCON.2010.5476320

Guha, S., Rastogi, R., & Shim, K. (1998). CURE: An efficient clustering algorithm for large databases. In *Proceedings of ACM SIGMOD International Conference on Management of Data*, (pp. 73 – 84). ACM.

Gunasekaran, A., & Ngai, E. W. (2007). Knowledge management in 21st century manufacturing. *International Journal of Production Research, 45*(11), 2391–2418. doi:10.1080/00207540601020429

Guo, A. (2004). A new framework for clustering algorithm evaluation in the domain of functional genomics. In *Proceedings of ACM Symposium on Applied Computing*, (pp. 143–146). ACM.

Guo, X. Yang., P., Chen, L., Wang, X. & Li, L. (2006). Study of the control mechanism of robot-prosthesis based-on the EMG processed. In *Proceedings of 6ᵗʰ World Congress on Intelligent Control and Automation*. IEEE.

Guo, X., Yu, H., Zhen, G., Liu, Y., Zhang, Y., & Zhang, Y. (2009). Artificial intelligent based human motion pattern recognition and prediction for the surface electromyographic signals. In *Proceedings of International Conference on Information Technology and Computer Science*, (pp.289-292). IEEE.

Gupta, J., & Sharma, S. (2004). *Creating knowledge based organization*. Boston, MA: Idea Group Publishing.

Gu, Z., & Siu, R. C. S. (2009). Drivers of job satisfaction as related to work performance in Macao casino hotels: An investigation based on employee survey. *International Journal of Contemporary Hospitality Management, 21*(5), 561–578. doi:10.1108/09596110910967809

Hakimi., S., & Chwa, K. (1981). Schemes for fault tolerant computing: A comparison of modularly redundant and t-diagnosable systems. *Inform. Contr.*, 212–238.

Hakimi, S. L., & Amin, A. T. (1975). Characterization of the connection assignment of diagnosable systems. *IEEE Transactions on Computers*, 1040–1042.

Hall, B. P. (2001). Values development and learning organizations. *Journal of Knowledge Management, 5*(1), 19–32. doi:10.1108/13673270110384374

Hall, M., & Lloyd, S. (1997). Feature subset selection: A correlation based filter approach. In *Neural information processing and intelligent information systems*. Berlin: Springer.

Hambaba, M. L. (1996). Intelligent hybrid system for data mining. In *Proceedings of the IEEE/IAFE 1996 Conference on Computational Intelligence for Financial Engineering, 1996*. IEEE. doi:10.1109/CIFER.1996.501832

Hamidzadeh, B., Atif, Y., & Lilja, D. (1995). Dynamic scheduling techniques for heterogeneous computing systems. *Concurrency (Chichester, England), 7*(7), 633–652. doi:10.1002/cpe.4330070705

Han, L. (2010). Research and implementation of an anomaly detection model based on clustering analysis. In *Proceedings of the 2010 International Symposium on Intelligence Information Processing and Trusted Computing (IPTC)*. IEEE. doi:10.1109/IPTC.2010.94

Hand, D. J., Mannila, H., & Smyth, P. (2001). *Principles of data mining*. Cambridge, MA: MIT Press.

Han, J., & Kamber, M. (2000). *Data mining: Concepts and techniques*. San Francisco: Morgan Kaufmann Publisher.

Hannaford, B., & Lehman, S. (1986). Short time Fourier analysis of the electromyogram: Fast movements and constant contraction. *IEEE Transactions on Bio-Medical Engineering, 33*(12), 1173–1181. doi:10.1109/TBME.1986.325697 PMID:3817851

Hanvanich, S., Sivakumar, K., Tomas, G., & Hult, M. (2006). The relationship of learning and memory with organizational performance: The moderating role of turbulence. *Journal of the Academy of Marketing Science, 34*(4), 600–612. doi:10.1177/0092070306287327

Hargrove, L., Englehart, K., & Hudgins, B. (2006). The effect of electrode displacements on pattern recognition based myoelectric control. In *Proceedings 28th Annual International Conference of the IEEE Engineering Medicine Biological Society*. IEEE.

Hargrove, L., Losier, L., Lock, B., Englehart, K., & Hudgins, B. (2007). A real-time pattern recognition based myoelectric control usability study implemented in a virtual environement. In *Proceedings of 29th Annual International Conference of the IEEE Engineering Medicine Biological Society*. IEEE.

Hargrove, L., Guangline, L., Englehart, K., & Hudgins, B. (2009). Principal components analysis preprocessing for improved classification accuracies in pattern-recognition-based myoelectric control. *IEEE Transactions on Bio-Medical Engineering*, 56(5), 1407–1414. doi:10.1109/TBME.2008.2008171 PMID:19473932

Harris, R. L. (1999). *Information graphics: A comprehensive illustrated reference*. Oxford, UK: Oxford Press.

Harris, S. G., & Mossholder, K. W. (1996). The affective implications of perceived congruence with culture dimensions during organizational transformation. *Journal of Management*, 22(4), 527–547. doi:10.1177/014920639602200401

Haupt, R. L., & Haupt, S. E. (2004). *Practical genetic algorithms*. New York: John Wiley & Sons.

Hauschild, S., Licht, T., & Stein, W. (2001). Creating a knowledge culture. *The McKinsey Quarterly*, 74(1), 74–82.

Hayes, M., & Walsham, G. (2003). Knowledge sharing and ICTs: A relational perspective. In M. Easterby-Smith, & M. A. Lyles (Eds.), *The Blackwell handbook of organizational learning and knowledge management* (pp. 54–57). Malden, MA: Blackwell.

Haykin, S. (2005). *Neural networks a comprehensive foundation*. Delhi, India: Pearson Prentice Hall.

Health Behavior in School-Aged Children (HBSC). (n.d.). Retrieved from http://www.hbsc.org

Heisig, P. (2009). Harmonisation of knowledge management: Comparing 160 KM frameworks around the globe. *Journal of Knowledge Management*, 13(4), 4–31. doi:10.1108/13673270910971798

Hestenes, M. R., & Stiefel, E. (1952). Methods for conjugate gradients for solving linear systems. *Journal of Research of the National Bureau of Standards*, 49, 409–436. doi:10.6028/jres.049.044

Hinneburg, A., & Keim, D. A. (1998). An efficient approach to clustering in large multimedia databases with noise. *Knowledge Discovery and Data Mining*, 58–65.

Hipp, J., Guntzer, U., & Nakhaeizadeh, G. (2000). Algorithms for association rule mining-A general survey and comparison. *SIGKDD Explorations*, 2(2), 1–58.

Hochbaum, D. S. (2003). *Approximation algorithms for NP-hard problems*. Thomson Asia Pte Ltd.

Hofstede, G., Neuijen, B., Ohayv, D. D., & Sanders, G. (1990). Measuring organizational cultures: A qualitative and quantitative study across twenty cases. *Administrative Science Quarterly*, 35(2), 286–316. doi:10.2307/2393392

Holm, C., & Nad Sander, L. (1996). Mapping the protein universe. *Science*, 2(273), 595–603. doi:10.1126/science.273.5275.595 PMID:8662544

Holowetzki, A. (2002). *The relationship between knowledge management and organizational culture: An examination of cultural factors that support the flow and management of knowledge within an organization*. Eugene, OR: Applied Information Management Program.

Hong, J. (2001). *Knowledge innovation and organization learning*. Taipei: Wu-Nan Publisher.

Horiuchi, J., Kikuchi, S., Kobayashi, M., Kanno, T., & Shimizu, T. (2001). Modeling of pH response in continuous anaerobic acidogenesis by an artificial neural network. *Biochemical Engineering Journal*, 9, 199–204. doi:10.1016/S1369-703X(01)00153-X

Horowitz, E., Sahni, S., & Rajasekaran, S. (2003). *Fundamentals of computer algorithms*. New Delhi: Galgotia Publications.

Horowitz, J. (1967). *Critical path scheduling management control through CPM and PERT*. New York: The Ronald Press Company.

Huang, H.-P., Liu, Y.-H., & Wong, C.-S. (2003). Automatic EMG feature evaluation for controlling a prosthetic hand using supervised feature mining method: An intelligent approach. In *Proceedings of IEEE International Conference on Robotics and Automation*. IEEE.

Huang, L. S., & Lai, C. P. (2012). An investigation on critical success factors for knowledge management using structural equation modeling. *Technology Management*, *40*, 24–30.

Huang, Y., Englehart, K., Hudgins, B., & Chan, A. D. C. (2005). A gaussian mixture model based classification scheme for myoelectric control of powered upper limb prostheses. *IEEE Transactions on Bio-Medical Engineering*, *52*(11), 1801–1901. doi:10.1109/TBME.2005.856295 PMID:16285383

Huber, G. P. (1991). Organizational learning: The contributing processes and the literatures. *Organization Science*, *2*(1), 88–115. doi:10.1287/orsc.2.1.88

Hudgins, B., Parker, P., & Scott, R. N. (1993). A new strategy for multifunction myoelectric control. *IEEE Transactions on Bio-Medical Engineering*, *40*(1), 82–94. doi:10.1109/10.204774 PMID:8468080

Hu, Q. H., Liu, J. F., & Yu, D. R. (2008). Mixed feature selection based on granulation and approximation. *Knowledge-Based Systems*, *21*, 294–304. doi:10.1016/j.knosys.2007.07.001

Hu, Q. H., Pedrycz, W., Yu, D. R., & Lang, J. (2010). Selecting discrete and continuous measures based on neighborhood decision error minimization. *IEEE Transactions on Systems, Man, and Cybernetics. Part B, Cybernetics*, *40*, 137–150. doi:10.1109/TSMCB.2009.2024166

Hu, Q. H., Yu, D. R., Liu, J. F., & Wu, C. X. (2008). Neighborhood rough set based heterogeneous feature selection. *Information Sciences*, *178*, 3577–3594. doi:10.1016/j.ins.2008.05.024

Hu, Q. H., Yu, D. R., & Xie, Z. X. (2008). Neighborhood classifiers. *Expert Systems with Applications*, *34*, 866–876. doi:10.1016/j.eswa.2006.10.043

Hutchison, D., Kanade, T., Kittler, J., Kleinberg, J. M., Mattern, F., & Mitchell, J. C. … Millán, R. (2010). Using regression analysis to identify patterns of non-technical losses on power utilities. In R. Setchi, I. Jordanov, R. J. Howlett, & L. C. Jain (Eds.), *Knowledge-based and intelligent information and engineering systems* (Vol. 6276, pp. 410–419). Berlin, Germany: Springer. Retrieved from http://www.springerlink.com/content/43m1340538478854/

Hu, V., Wang, W., & Zhao, K. (2011). The design and implementation of trusted communication protocol for intrusion prevention system. *Journal of Convergence Information Technology*, *6*, 55–62. doi:10.4156/jcit.vol6.issue3.7

Hwang, K. F., & Chang, C. C. (2002). A fast pixel mapping algorithm using principal component analysis. *Pattern Recognition Letters*, *23*(14), 1747–1753. doi:10.1016/S0167-8655(02)00148-4

Hwang, K., Fox, G., & Dongarra, J. (2012). *Distributed and cloud computing: From parallel processing to the internet of things*. San Francisco: Morgan Kaufmann.

Iglesias, J. M. (2006). Follow-up and preventive control of non-technical losses of energy in C.A. Electricidad de Valencia. In *Proceedings of the Transmission & Distribution Conference and Exposition: Latin America, 2006*. IEEE. doi:10.1109/TDCLA.2006.311381

Iqbal, M. K., Iqbal, M. B., Rasheed, I., & Sandhu, A. (2012). 4G evolution and multiplexing techniques with solution to implementation challenges. In *Proceedings of Cyber-Enabled Distributed Computing and Knowledge Discovery (CyberC), 2012 International Conference on* (pp. 485-488). IEEE.

Ito, K., Tsukamoto, M., & Kondo, T. (2008). Discrimination of intended movements based on nonstationary EMG for a prosthetic hand control. In *Proceedings of 3rd International Symposium on Communications, Control and Signal Processing*. IEEE.

Jaharah, A. G., Liang, Wahid, S. Z., Rahman, M. N. A., & Hassan, C. H. C. (2008). Performance of copper electrode in electrical discharge machining (EDM) of AISI H13 harden steel. *International Journal of Mechanical and Materials Engineering*, *3*(1), 25–29.

Jiang, M. W., Wang, R. C., Wang, J. Z., & Jin, D. W. (2005). A method of recognizing finger motion using wavelet transform of surface EMG signal. In *Proceedings of. 27ᵗʰ Annual International Conference of the IEEE Engineering Medicine Biological Society*. IEEE.

Jiang, N., Wu, W. X., & Mitchell, I. (2005). Protein folds recognition using neural networks and support vector machines. In *Proceeding of the 6ᵗʰ International Conference on Intelligent Data Engineering and Automated Learning-IDEAL*. Springer-Verlag.

Jie, V., Xiao, Z., Yabin, L., & Chenghui, S. (2009). Intrusion prevention in depth system research based on data mining. *International Journal of Distributed Sensor Networks, 5*(22).

Jin, S., So Yeung, D., Wang, X., & Tsang, E. C. (2005). A feature space analysis for anomaly detection. In *Proceedings of the 2005 IEEE International Conference on Systems, Man and Cybernetics*. IEEE. doi:10.1109/ICSMC.2005.1571706

Jin, W., Tung, A. K. H., Han, J., & Wang, W. (2006). Ranking outliners using symmetric neighborhood relationship. In *Proceedings of PAKDD*, (pp. 577–593). PAKDD.

Johannessen, J. A., Olsen, B., & Olaisen, J. (1999). Aspects of innovation theory based knowledge management. *Journal of International Management, 19*(2), 121–139.

John, G. H., Kohavi, R., & Pfleger, K. (1994). Irrelevant features and the subset selection problem. In *Proceedings of the Eleventh International Conference on Machine Learning*, (pp. 121-129). IEEE.

John, S. (2006). Adapting an enterprise software security framework. *IEEE Security and privacy Journal, 4*(2), 84-87.

John, S. (2011). Research challenges in the migration to future mobile systems. In *Proceedings of Current Trends in Information Technology (CTIT), 2011 International Conference and Workshop on* (pp. 92-96). IEEE.

Johnes, G., & Johnes, J. (n.d.). Measuring the research performance of UK economics departments: An application of data envelopment analysis. *Oxford Economics Papers, 4*(2), 332-347.

Johnes, J. (1993). *Measuring teaching efficiency in higher education: an application of data envelopment analysis to graduates from UK universities* (Working Paper 2003/007). JEL Classification: I21, C14.

Jones, D. T. (1999). GenTHREADER: An efficient and reliable protein folds recognition method for genomic sequences. *Journal of Molecular Biology, 287*, 797–815. doi:10.1006/jmbi.1999.2583 PMID:10191147

Jones, G. R. (2010). *Organizational theory, design, and change*. Upper Saddle River, NJ: Prentice Hall.

Joreskog, K. G., & Sorbom, D. (1993). *LISREL 8: User's reference guide*. Chicago, IL: Scientific Software International.

Jotsov, V. S. (2008). Novel Intrusion prevention and detection methods IS2008. In *Proceedings of IEEE Intl. Conference on Intelligent Systems*. IEEE Press.

Jung, K. K., Kim, J. W., Lee, H. K., Chung, S. B., & Eom, K. H. (2007). EMG pattern classification using spectral estimation and neural network. In *Proceedings of Annual Conference on Society of Instrumentation and Control Engineers*. IEEE.

Juran, J. M., & Gryna, F. M. (1988). *Juran's quality control handbook* (4th ed.). New York: McGraw-Hill.

Ju, T. L., Li, C. Y., & Lee, T. S. (2006). A contingency model for knowledge management capability and innovation. *Industrial Management & Data Systems, 106*(5/6), 855–877. doi:10.1108/02635570610671524

Kafil, M., & Ahmad, I. (1998). Optimal task assignment in heterogeneous distributed computing systems. *IEEE Concurrency, 6*(3), 42–50. doi:10.1109/4434.708255

Kakoty, N. M., & Hazarika, S. M. (2009). Classification of grasp types through wavelet decomposition of EMG signals. In *Proceedings of 2ⁿᵈ International Conference on Biomedical Engineering and Informatics*. IEEE.

Kalyanmoy, D. (2004). *Optimization for engineering design: Algorithms and examples*. PHI Learning Pvt. Ltd.

Kanagarajan, D., Karthikeyan, R., Palanikumar, K., & Sivaraj, P. (2008). Influence of process parameters on electric - Discharge machining of WC/30%Co composites. *Proceedings of the Institution of Mechanical Engineers. Part B, Journal of Engineering Manufacture*, *222*(7), 807–815. doi:10.1243/09544054JEM925

Kang, Q., He, H., & Song, H. (2011). Task assignment in heterogeneous computing systems using an effective iterated greedy algorithm. *Journal of Systems and Software*, *84*(6), 985–992. doi:10.1016/j.jss.2011.01.051

Kang, S. C., Morris, S. S., & Snell, S. A. (2007). Relational archetypes, organizational learning, and value creation: Extending the human resource architecture. *Academy of Management Review*, *32*(1), 236–256. doi:10.5465/AMR.2007.23464060

Kang, W.-J., Shiu, J.-R., Cheng, C.-K., Lai, J.-S., Tsao, H.-W., & Kuo, T.-S. (1995). The application of cepstral coefficients and maximum likelihood method in EMG pattern recognition. *IEEE Transactions on Bio-Medical Engineering*, *42*(8), 777–785. doi:10.1109/10.398638 PMID:7642191

Karatza, H. (2000). A comparative analysis of scheduling policies in a distributed system using simulation. *International Journal of Simulation Systems, Science & Technology*, 1–2.

Karatza, H., & Hilzer, R. (2002). Load sharing in heterogeneous distributed systems. In *Proceedings of Simulation Conference*, (Vol. 1, pp. 489–496). Academic Press.

Kargupta, H., Datta, S., Wang, Q., & Krishnamoorthy, S. (2003). On the privacy preserving properties of random data perturbation techniques. In *Proceedings of the ICDM 2003- 3rd IEEE International Conference on Data Mining* (pp. 99-106). Los Alamitos, CA: IEEE Computer Society.

Karlik, B., Tokhi, M. O., & Alci, M. (2003). A fuzzy clustering neural network architecture for multifunction upper-limb prosthesis. *IEEE Transactions on Bio-Medical Engineering*, *50*(11), 1255–1261. doi:10.1109/TBME.2003.818469 PMID:14619995

Karthikeyan, R., Lakshmi Narayanan, P. R., & Naagarazan, R. S. (1999). Mathematical modelling for electric - Discharge machining of aluminium-silicon carbide particulate composites. *Journal of Materials Processing Technology*, *87*, 59–63. doi:10.1016/S0924-0136(98)00332-X

Karypis, G., Eui-Hong, H., & Kumar, V. (1999). CHAMELEON: A hierarchical clustering algorithm using dynamic modeling. *IEEE Computer*, *32*(8), 68–75. doi:10.1109/2.781637

Kassar, M., Kervella, B., & Pujolle, G. (2008). An overview of vertical handover decision strategies in heterogeneous wireless networks. *Computer Communications*, *31*(10), 2607–2620. doi:10.1016/j.comcom.2008.01.044

Kasturi, J., & Acharya, R. (2004). Clustering of diverse genomic data using information fusion. In *Proceedings of the 2004 ACM Symposium on Applied Computing*, (pp. 116–120). ACM.

Kauffman, C., & Karypis, G. (2009). Librus: Combined machine learning and homology information for sequence-based ligand-binding residue prediction. *Bioinformatics (Oxford, England)*, *25*(23), 3099–3107. doi:10.1093/bioinformatics/btp561 PMID:19786483

Kaur, H., Chauhan, R., & Alam, M. A. (2010). An optimal categorization of feature selection methods for knowledge discovery. In Visual analytics and interactive technologies: Data, text and web mining applications. Hershey, PA: IGI Global Publishing.

Kaur, H., Chauhan, R., Alam, M. A., Aljunid, S., & Salleh, M. (2012). SpaGRID: A spatial grid framework for high dimensional medical databases. In *Proceedings of International Conference on Hybrid Artificial Intelligence Systems* (LNCS), (vol. 7208, pp. 690-704). Berlin: Springer.

Kaur, H. (2005). Actionable rules: Issues and directions. *World Academy of Science. Engineering and Technology*, *5*, 61–64.

Kaur, H., Chauhan, R., & Ahmed, Z. (2012). Role of data mining in establishing strategic policies for the efficient management of healthcare system–A case study from Washington DC area using retrospective discharge data. *BMC Health Services Research*, *12*(Suppl. 1), 12. doi:10.1186/1472-6963-12-S1-P12 PMID:22236336

Kaur, H., Chauhan, R., & Aljunid, S. (2012). Data mining cluster analysis on the influence of health factors in Casemix data. *BMC Health Services Research*, *12*(1), O3. doi:10.1186/1472-6963-12-S1-O3

Keim, D. A., & Kreigel, H. P. (1996). Visualization techniques for mining large databases: A comparison. *IEEE Transactions on Knowledge and Data Engineering*, 8.

Kerk, S. G. (2005). An AMR study in an Indian utility. In *Proceedings of the Power Engineering Conference, 2005*. IEEE. doi:10.1109/IPEC.2005.206894

Keskin, Y., Halkaci, H., & Kizil, M. (2006). An experimental study for determination of the effects of machining parameters on surface roughness in electrical discharge machinings (EDM). *International Journal of Advanced Manufacturing Technology*, *28*(11-12), 1118–1121. doi:10.1007/s00170-004-2478-8

Khan, A. (2008). Electrode wear and material removal rate during EDM of aluminum and mild steel using copper and brass electrodes. *International Journal of Advanced Manufacturing Technology*, *39*(5-6), 482–487. doi:10.1007/s00170-007-1241-3

Khan, A., Ali, M., & Haque, M. (2009). A study of electrode shape configuration on the performance of die sinking EDM. *International Journal of Mechanical and Materials Engineering*, *4*(1), 19–23.

Khilar, P. M., & Mahapatra, S. (2007). A distributed diagnosis approach to fault tolerant multi-rate real-time embedded systems. In *Proc. of 10th Intel Conf. on Information Technology,* (pp. 167–172). Academic Press.

Khilar, P. M., & Mahapatra, S. (2007). Two phase distributed diagnosis in dynamic fault environment. In *Proc. of International Conference on Advance Computing,* (pp. 120-124). Academic Press.

Khilar, P. M., & Punyotoya, S. (2009). A survey on system level diagnosis in distributed network. In *Proc. of International Conference on Information Technology,* (pp. 213-217). Academic Press.

Khilar, P. M., & Punyotoya, S. (2010). A novel fault diagnosis algorithm for k-connected distributed clusters. In *Proc. of IEEE International Conference on Industrial Electronics, Control and Robotics,* (pp. 101-105). IEEE.

Khilar, P. M., & Mahapatra, S. (2009). Time-constrained fault tolerant x-by-wire systems. *International Journal of Computers and Applications*, *31*(4), 231–238. doi:10.2316/Journal.202.2009.4.202-2391

Kiessling, T. S., Richey, R. G., Meng, J., & Dabic, M. (2009). Exploring knowledge management to organizational performance outcomes in a transitional economy. *Journal of World Business*, *44*(4), 421–433. doi:10.1016/j.jwb.2008.11.006

Kihara, D., & Skolnick, J. (2004). Microbial genomes have over 72% structure assignment by the threading algorithm PROSPECTOR_Q. *Proteins*, *55*, 464–473. doi:10.1002/prot.20044 PMID:15048836

Kim, J.-U., & Kim, Y.-D. (1996). Simulated annealing and genetic algorithms for scheduling products with multi-level product structure. *Computers & Operations Research*, *23*(9), 857–868. doi:10.1016/0305-0548(95)00079-8

Kirkpatrick, S., Jr, D. G., & Vecchi, M. P. (1983). Optimization by simmulated annealing. *Science*, *220*(4598), 671–680. doi:10.1126/science.220.4598.671 PMID:17813860

Kiyak, M., & Cakir, O. (2007). Examination of machining parameters on surface roughness in EDM of tool steel. *Journal of Materials Processing Technology*, *191*, 141–144. doi:10.1016/j.jmatprotec.2007.03.008

Kleinberg, J., & Tardos, E. (2006). *Algorithm design.* Upper Saddle River, NJ: Pearson Education Inc.

Klosgen, W. (1996). Explora: A multipattern and multistategy discovery assistant. In U. Fayyad, G. Piatetsky-Shapiro, P. Smyth, & R. Uthurusay (Eds.), *Advances in knowledge discovery* (pp. 249–272). Cambridge, MA: AAAI Press/The MIT Press.

Knox, R., & Brooks, D. H. (1994). Classification of multifunction surface EMG using advanced AR model representations. In *Proceedings of Bioengineering Conference*. IEEE.

Ko, J., Lee, D., Park, H., Coutsias, E. A., Lee, J., & Seok, C. (2011). The FALC-loop web server for protein loop modeling. *Nucleic Acids Research*, *39*, W210–W214. doi:10.1093/nar/gkr352 PMID:21576220

Kolinski, A., & Skolnick, J. (2004). Reduced models of proteins and their applications. *Polymer*, *45*, 511–24S. doi:10.1016/j.polymer.2003.10.064

Koller, R., Rangaswami, R., Marrero, J., Hernandez, I., Smith, G., & Barsilai, M. … Merrill, K. (2008). Anatomy of real time intrusion prevention system. In *Proceedings of International Conference on Autonomic Computing* (pp.151-160). IEEE Press.

Kondo, T., Amagi, O., & Nozawa, T. (2008). Proposal of anticipatory pattern recognition for EMG prosthetic hand control. In *Proceedings of IEEE International Conference on Systems, Man and Cybernetics*. IEEE.

Koptez, H., & Gruensteidl, G. (1993). TTP—A time-triggered protocol for fault-tolerant real-time systems. In *Proc. of IEEE Fault-Tolerant Computing Symp.*, (pp. 524-532). IEEE.

Kou, Y., Lu, C.-T., Sirwongwattana, S., & Huang, Y.-P. (2004). Survey of fraud detection techniques. In *Proceedings of the 2004 IEEE International Conference on Networking, Sensing and Control*. IEEE. doi:10.1109/ICNSC.2004.1297040

Kryszkiewicz, K. (1998). Rough set approach to incomplete information systems. *Information Sciences*, *112*, 39–49. doi:10.1016/S0020-0255(98)10019-1

Kumar Tripathi, A., Kumer Sarker, B., Kumar, N., & Vidyarthi, D. P. (2000). A GA based multiple task allocation considering load. *International Journal of High Speed Computing*, *11*(4), 203–214. doi:10.1142/S0129053300000187

Kumar, V., & Tyagi, N. (2010). Media independent handover for seamless mobility in IEEE 802.11 and UMTS based on IEEE 802.21. In *Proceedings of Computer Science and Information Technology (ICCSIT), 2010 3rd IEEE International Conference on* (Vol. 4, pp. 474-479). IEEE.

Kumar, R., Imam, S. A., & Khan, M. R. (2009). A critical review of taguchi gas sensor for the detection of VOC's. *MASAUM Journal of Reviews and Surveys*, *1*(2), 177–183.

Kung, K. Y., Horng, J. T., & Chiang, K. T. (2009). Material removal rate and electrode wear ratio study on the powder mixed electrical discharge machinings of cobalt-bonded tungsten carbide. *International Journal of Advanced Manufacturing Technology*, *40*(1-2), 95–104. doi:10.1007/s00170-007-1307-2

Kun, L., Hillol, K., & Jessica, R. (2006). Random projection-based multiplicative data perturbation for privacy preserving distributed data mining. *IEEE Transactions on Knowledge and Data Engineering*, *18*(1), 92–106. doi:10.1109/TKDE.2006.14

Kuppan, P., Rajadurai, A., & Narayanan, S. (2007). Influence of EDM process parameters in deep hole drilling of inconel 718. *International Journal of Advanced Manufacturing Technology*, *38*, 74–84. doi:10.1007/s00170-007-1084-y

Kurtanjek, Z. (1994). Modeling and control by artificial neural networks in biotechnology. *Computers & Chemical Engineering*, *18*, S627–S631. doi:10.1016/0098-1354(94)80102-9

Kyte, J., & Doolittle, R. F. (1982). A simple method for displaying the hydropathic character of a protein. *Journal of Molecular Biology*, *157*, 105–132. doi:10.1016/0022-2836(82)90515-0 PMID:7108955

Labedz, C., Cavaleri, S., & Berry, G. (2011). Interactive knowledge management: Putting pragmatic policy planning in place. *Journal of Knowledge Management*, *15*(4), 551–567. doi:10.1108/13673271111151956

Langley, P. (1994). Selection of relevant features in machine learning. In *Proceedings of the AAAI Fall Symposium on Relevance*. New Orleans, LA: AAAI Press.

Laskowski, R. A., Watson, J. D., & Thornton, J. M. (2003). From protein structure to biochemical function? *Journal of Structural and Functional Genomics*, *4*, 167–177. doi:10.1023/A:1026127927612 PMID:14649301

Le, A. AL-Shaer, E., & Boutaba, R. (2008). On optimizing load balancing of IDPS. In *Proceedings of IEEE Infocom Workshop* (pp.1-6). IEEE Press.

Lee, D. S., Sang, W. B., Minho, L., & Duk, D. L. (2005). Micro gas sensor array with neural network for recognizing combustible leakage gases. *IEEE Sensors Journal*, *5*(3), 530–536. doi:10.1109/JSEN.2005.845186

Lee, H. Y., & Ong, K.-L. (1996). Visualization support for data mining. *IEEE Intelligent Systems*, *11*(5), 69–75.

Lee, S., & Sardis, G. N. (1984). The control of a prosthetic arm by EMG pattern recognition. *IEEE Transactions on Automatic Control, 29*(4), 290–302. doi:10.1109/TAC.1984.1103521

Lee, W.-C., Wu, C.-C., & Chen, P. (2006). A simulated annealing approach to makespan minimization on identical parallel machines. *International Journal of Advanced Manufacturing Technology, 31*(3), 328–334. doi:10.1007/s00170-005-0188-5

Lee, W., Lee, I., Kwak, J. S., Ihm, B. C., & Han, S. (2012). Multi-BS MIMO cooperation: Challenges and practical solutions in 4G systems. *IEEE Wireless Communications, 19*(1), 89–96. doi:10.1109/MWC.2012.6155881

Lee, Y. C., & Lee, S. K. (2007). Capability, processes, and performance of knowledge management: A structural approach. *Human Factors and Ergonomics in Manufacturing, 17*(1), 21–41. doi:10.1002/hfm.20065

Lei, J. Z., & Ghorbani, A. A. (2012). Improved competitive learning neural networks for network intrusion and fraud detection. *Neurocomputing, 75*(1), 135–145. doi:10.1016/j.neucom.2011.02.021

León, C., Biscarri, F., Monedero, I., Guerrero, J. I., Biscarri, J., & Millán, R. (2011). Integrated expert system applied to the analysis of non-technical losses in power utilities. *Expert Systems with Applications, 38*(8), 10274–10285. doi:10.1016/j.eswa.2011.02.062

Leuski, A. (2001). Evaluating document clustering for interactive information retrieval. In *Proceedings of Tenth International Conference on Information and Knowledge Management,* (pp. 33–40). IEEE.

Levitt, B., & March, J. (1988). Organizational learning. *Annual Review of Sociology, 14*(3), 319–340. doi:10.1146/annurev.so.14.080188.001535

Li, J. (1993). A mixed gas sensor system based on thin film saw sensor array and neural network. In *Proceedings of the Twelfth Southern Biomedical Engineering Conference,* (pp. 179-181). doi:10.1109/SBEC.1993.247403

Liang, J. Y., & Li, D. Y. (2005). *Uncertainty and knowledge acquisition in information systems.* Beijing: Science Press.

Liang, J. Y., & Shi, Z. Z. (2001). The information entropy, rough entropy and knowledge granulation in rough set theory. *International Journal of Uncertainty. Fuzziness and Knowledge-Based Systems, 12*(1), 37–46. doi:10.1142/S0218488504002631

Liang, J. Y., Shi, Z. Z., Li, D. Y., & Wireman, M. J. (2006). The information entropy, rough entropy and knowledge granulation in incomplete information system. *International Journal of General Systems, 35*(6), 641–654. doi:10.1080/03081070600687668

Li, G., Tang, C., & Wei, Z. (2007). New conjugacy condition and related new conjugate gradient methods for unconstrained optimization. *Journal of Computational and Applied Mathematics, 202*(2), 523–539. doi:10.1016/j.cam.2006.03.005

Lim, D., & Klobas, J. (2000). Knowledge management in small enterprises. *The Electronic Library, 18*(6), 420–432. doi:10.1108/02640470010361178

Lin, G. P., Qian, Y. H., & Li, J. J. (2011). A covering-based pessimistic multi-granulation rough set. In *Proceedings of International Conference on Intelligent Computing.* Zhengzhon, China: IEEE.

Lin, T. Y. (2003). Neighborhood systems: Mathematical models of information granulations. In *Proceedings of 2003 IEEE International Conference on Systems, Man & Cybernetics,* (pp. 5–8). IEEE.

Lin, C. H., & Tseng, S. E. (2005). The implementation gaps for the knowledge management system. *Industrial Management & Data Systems, 105*(2), 208–222. doi:10.1108/02635570510583334

Lindell, Y., & Benny, P. (2009). Secure multiparty computation for privacy preserving data mining. *The Journal of Privacy and Confidentiality, 1*(1), 59–98.

Lin, G., Qian, Y., & Li, J. (2012). NMGRS: Neighborhood-based multigranulation rough sets. *International Journal of Approximate Reasoning, 53,* 1080–1093. doi:10.1016/j.ijar.2012.05.004

Lin, H., & Raghavendra, C. (1992). A dynamic load-balancing policy with a central job dispatcher (lbc). *IEEE Transactions on Software Engineering, 18*(2), 148–158. doi:10.1109/32.121756

Lin, K., May, A. C. W., & Taylor, W. R. (2002). Threading using neural network (TUNE), the measure of protein sequence-structure compatibility. *Bioinformatics (Oxford, England)*, *18*, 1350–1357. doi:10.1093/bioinformatics/18.10.1350 PMID:12376379

Linko, P., & Zhu, Y. H. (1992). Neural network modeling for real-time variable estimation and prediction in the control of glucoamylase fermentation. *Process Biochemistry*, *27*, 275–283. doi:10.1016/0032-9592(92)85012-Q

Lin, T. Y. (2001). Granular and nearest neighborhood: Rough set approach. In *Granulation computing: An emerging paradigm* (pp. 125–142). Berlin: Physica-Verlag. doi:10.1007/978-3-7908-1823-9_6

Liu, C. H., & Miao, D. Q. (2011). Covering rough set model based on multi-granulations. In *Proceedings of Thirteenth International Conference on Rough Sets, Fuzzy Set, Data Mining and Granular Computing* (LNAI), (vol. 6743, pp. 87 – 90). Berlin: Springer.

Liu, C. H., & Wang, M. Z. (2011). Covering fuzzy rough set based on multi-granulation. In *Proceedings of International Conference on Uncertainty Reasoning and Knowledge Engineering*, (vol. 2, pp. 146 – 149). Academic Press.

Liu, J., Yong, Z., Yonghuai, Z., & Ming, C. (2001). Cross sensitivity reduction of gas sensors using genetic algorithm neural network. In Proc. SPIE 4201, Optical Methods for Industrial Processes. doi: doi:10.1117/12.417392

Liu, Q., Li, T., & Xu, W. (2009). A subjective and objective integrated method for fraud detection in financial systems. In *Proceedings of the 2009 International Conference on Machine Learning and Cybernetics*. IEEE. doi:10.1109/ICMLC.2009.5212307

Liu, Y., Jiang, Y., & Lin, W. (2006). A rough set and evidence theory based method for fraud detection. In *Proceedings of the Sixth World Congress on Intelligent Control and Automation, 2006*. IEEE. doi:10.1109/WCICA.2006.1712608

Liu, C. (2013). On multi-granulation covering rough sets. *International Journal of Approximate Reasoning*.

Liu, G., Poh, K., & Xie, M. (2005). Iterative list scheduling for heterogeneous computing. *Journal of Parallel and Distributed Computing*, *65*(5), 654–665. doi:10.1016/j.jpdc.2005.01.002

Liu, K., Subrata, R., & Zomaya, A. (2007). On the performance-driven load distribution for heterogeneous computational grids. *Journal of Computer and System Sciences*, *73*(8), 1191–1206. doi:10.1016/j.jcss.2007.02.007

Liu, Y., & Storey, C. (1991). Efficient generalized conjugate gradient algorithms, part 1: Theory. *Journal of Optimization Theory and Applications*, *69*, 129–137. doi:10.1007/BF00940464

Livieris, I. E., & Panagiotis, P. (2011). *An advanced conjugate gradient training algorithm based on a modified secant equation*. International Scholarly Research Network ISRN Artificial Intelligence.

Locke, E. A. (1969). What is job satisfaction? *Organizational Behavior and Human Performance*, *4*(4), 309–336. doi:10.1016/0030-5073(69)90013-0

Locke, E. A. (1976). The nature and causes of job satisfaction. In M. P. Dunnette (Ed.), *Handbook of industrial and organizational psychology* (pp. 1297–1359). Chicago, IL: Rand McNally.

Long, D. D. (1997). *Building the knowledge-based organizations: How culture drives knowledge behaviors*. Cambridge, MA: Center for Business Innovation, Ernst & Young LLP.

Lönnqvist, A., & Laihonen, H. (2013). Managing regional development: A knowledge perspective. *International Journal of Knowledge-Based Development*, *4*(1), 50–63. doi:10.1504/IJKBD.2013.052493

Lopes, A., Lúcia, M., & Lanzer, E. A. (2002). Data envelopment analysis – DEA and fuzzy sets to assess the performance of academic departments: A case study at Federal University of Santa Catarina – UFSC. *PesquisaOperacional*, *22*(2), 217–230.

Lopez, S. P., Peon, J. M. M., & Ordas, C. J. V. (2004). Managing knowledge: The link between culture and organizational learning. *Journal of Knowledge Management*, *8*(6), 93–104. doi:10.1108/13673270410567657

Louta, M., & Bellavista, P. (2013). Bringing always best connectivity vision a step closer: Challenges and perspectives. *IEEE Communications Magazine*, *51*(2), 158–166. doi:10.1109/MCOM.2013.6461201

Ma, N., Kumar, D. K., & Pah, N. (2001). Classification of hand direction using multi-channel electromyography by neural network. In *Proceedings of 7th Australian and New Zealand Intelligent Information Systems Conference*. IEEE.

Maeng, J., & Malek, M. (1981). A comparison connection assignment for self-diagnosis of multiprocessor systems. In *Proc. of 11th Int. Symp. on Fault-Tolerant Comput.*, (pp. 173–175). Academic Press.

Magnani, M. (2003). *Technical report on rough set theory for knowledge discovery in data bases*. Bologna, Italy: University of Bologna.

Mahapatra, A., & Khilar, P. M. (2012). An energy-efficient distributed approach for clustering-based fault detection and diagnosis in image sensor networks. *International Journal of Wireless Sensor Systems*, *2*(4).

Mahapatra, A., & Khilar, P. M. (2012). On-line fault diagnosis of arbitrary connected networks. *International Journal on Network Security*, *3*(1), 10–13.

Maheswaran, M., & Siegel, H. (1998). A dynamic matching and scheduling algorithm for heterogeneous computing systems. In *Proceedings of Heterogeneous Computing Workshop, 1998*. Academic Press.

Maheswaran, M., Ali, S., Siegal, H., Hensgen, D., & Freund, R. (1999). Dynamic matching and scheduling of a class of independent tasks onto heterogeneous computing systems. In *Proceedings of Heterogeneous Computing Workshop, 1999*. Academic Press.

Maitrot, A., Lucas, M.-F., Doncarli, C., & Farina, D. (2005). Signal-dependent wavelets for electromyogram classification. *Journal of Medical and Biological Engineering and Computing*, *43*(4), 487–492. doi:10.1007/BF02344730 PMID:16255431

Makaya, C., & Pierre, S. (2011). *Emerging wireless networks: Concepts, techniques and applications*. Boca Raton, FL: CRC Press, Inc.

Malek, M. (1980). A comparison connection assignment for diagnosis of multiprocessor systems. In *Proc. of 7th Int. Symp. on Comput. Architecture*, (pp. 31–35). Academic Press.

Malekian, R. (2008). The study of handover in mobile IP networks. In *Proceedings of Broadband Communications, Information Technology & Biomedical Applications, 2008 Third International Conference on* (pp. 181-185). IEEE.

Mandal, D., Pal, S. K., & Saha, P. (2007). Modeling of electrical discharge machinings process using back propagation neural network and multi-objective optimization using non-dominating sorting genetic algorithm-II. *Journal of Materials Processing Technology*, *186*, 154–162. doi:10.1016/j.jmatprotec.2006.12.030

Manikopoulos, C. (2003). Early statistical anomaly intrusion detection of DOS attacks using MIB traffic parameters. In *Proceedings of IEEE Systems, Man and Cybernetics Society* (pp. 53-59). IEEE.

Mannila, H. (2002). Local and global methods in data mining: Basic techniques and open problems. In *Proceedings of Twenty-Ninth International Colloquium on Automata, Languages and Programming* (LNCS), (pp. 57-68). Berlin: Springer-Verlag.

Mansoor, M., & Tayib, M. (2010). An empirical examination of organizational culture, job stress, job satisfaction within the indirect tax administration in Malaysia. *International journal of Business and Social Sciences*, *1*(1), 81-95.

Markoc, Z., Hlupic, N., & Basch, D. (2011). Detection of suspicious patterns of energy consumption using neural network trained by generated samples. In *Proceedings of the ITI 2011 33rd International Conference on Information Technology Interfaces* (ITI). IEEE.

Marques, D. P., & Simon, F. J. G. (2006). The effect of knowledge management practices on firm performance. *Journal of Knowledge Management*, *10*(3), 143–156. doi:10.1108/13673270610670911

Marsch, P., Raaf, B., Szufarska, A., Mogensen, P., Guan, H., Farber, M., & Kolding, T. (2012). Future mobile communication networks: Challenges in the design and operation. *IEEE Vehicular Technology Magazine*, *7*(1), 16–23. doi:10.1109/MVT.2011.2179343

Martin, J., Amin, R., Eltawil, A., & Hussien, A. (2011). Limitations of 4G wireless systems. In *Proceedings of Virginia Tech Wireless Symposium*. Virginia Tech.

Martin, B. J. (1990). A successful approach to absenteeism. *Nursing Management, 21*(8), 45–48. doi:10.1097/00006247-199008000-00019 PMID:2381601

Martino, R. L. (1970). *Finding the critical path, project management and control*. New York: American Management Association.

Martin, S. (1993). What's wrong with MBA ranking surveys? *Management Research News, 16*(7), 15–18. doi:10.1108/eb028322

Marti-Renom, M. A., Madhusudhan, M. S., Fiser, A., Rost, B., & Sali, A. (2002). Reliability of assessment of protein structure prediction methods. *Structure (London, England), 10*, 435–440. doi:10.1016/S0969-2126(02)00731-1 PMID:12005441

Massa, S., & Testa, S. (2009). A knowledge management approach to organizational competitive advantage: Evidence from the food sector. *European Management Journal, 27*(2), 129–141. doi:10.1016/j.emj.2008.06.005

Matsumura, Y., Mitsukura, Y., Fukumi, M., & Akamatsu, N. (2002). Recognition of EMG signal patterns by neural networks. In *Proceedings of 9th International. Conference on Neural Information Processing*, (vol. 2, pp. 750-754). Singapore: IEEE.

McDermott, R., & O'Dell, C. (2001). Overcoming cultural barriers to sharing knowledge. *Journal of Knowledge Management, 5*(1), 76–85. doi:10.1108/13673270110384428

McGurk, J., & Baron, A. (2012). Knowledge management: Time to focus on purpose and motivation. *Strategic HR Review, 11*(6), 316–321. doi:10.1108/14754391211264776

McKenna, E. (2006). *Business psychology and organisational behaviour*. New York, NY: Psychology Press.

McKinlay, A. (2005). Knowledge management. In S. Ackroyd, R. Batt, & P. Thompson (Eds.), *The Oxford handbook of work and organization* (pp. 242–262). Oxford, UK: Oxford University Press.

McKinnon, J., Harrison, G., Chow, C., & Wu, A. (2003). Organizational culture: Association with commitment, job satisfaction, propensity to remain, and information sharing in Taiwan. *International Journal of Business Studies, 11*(1), 25–44.

McLaughlin, S., Paton, R. A., & Macbeth, D. K. (2008). Barrier impact on organizational learning within complex organizations. *Journal of Knowledge Management, 12*(2), 107–123. doi:10.1108/13673270810859550

Mcmillan, L. M., & Datta, D. (1998). The relative efficiencies of Canadian universities: A DEA perspective. *Canadian Public Policy – Analyse De Politiques, 24*(4), 485-511.

McMullen, P. R. (1997). Assessment of MBA programs via data envelopment analysis. *Journal of Business and Management, 5*(1), 77–91.

McShane, S. (2004). *Canadian organizational behavior*. Toronto, Canada: McGraw-Hill Ryerson.

Michalsky, E., Goede, A., & Preissner, R. (2003). Loops in proteins (LIP) - A comprehensive loop database for homology modeling. *Protein Engineering, 16*, 979–985. doi:10.1093/protein/gzg119 PMID:14983078

Miller, G. J., Bräutigan, D., & Gerlach, S. V. (2006). *Business intelligence competency centres: A team approach to maximising competitive advantage*. New York: Wiley and Sons.

Miller, H. J., & Han, J. (2001). *Geographic data mining and knowledge discovery*. San Francisco: Taylor and Francis. doi:10.4324/9780203468029

Miller, R. W. (1963). *Schedule, cost, and profit control with PERT a comprehensive guide for program management*. New York: McGraw-Hill Book Company.

Misener, T. R., Haddock, K. S., Gleaton, J. U., & Ajamieh, A. R. A. (1996). Toward an international measure of job satisfaction. *Nursing Research, 45*(2), 87–91. doi:10.1097/00006199-199603000-00006 PMID:8604370

Mishra, S., & Khilar, P. M. (2011). Heartbeat based error diagnosis framework for distributed embedded systems. In *Proceedings of International Conference on Software and Computer Technology*. Academic Press.

Mitra, P., Murthy, P. A., & Pal, S. K. (2002). Unsupervised feature selection using feature similarity. *IEEE Transactions on Pattern Analysis and Machine Intelligence, 24*(3), 301–312. doi:10.1109/34.990133

Moder, J. J., & Phillips, C. R. (1967). *Project management with CPM and PERT*. New York: Reinhold Publishing Corporation.

Mohamed, A., Bandi, A. F., Tamrin, A. R., Jaafar, M. D., Hasan, S., & Jusof, F. (2009). Telecommunication fraud prediction using backpropagation neural network. In *Proceedings of the International Conference of Soft Computing and Pattern Recognition, 2009*. IEEE. doi:10.1109/SoCPaR.2009.60

Moller, M. F. (1993). A scaled conjugate gradient algorithm for fast supervised learning. *Neural Networks, 6*. doi:525-533.0893-6080/93

Monedero, Í., Biscarri, F., León, C., Guerrero, J. I., Biscarri, J., & Millán, R. (2009). *New methods to detect non-technical losses on power utilities*. Paper presented at the IASTED - Artificial Intelligence and Soft Computing. Palma de Mallorca, Spain.

Montelione, G. T., Zheng, D., Huang, Y. J., Gunsalus, K. C., & Szyperski, T. (2000). Protein NMR spectroscopy in structural genomics. *Nature Structural Biology, 7*, 982–985. doi:10.1038/80768 PMID:11104006

Moore, R. A. Jr. (1996). *Controlled data-swapping techniques for masking public use microdata sets. Statistical Research Division Report Series RR 96-04*. Washington, DC: US Bureau of the Census.

Mosadeghrad, A. M. (2003). The role of participative management (suggestion system) in hospital effectiveness and efficiency. *Research in Medical Sciences, 8*(3), 85–89.

Moult, J., Fidelis, K., Rost, B., Hubbard, T., & Tramontano, A. (2005). Critical assessment of methods of protein structure prediction (CASP)–Round 6. *Proteins, 61*, 3–7. doi:10.1002/prot.20716 PMID:16187341

Moult, J., Fidelis, K., Zemla, A., & Hubbard, T. (2003). Critical assessment of methods of protein structure prediction (CASP)-Round V. *Proteins, 53*, 334–339. doi:10.1002/prot.10556 PMID:14579322

Mount, D. M. (2004). *Bioinformatics: Sequence and genome analysis* (2nd ed.). New York: Cold Spring Harbor Laboratory Press.

Munetomo, M., Takai, Y., & Sato, Y. (1994). A genetic approach to dynamic load balancing in a distributed computing system.[IEEE.]. *Proceedings of Evolutionary Computation, 1994*, 418–421.

Mwaura, F. M. (2012). Adopting electricity prepayment billing system to reduce non-technical energy losses in Uganda: Lesson from Rwanda. *Utilities Policy, 23*, 72–79. doi:10.1016/j.jup.2012.05.004

Nagaraju, M., & Tripathy, B. K. (2013). Covering based multi granulation rough sets and study of their topological properties. In *Proceedings of CCIIS 2013*. VIT University.

Nagi, J., Mohammad, A. M., Yap, K. S., Tiong, S. K., & Ahmed, S. K. (2008). Non-technical loss analysis for detection of electricity theft using support vector machines. In *Proceedings of the Power and Energy Conference, 2008*. IEEE. doi:10.1109/PECON.2008.4762604

Nagi, J., Yap, K. S., Nagi, F., Tiong, S. K., Koh, S. P., & Ahmed, S. K. (2010). NTL detection of electricity theft and abnormalities for large power consumers. In *Proceedings of the 2010 IEEE Student Conference on Research and Development* (SCOReD). IEEE. doi:10.1109/SCORED.2010.5704002

Nagi, J., Yap, K. S., Tiong, S. K., Ahmed, S. K., & Mohammad, A. M. (2008). Detection of abnormalities and electricity theft using genetic support vector machines. In *Proceedings of the TENCON 2008 - 2008 IEEE Region 10 Conference*. IEEE. doi:10.1109/TENCON.2008.4766403

Nagi, J., Siah Yap, K., Kiong Tiong, S., Ahmed, S. K., & Nagi, F. (2011). Improving SVM-based nontechnical loss detection in power utility using the fuzzy inference system. *IEEE Transactions on Power Delivery, 26*(2), 1284–1285. doi:10.1109/TPWRD.2010.2055670

Nagi, J., Yap, K. S., Kiong Tiong, S., Ahmed, S. K., & Mohamad, M. (2010). Nontechnical loss detection for metered customers in power utility using support vector machines. *IEEE Transactions on Power Delivery, 25*(2), 1162–1171. doi:10.1109/TPWRD.2009.2030890

Nahapiet, J., & Ghoshal, S. (1998). Social capital, intellectual capital, and organizational advantage. *Academy of Management Review, 23*(2), 242–266.

Narang, R., & Dwivedi, A. (2010). Managing the job satisfaction of knowledge workers: An empirical investigation. *Asia Pacific Journal of Business and Management, 1*(1), 1–14.

Nassu, B. T., Duarte, E. P., Jr., & Pozo, A. T. (2005). A comparision of evolutionary algorithms for system level diagnosis. In *Proc. of Genetic and Evolutionary Computation Conference*. Academic Press.

Natarajan, R. (2003). Quality and accreditation in technical & management education. *Productivity, 44*(2), 165–172.

Neilson, R. (1997). *Collaborative technologies & organizational learning*. Hershey, PA: Idea Group Publishing.

Nielsen, H., & Krogh, A. (1998). Prediction of signal peptides and signal anchors by a hidden Markov model. *Proc ISMB, 6*, 122–30.

Ninghui, L., Tiancheng, L., & Venkatasubramanian, S. (2007). t-Closeness: Privacy beyond k-anonymity and l-diversity. In *Proceeding of ICDE 2007 IEEE 23rd International Conference on Data Engineering* (pp. 106-115). Istanbul, Turkey: IEEE.

NIOSH. (2011). *Volunteer fire fighter dies during attempted rescue of utility worker from a confined space*. Retrieved from http://eww.cdc.gov/niosh/re/reports/face201031.html

Nishikawa, D., Yu, W., Yokoi, H., & Kakazu, Y. (1999). EMG prosthetic hand controller using real-time learning method. In *Proceedings of IEEE Systems Man and Cybernetics*. IEEE.

Nitin, G., Nitin, M., Kamal, T., & Pabitra, M. (2006). Mining quantitative association rules in protein sequences. *Lecture Notes in Computer Science, 3755*, 273–281. doi:10.1007/11677437_21

Nizar, A. H., & Dong, Z. Y. (2009). Identification and detection of electricity customer behaviour irregularities. In *Proceedings of the Power Systems Conference and Exposition, 2009*. IEEE. doi:10.1109/PSCE.2009.4840253

Nizar, A. H., Dong, Z. Y., & Zhao, J. H. (2006). Load profiling and data mining techniques in electricity deregulated market. In *Proceedings of the IEEE Power Engineering Society General Meeting, 2006*. IEEE. doi:10.1109/PES.2006.1709335

Nizar, A. H., Dong, Z. Y., Jalaluddin, M., & Raffles, M. J. (2006). Load profiling method in detecting non-technical loss activities in a power utility. In *Proceedings of the Power and Energy Conference, 2006*. IEEE. doi:10.1109/PECON.2006.346624

Nizar, A. H., Dong, Z. Y., Zhao, J. H., & Zhang, P. (2007). A data mining based NTL analysis method. In *Proceedings of the IEEE Power Engineering Society General Meeting, 2007*. IEEE. doi:10.1109/PES.2007.385883

Nizar, A. H., Hua Zhao, J., & Yang Dong, Z. (2006). Customer information system data pre-processing with feature selection techniques for non-technical losses prediction in an electricity market. In *Proceedings of the International Conference on Power System Technology, 2006*. IEEE. doi:10.1109/ICPST.2006.321964

Nizar, A. H., Yang Dong, Z., & Zhang, P. (2008). Detection rules for non technical losses analysis in power utilities. In *Proceedings of the 2008 IEEE Power and Energy Society General Meeting - Conversion and Delivery of Electrical Energy in the 21st Century*. IEEE. doi:10.1109/PES.2008.4596300

Nizar, A. H., Dong, Z. Y., & Wang, Y. (2008). Power utility nontechnical loss analysis with extreme learning machine method. *IEEE Transactions on Power Systems, 23*(3), 946–955. doi:10.1109/TPWRS.2008.926431

Nykodym, N., Longenecker, C., & Ruud, W. (2008). Improving quality of work life with transactional analysis as an intervention change strategy. *Applied Psychology, 40*(4), 395–404. doi:10.1111/j.1464-0597.1991.tb00999.x

O'Reilly, C. A., & Chatman, J. A. (1996). Culture as social control: Corporation, cults, and commitment. In B. M. Staw, & L. L. Cummings (Eds.), *Research in organizational behavior* (pp. 157–200). Greenwich, CT: JAI Press.

Offsey, S. (1997). Knowledge management: Linking people to knowledge for bottom line results. *Journal of Knowledge Management, 1*(2), 113–122. doi:10.1108/EUM0000000004586

Oh, S. H., & Lee, W. K. (2003). An anomaly intrusion detection method by clustering normal user behavior. *Computers & Security, 22*, 596–612. doi:10.1016/S0167-4048(03)00710-7

Oluikpe, P. (2012). Developing a corporate knowledge management strategy. *Journal of Knowledge Management, 16*(6), 862–878. doi:10.1108/13673271211276164

Openshaw, D. (2008). Smart metering an energy networks perspective. In *Proceedings of the 2008 IET Seminar on Smart Metering - Gizmo or Revolutionary Technology*. IET.

OSHA. (2009). *OSHA fact sheet: Carbon monoxide*. OSHA.

Pace, R. W., Regan, L., Miller, P., & Dunn, L. (1998). Natural growth goals and short-term training: A boomerang effect. *International Journal of Training and Development, 2*(2), 128–140. doi:10.1111/1468-2419.00041

Page, A., & Naughton, T. (2005). Dynamic task scheduling using genetic algorithms for heterogeneous distributed computing. In *Proceedings of Parallel and Distributed Processing Symposium, 2005*. IEEE.

Page, A., & Naughton, T. (2005). Framework for task scheduling in heterogeneous distributed computing using genetic algorithms. *Artificial Intelligence Review, 24*(3), 415–429. doi:10.1007/s10462-005-9002-x

Paint, F., Engelstad, P., Vanem, E., Haslestad, T., Nordvik, A. M., Myksvoll, K., & Svaet, S. (2002). *Mobility aspects in 4G networks* (White Paper).

Palte, R., Hertlein, M., Smolnik, S., & Riempp, G. (2011). The effects of a knowledge management strategy on KM performance in professional services firms. *International Journal of Knowledge Management, 7*(1), 16–34. doi:10.4018/jkm.2011010102

Pan, W., Ning, L., & Pandeng, L. (2009). Application of electronic nose in gas mixture quantitative detection. In *Proceedings of IC-NIDC*, (pp. 976-980). IEEE.

Panda, D. K., & Bhoi, R. K. (2005). Artificial neural network prediction of material removal rate in electro - discharge machining. *Materials and Manufacturing Processes, 20*, 645–672. doi:10.1081/AMP-200055033

Panda, M., Abraham, A., Das, S., & Patra, M. R. (2011). Network intrusion detection system: A machine learning approach. *Intelligent Decision Technologies Journal, 5*(4), 347–356.

Panda, M., Abraham, A., & Patra, M. R. (2012). *Hybrid intelligent systems for detecting network intrusions*. Wiley Security and Communication Network Journal. doi:10.1002/sec.592

Pandey, S. C., & Dutta, A. (2013). Role of knowledge infrastructure capabilities in knowledge management. *Journal of Knowledge Management, 17*(3), 435–453. doi:10.1108/JKM-11-2012-0365

Pantouvakis, A., & Bouranta, N. (2013). The link between organizational learning culture and customer satisfaction: Confirming relationship and exploring moderating effect. *The Learning Organization, 20*(1), 48–64. doi:10.1108/09696471311288528

Pantouvakis, A., & Mpogiatzidis, P. (2013). The impact of internal service quality and learning organization on clinical leaders' job satisfaction in hospital care services. *Leadership in Health Services, 26*(1), 34–49. doi:10.1108/17511871311291714

Parasuraman, A., Zeithaml, V. A., & Berry, L. L. (1985). A conceptual model of service quality and its implication for future research. *Journal of Marketing, 49*, 41–50. doi:10.2307/1251430

Park, H., Ribiere, V., & Schulte, W. D. (2004). Critical attributes of organizational culture that promote knowledge management technology implementation success. *Journal of Knowledge Management, 8*(3), 106–117. doi:10.1108/13673270410541079

Patel, A., Juir, J. C., & Pedersen, J. M. (2013). *An intelligent collaborative IDPS for smart grid environments*. Computer Standards and Interface Journal.

Patel, A., Taghavi, M., Bakhtiyari, K., & Juier, J. C. (2013). An IDPS in cloud computing: A systematic review. *Journal of Network and Computer Applications, 36*, 25–41. doi:10.1016/j.jnca.2012.08.007

Patel, M. R., Maria, B. A., Eubank, P. T., & DiBitonto, D. (1989). Theoretical models of the electrical discharge machining process II - The anode erosion model. *Journal of Applied Physics, 66*(9), 4104. doi:10.1063/1.343995

Patil, S., & Meshram, B. B. (2012). Network intrusion detection and prevention technique for DOS attack. *Intl. Journal of Scientific and Research Publications*, *2*(7), 1–4.

Pauling, L., Corey, R. B., & Branson, H. R. (1951). The structure of proteins, two hydrogen-bonded helical configurations of the polypeptide chain. *Proceedings of the National Academy of Sciences of the United States of America*, *37*(4), 205–211. doi:10.1073/pnas.37.4.205 PMID:14816373

Pawlak, Z. (1982). Rough sets. *International Journal of Computer and Information Sciences*, *11*, 341–356. doi:10.1007/BF01001956

Pawlak, Z. (1983). Rough classifications. *International Journal of Man-Machine Studies*, *20*, 469–483. doi:10.1016/S0020-7373(84)80022-X

Pawlak, Z. (1991). *Rough sets: Theoretical aspects of reasoning about data*. Dordrecht, The Netherlands: Kluwer Academic Publishers.

Pedrycz, W. (2007). Granular computing: The emerging paradigm. *Journal of Uncertain Systems*, *1*(1), 38–61.

Pedrycz, W., & Bargiela, A. (2002). Granular clustering: A granular signature of data. *IEEE Transactions on Systems, Man, and Cybernetics. Part B, Cybernetics*, *32*(2), 212–224. doi:10.1109/3477.990878 PMID:18238121

Pelc, A. (1992). Optimal fault diagnosis in comparison models. *IEEE Transactions on Computers*, *41*(6), 779–786. doi:10.1109/12.144631

Penmatsa, S., & Chronopoulos, A. (2007). Dynamic multi-user load balancing in distributed systems. In *Proceedings of Parallel and Distributed Processing Symposium, 2007*. IEEE.

Perez-Lopez, S., & Alegre, J. (2012). Information technology competency, knowledge processes and firm performance. *Industrial Management & Data Systems*, *112*(4), 644–662. doi:10.1108/02635571211225521

Perry, A. (1978). A modified conjugate gradient algorithm. *Operations Research*, *26*, 1073–1078. doi:10.1287/opre.26.6.1073

Peter, C. (2012). A survey of indexing techniques for scalable record linkage and deduplication. *IEEE Transactions on Knowledge and Data Engineering*, *24*(9), 1537–1555. doi:10.1109/TKDE.2011.127

Peters, T. J., & Waterman, R. H. (1982). *In search of excellence*. New York: Harper and Row.

Peters, T. J., & Waterman, R. H. (1982). *In search of excellence: Lessons from America's best run company*. New York, NY: Harper & Row.

Phillips, D. T., & Garcia-Diaz, A. (1981). *Fundamentals of network analysis*. Upper Saddle River, NJ: Prentice Hall Inc.

Piatetsky-Shapiro, G., Brachman, R., Khabaza, T., Kloesgen, W., & Simoudis, E. (1996). An overview of issues in developing industrial data mining and knowledge discovery application. In *Proceedings of Second International Conference on Knowledge Discovery and Data Mining*. Portland, OR: AAAI Press.

Piri, E., & Pentikousis, K. (2009). IEEE 802.21: Media independent handover services. *The Internet Protocol Journal*, *12*(2), 7–27.

Plessis, M. D. (2005). Drivers of knowledge management in the corporate environment. *International Journal of Information Management*, *25*(3), 193–202. doi:10.1016/j.ijinfomgt.2004.12.001

Polak, E., & Ribiere, G. (1969). Note sur la convergence de methods de directions conjuguees. *Revue Francais d'Informatique et de Recherche Operationnelle*, *16*, 35–43.

Pool, S. (2000). The learning organization: Motivating employees by integrating TQM philosophy in a supportive organizational culture. *Leadership and Organization Development Journal*, *21*(8), 373–378. doi:10.1108/01437730010379276

Pool, S., & Pool, B. (2007). A management development model: Measurement organizational commitment and its impact on job satisfaction among executives in a learning organization. *Journal of Management Development*, *26*(4), 353–369. doi:10.1108/02621710710740101

P-pale. T.K. (2007). Optimization of firewall rules. In *Proc. of ITI 29ᵗʰ Intl. Conf. on Information Technology Interfaces*, (pp. 685-690). IEEE.

Pradhan, B. B., & Bhattacharyya, B. (2009). Modelling of micro-electrodischarge machining during machining of titanium alloy Ti-6Al-4V using response surface methodology and artificial neural network algorithm. *Proceedings of the Institution of Mechanical Engineers. Part B, Journal of Engineering Manufacture, 223*(6), 683–693. doi:10.1243/09544054JEM1343

Pradhan, M. K., & Biswas, C. K. (2009). Neuro-fuzzy model and regression model a comparison study of MRR in electrical discharge machining of D2 tool steel. *International Journal of Mathematical. Physical and Engineering Sciences, 3*, 48–53.

Pradhan, M. K., Das, R., & Biswas, C. K. (2009). Comparisons of neural network models on surface roughness in electrical discharge machining. *Proceedings of the Institution of Mechanical Engineers. Part B, Journal of Engineering Manufacture, 223*(7), 801–808. doi:10.1243/09544054JEM1367

Pradhan, M. K., Das, R., & Biswas, C. K. (2010). Prediction of material removal rate using recurrent Elman networks in electrical discharge machining of AISI D2 tool steel. *International Journal of Manufacturing Technology And Industrial Engineering, 1*, 29–37.

Pradhan, M., & Biswas, C. (2010). Neuro-fuzzy and neural network-based prediction of various responses in electrical discharge machining of AISI D2 steel - NF and NN based prediction of responses in EDM of D2 steel. *International Journal of Advanced Manufacturing Technology, 50*, 591–610. doi:10.1007/s00170-010-2531-8

Pramanik, K. (2004). Use of artificial neural networks for prediction of cell mass and ethanol concentration in batch fermentation using saccharomyces cerevisiae yeast. *Institution of Engineers Journal, 85*, 31–35.

Preparata, M. G., & Chien, R. (1967). On the connection assignment problem of diagnosable systems. *IEEE Trans. Comps, 16*(6), 848–854.

Pritsker, A.A.B. (1966). *GERT: Graphical evaluation and review technique, memorandum*. RM-4973-NASA.

Pritsker, A. A. B. (1968). *GERT networks*. New York: The Projection Engineer.

Pritsker, A. A. B. (1977). *Modeling and analysis using Q-GERT networks*. New York: John Wiley & Sons.

Puertas, I., Luis, C. J., & Alvarez, L. (2004). Analysis of the influence of EDM parameters of surface quality, MRR and awe of WC-Co. *Journal of Materials Processing Technology, 153-154*(1-3), 1026–1032. doi:10.1016/j.jmatprotec.2004.04.346

Punyotoya, S., & Khilar, P. M. (2009). Distributed microcontroller-based actuator fault diagnosis in multi-rate fly-by-wire system. In *Proc. of 12th International Conference on Information Technology*, (pp. 17-22). Academic Press.

Qian, Y. H., & Liang, J. Y. (2006). Rough set method based on multi-granulations. In *Proceedings of the 5th IEEE Conference on Cognitive Informatics*, (Vol. 1, pp. 297 – 304). IEEE.

Qian, Y. H., Liang, J. Y., & Dang, C. Y. (2007). MGRS in incomplete information systems. In *Proceedings of IEEE Conference on Granular Computing*, (pp. 163 – 168). IEEE.

Quinn, R. E., & Cameron, K. (1983). Organizational life cycles and sifting criteria of effectiveness: Some preliminary evidence. *Management Science, 29*(1), 33–51. doi:10.1287/mnsc.29.1.33

Raghavan, R., & Tripathy, B. K. (2011). On some topological properties of multigranular rough sets. *Journal of Advances in Applied Science Research, 2*(3), 536–543.

Raghavan, R., & Tripathy, B. K. (2013). On some comparison properties of rough sets based on multigranulations and types of multigranular approximations of classifications. *International Journal of Intelligent Systems and Applications, 6*, 70–77. doi:10.5815/ijisa.2013.06.09

Raghunath, B. R., & Mahadeo, S. N. (2008). Network intrusion detection system (NIDS). In *Proceedings of the First International Conference on Emerging Trends in Engineering and Technology, 2008*. IEEE. doi:10.1109/ICETET.2008.252

Rahmani, A. M., & Rezvani, M. (2009). A novel genetic algorithm for static task scheduling in distributed systems. *International Journal of Computer Theory and Engineering, 1*(1), 1793–8201.

Rakesh, A., & Ramakrishnan, S. (2000). Privacy-preserving data mining. In *Proceedings of the 2000 ACM SIGMOD International Conference on Management of Data* (pp. 439-450). New York: ACM.

Ramakrishnan, S., & Rakesh, A. (1996). Mining quantitative association rules in large relational table. *SIGMOD Record*, *25*(2), 1–12. doi:10.1145/235968.233311

Ramanathan, R. (2001). A data envelopment analysis of comparative performance of schools in Netherland. *Opsearch*, *38*(2), 160–182.

Ramos, C. C. O., Papa, J. P., Souza, A. N., Chiachia, G., & Falcao, A. X. (2011). What is the importance of selecting features for non-technical losses identification? In *Proceedings of the 2011 IEEE International Symposium on Circuits and Systems* (ISCAS). IEEE. doi:10.1109/ISCAS.2011.5937748

Ramos, C. C. O., Souza, A. N., Papa, J. P., & Falcao, A. X. (2009). Fast non-technical losses identification through optimum-path forest. In *Proceedings of the 15th International Conference on Intelligent System Applications to Power Systems, 2009*. IEEE. doi:10.1109/ISAP.2009.5352910

Ramos, C. C. O., de Sousa, A. N., Papa, J. P., & Falcão, A. X. (2011). A new approach for nontechnical losses detection based on optimum-path forest. *IEEE Transactions on Power Systems*, *26*(1), 181–189. doi:10.1109/TPWRS.2010.2051823

Ramraj, R., Ahmad, I., & Habibi, D. (2011). *Multi-access environments in next generation networks.*

Randeree, K., & Chaudhry, A. (2007). Leadership in project managed environments: Employee perceptions of leadership styles within infrastructure development in Dubai. *International Review of Business Research Papers*, *3*(4), 220–232.

Rao, M. (2002). *Knowledge management tools and techniques: Practitioners and experts evaluate KM solutions.* Amsterdam, The Netherlands: Elsevier.

Rastogi, P. (2000). Knowledge management and intellectual capital: The new virtuous reality of competitiveness. *Human Systems Management*, *19*(1), 39–49.

Rathore, A. K., Chaurasia, R. K., Mishra, R., & Kumar, H. (2012). Road map and challenges in 4G wireless system. *J Elec Electron*, *1*(104), 2.

Ravasi, D., & Schultz, M. (2006). Responding to organizational identity threats: Exploring the role of organizational culture. *Academy of Management Journal*, *49*(3), 433–458. doi:10.5465/AMJ.2006.21794663

Ray, C. S., & Yongil, J. (2003). *Reputation and efficiency: A nonparametric assessment of America's top-rated MBA programs* (Working Paper 2003-13). Retrieved from http://www.econ.uconn.edu/

Ray, S. K., Pawlikowski, K., & Sirisena, H. (2010). Handover in mobile WiMAX networks: The state of art and research issues. *IEEE Communications Surveys & Tutorials*, *12*(3), 376–399. doi:10.1109/SURV.2010.032210.00064

Rebahi, Y., Nassar, M., Magedanz, T., & Festor, O. (2011). A survey on fraud and service misuse in voice over IP (VoIP) networks. *Information Security Technical Report*, *16*(1), 12–19. doi:10.1016/j.istr.2010.10.012

Ren, X., Huang, H., & Deng, L. (2009). MUAP classification based on wavelet packet and fuzzy clustering technique. In *Proceedings of 3rd International Conference on Bioinformatics and Biomedical Engineering*. IEEE.

Ren, Y. S., Shang, F. J., & Lei, Y. (2008). Survey of mobility management and mobile IP technique. *Application Research of Computers*, *12*, 9.

Reynolds, S. M., Ka, L., Riffle, M. E., Bilmes, J. A., & Noble, W. S. (2008). Transmembrane topology and signal peptide prediction using dynamic bayesian networks. *PLoS Computational Biology*, *4*(11), e1000213. doi:10.1371/journal.pcbi.1000213 PMID:18989393

Rhodes, E. Y., & Southwick, L. (1986). *Determinants of efficiency in public and private universities*. Department of Economics, University of South Carolina.

Richardson, R. (1997). Neural networks compared to statistical techniques. In *Proceedings of the Computational Intelligence for Financial Engineering (CIFEr)*. IEEE.

Robbins, S. P., & Judge, T. (2009). *Organizational behavior*. Upper Saddle River, NJ: Pearson Prentice Hall.

Robert, J., & Schalkof. (2001). *Artificial neural network*. New York: McGraw-Hill.

Roche, D. B., Buenavista, M. T., Tetchner, S. J., & Mc-Guffin, L. J. (2011). The IntFOLD server: An integrated web resource for protein fold recognition, 3D model quality assessment, intrinsic disorder prediction, domain prediction and ligand binding site prediction. *Nucleic Acids Research*, 39, W171-6. doi:10.1093/nar/gkr184 PMID:21459847

Roche, D. B., Tetchner, S. J., & McGuffin, L. J. (2010). The binding site distance test score: A robust method for the assessment of predicted protein binding sites. *Bioinformatics (Oxford, England)*, 26(22), 2920–2921. doi:10.1093/bioinformatics/btq543 PMID:20861025

Rohl, C. A., Strauss, C. E. M., Misura, K. M. S., & Baker, D. (2004). Protein structure prediction using rosetta. *Methods in Enzymology*, 383, 66–93. PMID:15063647

Ruiz-Mercader, J., Merono-Cerdan, A. L., & Sabater-Sanchez, R. (2006). Information technology and learning: Their relationship and impact on organizational performance in small business. *International Journal of Information Management*, 26(1), 16–29. doi:10.1016/j.ijinfomgt.2005.10.003

Rummelhart, D., Hinton, G., & Williams, R. (1986). Learning representations by back propagation errors. *Nature*, 323, 533–536. doi:10.1038/323533a0

Sabir, H. M., & Kalyar, M. N. (2013). Firm's innovativeness and employee job satisfaction: The role of organizational learning culture. *Interdisciplinary Journal of Contemporary Research in Business*, 4(9), 670–686.

Sahah, K., & Kahtani, A. (2010). Performance evaluation comparison of snort NIDS under LINUX and windows server. *Journal of Network and Computer Applications*, 33, 6–15. doi:10.1016/j.jnca.2009.07.005

Sahin, Y., & Duman, E. (2011). Detecting credit card fraud by ANN and logistic regression. In *Proceedings of the 2011 International Symposium on Innovations in Intelligent Systems and Applications* (INISTA). IEEE. doi:10.1109/INISTA.2011.5946108

Sahin, Y., Bulkan, S., & Duman, E. (2013). A cost-sensitive decision tree approach for fraud detection. *Expert Systems with Applications*, 40(15), 5916–5923. doi:10.1016/j.eswa.2013.05.021

Sahoo, B., Kumar, D., & Jena, S. K. (2013). Analysing the impact of heterogeneity with greedy resource allocation algorithms for dynamic load balancing in heterogeneous distributed computing system. *International Journal of Computers and Applications*, 62(19), 25–34. doi:10.5120/10190-5070

Sajeva, S. (2010). The analysis of key elements of socio-technical knowledge management system. *Economics and Management*, 15, 765–774.

Saleem, D. M. A., Acharjya, D. P., Kannan, A., & Iyengar, N. C. S. N. (2012). An intelligent knowledge mining model for kidney cancer using rough set theory. *International Journal of Bioinformatics Research and Applications*, 8(5/6), 417–435. doi:10.1504/IJBRA.2012.049625 PMID:23060419

Sali, A. (1995). Comparative protein modeling by satisfaction of spatial restraints. *Molecular Medicine Today*, 1, 270–277. doi:10.1016/S1357-4310(95)91170-7 PMID:9415161

Salleh, K., Chong, S. C., Syed Ahmad, S. N., & Syed Ikhsan, S. O. (2012). Learning and knowledge transfer performance among public sector accountants: An empirical survey. *Knowledge Management Research and Practice*, 10(2), 164–174. doi:10.1057/kmrp.2011.46

Salonitis, K., Stournaras, A., Stavropoulos, P., & Chryssolouris, G. (2009). Thermal modeling of the material removal rate and surface roughness for die-sinking EDM. *International Journal of Advanced Manufacturing Technology*, 40(3-4), 316–323. doi:10.1007/s00170-007-1327-y

Sanchez, R. (1996). *Strategic learning and knowledge management*. Chichester, UK: John Wiley & Sons.

Sandhu, U. A., Haider, S., Naseer, S., & Ateeb, O. U. (2011). A survey of Intrusion detection and prevention technology. In *Proceedings of Intl. Conf. on Information Communication and Management*. IACSIT Press.

Sandhu, P. S., & Shalini, C. (2011). A comparative analysis of conjugate gradient algorithms & PSO based neural network approaches for reusability evaluation of procedure based software systems. *Chiang Mai Journal of Science*, 38, 123–135.

Sandhu, U. S., Haider, S., Naseer, S., & Ateeb, O. U. (2011). A study of novel approaches used in intrusion detection and prevention system. *Intl. Journal of Information and Education Technology*, *1*(5), 426–431. doi:10.7763/IJIET.2011.V1.70

Santos-Vijande, M. L., Lopez-Sanchez, J. A., & Trespalacios, J. A. (2012). How organizational learning affects a firm's flexibility, competitive strategy, and performance. *Journal of Business Research*, *65*(8), 1079–1089. doi:10.1016/j.jbusres.2011.09.002

Sardis, G. N., & Gootee, T. P. (1982). EMG pattern analysis and classification for a prosthetic arm. *IEEE Transactions on Bio-Medical Engineering*, *29*(6), 403–412. doi:10.1109/TBME.1982.324954 PMID:7106790

Sattar, A., Khan, S., Nawaz, A., & Qureshi, Q. (2010). Theories of job satisfaction: Global applications and limitation. *Gomal University Journal of Research*, *26*(2), 45–62.

Sattar, A., & Nawaz, A. (2011). Investigating the demographic impacts on the job satisfaction of district officers in the province of KPK, Pakistan. *International Research Journal of Management and Business Studies*, *1*(2), 68–75.

Saxena, N., Sengupta, S., Wong, K. K., & Roy, A. (2013). Special issue on advances in 4G wireless and beyond. *EURASIP Journal on Wireless Communications and Networking*, (1): 1–3.

Scarfone, K., & Mell, P. (2007). *Guide to Intrusion detection and prevention system (IDPS)*. Retrieved from http://csrc.nist.gov/publications/nistpubs/800-94/sp800-94.pdf

Schein, E. H. (1992). *Organizational culture and leadership: A dynamic view*. San Francisco, CA: Jossey-Bass.

Schwede, T., Sali, A., Honig, B., Levitt, M., Berman, H. M., & Jones, D. et al. (2009). Outcome of a workshop on applications of protein models in biomedical research. *Structure (London, England)*, *17*(2), 151–159. doi:10.1016/j.str.2008.12.014 PMID:19217386

Seddigh, N., Nandy, B., Makkar, R., & Beaumont, J. F. (2010). Security advances and challenges in 4G wireless networks. In *Proceedings of Privacy Security and Trust (PST), 2010 Eighth Annual International Conference on* (pp. 62-71). IEEE.

Sehgal, A., & Agrawal, R. (2010). QoS based network selection scheme for 4G systems. *IEEE Transactions on Consumer Electronics*, *56*(2), 560–565. doi:10.1109/TCE.2010.5505970

Seidler-de Alwis, R., & Hartmann, E. (2008). The use of tacit knowledge within innovative companies: Knowledge management in innovative enterprises. *Journal of Knowledge Management*, *12*(1), 133–147. doi:10.1108/13673270810852449

Senge, P. M. (1990). *The fifth discipline: The art & practice of the learning organization*. London, UK: Random House.

Sengupta, A., & Dahbura, A. T. (1989). On self-diagnosable multiprocessor systems: Diagnosis by the comparison approach. In *Proc. IEEE Symp. on Fault-Tolerant Computing*, (pp. 54-61). IEEE.

Seo, D., Lee, H., & Nuwere, E. (2013). SIPAD: SIP–VoIP anomaly detection using a stateful rule tree. *Computer Communications*, *36*(5), 562–574. doi:10.1016/j.comcom.2012.12.004

Serenko, A., & Bontis, N. (2004). Meta-review of knowledge management and intellectual capital literature: Citation impact and research productivity rankings. *Knowledge and Process Management*, *11*(3), 185–198. doi:10.1002/kpm.203

Seyedhossein, L., & Hashemi, M. R. (2010). Mining information from credit card time series for timelier fraud detection. In *Proceedings of the 2010 5th International Symposium on Telecommunications* (IST). IEEE. doi:10.1109/ISTEL.2010.5734099

Shabtai, A., Fledel, Y., Kanonov, V., Elovici, Y., Dolev, S., & Glezer, C. (2010). Google Android: A comprehensive security assessment. *IEEE Security and Privacy*, *8*, 35–44. doi:10.1109/MSP.2010.2

Shadur, M. A., Kienzle, R., & Rodwell, J. J. (1999). The relationship between organizational climate and employee perceptions of involvement. *Group & Organization Management*, *24*(4), 479–503. doi:10.1177/1059601199244005

Shahzad, F., Luqman, R. A., Khan, A. R., & Shabbir, L. (2012). Impact of organizational culture on organizational performance: An overview. *Interdisciplinary Journal of Contemporary Research in Business*, *3*(9), 975–985.

Sharma, S. G. (2010). *Implementation of artificial neural network for odours identification using E-NOSE.* Paper presented at the National Conference on Computational Instrumentation CSIO. Chandigarh, India.

Sharma, R. S., & Djiaw, V. (2011). Realising the strategic impact of business intelligence tools. *Vine, 41*(2), 113–131. doi:10.1108/03055721111134772

Shin, D. H. (2010). Challenges and drivers in the 4G evolution in Korea. *International Journal of Mobile Communications, 8*(3), 297–312. doi:10.1504/IJMC.2010.032976

Shragai, A., & Schneider, M. (2001). Discovering quantitative associations in databases. In *Proceedings of IFSA World Congress and 20th NAFIPS International Conference* (pp. 423-428). Vancouver, Canada: IEEE.

Shrikant, A., Tanu, S., Swati, S., Vijay, C., & Abhishek, V. (2010). Privacy and data protection in cyberspace in Indian environment. *International Journal of Engineering Science and Technology, 2*(5), 942–951.

Sibanda, B. L., Blundell, T. L., & Thornton, J. M. (1989). Conformation of hairpins in protein structures: A systematic classification with applications to modeling by homology, electron density fitting and protein engineering. *Journal of Molecular Biology, 206*, 759–777. doi:10.1016/0022-2836(89)90583-4 PMID:2500530

Siegel, H. J., & Ali, S. (2000). Techniques for mapping tasks to machines in heterogeneous computing systems. *Journal of Systems Architecture, 46*(8), 627–639. doi:10.1016/S1383-7621(99)00033-8

Simons, K. T., Strauss, C., & Baker, D. (2001). Prospects for ab initio protein structural genomics. *Journal of Molecular Biology, 306*, 1191–1199. doi:10.1006/jmbi.2000.4459 PMID:11237627

Singh, M. D., Shankar, R., Narain, R., & Kumar, A. (2006). Survey of knowledge management practices in Indian manufacturing industries. *Journal of Knowledge Management, 10*(6), 110–128. doi:10.1108/13673270610709251

Skolnick, J., Fetrow, J. S., & Kolinski, A. (2000). Structural genomics and its importance for gene function analysis. *Nature Biotechnology, 18*(3), 283–285. doi:10.1038/73723 PMID:10700142

Skorin, K. J., & Wendy, K. T. (2001). Training artificial neural networks: Backpropagation via nonlinear optimization. *Journal of Computing and Information Technology, 9*, 1–14. doi:10.2498/cit.2001.01.01

Slater, S. F., & Narver, J. C. (1995). Market orientation and the learning organization. *Journal of Marketing, 59*(3), 63–74. doi:10.2307/1252120

Smyth, P. (2001). Breaking out of the black-box: Research challenges in data mining. In *Proceedings of ACM SIGMOD International Workshop on Research Issues in Data Mining and Knowledge Discovery* (DMKD'01). ACM.

Snoeren, A. C., & Balakrishnan, H. (2000). An end-to-end approach to host mobility. In *Proceedings of the 6th Annual International Conference on Mobile Computing and Networking* (pp. 155-166). ACM.

Soares, A., Andrade, A., Lamounier, E., & Carrijo, R. (2003). The development of a virtual myoelectric prosthesis controlled by an EMG pattern recognition system based on neural networks. *Journal of Intelligent Information Systems, 21*(2), 127–141. doi:10.1023/A:1024758415877

Sohani, M., Gaitonde, V., Siddeswarappa, B., & Deshpande, A. (2009). Investigations into the effect of tool shapes with size factor consideration in sink electrical discharge machining (EDM) process. *International Journal of Advanced Manufacturing Technology*, 1–15.

Soliman, H., Bellier, L., Elmalki, K., & Castelluccia, C. (2008). *Hierarchical mobile IPv6 (HMIPv6) mobility management.*

Sonnhammer, E., von Heijne, G., & Krogh, A. (1998). A hidden Markov model for predicting transmembrane helices in protein sequences. *Proc ISMB, 6*, 175–182.

Sotarauta, M., Horlings, L., & Liddle, J. (2012). *Leadership and change in sustainable regional development.* London, UK: Routledge.

Sotiropoulos, D. G., Kostopoulos, A. E., & Grapsa, T. N. (2002). A spectral version of perry's conjugate gradient method for neural network training. *Proceedings of 4th GRACM Congress on Computational Mechanics, 1*, 291-298.

Spector, P. (1997). *Job satisfaction: Application, sssessment, sauses, and consequences*. Thousand Oaks, CA: Sage Publications.

Spies, F. (1996). Modeling of optimal load balancing strategy using queueing theory. *Microprocessing and Microprogramming, 41*(8), 555–570. doi:10.1016/0165-6074(95)00006-2

Sreekumar, & Patel, G. (2007). Comparative analysis of b-school rankings and an alternate ranking method. *International Journal of Operations and Quantitative Management, 13*(1), 33-46.

Sreekumar, & Patel, G.N. (2005). Measuring the relative efficiency of some Indian MBA programmes- A DEA approach. *Business Perspective, 7*(2), 47-59.

Srivastava, A. K., Srivastava, S. K., & Shukla, K. K. (2000). *On the design issue of intelligent electronic nose system.* IEEE. doi:10.1109/ICIT.2000.854142

Stakhanova, N., Babu, S., & Wong, J. (2007). A taxonomy of intrusion response system. *International Journal of Computer Security, 1*, 169–184. doi:10.1504/IJICS.2007.012248

Stella, A., & Woodhouse, D. (2006). Australian universities quality agency. *Occasional Publications, 6*, 1446–4268.

Stevens-Navarro, E., & Wong, V. W. (2006). Comparison between vertical handoff decision algorithms for heterogeneous wireless networks. In *Proceedings of Vehicular Technology Conference, 2006* (Vol. 2, pp. 947-951). IEEE.

Struttmann, T. et al. (1998). Unintentional carbon monoxide poisoning from an unlikely source. *The Journal of the American Board of Family Practice, 11*(6), 481–484. doi:10.3122/jabfm.11.6.481 PMID:9876005

Suarez, A., & Macias, E. (2010). Video streaming based services over 4G networks: Challenges and solutions. In *Fourth-generation wireless networks: Applications and innovations* (pp. 494–525). Academic Press.

Sueaseenak, D., Wibirama, S., Chanwimalueang, T., Pintavirooj, C., & Sangworasil, M. (2008). Comparison study of muscular-contraction classification between independent component analysis and artificial neural network. In *Proceedings of International Symposium on Communications and Information Technologies*. IEEE.

Suehring, S., & Ziegler, R. L. (2006). *LINUX firewalls* (3rd ed.). Pearson Education Inc.

Suman, B., & Kumar, P. (2005). A survey of simulated annealing as a tool for single and multiobjective optimization. *The Journal of the Operational Research Society, 57*(10), 1143–1160. doi:10.1057/palgrave.jors.2602068

Sweeney, L. (2001). *Computational disclosure control: A primer on data privacy protection.* (Ph.D. Thesis). Massachusetts Institute of Technology. Cambridge, MA.

Sweeney, L. (1997). Guaranteeing anonymity when sharing medical data the Datafly system. In *Proceedings Journal of the American Medical Informatics Association* (pp. 51–55). Washington, DC: AMIA.

Sweeney, L. (2002). Achieving k-anonymity privacy protection using generalization and suppression. *International Journal on Uncertainty. Fuzziness and Knowledge-Based Systems, 10*(5), 571–588. doi:10.1142/S021848850200165X

Taminiau, Y., Smit, W., & De Lange, A. (2009). Innovation in management consulting firms through informal knowledge sharing. *Journal of Knowledge Management, 43*(1), 42–55. doi:10.1108/13673270910931152

Tang, H. K. (1999). An inventory of organizational innovativeness. *Technovation, 19*(1), 41–51. doi:10.1016/S0166-4972(98)00077-7

Taniguchi, M., Haft, M., Hollmen, J., & Tresp, V. (1998). Fraud detection in communication networks using neural and probabilistic methods. In *Proceedings of the 1998 IEEE International Conference on Acoustics, Speech and Signal Processing.* IEEE. doi:10.1109/ICASSP.1998.675496

Taniuchi, K., Ohba, Y., Fajardo, V., Das, S., Tauil, M., Cheng, Y. H., & Famolari, D. (2009). IEEE 802.21: Media independent handover: Features, applicability, and realization. *IEEE Communications Magazine, 47*(1), 112–120. doi:10.1109/MCOM.2009.4752687

Tao, Z., & Wang, L. (2009). Mixed gases recognition based on feedforward neural network. In *Proceedings of Second International Symposium on Intelligent Information Technology and Security Information.* IEEE. DOI 10.1109/IITSI.2009.35

Tenore, F., & Ramos, A. (2007). Towards the control of individual fingers of a prosthetic hand using surface EMG signals. In *Proceedings of 29th Annual International Conference of the IEEE Engineering Medicine Biological Society*. IEEE.

Terpstra, J. H., Love, P., Reck, R. P., & Scanlon, T. (2004). *Hardening LINUX*. New York: McGraw-Hill.

Theys, M. D., Braun, T. D., Siegal, H., Maciejewski, A. A., & Kwok, Y. (2001). Mapping tasks onto distributed heterogeneous computing systems using a genetic algorithm approach. In *Solutions to parallel and distributed computing problems: Lessons from biological sciences* (pp. 135–178). Academic Press.

Thompson, J., & Cavaleri, S. (2010). Dynamic knowledge, organizational growth, and sustainability: The case of Prestwick memory devices. *International Studies in Management and Organization, 40*(3), 50–60. doi:10.2753/IMO0020-8825400303

Tian, J., Zheng, X., Hu, H., & You, X. (2011). A survey of next generation mobile communications research in China. *Chinese Science Bulletin, 56*(27), 2875–2888. doi:10.1007/s11434-011-4658-x

Tong, X., & Shu, W. (2009). An efficient dynamic load balancing scheme for heterogenous processing system.[]. Academic Press.]. *Proceedings of Computational Intelligence and Natural Computing, 2*, 319–322.

Tridandapani, S., Somani, A. K., & Reddy, U. (1995). Low overhead multiprocessor allocation strategies exploiting system spare capacity for fault detection and location. *IEEE Transactions on Computers, 44*(7), 865–877. doi:10.1109/12.392845

Tripathy, B. K. (2012). On some topological properties of pessimistic multigranular rough sets. In *Proceedings of the UGC Sponsored National Conference in Seemanta College*. UGC.

Tripathy, B. K., & Mitra, A. (2013). On the approximate equalities of multigranular rough sets and approximate reasoning. In *Proceedings of 4th IEEE Conference on Computing, Communication and Network Technologies*. Tamil Nadu, India: IEEE.

Tripathy, B. K., & Nagaraju, M. (2011). Topological properties of incomplete multigranulation based on fuzzy rough sets. In *Proceedings of ObCom 2011 Conference*. VIT.

Tripathy, B. K. (2011). An analysis of approximate equalities based on rough set theory. *International Journal of Advances in Science and Technology, 31*, 23–36.

Tripathy, B. K., & Acharjya, D. P. (2010). Knowledge mining using ordering rules and rough sets on fuzzy approximation spaces. *International Journal of Advances in Science and Technology, 1*(3), 41–50.

Tripathy, B. K., & Acharjya, D. P. (2011). Association rule granulation using rough sets on intuitionistic fuzzy approximation spaces and granular computing. *Annals Computer Science Series, 9*(1), 125–144.

Tripathy, B. K., Mitra, A., & Ojha, J. (2008). On rough equalities and rough equivalence of sets. In *Rough sets and current trends in computing (LNAI)* (Vol. 5306, pp. 92–102). Berlin: Springer. doi:10.1007/978-3-540-88425-5_10

Tripathy, B. K., & Raghavan, R. (2013). Some algebraic properties of multigranulations and an analysis of multigranular approximations of classifications. *International Journal of Information Technology and Computer Science, 7*, 63–70. doi:10.5815/ijitcs.2013.07.08

Trivedi, K. S. (2001). *Probability and statistics with reliability, queuing and computer science applications*. Upper Saddle River, NJ: Prentice Hall.

Tsang, E. C. C., Yeung, D. S., & Wang, X. Z. (2003). OFFSS: Optimal fuzzy-valued feature subset selection. *IEEE Transactions on Fuzzy Systems, 11*(2), 202–213. doi:10.1109/TFUZZ.2003.809895

Tseng, L., Chin, Y., & Wang, S. (2009). A minimized makespan scheduler with multiple factors for grid computing systems. *Expert Systems with Applications, 36*(8), 11118–11130. doi:10.1016/j.eswa.2009.02.071

Tsenov, G., Zeghbib, A. H., Palis, F., Shoylev, N., & Mladenov, V. (2006). Neural networks for online classification of hand and finger movements using surface EMG signals. In *Proceedings of 8th Seminar on Neural Network Applications in Electrical Engineering*. IEEE.

Tsirigotis, G., Laure, B., & Maria, G. (2003). Neural network based recognition, of CO and NH_3 reducing gases, using a metallic oxide gas sensor array. *Scientific Proceedings of RTU, Telecommunications and Electronics, 3*(7), 6-10.

Tsuji, T., Fukuda, O., Kaneko, M., & Koji, I. (2000). Pattern classification of time-series EMG signals using neural networks. *International Journal of Adaptive Control and Signal Processing, 14*(8), 829–848. doi:10.1002/1099-1115(200012)14:8<829::AID-ACS623>3.0.CO;2-L

Tuan, L. T. (2013). Leading to learning and competitive intelligence. *The Learning Organization, 20*(3), 216–239. doi:10.1108/09696471311328460

Tusnady, G., & Simon, I. (1998). Principles governing amino acid composition of integral membrane proteins: Application to topology prediction. *Journal of Molecular Biology, 283*, 489–506. doi:10.1006/jmbi.1998.2107 PMID:9769220

Ucar, B., Aykanat, C., Kaya, K., & Ikinci, M. (2006). Task assignment in heterogeneous computing systems. *Journal of Parallel and Distributed Computing, 66*(1), 32–46. doi:10.1016/j.jpdc.2005.06.014

Uchida, N., Hiraiwa, A., Sonehara, N., & Shimohara, K. (1988). EMG pattern recognition by neural networks for multi fingers control. In *Proceedings of Annual International Conference of the IEEE Engineering Medicine Biological Society*. IEEE.

Uotila, T., Melkas, H., & Harmaakorpi, V. (2005). Incorporating futures research into regional knowledge creation and management. *Futures, 37*(8), 308–317. doi:10.1016/j.futures.2005.01.001

USEPA. (1980). *Health and environmental effects problem for hydrogen sulfide*. USEPA.

Valentincic, J., & Junkar, M. (2004). A model for detection of the eroding surface based on discharge parameters. *International Journal of Machine Tools & Manufacture, 44*, 175–181. doi:10.1016/j.ijmachtools.2003.10.013

Valez, G. V. (1972). A study of faculty satisfaction and dissatisfaction with the intrinsic and extrinsic job factors in Columbia University. *Dissertation Abstracts International, 33*(3), 997-A.

Van der Heijden, K. (2004). Can internally generated futures accelerate organizational learning? *Futures, 36*(2), 145–159. doi:10.1016/S0016-3287(03)00143-5

Van Dyke, N. (2005). Twenty years of university report cards. *Higher Education in Europe, 30*(2), 103–124. doi:10.1080/03797720500260173

Venmani, D. P., Gourhant, Y., Reynaud, L., Chemouil, P., & Zeghlache, D. (2013). Substitution networks based on software defined networking. In *Ad hoc networks* (pp. 242–259). Berlin: Springer. doi:10.1007/978-3-642-36958-2_17

Verykios, V. S., Bertino, E., Fovino, I. N., Provenza, L. P., Saygin, Y., & Theodoridis, Y. (2004). State-of-the-art in privacy preserving data mining. *SIGMOD Record, 33*(1), 50–57. doi:10.1145/974121.974131

Vidyarthi, D. P., & Tripathi, A. K. (2001). Maximizing reliability of distributed computing system with task allocation using simple genetic algorithm. *Journal of Systems Architecture, 47*(6), 549–554. doi:10.1016/S1383-7621(01)00013-3

Vijay, K. G., & Radha, K. P. (2008). A novel approach for statistical and fuzzy association rule mining on quantitative data. *Journal of Scientific and Industrial Research, 67*, 512–517.

Wakako, H. (2002). Separation of independent components from data mixed by several mixing matrices. *Signal Processing, 82*(12), 1949–1961. doi:10.1016/S0165-1684(02)00197-4

Wallach, E. (1983). Individuals and organizations: The cultural match. *Training and Development Journal, 37*(2), 29–36.

Walter, C. J., Lincoln, P., & Suri, N. (1997). Formally verified on-line diagnosis. *IEEE Transactions on Software Engineering, 23*(11), 684–721. doi:10.1109/32.637385

Wang, J. Z., Wang, R. C., Li, F., Jiang, M. W., & Jin, D. W. (2005). EMG signal classification for myoelectric teleoperating a dexterous robot hand. In *Proceedings of. 27th Annual International Conference of the IEEE Engineering Medicine Biological Society*. IEEE.

Wang, S. L., & Jafari, A. (2005). Hiding sensitive predictive association rules. In *Proceedings of IEEE International Conference on Systems, Man and Cybernetics*, (pp. 164-169). IEEE.

Wang, S. L., Lee, Y. H., Billis, S., & Jafari, A. (2004). Hiding sensitive items in privacy preserving association rule mining. In *Proceedings of International Conference on Systems, Man and Cybernetics*. IEEE.

Wang, C. C., & Lin, Y. (2009). Feasibility study of electrical discharge machining for W/Cu composite. *International Journal of Refractory Metals and Hard Materials*, 27(5), 872–882. doi:10.1016/j.ijrmhm.2009.04.005

Wang, H. (2006). Nearest neighborhood by neighborhood counting. *IEEE Transactions on Pattern Analysis and Machine Intelligence*, 28, 942–953. doi:10.1109/TPAMI.2006.126 PMID:16724588

Wang, K., Gelgele, H. L., Wang, Y., Yuan, Q., & Fang, M. (2003). A hybrid intelligent method for modelling the EDM process. *International Journal of Machine Tools & Manufacture*, 43, 995–999. doi:10.1016/S0890-6955(03)00102-0

Wang, P.-J., & Tsai, K.-M. (2001). Semi-empirical model on work removal and tool wear in electrical discharge machining. *Journal of Materials Processing Technology*, 114(1), 1–17. doi:10.1016/S0924-0136(01)00733-6

Wang, Y. L., & Ellinger, A. D. (2011). Organizational learning: Perception of external environment and innovation performance. *International Journal of Manpower*, 32(5-6), 512–536. doi:10.1108/01437721111158189

Wasniowski, R. (2006). Data mining support for intrusion detection and prevention. In *Proc. of the 6th WSEAS Intl. Conf. on Applied Computer Science* (pp. 392-396). Tenerife, Spain: WSEAS.

Watts, J., & Taylor, S. (1998). A practical approach to dynamic load balancing. *IEEE Transactions on Parallel and Distributed Systems*, 9(3), 235–248. doi:10.1109/71.674316

Weatherford, M. (2002). Mining for fraud. *IEEE Intelligent Systems*, 17(4), 4–6. doi:10.1109/MIS.2002.1024744

Weiss, D., Dawis, R., England, G., & Lofquist, L. (1967). *Manual for the Minnesota satisfaction questionnaire*. Minneapolis, MN: University of Minnesota Industrial Relations Center.

Weiss, H. (2002). Deconstructing job satisfaction: Separating evaluations, beliefs and affective experiences. *Human Resource Management Review*, 12(2), 173–194. doi:10.1016/S1053-4822(02)00045-1

Whitley, D. (1994). A genetic algorithm tutorial. *Statistics and Computing*, 4(2), 65–85. doi:10.1007/BF00175354

Wickramasinghe, N. (2007). Fostering knowledge assets in health with the KMI model. *International Journal of Management and Enterprise Development*, 4(1), 52–65. doi:10.1504/IJMED.2007.011455

Widyanto, M. R., Benyamin, K., Hajime, N., Kazuhiko, K., & Kaoru, H. (2006). A fuzzy-similarity-based self-organized network inspired by immune algorithm for three-mixture-fragrance recognition. *IEEE Transactions on Industrial Electronics*, 53(1), 313–321. doi:10.1109/TIE.2005.862212

Wiest, J. D., & Levy, F. K. (2008). *A management guide to CPM/PERT with GERT/PDM/DCPM and other networks*. New Delhi, India: Prentice-Hall of India.

Wilks, A. J. (1990). Hall effect based electrical energy metering device with fraud detection and instantaneous voltage, current and power outputs. In *Proceedings of the Sixth International Conference on Metering Apparatus and Tariffs for Electricity Supply*. IET.

Williams, L. J., & Hazer, J. T. (1986). Antecedents and consequences of satisfaction and commitment in turnover models: A reanalysis using latent variable structural equation methods. *The Journal of Applied Psychology*, 71(2), 219–231. doi:10.1037/0021-9010.71.2.219

William, W., Cooper, L., Seiford, M., & Zhu, J. (2011). Data envelopment analysis history, models and interpretations. *International Series in Operations Research & Management Science*, 16(4), 1–39.

Wilson, A. M. (2001). Understanding organizational culture and the implication for corporate marketing. *European Journal of Marketing*, 35(3-4), 353–367. doi:10.1108/03090560110382066

Witten, I. H., & Frank, E. (2005). *Data mining: Practical machine learning tools and techniques* (2nd ed.). San Francisco: Morgan Kaufmann.

Wolfe, P. (1969). Convergence conditions for ascent methods. *SIAM Review, 11*(2), 226–235. doi:10.1137/1011036. JSTOR 2028111

Wolfe, P. (1971). Convergence conditions for ascent methods: II: Some corrections. *SIAM Review, 13*(2), 185–188. doi:10.1137/1013035

Won, S., Dongil, S. Y., & Jamin, K. (2010). The estimation of hazardous gas release rate using optical sensor and neural network. In *Proceedings of European Symposium on Computer Aided Process Engineering, ESCAPE20.* Elsevier B.V.

Wongchoosuka, C., Wisitsoraatb, A., Tuantranontb, A., & Kerdcharoena, T. (2010). Portable Electronic nose based on carbon nanotube-sno$_2$ gas sensors and its application for detection of methanol contamination in whiskeys. *Sensors and Actuators. B, Chemical.* doi:10.1016/j.snb.2010.03.072

Wu, L., Ping, R., Ke, L., & Hai-xin, D. (2011). Intrusion detection using SVM. In *Proceedings of the 2011 7th International Conference on Wireless Communications, Networking and Mobile Computing* (WiCOM). IEEE. doi:10.1109/wicom.2011.6040153

Wu, M., & Kou, G. (2010). Fuzzy rough set model on multi-granulations. In *Proceedings of the 2nd International Conference on Computer Engineering and Technology,* (Vol. 2, pp. 72–75). IEEE.

Wu, J. (1999). *Distributed system design.* Boca Raton, FL: CRC Press.

Xie, J., & Akyildiz, R. (2002). An optimal location management scheme for minimizing signaling cost in mobile IP. In *Proceedings of Communications, 2002* (Vol. 5, pp. 3313–3317). IEEE.

Xinyou Zhang, W. Z., & Li, C. (2004). Intrusion prevention system design. In *Proceedings of Computer and Information Technology* (pp. 386–390). CIT.

Xu, W., Pang, Y., Ma, J., Wang, S.-Y., Hao, G., Zeng, S., & Qian, Y.-H. (2008). Fraud detection in telecommunication: A rough fuzzy set based approach. In *Proceedings of the 2008 International Conference on Machine Learning and Cybernetics.* IEEE. doi:10.1109/ICMLC.2008.4620596

Xu, C., & Lau, F. (1994). Iterative dynamic load balancing in multicomputers. *The Journal of the Operational Research Society,* 786–796.

Xue, M., & Zhu, C. (2009). Applied research on data mining algorithm in network intrusion detection. In *Proceedings of the International Joint Conference on Artificial Intelligence, 2009.* IEEE. doi:10.1109/JCAI.2009.25

Xu, J. (2005). Fold recognition by predicted alignment accuracy. *IEEE/ACM Transactions on Computational Biology and Bioinformatics, 2,* 157–165. doi:10.1109/TCBB.2005.24 PMID:17044180

Xu, L. Z., S'anchez, R., Sali, A., & Heintz, N. (1996). Ligand specificity of brain lipid binding protein. *The Journal of Biological Chemistry, 271,* 24711–24719. doi:10.1074/jbc.271.40.24711 PMID:8798739

Yamane, T. (1970). *Statistics – An introductory analysis.* Tokyo, Japan: John Weatherhill.

Yang, K., Gondal, I., Qiu, B., & Dooley, L. S. (2007). Combined SINR based vertical handoff algorithm for next generation heterogeneous wireless networks. In *Proceedings of Global Telecommunications Conference, 2007* (pp. 4483-4487). IEEE.

Yang, J. C. Y., & Clarke, D. W. (1999). The self-validating actuator. *Control Engineering Practice, 7*(3), 249–260. doi:10.1016/S0967-0661(98)00148-8

Yao, Y. Y. (2005). Perspectives of granular computing. In *Proceedings of 2005 IEEE International Conference on Granular Computing,* (pp. 85 – 90). IEEE.

Yao, Y. Y. (2007). The art of granular computing. In *Proceedings of the International Conference on Rough Sets and Emerging Intelligent Systems Paradigms,* (pp. 101 – 112). IEEE.

Yao, J. T., Vasilakos, V., & Pedrycz, W. (2013). *Granular computing: Perspectives and challenges.* IEEE Transactions on Cybernetics.

Yao, Y. Y. (1998). Relational interpretations of neighborhood operators and rough set approximation operators. *Information Sciences, 111,* 239–259. doi:10.1016/S0020-0255(98)10006-3

Yao, Y. Y. (2008). A unified framework of granular computing. In *Handbook of granular computing* (pp. 401–410). Academic Press. doi:10.1002/9780470724163.ch17

Yao, Y. Y., & Yao, B. (2012). Covering based rough set approximations. *Information Sciences, 200,* 91–107. doi:10.1016/j.ins.2012.02.065

Yeo, R. K., & Li, J. (2013). In pursuit of learning: Sensemaking the quality of work life. *European Journal of Training and Development, 37*(2), 136–160. doi:10.1108/03090591311301662

Yeo, S. H., Kurnia, W., & Tan, P. C. (2008). Critical assessment and numerical comparison of electro-thermal models in EDM. *Journal of Materials Processing Technology, 203*(1-3), 491. doi:10.1016/j.jmatprotec.2007.10.026

Yiping, K., James, C., & Wilfred, N. (2008). An information-theoretic approach to quantitative association rule mining. *Knowledge and Information Systems, 16*(2), 213–244. doi:10.1007/s10115-007-0104-4

Yonatan, A., & Yehuda, L. (2003). A statistical theory for quantitative association rules. *Journal of Intelligent Information Systems, 20*(3), 255–283. doi:10.1023/A:1022812808206

Yu, L., & Liu, H. (2003). Feature selection for high-dimensional data: A fast correlation-based filter solution. In *Proceedings of Twelfth International Conference on Machine Learning.* San Francisco: Morgan Kaufmann.

Yu, D., Chatterjee, S., Sheikholeslami, G., & Zhang, A. (1998). *Efficiently detecting arbitrary shaped clusters in very large datasets with high dimensions.* Buffalo, NY: State University of New York at Buffalo.

Yue, D., Wu, X., Wang, Y., Li, Y., & Chu, C.-H. (2007). A review of data mining-based financial fraud detection research. In *Proceedings of the International Conference on Wireless Communications, Networking and Mobile Computing.* IEEE. doi:10.1109/WICOM.2007.1352

Zadeh, L. A. (1965). Fuzzy sets. *Information and Control, 8*(11), 338–353. doi:10.1016/S0019-9958(65)90241-X

Zahran, A. H., & Liang, B. (2005). Performance evaluation framework for vertical handoff algorithms in heterogeneous networks. In *Proceedings of Communications, 2005* (Vol. 1, pp. 173–178). IEEE. doi:10.1109/ICC.2005.1494342

Zaim, H., Ekrem, T., & Selim, Z. (2007). Performance of knowledge management practices: A casual analysis. *Journal of Knowledge Management, 11*(6), 54–67. doi:10.1108/13673270710832163

Zakowski, W. (1983). Approximations in the space (U II). *Demonstration Mathematics, 16,* 761–769.

Zardoshti-Kermani, M., Wheeler, B. C., Badie, K., & Hashemi, R. M. (1995). EMG feature evaluation for movement control of upper extremity prosthesis. *IEEE Transactions on Rehabilitation Engineering, 3*(4), 324–333. doi:10.1109/86.481972

Zellmer-Bruhn, M., & Gibson, C. (2006). Multinational organization context: Implications for team learning and performance. *Academy of Management Journal, 49*(3), 501–518. doi:10.5465/AMJ.2006.21794668

Zeng, Z., & Veeravalli, B. (2006). Design and performance evaluation of queue-and-rate-adjustment dynamic load balancing policies for distributed networks. *IEEE Transactions on Computers, 55*(11), 1410–1422. doi:10.1109/TC.2006.180

Zhang, T., Ramakrishnan, R., & Livny, M. (1996). BIRCH: An efficient data clustering method for very large databases. In *Proceedings of SIGMOD International Conference,* (pp. 103–114). ACM.

Zhang, Y., Chen, W., & Black, J. (2011). Anomaly detection in premise energy consumption data. In *Proceedings of the 2011 IEEE Power and Energy Society General Meeting.* IEEE. doi:10.1109/PES.2011.6039858

Zhang, C., Ariyavisitakul, S. L., & Tao, M. (2012). LTE-advanced and 4G wireless communications. *IEEE Communications Magazine, 50*(2), 102–103. doi:10.1109/MCOM.2012.6146488

Zhang, Q., Haigang, L., & Zhongyu, T. (2010). *Knowledge-based genetic algorithms data fusion and its application in mine mixed-gas detection.* IEEE.

Zhang, X., Shira, L. B., & Patrick, J. F. (2002). A con-njugate gradient neural network technique for ultrasound inverse imaging. *Journal of Computational Acoustics*, *10*(2), 243–264.

Zhang, Y. (2008). Progress and challenges in protein structure. *Current Opinion in Structural Biology*, *18*(3), 342–348. doi:10.1016/j.sbi.2008.02.004 PMID:18436442

Zhao, J. Xie, Z., Jiang, L., Cai, H., Liu, H., & Hirzinger, G. (2005). Levenberg-Marquardt based neural network control for a five-fingered prosthetic hand. In *Proceedings of IEEE International Conference on Robotics and Automation*. IEEE.

Zhao, J., Jiang, L., Cai, H., Liu, H., & Hirzinger, G. (2006). A novel EMG motion pattern classifier based on wavelet transform and nonlinearity analysis method. In *Proceedings of IEEE International Conference on Robotics and Biomimetics*. IEEE.

Zhao, J., & Ordóñez de Pablos, P. (2011). Regional knowledge management: The perspective of management theory. *Behaviour & Information Technology*, *30*(1), 39–49. doi:10.1080/0144929X.2010.492240

Zhao, Y., & Karypis, G. (2002). Evaluation of hierarchical clustering algorithms for document datasets. In *Proceedings of Information and Knowledge Management*. McLean, VA: Academic Press.

Zhou, H., Pandit, S. B., Lee, S. Y., Borreguero, J., Chen, H., Wroblewska, L., & Skolnick, J. (2007). Analysis of TASSER-based CASP7 protein structure prediction results. *Proteins*, *69*(8), 90–97. doi:10.1002/prot.21649 PMID:17705276

Zhou, H., & Zhou, Y. (2002). Distance-scaled, finite ideal-gas reference state improves structure-derived potentials of mean force for structure selection and stability prediction. *Protein Science*, *11*, 2714–2726. doi:10.1110/ps.0217002 PMID:12381853

Zomaya, A., & Teh, Y. (2001). Observations on using genetic algorithms for dynamic load-balancing. *IEEE Transactions on Parallel and Distributed Systems*, *12*(9), 899–911. doi:10.1109/71.954620

About the Contributors

B. K. Tripathy a senior professor in the school of computing sciences and engineering, VIT University, at Vellore, India. He has published more than 190 technical papers in various international journals, conferences, and book chapters and has guided 14 scholars for their PhD degrees in both mathematics and computer science. He is associated with many professional bodies like IEEE, ACEEE, ACM, IRSS, AISTC, ISTP, CSI, AMS, and IMS. He is in the editorial board of several international journals like CTA, ITTA, AMMS, IJCTE, AISS, AIT, and IJPS and is a reviewer of over 40 international journals like *Mathematical Reviews, Information Sciences, Analysis of Neural Networks, Journal of Knowledge Engineering, Mathematical Communications, IEEE Transactions on Fuzzy Systems*, and *Journal of Analysis*. His research interest includes fuzzy sets and systems, rough sets and knowledge engineering, data clustering, soft computing, granular computing, theory of multisets, list theory, content-based learning, remote laboratories and social networks.

D. P. Acharjya received his Ph. D in computer science from Berhampur University, India; M. Tech. degree in computer science from Utkal University, India in 2002; and M. Sc. from NIT, Rourkela, India. He has been awarded with Gold Medal in M. Sc. Currently he is an Associate Professor in the school of computing sciences and engineering, VIT University, Vellore, India. He has authored many national and international journal papers and five books: *Fundamental Approach to Discrete Mathematics, Computer Based on Mathematics, Theory of Computation; Rough Set in Knowledge Representation and Granular Computing; Introduction to Information Technology and Computer Programming* to his credit. He is associated with many professional bodies CSI, ISTE, IMS, AMTI, ISIAM, OITS, IACSIT, CSTA, IEEE and IAENG. He was founder secretary of OITS Rourkela chapter. His current research interests include rough sets, formal concept analysis, knowledge representation, data mining, granular computing and business intelligence.

* * *

Vikramaditya Bhandari obtained his B. Tech. (Chemical Engineering) from VIT University, India. He started his professional career as a graduate engineer trainee with Nutra Specialties Pvt Ltd, India and later joined Sanskar Chemicals and Drugs Pvt Ltd., India as project engineer where he was involved in production planning, process scheduling, optimization and defining standards for quality control and assurance. He is currently working as process engineer for Shasun Pharma Solutions Limited, Dudley, UK. His areas of work include designing process streams for new product introduction, preparing engineering flow diagrams, carrying out environmental impact assessment, modeling emission rates for submission to environmental authorities, solvent management, scaling up processes from lab scale to plant scale, equipment mapping along with initiation time, scheduling time cycle and performing utility requirement calculations.

Félix Biscarri received the B.Sc. degree in electronic physics and the Ph.D. degree in computer science from the University of Seville, Seville, Spain, in 1991 and 2001 respectively. He is currently a coordinating professor of power electronic with the polytechnic, University School of Seville. His research areas include electricity markets, electrical customer classification, and fraud detection in the power electric industry.

Jesús Biscarri received the B.Sc. and Ph.D. degrees in electronic physics from the University of Seville, Seville, Spain, in 1982 and 2001, respectively. He has been working in Endesa since 1985 at IT, Measure and Non Technical Losses Control Areas. Currently, he is also collaborating as an associate professor at the Polytechnic University School of Seville.

Ritu Chauhan is currently working as assistant professor in department of biotechnology, Amity University, India. Her Ph.D. research area includes Spatial Data Mining; concentrating on clustering data mining under the supervision of Dr. Harleen Kaur in computer science at the Hamdard University, India. She has published numerous research papers in international journals and chapter in an edited book. Her main research interests area include analysis of data using retrieval process with application towards clinical databases, decision making healthcare databases and several visualization techniques.

David K. Daniel obtained his B. Tech (Chemical Engineering) from the University of Kerala, India; M. Tech (Chemical Engineering) from Calicut University, India. He received his Ph. D (Biotechnology) from the IIT-Kharagpur, India. At present, he is working as professor in the chemical engineering division, School of Mechanical and Building Sciences, at VIT University, Vellore, India. His research interests include bioprocess development, optimization and modeling, alternate fuels, microbial fuel cells and biosensors development. He is the recipient of the best teacher award by the VIT University followed by the certificate of appreciation from VIT University in recognition of the research efforts for publishing in refereed journals. He has also received JEC-Asia 2013 innovation award for recycling category. Dr. David is an active member of the IE, IICE and Biotech Research Society of India.

Raja Das is an assistant professor in the school of advanced sciences, VIT University, India. He received his M. Sc. (Applied Mathematics) from National Institute of Technology, Rourkela, India; and PhD from Sambalpur University, India. His area of research interest includes mathematical modeling, optimization and soft computing. He has published more than ten research papers in the international journals and presented more than four articles at different international and national conferences.

Paramartha Dutta did his Bachelors and Masters in Statistics from the Indian Statistical Institute, Calcutta, India. He afterwards completed his M. Tech. (Computer Science) from the same institution. He received PhD (Engineering) from the Bengal Engineering and Science University, Shibpur. At present, he is working as a professor in the department of computer and system sciences of the Visva Bharati University, India. He has coauthored four books and has also one edited book to his credit. He has published about hundred papers in various journals and conference proceedings, both international and national. Dr. Dutta is a life member of OSI, CSI, ISCA, ISTE, IUPRAI; member of ACM and IEEE.

P. Geethanjali received her B.E. (Electrical and Electronics Engineering) from University of Madras, Tamilnadu, India. She obtained M. Tech (Electrical Drives and Control) from Pondicherry Engineering College, Pondicherry University, Puducherry, India; and Ph. D from VIT University, Vellore in 2012. At present, she is working as an associate professor in school of electrical engineering, VIT University, Vellore, India. Her research interests include bio-signal processing using soft computing techniques, development of assistive devices, renewable energy, and applications of renewable energy.

Juan Ignacio Guerrero received the Ph.D. Degree in industrial informatics from the University of Seville, Spain, in 2011; and the B.Sc. Degree in computer science from University of Seville, in 2006. He works as professor and researcher in University of Seville. His research areas include artificial intelligence, neural networks, expert systems, data mining and evolutionary computation focus on utilities and smart grids.

D. H. Manjaiah is currently working as a professor at the department of computer science, Mangalore University, India. In addition, he is the board of studies of Mangalore University, India. He received PhD from Mangalore University, India; M. Tech. from National Institute of Technology, Surathkal, India, and B.E. from Mysore University, India. He has authored more than 70 research papers in international and national reputed journals and conferences. His name appears in the editorial board of many international journals and is a committee member of various technical bodies like AICTE, UGC. His research interest includes advanced computer networking, mobile / wireless communication, wireless sensor networks.

Arun G Ingale obtained his PhD (Biotechnology) from Sant Gadge Baba Amravati University, India. He was the founder head of department of biotechnology, Dr. Babasahed Ambedkar Marathwada University, India. Dr. Ingale is president of society for biotechnology and bioinformatics, India. His name appears in the editorial board of many international journals. In addition, he has published many research papers of international repute. He has received the award as a Fellow of Society of Sciences (FSSc), Dumka and MIF fellowship by Matsuame International Foundation, Japan. His research interest includes immunology, structure-function prediction, lectin biosensor, glyco nanobiotechnology, genomics, proteomics, and bioinformatics. He has submitted protein and nucleotide sequences on NCBI and viral protein models are being submitted in PDB database.

Sanjay Kumar Jena is professor in the department of computer science and engineering, National Institute of Technology, Rourkela, India. His areas of research interest include database engineering, parallel algorithm, artificial intelligence and neural computing, computational machines, Network security. He is the principal investigator of information security education and awareness project for MIT, Government of India at National Institute of Technology, Rourkela, India.

Ramesh Kannan obtained his Bachelor's degree in civil engineering from Hindustan College of Engineering, Chennai and master's degree from college of engineering, Guindy, Chennai. He is currently working as assistant professor in the department of civil engineering, VIT University, India. His area of research includes constructability assessment, concrete formwork systems, structural optimization and network based project management. He is currently pursuing his Ph. D in VIT University, India. He has published many research papers in international, national and international conferences. He is also interested in the Digital Typography and Photography.

Kijpokin Kasemsap received his BEng degree in Mechanical Engineering from King Mongkut's University of Technology Thonburi, his MBA degree from Ramkhamhaeng University, and his DBA degree in Human Resource Management from Suan Sunandha Rajabhat University. Now he is a special lecturer at Faculty of Management Sciences, Suan Sunandha Rajabhat University based in Bangkok, Thailand. He has 17 years of engineering and management experiences in multinational corporations. He has numerous original research articles in top international journals, conference proceedings, and book chapters on business management, human resource management, and knowledge management published internationally.

Harleen Kaur works in the Hamdard University, India. She has served in United Nations University – IIGH, Malaysia as a research fellow focusing on information technology in Healthcare. She holds a Ph.D. in Computer Science on the topic of applications and social impact of data mining techniques in health care management. She researches broadly in the fields of information technology in healthcare, big data analytics, knowledge discovery, data mining and its applications. She serves as an editorial board member of the peer-reviewed journals and a member of several international bodies like ACUNS. She has contributed to several international publications in refereed journals, conferences, books and is the editor of the book on *ICTs and the Millennium Development Goals: A United Nations Perspective* published by Springer.

Pabitra Mohan Khilar has completed his B. Tech. (CSE) from Mysore University, India; M. Tech. (CSE) from NIT, Rourkela, India; and Ph.D. (Distributed Computing) from IIT, Kharagpur, India. He has been working as a faculty in the department of computer science & engineering, at NIT, Rourkela, India. He has published a number of books and book chapters in various reputed publishers around the globe. His area of interest is fault tolerant computing, high performance computing and distributed wired and wireless networks. He has guided one Ph.D. and more than 100 under graduate and post graduate students in computer science and engineering. He is member of various professional bodies such as IEEE, CSI, IETE, IE, OBA, and ACS. He has been awarded with IBM faculty award and IE Gold Medal. He has served in the capacity of editor-in-chief, editor, reviewer in many reputed international and national journals.

Geetha Mary A. received her M. Tech. in computer science and engineering from VIT University, Vellore, India in 2008 and B.E. from University of Madras, Tamil Nadu, India in 2004. At present, she is working at VIT University as Assistant Professor-Senior. She is currently doing her PhD at VIT University. Her field of interest spans and is not limited to computer science and health care management. Her research interests include security for data mining, databases and intelligent systems. Ms Geetha is associated with professional bodies IAENG and CSTA.

Carlos Leon de Mora received the B.Sc. degree in electronic physics in 1991 and his Ph.D. degree in computer science in 1995, both from the University of Seville, Seville, Spain. At present, he is working as a full professor of the electronic technology department at the University of Seville. He is acting as an advisor of 6 doctoral thesis dissertations; professor of the "Chair Telefonica" and chief information officer at the University of Seville; head of more than 30 research projects, head of the research group of electronic technology and industrial informatics (15 PhDs); and Vice-rector. He has published more than 100 papers and conference contributions, and member of the International Program Committee in more than 50 international scientific meetings. His research areas include knowledge-based systems, data mining and computational intelligence focus on utilities system management. Dr Leon is IEEE senior member.

Sudipta Mahapatra obtained his M. Tech. and Ph.D. degree in Computer Engineering from IIT, Kharagpur. He was in the electronic systems design group of Loughborough University, UK, as BOYSCAST fellow of DST Government of India. He is presently working as an associate professor in the electronics and electrical communication engineering department of IIT, Kharagpur. His areas of research interest include image and video compression, optical and wireless networks, parallel and distributed Systems.

Rocío Millán received the B.Sc. degree and the Ph.D. degree in economics and business administration from the University of Seville, Seville, Spain, in 1985 and 1996, respectively. She worked as professor of economic theory and finance in this university for more than ten years and is working for Endesa as Metering Control Deputy Director. Her research areas include public deficit, energy futures markets, and NTLs detection in electricity companies.

Iñigo Monedero received the B.Sc. and Ph.D. degrees in computer science from the University of Seville, Seville, Spain, in 1994 and 2004, respectively. He joined the automatics and robotics department for two years and he has been a professor in the electronic technology department of the University of Seville since 1998. His research areas include artificial intelligence, expert systems, and data mining in the power electricity industry.

Varun Kumar Ojha did his B. Tech. (CSE) from West Bengal University of Technology, India and did his M. Tech. (CSE) from Kalyani Government Engineering College, India. He is pursuing his PhD in Computer Science & Engineering from Jadavpur University, India. He is working as fulltime research fellow at Visva-Bharati University, India. He has published one book, one chapter and about eight research articles in international journals and conferences. He is associated with ACM and IEEE.

Mrutyunjaya Panda received his PhD (Computer Science) from Berhampur University, India; Master in communication system engineering from Sambalpur University, India; MBA in HRM from IGNOU, India; and BE (ETC Engineering) from Utkal University, India. He is presently working as a professor in the department of ECE, Gandhi Institute for Technological Advancement, India. He has published about 45 papers in international and national journals and conferences, and 5 book chapters. He is acting as a member of various international journals. His active area of research includes data mining, intrusion detection and prevention, social networking, mobile communication, wireless sensor networks, trust management. He is a member of various professional bodies such as IEEE, MIR Labs, KES, IAENG, ACEEE, IETE, CSI, and ISTE.

G. N. Patel is currently working as senior professor at Birla Institute of Management Technology (BIMTECH) a leading B-School in India in the area of decision science. He has published more than 100 research papers in leading national and international journals. He guided 8 candidates for their Ph.D and currently 10 students are working under him for their doctoral degree. His area of interest includes frontier analysis and mathematical programming. He is invited by many Indian and overseas universities and institutions for his talk.

Manas Ranjan Patra holds a Ph.D. degree in computer Science from the Central University of Hyderabad. Currently, he is the director of the computer centre at Berhampur University in addition to his teaching assignment in the PG department of computer science. He is actively engaged in research and teaching for more than 25 years. As a United Nations Visiting Fellow, he worked at the International Institute for Software Technology, United Nations University, Macau; and Institute for Development and Research in Banking Technology, Hyderabad. His research interests include service based computing, applications of data mining, and e-Governance. He has supervised 5 Ph.D. students and has more than 100 publications in journals and international conferences to his credit. He is a life member of CSI, ISTE and OITS, and a fellow of ACEEE.

P. Payaswini received her M. Sc. (Computer Science) from Mangalore University, Mangalore, India and at present perusing her Ph. D (Computer Science) at Mangalore University, India. She is awarded with DST - INSPIRE fellowship available for first rank holders in master degree for pursuing Ph.D. Her research areas are advanced computer networks and mobile communication system. She has authored many research papers in international, national journals and conferences to her credit.

M. K. Pradhan is an assistant professor in the department of mechanical engineering, Maulana Azad National Institute of Technology, Bhopal, India. He received his M. Tech and PhD from National Institute of Technology, Rourkela, India. His area of research interest includes modeling, analysis and optimization of manufacturing processes and systems. He has published more than 25 research papers in the international journals and presented many articles at international and national conferences. He is a life member of ISTE, IACSIT, IAENG and IE (I).

Bibhudatta Sahoo is an assistant professor in the department of computer science and engineering, NIT Rourkela, India. His technical interests include performance evaluation methods and modeling techniques in distributed computing systems, networking algorithms, scheduling theory, cluster computing and Web engineering. He is associated with several R & D projects sponsored from Government of India.

Sreekumar is currently working as an associate professor in the area of decision science at Rourkela Institute of Management studies, Rourkela in India. He obtained his PhD from Sambalpur University, India; and M. Sc. (Applied Mathematics) from NIT, Rourkela, India. He has published more than 40 research papers in leading national and international referred journals. He participated and presented papers in both national and international conferences. His area of interest includes application of DEA for efficiency measurement, multi criteria decision making and supply chain management. He is associated with professional bodies OITS and CSI.

Index